AMERICAN
GRAND JURY
FOUNDATION

This copy of

Grand Juries in California:
A Study in Citizenship

by
Bruce T. Olson

is a gift by the author
for scholars, students, and other citizens
who share an interest in grand juries
and self-government

GRAND JURIES
in
California

GRAND JURIES

a study in citizenship

in

California

BRUCE T. OLSON

American Grand Jury
Foundation

Modesto, California

University of the Pacific Library

THE AMERICAN GRAND JURY FOUNDATION
P.O. Box 1690
Modesto CA 95353-1690
www.grandjuryfoundation.org

Cover illustration © 2000 www.arttoday.com

Editor	Carolyn Acheson, Aurora, Colorado
Book Design	Denise Metzger, *Accent on Words,* Modesto, California
Cover Design	TLC Graphics, *www.TLCGraphics.com*
Proofreading	Ruth E. Stevens, San Jose, California
Printing	Jostens Printing & Publishing, Visalia, California

Manufactured in the United States of America

10 9 8 7 6 5 4 3 2 1

Olson, Bruce T.
    Grand juries in California: a study in citizenship / Bruce T. Olson —
1st ed.
        p.   cm.
    Includes bibliographical references and index.
    ISBN 0-9702322-0-9
    1. Grand juries—California.   2. Justice, Administration of—
California.   3. Courts—California.   I. Olson, Bruce T.   II. Title.

Library of Congress Card Number: 00-105328

The paper used in this publication is both acid free and totally chlorine
free (TCF). It meets the minimum requirements of the ANSI/NISO
Z39.48-1992 (R 1997) (*Permanence of Paper*).

Contents

List of Tables

List of Figures

Preface

Each year California laws require superior court judges to impanel civil grand juries in every California county. Briefly stated, civil grand juries investigate certain local-government activities and, at the end of their year, publish reports about what they have found. In this book I evaluate how effectively California citizens fulfill their responsibilities as civil grand jurors.

For many years the American Grand Jury Foundation has offered annual training programs for newly appointed civil grand jurors. My fellow Directors and I design and present the seminars. Several years ago, at the end of a seminar, a member of the audience, perhaps anxious about the year ahead, asked me this question: "In an era of experts, professional administrators, and increasingly complex government, is there a need for the civil grand jury, and what is its future?" The question was asked about two minutes before the conclusion of a busy two days, when everyone was ready to go home.

Although the question seemed simple, I recall feeling caught off guard for several reasons. *First,* not enough time remained to answer the question satisfactorily. "Why," I wondered, "would anyone wait to ask such a broad question two minutes before the seminar ends?" No conscientious trainer enjoys finding himself in such an awkward spot.

Second, the grand juror asked the question in the accent of someone whose native language was not English, and who probably had obtained his formal education in Great Britain. That observation introduced some complexity into the situation. I shall comment more about that point shortly.

Third, newly appointed grand jurors rarely ask questions about political philosophy. Usually they are concerned about matters such as, "Why do we get only fifteen dollars for attending grand jury meetings?" Or, "Is it legal for our city treasurer to serve on the grand jury?" Or, "Who appointed me to the grand jury, and why?"

Questions like these usually can be answered briefly, and often with specific references to a law. A question about the future of the civil grand jury is another matter, particularly because it raises issues about the future of citizenship and representative government itself, as I hope to convince you in this book.

Recalling Mark Twain's definition of repartee as "the reply you thought of too late," I stumbled through an answer that, mercifully, I have forgotten. Although I do not recall my impromptu response, the question has stayed with me for years. This book is my belated—and I hope more thoughtful—answer to the questioner's provocative query about an unusual American institution.

Something else came to mind as I stood at the lectern scrambling mentally for inspiration. I thought of how often I have heard profound questions about our political system asked in accented voices. Naturalized Americans, after all, have lived previously in other regimes, and many of them have a deep interest in the future of the government they adopted. As I continued to gather my wits, I recalled listening late at night, as a child, to my foreign-language-speaking uncles and aunts arguing with each other in broken English about political issues. The lesson I was learning, although I did not realize it then, was that new Americans often take their citizenship seriously.

Later I learned that the questioner was a physician practicing in a Northern California county. Because I recalled his name, I sent a copy of this book to him with an apology for taking so long to revise my original answer. As good as his question was, however, I now think that he missed an important point, just as I probably did with my impromptu answer. The question should not be about the future of the civil grand jury. That institution is merely an abstraction. Even if it is nearly a thousand years old, it is, good or bad, only what grand jurors make of it.

At the dawn of a new era, the question we all should be asking is not whether we need the civil grand jury, or campaign finance reform, or term limits but, instead, whether the kind of citizenship we practice in the United States is equal to the challenge of the modern American state and the rapidly changing social trends that shape it. If we are not up to that challenge, the future is not rosy for either the civil grand jury or for representative government.

As I explain in later chapters, if you wish to know whether American citizenship is equal to the challenge of modernity, the civil grand jury is a convenient lens through which to study that question. Some readers, of course, will insist on a short answer, and I invite them to read the last paragraph of Chapter 8. Those who would prefer more than "yes," "no," or "maybe" will find throughout this book the ingredients of an answer they can construct for themselves.

Bruce T. Olson
Executive Director
American Grand Jury Foundation
Modesto, California
October 2000

1

Citizenship and the
Spirit of the Institution

The civil function of the California grand jury is as old as the State itself. Each year for decades, the 58 county civil grand juries of California have issued final reports of their findings and recommendations concerning local government.[1] In performing this function for their communities, civil grand jurors are informally said to be exercising their watchdog, rather than indictment, function.[2]

To the extent that California citizens know anything about the civil function of the grand jury, they associate it with the annual publication of grand jury final reports. Final reports in some counties are included as inserts in newspapers. In other counties, newspapers merely summarize only a few of many investigations that the grand jury reported. Elsewhere, grand juries issue so few copies of their final reports that most citizens are unaware that the reports exist, especially when newspapers ignore them.

Some public officials are pleased with a grand jury's findings and recommendations about the local-government agencies they manage. Others are disappointed or angry concerning what grand juries have reported about them. Each year, at least one local-government official somewhere in California expresses outrage about what a grand jury has reported about the local-government functions he or she administers. In expressing anger, an official may receive strong editorial support from one of the community's newspapers. Another newspaper in the same county, however, might commend the grand jury for the same investigation that its competitor deplored.

Objectives of the Study

Despite the publicity that often surrounds the California civil grand jury, the institution is a mystery to many citizens. The first objective of this book, therefore, is to answer a question that newly selected California grand jurors often ask early in their term of service: "What is the civil grand jury, and what does it do?" This book also will answer similar questions that public officials and other citizens might ask about the institution, such as:

- What is a grand jury final report? Is it the product of a completely independent body, or are grand juries responsible to some higher authority? What kinds of issues interest grand jurors, and how do they organize themselves to accomplish their objectives?

- Why do grand juries issue reports? Are their reports based on law, or do grand juries publish them with no authority to do so? May grand juries issue reports about any subject, or do they have limits as to what they may report?

- Why are only local governments the subjects of grand jury reports? May grand juries investigate private persons or businesses? Are grand juries part of county government, and if they are, on what basis do they issue reports about cities, special districts, and other local governments?

- Must all grand jurors approve final reports, or are final reports the products of one or two dominant grand jurors? Can a grand jury foreman decide what grand juries investigate and report? May several grand jurors issue a dissenting report apart from the report of the entire body?

- Are grand jury investigations factual and impartial, or are they based on whim and conjecture? What happens if a grand jury report is unfair? Under what circumstances can someone sue a grand jury for what it has written in a report? Have any California grand juries been successfully sued for libel?

- Shouldn't public officials have the right to review drafts of grand jury reports about their departments before the reports are made public? What happens if a public official ignores a grand jury report or disagrees with it?

The second objective of the book is to report my evaluation of all 58 county final reports for one year and, in doing so, report my assessment of the citizenship skills of grand jurors. In particular, I am concerned with whether news reports of grand jury controversies represent only occasional problems in a few counties or whether they exemplify institutionalized defects Statewide. News-media reports of grand jury controversies, rare though they might be, create much of the ambiguity, confusion, and distrust surrounding the institution. These stories often inspire widespread sentiment either to eliminate the grand jury or to severely restrict its powers. Fair-minded citizens, of course, would not support such drastic legislation merely because of occasional blunders by grand jurors. Unfortunately, however, real or suspected abuse of power, privilege, or professional practice in only one instance can deeply tarnish the reputation of any institution, profession, or craft.

Although the Rodney King episode of 1991 involved only a few peace officers, it affected the attitudes of many citizens about law enforcement in general. Similarly, Watergate was the act of only a few of the nation's hundreds of thousands of public officials, but our memory of the dishonor associated with it is revived frequently in the use of the "-gate" suffix in news accounts of actual or suspected unethical political behavior. In a like manner, people who complain about the widespread decline of ethics in journalism support their criticism by referring to rare episodes of unethical acts committed by news-media reporters. Thus, the human tendency to draw broad conclusions from inadequate samples affects grand juries just as much as it affects other institutions.

Each year in California, newspapers publish accounts of episodes in which grand jurors have intentionally or inadvertently abused the institution, sometimes with spectacular consequences. The full implications of these abuses may not be obvious to readers, depending on their depth of knowledge of grand jury laws. In writing stories about actual or possible abuses of the grand jury, some newspaper reporters fail to understand the significance of what they have written. Quoting persons who have little knowledge of the laws governing the institution or failing to check applicable statutes could mean the difference between thoughtful, well-documented reporting and a shallow, weak story that confuses rather than illuminates. No matter what the particulars are regarding news stories about occasional grand jury controversies, they shape the body of public opinion held by public officials, the news media, and other citizens concerning the institution.

Five Examples of an Institutionalized Problem

As I explain later in this chapter, most of the data in this study are from California civil grand jury final reports released in 1992. In a strict temporal sense, the data are not current. My purpose in conducting the research for this book, however, was not merely to create an inventory of civil grand jury final reports, current or otherwise. Rather, my objective was to examine the problems that persist year after year in civil grand jurors' reports of their inquiries into California local government. In particular, I desired first to evaluate the recurring problems in terms of the relevant laws governing the civil grand jury. Second, I wanted to determine the extent of each of the persistent problems.

By accomplishing these two objectives, I believed that I could develop statutory and other guidelines to help grand jurors improve future investigations and reports. I also hoped that a systematic analysis of grand jurors' commentary about local governments in their communities would reveal insights about the practice of citizenship in the nation's most populated state. Throughout this study, and particularly in Chapters 7 and 8, I therefore comment about citizenship in the context of recurring problems in the final reports of civil grand juries in California.

To help readers understand what I mean by "persistent problems," I present in the next section five brief accounts of grand jury controversies that have occurred in recent times. Though these incidents vary in their implications, intensity, and seriousness, they share this characteristic: They reveal important insights into how the behavior and attitudes of grand jurors may affect the integrity and independence of the grand jury. In this sense, the five examples will serve to describe further the study's objectives.

THE MARIPOSA COUNTY GRAND JURY OF 1994–1995

Just before their term ended, the 10 members of the Mariposa County Grand Jury of 1994–1995 filed indictments against certain public officials of Mariposa County, a member of the Office of the Attorney General of California, and the superior court judge who appointed the jurors.[3] In the final report they filed after issuing indictments, the Mariposa County grand jurors claimed that specifically named public officials were guilty of a variety of corrupt acts. Later in the summer of 1995, a superior court judge in another county declared the indictments to be filed improperly and therefore unlawful.

The controversy that arose from this incident lasted through early fall of 1995. The incident resulted in several television stories, many letters to the editor in the local newspapers of Mariposa and adjoining counties, and reports in other newspapers in California. Hoping to settle the controversy, the Mariposa County Board of Supervisors urged the panel of 1995–1996 to investigate the work of its predecessor for two purposes: to review the evidence upon which the previous Grand Jury based its indictment, and to determine whether the indictment procedures the earlier panel used were lawful. The Grand Jury of 1995–1996 thereafter issued a 27-page report that it believed repudiated the findings of its predecessor.[4]

The Mariposa County Grand Jury incident involves too many twists and turns to be summarized further for this study; however, the news accounts of the matter and the information the 1995–1996 Grand Jury included in its report demonstrate that factuality, or the lack of it, was at the heart of the episode. For example, in reviewing the events leading up to the filing of indictments by its predecessor, the 1995–1996 Grand Jury included comments such as this:

> None of the indictments was supported by evidence of criminal activity by those indicted. The evidence adduced by the 95–96 Grand Jury investigation exonerates and disproves the charges alleged against them.

The intrigue surrounding the 1994–1995 Mariposa County Grand Jury Final Report is heightened by one more complication—that the Mariposa County Grand Jury Final Report of 1995–1996 did not cite the authority under which it investigated the acts of its predecessor. According to an opinion that the

Attorney General of the State of California issued in 1993, grand juries have no jurisdiction in the courts.[5] If, therefore, in issuing indictments, grand juries are functioning as organs of the courts, it follows that no authority exists for one grand jury to investigate another for the indictments it has issued. If my logic is correct, the situation in Mariposa County would be that of one grand jury unlawfully investigating what it considered to be the unlawful acts of another, thereby further contributing to the confusion concerning the institution.[6]

THE ORANGE COUNTY GRAND JURY OF 1984–1985

In publishing their final report, the Orange County grand jurors of 1984–1985 probably did not realize that they had missed an opportunity to prevent one of the largest debacles in the history of American public finance: the Orange County financial scandal of 1994 and 1995. This episode resulted in dozens of embarrassing newspaper headlines in California and across the country, such as: "Orange County Teaches Investors What Not To Do."[7] In a three-page report of their study of the Office of the Orange County Treasurer and Tax Collector in 1985, grand jurors of that year offered only a mildly worded recommendation that the County Treasurer "… develop and maintain written procedures covering all major areas of the investment and cash management functions." Unfortunately, the Grand Jury provided little information to document its recommendation and explain its implications. In the absence of a thorough discussion by the panel of the significance of its finding, most newspaper reporters reading the perfunctory Grand Jury report would not see in it the red flags of an impending financial disaster.

Even worse, the Orange County grand jurors' restrained expressions of concern about the office of County Treasurer and Tax Collector were softened further by the use of complimentary terms elsewhere in the same three-page document, such as "the smooth functioning of this office," the office being "conducted in a capable manner," that "Cash forecasting is managed well and with a high degree of accuracy," and that "Securities settlement procedures and safekeeping appear to be well controlled." Indeed, the panel commended the County Treasurer for "making effective use of the variety and sophistication of the broad range of investment instruments available in the money market."[8]

Because the commendatory words and phrases in the report are more abundant than the few restrained cautionary comments, many citizens reading it probably concluded that the panel thought the office of the County Treasurer was generally well managed. A few persons knowledgeable about the investment of public funds might have wanted more specific information about what the Grand Jury described as sophisticated "investment instruments." Still other readers might have been puzzled by the fact that, although grand jurors claimed that "this report has been a cooperative effort between the

Orange County Grand Jury and their contract auditor," grand jurors included in their report no findings, recommendations, or other information from the report of the auditing firm.

Ten years later, while still in shock from threats of the bankruptcy of County government, severe cutbacks in public services, and reports that the some of the investment decisions the County Treasurer made were guided by the signs of the Zodiac, a few Orange County citizens might have remembered the 1984–1985 Grand Jury Final Report. If so, they might reasonably have asked whether, by not including in its report the findings and recommendations of its independent auditor, the panel inadvertently or intentionally suppressed its consultant's investigation.

Certainly nothing in the Grand Jury report would have inspired most news reporters or citizens to probe more deeply into the County Treasurer's Office. Thus, the principal deficiency of the Grand Jury report was that its bland, undocumented tone did little to motivate citizens, the press, or public officials to probe more deeply into the matter. As a result of the national controversy that came to light 10 years after the Grand Jury issued its report, Orange County now has the unenviable reputation of being widely cited as a spectacular confirmation of the ancient saying that high yield means high risk.[9]

The San Joaquin and Tehama County Grand Juries of 1992–1993

The third example differs from the previous two in at least one important respect: It generated no extensive publicity. Nevertheless, from the perspective of the integrity of the institution, this example is as important as the Mariposa and Orange County incidents. In fact, the important deficiency in the third example is at the root of most of the problems in the first two examples and, for that matter, many of the problems in other examples of grand jury investigations and reports that I shall discuss.

Because most citizens read only the final reports of their home counties, they would not know that two California grand juries (San Joaquin and Tehama Counties) in the same year published opposing conclusions from the same data. Unfortunately, in neither case did grand jurors adequately report the original facts that led them in their respective investigations to contradictory conclusions. Rather, the information was reported in brief commentaries concerning an issue of interest for many grand jurors: the wisdom of the statutory provision for carry-over grand jurors.[10]

Although the Tehama County Grand Jury did not reveal how it obtained the data, the panel used information the San Joaquin County Grand Jury had gathered by conducting a survey among other grand juries to determine the attitudes of grand jurors concerning the use of the carry-over statute in their respective counties. After discussing what it considered to be the advantages and disadvantages of "carry-over grand jurists [*sic*]," the San Joaquin County Grand Jury came to the following conclusion based on its unreported survey data:

> Statistical analysis revealed that 65% of the Grand Juries polled currently "carry over" grand jurists. More significantly, *the number of Grand Juries which previously used "carry-over" grand jurors but no longer do so was down 84%* [emphasis added]. It was this downward trend of the "carry over" practice among California Grand Juries which convinced us that the practice is not meeting with success and should *not* be recommended for San Joaquin County. Rather, a voluntary practice of making available key members of the outgoing Grand Jury to assist the new Grand Jury is highly recommended.

Citing the same data in its final report, the Tehama County Grand Jury concluded:

> Forty-four of California's fifty-eight grand juries responded to a short questionnaire [about] carry-over jurors. Some of the data follows:
>
> 64% of the counties now have carry-over jurors
>
> *85% of the counties have used them in the past* [emphasis added]
>
> 96% found carry-over jurors beneficial
>
> Having just spent a busy year on the 1992–1993 Grand Jury, we feel the advantages of carry-over jurors far outweigh the disadvantages.[11]

Because few citizens would have read both final reports, the significance of these two divergent conclusions would not be generally understood. Nevertheless, the implications for the institution of two panels of grand jurors deriving contradictory conclusions from the same data are significant. The most important shortcoming in both instances is that neither grand jury fully described how the survey was conducted, nor did either grand jury disclose all the data the questionnaire generated, thereby depriving readers of the means for evaluating the soundness of each conclusion. Barring a concern for confidentiality or secrecy, full disclosure of survey data is an ethical imperative in survey research.[12]

The way the data were collected also could have biased the survey results. For example, in some counties only one person (the foreman or forewoman) might have answered the questionnaire the grand jury received. Unfortunately, neither grand jury included information in its report about how the questionnaires were distributed and, in particular, what was done to ensure that they represented the responses of entire panels rather than one or two members. In the absence of such information, readers of the final reports have no way of deciding what the data represented: the opinions of grand jurors in a carefully constructed sample, the opinions of county staff members who might have intercepted and answered the questionnaire, the opinions of judges who might have completed it, or the opinions of foremen and forewomen who might have had a vested interest in supporting or opposing the carry-over statute.

Similarly, the wording of questions in the mailed questionnaire could have been a source of bias. Because neither grand jury included the questionnaire in its report, readers have no way of determining whether bias may have existed. A question reading, "It is widely known that the carry-over system has greatly improved the quality of final reports. Do you oppose or support it?" might yield a different result from a more objectively phrased question.

Neither grand jury identified the counties that returned or did not return completed questionnaires. What, therefore, does the phrase, "65% of the grand juries polled currently 'carry over' grand jurists" mean? If only 25 percent of the grand juries in California were "polled," 65 percent might be a negligible figure. Because information about response was missing in both studies, readers were deprived of information that should be included routinely in reports of survey data and that would have allowed them to judge the validity of the data.

Because of incomplete information in each grand jury report, I cannot explain how two panels could have drawn exactly opposite conclusions from the same data. On several occasions I contacted the San Joaquin County Grand Jury office for permission to examine the original questionnaires and to study the wording of the questionnaire. I was unsuccessful in gaining access to that information. Later, a member of the San Joaquin County court staff told me that the completed questionnaires had been discarded.

A number of explanations can be advanced to explain tentatively the differences in the data and the conclusions reported by these two grand juries. It is possible, for example, that grand jurors in one of the counties were so committed to a position about the carry-over statute that they misread the data. Or, perhaps for the same reason, one of the grand juries falsely reported the results. If this is so, one of the reports must be regarded as an example of ax-grinding. If a grand jury falsified data in one instance, what would prevent it from falsifying data in others? The slipshod manner in which both grand juries reported their data and conclusions suggest the most likely explanation: Grand jurors in both counties were unfamiliar with the rudimentary principles of objective analysis and reporting, a deficiency that raises serious questions about their citizenship skills.

DISSOLUTION OF THE SANTA CLARA COUNTY GRAND JURY OF 1998–1999

In December 1998, a superior court judge of Santa Clara County issued a "scathing order" dismissing several civil grand jurors for violating their oath. The judge also discharged without censure the remaining grand jurors because, according to news recounts, internal controversy fragmented the panel so badly that it could not function. Not only did the first group of dismissed grand jurors complain to the County Human Relations Commission of mistreatment by fellow grand jurors, but they also demanded that the Board of Supervisors of Santa Clara County order an audit of the Grand Jury. The dissenting members further complained that other grand jurors were "covering up" audits, that the District Attorney was blocking investigations, and that "a civil grand jury hierarchy ... weeded out and isolated minority members and others who dared speak up, eliminating them from committees or refusing to allow them to vote on key issues."

Because of grand jury secrecy provisions, little information is publicly available about the causes of the controversy. The incident spawned at least 10 newspaper articles, letters to the editor, and editorials between November 1998 and February 1999. Although the press did not report specific details about the inner workings of the Grand Jury during the controversy, one editorial rebuked the judge who impaneled the Grand Jury for appointing his former clerk as foreman. A later editorial commended the presiding judge of the Superior Court for announcing his intention to involve all 79 superior court judges and 10 jury commissioners in selecting future grand juries and for "... working with the district attorney and county counsel to design [training programs] for future grand juries."[13]

Similar grand jury controversies in other counties have led occasionally to the discharge of entire panels. The publicity that follows such drastic actions takes a toll on the prestige of the institution, causing citizens to wonder why these incidents occur, what can be done to prevent them, and what they imply about their communities.

THE YUBA COUNTY DEFAMATION LAWSUIT OF 1993–1994

In 1994, the Yuba County Grand Jury included in its final report two separate critical reports about the County Building and Planning Department.[14] The reports included allegations of inept administrative decision making, false filing of expense accounts, lax supervision, and other examples of alleged mismanagement and irregularities. Thereafter, two leading Department officials named in the report attempted to sue grand jurors of that year for defamation.

The case eventually was appealed to the Third Appellate District Court of California. That Court ruled that a lower court had properly dismissed the defamation suit filed against the Yuba County grand jurors. The Appellate Court stated that the two public officials failed to prove "with clear and convincing evidence" that "actual malice" motivated the grand jurors who prepared the two reports.[15]

The Yuba County defamation lawsuit raises several issues that are relevant for the present study, which I discuss in later chapters. In particular, the episode illustrates the problem of subjectivity in grand jury final reports, a quality that causes perennial criticism of grand jurors. The incident is important for another reason: Although the two lawsuits caused much grief, confusion, and anguish for the affected parties, it settled little in terms of the California civil grand jury as an institution. Moreover, because of the manner in which the Appellate Court disposed of this case, it could lead to more harm than good.

Because the effect of the Appellate Court's ruling was to end the lawsuit, at least at this writing, future grand jurors might conclude that the decision created a standard concerning the kind of criticism about public officials that courts will tolerate in grand jury final reports. That conclusion would be erroneous; in its holding, the Court did not specifically address issues of factuality in the two final reports. The Appellate case is of limited value for another reason: It was not officially published. Thus, the case cannot be used to decide similar future defamation lawsuits against grand jurors. The case therefore has left unsettled important issues about grand jury criticism in final reports of public officials.

As knowledge of the case enters the civil grand jury culture, many grand jurors will understand it merely as an example of a court rejecting a suit for defamation. Only the few grand jurors, or their legal advisors, who take the time to review the trial history of the case, the 20-page Appellate ruling, the two grand jury reports in question, and the controversy surrounding the practice of depublication will understand that the Appellate ruling is an anomaly in the judicial system. Because of its depublished nature, the case will have little bearing on future defamation lawsuits, if any, that public officials may initiate against grand jurors.[16]

The case nevertheless is important for purposes of this study. For example, it raises questions about the adequacy of modern civic education and the need to prepare citizens to exercise the skills of fact finding that are crucial not merely for grand jury service but for self-government in general. Similarly, the incident emphasizes the need to examine civil grand jury statutes to determine whether they can be modified to prevent it from happening again.

One possible result of the Yuba County defamation suit was the enactment into law of Penal Code Section 929 in 1998. Among other provisions, this statute permits superior court judges to expunge before publication "any testimony or materials of a defamatory or libelous nature" from civil grand jury final reports. For this statute to work, the courts must, of course, review final reports carefully. Under pressure of time, it is possible that a judge might overlook defamatory material. Likewise, because the statute merely permits judges to expunge such material, there is no duty to do so. Finally, the fact that a judge has authorized the publication of a final report does not prevent the initiation of a libel suit. In Chapter 7, I therefore offer suggestions for legislation that would go farther than Penal Code Section 929 in preventing the occurrence of subjectivity, an important issue in defamation lawsuits, in civil grand jury final reports.

Grand Jury Blunders: Few or Many?

The preceding accounts by no means exhaust the examples of the unfavorable publicity that many grand juries have received during the time I have been observing them. Whatever reasons might be advanced to explain these unfortunate incidents, an important question remains: How common are they? Finding an answer to that question is this study's third objective. To accomplish that objective, I decided to evaluate in detail the grand jury final reports of each one of California's counties for one year. For that purpose, I used a computer to store information extracted from 58 grand jury final reports, using the method I describe in Appendix A, "Some Notes About the Study and Its Method." Unlike a study of grand jury final reports I conducted in the early 1960s,[17] this project was concerned with the legality of the final reports of civil grand juries in California, as I explain in Chapter 2.

As I refined and tested the method I used to collect the data for this study, I discovered that as the volume of information grew, it gave rise to questions about how grand jurors as citizens conceive of their relationship to the grand jury as an institution. Therefore, what began as a project to find answers to the questions I posed earlier broadened into a fourth objective: to learn what grand jury final reports reveal about the practice of citizenship. Just as William Blake marveled at the prospect of understanding the world by studying a grain of sand,[18] I learned that the grand jury, though it is a relatively small institution, exhibits many of the same problems and accomplishments found in much larger political bodies such as state governments and the United States Congress.

Consider, for example, the question of how far governmental institutions stray from their legislated boundaries. A Statewide assessment of the civil grand jury in California could reveal whether a significant gap exists between what the Legislature intends the institution to be each year and what it actually becomes in the hands of citizens appointed to it. Of course, some flexibility in any political body is an asset. Nevertheless, when a creature of a legislative body drifts too far from its statutory or constitutional framework, it is cause for concern. In the case of the grand jury, that concern is especially pressing because the mandate of the institution is, after all, to assess the effectiveness of local-government services, functions, and departments.

Discovering the divergence, if any, between the authority and jurisdiction the Legislature has granted the grand jury and how grand jurors interpret their mandate is important for another reason. As I show in the next chapter, the legal framework of the California grand jury consists of relatively few statutes. The extent to which grand jurors understand and adhere to the law governing the institution and, as needed, apply it during their term of service is a function of their conception of what it means to be citizens.

The legality and effectiveness of grand jury final reports depend, therefore, almost entirely on the citizenship knowledge, skills, and attitudes of grand jurors, just as the practice of citizenship is important for governing any other political system. In this sense, final reports are the product of, so to speak, the art of citizenship. Accordingly, one of the purposes of this study is to determine what final reports reveal about citizenship in contemporary California. Because of this objective, a review of the literature of citizenship, particularly as it is relevant to the study's objectives, will be helpful.

Citizenship: Selected Definitions and Literature

Most people reading books, newspaper articles, and academic studies of citizenship will be struck by the many meanings attached to the word. One would think that, given the massive outpouring of books, newspaper articles, and editorials concerning contemporary American society and government, a well-developed citizenship terminology would have emerged. The lack of a coherent theory of citizenship, however, is responsible for imprecision in the use of the word not only in scholarly writings but in everyday life as well.[19]

During a conversation with a former grand juror, I mentioned that I was writing a book about California grand juries. "What will its title be?" he asked. When I replied, "Probably something like *Grand Juries in California: A Study in Citizenship*," he seemed perplexed and said that he could not see the connection between immigration and grand juries. His comment reminded me of my own puzzlement about the term *citizenship* when I first began reading its literature and discovered, as I shall describe below, that writers rarely define what they mean by the word.[20]

One advantage of the semantic richness of the word is that it can be discussed productively in many contexts. The statement by my former-grand-juror acquaintance, however, emphasizes that, given the variability in use of the term and the institutional characteristics of the grand jury, I must explain how I use *citizenship* in this study. This is particularly important because the meaning I attach to the word is rarely encountered in the literature of citizenship. Later in this section, I therefore define the kind of citizenship I refer to in the context of the civil grand jury. First, however, a review of some of the literature of citizenship and its related concerns will be helpful.

Renewed Interest in Citizenship

Not since the founding of the United States and the Progressive Era has citizenship received so much attention by the news media and observers of politics. Indeed, a comprehensive treatment of the social, economic, and political pressures behind this broadening wave of interest would require far more attention than I can give it in this book. Among the concerns expressed in the growing body of literature[21] concerning how social, economic, and political trends affect citizenship and American society are:

- Globalism and the increased size and power of government and monopolistic corporations
- The rise of mass society and popular culture
- Declining citizen support of government and its officials
- Contemporary trends in immigration to the United States and cultural problems associated with the assimilation of new Americans
- Radical changes in the funding, organization, and methods of the news media
- The consequences of professionalism, expertism, and elitism in government and the news media
- The influence of television, loss of leisure time, falling rates of newspaper readership, and advent of the Internet
- Development of an "inside-the-Beltway" culture and the growing sense of distance between the rulers and the ruled

Even the so-called breakup of the Soviet Union, according to some observers, has affected the American notion of citizenship. Whatever its evils might have been, the argument runs, the Cold War provided a common focus for American citizens: their survival. The loss of a unifying interest for Americans, therefore, is partly responsible for expanding social divisions and problems. The decline of a national purpose also is attributed to public anxieties and suspicions surrounding diverse influences such as the assassination of the Kennedy brothers and Martin Luther King, Jr., the rise of the "counterculture" in the 1960s and 1970s, American military involvement in Vietnam, the advent of affirmative action, and a host of other controversies following World War II. Though no one has yet proposed a general theory that explains how the various strains and stresses in recent years have affected our concept of citizenship, some of the consequences are said to be:

- Low rates of voter turnout
- The reluctance of qualified citizens to seek public office
- Growing ignorance, fear, and suspicion of government and its officials, leading to the rise of the "tax protest" movement and related phenomena
- The increasing inability of legislative bodies to conduct the business of government
- The decline of a sense of community

CONCERNS ABOUT CITIZEN DISCONTENT

Some of the evidence concerning the morale of Americans as citizens is found in national surveys. For example, the National Civic League, one of the oldest civic associations in the United States, commissioned public-opinion surveys in 1990 and 1994 and concluded that

> above all else, Americans have confidence in one institution—themselves and others like them. They distrust every other institution be it public, private, or nonprofit, with each of these sectors enjoying the confidence of less than 50 percent of Americans. Citizens are tired and distrustful of people and organizations that are distant from themselves, or people like themselves, who are deciding things for them. They want to decide things for themselves.[22]

No one who is familiar with political or social philosophy should be surprised at the recent flood of literature concerning citizen unrest. More than one hundred years ago, Alexis de Tocqueville and Emile Durkheim wrote about what they foresaw as the consequences of mass society and its culture. Durkheim predicted that as society becomes more complex, citizens will need new social mechanisms to express their needs to the larger political systems upon which they will become increasingly dependent and which will envelop their lives. But he did not describe how an institution such as the grand jury could intervene between citizens and government. Tocqueville referred to grand juries, but only briefly, and few other social commentators since his time have speculated on the function of grand juries as mediating institutions.[23]

Even a brief listing of the social, political, economic, and cultural concerns that often are interwoven in discussions of citizenship suggests why its study has resulted in a hodgepodge of explanations for the increasing discontent of many Americans with the civic dimension of their lives. Theory-building is never easy in subjects such as citizenship when variables can be causes or effects, or both, depending on circumstances. In trying to bring order into the study of citizenship, some writers have attempted to understand how it changed through several epochs and to find ways to classify the various types of citizenship in various political systems.

PERSPECTIVES ON CITIZENSHIP AND CITIZEN COMPETENCE

One of the most frequently cited treatments of citizenship is by a writer who claims that citizenship in England passed through three stages, each of which arose in successive centuries: (1) civil stage (eighteenth century); (2) political stage (nineteenth century); (3) social stage (twentieth century). Thus, the form of citizenship that arose during the expansion of the welfare state is quite different from that of the two previous centuries. Other observers are interested in the variation of citizenship among different types of political regimes such as monarchies, fascist and socialist governments, and capitalist systems.[24] In this context, the definition of citizenship is that which the state prescribes.

In an unusual cross-cultural focus-group study of how people "actually understand their rights, duties, and identities" as citizens, three researchers reported that they found distinct differences in the language that American and English citizens used to express their conceptions of citizenship. Whereas the American respondents emphasized civil rights, the English citizens rarely referred to individual rights; rather, they spoke of the rights of groups of which one might be a member. The tendency of American participants to speak of duties (for example, paying taxes or defending their country in wartime) differed somewhat from words the English citizens used, such as referring to themselves as "subjects," and other linguistic conventions that denote obeying the law and respecting community norms and civility.[25]

Another observer asserted that the conception of citizenship within the same country might vary regionally in that country according to the residual influences of the social, economic, and political characteristics of earlier times. Thus, citizens in the northern section of a nation may have developed citizenship traditions and practices quite different from those of citizens of its southern communities.[26]

Of the various concerns found in the literature of citizenship, three are particularly suggestive for assessing investigations and reports of California grand juries:

- Self-interest and common-good citizenship
- Active or passive citizenship
- Citizen competence

Although the first two concepts often are expressed as clear-cut opposites, I know no one who claims that they exist in pure forms. For example, few citizens participate in the political lives of their communities solely for self-interest. Similarly, few citizens are dedicated unreservedly to the common good, though occasionally statues are erected and awards are conferred for that virtue. Nor are people consistently either active or passive throughout their lives in the practice of citizenship. Citizens who have been passive for years might become active if issues arise in their communities that either conflict with their self-interest or offend their sense of the common good.

Other citizens explain that, although they realize they should participate in the civic life of their communities, they have too few leisure hours to do so. Or, like Oscar Wilde, who complained that the trouble with socialism is that it requires too many evenings, they might prefer to spend their spare hours pursuing other interests.[27] One contemporary social analyst, however, contends that the complaint of too few hours might be explained by too much television watching.[28]

Citizens also vary in what they identify as appropriate activities for practicing their preferred brand of citizenship. One person might think of himself as an active, common-good citizen because he dutifully votes in every election, yet he participates in no other way in the political life of his community. Some citizens might argue that the practice of citizenship should be restricted to voting to renew or cancel the mandate they have granted to elected officials to govern them. In this conception, any other kind of direct participation in public affairs must be avoided because it interferes with the orderly administration and management of government.[29] Another citizen might argue that an active, common-good citizen must do more than vote and that a person does not contribute to the common good unless he runs for office, serves as a reserve peace officer in his city's police force, or in some other way is directly, but voluntarily, involved in public service.

Other citizens might not wish to serve as volunteer workers in a governmental setting. Instead, they define good citizenship in terms of charitable activities in private settings, such as working as a volunteer in a privately funded community hospice. In contrast, some citizens do not equate activities of that kind, laudatory as they are, with the practice of citizenship but, rather, see them as an expression of a humanitarian spirit. Active citizenship, they contend, is a term that should be restricted to direct involvement in the politics of a community by serving, for example, on the county central committee of their political party. Still other people suggest that serving on the central committees of political parties is a waste of citizenship energy because those bodies are controlled by powerful interests outside the community.

Although the active-passive conception is a useful way of thinking about citizenship in terms of expending energy, it has limited use for describing the ideological element of citizenship. To illustrate, an active socialist might support a method of financing the construction of a public building that an active full-market enthusiast would oppose. Both might be equally active, but the political basis of their citizenship is quite different. In attempting to explain the values inherent in different kinds of citizenship, some writers identify types of citizenship. For example, Professor Adrian Oldfield describes two views of citizenship (liberal-individualist and civic-republican) that differ radically in their assumptions:[30]

Liberal-Individualist	Civic-Republican
1. Citizenship is a status characterized by individualism	1. Citizenship is a role, i.e., a constellation of obligations,
2. based on contractual social bonds with few obligations,	2. community based and shared,
3. employing a language of "needs" and "rights."	3. employing a language of "duties."

Although I have somewhat revised and summarized Professor Oldfield's more elaborate formulation, one can see that these two views of citizenship would result in quite different beliefs about the proper role of government and its methods.

Considering the large number of books, scholarly papers, and monographs decrying the degradation of American culture and the consequent loss of a sense of community, one would expect to find more commentary about citizen competence. If society can be no better or worse than its citizens make it, the issue of citizen competence should receive more attention, yet it is rarely addressed. Indeed, many political theorists seem to have assumed that the extent of civic knowledge that citizens desire or believe they need is little more than understanding the obligation to vote.

The skills required to implement this knowledge are only those for finding one's way to the polling place, reading ballots, and pulling the necessary voting-machine levers on behalf of self-interest. These people are what Professor Robert Dahl calls "good enough" citizens, individuals who "possess sufficiently strong incentives to gain a modicum of knowledge of their own interests and of the political choices most likely to advance them, as well as sufficiently studying incentives to act on behalf of these choices."[31]

By no means does Professor Dahl propose that "good enough" citizens are adequate for the requirements of a modern democracy. Indeed, he laments that "the practices and institutions of modern democratic countries seem to be failing to produce even the 'good-enough' citizens envisioned in this formulation."[32] If our educational institutions, news media, and even our child-rearing practices cannot create a recruitment pool of even minimally competent and informed lever pullers, where will we find enough qualified citizens for grand jury service?

If, after conducting a "citizenship manpower survey," we decide that too few citizens are qualified to serve as grand jurors, we shall have arrived at a conclusion of tragic significance. We might be forced to concede that our government is in jeopardy, for it consists of only a few people who have acquired the skills needed to become rulers and a much larger mass of ignorant, uninterested, and apathetic people whose political socialization is sufficient only for the purpose of pursuing their self-interest in the voting booth.

Suppose, however, that our manpower survey reveals that many people are available who, when the situation demands, can function well as civic troubleshooters; they would be ideal members of civil grand juries. More important, that discovery would assure us that our population indeed includes a substantial body of citizens who think independently, are not afraid to speak their minds, and can rise above factionalism and self-interest to serve their fellow citizens as civic watchdogs.

This finding would be greatly encouraging. For example, it would assure us that our educational systems create truly active, informed citizens who understand and practice the ideal of the common good. Even if we discover that the classical virtues of active citizenship are not in full flower, at least we would be heartened to learn that some seeds might be found to produce an occasional crop of concerned, independently thinking citizen activists. We also might be comforted by the thought that enough people exist in the our political system to raise a hue and cry against any fraud, graft, corruption, and inefficiency in government that they might discover. The thought would be reassuring that our civic troubleshooters would awaken the rest of us if they were to detect signs of tyranny, totalitarianism, or repression in the body politic. Framed in this manner, governance and citizen competence should be an important field of inquiry in the social sciences.

In practice, social science has assigned little importance to studying what happens when, for one reason or another, citizens directly attempt to evaluate the mechanisms of government. Moreover, if social scientists explore the issue at all, they do so at the state and federal levels of government. The fixation of American social scientists on our federal government and on foreign governments is itself a topic that deserves examination. For the purpose of this study, however, it is sufficient to say that social scientists rarely study the direct involvement of citizens in local government, either through the means of grand juries or any other mechanism. Another purpose of this book, therefore, is to examine the California grand jury to see what kinds of issues it, as a small-scale political system, might reveal to social scientists who wish to study citizen competence in the context of the forms of government closest to citizens.[33]

This brief summary of selected concerns in the literature of citizenship and its definitions reveals how large or small a claim the concept may have on the identity, self-concept, or personality of citizens. Almost everyone with experience in community life has known people who were so dominated by their sense of citizenship that it endangered their family life, their health, or their livelihood. On the other hand, some people are found in any community whose identities as citizens are so undeveloped that they cannot name even one of the local governments in which they live, let alone all of them.

In theory, American government is said to be an experiment in self-government. If this is so, one would expect social scientists to have produced a body of literature concerning what skills, attitudes, and beliefs American citizens need so they can effectively practice the self-governance implied by the United States Constitution. Two hundred years after the founding of our country, we should know much more than we do about what we ought to require of ourselves, our educational system, our news media, and our legislators to maintain representative government.

Unfortunately, an expanding body of evidence supports the contention that most Americans, in the manner of the people in the popular song of the 1960s who "don't know much about geography," also know little about the way in which their government works: "[I]ndividuals emerge from the educational system with lower levels of knowledge about current political figures and alignments than 30 or 40 years ago."[34] One of the questions with which this study is therefore concerned is whether the conceptions of citizenship among citizens who are impaneled for grand jury service hinder or enhance the work of the civil grand jury in California.

Significance of Citizenship for the Grand Jury

A proposal by a legal scholar illustrates why citizen competence is significant for the California civil grand jury. Professor Ronald F. Wright advocates creating administrative grand juries to review the administration of local, state, and federal governments.[35] Although Professor Wright concedes the problems involved in finding motivated and qualified persons to impanel as administrative grand jurors, his idea has considerable promise. By involving citizens more directly in the oversight of their government, administrative grand juries might encourage public officials to manage public services more effectively, thereby increasing in citizens a sense of meaningful involvement and participation in their government.

Involving citizens directly in reviewing administrative practices, however, has merit only to the extent that citizens are qualified to do so. If too few citizens are available who have the requisite skills, knowledge, and sense of independence needed to be competent panel members, administrative grand juries could become little more than pawns of their appointing authorities and the officials whose practices they review.

As an institution, of course, a grand jury cannot itself select men and women whose sense of citizenship comports with its statutes and traditions. It must accept the people whom the courts appoint to it. If the selection of grand jurors were completely random among statutorily qualified adult citizens, chance would ensure that a grand jury would consist of people who represent the variety of citizenship self-concepts in the community at large. In a sense, therefore, the civil grand jury's greatest challenge is similar to that of its criminal counterpart: to survive whatever tensions might arise among the varieties of citizenship that are expressed by its members and the imperatives of its statutory framework and traditions.

Ideally, the statutes and traditions upon which the California civil grand jury rests require a form of citizenship that rarely is treated in the literature of the subject: the assertive, open-minded, common-good citizenship needed for self-government. Some people, on reading the previous sentence, might argue that men and women who for purely altruistic reasons join the Peace Corps are active, common-good citizens, and so they are. Similarly, a person who, as an unpaid advocate of animal rights, attends without fail every local-government board meeting in his community to speak for the welfare of animals might properly be said to be an active, common-good citizen. A young man who joins a military service solely for patriotic reasons also might be thought of as an active, common-good citizen.

Although the citizenship self-concept of these individuals approaches that needed for grand jury service, one more element is required: the will and desire to determine whether the business of government is being conducted lawfully, effectively, openly, and equitably. This is not a conception of citizenship that argues whether government should or should not do something, whether its policies are ill conceived or poorly advised, or whether its reach should be broadened or restricted. Policy matters are the province of elected officials and, therefore, are beyond the statutory scope of the civil grand jury.

Rather, the form of citizenship implicit in the statutes governing the civil grand jury in California is that which insists on procedural fairness, effectiveness, compliance, and accountability. These concerns are, of course, essential ingredients of self-government: "the rule-governed practices that make democracy work."[36] This conception of civil grand jury service contrasts sharply with a view of citizens as merely passive recipients of "certain benefits that the State, and no other social or political organization, provides."[37] It is, instead, the practice of a type of citizenship that understands that by insisting on accountability in

> ... government, by opening its operations to the fresh breezes of public discussion and inquiry and by its periodic activity in changing its leaders, it furnishes the surest medicine against the perpetuation of bureaucracy. Its success in this enterprise depends on its alertness, on the level of public education [and it recognizes that] democracy in this respect [is] also unlike other forms of government, in that its very existence is a function of the social awareness, the vigilant spirit of its citizens.[38]

In describing the kind of citizenship that grand jury statutes and its tradition imply, I do not propose that every grand juror on each panel must be of that variety. Nor do I suggest that either passive or active self-interest grand jurors have nothing to contribute. In certain circumstances, these persons can be valuable panel members. I do contend that each grand jury should have *some* grand jurors of the active, self-government, procedural-accountability variety. By their conduct, they would set a standard for their colleagues.

For example, they would help their colleagues understand that the civil grand jury is not like any other institution with which they have had experience. They also might inspire the panel to develop a thorough understanding of grand jury statutes, traditions, and case law early in its term. These grand jurors also could explain to their colleagues what "conflict of interest" means and that for the grand jury to be effective, real or potential conflict of interest within the panel must be understood and dealt with, just as it must be within local government itself.

Similarly, grand jurors committed to the concept of self-government and procedural accountability would help their colleagues understand why independence is the institution's greatest asset, why they must ensure that every assertion grand jurors make in their final reports must be based on at least one documented fact, and that the institution can be as quickly discredited by grand jurors who adopt a fawning, servile attitude in their relationship to public officials as it can be by grand jurors who condemn government and its public officials and employees for no reason other than that they despise all government as tyrannical.

The form of citizenship that the civil grand jury requires is important for one more reason: Grand juries become what their members want them to be. The California Legislature permits grand jurors great discretion in how they organize themselves for their year of service, in deciding what kinds of procedures to establish, and in deciding which local governments to study. Grand jurors are able to decide matters such as the system they use for establishing their priorities, whether they will accept or reject anonymous complaints from citizens, and whether they will issue only one report during the year, or several.

Clearly, the nature and quality of these decisions depend on the concept each grand juror has of the duties, rights, and obligations of citizenship. Grand jury final reports, therefore, are much more than merely accounts of what citizens did during their year of grand jury service. They are, rather, documents that offer rare insights into how well prepared citizens are for the practice of self-government.

Method

Readers who are interested in the data-collection and analysis phase of this study will find this information in Appendix A. In this section I provide information to assist the reader in understanding the scope of the study and the significance of the tables and charts that reveal the principal findings of the project in this and subsequent chapters.

NUMBER OF FINAL REPORTS

Much of the data in this book are from the 58 California grand jury final reports of 1991–1992.[39] Table 1, "Number of Fiscal- and Calendar-Year Grand Jury Final Reports Reviewed," shows how many final reports reviewed in this study were issued by grand juries of the study period serving either fiscal- or calendar-year terms.[40]

TABLE 1
Number of Fiscal- and Calendar-Year
Grand Jury Final Reports Reviewed

Fiscal Year	52
Calendar Year	6
Total	58

ORGANIZING PROJECT DATA

Accomplishing the project objectives required a method for collecting and classifying several kinds of textual materials developed from reviewing the final reports of the study period. Examples of materials used are:

- Summaries of investigations
- Observations about investigations and other matters in the final reports
- Quotations, figures, references, and the like from the final reports

These and other related materials I entered as "notes" into a computer. In all, I collected nearly 2,000 notes from reading the 58 final reports. Notes ranged from several sentences to two or three pages. In some cases, the project notes were direct quotations of textual or numerical information. In other cases, the notes were paraphrases of larger amounts of original text. Thus, the "summaries" in Chapters 3, 4, and 5 are often abbreviated versions of investigative reports that were two or more pages long.

EVALUATIVE CRITERIA

The study of the civil function of the California grand jury that I conducted 30 years ago was descriptive; I merely summarized and classified grand jury investigations rather than evaluate their quality, legality, or validity. In the years following that study, I noticed that certain types of problems occurred year after year in many final reports. I do not mean that every grand jury in each county issued defective reports each year. In no county do grand jurors issue reports of an identical quality year after year. For example, in one county, for three or four consecutive years, final reports may be objective, significant, and comprehensive. Thereafter, grand jurors in the same county might issue subjective or trivial reports for one or more years. Statewide, however, the most noticeable characteristic of final reports is the regularity with which certain problems recur.

Accordingly, I designed this study to test a method for identifying the problems and determining their frequency. Although I realized that the secrecy and confidentiality of the institution's proceedings would not permit anyone to discover the actual causes of the repeated problems, I believed it might be possible to infer tentatively some of them. To do so, however, would require me to discover the patterns of the problems and their frequency. This necessitated the development of criteria to identify the gap between *what is* and *what should be*.

Study Criteria in Brief

In the next chapter, I describe how I developed the project's evaluative criteria. Nevertheless, a brief discussion of the criteria and their rationale now will help readers orient themselves to the study. I chose the criteria from many sources and experiences, such as:

- observing and consulting with grand juries
- reading newspaper stories about their achievements and problems
- conversing with California grand jurors
- answering questions that grand jurors have asked me in training sessions
- talking to legal advisors about the meanings of statutes affecting the grand jury
- reading what judges write about grand juries when they decide cases involving them
- reviewing applicable statutes
- reading historical works

My focus for this project was not primarily on individual facts but, rather, the repetitive occurrence of issues, problems, or achievements that a body of text (in this case, grand jury final reports of one year) might reveal. Isolated facts, after all, have only limited use for understanding institutions, organizations, or groups of people. My data-gathering strategy therefore became one of searching for recurring patterns in final reports, using three types of criteria:

- Lack of compliance with statutes and case law
- Errors of judgment
- Ineffectively written or designed final reports

The term "criteria" refers to certain qualities or characteristics I used for assessing investigations, reports, and the citizenship skills that created them. I do not think of the criteria as standards, though some might be used as such. In some cases, the criteria are based on applicable grand jury law. In other cases, they are merely categories for organizing similar materials under one name.

Although the law-related criteria are of primary importance, I used two additional sets of criteria for assessing grand jury investigations and reports. The first set (community criteria) refers to the grand jury's relationship to its community. The second set (technical criteria) was used to evaluate grand jury final reports as community documents. I developed these secondary two sets of criteria for the following reasons.

First, some grand jury final reports that are issued each year violate few, if any, legal criteria but nevertheless have limited value for the citizens of the communities in which they are issued and little more for local-government officials. These reports result in no improvement in governance. Second, some final reports contribute to the problem cited earlier: citizens' lack of information about grand juries. For example, although no statute requires grand jurors to account for their workload in their reports to their communities, panels should describe their work, even if only briefly, to inform citizens about the role of the institution in their communities.

These, and the other examples of community criteria I discuss in Chapter 2, provide a basis for assessing how effectively citizens selected for grand jury service permit the civil function of the institution to achieve its purpose. Even though grand jurors might conduct well-conceived and thoroughly planned investigations during their term of service, the investigations will have little value unless final reports are well written and organized, easy to read and understand, and competently designed, printed, and distributed. To assess final reports in these terms, I developed the technical criteria I discuss more fully in Chapter 2.

I explain in detail in Chapter 2 the rationale for each of the study's criteria. In the next section, I show how many examples of each criterion were entered into the computer. I also explain why readers should not assume that the numbers for each criterion are exact counts of their incidence in final reports for the study period.

Number of Examples of Criteria

As I discuss in Appendix A, some of the project data pertaining to final reports of the study period are reasonably accurate counts of the incidence of examples representing the various criteria. For example, the data in Chapter 3, Table 10, pertaining to the number of investigations by county and by topic are generally accurate because the classification categories used to collect these data had been developed for an earlier project.

Although slight discrepancies exist between totals in some of the tables the computer generated for this project, these generally are attributable to refinements I made in the coding guide as the project progressed. Thus, the totals for some of the criteria in Table 2, "Number of Examples for Each of the Criteria," should not be understood to be a measure of the actual incidence of examples of the criteria and other features of final reports of the study period. In some cases, as I explain in Appendix A, the actual incidence in final reports of the problems represented by the criteria may be larger than what is shown in Table 2. In cases where I began the project with criteria that were not subsequently modified (such as jurisdiction and independence, emphasizing procedures rather than policies, achievements of grand juries), the counts are accurate.

TABLE 2
Number of Examples for Each of the Criteria

Criterion	Number of Examples in the Database
Law-related criteria	
Jurisdiction and independence	
Jurisdiction	71
Independence	18
Fair comment	22
Conducting justified investigations	6
Emphasizing procedures rather than policies	27
Validity of investigations and reports	36
Legality and effectiveness of findings and recommendations	43
Confidentiality and secrecy	6
Collegial nature of the grand jury	25
Community criteria	
Achievements	27
Conflict resolution	9
Bureaucratic encounters	11
Examples of well-reported investigations	13
Indictment commentary	11
Significance	7
Accountability	14
Continuity	52
Technical criteria	36
Total	434

The tally for "legality and effectiveness of findings and recommendations" is an example of a criterion that certainly is much smaller than the actual incidence of problems it represents.[41] When I made notes from final reports of sufficient examples to represent this criterion adequately, I stopped entering additional examples of it into the computer. The count (7) for "Significance" in Table 2 also is much lower than a complete census of that criterion would yield. The number shown means that I entered into the computer only seven examples for the criterion. In fact, far more examples of triviality are contained in the final reports of the study period than this number implies.

In its present form, the revised classification guide could be used in a future study to obtain an accurate count of the various types of problems and other concerns represented by project criteria. Though I cannot predict what the actual number for each criterion might be, I am certain that the grand total of the problems shown in Table 2 would be somewhat larger than it now is. In later chapters, I offer suggestions for eliminating the problems that the evaluative criteria represent.

USE OF FINAL REPORTS

Most of the information in this study was obtained by reading final reports rather than by interviewing grand jurors or by observing grand jury proceedings. Interviewing sitting grand jurors about their investigations and observing their deliberations would have added much to the study. The nature of the institution, however, forbids using such methods. The statutes and case law render the internal workings and deliberations of grand juries inaccessible to scholars, news-media representatives, and other persons who might wish to observe panel members at work.[42]

Some other sources of information about grand juries are, of course, available—for example, newspaper stories about internal grand jury problems,[43] anecdotal information from former grand jurors,[44] and the recollections of public officials or other citizens who have had dealings with grand juries.[45] This sort of material, however, is frequently difficult to obtain and verify or is otherwise limited and may not fairly represent the activities of grand juries throughout the State. The main reason, however, for using final reports as this study's chief source of data is that these reports are the official public records of grand jury activity. They also are the most important product of the institution.

Scope, Limitations, and Validity

Although the final reports represented in this study were released early in the decade of the 1990s, the problems of the study period would not likely be different in kind or quantity if the study were repeated today. Indeed, a perusal of grand jury final reports that were issued in the years following the study period confirms a major project finding that I discuss in Chapters 7 and 8: Many of the institution's problems are deeply rooted in the traditions that grand jurors, public officials, and other people have created for it. Furthermore, the passage of time has permitted some of the project data to acquire significance that would not otherwise be possible. For example, readers will see that an example, during the study period, of rarely reported ill will between a grand jury and a public official resulted in a major legislative setback for the institution several years later.

Scope and Limitations

The data from final reports in this study are from California's 57 counties for the fiscal year 1991–1992 and calendar year 1992. The study also includes information from the Grand Jury of the City and County of San Francisco for fiscal year 1991–1992. Occasionally I cite references to grand jury reports or other materials outside of the study period, but in general, the examples from grand jury investigations are confined to that time. The study also contains references to correspondence, grand jury procedures manuals, case law, statutes affecting grand juries, and quotations from newspaper stories. Although anecdotal comments by former grand jurors occasionally are included, these are anonymous. Citations from various legal periodicals and related publications also are included in the study.

The focus of this research generally is limited to the so-called civil authority of California grand juries. Most of the literature and many of the grand jury handbooks or procedures manuals characterize the grand jury as having three types of authority:

1. Issuing or declining to issue true bills of indictment (Penal Code Section 889)
2. Hearing testimony and considering evidence that may result in the removal, by accusation, of public officers from office if they are subsequently found guilty of willful misfeasance, malfeasance, or nonfeasance (Government Code Section 3060)
3. Reporting the results of investigations into designated local governments as authorized in the statutes described in Chapter 2.

This study is concerned with the third power, sometimes informally referred to as the "watchdog function." Though these three powers often are treated as separate functions, in specific cases they may be related. For example, a grand jury might discover indications of criminal wrongdoing, or mis-, mal-, or nonfeasance while investigating local governments. Thus, what might begin as a routine concern about the efficiency, effectiveness, systems, or procedures of a local government could result in a trial under the indictment or accusation statutes. From the point of view of some public officials, the possible exercise of the first two powers is what makes the exercise of the last power significant.

Some readers might be surprised that the study includes only meager information about grand jury indictments. Grand jury indictments certainly are a subject of interest and significance in the California criminal justice system; however, they usually have little to do with the civil function. Essentially, indictments are legal proceedings involving grand juries by which a district attorney might initiate a prosecution against someone suspected of committing a felony. By using indictments, prosecutors need not bring their cases to preliminary hearings. From a prosecutor's point of view, this has some advantages. From a broader social perspective, indictments play a numerically insignificant role in the administration of criminal justice. Of the tens of thousands of felony arrests that peace officers make each year in California, only a small percentage leads to indictments.[46]

Unlike panels of earlier times, California grand juries do not customarily initiate indictments. According to an opinion of the Attorney General of California, grand juries have no choice but to hear an indictment when a prosecutor so demands.[47] Because indictments are criminal matters, I have included in this study only a few references to them. Readers likewise will find only minor references to the accusation function because I found only one reference to them in final reports of the study period.[48] The study, however, will include several quotations from final reports in which grand juries commented about the relationship of indictments to the grand jury's civil function or about the advantages and disadvantages of indictments.

The study also excludes or treats only briefly other important facets of the California grand jury. For example, I include little about the methods grand juries use in their civil investigations. Grand juries themselves rarely provide information about these matters in their final reports. The study similarly excludes a Statewide analysis of a matter of great interest to many people: methods for selecting the men and women who serve on grand juries.[49]

Grand jury selection is a politically sensitive issue in many counties, and as many systems exist for selecting grand jurors as there are counties. In some counties, the method used each year varies according to which judge is responsible that year for selecting grand jurors. If the question is asked, "How are grand juries in a given county actually selected?" rather than "What does the law say about the selection of grand jurors?" research techniques entirely different from those used in this study must be employed to obtain an answer.

Unfortunately, the research methods required to answer the first question on a Statewide basis require far more resources and insider information than is needed to answer the second question. Because the method used to select grand jurors could affect how they choose investigative topics and what they say in their reports about them, I will discuss briefly several aspects of grand jury selection. In doing so, I emphasize the political rather than the statutory reality of the process.

If the realities of grand jury selection defy documentation, some insight into the controversy that swirls each year about grand jury selection can be sensed from newspaper stories about this issue in recent years. The headlines of these stories included concerns about the political-party makeup of grand juries, their racial composition, and purported nepotism in grand jury selection.[50]

At the beginning of the grand jury year in some counties, the press traditionally reports the names of persons whom the courts have impaneled for grand jury service. News stories, unfortunately, rarely describe the specific procedures officials use to nominate citizens for grand jury service. If reporters do attempt to describe grand jury selection, most of them accept without verification the explanations that court administrative officers or judges offer. Thus, many news stories about grand jury selection may employ such terms as "random" or "representative" without inquiring more deeply into the methods actually used. Given the vagueness of the current statutes governing the selection of grand jurors for the civil function,[51] a completely unrepresentative body of grand jurors may be lawfully impaneled. A grand jury might, for example, consist entirely of the business associates of one or two county supervisors; or grand jurors might all be the friends, relatives, and campaign workers of the elected officials of cities, school districts, special districts, and other institutions within the jurisdiction of grand juries. In some counties, several members of panels are often employed by, or recently retired from, local governments over which grand juries have statutory authority. If challenged, public officials and judges who nominated or impaneled these persons for grand jury service can truthfully say, "We followed the law."

Readers interested in how the courts select grand juries in their counties may themselves conduct research into this matter using some information in final reports. For example, all civil grand juries in California list the names of grand jurors in their final reports, and some final reports include information about the occupations of panel members. An inspection of these lists might reveal certain patterns in grand jury selection, such as how many men and women are selected,[52] or whether an unusually large number of current or former public employees constitutes the panel. Some grand juries identify in final reports the names of the communities in which grand jurors reside; a review of this information might disclose how representative the grand jury is of the entire county or whether most grand jurors live in the district of a certain county supervisor or some other elected official who could have nominated them for grand jury service.

Even this brief discussion of selecting grand jurors illustrates its implications for grand jury investigations and reports. Because final reports reveal little about the representativeness of civil grand juries, I include nothing more about the matter in this chapter. In Chapter 7, however, I discuss several implications of grand jury selection for the validity of final reports.

Because this study employs legal criteria to evaluate investigations and final reports, it necessarily focuses on the grand jury's problems rather than its accomplishments. I would like to have included more information about the achievements of grand juries, but documented proof of achievements is difficult to find either in final reports or elsewhere. Grand jurors often provide oral accounts at the Grand Jury Exchange Seminars about grand jury accomplishments, but these appear only rarely in final reports. Newspaper reporters also write stories occasionally about grand jury accomplishments, but no single source of news stories about grand jury achievements each year in California is available. The impression that grand juries accomplish little is thereby reinforced because grand jurors have developed no tradition of accumulating and reporting evidence of the institution's accomplishments.[53]

A discussion about orienting the book toward the grand jury's problems raises a point closely connected to the essence of the institution: the emotional investment of many grand jurors in their year of service. At the Grand Jury Exchange Seminars, some grand jurors occasionally object to the problem orientation of the workshops and forums. As one person wrote in an evaluation, "It is difficult enough being a grand juror without hearing about all these problems. We need support, not criticism." Comments such as this could compromise the integrity of the institution to serve the emotional needs of grand jurors. Most of the problems this book addresses are created by grand jurors, not the institution.

As subsequent chapters will show, to function effectively, the grand jury requires the selection of jurors who are willing and competent to learn the statutory scheme of the institution and to subordinate their personal desires and expectations to the statutory reality of its powers. Grand jurors who do not accept responsibility for understanding equally well the breadth and limitations of the institution's powers have failed to honor the requirement of diligence they affirmed in taking the grand juror's oath.

The authors of some examples discussed in this study might object that information about the context of an investigation or report, or other information that was not revealed in the reports, would cast the examples in a more favorable light. I have tried to take context into account, insofar as it was revealed in reports. The explanation that a more thorough understanding of information not published might justify a finding or recommendation raises an interesting point—namely, that readers can draw conclusions only from what they read, not from what might have been written but was not.

Some of the criticisms in this study are about grand jury activities for which there is no statutory authority. Consider, for example, grand juries that recommend, oppose, or support legislation. Some grand jurors or other citizens attempt to justify this practice as a common-law function of grand juries. This study, however, follows the holdings of several courts that grand juries may exercise only those powers that the Legislature has granted them.[54] If, therefore, no statute authorizes grand juries to oppose, support, or propose legislation, that activity would be extra-legal. Just because some grand juries have engaged in this practice for years, even to the point of creating standing committees for this purpose, that is not sufficient reason to justify it.

I offer one more explanation of the problem orientation of this study. Notwithstanding the low estate to which it occasionally falls, the California grand jury as an institution has remarkable potential. It is one of the few institutions today in the United States that allow citizens to study government firsthand and to propose recommendations to improve it. Given the range of its powers and jurisdiction, the grand jury is, or could be, a force for civic improvement. When a grand jury in a county fails to achieve this potential, a defect of knowledge, strategy, judgment, motivation, fairness, or energy of individual grand jurors is often the reason. To those who advocate ignoring these defects, I commend the words of C. S. Lewis: "The real traitor to our order is not the man who speaks within that order of its faults, but the man who flatters our corporate self-complacency."[55]

Validity

The validity of grand jury investigations and reports is difficult to assess using only what grand jury final reports contain. As will be explained in later chapters, findings in final reports are frequently undocumented. Similarly, many grand jury recommendations are not supported by findings. Unsubstantiated conclusions also are the basis of many grand jury recommendations, and the investigative principle of corroboration often is not followed, or if it is followed, it is not reported. Or a report might seem to be well documented, but someone analyzing it with knowledge of local circumstances might be able to refute one or more of its facts in whole or in part.

In assessing the validity of final reports, I could not, and therefore did not, verify that every purported fact in each report was accurate. Instead, I employed a definition of factuality advanced by a leading authority of general semantics: A factual statement is one that is written so it is verifiable.[56] Thus, if a finding in a routine report of a civil inquiry is not documented with at least one verifiable fact, I consider the finding, and any recommendation derived from it, invalid.

The study relies on what grand juries reported and assumes, barring evidence to the contrary, that grand juries and their legal advisors have taken appropriate safeguards to issue valid reports. Besides any internal procedures that grand juries might adopt to ensure it, three other important determinants of the validity of reports are:

- Section 916 of the Penal Code, which requires grand juries to include in final reports only data that have been approved by the number of grand jurors appropriate for the size of the panel[57]
- Penal Code Sections 914 and 914.1, which direct superior court judges to call grand jurors' attention to the need to conduct investigations in compliance with applicable statutes

- Penal Code Section 933(a), which requires grand juries to send their final reports to the presiding judges before they are publicly distributed[58]

Readers familiar with statutes governing California grand juries might wonder why I did not include in this study the comments that local-government officials are required to make about findings and recommendations affecting them or their departments.[59] These comments certainly would have increased readers' understanding of how local-government officials react to grand jury reports. For reasons I shall discuss later, however, obtaining copies of the comments is costly and difficult. Similarly, few final reports contain information about what grand juries discovered if they studied the comments by public officials concerning the findings and recommendations in the reports of their predecessors.

The study also includes little information about the politics, conflicts, or controversies of grand jury service. Final reports rarely include this sort of information, and although the press occasionally reports such incidents, I know of no practical way routinely to collect news reports about these matters from the several hundred California daily and weekly newspapers.

OTHER RESEARCH STRATEGIES

Although this study evaluates investigations in final reports for their compliance with legal criteria, grand juries could be assessed from other perspectives. For example, a benefit-cost approach would consider whether expenditures for grand juries are offset by the amount of money grand juries save local governments by offering effective recommendations to improve services or procedures. Even though this method has considerable appeal, the logistics required to document and verify the acceptance or rejection of grand jury recommendations were beyond the resources of the project.

Still another approach would be to send a questionnaire to grand jurors seeking their opinions about selected matters concerning their service as grand jurors. Although a mailed questionnaire might yield interesting information, the methods and results of that type of survey would be subject to limitations even more serious than those of the present study. Even if it were possible to obtain their home addresses, many grand jurors would be concerned that someone was able to do so.

Other problems arise in mailing questionnaires to grand jury offices in county government, not the least of which is that, for one reason or another, each grand juror might not receive his or her copy. Second, the opinions of grand jurors and their knowledge or beliefs about the institution would differ according to the stage during their term of service when they received their questionnaires. Responses to a questionnaire received at the end of their term might be better informed, in some cases, than those obtained at the beginning of their term.

If grand jurors were to receive questionnaires during their last few months of service, however, they might be so involved in the details of producing their final report that their willingness to answer a questionnaire would be affected. Indeed, a high return rate from grand jurors during this period might be of questionable validity if the respondents were grand jurors who accomplished so little during their term that they had time for participating in a survey. Thus, a high rate of returned questionnaires between March and May might mean a bias in the direction of apathetic panels. Finally, given the large number of trivial investigations and reports the project disclosed, answers from persons responsible for them would seem to have limited value in contrast to a research strategy based on final reports that reveal what grand jurors actually accomplished rather than what they claim to have achieved.

One of America's most astute observers of bureaucracy recommends that we "judge organizations by their results."[60] Although a pragmatic approach is useful, for this study I modified that suggestion to read, "Judge the grand jury by its compliance with the laws that govern how it attains its objectives." Evaluating grand juries by the results they achieve presents a considerable logistic problem because grand jurors rarely document their achievements in final reports. Even if grand juries were to record their achievements and those of their predecessors, the volume of findings and recommendations in final reports Statewide is so large that much time, effort, and money would be required for independent corroboration of even a representative sample of grand jury claims of accomplishments.

Ideally, of course, a combination of a legal- and a results-oriented method would have provided a more comprehensive assessment of the institution. My resources for the project, however, did not permit an independent assessment of each grand jury finding and recommendation in terms of their effects on the local governments of each of the 57 counties of California and the City and County of San Francisco.

Definitions and Organization

The Glossary contains definitions of selected technical terms used in this book or that are otherwise associated with grand jury service. I have prepared the Glossary for the use of citizens who have no formal background in criminal justice. Therefore, some of the definitions lack the technical exactitude one would find, for example, in a dictionary of legal terms. In most cases, however, the Glossary should assist readers in understanding certain words and phrases of legal origins that are used in this book.[61]

DEFINITIONS

Readers will be assisted by understanding several conventions I follow in using certain words and phrases in this study. For example, throughout the book I refer to "the panel" or "panels" to relieve the monotony of using "grand jury" or "grand juries." Occasionally I use the term "the grand jury" in reference to the institution in general rather than a specific county grand jury. The term should not be understood to refer to a State grand jury, as none exists in California.

I also hope readers will avoid the word-use traps into which some grand jurors occasionally fall. Of these, the "allness" problem is especially serious.[62] For example, in referring to the grand jury's authority or to the local governments over which it has jurisdiction, I often refer to "designated powers" or "designated local governments." In using these terms, I emphasize that California grand juries do not have broad, unlimited authority, nor do they have powers in every aspect of local government, nor in State or federal government. In like manner, I have avoided referring to the grand jury as "a court of last resort," or as an "ombudsman." These terms convey an unrealistic impression of the grand jury. Similarly, I use "civil function" rather than "watchdog powers" because the latter, I believe, is a somewhat misleading, romanticized characterization of the institution.

The use of "county government" as a synonym for local government is a variant of the allness problem. In grand jury handbooks and final reports, readers frequently encounter assertions such as, "Grand juries are the watchdogs of county government." If grand juries are indeed watchdogs, this responsibility extends beyond county government, for counties are but one type of local government in California. I believe the imprecise use of "county government" for "local government" is one reason why grand juries spend more of their time and resources in county government than in any of the other local governments over which they have jurisdiction.[63]

Throughout this study, I use "spirit of the institution" as a general term for how the common law, California statutes, and its lawful traditions and practices have defined the grand jury. Although the phrase cannot be found in the statutes, the courts occasionally have expressed a similar concept in case law; for example:

> In our system of government, a grand jury is the only agency free from possible political or official bias that has an opportunity to see the picture of crime and the operation of government relating thereto on any broad basis. It performs a valuable public purpose in presenting its conclusions drawn from that overview.[64]

An important implication of statements such as these is that certain practices must be followed to preserve institutional integrity. For example, freedom from "possible political or official bias" has significance for how courts select grand jurors. Thus, to the extent that grand jurors are the friends, political allies, relatives, or campaign managers of local-government officials or judges themselves, the spirit of the institution is tarnished. Similarly, if the grand jury must have a disinterested view of the "operation of government," appointing large numbers of public employees to a panel raises questions about its impartiality in investigating the local governments employing them.

If conclusions of grand juries are to provide a "valuable public purpose," the facts and findings underlying them must be drawn objectively and fairly. Moreover, nothing should interfere with how grand jurors decide which issues to investigate and the proper methods to use for investigations. Panel members should, in short, have complete independence in these matters. In this context, the relationships of grand jurors to district attorneys, other county staff members, former grand jurors, or other private persons or organizations is potentially corrupting. If, even with the best of intentions, these persons influence the grand jury, its independence is in jeopardy, if not entirely subverted. Similarly, if grand jurors enter into "partnerships" with local-government officials, represent their panels on local-government decision-making bodies, or accept the hospitality of public officials at receptions, retreats, or entertainment events, independence is further compromised and the spirit of the institution thereby sullied.

Brochures that grand jurors distribute throughout their communities occasionally contain terms such as "conscience of the community" or "cross-section of the people" to characterize the institution. These terms imply a broadly represented, annual fresh outlook on local-government affairs. Any practice, therefore, by which the same people are repeatedly appointed to grand juries tarnishes the spirit of the institution. Similarly, if grand jurors do not do everything feasible to avoid the influence of self-interest and self-aggrandizement, or the signs thereof, the institution is blemished.

Corruption may not be intentional in the criminal sense. Ignorance, unwillingness to take time to read and understand the statutes governing the institution, or acting on expedience rather than on principle are not felonies or misdemeanors. Even so, they do little to honor the institution. Unlike the legal criteria discussed in Chapter 2, the *spirit of the institution* is a broader and more abstract criterion but, nonetheless, is important. I do not mean the phrase to have deeply philosophical or idealistic significance, nor do I intend it to glorify the institution. I use *spirit of the institution* merely to represent briefly the ethical, moral, and legal foundations of the institution. In Chapter 7, I discuss this criterion further in the context of citizenship.

Readers will encounter one more term later in this book that requires explanation: *civic values*. By this term, I refer to certain basic propositions of civic life. Rather than quote a definition of this term from a dictionary, a political science textbook, or a scholarly work about constitutional law, I offer a hypothetical discussion between two civil grand jurors. Although this imaginary discussion is not a technical definition of civic values, it illustrates how they might arise in grand jury service and how they might affect grand jury deliberations.

Assume that our fictional grand jurors have just learned about an amendment to Penal Code Section 914. The amendment, subsection b, requires the superior court of each county, "in consultation with the district attorney, the county counsel, and at least one former grand juror," to ensure that civil grand jurors receive "training that addresses, at a minimum, report writing, interviews, and the scope of the grand jury's responsibility and statutory authority."

One of our two fictional grand jurors begins the discussion about the amendment with this comment: "What a wonderful idea! The judge, the district attorney, and the county counsel are just the people to help us learn our job."

The second grand juror replies, "Well, that may be, but aren't the district attorney and the county counsel public officials? And isn't it the job of the grand jury to see that public officials perform their duties effectively and honestly? Can we rely on them to train us objectively?"

The first grand juror might reply, "Surely one can be too suspicious. Besides, who else is better qualified to train us? This new law requires these officials to take time out of their busy workday to help us keep out of trouble. I think we should be thankful that the law exists rather than question its intent."

Pausing for a moment, the second grand juror answers, "It's not a question of suspicion. The point is that the county counsel is the official lawyer for the very people whose offices we're going to study. And yet he's involved in training us about how to review his clients' official activities. If he's supposed to look out for his clients' best interests, how can he train us objectively? There's something odd about this arrangement."

To this, the first grand juror counters, "Look, we've got to assume that these officials are honest, sincere, and dedicated. You're starting your term as a grand juror with a prejudiced attitude toward public officials. With that attitude, you can't be very objective yourself."

"Prejudice works both ways," the second grand juror responds. "You seem to be starting your year of service with your own preconceptions. I'm just saying that we need to recognize that it might be a good idea to do some studying on our own. Besides, I'm not too comfortable with having a former grand juror involved in training us. Aren't we supposed to be a new grand jury with no ties to the old? Why should we assume that just because a former grand juror had a year on the grand jury before us, he learned anything? You may think the new law is a blessing, but I think it can be potentially corrupting for grand juries. After all, the judge urged us to remember that the grand jury is an independent body."

The conversation need not be extended. It should be obvious that both grand jurors' arguments reveal underlying beliefs about citizenship, grand jury service, and the nature of government. In this brief conversation, for example, one can detect several civic values at work: attitudes about the nature of government and public officials, citizenship, and the purpose of grand jury service. More will be said of other civic values in Chapters 7 and 8.

ORGANIZATION

In Chapter 2, I describe the development of the criteria used to evaluate grand jury investigations and reports discussed in Chapters 4 and 5. It is based on statutes and case law that directly or indirectly affect the grand jury's civil function. The chapter also includes a discussion of selected opinions by grand jury legal advisors concerning the civil powers of grand juries. Similarly, Chapter 2 briefly covers what grand jurors learn about their powers from their procedures manuals and the judicial charges they receive at the beginning of their year of service.

Chapter 3 presents data regarding the numbers and types of investigations in grand jury final reports for the study period and includes examples of the meager information in final reports about grand jury achievements. The chapter also provides summaries of grand jury investigations that illustrate exceptionally well-conceived and executed investigations.

Chapters 4 and 5 provide information about grand jury organization and procedures and give examples of problems grouped according to the criteria described in Chapter 2. Chapter 6 offers suggestions that are within the discretion of grand jurors to improve grand jury investigations and reports. In Chapter 7, I discuss the history of the grand jury, including the spirit of the institution and its relationship to the grand jury culture and selected institutionalized problems and their solutions. Comments about selecting grand jurors are followed by suggestions for legislation to improve grand jury investigations and reports. The suggestions are organized according to the criteria developed in Chapter 2. Chapter 8 concludes the study with a discussion of implications of grand jury investigations and reports for self-government, citizen competence, and the institutional future of the grand jury. Following the text, the end matter contains an index, a glossary, appendices, and suggestions for additional reading.

Summary and Conclusion

The California civil grand jury provides an unusual opportunity for people conducting research in citizenship, self-government, and citizen competence. To the extent that grand jurors achieve the full potential of the statutes defining the institution, it is in the hands of capable people with well-developed skills of self-government. On the other hand, if the institution is abused by the pursuit of trivial problems, is degraded by the misuse of its powers, and is compromised by an inadequate understanding of its independence, the lack of the citizenship skills of self-government could be an important cause.

Using grand jury final reports, this study examines how effectively California grand jurors during the study period created procedures that resulted in final reports within the institution's statutory framework. Similarly, the study's evaluative criteria are concerned with how effectively final reports during the study period documented the workload of the institution and informed citizens in the community of grand jury findings and recommendations. To achieve the study's objectives, I evaluated grand jury investigations and final reports by using two types of criteria: legal and nonlegal.

Grand jury final reports were the chief source of data for this study. Legal restrictions prohibit researchers and other citizens from observing grand jury meetings and asking grand jurors about the work of the institution. Grand jury final reports are the institution's most important means of accomplishing its objectives. Because they may be published only after the courts ascertain that they have complied with certain statutory requirements, the reports are the most readily available and reliable insight into how effectively grand jurors use their citizenship skills to fulfill the institution's potential.

2

Legal Aspects of the Grand Jury's Investigating and Reporting Powers

When California grand juries issue reports of civil investigations, they exercise an ancient power. In their history of local government in England, Sidney and Beatrice Webb present evidence that English grand juries conducted civil investigations before the Industrial Revolution. This quotation, for example, is a brief account of grand jury investigations in late seventeenth-century England:

> Yet, even in 1689, it was still taken for granted that, when the county gaol or the county hall was out of repair, or the county bridges needed amendment, it was for the grand jury to initiate the proceedings by a formal presentment, before any action was taken by the justices.[1]

The grand jury that the Webbs wrote about was a common-law institution, deriving its powers from tradition and precedent rather than statutes. The California grand jury of today is not, however, a common-law body and may exercise only the investigating and reporting powers the Legislature has granted it.[2] Because the California Legislature, rather than tradition, is today the source of the grand jury's civil investigating and reporting powers, an assessment of the grand jury's effectiveness must consider the institution's adherence to the law. The purpose of this chapter is to survey the law governing grand jury investigating and reporting powers to create a framework of legal criteria for the next two chapters.

Although I have limited my inquiry to laws directly governing the grand jury's investigating and reporting powers, other grand jury statutes affect these powers, if only indirectly. For example, the effectiveness of a final report depends on how judges apply laws governing the selection of grand jurors. A final report of a grand jury dominated by retired county employees may be markedly different from reports of grand juries dominated by farmers, business owners, medical doctors, or retired military officers. Similarly, a grand jury whose members average 65 years of age may produce a final report different in some respects from that of a panel of much younger persons. Although these matters are of considerable interest, they require exposition beyond the scope of this study. Instead, this chapter is restricted to developing criteria for assessing grand jury investigations and reports.

Legal Sources of Grand Jury Authority to Investigate and Report

The grand jury derives its authority from three legal sources:
- The California Constitution
- Statutes
- Case law (sometimes called "decisional" law)

We shall consider each of these in turn. Because many grand juries also rely on handbooks, guides, or procedures manuals as compendia of applicable laws, we also shall briefly review examples of these materials. This section also includes selected opinions by legal advisors for grand juries and examples of charges (instructions) that judges give to California panels.

Before beginning our review of laws governing the California grand jury's investigating and reporting powers, several matters must be understood. *First,* not all the grand jury's reporting authority is stated explicitly in the statutes. For example, grand juries may lawfully issue reports about school districts, yet the words "school districts" are not found in grand jury statutes. We shall see later how grand juries nevertheless can lawfully exercise designated investigating and reporting powers in school districts.

Second, the Legislature has given grand juries little guidance in how to use their investigating and reporting powers. For instance, panels are left to decide the format of reports, how much time to spend on each type of local government, and how to select issues or topics to investigate.

Third, the Legislature did not grant investigating and reporting powers to the grand jury in one legislative session. The powers we shall review developed over many years.

The patchwork manner in which the modern grand jury acquired its powers has more than historical significance. Because the grand jury first exercised its civil investigating and reporting powers in county government, for example, that form of government first captured grand jurors' attention and continues to dominate it today. It might also explain why public officials in some of the newer forms of local government (local agency formation commissions, business improvement districts, and redevelopment agencies, for example) may at times express surprise when they learn that a grand jury is investigating their agencies.

When we consider the principle that the grand jury may do only what the Legislature authorizes, we refer to the grand jury's *jurisdiction.* Jurisdiction also has a geographical sense. Thus, the physical borders of a grand jury's work are the boundary lines of each county; again, this principle has minor exceptions.[3] An Attorney General's opinion, for example, defines a circumstance in which grand jury committees of two or more counties may lawfully meet together, but not the entire panels.[4]

In reading the remainder of this chapter, readers are cautioned that although the laws and legal opinions affecting the civil grand jury change slowly, they do change. For example, the holdings of several important appellate cases of recent decades are not yet incorporated into the statutes. Similarly, in a few cases, statutes have made obsolete certain opinions of the Attorney General of the State of California. As needed, I shall comment about changes in statutes that occurred after the study period, and in Chapter 7, I offer suggestions to align statutory law concerning the civil grand jury with case law.

COMMON-LAW ORIGINS

Before continuing, we must return briefly to the concept of the "common law."[5] As a common-law institution, the English grand jury developed slowly by acquiring its duties and powers by the accretion of hundreds of years of custom and tradition rather than from legislation. As the grand jury slowly expanded its scope, a tradition emerged that was common to each of the counties of England. Thus, few, if any, of the English grand jury's powers were formalized as written laws. The common law was the unwritten but accepted authority for the institution's existence. When the grand jury arrived in America, it continued to exercise its investigating and reporting authority under common law rather than statutes. Because statutes define the structure of so much of American government, legislatures slowly eliminated, severely curtailed, or codified in statutes many of the grand jury's ancient common-law investigating and reporting powers.

By enacting statutes to define the grand jury's powers, the Legislature substituted itself for tradition and common law and thereby established itself as the sole authority for deciding which powers grand juries shall or shall not exercise.[6] Accordingly, we review these legislative grants of authority to extract from them criteria for assessing how grand juries use their powers.

THE CALIFORNIA CONSTITUTION

Although one might think that the California Constitution is the grand jury's primary authority for reporting its findings and recommendations about local government, the Constitution contains nothing regarding the grand jury's investigating and reporting powers. Article 1, Section 23, of the California Constitution merely provides that at least one grand jury shall be drawn and summoned in each county each year. No Constitutional barrier, therefore, would prevent the Legislature from eliminating the statutes defining the grand jury's investigating and reporting powers.

STATUTES IN THE PENAL CODE

Most of the investigating and reporting powers of the California grand jury are defined in statutes between Penal Code Sections 888 and 940.[7] The grouping of the statutes, the wording of their titles, and their sequence make them awkward to read for people who are inexperienced in legal terms and concepts.[8] As a result, few grand jurors learn their responsibilities by reading statutes; instead, most of them rely on local-government officials to explain the duties and responsibilities of the institution.

Another problem for persons trying to find statutes regarding specific grand jury powers is that the index to the Penal Code uses legal terms rather than commonly understood words or phrases. For example, a layman who wants to find the statute concerning libel or unauthorized comment about public officials in final reports probably would look for "libel" in the Penal Code index. Curiously, neither the index nor Penal Code Section 930 contains "libel" or any other word that a layman might use in discussing the matter. A reader must be a lawyer, or at least have some training in legal terminology, to associate the statute with the word it employs: *privilege*. Similarly, the word *plagiarism* is not in the index to the Penal Code, nor is the word used in the statute that forbids it: Penal Code Section 939.9.

Authority for Investigations and Reports

One way to survey the investigating and reporting powers of the grand jury is to scan applicable statutes for their key nouns or verbs. This technique must not replace a close reading of the statutes and case law but is useful as a preliminary review of grand jury law. Table 3, "Civil Jurisdiction and Methods of the California Civil Grand Jury, with Applicable Code Section(s)," shows the key words or phrases authorizing the grand jury's investigating and reporting powers. The first section of Table 3 (Jurisdiction) displays words or phrases concerning the jurisdiction of the grand jury. The second section (Methods) lists words or phrases describing the authorized methods for executing the investigating and reporting powers.

TABLE 3
Civil Jurisdiction and Methods of the California Civil Grand Jury, with Applicable Code Section(s)

Jurisdiction	Code Section(s)
Abolition or creation of agencies or offices	888; 925(a)*; 928*
City or incorporated city; cities	925(a)*
County assessor	926(b)
County matters of civil concern	888
County officers, departments, functions	888; 914.1; **925***; 928*
Districts, other	**925***
Equipment	888; 925(a)*; 928*
Housing affairs and authority	933.1
Jails	919(a)
Joint powers agency, authority	925(a)*; 933.1
Land, sales and transfers, escheat; escheat proceedings	920*
Local Agency Formation Commission	933.5
Method or system of performing duties	888; 925(a)*; 928*; 933.1; 933.5; 933.6*
Needs of county officers, books, documents	888; 928*
Nonprofit corporation ... established by or operating on behalf of public entity	933.6
Operations, accounts, records; books, documents	925(a)*; 926; 933.1; 933.5; 933.6
Peace officer personnel records, grand jury access to	832.7
Performance of duties	888; 933.1; 933.5; 933.6
Persons imprisoned but not indicted	919(a)
Prisons, grand jury entitled to free access	921
Prisons, public, condition and management	**919(b)***; 921
Public offenses, indictment	917
Public offense, individual juror, declares	918
Public officers (removal of district, county, city officers for willful, corrupt misconduct)	**919(c)***; 922; G.C. 3060
Purchase, lease, or sale of equipment	888
Redevelopment agency	933.1
Salaries of county-elected officials (*Shall*, if requested)	927*
School districts (not specifically mentioned; see endnote 11)	
Special legislative district or other district in the county	**925**
Special-purpose assessing or taxing district	933.5

(Table Continued)

TABLE 3, *Continued*

Methods	Code Section(s)
Ascertain	914.1
Documented evidence	916*
Findings	933*
Inquire	888; 914.1
Interviews	916*
Investigate and report; investigation	914.1; 925(a)*; 918; 920*; 928*; 933.6
Recommendations	933*
Records, public; access to	921
Report	**925***
Selective basis (for deciding what to investigate)	925*; **928***
Suit, to recover money	932

*Note: Statute section numbers in bold print are mandated responsibilities. Asterisks identify discretionary authority. Statute includes the word "shall" either in connection with a mandated grand jury investigation or in connection with some other duty related to the investigation.

Table 3 may be thought of as the skeleton of the grand jury's investigating and reporting jurisdiction. It presents in abbreviated form the investigating and reporting authority the Legislature has given the grand jury. If the Legislature has not designated in a statute a certain grand jury activity or a specific local-government service or function, the grand jury has no authority in the matter. Thus, what is not in Table 3 is as important as what is in it. For example, no words in the table authorize the grand jury to recommend, support, or oppose legislation. It also includes no reference to State[9] or federal government, and no reference to private individuals may be found. Similarly, the words or phrases in the table give grand juries no power to enforce the implementation of their recommendations.

The key words in Table 3 refer to matters such as "equipment," "methods or systems," "books, documents," and so on. These words give the grand jury no authority in matters of public policy; the grand jury's investigating and reporting powers are defined by words referring to economy, effectiveness, and efficiency rather than approving or condemning the wisdom or social value of local-government policies. Essentially, the grand jury's jurisdiction lies in the means rather than the ends of designated local governments.

Thus, grand juries are authorized to criticize only the procedures, not the policies, of local governments. This limitation of grand jury powers demoralizes some newly appointed grand jurors who do not understand the difference between policy and procedures. The distinctions between policy and procedure, policy and method, or policy and operations are often subtle. Even superior court judges occasionally express frustration in explaining to grand jurors the panel's lack of authority to criticize, challenge, question, or support local-government policies:

> You are not there, please keep in mind, to second guess decisions. Most agencies and people in government are given by the laws that govern their activities a certain latitude or discretion to act. So long as they act properly, that is, without bias and without prejudice and with some reasonable basis, they may come up with a decision with which you disagree, with which another person in their position might disagree, but if it is a decision that is within the discretion that they are vested to reach, and if they have acted properly, they haven't been bribed, they didn't flip a coin, they investigated reasonably well, then the Grand Jury has no business investigating that decision unless, of course, it is a pattern of wrongness that obviously means something else. The distinction I am drawing—I assume I am communicating, while it is difficult for me to find the words—that there is a difference between inefficiencies or ineffectiveness in government or improper conduct, and simply decisions that are controversial or with which people have disagreement.[10]

Like most citizens, many grand jurors have had no reason before grand jury service to think about such distinctions unless they had served as public officials or had studied these matters in civics or public administration courses. Even with careful study, the distinction between what is policy and what is procedure is, in some cases, elusive. One county counsel explained the difference using this illustration:

> [A]s is the case generally with grand jury civil jurisdiction, there is no authority to "second guess" a substantive exercise of judgmental discretion by a school district governing body. For example, a school district governing board might decide to buy ten buses, and a grand jury might think that eight was adequate. So long as the purchase of ten buses was reasonably debatable and within the authority of the governing board, the jury would have no jurisdiction on the question of the number of buses to be purchased. On the other hand, if the governing board used an improvident method to buy the buses, then that would be a proper subject of grand jury inquiry under the "method or system" language of [the applicable statutes].[11]

No words or phrases in Table 3 suggest that the Legislature intends the grand jury to exercise unlimited authority as an "ombudsman" or a "court of last resort." Although one can find such lofty phrases in grand jury handbooks, procedures manuals, final reports, or brochures, these conceptions are in the minds of grand jurors rather than in the statutes. In the absence of legislative authority to criticize local-government policies or to overturn administrative or legislative decisions, grand juries exceed their jurisdiction by addressing such matters in their reports.

Although the legislature has given grand juries the authority designated in Table 3, the words and phrases of these statutes are left to grand jurors and their legal advisors to construe. For example, Penal Code Section 888 allows the grand jury to "investigate or inquire into" the "abolition or creation of offices." That section, however, provides no definition or examples of what these words mean. Grand jurors occasionally wonder if the statute permits grand juries to recommend the consolidation or elimination of school districts or the disincorporation of cities. Whether the Legislature intended the word "offices" to include cities or school districts is for grand jury legal advisors to interpret.

The statute granting authority to grand juries in matters involving nonprofit corporations (Penal Code Section 933.6) is another example of ambiguity regarding the grand jury's investigating and reporting authority. When it enacted this statute, the Legislature granted the grand jury jurisdiction in some, but not all, nonprofit corporations. The statute addresses only those "established by or operated on behalf of a public entity the books and records of which it is authorized by law to examine." The statute might seem clear enough, but that clarity might disappear when a grand jury attempts to apply the statute to an actual case.

Consider, for example, a small nonprofit corporation dispensing counseling services to its clients. Some clients pay fees to the corporation from their own resources, whereas others pay fees with tax money the county gives them. Is the corporation operating on behalf of a public entity? The answer might depend on whether the nonprofit corporation had a contract with the county and what the contract specified. Suppose further that the nonprofit corporation receives no funds from the county, but that the county permits it to use an office in a county building in exchange for occasionally providing limited services to the county. Would the nonprofit corporation be within the grand jury's jurisdiction? Questions about what the Legislature may have meant in creating Penal Code Section 933.6 illustrate the occasional confusion that grand juries encounter in exercising their authority to investigate and report. Later we shall consider examples of how legal advisors and appellate courts have resolved some of this confusion.

A casual reader of civil grand jury statutes might not notice that "shall" appears in some statutes and that "may" is used in others. "Shall" means that the Legislature intended that the grand jury *must* do something. The Legislature uses "may" twice as often as it uses "shall" in grand jury statutes, thereby leaving the execution of many grand jury powers to the discretion of grand jurors.

For example, Penal Code Section 928 requires grand juries to conduct their investigations "selectively each year" in county government. Because many grand juries ignore this provision, some county-government offices escape routine inquiry year after year, though the Legislature evidently intended that the grand jury should not overlook such offices. What is meant, however, by "selectively"? Does this refer to how often the investigations are conducted or to investigating only departments with large budgets? These, too, are questions for grand jurors or their legal advisors to resolve.

In general, the grand jury may exercise its investigating and reporting powers in an identical way among most local governments designated in the statutes. This was not always so. For many years, for example, the grand jury's authority in cities was more limited than its jurisdiction in counties. Although statutes authorized grand jury inquiry into the books, records, and accounts of both types of local government, grand juries could examine methods or systems of performing duties only in county government. In 1983, the Legislature amended Penal Code 925(a) to authorize grand juries to exercise the latter power in cities, thereby bringing both cities and counties within the scope of identical grand jury investigating and reporting authority. Similarly, the civil-investigation authority of grand juries in special districts, redevelopment agencies, housing authorities, joint powers agencies, and non-profit corporations equals that authorized for cities and counties because the words "may investigate and report upon the method or system of performing duties" appear in the statutes concerning these functions.

Readers might notice that Table 3 qualifies its reference to school districts. The lack of an explicit designated grant of authority for grand juries in school districts sometimes confuses grand jurors and school district officials about the panel's jurisdiction. In a later section we shall review an appellate case and a county counsel's opinion concerning the jurisdiction of grand juries in school districts.[12]

Table 3 shows that the Legislature has authorized the grand jury to exercise its investigating and reporting powers in most of the entities that constitute local government today in California. "Entities" is the term local-government officials often use to embrace in one word the various organizations, functions, and contractual arrangements that constitute local government in California.

The first form of government in which the grand jury exercised its reporting power was the county.[13] As California's population grew and the State shifted from a rural to an urban-industrialized economy, the grand jury's investigating and reporting powers broadened. Thus, the addition of special districts (Penal Code Section 933.5, 1961), redevelopment agencies (Penal Code Section 933.1, 1979), local agency formation commissions (Penal Code Section 933.5, 1979), joint powers authorities (Penal Code Section 933.1, 1986), and designated non-profit corporations (Penal Code Section 933.6, 1986) follows the urbanization and increasing differentiation of California local government in the expansive post–World War II years.[14]

Although the statutes assign no investigating and reporting priorities for grand jurors, county government is by custom the focus of their work in local government for several reasons. *First,* in early California, counties were the dominant local governments. Grand juries therefore are preoccupied with county government as a matter of tradition rather than for any more objective reason.[15]

Second, some grand jurors think of the grand jury as a function of county government rather than of the courts. Examples of this misconception can be found in final reports whose covers or inside pages bear the seal of the county and in some cases display the names and photographs of county supervisors or in other respects seem to be little more than "state-of-the-county" memoranda to county officials. This misconception undermines the independence of the grand jury and might be attributable to the close political ties between some grand jurors and the county supervisors who have nominated them for grand jury service.[16]

Lack of knowledge among grand jurors about local government also could be an explanation. Final reports occasionally show examples of grand juries whose members do not understand the relationship of the grand jury to local government or the relationships of one local government to another.[17] Even the language grand jurors use when talking about local government restricts their conception of it. For example, grand jury manuals and handbooks frequently speak of the panel's responsibilities in "county government" when context suggests that the term "local government" should be used.

Third, the preoccupation of grand juries with county government might arise from their being headquartered in county-government buildings. Similarly, their budgets are included in county-government budgets. In some cases, county-government officials assign staff members to provide secretarial and other related services to grand juries. Given these circumstances, one can understand why grand jurors sometimes think of themselves as part-time county employees or otherwise assume that the grand jury is a county department rather than an arm of the court.[18]

We have considered so far only the local governments that statutes have subjected to the grand jury's civil investigation powers. Within these governments, the grand jury is limited to activities the Legislature has authorized, which the key words in Table 3 describe. The sense of most of these words is that the grand jury is an investigating (sometimes referred to as "inquisitorial"), deliberating, and reporting body. The words "ascertain," "inquire," "examine," and "investigate" make clear that the California Legislature intends the grand jury to be such an institution. The absence of words or phrases authorizing grand juries to enforce their recommendations or findings shows that the Legislature intended the grand jury to have no executive or administrative powers.[19]

A grand jury's success or failure in an investigation might depend on whether the panel's members understand thoroughly a relatively brief statute: Penal

Code Section 916. Line for line, this statute contains more implications for the grand jury's reporting and investigating function than any other Penal Code Section. The independence and integrity of the grand jury underlie the words that constitute this statute and provide several important criteria for evaluating the investigating and reporting powers of the grand jury. Table 4, "An Analysis of Penal Code Section 916," displays the meaning of Penal Code Section 916 in two columns. The first column consists of the words in the statute; the second column discusses possible effects or implications of each provision.

TABLE 4
An Analysis of Penal Code Section 916

Provisions	Effects
Each grand jury shall choose its officers, except the foreman, and shall determine its rules of proceeding.	This provision requires that the panel, rather than the foreman, one or two dominant members, or a clique, decides crucial matters such as naming and appointing committees, preparing the next year's budget for the grand jury, planning investigations, or developing a distribution plan for a final report; the statute also means that the foreman of the grand jury has no more power or authority than the grand jury delegates to him or her.
Adoption of its rules of procedure and all public actions of the grand jury, whether concerning criminal or civil matters unless otherwise prescribed by law, including adoption of final reports, shall be only with the concurrence of that number of grand jurors necessary to find an indictment pursuant to Section 940.	This requires the panel, not individual grand jurors, to be responsible each year for developing and adopting administrative, investigative, and reporting procedures; it ensures that the grand jury deliberates and votes upon procedures, public actions, and reports. Implications include reviewing and revising a procedures manual each year, thoroughly discussing drafts of final reports before publishing them, and ensuring the independence of the grand jury by preventing its domination by one person, a clique, or carry-over grand jurors.*

(Table Continued)

TABLE 4, *Continued*

Provisions	Effects
Rules of procedure shall include guidelines for that grand jury to ensure that all findings included in its final reports are supported by documented evidence, including reports of contract auditors or consultants, official records, or interviews attended by no fewer than two grand jurors ...	This requires the grand jury to develop guidelines to ensure the validity of findings. Implications include providing the factual basis of findings from sources such as reports of contract auditors or other consultants, official (public) records, and ensuring that no one can challenge one or more findings in a grand jury report by claiming that "I didn't say that in the interview." It restricts grand juries from publishing reports based on information obtained by only one grand juror.
... and that all problems identified in a final report are accompanied by suggested means for their resolution, including financial, when applicable.	This requires the grand jury ("when applicable") to consider, discuss, and suggest means for solving problems identified in final reports, including possible sources of revenue for recommended solutions. Implications also include the encouragement of practical solutions, requiring panels to recognize fiscal limits of recommendations, thereby improving the quality of final reports and providing estimates of the costs of implementing recommendations.

*Penal Code Section 901(b) permits judges to retain up to 10 grand jurors for the following year.

Penal Code Section 916 is the grand jury's charter for self-government. By making grand juries rather than judges or other public officials responsible for developing rules of procedure, the Legislature has placed the destiny and independence of the institution in the hands of grand jurors. Using Penal Code Section 916, grand jurors therefore may enact internal policies to implement applicable statutes. As an example, grand juries might embody the several statutes concerning grand jury secrecy[20] into several sections of a code of conduct that grand jurors may be required to sign:

> I will not discuss grand jury matters with friends, relatives, business acquaintances, the news media, or other persons.

I will not make public statements concerning grand jury matters approving or disapproving of agencies, departments, or public issues.

I will not discuss grand jury matters with fellow grand jurors outside the jury room except where privacy is assured.[21]

Establishing effective procedures to guide the development of investigations and reports is especially important for an institution consisting of people of varying backgrounds, education, and experiences. Well-conceived procedures assist grand juries in using internal resources as effectively as possible within the constraints imposed on them. Because many grand juries receive no funds to hire consultants to assist them,[22] they must depend on their own resources, and they occasionally receive criticism for the poor quality of their investigations and reports.[23]

Penal Code Section 916 is the means by which grand jurors can fashion the internal procedures and mechanisms to ensure valid investigations, collegial relationships, and productive coordination of effort. Thus, more than any other statute, Penal Code Section 916 embodies the spirit of the institution.

Issuing Reports

Statutes specify three steps for developing and issuing reports. As a first step, the grand jury prepares the final draft of its report. The law requires the grand jury to submit its report to a judge of the superior court.[24] Statutes and case law permit the court to review the report for four purposes:

- It may accept only reports about an "appropriate subject."[25]
- It must determine that the report is within the jurisdiction of the grand jury.[26]
- It may accept only a "report, declaration, or recommendation" based on the grand jury's independent investigation.[27]
- To discover whether the report contains "evidentiary material, findings, or other information" or "the identity of witnesses and any testimony or materials of a defamatory or libelous nature" that require "redaction or masking."[28]

The implication of Penal Code Section 933 is that the court independently verifies the originality of findings and recommendations. This indeed would be an onerous task. In practice, most judges accept reports from grand juries, trusting that panels have complied with the law. Presumably, the court also should review the final report to see that it has met the applicable requirements of Penal Code Section 916 (such as provisions for voting, supporting findings with documented evidence, and offering solutions for problems). If the court finds that a report does not conform to one or more of these criteria, it probably would return the report with appropriate comment to the grand jury.

The second step in promulgating final reports occurs after the court has reviewed the report to ensure its compliance with Title 4 (Grand Jury Procedures) of the Penal Code. The court then files one copy of the report with the county clerk.[29] In the third step, the grand jury releases its report to the public.[30] Many grand juries send copies of reports to local-government officials affected by the reports. Although most grand jurors and many local-government officials speak of "responding" to findings and recommendations in final reports, the applicable statute rarely uses this word but more generally employs "comment" instead. The statute does not specify how thorough or factual comments shall be, nor does it provide sanctions against local-government officials who do not comply with it.[31]

Comments by Officials About Findings and Recommendations

Many grand jurors, local-government officials, and news-media staff conceive of commenting about findings and recommendations in final reports as something that occurs between two parties: the officials and the grand juries. The language of the statutes, however, depicts a different process: The grand jury sends its final report to the presiding judge, the judge files the final report with the county clerk, and local-government officials send their comments to the judge. In theory, if not in practice, this means that a judge could treat as contempt of court the willful refusal of public officials to comment about findings or recommendations affecting them in a grand jury final report. Similarly, a judge could issue an order of the court to enforce compliance. Finally, some other party (such as a citizen or another official) could file a writ of mandate (Code of Civil Procedure 1085) to force compliance.[32]

Although some grand juries use the term "interim" in the titles of reports they issue before the end of their term, no law authorizes this practice. Because the statutes do not mention interim reports, local-government officials are not obliged to comment about recommendations or findings in them. Recognizing this limitation, some grand juries issue final reports about the same subject at two or three different times during a year, a practice that Penal Code Section 933(a) supports: "Final reports on any appropriate subject may be submitted to the presiding judge of the superior court at any time during the term of service of a grand jury." Publishing final reports before the end of the grand jury's year permits grand juries to initiate a cycle of reports and comments to findings and recommendations.

The statutes do not give grand juries power to force local-government officials to comply with grand jury recommendations. The only power the grand jury has in respect to its findings and recommendations is to report them to the community. If local-government officials agree with the findings of grand juries or comply with grand jury recommendations, they do so voluntarily. Grand jurors sometimes complain that local-government officials ignore their reports, including their findings and recommendations. Among the reasons that grand juries express dissatisfaction with the reactions of local-government officials to findings and recommendations are these:

- The unwillingness of local-government officials to comment adequately about findings and recommendations[33]
- Grand juries incorrectly assuming that Penal Code Section 933 applies to so-called interim reports[34]
- Officials claiming they could not identify findings and recommendations in reports[35]

CASE LAW

Within the provisions of the Penal Code, grand juries exercise considerable discretion in using their investigating and reporting powers. The choice of investigative topics, what kinds of data to use, deciding whom to interview in an investigation, what conclusions and findings to present in final reports, and related issues are, with few exceptions, matters of judgment.[36] Because the stakes in local-government politics are often high, appointed and elected officials sometimes challenge the authority of grand juries. Examples of challenges are:

- Refusing to give grand juries requested public information because an official claims the information is his or her personal property[37]
- Challenging a grand jury as having no jurisdiction in an investigation[38]
- Refusing to give grand juries documents to review because grand jurors would be "incapable" of understanding them[39]

Most of the challenges to grand jury authority are resolved easily and informally. A legal advisor or other person might refer someone challenging the grand jury's authority to read a statute or an appellate case. Usually this will solve the problem. Sometimes, however, a disputed issue is the subject of a superior court trial. In some cases, people who are dissatisfied with the decision of a superior court or appellate court appeal it to a higher court. Although most of the cases regarding the grand jury's authority have been concerned with the indictment function, a few cases have directly concerned the grand jury's investigating and reporting powers. In this section we briefly review examples of these cases according to the recency of their occurrence.

The legality of issuing minority reports is the subject of a case published in 1989.[40] The case arose when several grand jurors, having taken exception to the majority of the panel regarding a matter, tried to issue a minority report independently. After a superior court judge refused to file the minority report, the grand jurors retained an attorney to force the court to accept their report. An appellate court supported the superior court, ruling that because the minority report was not submitted to the full membership of the grand jury for approval by a majority, it could not be published.

In 1988, an appellate court ruled in a contested matter regarding the authority of a superior court judge to delete material from a final report. The case concerns the legality of including "raw evidentiary material" in final reports. In the context of the case, raw evidentiary material seems to refer to facts disclosed by witnesses in sworn secret testimony. Reasoning that quoting such testimony in a final report would violate grand jury secrecy and confidentiality, the court held that a superior court judge acted properly in expunging raw evidentiary materials from a final report.[41]

Because of uncertainty about what "raw evidentiary material" means, many grand juries exclude from their reports routinely obtained supporting data such as organization charts, staffing patterns, crime rates, revenue, expenditures, and other budgetary information. As I discuss in Chapter 7, the raw-evidentiary-material holding caused confusion among grand jurors and some of their legal advisors. Although it was not solely responsible for many of the problems in final reports that I describe in later chapters, it aggravated them.

The California Legislature in 1998 enacted Penal Code Section 929 to offset the confusion that the raw-evidentiary-material problem created. Unfortunately, the wording and scope of the statute will do little to solve the subjectivity problem in civil grand jury reports. In Chapter 7, therefore, I offer suggestions for legislation that will address that issue more directly and emphatically.[42]

Besides its ruling about raw evidentiary material, the court strongly affirmed that secrecy in grand jury proceedings is necessary for a variety of reasons, including:

- encouraging witnesses such as public employees to testify without fearing retaliation
- protecting grand jurors from pressure, threats, or influence
- protecting from public ridicule accused persons who are later exonerated

Another important case concerning the grand jury's reporting power involved libel. Briefly stated, libel is the defaming of character by use of the written word. The only known instance of a successful libel suit against California grand jurors engaged in the civil function was decided by an appellate court in 1978.[43] Although this case concerned a private corporation rather than a public official, its implications are important for public officials and other citizens who might be criticized in grand jury reports. The case involves the concept of "privilege," a legal principle that grants certain rights, exemption from prosecution, or benefits to certain persons. Like judges or prosecutors in criminal matters, grand jurors are exempt from lawsuits for what they may say during indictment proceedings. Section 930 of the Penal Code, however, removes this immunity from grand jurors in the exercise of their civil function.

When the Grand Jury used the words "negligent," "incompetent," and "wrong" to describe what it believed was the failure of an engineering firm to perform its duties properly for a county, the firm's attorneys sued the Grand Jury for defaming it. A superior court judge attempted to dismiss the suit, ruling that Penal Code Section 930 was unconstitutional, and grand jurors therefore enjoyed immunity from a lawsuit for libel arising from a civil investigation. In his decision, the Superior Court judge held that the Legislature did not have the constitutional authority to remove immunity from grand jurors by enacting Penal Code Section 930. The engineering firm appealed this ruling to a higher court, which reversed the decision of the Superior Court, holding that the Legislature had properly enacted Penal Code Section 930.[44]

A 1975 case addressed another facet of a judge's authority with regard to a final report. In this case, a grand jury attempted to issue a report about local government that the superior court believed exceeded the grand jury's jurisdiction. When the superior court refused to file the report, the matter came before a higher court for review.

The higher court upheld the superior court and ruled that the judge acted properly in refusing to file a report that exceeded the Grand Jury's established legal limits. The appellate court emphasized, however, that a judge's authority to review the Grand Jury's civil function is limited and does not include editing or sealing a report merely because a judge believes a grand jury's recommendations are unjustified or hastily developed; nor until 1998 could judges edit or redact reports because they believed such reports were libelous.[45]

A 1968 case ruled on a question that grand jurors face each year: Under what circumstances may a grand jury initiate an investigation? Part of the answer lies in a well-settled principle of common law that prohibits grand juries from indiscriminately intruding into public affairs to discover wrongdoing—conducting a "fishing expedition." A court applied this principle to an attempt by a grand jury to subpoena personnel records pertaining to two school administrators (a principal and a vice principal). When a school board challenged the Grand Jury, the court ruled that in the absence of a legally defensible reason for the Grand Jury to believe that wrongful misconduct or criminal activities may have occurred, the Grand Jury had no authority to obtain such records.[46]

In this case, the court did not exempt school districts from grand jury inquiry. In fact, the court held that a grand jury may properly examine the books and records of the districts. The court reasoned that because school districts were special districts, they thereby were subject to Section 933.5 of the Penal Code that grants designated authority to grand juries in such districts. At the time of this case, the grand jury's civil investigative authority in special districts was limited to examining books and records. In 1969, the Legislature amended Penal Code Section 933.5 to include the words, "… and, in addition to any other investigatory powers granted by this chapter, [the grand jury] may investigate and report upon the method or system of performing the duties of such district or commission." In so doing, the Legislature extended the grand jury's civil jurisdiction in school districts.[47]

The idea of the fishing expedition is abhorrent to the American character. Searching passport files for "dirt" to use in a political campaign, snooping in garbage cans for incriminating evidence, or installing electronic equipment to observe employees secretly leads, when exposed, to public condemnation. Unfortunately, no case has provided specific guidelines to help grand juries avoid fishing expeditions. Occasionally a grand jury encounters a local-government official who is unaware of the Constitutional provision for grand juries and their legislative grants of investigating and reporting powers. In these circumstances, an official might respond defensively to a grand jury inquiry and raise the issue of fishing expeditions.

In other instances, grand juries may not clearly explain their jurisdiction before beginning an investigation, and thereby provoke the defensive response of conducting fishing expeditions. In other cases, a grand jury may begin an inquiry without proper cause, thereby justifying such charges. Because the phrase is subject to interpretation, disputes occasionally arise about the grand jury's authority to initiate investigations. Questions of this nature can be resolved by referring to the statutes listed in Table 3 to see what investigations the legislature has authorized. Other examples of statutory authority for grand jury investigations include:

- the grand juror's oath and its requirement that grand jurors "diligently inquire into, and true presentment make, of all public offenses against the people of the state, committed or triable within this county, of which the grand jury shall have or can obtain legal evidence."[48]
- the authority for "a member [of a grand jury who] knows, or has reason to believe, that a public offense, triable within the county has been committed [to] declare it to his fellow jurors, who may thereupon investigate it."[49]

In late 1937, A California appellate court decided a case that has had important implications for grand jury reports and investigations.[50] This case arose when a Los Angeles grand juror named Clinton tried to use a legal procedure to force fellow grand jurors to hear "his case." Clinton previously attempted to bring to the attention of his colleagues an allegation of extensive vice and corruption in local government. His fellow grand jurors agreed to hear Clinton's charges but only if he would identify by name the witnesses he intended to produce. When Clinton refused to reveal the names of the witnesses in advance of their appearing before the panel, the grand jurors declined to consider the case further. Clinton hired an attorney who tried to obtain a court order to compel the Grand Jury to hear his case. When the Superior Court refused to grant Clinton's request, his attorney appealed the matter to an appellate court.

Noting that Clinton had attempted to present "his case" "in his own way and as he desired and according to his own opinion and sole judgment," the appellate court denied Clinton's appeal. In doing so, the court emphasized that Clinton misunderstood the nature and purpose of the grand jury and the relationship of individual grand jurors to the panel.

The main principle in the court's decision was that only the grand jury, and not individual members, may exercise grand jury powers. The *Clinton* case, although it did not use the phrase, affirmed the grand jury as a collegial body rather than as an administrative convenience for grand jurors pursuing individual interests and objectives or whose allegiance is to autonomous committees of their panel.

When considered in the context of Penal Code Section 916, the *Clinton* case has several implications for the grand jury's investigating and reporting authority. *First,* only the entire panel, not a committee or a single grand juror, may issue a report. *Second,* the entire panel must review and vote upon grand jury investigations before they are reported.[51] *Third,* no individual grand juror or grand jury officer has authority to decide what should or should not be in a report. In short, a grand jury report must be the product of a quorum of the entire panel rather than that of one grand juror (such as the foreman) or a group of grand jurors smaller than the number needed to approve a report.

Opinions

Legal advisors to grand juries (the district attorney or county counsel) occasionally write opinions to resolve disagreements about the meaning of statutes or cases concerning the civil grand jury. In California, the county counsel (the chief lawyer for the civil affairs of county government) writes most of the opinions affecting civil grand juries. Because no central depository of county counsels' opinions is publicly available, the examples I have cited in this section were obtained directly from county counsels or grand juries.[52]

We also shall consider several examples of opinions concerning grand jury civil powers that the Office of Attorney General has issued in recent years. Although opinions are not laws in the sense of statutes, constitutions, or ordinances, local-government officials, their legal advisors, and judges often consider them to be persuasive.

Opinions of the Office of Attorney General of the State of California

The Office of Attorney General of the State of California has issued few opinions directly addressing the grand jury's investigating and reporting powers. Examples of these opinions, either directly or indirectly applicable to the civil grand jury, are as follows:

- A county is required to provide indemnification and defense for grand jurors who are sued for statements they have made in a final report issued within the lawful scope of their reporting duties (Opinion No. 97-1210, June 2, 1998, Vol. 81, p. 199).

- When a grand jury is conducting a civil "watchdog" investigation of a local police agency, it has the right to examine peace officer personnel records, including citizens' complaints, or information compiled from such records, without first obtaining issuance of a subpoena or court order, etc. (Opinion No. 96-307, September 1996, Vol. 79, p. 185).

- A grand jury may not exercise its oversight function with respect to the superior court and executive officer because the "grand jury no longer has oversight of the trial courts and their officers since that now reposes in state officers, the Judicial Council, and the Legislature itself. Treated as state agencies rather than county agencies for the purposes of auditing their operations, the trial courts are outside the scope of Penal Code Sections 925, 928, and 933" (Opinion No. 92-1204, May 4, 1993, Vol. 76, p. 70).

- Penal Code Section 904.6 authorizes an additional grand jury in each county, but that grand jury may not exercise civil investigation and reporting powers (Opinion No. 93-505, August 25, 1993, Vol. 76, p. 181).

- Payment of per-diem expenses to grand jurors under Penal Code Section 890 is only for attendance at a called grand jury meeting of the entire panel, including indictment proceedings (Opinion No. 93-514, August 25, 1993, Vol. 76, p. 187).

- The Atascadero State Hospital is not included within the meaning of Penal Code Section 919(b) (Opinion No. 79-313, May 18, 1979, Vol. 62, p. 268).

- Except for information relating to criminal investigations, or that could form part or all of the basis for issuing an indictment, sitting grand juries may transmit to succeeding grand juries information or evidence acquired during the course of any investigation they have conducted (Opinion No. 88-703, August 3, 1989, Vol. 72, p. 128).

- Grand jury committees from different counties may lawfully meet together to conduct a joint investigation of a multi-county taxing district that includes such counties for limited purposes to assist their respective grand juries in performing their functions (Opinion No. 83-903, February 24, 1984, Vol. 67, p. 58).

- Grand juries may investigate only the operational procedures, not the substantive policy concerns, of special-purpose assessing or taxing districts located wholly or partly in the county (Opinion No. 81-1015, December 29, 1981, Vol. 64, p. 900).
- In the absence of cause to believe that school-district officials are guilty of any crime or of misconduct in office, no statutory authority exists for a grand jury to investigate the evaluation of teachers and principals by school district officials (Opinion No. 64-265, December 22, 1965, Vol. 46, p. 144).

Opinions of County Counsels

The following examples of opinions of county counsels concerning civil grand juries are offered merely as illustrations. They might have been modified subsequently either by opinions of the Attorney General of the State of California or by legislation:

- An explanation of the meaning of "shall" and "will" as these words appear in certain statutes pertaining to the jurisdiction of civil grand juries in California (Office of County Counsel, Amador County, May 7, 1999).
- Only the grand jury, and not one of its committees, may request the issuance of a subpoena through its foreman (Office of County Counsel, Tulare County, August 5, 1992).
- The grand jury cannot investigate and report on the judicial actions of the municipal court, nor may it investigate and report on the clerical and administrative aspects of the municipal court (Office of County Counsel, Merced County, April 3, 1992).
- The grand jury has the same jurisdiction, for purposes of the exercise of its civil function in public school districts, that it has in cities, counties, and special districts; and other matters (Office of County Counsel, Sonoma County, July 6, 1990).
- The grand jury may exclude the district attorney from its sessions under certain circumstances (memorandum to Foreman of the 1984–1985 Orange County Grand Jury, prepared by the Office of County Counsel, Orange County, June 5, 1986).

CHARGES TO GRAND JURIES

One of the oldest grand jury traditions is the ceremony of the judge's charge. "Charging" a grand jury means that a judge informs newly selected grand jurors of the panel's authority, defines its jurisdiction, cautions grand jurors about possible abuses of their authority, and other matters. In eighteenth-century England, judges often included in their charges comments about public morality, political corruption, and blasphemy.[53]

California law does not authorize judges, as they did occasionally in earlier times, to engage in political digressions when charging grand juries, though Penal Code Section 914 directs judges to "give the grand jurors such information as [the judge] deems proper, or as is required by law." Penal Code Section 914.1 specifies the topics that judges must address. Sixteen topics from charges that judges in eight counties gave to grand juries in the early 1960s are valid today:[54]

- statutory duties
- grand juror's oath
- suggestions for committee organization
- suggested procedure for meetings
- frequency and location of meetings
- procedure for accusation and indictments
- relationships with the district attorney
- civil liability of grand jurors
- limitations of investigatory power
- press relationships and publicity
- index to statutes or copies
- format for grand jury meetings
- duties of foreman
- duties of secretary
- handling witnesses
- history of grand juries

Superior court judges vary in how they prepare the ceremony for charging the grand jury. Some judges are formal, brief, and restrictive in delivering a charge, and others are informal, yet comprehensive and humorous. One five-page charge[55] was admonitory in tone and general in scope; its three main headings were:

History of the Civil and Criminal Function
Independence and Secrecy
Threats to the Grand Jury System

A charge of 35 pages balanced a light, informal style with a positive, yet cautionary tone. The main points were:[56]

- Grand jurors should read last year's final report "cover to cover."
- The grand jury procedures manual should be read carefully.
- A description of the three important functions of the modern grand jury.
- The grand jury has only the authority the Legislature has granted it.
- Before starting an investigation, the jurisdiction to do so should be discussed.
- The grand jury exists only as a body.
- Facts must be verified.

- Grand jurors must not interfere with the daily work of local-government employees.
- Reporting favorable findings is as important as reporting unfavorable findings.
- Conducting several investigations thoroughly is better than conducting a large number of investigations poorly.
- Indictments should be used properly.
- Merely because grand jurors disagree with administrative acts or decisions does not necessarily mean they are unlawful.
- Maintaining a constructive relationship with legal advisors is important.
- Suggestions for preventing lawsuits.

HANDBOOKS, GUIDES, AND PROCEDURES MANUALS

Legal advisors, court staff, and grand jurors in some counties have individually or collectively prepared handbooks, guides, or procedures manuals for grand jurors to refer to during their year of service. Examples of materials in these documents include:

- photocopies of applicable statutes
- information about administrative matters, such as how to complete claims for expense reimbursement
- duties of grand jury officers
- descriptions of grand jury committees
- investigating and interviewing procedures

The usefulness of these reference materials depends on the knowledge, skills, and experience of the people who prepare them. If these documents are not revised each year, they might contain outdated, and therefore incorrect, information. Although handbooks, procedures manuals, and guides are useful, they are not substitutes for statutes and case law. Indeed, the number and types of errors in some of these materials is surprising, and for grand jurors who rely on such materials instead of reading the statutes or case law, they can be misleading, if not dangerous. Examples of errors in handbooks will be cited later.

Criteria for Evaluating Investigations and Final Reports

The purpose of the preceding review of selected statutes, case law, and legal opinions was to identify legal criteria for evaluating the investigating and reporting powers of the California grand jury. The review also shows that, although the grand jury's civil powers are statutory, case law and legal opinions illuminate several of them. Each of the eight legal criteria I shall use, therefore, is based on or related to at least one statute or appellate case. I supplement the eight legal criteria with two nonlegal but nonetheless important groups of criteria that neither case law nor statutes address: (a) the value of final reports to citizens who read them, and (b) the effectiveness of final reports as the means by which grand juries inform the community of their findings and recommendations.

Several comments about grand juries and the laws governing them will assist readers in considering the ten criteria. *First,* examining the statutes upon which Table 3 is based is only a beginning step for understanding the civil investigating and reporting powers of the California grand jury. Unless one also reads applicable case law, reading only the statutes yields limited information about grand jury powers.

Consider, for example, the concept of grand jury independence. Nowhere in Penal Code statutes concerning grand juries does the word "independence" appear. Although grand jury independence is firmly rooted in the common law, that body of law is somewhat diffuse, and within it, discussions of concepts such as independence are rarely found in one place.

Similarly, no one case fully develops the concept with respect to civil investigations and reports. Although grand jury independence is, of course, implicit in Penal Code Section 916, the statute does not name and address it. And no statute directly describes the criterion referred to in this section as the "collegial nature of the grand jury." This concept acquires meaning only upon reading certain case law. Except for the requirement in Penal Code Sections 916 and 940 concerning the number of votes required for panel decision making, no other statutes convey the principle that the grand jury may exercise its powers only as a body.

Second, understanding the grand jury's civil investigating and reporting powers depends not only on reading statutes and case law but also requires a sense of semantics. Penal Code Section 930 illustrates this point. That statute is concerned with two matters: (a) providing grand jurors with immunity for what they may say or write in the exercise of the indictment function, but (b) denying them that protection in the exercise of the civil function.

A reading of Penal Code Section 930 will disclose that the statute does not refer to the accusation function of the California grand jury (Penal Code Section 919(c) and Government Code Section 3060). No other statute can be found that extends immunity to grand jurors in the exercise of the accusation function, nor are the applicable appellate cases clear about the matter. Nevertheless, many grand jury handbooks, guides, or procedures manuals advise grand jurors that they enjoy immunity during the exercise of the accusation function.

Third, the absence of explicitly stated legislative intent in most grand jury statutes leaves room for speculation and interpretation as to their purpose and application. When, for example, the Legislature created Penal Code Section 933(c) requiring public officials to comment about grand jury findings and recommendations, a statement of legislative intent might have provided assistance to local-government officials who, as matters now stand, can only speculate about its meaning.

The foregoing review is not a substitute for firsthand reading of statutes, case law, and opinions concerning the investigating and reporting authority of the California grand jury. The review, however, does reveal the criteria I shall use to evaluate investigations that grand juries published in their final reports during the study period. Similarly, the criteria also set the stage for suggestions I offer in Chapter 7 to reform the civil grand jury in California.

LAW-RELATED CRITERIA

For convenience, I created the following eight categories of statutory criteria pertaining to the California civil grand jury. The California Penal Code neither uses these terms nor organizes the statutes in the manner shown. What follows is merely a brief explanation of these categories as they are used and are explained in more detail throughout this book.

Jurisdiction and Independence

Grand juries must exercise their powers only within designated local governments. In brief terms, *jurisdiction* means that grand juries may do only what the law permits them to do. Statutes do not authorize findings and recommendations directed to State and federal governments, superior and municipal courts, and private persons. Similarly, findings and recommendations supporting or opposing legislation, or broad commentary about social, economic, or political issues and policies are outside the purview of grand juries.

Within their legal boundaries, grand juries have almost complete *independence* from the courts and legislative or administrative bodies. By exercising independence wisely, they may issue reports free of bias or subjectivity and therefore achieve community support. Practices threatening or jeopardizing grand jury independence include establishing alliances with public officials, private persons, or organizations; confusing the grand jury's identity with that of other bodies; and appearing to be subordinate to, or influenced by, public officials or other branches of government.

Fair Comment

Penal Code Section 930 exempts grand juries from immunity in the exercise of their civil function if they include libelous statements in their reports. Gratuitous, subjective, sweeping condemnations of public officials or private persons, therefore, may be the basis of libel suits against grand jurors. Similarly, obsequious commendations or endorsements of public officials or employees without justification degrade grand jury independence.

Exercise of the civil function sometimes requires grand juries to comment unfavorably about local-government practices, procedures, and the persons responsible for them. Such comments, when fairly expressed (factually and without malice) are necessary in a democracy, and the courts are unlikely to declare them libelous. Nevertheless, because community support of the grand jury is important, and most citizens deplore abuses of governmental power, this study defines negative, subjective grand jury commentary as a violation of the principle of fair comment even if it is not technically libelous.

The examples cited in Chapter 4 representing this criterion are not referred to by the word "libel." That word should be reserved for matters that have been adjudicated. Possibly one or more of the examples we will examine were libelous as the law defines that term, but libel would be the appropriate word only after all the attendant circumstances were reviewed in a trial. Libelous or not, however, the examples represent ill-advised language. Even in the few instances in which grand juries offered some evidence to support their criticisms, it was not substantial enough to justify the language used.

Conducting Justified Investigations

Grand juries may not use their powers indiscriminately and without cause to search for wrongdoing. These practices abuse grand jury independence, violate individual liberties, and discredit the institution. Although statutes confer upon grand juries many different discretionary and mandatory powers, the lack of justification for exercising them may cause citizens and public officials to question grand jurors' motives.

Clear explanations, within the limits of statutorily imposed secrecy and confidentiality, of the reasons for conducting civil investigations assure citizens that panels have exercised their powers wisely and for good cause. These explanations also prevent unnecessary animosity, suspicion, or threats by clearly explaining the link between a reported investigation and the law granting jurisdiction in the matter. Similarly, identifying whether grand jury investigations were initiated by complaints from citizens, officials, or individual grand jurors can add to the validity of grand jury investigations and reports in certain circumstances. These and related matters are the foundation for deciding whether grand jury investigations, based on what grand juries have reported, were justified.

Emphasizing Systems, Methods, and Procedures

No California case law directly explains why grand juries must not challenge or support the lawful decisions of legislative bodies or administrative officials. On the other hand, grand juries may properly review the procedures under which decisions have been made or, with good cause, investigate violations of criminal law that officials or other persons may have committed in connection with those decisions. The words the California Legislature chose to define the grand jury's civil jurisdiction, however, require panels to focus on the systems, methods, and procedures of designated local governments. Criticizing the lawful decisions of legislative bodies, recommending changes in public-school curricula, or challenging lawful policy determinations of appointed officials are examples of grand jury actions that try to, or do, usurp the policy-formation responsibilities of local-government officials.

Validity of Investigations and Reports

Critics of grand juries sometimes cite the subjectivity of investigations and reports as sufficient reason for eliminating the institution. In one sense, this study cannot definitively address validity without independent verification and corroboration of investigations and reports. Instead, the criterion of validity is concerned with whether reports are documented adequately for persons who may have the time or resources to verify facts or findings in final reports.

By enacting the several statutes authorizing or requiring civil investigations, the Legislature presumably expected grand juries to support their findings in final reports with independently developed documented evidence. One statute, therefore, prohibits grand juries from making reports, declarations, or recommendations without independent investigation or adopting as their own the recommendations of other grand juries without independent investigation.

Decisional law restricts grand juries from publishing "raw evidentiary data" but does not define its nature. In addition, grand jurors must observe certain restrictions on asking public officials or other people to review drafts of their investigative reports for accuracy. Legal requirements such as these oblige grand juries to take special care to ensure that they have developed internal procedures for verification, corroboration, and documentation.

We shall examine other issues of validity in final reports. These include whether grand juries provide information in their reports that assure readers of their objectivity, whether grand juries document sources from which reported facts have been taken; whether they interview a variety of employees in an organization or obtain information from only one of its levels; and whether they have cited any laws, ordinances, or regulations they claim have been ignored.

Legality and Effectiveness of Findings and Recommendations

Other than authorizing the reporting of findings and recommendations, statutes offer little guidance to grand juries for issuing them. Supporting findings with documented evidence, including in final reports only findings based on interviews conducted by two or more grand jurors, and not adopting recommendations of other grand juries or other organizations are statutory mandates. The Legislature, however, requires grand juries, as collegial bodies, to determine rules of procedure for receiving complaints, for deliberating about them, for planning and managing investigations, and for deciding what to report about them. Grand juries, nevertheless, have discretion for deciding how to express their recommendations and findings, how to display them in reports, and whether they should review the comments of local-government officials concerning the findings and recommendations of their predecessors.

Statutorily correct findings and recommendations, of course, are of little value if local-government officials cannot identify them in final reports, if they are addressed incorrectly, or if they are written confusingly or vaguely. Other issues for assessing the effectiveness of findings and recommendations include whether grand juries have complied with the requirement to provide, as applicable, cost estimates to accompany them; whether they were displayed conspicuously in reports; and whether grand jurors correctly used the terms "findings" and "recommendations" as these terms are used in scientific, legal, and technical reporting.

Confidentiality and Secrecy

Because issues about confidentiality and secrecy are often clear-cut, few problems concerning them likely will be found in final reports, especially if legal advisors have reviewed them carefully. An example of a breach of confidentiality might be identifying complainants who have requested anonymity. Breaches of secrecy also would include revealing the identity of individuals who provided sworn, secret testimony and publishing quotations attributed to them. Other examples of the violation of confidentiality and secrecy include revealing information that, because of security reasons, might better be undisclosed, or naming local-government employees or other citizens in final reports who have complained to grand juries and who thereby may be subjected to possible recriminations or harassment.

Practices Related to the Collegial Nature of the Grand Jury

Like trial juries, grand juries are deliberative bodies in which no grand juror, including the foreman, has more or less authority, power, status, or responsibility than fellow grand jurors. The definition of the Latin word from which "colleague" has been derived summarizes the nature of a *collegial organization:* one chosen to serve with another. This definition denotes equivalency of rank, power, prestige, and authority.

The collegial nature of the grand jury is necessary for grand jurors to become a deliberating body of equals, and practices that detract from collegiality erode validity and independence. These practices include foremen who assume power and authority that a grand jury has not delegated to them, issuing reports that seem to be the products of individuals or groups within the body, and praising named individual grand jurors for their achievements.

COMMUNITY CRITERIA

Community criteria consist of significance of investigations, accountability to citizens, and continuity. Of these criteria, significance (the importance of investigations for the community) is the most subjective. Conceivably, a significant grand jury investigation might seem to be trivial because a panel reported it inadequately. Nevertheless, its actual but unreported benefits to the community can have considerable consequence.

Significance

Insignificant investigations bring grand juries into disrepute by exposing them to ridicule. Disrepute, in turn, undermines the grand jury's community support, and the lack of community support lessens the independence of the institution. Statutes do not require grand juries to conduct significant investigations. Only the grand jurors themselves are responsible for deciding whether to use their powers for trivial or for important purposes.

Accountability

Accountability is defined as how much information grand juries include in their final reports about achievements, problems, and workload. Grand jurors frequently complain that few citizens are aware of what grand juries do. If grand jurors desire citizens to be better informed about the institution, we should expect to find in final reports statistical information such as numbers, types, and dispositions of complaints received from citizens, public officials, and other sources; how many meetings grand jurors attended; and the numbers and types of persons (unless otherwise forbidden by secrecy requirements) whom grand jurors interviewed during the year.

Continuity

The Constitutional premise of grand juries is that each year the courts impanel a new group of men and women. This group is likely to have fewer preconceived views and fixed opinions than is a group of people who are, so to speak, professional grand jurors with many terms of service. This premise, of course, results in forming grand juries that consist of men and women with little or no experience as grand jurors.

Arguments can be made against the "blank slate" theory of grand jury impanelment. Its practice, however, need not detract from institutional efficiency. To a considerable extent, an accurate, readable grand jury manual, a well-planned grand jury library, and an effective method of tracking and reviewing civil investigations of previous years will offset the limitations of impaneling a fresh group of grand jurors each year.

Of course, any provision for an institutional memory will be weakened by inadequate meeting space and the absence of staff, a permanent office, and filing cabinets. Many grand juries, therefore, begin their terms by finding no records of grand jury activities in previous years or copies of correspondence, reference materials, and final reports of predecessors. Some grand juries, however, have developed methods for providing continuity between grand juries. My assessment accordingly includes consideration of institutional memory systems that grand juries have created.

TECHNICAL CRITERIA

The internal and external features of final reports help or hinder grand juries in reporting to the community. Simple matters, such as how final reports are bound, influence whether citizens can find them easily on library shelves. For example, some libraries do not catalog books or other publications that do not have a title on the spine. News-media representatives working against deadlines may be less likely to read final reports that are confusingly written, poorly organized, or lack summary information about investigations.

Similarly, final reports filled with unnecessary or undigested data can overwhelm or intimidate readers. Other impediments to reading and comprehending final reports include

- the absence of tables of contents and indexes
- poor reproduction, difficult-to-read typestyles, and visually challenging paper colors
- obscure abbreviations, legalese, and bureaucratic language, which create the impression that the civil grand jury is a local-government bureaucracy rather than an independent institution

The number of reports printed, to whom they are distributed, and the ease with which citizens can obtain them are additional matters grand jurors must attend to if they expect citizens to read their final reports.

Summary and Conclusion

The civil investigation and reporting powers of the California grand jury have origins in remote times. Although the grand jury in England developed as a common-law institution, it no longer is so in California. As broad as its scope may be, the grand jury must work within limits that the courts and the Legislature have decreed. The jurisdiction of grand juries in designated local governments is represented by words such as "procedures," "methods," "operations," "books and records," and "systems."

The Legislature has slowly standardized the grand jury's civil investigation and reporting powers in designated local governments. Whereas the grand jury of 50 or 75 years ago was concerned with "books, records, and accounts," the Legislature has broadened the jurisdiction of the modern panel to issues of effectiveness and efficiency. Among all other statutes, Penal Code Section 916 most decisively places the grand jury's destiny in the hands of grand jurors. From its several provisions, only sitting grand jurors, not former grand jurors, local-government officials, or their legal advisors, create the internal procedures and systems upon which a successful year of grand jury service depends.

Because grand jury handbooks, guides, and procedures manuals are obsolete the day a new grand jury is impaneled, grand jurors must revise them each year. Only grand juries have statutory authority for performing these tasks. Whether the new grand jury functions effectively and in a collegial manner depends on how quickly and wisely its members blend into a body of equals who investigate and deliberate carefully and objectively.

Penal Code Section 933 requires local-government officials to comment about findings and recommendations affecting them. This commentary may refute or correct actual or imagined inaccuracies in grand jury reports. Local-government officials also may use the Comment statute to acknowledge their compliance with grand jury findings and recommendations. The Legislature has withdrawn from grand jurors any immunity from prosecution for what they may say or write in their civil investigations and reports concerning local-government officials or other citizens. Thus, the civil authority of the grand jury falls short of the power of rebuking, condemning, or maligning local-government officials gratuitously or without justification. Grand juries also are required to publish findings and recommendations that are supported by documented evidence and to propose, when applicable, solutions (including financial) for problems identified in reports. Similarly, grand juries may not issue final reports containing findings and recommendations that are not supported by evidence obtained in interviews with at least two grand jurors present.

Although grand jury reports are the principal tool that panels have by which to accomplish their objectives, the power to report can be, in a democracy, an important means for civic improvement. The reporting power also is enhanced by the subpoena power, the power to indict, and the power to file accusations for misfeasance, malfeasance, or nonfeasance in public office. Even though these powers are important, I restrict my evaluation of how effectively grand juries used their investigating and reporting powers during the study period to two kinds of criteria: (a) those derived from statutes and case law, and (b) criteria concerning the institution's relationship to citizens in its community and its ability to inform them of its work.

3

Grand Jury Investigations and Reports About Local Governments and Public Officials

As is often the case in organizations, the leadership, division of labor, limitations of time and resources, and related matters affect the quality of their products—in this case, grand jury reports. One of the purposes of this chapter, therefore, is to describe how civil grand jurors in California organize and govern themselves, including matters such as the names of committees, the role of foremen, and how panels obtain their resources. A second objective of the chapter is to look broadly at the types of topics that commanded the attention of grand jurors in the study period.

Several tables in this chapter list the topics that grand jurors chose to investigate in the study period, and their frequency. Unless readers understand certain statutes pertaining to the California civil grand jury, they would not know that some investigations summarized in this chapter have no statutory basis. Merely because an investigation has been included in a grand jury final report does not make it lawful. Also, because they are necessarily brief, the summaries often do not contain enough information for readers to judge whether the investigations were well planned and conducted, significant, or effectively reported.

This chapter also presents information about certain tensions between grand juries and public officials. One conflict that I summarize in this chapter occurred between a grand jury and a public official during the study period. It is of particular importance for this study because it resulted in several legislative attempts after the study period that would have diminished the independence of the institution. For this reason, the account of that controversy in this chapter will assist readers in understanding the consequences of this conflict, which I discuss later in this chapter and in Chapter 6.

The discussion in this chapter also will help readers determine the soundness of some of the suggestions to improve the investigations and reports that I present in Chapter 6. For example, by understanding what grand jury reports and procedures manuals reveal about the foreman's role, readers will understand the basis for my comments concerning that role. Similarly, to understand why I recommend abandoning the conventional form of committee organization, readers first must understand how grand jurors have traditionally named their committees. This chapter, therefore, presents descriptive information about grand jury committees.

To balance the focus in Chapters 4 and 5 on certain deficiencies in grand jury investigations and reports, this chapter summarizes positive information about grand jury achievements and investigations. Examples of newspaper accounts of grand jury contributions to their communities support the positive emphasis. In this chapter I also explain the basis for the suggestions I offer in Chapter 6 with respect to documenting and reporting grand jury workloads.

Readers will find in this chapter only meager information about how grand juries consider and respond to complaints they receive from citizens, because final reports generally are silent about these matters. Accordingly, the chapter excludes detailed information about issues such as how grand juries differ in their method of receiving complaints from citizens, the practice of accepting only signed complaints, and controversies about whether grand juries should actively encourage citizens to send them complaints.

The summaries of investigations that this chapter presents are not, generally, quotations from final reports; rather, they are abstracts I prepared of grand jury investigations during the study period. Readers are cautioned to consider none of the quotations from, or summaries of, grand jury reports in this chapter as definitive. Although one hopes that all the findings in final reports are documented with facts, that all conclusions are reasonable, and that all recommendations are practical, one also must recognize that grand jurors, like public officials and other citizens, make mistakes. Thus, a more comprehensive understanding of any of the summaries in this report would require one to read comments by public officials in regard to the reports they represent. Evaluating such information, as I explained previously, is beyond the scope of this project.

Producing Reports

Immediately following impanelment and any training that grand jurors receive, they learn that their most pressing problem is to organize themselves to overcome obstacles resulting from the nature of the institution—namely, that grand juries are not permanent bureaucracies. Thus, "How do we get started?" is the first question many grand jurors ask immediately after impanelment.[1]

Getting Started

Grand jurors never will be more aware than they are at their first meeting of the consequences of the tradition that the grand jury is a body of citizens drawn representatively from the community. To the extent that superior court judges impanel grand juries in this manner, the group of men and women who are assembled will not be, so to speak, professional grand jurors.[2] They will be, as is their community, a diverse group, characterized by varying interests, skills, and motives as their differing social, economic, and political circumstances dictate. Indeed, if they are drawn as randomly as possible, only a few grand jurors will be acquainted personally with local-government officials and employees. Like most Americans, they will also not possess detailed knowledge of local government. These factors are consistent with the spirit of the institution.

In a sense, impaneling grand jurors who have no formal training in the law and the rules of evidence, in organizing written materials, in understanding the distinction between a finding and a conclusion, and in planning and managing investigations could be considered a sign of impartial grand jury selection. These are competencies that, after all, citizens do not widely possess. Unfortunately, limitations such as these also expose grand jurors to becoming dependent for information and technical assistance upon many of the same local-government officials or agencies over which they have statutory authority.

The Penal Code has no provisions to help grand jurors overcome many of the obstacles they will encounter early in their term. Although Penal Code Section 916 authorizes grand jurors to adopt their own procedures, it does not specify which procedures may or may not be useful, nor does it recommend when and how to use them. Each grand jury, therefore, is left to its own devices to deal with the limitations of its members. Even if a grand jury manual or handbook is available, that document has no authority over a new grand jury unless that specific panel formally adopts it. Moreover, handbooks might contain factual errors and misunderstandings about grand jury authority, or they might be written in a legal style that renders them of little use to citizens who have no background in legal terms and concepts.[3]

By no means are the problems we have just reviewed a complete accounting of all the obstacles grand jurors face when they are first impaneled. They do illustrate, however, that effective grand juries are those whose members, early in their terms, discuss and establish priorities and agree upon methods for organizing themselves efficiently.

ORGANIZING FOR INVESTIGATIONS

Grand jurors have only about six months during their year of service in which to conduct investigations. Their first three months typically are used for organizing the panel, deliberating about internal policies, and learning about local government. The last three months of grand jury service are devoted mostly to reviewing and discussing the results of investigations and writing, editing, and producing a final report. Whether grand jurors understand this reality early in their terms, and what they do about it, depends on whether the courts have impaneled people with backgrounds in time management, organizational planning, and establishing workload priorities.

Like many Americans in organizational settings, grand jurors respond to the challenge of their work by forming committees. Although no statute requires that they be created, at least four committees are formed early in the terms of most grand juries. Beyond several statutes that specify what grand jurors "may" do or "shall" do, Penal Code Section 916 grants them authority to perpetuate the committees of their predecessors, eliminate them, or continue some committees and discontinue others.[4]

Many grand jury handbooks or procedures manuals include lists of names of committees for grand juries to create. Some handbooks include cautions that committee names are only suggestions. In other counties, handbooks "recommend" the formation of specific committees and provide detailed descriptions of committee responsibilities.[5] Despite the freedom that grand jurors have in deciding the names of their committees, little variation in committee organization occurs in most counties from one year to the next. The names of grand jury committees during the study period are remarkably similar to those of the early 1960s.

The Persistence of Committee Names

Table 5, "Most Frequent Primary Names of Grand Jury Committees: 1991–1992 and 1992–1993," shows the primary names of committees for grand juries of the study period and for the grand juries of the following year.[6]

Table 6, "Frequency of Grand Jury Committee Assignments in 1963," shows the names of committees in grand jury final reports more than 30 years ago.[7] Although tallying only primary names results in some loss of detail, the data in Tables 5 and 6 nevertheless illustrate the persistence of names of grand jury committees. Some of this stability no doubt is attributable to the social, political, and economic significance of the topics designated in committee names. In California's rapidly changing society, the issues surrounding education, health, law enforcement, and planning, for example, have been in the

TABLE 5
Most Frequent Primary Names of Grand Jury Committees:
1991–1992 and 1992–1993

Primary Committee Name	Number in 1991–1992	Primary Committee Name	Number in 1992–1993
Administration	13	Ad Hoc	6
Audit	26	Administration	11
Cities	15	Audit	17
Continuity	5	Cities	9
County	14	County	6
Criminal Justice	13	Criminal Justice	10
Editorial	9	Editorial	5
Education	26	Education	17
Environment	6	Environment	9
General Services	5	Government	9
Government	6	Health	27
Health	36	Law and Justice	8
Law	9	Law Enforcement	11
Law Enforcement	14	Planning	9
Planning and Environment	10	Public Works	6
Public Works	11	Special Districts	8
Social and Human Services	6		
Special Districts	8		

forefront for decades. Tables 5 and 6 show that, although a few topics changed over the years, most remained stable:

- Health and education are leading concerns in both tables.
- In both tables, topics related to law enforcement are shown to be of high interest.
- Some of the changes in the two tables express the concerns of the two periods; as examples, environment is not in the 1963 list, and welfare lost its earlier prominence for grand juries of the study period.
- Although "public works" as a committee name is missing from the 1963 list, more specific terms such as "buildings and grounds," "county roads," and "flood control" represented public works that year.
- The term "taxes and assessments" is not present in the more recent table.

TABLE 6
Frequency of Grand Jury Committee Assignments in 1963

Committees	Number of Committee Assignments
Education	36
Audit	32
Welfare	31
Buildings and Grounds	30
County Roads	29
Health and Sanitation	27
Law Enforcement	26
County Offices	26
Hospitals	24
Planning	17
Jails	16
Probation	15
Criminal Complaints	12
Recreation	9
Juvenile	7
Government Efficiency	5
Complaints (other than criminal)	5
Special Districts	5
Taxes and Assessments	5
Flood Control	4
Public Safety	3

Emphasizing County Government

In Table 5, "County" refers to committees whose members studied county government. Examples of the full names of these committees are County Administration, County Government, and County Administration and Government. Grand juries, however, spent more time on county government than the single term "County" implies. For example, most of the investigations conducted by committees named Criminal Justice, Administration, General Services, Public Works, and Law Enforcement involved agencies of county government. Cities, of course, are missing from the 1963 list because city government was not then within the grand jury's jurisdiction as it now is under Penal Code Section 925(a).

Committee Names and Workload

With a few exceptions (such as Cities, County, and Special Districts), committee names designate the nature of a public service or function rather than a type of local government. Deciding the names of committees is more than an idle linguistic exercise. For example, the tradition of adopting without question the committee names and organization of its predecessor could commit a newly impaneled grand jury to a predetermined focus.

Another problem with this practice is that it could encourage ax-grinders to apply for grand jury service. A retired nurse might desire to be a member of a Health and Hospitals committee; a retired peace officer might wish to be the chairman of the Law Enforcement or Criminal Justice committee; a retired county or city director of public works might seek membership on the Public Works committee. A suggestion I offer in Chapter 6 will reduce both effects of predetermined committee names.

Grand Jury Committee Names in the Study Period

Most names of grand jury committees denote one or two topics. To illustrate, 18 counties during the study period had Education committees; 8 counties joined education with some other topic: Education and Libraries; Education, Youth, and Library; and the like. Similarly, 6 of the 11 Public Works committees were so titled; the remaining 5 were joined with some other topic: Public Works, Parks, and Recreation; Public Works/Special Districts; and Public Works/Water Agencies.

In the present era, "criminal justice" is the term often used to embrace the various public agencies and services concerned with crime in society. Some grand juries used this term in their committee organization, and other terms also were used, as this list reveals:

Administration of Justice	Justice System
Court and Law Enforcement	Juvenile
Crime and Delinquency	Law and Justice
Detention Facilities	Law and Safety
Jails	Law Enforcement
Judicial	Public Safety
Justice	Safety, Protection, and Justice

Grand juries during the study period created 14 Administration of Justice and Law Enforcement committees. The next most frequent term for this local-government function was Law and Justice, used 7 times. Most of the remaining terms appeared only once in the 58 final reports. Two or more of the above terms appeared in some final reports. The total number of committee names represented by the above list in the study period was 51. Thus, grand juries during the study period created more criminal-justice-related committees than committees of any other topic.

Most committee names referred to no more than two topics. Occasionally, however, committee names were more complex; for example:

- County Social Services, Education, Library, Parks and Recreation
- Health, Hospital, Sanitation and Public Assistance/Welfare
- Technical, Public Works, Planning and Agriculture

Trends in Grand Jury Committee Organization

Table 7, "Trends in Grand Jury Committee Organization: 1991–1992 and 1992–1993," shows two types of data: (a) the number of changes in grand jury committees of 1992–1993 compared to those of 1991–1992, and (b) the number of committees each grand jury organized for each of the two years. Of the 34 grand juries for which data were available for both years, 88 percent of the grand juries had only one or two changes in 1992–1993 compared to 1991–1992. No grand juries completely changed all their committee names in the latter year compared to the previous year; and only four grand juries made four or five changes in committee names in the year following the study period.

The average number of committees for each grand jury in both years was the same (seven). Nine grand juries in 1992–1993 did not identify committees in their reports, though they did in 1991–1992. This suggests a trend toward more cohesive final reports.[8]

One grand jury identified committee names in 1992–1993 but did not do so in 1991–1992. The grand jury final reports in which committee names and their members were not identified during the study period were in Northern California. The Los Angeles County Grand Jury created the most committees (14) during the study period, and the Santa Cruz panel formed the fewest committees (3). In most counties, the number of committees varied little from one year to the next. In 14 of the 34 counties for which committee information was available for both years, the number of committees was the same.

MANAGING COMPLAINTS AND WORKLOAD

The system the grand jury establishes to receive, consider, and assign complaints for investigation is the heart of its investigative process. If grand jury procedures are poorly planned, are ambiguous, or become the captive of one or two dominant grand jurors, internal dissension arises sooner or later.

Occasionally a newly impaneled foreman will assume that the term "foreman" has the same meaning in grand jury service that it has at a ranch, on a

TABLE 7
Trends in Grand Jury Committee Organization: 1991–1992 and 1992–1993

County	Number of Changes: 1992–1993 Compared to 1991–1992 — Identical or Only 1 Change	2–3	4–5+	Number of Committees '91–'92	'92–'93
Alameda		X		8	7
Alpine					
Amador	X			6	6
Butte	X			8	8
Calaveras	X			6	6
Colusa	X			7	6
Contra Costa					
Del Norte				4	N/A
El Dorado		X		7	9
Fresno	X			6	6
Glenn		X		7	5
Humboldt					
Imperial				7	N/L
Inyo				7	N/A
Kern		X		10	13
Kings		X		7	7
Lake	X			6	6
Lassen			X	6	4
Los Angeles			X	14	11
Madera		X		7	5
Marin		X		7	5
Mariposa				7	N/L
Mendocino	X			6	6
Merced				5	N/L
Modoc	X			6	6
Mono		X		7	7
Monterey				6	N/L
Napa				6	N/A
Nevada					
Orange		X		8	6
Placer	X			8	9
Plumas				6	N/L
Riverside		X		7	5
Sacramento	X			6	5
San Benito				6	N/A

(Table Continued)

TABLE 7, *Continued*

| County | Number of Changes: 1992–1993 Compared to 1991–1992 | | | Number of Committees | |
	Identical or Only 1 Change	2–3	4–5+	'91–'92	'92–'93
San Bernardino	X			11	11
San Diego	X			6	5
San Francisco					
San Joaquin					
San Luis Obispo	X			6	6
San Mateo		X		7	8
Santa Barbara				10	N/L
Santa Clara	X			4	4
Santa Cruz	X			3	3
Shasta					
Sierra					
Siskiyou					3
Solano	X			8	7
Sonoma					N/L
Stanislaus				7	
Sutter			X	8	5
Tehama				8	
Trinity			X	9	5
Tulare	X			7	7
Tuolumne					
Ventura	X			6	7
Yolo	X			12	11
Yuba				7	N/L
Totals	19	11	4	$\overline{x}$=7	$\overline{x}$=7

Note: "N/A" means "not available"; "N/L" means "not listed"; "$\overline{x}$" is the symbol for "average."

construction crew, or in other industrial settings. Some former military officers whom judges appoint as foremen, for example, attempt to organize the grand jury along military lines. Similarly, some retired professional people (such as lawyers, medical doctors, and college professors) appointed as foremen assume that their social status justifies their taking charge of the grand jury. If this person is sufficiently dominant and persuasive, and if grand jurors are apathetic, easily influenced, or uninformed about the meaning of collegiality, a foreman might control a grand jury throughout its term.

Procedures manuals sometimes encourage this behavior by designating foremen exclusively to accept or reject citizen complaints and by giving foremen sole authority to assign complaints to committees. In some cases, a foreman usurps the grand jury's powers to the extent that he or she creates committees without the panel's approval, assigns grand jurors to them, and removes jurors from them at will.[9] Indeed, foremen have been known to attempt to discharge grand jurors; however, courts usually intervene in such ill-advised efforts.

In theory, Penal Code Section 916 may be understood as permitting a grand jury to delegate complete authority for decision making to a foreman or a grand jury committee; to do so, however, would negate the principles of grand jury independence and the collegial nature of the institution. Although the courts have not ruled directly on the role of foremen or committees in civil grand jury decision making, the *Clinton* case would seem to support the principle that grand jury foremen and committees cannot exercise grand jury powers, as individuals or small groups, without the required vote of the panel.[10]

Complaints come from many sources and are motivated by many desires. Grand juries rarely list the numbers and types of complaints they receive. Only under unusual circumstances do grand juries identify complainants by name. To do so might constitute a breach of confidentiality, and the practice likely would be risky for the complainant. Because grand jury reports include little information about the demographic characteristics of complainants (sex, age, occupation, community of residence, and so on), little is known about their life circumstances. Nor is information available in most final reports about whether grand jurors themselves initiate many or few complaints or whether some kinds of investigations are more likely than others to be the result of citizens' complaints.[11]

Penal Code Section 918 authorizes sitting grand jurors to bring "public offenses" to the attention of fellow panel members, who may decide to accept or reject such complaints. Many grand juries therefore adopt procedures that permit individual grand jurors to file complaints about noncriminal matters such as possible civil investigations. Individual grand jurors, however, have no more power than other citizens to compel grand juries to conduct these investigations.[12]

Community disputes, tragedies, or catastrophes sometimes create the need for grand jury investigations. Similarly, some citizens turn to the grand jury as a "court of last resort" if they have been denied other remedies. Other persons urge a grand jury to mediate disputes between them and government agencies or within government agencies.[13]

Grand juries at times start investigations based on information reported by the news media, and they also can accept for investigation complaints that previous grand juries have recommended, though they have no obligation to do so. Additional sources of investigative leads for grand juries are financial audit reports, reports of performance auditors, and, occasionally, memoranda exchanged between public officials.[14]

Although the Penal Code requires grand juries to perform some duties (see the references to "shall" in Table 3, Chapter 2), most of the grand jury's workload is within the panel's control. Grand jurors as a body can accept or reject complaints as they please, and no statute requires them to justify their reason for doing so. Some grand jury handbooks nevertheless list reasons that can be offered to complainants to explain why a complaint was not accepted for investigation. Examples of reasons that grand juries cite to explain why they rejected complaints from citizens include the following:

- Another agency is considering the complaint or has resolved it.
- The grand jury has no jurisdiction in the complaint.
- The complainant has not given an official or agency an opportunity to correct the alleged wrong.
- The complaint is about a matter that should be pursued through private counsel.
- The complainant provided no facts to substantiate the complaint.

EFFECTS OF THE INDICTMENT FUNCTION ON THE GRAND JURY'S CIVIL WORKLOAD

In June 1990, California voters passed Proposition 115, the so-called Victims' Rights Law. As a result, California district attorneys have increasingly used the indictment to initiate prosecutions. Because of the *Hawkins* case (*Hawkins v. Superior Court* (1978) 22 Cal.3d 584, 592–593 [150 Cal.Rptr. 435]), district attorneys rarely used grand jury indictments to initiate prosecutions between 1978 and 1990. Table 8, "Grand Jury Indictments in California: 1973–1997," shows the number of indictments for each of the five years preceding the *Hawkins* decision (1978), for the years during which *Hawkins* prevailed (1978–1990), and the years for which Statewide indictment data are available following the increased use of the indictment.[15] Even before *Hawkins*, one study claimed that grand juries spent most of their time on civil investigations.[16]

Although few grand juries include in their reports detailed descriptions of their workloads, they sometimes offer comments about the increased use of the indictment and its effect on the time available for civil investigations, as these two examples show:

> This Grand Jury spent much of its time in indictment hearings. This was particularly true in the latter part of the year, when one particular indictment occupied more than 20 full days of testimony. This indictment greatly impacted the time normally spent finishing final reports. As a result, most of the jurors spent many extra hours completing their work.[17]

TABLE 8
Grand Jury Indictments in California: 1973–1997

Year	Number	Year	Number
1973	1,943	1986	25
1974	1,902	1987	6
1975	1,192	1988	23
1976	841*	1989	20
1977	689*	1990	36
1978	615	1991	264
1979	439	1992	540
1980	113	1993	1,104
1981	102	1994	842
1982	36	1995	610
1983	33	1996	829
1984	18	1997	691
1985	35		

*Excludes Santa Clara County

In April the Grand Jury was part of a criminal indictment. While based on the evidence the Grand Jury was presented, a vote for indictment was returned [leaving most grand jurors] uneasy about the system and caus[ing] many to be taken off course as to their role of "citizen watchdog."[18]

The strain between grand juries and district attorneys concerning intrusion of the indictment function on the grand jury's civil investigative duties is longstanding.[19] For example, 30 years ago a California legislative hearing disclosed the theory that some district attorneys distract grand juries from their civil investigative functions by occupying them with the indictment function:

Chairman Winton: I think this [the watchdog function] is an area, coming from a district which has three small counties in it, that causes most of the problems with the grand jury. In our counties—all three of them—I think the principal effort of the grand jury is directed towards some of these checking of county votes and school district votes and various public agency functions rather than the criminal side, and sometimes I think they tend to get way out on a limb on some of their investigations.

Mr. Smith: There is what we used to call the Lynch-Price theory— Tom Lynch and John Price [former district attorneys of Sacramento County].... They always keep their grand juries extremely busy.

Chairman Winton:	With criminal matters, that is.
Mr. Smith:	Criminal matters.
Chairman Winton:	I think this is a pretty good theory.[20]

Current law (Penal Code Section 904.6) allows a superior court to establish a second grand jury in the county for indictment purposes. Some grand juries believe this provision would conserve time for use in the civil function:

> As California statutes now allow, it is the recommendation of this Grand Jury that future criminal matters be taken before a specially selected Grand Jury specifically designated only for each criminal matter. This procedure would allow the members of the original Grand Jury to devote their time and efforts solely to matters regarding government activities and governmental expenditures.[21]

Grand jury reservations about the indictment are by no means held universally. Final reports occasionally express concern that the grand jury was not involved in indictments, and one grand jury demanded an explanation of why "some court cases were 'thrown out' of court simply because they originated with a grand jury indictment."[22]

Readers who would like more information about how grand juries assess their role in the indictment function will find ample commentary about this matter in final reports during the study period. Examples of these discussions include:

- A summary of the Grand Jury's involvement in indictments (Alameda; 1991–1992; 1:0)
- Report of use of the indictment (Los Angeles; 1991–1992; 5:0)
- The need for a second Grand Jury; financial consequences; housing of second Grand Jury; availability of qualified citizens; effects on District Attorney, Court, Public Defender, and other matters (Orange; 1991–1992; 32:3)
- Brief description and summary of indictment hearings (Riverside; 1991–1992; 2 pp.)
- Discussion of Proposition 115; Grand Jury accepted requests to present indictments from the District Attorney and the Attorney General (Sacramento; 1991–1992; 2:0)
- Summary of indictment brought against a law enforcement officer (San Benito; 1992; 2:0)
- Review of indictment function of Grand Jury; summary of Grand Jury's involvement in indictments; description of the indictment process (Santa Cruz; 1991–1992; 6:0)

- Description of indictments heard by the Grand Jury; reasons the indictment process is used; comments about impanelment of second Grand Jury (Shasta; 1991–1992; 2:0)
- Discussion of why a second Grand Jury was impaneled for indictments (Stanislaus; 1991–1992; 2:0)

GRAND JURY EXPENDITURES AND OTHER RESOURCES

Grand jury costs are paid from the general fund of county governments. In effect, grand jury investigations of the different types of local government (for example, cities, special districts, and redevelopment agencies) are therefore financed by county taxpayers. Citizens who wish to examine grand jury budgets will find them, in most counties, in the same financial documents (preliminary and final budgets) that contain budgetary information about other county functions. Typically, information about expenditures concerning grand juries will be found in the superior court section of county budgets.

Establishing Grand Jury Budgets

Grand jurors work within budgets that were approved the year before they were impaneled. In all California counties, grand jurors have no direct authority to authorize expenditures for themselves or budgets for their successors. In some counties, however, grand jurors create committees to prepare a tentative budget for next year's panel. After the grand jury has reviewed its budget committee's findings, the panel sends the budget request to the superior court for review. In other counties, grand juries by tradition are not involved in preparing budgets; instead, a superior court secretary, for example, has that responsibility.

In theory, if not in practice, the court is responsible for the formal review and approval of a grand jury budget before a board of supervisors considers it. The board of supervisors may approve or reject the request, or it may ask the county administrative officer to obtain additional information about the budget proposal. Eventually, the board of supervisors in most counties makes the final decision about the grand jury's budget for the following year.

The budgetary process I have just described varies among counties, depending on the relationships between the superior court and the board of supervisors and the historical role of grand jurors in budget preparation. The standing of the grand jury in the community and other forces also affect the process, and, in the broadest sense of the word, decisions about grand jury budgets and other resources are political, though they are made within a statutory context.

Statutes Concerning Grand Jury Finances

One might conclude that because boards of supervisors decide grand jury budgets, panels, even though they are judicial bodies, are helpless dependents of the legislative branch of government. With their hands on the institution's purse strings, county supervisors determine each year how much or how little the term "grand jury independence" means. Boards of supervisors also must approve the budgets of superior courts. Superior court judges, however, are better equipped than are grand jurors, in several ways, for the political infighting of the annual budgetary process.

First, the judiciary, the legislative, and the executive branches of government understand that Constitutional remedies prevent the latter two branches from tampering with the judicial branch. *Second*, to some extent, the State of California augments and therefore influences superior court budgets. *Third*, in many counties the administrative and negotiating details of superior courts are in the hands of professional court administrators. These persons are often at least as well trained, highly skilled, and persuasive as the county administrative officers who constitute the executive staff of county supervisors. Moreover, because these persons are employees of the courts, they possess, as do the courts themselves, certain advantages in budgetary battles.

Depending on circumstances and the personalities involved, grand juries might benefit from one or more important statutory resources. Penal Code Section 931, for example, authorizes judges to order the county treasurer and county auditor to process payment for whatever expenses grand juries incur for their exercise of powers under Article 2, Title 4, of the Penal Code (the so-called civil powers). In theory, this statute can be used if a court believes a grand jury is justified in employing one of the "experts," "assistants," "auditors," or "appraisers" that Penal Code Section 926 authorizes, even though no funds have been budgeted for those purposes or when a board of supervisors has refused to grant a supplemental budget.

In practice, Penal Code Section 931 is used rarely, for several reasons. Some courts are reluctant to use it because of the tension that doing so is apt to incite in their relationships with boards of supervisors. In other cases, boards of supervisors prefer to take the initiative to allocate a moderate amount of money for a grand jury investigation rather than run the risk of a court issuing an order raising a larger sum to support a full-scale investigation into a potentially embarrassing matter. Examples of the use of Penal Code Section 931 in recent years include ordering the augmentation of grand jury budgets to:

- supplement a grand jury budget so a panel could continue an investigation into expense accounts of public officials
- contract with an auditing firm to study procedures in the office of a county clerk
- hire special counsel to assist a sitting grand jury in investigating suspected improper activities of a previous grand jury.

Several years after Penal Code Section 931 was enacted, the Legislature created Penal Code Section 914.5, forbidding grand juries from spending beyond their budgets for their investigative activities. The statute further provides, however, that additional expenditures may be allowed if the court approves them in advance and if the board of supervisors has been advised of the requested additional monies. The statute does not permit boards of supervisors to deny the requested additional funds, nor does it provide a penalty for grand juries that improperly exceed their budgets.

Trends in Expenditures

One way to assess the standing of panels in their communities is to examine trends in grand jury expenditures. One would expect that effective grand juries would enjoy more financial support than would mediocre panels. Or, in market-theory terms, the demand for ineffective civil grand jury products would be negligible. Of course, financial data by themselves provide few conclusive explanations for variations that might exist Statewide in grand jury finances. Nevertheless, some insights into community support for panels may be obtained by examining grand jury expenditures for an extended period.

Grand Juries and Boards of Supervisors

The analysis would be more illuminating if grand jury expenditures were compared to those for some other county function. Of several possibilities (such as comparing grand jury expenditures to those of superior courts, county auditors, or district attorneys), the one that seems most promising is to compare the expenditures of grand juries to those of county boards of supervisors. Comparing expenditures between the two bodies is of particular interest for three reasons:

- Boards of supervisors establish the budgets of grand juries.
- No federal or State laws, rules, or regulations control how much money boards of supervisors appropriate for themselves or for grand juries.
- The expenditures of boards of supervisors are more similar in magnitude to grand jury expenditures than those of many other county functions.

Although the grand jury is an arm of the superior court, judges in California rarely are involved personally in grand jury budgets. Except in unusual circumstances, superior courts do not interfere with decisions of county boards of supervisors, a local-governmental function that is subject to civil grand jury review, concerning grand jury budgets. Thus, many of the political considerations that affect other county departments under the control of county supervisors also might influence decisions about grand jury budgets. For this reason, a comparison of grand jury expenditures to those of county boards of supervisors could reveal how the former body appraises the worth of the latter.

If in a given county, for example, expenditures increase steadily every year for county supervisors but decline for the grand jury, one need not look beyond the relationship between the two bodies to find reasons for this disparity. This trend might be of particular interest in counties in which enmity exists between the two bodies. On the other hand, if trends in expenditures elsewhere show that those of county supervisors remain constant while those of grand juries increase annually, one might conclude that the county supervisors either think highly of the institution or the panels enjoy strong citizen support, or both. In still other counties, the expenditure trends for grand juries might follow the same pattern as the trends for county supervisors. In this case, we might conclude tentatively that county supervisors respect the independence of the grand jury.

Differences in expenditure trends between the two bodies also might be attributed to other influences. For example, in some counties, grand jury budgets traditionally include money for the services of contract auditors who report their findings directly to grand juries. In other counties, practice dictates that financial and performance auditors work independently of the grand jury, reporting instead to the board of supervisors. Similarly, grand juries that are frequently involved in indictments tend to have larger budgets than panels that rarely hear them. Counties also vary in how much money boards of supervisors allow grand jurors to receive for attending meetings, as we shall soon see in the discussion of "Fees and Mileage." For reasons such as these, grand jury expenditures by themselves, or in comparison to expenditures of boards of supervisors, should be regarded only as leads for further inquiry.

STATEWIDE TRENDS

As the Statewide expenditure table shows in Appendix A, "Some Notes About the Study and Its Method," grand jury expenditures and those of boards of supervisors increased between 1984 and 1996. Of course, if these dollars were adjusted for inflation, the actual increases for both bodies would be smaller in dollar buying power. I have not made this adjustment because both bodies would have been affected equally by inflation. For the purposes of this section, the relative standing between the two bodies is of more concern than how the buying power of the dollar affected them during that period.[23]

Statewide, grand jury expenditures between 1984 and 1996 increased at a smaller magnitude (44.1 percent) than did expenditures for boards of supervisors (87.4 percent) for the same period. The fourth column in the expenditure table in Appendix A provides another view of this long-term trend: Year by year, grand jury expenditures typically diminish as a proportion of expenditures for boards of supervisors. These figures are, of course, averages. County by county, we would expect to find different patterns between the two bodies: The expenditure trends for some grand juries may be up; the trends for others may be down; and the trends for both bodies elsewhere may be identical. In any case, on the basis of the Statewide expenditure data, grand juries seem to be losing ground compared to boards of supervisors.

Neither of these expenditure trends, expressed in actual dollars, proceeds at the same annual rate. Figure A, "Overall Patterns of Expenditures by Grand Juries and by Boards of Supervisors," shows the "best fit" trend lines for the actual dollar amounts of expenditures for the two bodies in the 13-year period. Graph lines representing actual dollar amounts would be much more jagged. One can see that the trend line for boards of supervisors is increasing more sharply than the trend line for grand juries.

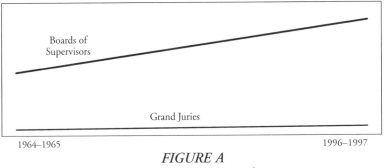

FIGURE A
Overall Patterns of Expenditures
by Grand Juries and by Boards of Supervisors

Figure B, "Grand Jury Expenditures Statewide as a Percentage of Expenditures for Boards of Supervisors," shows year-by-year variations. This graph is based on the far-right column of the expenditure table in Appendix A. The general trend of this measure of the relationship of grand jury expenditures to those of county boards of supervisors is steadily down for the 13-year period.

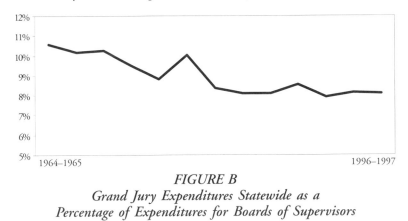

FIGURE B
Grand Jury Expenditures Statewide as a
Percentage of Expenditures for Boards of Supervisors

Still another view of grand jury finances is provided by calculating for each county in the 13-year period the percentage that grand jury expenditures were of expenditures for boards of supervisors. Because of space limitations, the individual graphs for each of the counties are not shown in this study; however, a visual inspection of the "best-fit" lines for county supervisors and grand juries in each county for the 13-year period illustrates how each panel fared yearly compared to its board of supervisors. The following tally reveals that the number (14) of upward trends for grand juries relative to expenditures for county supervisors is somewhat smaller than the number (18) of downward trends.

Description of Trend	Number of Grand Juries
Generally or slightly upward	14
Flat	21
Generally or slightly downward	18
Erratic	4
Total	57

In this list, "flat" means that grand jury budgets fluctuated little from one year to the next. Of course, a flat expenditure trend for the period indicates an actual decline in budgetary resources. "Downward" and "upward" are subjective terms, based on a visual inspection of trend lines rather than mathematical computations.

EXAMPLES OF INDIVIDUAL COUNTY TRENDS

Figure C, "Expenditures for Grand Juries and Boards of Supervisors in Five Counties," depicts several of the individual county trends discussed in the previous paragraph. Counties A and B are similar in that the trends for grand juries and county supervisors are generally upward. County A, however, has a somewhat more erratic pattern for both bodies than does County B. The trends for the boards of supervisors in Counties C and D are likewise upward, whereas the grand jury trends are down for County C and somewhat flat for County D.

County C is one of several California counties that have been reported to consider bankruptcy in recent years. In this county, however, the grand jury has been more affected by concern about scarce revenues than have county supervisors. The upward turn in the best-fit line for County C in 1996–1997 coincides with, but is not necessarily related to, the retirement of a superior court judge who served for many years. The pattern of County E is unusual: a long-term decline for the board of supervisors but an upturn in recent years for the grand jury. By the end of fiscal year 1996–1997, grand jury expenditures in County E became more like those of grand juries in counties of a similar population size. Unlike the case of County A, however, the board of supervisors reduced its own expenditures considerably in the same period. The trends for both bodies in County E are unique among California counties in the expenditure patterns for the 13-year period.

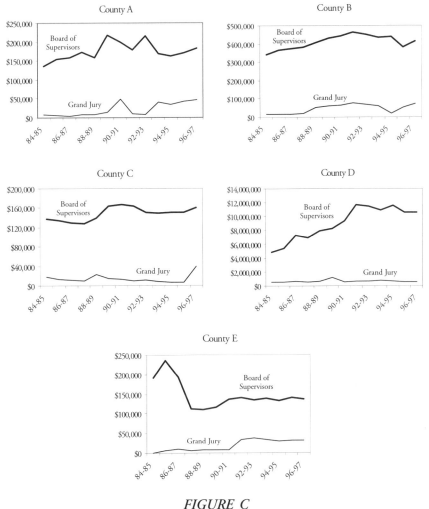

FIGURE C
Expenditures for
Grand Juries and Boards of Supervisors
in Five Counties

Table 9, "Expenditures for Grand Juries and County Boards of Supervisors in Five California Counties: Percentage Changes for 1996–1997 over 1984–1985," shows the changes in percentage increases for the last fiscal year over the first fiscal year depicted in the five graphs in Figure C. Of course, the scale of the actual dollar amounts is quite different in each of the counties. For example, the large increase in grand jury expenditures in County A is unusual. In this county, grand jury expenditures in the base year were only several hundred dollars. By the end of the period, the expenditures increased to an amount that is still considerably smaller than the budgets of grand juries in counties of a similar population size, although the percentage increase is large. Similarly, the very large percentage increase in County E is attributable to an unusually small expenditure in the panel's base year. Unlike the pattern in County A, however, expenditures for the grand jury in County E rose to a level in the upper range of expenditures in counties of similar size.

TABLE 9
Expenditures for Grand Juries and County Boards of Supervisors in Five California Counties: Percentage Changes for 1996–1997 over 1984–1985

	Percentage Change
County A	
Grand jury	445.9
Board of supervisors	34.8
County B	
Grand jury	367.5
Board of supervisors	22.5
County C	
Grand jury	111.8
Board of supervisors	17.5
County D	
Grand jury	15.4
Board of supervisors	117.8
County E	
Grand jury	8,696.5
Board of supervisors	-28.2

Fees and Mileage

Grand jurors in California do not receive salaries for grand jury service. One statute (Penal Code Section 890), however, requires that they receive payment of $10 for each day's attendance as a grand juror and mileage reimbursement of 15¢ per mile "in going only." The reimbursement provisions of this statute have not changed in many years. Government Code Section 68091, however, authorizes boards of supervisors to establish fees and mileage reimbursements higher than those the Legislature authorizes. In some counties, grand jurors therefore receive higher fees and mileage than Penal Code Section 890 requires. In 1992, the Resources Committee of one grand jury reported a 70 percent response to its survey of California grand juries.[24] The survey revealed that counties reimburse some grand juries for general grand jury meetings and committee meetings, as follows:

General Meetings	Number Responding		Committee Meetings	Number Responding
$25.00	6		$25.00	4
20.00	4		20.00	2
15.00	9		15.00	6
11.00	1		12.00	1
10.00	21		11.00	1
			10.00	11
			9.00	1
			6.00	1
			0 (or N/R)	14

Of the grand juries providing information about mileage reimbursement, most grand juries reported that they received higher mileage reimbursement than the 15¢ minimum figure required by Penal Code Section 890:

Amount Reimbursed Per Mile	Number Responding
37¢	1
32¢	1
30¢	1
29¢	1
28¢	8
27¢	1
26¢	3
25¢	3
24¢	1
20¢	1
15¢	1
"Yes" but no amount shown	14
No response	5

Grand Jury Comments About Resources

This summary of an investigation in a grand jury report refers to the frustration of a panel in attempting to obtain an appropriate setting for deliberations:

> Exchange of correspondence between the grand jury and the county administrator regarding the former's attempt to obtain a meeting room, a small office, locking file cabinets, table, desk, chairs, and a telephone.[25]

Most grand juries have no secretarial staff, and only a few have budgets for hiring employees. If the salaries for these employees are in the budgets of departments for which grand juries have statutory authority, a problem of divided allegiance may arise. If a county staff member assigned to the grand jury is a long-time employee, he or she may encounter peer-group pressure, or pressure from department heads, to discuss grand jury activities.[26]

Grand Jury Expenditures and the Spirit of the Institution

As is the case with boards of supervisors themselves, size of budget does not guarantee high performance. Well-planned and executed grand jury investigations and clear, concise, and complete reports of them depend far more on the character of grand jurors than on their budgets. The grand jury tradition argues against salaried panel members, well-appointed offices and vehicles, and large staffs. Nevertheless, phone bills must be paid, documents must be typed, and file cabinets must be available. The expenditure data discussed here reveal considerable variation in the willingness of boards of supervisors to provide support for the institution.

Reports About Local Government

In this section we will examine information from the project database about the numbers and types of grand jury investigations, the most and least frequent investigative topics, how grand juries allocate their investigative resources, grand jury claims of achievements, summaries of soundly conceived and executed investigations, and local-government officials' comments about findings and recommendations. The discussion includes summaries of occasional grand jury conflicts with elected or appointed officials.

OVERVIEW OF THE DATABASE

The project database yielded data about the numbers and types of investigations during the study period Statewide and by individual county. Most of the data in this section are quantitative: They reveal, so to speak, the workload of grand juries as they exercise their civil function.

Number of Investigations by Year and by County

Nearly 1,000 summaries of investigations conducted during the study period were entered into the database. The number of investigations for the two grand jury years (fiscal and calendar) is:

1991–1992	862
1992	109
Total	971

The number of investigations included in final reports varied by grand jury. Table 10, "Number of Investigative Topics by County," shows how many summaries of investigations the database contains, by county. Discrepancies in the totals for several tables in this section are a result of my adding or modifying computer codes as I proceeded through the data-entry phase of the study. For example, about halfway through the project, I decided to discontinue entering information about perfunctory tours or visitations and brief, particularly insignificant "investigations" with no findings and recommendations. In some

TABLE 10
Number of Investigative Topics by County

County	Number of Topics	County	Number of Topics
Alameda	14	Placer	24
Alpine	19	Plumas	5
Amador	20	Riverside	45
Butte	16	Sacramento	14
Calaveras	17	San Benito	15
Colusa	7	San Bernardino	25
Contra Costa	18	San Diego	19
Del Norte	14	San Francisco	5
El Dorado	20	San Joaquin	12
Fresno	17	San Luis Obispo	21
Glenn	23	San Mateo	20
Humboldt	15	Santa Barbara	16
Imperial	7	Santa Clara	22
Inyo	8	Santa Cruz	31
Kern	29	Shasta	15
Kings	25	Sierra	14
Lake	26	Siskiyou	16
Lassen	16	Solano	10
Los Angeles	23	Sonoma	16
Madera	6	Stanislaus	15
Marin	13	Sutter	23
Mariposa	31	Tehama	9
Mendocino	19	Trinity	13
Merced	12	Tulare	17
Modoc	15	Tuolumne	17
Mono	13	Ventura	23
Monterey	21	Yolo	19
Napa	13	Yuba	29
Nevada	20		
Orange	16	Total	1,023

cases I created new codes for two or three topics that I originally had entered as one topic, and so on. Because the study was exploratory, I elected not to spend time modifying the database to conform to the coding guide as it existed at the end of the project.

Frequency of Grand Jury Investigative Topics

Table 11, "Range in Production of Grand Jury Investigative Reports," shows the range of grand juries in the production of reports. During the study period, the grand juries published between 11 and 25 reports of investigations in their final reports. Quality and quantity have no necessary relationship in producing final reports. In some cases, a low number of investigations means that grand jurors decided to conduct a few investigations well rather than many investigations poorly. In other cases, a large number of reports means that a grand jury conducted many superficial investigations.

TABLE 11
Range in Production
of Grand Jury Investigative Reports

No. of Reports	Number of Counties
1–5	2
6–10	6
11–15	15
16–20	19
21–25	10
25+	6
Total	58

Number of Investigative Topics
by Type of Local Government

Anyone reading grand jury final reports will conclude that grand jurors focus almost entirely on county government. In doing so, grand jurors do not seem to understand that, numerically, counties are a small segment in the array of all types of local governments in California. Unfortunately, a flaw in the first version of the coding guide prevented a precise tally of the numbers of investigations by type of local government. Table 12, "Number of Investigative Topics by Type of Local Government," nevertheless, shows a fairly valid picture of the tendency of grand jurors to direct their attention to county governments rather than the far more numerous other local governments in California.

TABLE 12
Number of Investigative Topics by Type of Local Government

Type of Local Government	Number of Investigations
Cities	27
Education (government schools only)	40
Housing	7
Joint Powers Agencies	3
Local Agency Formation Commissions	3
Nonprofit Corporations	16
Redevelopment Agencies	14
Special Districts	40
Total	150

A CLOSER LOOK AT THE DATABASE

The term "topics" refers to the general subject of an investigation. For example, in the example of a summary provided in Appendix A, "Some Notes About the Study and Its Method," the topic of the investigation was a sheriff's department. The names of the topics are, in general, my own creation. They are not necessarily identical to the names of grand jury committees, nor are they prescribed by law for grand jury usage.

Number of Investigations by Topic

Table 13, "Number of Investigations by Topic," identifies the 70 specific topics about which grand jurors issued reports during the study period. The number of investigations shows how many I summarized for the database.

Most Frequently Investigated Topics

Table 14, "Seventeen Most Frequent Investigative Topics," shows the investigative topics that were tallied more than 20 times in the database. I selected the number 20 as an arbitrary criterion for frequently reported investigations. The table shows that nearly all grand juries reported at least one investigation into county or city jails that resulted in one or more recommendations. Of the 17 topics in the table, 10 topics, designated with an asterisk, are entirely or chiefly functions of county government.

TABLE 13
Number of Investigations by Topic

Topic	Number of Investigations
Agriculture, sealer of weights and measures	5
Airports or aviation	9
Alcohol, drugs, narcotics, etc.	7
Animal control	11
Assessor, assessments, etc.	5
Audit by grand jury, audit review, etc.	16
Auditor, auditor-controller	10
Brown Act	7
Child protective services, children's services, etc.	22
Cities, city government	27
Civil service, merit system, personnel, etc.	30
Communications, electronic equipment	4
Community services	1
Conflict of interest, abuse of office, etc.	9
Contract review, contract services, franchises, etc.	17
County clerk, city clerk, clerk-recorder, etc.	5
County fairs	1
County government or administration, etc.	36
County or city counsel	5
County superintendent of schools	6
Crime, criminal justice, crime prevention	3
Data processing	8
District attorney, family support	20
Education, school districts, community colleges	40
Elections, registrar of voters, etc.	11
Emergency services, disaster preparedness, etc.	18
Expenses, expense accounts, misuse of funds, etc.	12
Finance, fiscal, budgeting, etc.	9
Fire districts, fire departments, etc.	28
Foster care, adoptions, group homes, etc.	4
Gangs	6
General services, county garage, etc.	5
Grand jury review, continuity, procedures, etc.	24
Guardian-conservator, public administrator	8
Hazardous and toxic waste, air pollution, etc.	35

(Table Continued)

TABLE 13, *Continued*

Topic	Number of Investigations
Health, hospitals, AIDS	37
Housing, public housing	7
Jails and prisons	55
Joint powers agencies and authorities	3
Judicial (superior court; not municipal court)	4
Juvenile, juvenile halls, institutions	26
Law enforcement, other, coroner, marshal, etc.	11
Legislative procedures, etc.	19
Libraries	17
Local agency formation commissions	3
Mental health, adult protective services	9
Municipal courts, justice courts	12
Nonprofit corporations	16
Parks and recreation, museums, county fairs	11
Performance audits or other special audits	13
Planning, land use, zoning, etc.	41
Police departments	29
Probation	9
Public defense, public defender	7
Public works, etc.	13
Purchasing department, etc.	10
Redevelopment agencies, etc.	14
Risk management, safety issues, etc.	6
Salary review of public officers	4
Sanitation, sewers, flood control	2
Senior citizens, nursing homes, etc.	4
Sheriffs' departments	37
Special districts, special taxing authorities, etc.	40
Taxation, fairness of rates, charges	2
Transportation, traffic, improvement of roads, etc.	6
Treasurer, treasurer-tax collector, etc.	11
Utilities	1
Veterans' affairs	3
Water	6
Welfare (social services), homeless, fraud, etc.	30
Other (unclassified)	8
Total	990

TABLE 14
Seventeen Most Frequent Investigative Topics

Topic	Number of Reports
*Jails and prisons	55
*Planning; land use, zoning, etc.	41
Special districts, special taxing authorities	40
Education, school districts; community colleges	40
*Sheriffs' departments	37
*Health, hospitals, AIDS	37
*County government or administration	36
*Hazardous and toxic waste; air pollution	35
*Welfare (social services); homeless; fraud, etc.	30
Civil service, merit system; personnel, etc.	30
Police departments	29
*Juvenile; juvenile halls, institutions	26
Grand jury review, continuity, procedures	24
Cities, city government	27
*Child protective services; children's services, etc.	22
Fire districts, fire departments, etc.	28
*District attorney; family support	20
Total	557

*Functions of county government

Types of Investigations

Table 15, "Examples of Nine Types of Grand Jury Investigations," presents the database from a different perspective than we have considered so far. This table shows the number of topics by type, rather than by topic, that are in the database. "Type," as the word is used in Table 15, is not a legal term. It signifies the effect an investigation produced, or what its actual result was, rather than its statutory purpose. The nine types in Table 15 were developed subjectively; the types are names selected to identify what seem to be "families" or categories of investigations in the database.[27]

In some cases, type of investigation might be directly related to one or more Penal Code statutes. In other cases, the type might be a derivative of one or more statutes, although they might not actually mention the words or terms used to express the type. The examples provide readers insight into the grand jury's civil function more conveniently than reading the summaries of all investigations in the project database.

TABLE 15
Examples of Nine Types of Grand Jury Investigations

Type of Investigation	Number of Investigations in the Study Period
1. Government Review and Inspection	498

Need for computer system, relocation of office, and pursuit of alternatives to chemical pest control by the Office of the County Agricultural Commissioner; Napa; 1991–1992; 3:4.

Review of span of control in County departments; includes response of County Administrator; San Luis Obispo; 1991–1992; 3:1.

Follow-up of a previous Grand Jury inquiry into how the County contracts for services; Santa Barbara; 1991–1992; 4:5.

Review of County-owned Nut Tree Airport; inadequacy of airport office; "self-sustaining" revenues; other matters; Solano; 1992; 2:6.

Study of a nonprofit corporation that provides 24-hour shelter for battered women and children; Sutter; 1991–1992; 2:0.

2. Governance   174

Investigation of a complaint that a member of the Board of Supervisors holds an incompatible office as Fire Chief in a local fire district; Calaveras; 1991–1992; 2:1.

Investigation of a complaint that a Supervisor assigned irrigation-district staff to work on the Supervisor's personal project during working hours, that proceeds from the sale of district scrap metal were retained by a Supervisor, and that the Supervisor ordered district tires and parts installed on a private vehicle; Merced; 1991–1992; 2:3.

Inquiry into a complaint from a citizen of Rohnert Park concerning the way the City conducts its business and an allegation that one developer receives preferential treatment; Sonoma; 1992; 31+:9.*

3. Resource Needs   72

Inquiry into the level of support services available for the elderly in Los Angeles County; Los Angeles; 1991–1992; 6:3.

Age of the building and the electrical system of the John C. Fremont Hospital District; the need for a larger emergency room; the need for coordination between the County and hospital service; Mariposa; 1991–1992; 2:4.

The need for an approved storage facility at Olivehurst Public Utilities District; Yuba; 1991–1992; 1:1.

(Table Continued)

TABLE 15, Continued

Type of Investigation	Number of Investigations in the Study Period
4. Organizational Assessment	55

Review of major revisions in the Sheriff's Department; El Dorado; 1991–1992; 5:0.

Report of an investigation into certain "limitations" of the current County computerized information system; San Luis Obispo; 1991–1992; 1:1.

A Study of Welfare Fraud; San Diego; 1991–1992; 18:22.

5. Employee Benefits and Welfare	48

Report on the County sick-leave program; Contra Costa; 1991–1992; 2:4.

Investigation into the Income Division of the County Welfare Department, including cramped working space, morale problems, unhealthful working conditions and the manner of making promotions; Siskiyou; 1991–1992; 5:?

The need for a retirement plan for all employees of the City of Wheatland and resolution of communication problems with Yuba County; Yuba; 1991–1992; 1:2.

6. Conflict Resolution	37

Expression of concern about reports of sexual harassment at Imperial Valley College; Imperial; 1991–1992; 3:0.

Review of the County Counsel's "Impartial Analysis" of a bond issue; San Luis Obispo; 1991–1992; 12:3.

History of 21-year dispute regarding a veterinary clinic in Ben Lomond; loss of citizens' faith in code enforcement; supervisorial influence and intervention, and other matters; Santa Cruz; 1991–1992; 7:8.

7. Social Issues and Trends	22

Report of an investigation into what local government in Los Angeles County is doing to address the problem of the "General Exodus of Businesses from Los Angeles County"; Los Angeles; 1991–1992; 51+:3.

Expression of concern about the emergence of gang activity in the County; effects of gang activity on schools and citizens; review of efforts by law enforcement to deal with the problem; Placer; 1991–1992; 5:9.

Effect of migrants trespassing on the community of Alpine and other locales in San Diego County; San Diego; 1991–1992; 4:4.

(Table Continued)

TABLE 15, *Continued*

Type of Investigation	Number of Investigations in the Study Period
8. Reorganization	17

Restructuring of the County Hospital to an Alternative Rural Model Facility; availability of language interpreters; recruitment of professional personnel; Glenn; 1991–1992; 2:2.

Need for "the emergence of a new type of public institution" to replace the traditional form of "bureaucratic county government"; County government should become more "entrepreneurial"; the need for clear mission statements; regarding citizens as customers, and related recommendations; Monterey; 1992; 3:4.

The need for greater efforts and coordination of child-abuse prevention training; Placer; 1991–1992; 6:4.

9. Accountability	17

The lack of inventory control over stores invites the misuse or misappropriation of assets; Calaveras; 1991–1992; 1:1.

An investigation into a complaint that a County water district did not comply with Government Code Section 25909 that requires the filing of a yearly audit; Mendocino; 1992; 2:2.

Following a request by an unidentified official or department, the Grand Jury completed the first formal independent audit in 35 years of the Museum of Natural History of the City of Pacific Grove; Monterey; 1992; 2:4.

Total	940

*This investigation illustrates how some grand jury investigations result in a flurry of newspaper articles and other reactions: "Don't ignore the grand jury: an editorial comment" (*Petaluma Argus-Courier*, January 24, 1993, n.p.); "The grand jury—a citizen's tool" (*Environmental Impact Reporter*, January–February 1993, p. 10); "RP council in tiff over reply to grand jury report" (*Press Democrat*, March 11, 1993, B-1); "Developer files claim against R.P." (*Petaluma Argus-Courier*, March 22, 1993, p. 1); "FBI inquiry targets Rohnert Park officials" (*Press Democrat*, May 8, 1993, p. A-1).

Five examples are provided for the first type because of its size. Thereafter, three examples are provided for each of the types. The examples were chosen as neither good nor bad investigations. They are merely representative. Most of them appear to be within the statutory jurisdiction of the grand jury, with the possible exception of the first example in "Social Issues and Trends." Reading that report, one wonders what the basis was for grand jury intervention into a matter that more properly is within the province of a chamber of commerce or taxpayers' association. In any case, none of the statutes granting the grand jury its authority seems directly related to this category.

The first and most frequent type, "Government Review and Inspection," includes investigations that many people refer to as the grand jury's watchdog function. This type includes reviews of administrative procedures, methods, practices, and operations. In these investigations, grand juries often express the need for improved methods and practices based on information acquired during on-site tours, inspections, and visits. This type also includes routine monitoring of legislative meetings, elections, and other official events. Also included in this category are follow-up studies of previous grand jury recommendations concerning this type of investigation.

The second most frequent type is designated as "Governance." In this type, one finds investigations concerning allegations of misuse of equipment or other resources and inquiries into complaints that officials failed to comply with statutes, ordinances, regulations, or approved procedures. This type also includes investigations into allegations of official conflict of interest; reports of abuse of power, office, or authority; and criminal acts, ethical transgressions, and unprofessional conduct or inadequate response or services by officials.

"Resource Needs," the third most frequent type, encompasses investigations concerning the adequacy of staffing levels, facilities, property, equipment, and budgets. The fourth type, "Organizational Assessment," is similar to "Government Review and Inspection" except that the former investigations are more detailed than the latter. Whereas the latter type of investigation is routine and sometimes perfunctory, "Organizational Assessment" investigations often involve the extensive investigation and analysis of interview, documentary, budgetary, survey research, and statistical information. When grand juries conduct this type of investigation well, they are similar to those conducted by professional internal auditors, performance analysts, and the like. This type of investigation also may contain data from fiscal and management audits and findings and recommendations concerning interorganizational relationships.

The fifth most frequent type, "Employee Benefits and Welfare," consists of studies or comments about salaries or other benefits for local-government elected and appointed officials. The most frequent category of investigation within this type concerns matters such as job safety, employee job satisfaction, training, and performance evaluation. Also included are investigations about procedures and practices for hiring, promoting, and terminating employees, chiefly at mid-management and line levels.

Grand juries occasionally report the results of their inquiries into community controversies, including

- how they arbitrated inter-governmental disagreements
- expressions of concern about dissension within local-government bodies

- investigations into arguments concerning the causes of highly publicized matters such as riots on government sites
- the results of their meetings with citizens who claim that a public official or employee has abused them.

In the table, this type of grand jury activity is referred to as "Conflict Resolution," the sixth most frequent category.

"Social Issues and Trends" refers to a type of investigation for which the statutory basis is more difficult to justify than any other type of grand jury investigation. As the third least-frequent type of investigation, it includes commentary about matters such as population growth; immigration; environmental issues; diseases; and other social, political, and economic trends, issues, and problems.

The last two types, "Reorganization" and "Accountability," include, respectively, reports about adding, eliminating, or reorganizing local-government services, functions, and departments and improper or inadequate inventories, accounting, or recording practices for public properties, equipment, and other physical resources.

A More Detailed Look at an Investigative Topic: Police Departments

Another view of grand jury investigations and reports can be obtained by examining summaries of one topic. We will use police departments for this purpose. The reason for choosing this topic for the reader's inspection is that the police service is one of the most basic functions of local government—and one in which many citizens have considerable interest. The following summaries reveal several aspects of grand jury investigations that also may be found in other topics:

- Routine visits to local law enforcement agencies; use of building space; adequacy of staffing; operation of the County kitchen facility; Amador; 1991–1992; 3:2.
- Report of a meeting with the Chief of Police and the Lieutenant of Police of the City of Colusa; Colusa; 1992; 1:?
- Report of an unannounced, on-site inspection at the South Lake Tahoe Police Department of all the records pertaining to the Asset Forfeiture Funds; El Dorado; 1991–1992; 2:1.
- An interview with the Chief of Police of Willows; inspection of the facilities; review of how evidence is handled and stored; Glenn; 1991–1992; 2:1.
- Comments regarding storage of evidence, controlled substances, and vehicles seized in the commission of a crime; Fresno; 1991–1992; 2:8.

- Methods and procedures that three cities used to handle citizen complaints about police officers; the lack of understanding that Penal Code Section 832.7 allows otherwise confidential law enforcement records to be examined by a grand jury; Humboldt; 1991–1992; 7:1.
- Report of an inquiry into a complaint from a citizen alleging that law enforcement agencies are delaying the investigation and prosecution of a case; Imperial; 1991–1992; 6:0.
- Reviews of citizen complaints alleging violations of civil rights by the California City Police Department; Kern; 1991–1992; 3:1.
- Inspection of the Hanford Police Department; Kings; 1991–1992; 2:0.
- Report of an inspection of the facilities of the Lakeport Police Department; Lake; 1991–1992; 2:0.
- Review of a citizen's complaint concerning alleged ethnic favoritism and sales of seized property by members of a police department; allegation not sustained; Lake; 1991–1992; 1:0.
- Review of procedures that local law enforcement agencies use to investigate citizen complaints against peace officers; the need for standard Countywide procedures; Marin; 1992; 23+:65.
- Investigation of a complaint regarding continuing internal problems and dissension within the Greenville Police Department; Monterey; 1992; 3:6.
- Response to citizen complaints regarding the Nevada City Police Department and follow-up by the previous Grand Jury to investigate the department; Nevada; 1991–1992; 4:8.
- Review of morale, allegations of quotas, unfair disciplinary actions, and unfair dismissals of police officers; Nevada; 1991–1992; 3:5.
- Comments about the age of buildings, termites, plans to equip vehicles with computers within five years, and other observations concerning several city police departments; Riverside; 1991–1992; 2:4.
- Inquiry into reasons why Hollister Police Department has curtailed certain services; hazardous highway condition aggravated by inadequate "Left Turn Ahead" signs; implementation of recommendations in a recent management study of the Police Department; San Benito; 1992; 5:4.
- Review of how peace officers use lethal force; San Diego; 1991–1992; 13:37.
- Police Facilities Improvement Bonds; educational incentives; the Police Stable; Central Station parking; tenure of the Police Chief; San Francisco; 1991–1992; 5:11.
- Visits to eight law enforcement agencies concerning officer-involved shootings, citizen complaints, abandoned property, disposal of illicit drugs, disposal of confiscated firearms; San Joaquin; 1991–1992; 2:2.

- Inspection and tour of the San Luis Obispo Police Department; San Luis Obispo; 1991–1992; 1:0.
- Follow-up of an investigation by the previous Grand Jury into towing contracts, evidence rooms, turnover rates of police officers, training, and other matters in the Paso Robles Police Department; San Luis Obispo; 1991–1992; 4:1.
- The need for the City of East Palo Alto to "allocate sufficient funding" to provide better salaries for the Police Department; the Department should "seek new and innovative resources and cooperation of nearby communities in crime control and reduction programs"; San Mateo; 1992; 2:4.
- Review of procedures by which police departments receive complaints about officers from citizens; Santa Clara; 1991–1992; 8:0.
- Review of the relationship between the City of San Jose Police Department and the U.S. Immigration and Naturalization Service with regard to alleged "sweeps" that the latter conducts; Santa Clara; 1991–1992; 3:0.
- Report of an investigation into an allegation of misuse of force by a deputy sheriff who accompanied a Child Protective Services worker on a visit to the home of a purported victim of child molestation; Santa Cruz; 1991–1992; 7:4.
- Review of the process for complaining against police at the West Sacramento Police Department; Yolo; 1991–1992; 2:1.
- The effect of booking fees on arrests by the Marysville Police Department; Yuba; 1991–1992; 1:1.

These summaries represent most of the nine types of grand jury activities discussed in the previous section, including routine inspections, responding to complaints from citizens, and detailed investigations of systems and procedures. This group of grand jury investigations also includes many of the leading issues in contemporary police administration, such as evidence and property-management problems, the use of force, and the procedures the police develop for investigating complaints about them from the community. In one investigation, a grand jury reported how it handled a problem many grand juries face: internal conflict of interest. In this case, a grand juror was a former law enforcement officer previously employed by the department the grand jury investigated. The panel attempted to assure readers that it had recognized and accounted for this relationship, in a paragraph immediately under the title of the report:

> This report of the Grass Valley Police Department is issued by the 1991–1992 Grand Jury with the exception of one member of this Grand Jury who is a former employee of the Grass Valley Police Department. This Grand Juror was excluded from all parts of the investigation, which included interviews, deliberations and the making and acceptance of this report. This report is

made based on information obtained from outside sources with none of the information being obtained from the excluded Grand Juror. (Nevada County Grand Jury Final Report, 1991–1992, p. 52)

The Audit Function

Many grand juries conduct their investigations largely without professional assistance. Under certain circumstances, however, panels become involved in audits in several ways:

- Grand juries might employ auditing firms to conduct financial audits.
- In some counties, grand juries and boards of supervisors jointly employ auditing firms to conduct financial audits.
- Some grand juries contract with auditing firms for performance or management audits; these audits are concerned with considerations of organizational efficiency and effectiveness rather than the integrity and accuracy of financial records and transactions.
- Grand juries also may use audit reports as sources of information and ideas for grand jury investigations.

We shall first consider summaries of grand jury reports about financial audits; following this list are summaries of performance audits that grand juries referred to in their reports.[28]

FINANCIAL AUDITS

The following summaries reveal the kinds of concerns and comments that grand juries make in their final reports regarding their involvement in financial audits of local government:

- The desirability of continuing to contract with an auditing firm to conduct an audit next year; Alameda; 1991–1992; 2:1.
- Review of an audit of the County; the need for a check protector and a uniform write-off policy; Butte; 1991–1992; 4:3.
- Review of an external audit of the County; Contra Costa; 1991–1992; 8:2.
- Review of an audit of the Auditor-Controller's Office; Lake; 1991–1992; 2:1.
- Review of audit recommendations and implementation; Mariposa; 1991–1992; 2:4.
- While reviewing a statement-of-delinquent-accounts report, the Grand Jury noticed that the statement was incompatible with the County's latest financial statement; reconciliation is important to determine accurately how much money is owed to the County; Monterey; 1992; 1:1.
- Analysis of why County financial statements are not completed within a reasonable time after the close of the fiscal year; Monterey; 1992; 4:4.

- Review of findings of a joint audit by the Grand Jury and the Board of Supervisors; Napa; 1991–1992; 2:4.
- Review of the County's annual budget process; the Grand Jury's participation in biweekly meetings between County staff and the auditing firm; the need for internal audits of 90-plus trust funds and for placement of purchasing orders, receiving materials and services, and handling of invoices; Placer; 1991–1992; 4:6.
- Audit of a Placer County department's trust funds and other agency funds; Placer; 1991–1992; 3:3.
- Review of reports of an audit of last year; studied implementation of recommendations of auditors; Plumas; 1991–1992; 1:9.
- Review of internal audits by the County of Santa Clara and financial and performance audits of private firms; Santa Clara; 1991–1992; 6:1.
- Discussion of the advisability of competitive bidding for an annual Grand Jury audit; Santa Cruz; 1991–1992; 1:1.
- The need for additional internal auditors; internal controls in the Public Guardian's office appear to be inadequate; Stanislaus; 1991–1992; 5:1.
- Bids on tax forms; bank charges seem excessive; credit cards are difficult to trace by employee name; no set spending limit for meal expenses and travel reimbursements; Tulare; 1991–1992; 4:4.

Performance Audits

Although grand jurors in many counties conduct most of their civil investigations themselves, they occasionally hire professional performance and management auditors. The use of contract auditors might be necessary when highly technical assistance is required, for example, to review leases, to study complex administrative practices, or to analyze how effectively a local government uses computers, as these summaries illustrate:

- Study of waste reclamation; contract audit; Los Angeles, 1991–1992; n.p.
- Audit of the Los Angeles County administrative office; contract audit; Los Angeles; 1991–1992, n.p.
- Business exodus from Los Angeles County; contract audit; Los Angeles, 1991–1992, n.p.
- Study and prevention of gang membership; contract audit; Los Angeles, 1991–1992, n.p.
- Cost impact of illegal aliens on County services; contract audit; Los Angeles, 1991–1992, n.p.
- Review of Juvenile Dependency Court legal representation; contract audit; Los Angeles, 1991–1992, n.p.

- Management audit of the Chief Administrative Officer's department; roles and responsibilities of the CAO; review of management controls of the CAO's multimillion-dollar office-refurbishment program; management of special accounts; Los Angeles; 1992; 96:5.
- Review of lease between the County of Orange and a private firm that manages an aquatic park; Orange; 1991–1992; 30:8.
- Investigation into the Office of Public Administrator/Public Guardian; need for a policies-and-procedures manual; study of the reason for lack of timely visits by social workers; compliance with Probate Code 8800; Orange; 1991–1992; 33:4.
- Special review related to Sacramento Regional County Sanitation District; the audit was concerned with fees the District charged; overall revenue controls; the level of reserves; rapid increases in budget, and other matters; Sacramento; 1991–1992; 40:13.
- The Grand Jury employed two accounting firms to conduct management audits: the Communications Division of the Office of Management Services; and the Chino Airport and Chino Airport facilities leased to Lockheed Aircraft Services; San Bernardino; 1991–1992; 18:29.
- Data Processing Management Study; Norris Consultants, Inc.; Sonoma; 1992; 49 pp.
- Agreed-Upon Procedures Report [of the County Purchasing Office]; Background, Staffing, Interactions with County Departments, Testing of Purchase Orders, Responsibilities, Policies and Procedures, Centralized Inventories; November 14, 1991; Tuolumne; 1991–1992; 100+ pp.

Examples of Statutorily Justified Investigations

In the next chapter we shall consider examples of grand jury investigations that, as reported, are outside the grand jury's jurisdiction. Though these investigations are ill-advised and potentially risky for the institution, they are relatively infrequent. In contrast, the following summaries exemplify investigations with clear statutory justification:

- Methods and procedures that three cities used to handle citizen complaints about police officers; the lack of understanding that Penal Code Section 832.7 allows the Grand Jury to examine otherwise confidential law enforcement records; Humboldt; 1991–1992; 7:1.
- Results of tests by the Grand Jury of security of County buildings; apathy concerning security; ease with which equipment may be removed; no identification system for employees; delivery of mail by persons assigned to serve community-service hours; Madera; 1991–1992; 4:9.

- Identification of joint powers agencies in Mendocino County; lack of accountability of these entities to the electorate; recommendations to the County Clerk to improve the system for inventorying such entities; Mendocino; 1992; 8:2.
- Report of a study of financial audits and internal control systems of five cities; Placer; 1991–1992; 29:48.
- Review of a process by which several key departments were combined into one agency; Riverside; 1991–1992; 4:5.
- Investigation into the performance of the County Fire Department during a fire in which a young girl died; San Luis Obispo; 1991–1992; 3:1.
- Investigation of sole-source contracts and the Request For Proposal process; Santa Clara; 1991–1992; 13:1.
- Review of the process by which victims of the Loma Prieta earthquake attempted to obtain permits from the County Planning Department to repair and reconstruct their homes; Santa Cruz; 1991–1992; 7:8.
- Review of lease specifications, including fee-adjustment clauses or penalty fees that the City of Redding uses for airport lessee; Shasta; 1991–1992; 2:4.
- Report of a management review of the existing data-processing operational processes and the data-processing management plans and goals for Sonoma County; Sonoma; 1992; 24+:9.

In reporting these investigations, the grand juries described the methods they used in obtaining information, explained the necessity and implications of the investigations, and reported them clearly and logically. One or more of the following qualities also characterize each of the examples listed above:

- The exercise of grand jury initiative and sound judgment in selecting feasible topics
- Emphasis on systems, methods, and processes, rather than policies and people
- A concern with the responsiveness and accountability of local government to the community
- Emphasizing the effective, economical, and humane provision of local-government services
- Selecting investigative topics with a potential for broad public benefit

Grand Jury Achievements

Grand juries inadvertently encourage criticism that they are ineffective and unnecessary by rarely documenting their achievements or those of their predecessors. Because the documents in which local-government officials report whether they accepted or rejected grand jury findings are distributed separately from the grand jury reports containing their findings and recommendations, citizens rarely learn the results of grand jury investigations.[29] Occasionally, however, grand juries report the positive results of their work in final reports. The database contains 27 references to grand jury achievements, of which the following notes from the database are examples:

- Investigation into hazardous driving conditions on a County road; decision of a School Board to end bus service on the road; a survey of residents along the road; agreement of the County Public Works Committee to commit the County to a specific date for improving the road; Amador; 1991–1992; 7:4.
- Follow-up inquiry into the Welfare Department regarding the previous Grand Jury's recommendation concerning removal of the Welfare Director; most Grand Jury recommendations of 1990–1991 have been completely or partly implemented; El Dorado; 1991–1992; 5:3.
- Inquiry into the assignment of court-mandated community-service workers to for-profit organizations; practice discontinued; Fresno; 1991–1992; 1:6.
- The Grand Jury could find no evidence that improper issuance of concealed-gun permits continues; the practice was discontinued after the 1989–1990 Grand Jury disclosed it; Glenn; 1991–1992; 2:0.
- Tours and visits of various school sites; Office of the County Superintendent of Schools; County Office of Education has followed a Grand Jury recommendation to list its toll-free telephone number in the current directory; Inyo; 1991–1992; 4: numerous unnumbered recommendations.
- Study of the Weed and Nuisance Abatement Program of the City of Madera; fees charged by contractors; need for improvement in public notification; the report includes copies of correspondence between the Grand Jury and the City of Madera that document improvements made in response to Grand Jury recommendations; Madera; 1991–1992; 15:5.
- Investigation of an allegation of conflict of interest concerning a member of the Board of the Mariposa County Redevelopment Agency; the member subsequently resigned; Mariposa; 1991–1992; 2:2.
- Investigation into a complaint that a member of the Board of Supervisors had incorrectly received an additional $7,000 homeowners' exemption; the spouse of a Supervisor canceled the exemption after the Grand Jury inquiry; Nevada; 1991–1992; 1:0.
- Overcrowding of jails; educational programs at the jails; implementation of tuberculosis screening following a Grand Jury interim report; San Francisco; 1991–1992; 8:16.
- Investigation of a "highly publicized case of three children whose parents were accused of severely neglecting them and whose mother had been convicted previously of child abuse"; subsequent review of Grand Jury recommendations implemented since the first report; Santa Cruz; 1991–1992; 16:16.

- A review of the responses of the Board of Supervisors showed that "the majority of the recommendations [of the 1991–1992 Grand Jury] had been acted upon"; of 10 recommendations the previous Grand Jury made about the Public Works Department, "the Board agreed with nine of the recommendations, some of which had been implemented by the time the response report was issued in November, 1991"; Sierra County; 1991–1992; p. 22.
- Investigation into the propriety of using education funds for the production of a video; creation of a new administrative position; the Superintendent implemented a Grand Jury recommendation to tell the public the reason for producing the video; Siskiyou; 1991–1992; 4:0.
- Following a citizen's complaint, the Grand Jury reported that the Sonoma County Director of Public Health sent a letter to city managers of cities that did not have current agreements with the County to perform the Health Officer functions. As a result, cities are now in compliance. Expression of commendation to the County Health Officer for correcting this long-existing oversight when he was alerted by the Grand Jury; Sonoma; 1992; p. 152.
- The 1991–1992 Grand Jury reported that "of the 32 recommendations made [in the final report of the previous year], 27 have, or are in the process of, being followed"; Stanislaus; 1991–1992, p. 81.
- At the Grand Jury's request, the School District staff assured a buyer of a mobile home that the dealer paid the necessary facility fees to the School District; Tehama; 1991–1992; 3:0.

Newspapers occasionally report grand jury achievements, as these examples illustrate:

- After the Grand Jury disclosed that two employees of a City building division had accepted gifts from developers, the City "laid off" the employees, and the City Council adopted a policy governing how City employees may accept gifts (*Five Cities Times Press Recorder*, January 10, 1991, n.p.).
- A Grand Jury indicted the Chief of a Fire District for "grand theft" in a case involving "between $8,000 and $14,000" worth of cash and household items; the District Attorney praised the indicted Chief for "accepting responsibility for his actions" and commented that "this case is an example of why we have grand juries acting as overseers of governmental agencies and special districts" (*Nevada Union*, March 2, 1991, n.p.).
- "We credit the [grand] jury highly for its report released Tuesday detailing possible steps to improve [the operations of Child Protective Services in Santa Cruz County]"; editorial, "Grand Jury Report Packs Some Wallop" (*Santa Cruz Sentinel*, October 2, 1991, n.p.).

- The Alameda County Board of Supervisors voted to add 12 investigators to strengthen the County's welfare-fraud investigation efforts: "The new team was spurred by state and grand jury reports suggesting that millions of dollars in welfare fraud goes undetected in Alameda County because of understaffing in the current fraud unit" (*San Jose Mercury News*, November 28, 1990, p. B-3).
- Following a grand jury investigation about assigning a county automobile to top management staff as part of its "compensation package," the County Executive Officer informed "administrators in non-law-enforcement posts that they will be required to turn their cars back in" (*San Jose Mercury News*, March 28, 1993, n.p.).

BUREAUCRATIC ENCOUNTERS AND CONFLICTS

The coding guide I developed for this study included at the outset of the project a code for references in final reports to conflicts between grand juries and local-government officials. If strains occur, grand juries report them infrequently; only 11 examples were entered into the database. Several of these, however, are of particular interest. The summary of a lengthy report of grand jury–public official conflict reveals only the outline of an investigation concerning

> problem areas in the Office of County Counsel; reviews Grand Jury–County Counsel relationships; includes statistics regarding minority employment in Office of County Counsel; San Diego; 1991–1992; 21:5.

Strained relations between the San Diego County Grand Jury and the County Counsel arose from an extensive Grand Jury investigation into Children's Protective Services in that county. The Grand Jury commented at length about what it believed was the County Counsel's inappropriate role in the investigation. Another view of a grand jury's perception of strains between it and a county counsel may be found in the Trinity County Grand Jury Final Report for 1991–1992. The Trinity County panel recited grievances that arose from an

> inquiry into a pending upgrade of the retirement plan for County employees; exchange between the Grand Jury and County Counsel regarding the propriety of the Grand Jury's investigation; Grand Jury's questioning of propriety of "retroactive payments" and decision-making process; allegation of Brown Act violation in connection with adoption of upgraded plan; expression of concern that the Board of Supervisors, the County Administrative Officer, and the County Counsel had a conflict of interest in implementing the program; other matters; Trinity; 1991–1992; 50:1.

The Trinity County Grand Jury had inquired into a decision of the Board of Supervisors to improve the County employees' retirement program. The Grand Jury's stated concern was the cost of the program and the method the Supervisors used to adopt it. The County Administrator, the Board of Supervisors, and the County Counsel argued that, notwithstanding its costs, advantages of the retirement program outweighed its disadvantages. The Grand Jury expressed two concerns about this issue: It arose during a recessionary period, and some of the officials who would benefit from the improved retirement plan were promoting its adoption. Accordingly, the Grand Jury raised questions about the method used to justify the change in the retirement system.

The final report of the Trinity County Grand Jury included a spirited exchange of letters, position papers, and memoranda between the panel and various County-government officials. The exchange began with an "Ad Hoc Committee Final Report" expressing the panel's concerns about changes in the County employees' retirement system. The dispute continued with the issuance of a second report that included the panel's rebuttal to officials' comments to the original report. The Grand Jury's last word about the controversy was the final report it issued on August 3, 1992.

Among the many charges and counter-charges between the panel and various public officials are two rebuttals by the Trinity County Counsel to the panel's first two reports about the County retirement system. Examples of the County Counsel's refutations of the Grand Jury's "many erroneous statement [*sic*] of the facts in the initial report [and] some new ones [in the subsequent report]," include

- the panel's misunderstanding of the contract-negotiation process;
- a denial that closed-session deliberations about changes in the retirement system were unlawful; and
- a charge that the panel "recommend[ed] that the Board of Supervisors intentionally breach lawful contracts."

The Sonoma County Grand Jury's final report documented another example of conflicts with some County government officials; for example:

> During this investigation, a number of employees on numerous occasions demonstrated a flippant attitude, lack of respect, "not my responsibility," or "not my job" syndrome to both the complainant and the Grand Jury.[30]

Looking back on the Grand Jury year, the Forewoman observed:

> This was a very difficult year. This Grand Jury hopes that in the future the volunteers who serve on the Grand Jury will be given the respect they deserve for the thousands of hours of service they render to their State, County and community. The Grand Jury should have the right to conduct their service without fear of political pressure.[31]

For a grand jury to be effective, grand jurors must have neither a subservient nor an overbearing relationship with local-government officials. Occasionally, grand jury reports reveal insights into how grand jurors and local-government officials view each other. Grand jurors' conceptions of their relationships to officialdom are by no means consistent Statewide. Consider, for example, the contrasts in attitudes toward officials that these two grand jury observations imply:

> Obviously, it is rare for a grand juror to possess the depth of knowledge that a professional in government service has. Our role is not to second guess local government officials but to offer our perspective as ordinary citizens.[32]

> Some [County government] departments hesitated to release documents to grand jurors because they judged jurors to be incapable of comprehending the language.[33]

The contrasts in perspective between officials in government and citizens is of interest to political scientists, sociologists, and others who study bureaucracy. In particular, the problem of "professionalism" is often cited as a major barrier between the rulers and the ruled.[34] Because the problem arises occasionally in grand jury service, a member of the California judiciary several years ago informed an audience of grand jurors that they could expect to encounter the sentiment that "the functioning of government has become so complicated and specialized that lay people such as ourselves can never hope to understand it sufficiently to evaluate it and make any kind of constructive and productive criticism aimed at improving the system." Grand jurors will discover, the judge continued, that government is not so complicated that

> people with ordinary intelligence cannot understand [it], particularly if those people are dedicated and conscientious and will put forth the effort and time to acquaint themselves with the overall functioning of local governments. In my opinion, it does not take a particularly sophisticated person to ask appropriate questions about whether county assets are being misused, whether county cars are being used for private purposes, whether county employees are using county equipment and personnel for their own person gain, whether elected officials are using their staff for purely political purposes, whether county employees are using county telephones for private long-distance calls, etc., etc., almost *ad infinitum*.[35]

The most specific and intense example of rarely reported conflicts between grand juries and public officials during the period of this study was found in the El Dorado County Grand Jury Final Report of 1991–1992. The document reveals much information about the inner workings of County government; the dynamics of making decisions such as granting bonuses to department heads; and the concerns of grand jurors who encounter a District Attorney they believe is unwilling to cooperate with grand juries to investigate allegations of conflict of interest involving public officials. The incident also illustrates a grand jury's concern with the suspected use of public resources for private purposes and the creation of barriers to the accomplishment of the Grand Jury's work.

The report also reveals the intriguing complexities of establishing non-profit corporations for the apparent purpose of diverting public monies for questionable uses, serving as forums to avoid the requirements of public-meeting laws, and providing a publicly funded coordinating apparatus for political allies. This account of one grand jury's relationship with a district attorney gives little support to critics who argue that grand juries are invariably the pawns of district attorneys.[36] Moreover, this episode resulted in legislative attempts to curtail grand jury independence severely, an effort I discuss in more detail in Chapters 6 and 7.

Our concluding example of grand jury intervention in bureaucracy is taken from the final report of a small Northern California county. The Sierra County Grand Jury reported a curious finding that "on June 24, 1992, there was a special committee created by the Board of Supervisors to aid the District Attorney in making determinations regarding prosecutable charges." The Grand Jury recommended

> that the Board of Supervisors consider that this committee may create the appearance of jeopardizing the constitutional rights of the accused, by diluting the separation of powers and independent judgment of offices created by the Constitution and mandated to be distinct departments of the Criminal Justice System.[37]

Summary and Conclusion

Penal Code 916 allows grand juries almost complete independence in organizing themselves to conduct investigations, write reports, and promulgate them. As a deliberative body, the grand jury is an institution in which each panel member contributes to developing and approving its procedures. None of the procedures that a grand jury develops in one term, however, may bind the grand jurors of succeeding terms. For this reason, grand jury procedures manuals or handbooks are, in a sense, out of date at the end of each grand jury year.

Unlike many of the local governments over which they have oversight, grand juries must spend some of their relatively meager resources creating themselves each year. In contrast, the "costs" of organizing local-government agencies have been paid in previous years, and even the complex but invisible webs of social relationships within such offices are well established, for the most part. Newly impaneled grand jurors, in contrast, must spend considerable time and effort at the beginning of their year in creating their social organization. The grand jury's success depends upon whether its members endow it with sufficient flexibility to absorb a workload that cannot be foreseen at the time of impanelment.

In recent years, the California grand jury has directed its time and resources almost exclusively to its civil function. In theory, however, a district attorney could occupy a grand jury so completely with indictments that it could not discharge even its statutorily mandated duties. A recent statute authorizing the establishment of a criminal grand jury has reduced the possibility of stifling the civil investigation function in some counties.

Grand juries focus most of their investigative resources on county government. Seventeen topics, about half of them county functions, accounted for approximately 25 percent of all grand jury investigative topics during the period of this study.

An analysis of the summaries of investigative reports in the database revealed nine types of grand jury investigations. Most of the nine types are related to one or more of the statutes cited in Chapter 2. The exception to this generalization is the social-trends-and-issues type, a category that carries grand juries into the political arena, or close to it.

Grand juries reported relatively few examples of achievements attributable to them or their predecessors. For many citizens, newspapers, not final reports, are the chief source of information about grand jury achievements. Most grand jury investigative reports are concerned with issues such as system effectiveness, employee concerns, local-government resources, and obtaining information or responses from local government on behalf of citizens. In general, this chapter presented only descriptive information about grand juries and California local government. In the next chapter, we shall review grand jury commentary that represent the legal criteria discussed in Chapter 2.

4

Evaluating Investigations and Reports Using Law-Related Criteria

Chapter 2 revealed that in California the civil grand jury's inquiries into statutorily designated local governments are restricted to the methods, systems, operations, books, records, and accounts of those entities. In selecting such words and phrases, the Legislature confined the institution essentially to questions of efficiency and effectiveness. This being so, one would expect grand jurors to ensure that the institution they themselves create each year exemplifies sound governance. Indeed, the integrity of the institution and the value that public officials, California legislators, and other citizens accord it is at stake when grand jurors improperly execute the civil function.

If the mandate of the grand jury is to reveal instances of slipshod, wasteful, or corrupt governance and offer recommendations to correct those derelictions, grand jurors must ensure that the institution of which they are temporary custodians is itself a model of effective governance. As this discussion will show, however, most final reports each year reveal at least one example, and often many, of how grand jurors mismanaged the institution.

Law-Related Criteria

In this chapter, I identify and discuss examples of problems in final reports using the law-related criteria presented in Chapter 2. The examples cited in this chapter are not exhaustive. I selected only those that best seemed to illustrate the recurring nature of problems in grand jury investigations and final reports. In some cases, I have not identified final reports from which the examples were taken. The sources of possibly libelous material are undisclosed, as are the sources of examples of the confidentiality and secrecy criterion. The conditions this latter criterion represents may still exist and thereby endanger the physical security of local-government employees, buildings, or property.

After presenting examples, I discuss several of their implications for the spirit of the institution, a theme that I develop more fully in Chapter 7, particularly as the examples reveal how grand jurors practice citizenship skills. My concern for now is to define and illustrate these recurring problems so readers might more readily comprehend their implications for the institution.

JURISDICTION AND INDEPENDENCE

Jurisdiction and independence are combined as a topic because of their relatedness. For example, grand juries can properly exercise their independence only when they stay within their jurisdiction. Similarly, the exercise of independence means little if grand juries ignore or are unaware of the breadth of their powers and the variety of local governments within their jurisdiction.

The final reports each yielded an average of four examples of problems with independence or jurisdiction. Some final reports revealed none of these problems, and others had as many as a half dozen or more. The number of jurisdiction and independence summaries would have been larger if forays into policy issues had been included in the jurisdiction category. I decided to create a separate criterion for this latter problem, though, because of its crucial character.

Jurisdiction

The first type of jurisdiction problem includes comments, findings, and recommendations about federal and state agencies. Although no statutory provision exists for those matters, one grand jury reported that it considered a request by "a large delegation of Native Americans and leaseholders from the Havasu Landing Chemehuevi Indian Reservation" who sought the Grand Jury's help "in solving a long list of grievances and problems."

The account of the investigation summarized a complex dispute between competing factions. From this controversy arose allegations of "abuse of civil rights, election fraud, misuse of Federal grant money, financial irresponsibility, sewage spills" and other matters. The Grand Jury offered no justification for reporting its observations about these issues, conceding that it realized that "County agencies and authorities have no jurisdiction on reservation land to act on or enforce State statutes or County Codes."

Moreover, the Grand Jury reported, "The Federal Government has the only power to act, if it chooses to, through the Department of the Interior, Bureau of Indian Affairs, and the Environmental Protection Agency." Nevertheless, the Grand Jury stated that one of its committees "investigated every possible avenue for solution." The panel ended its report with three recommendations directed to no named person or agency, calling for the exertion of "every possible pressure on Federal Authorities" for various purposes, and for an unnamed person or persons to "Request the Governor to exercise his authority in regulating and enforcing the Indian Gaming Regulatory Act of 1988."[1]

If the Grand Jury had been advised that it had jurisdiction in a federal matter, it did not report who gave it that advice. Judging by the Grand Jury's report, most of the problems in this matter were intra-tribal, and the Grand Jury did not report what it thought it could accomplish, if anything, by becoming involved in the controversy.

Just as California grand juries have no civil jurisdiction in federal matters, they also have no civil investigative authority over the actions of State officials. Nevertheless, several grand juries in the study period attempted to intervene in or influence the decisions of State officials. For example, when it learned that a State institution in its County might be closed, a Grand Jury included in its final report a copy of a letter it sent to the Director of the California Youth Authority protesting the closing of a State-financed-and-staffed camp.[2]

The second type of jurisdiction problem is reporting about private agencies or persons in noncriminal matters. In one instance, a panel reported that it met with a private group "for information only" and summarized in its final report interviews with several of the organization's members. The Grand Jury lauded the group's efforts to take action against "rampant drug activity in their neigh-borhood" and directed a recommendation to the City of Stockton to "provide support [for the group] in its quest for a drug-free neighborhood."[3] The Grand Jury did not discuss why it selected one private organization among many to commend, whether any of its members were involved in the organization, or how it justified endorsing the goals of a private organization when no statutory authority exists to do so. Although it did not explain its reason for doing so, another Grand Jury reported a different kind of incursion into a private activity:

> On [date and time] the [Education, Youth, and Library] committee went to ___'s Flea Market.... The committee spent about 1½ hours strolling through the area, watching buyers and sellers. During the course of this time period, members witnessed about 30 school-age children shopping at the "market." The younger children were with adults and high-school-age students were in groups of two or three.
>
> Members [of the Grand Jury] asked a couple of the children what schools they attended only to have adults speak for them and drag them off in a huff.[4]

The Grand Jury identified the flea market by name in its committee report and in the table of contents of the final report. Although the focus of the investigation was on school attendance, identifying a private business in that connection in a final report served no useful purpose.

Recommending, promoting, supporting, or opposing legislation is a third variety of grand jury activity for which no statutory authority exists. Most of the examples of this type of problem occurring during the study period were found in Southern California grand jury final reports; for example:

> It is recommended that the County of Ventura, through legislative means, seek the inclusion of language in the voter registration form whereby a person registering to vote must show valid evidence of U.S. Citizenship.[5]

Two even more striking examples of incursions into legislative matters were in the Orange County Grand Jury Final Report of 1991–1992. First, the Grand Jury reported that it sent two letters to various elected California and federal officials, having obtained for that purpose "neither comment nor concurrence … from County Counsel or the Grand Jury Judge." One letter expressed the Grand Jury's support of the "Foreign Felon Deportation Act," proposed as Bill Number 3364. The second example, from the same Grand Jury, takes its lead from a letter dated May 8, 1992, which it received from the Kern County Grand Jury, and reported that it therefore

> decided to write a letter to Orange County legislators regarding [HIV Infection and AIDS]. The intent of such a letter was, by Jury agreement, to identify our sympathetic attitude with the substance of the Kern County Grand Jury's letter and make our opinion in the matter known to selected California officials, including Orange County legislators.

As it did in the first example, the Grand Jury conceded that "Approval of Counsel and Grand Jury Judge was not sought in this delimited action."[6]

The desire to support or oppose legislation motivates some grand jurors to establish standing committees to review legislation. Two grand juries reported the existence of such committees. The San Diego County Grand Jury described the purpose of its Legislative Committee as

> monitoring state, county and city legislation as it affects the operation of the Grand Jury and on those areas of interest and study by the action committees.

This same Grand Jury described a number of activities in which its Legislative Committee engaged, including maintaining

> liaison with the legislative affairs offices of the county and city to stay aware of any pertinent pending or passed law, ordinance or regulation and to distribute these to jurors as applicable.

The committee's work also included "various … recommendations … for legislative actions" in welfare assistance, welfare fraud, "mismanagement by the school board," and other matters.[7]

In a letter accompanying a position paper dated and apparently mailed two days after the end of the controversial 1991–1992 San Diego County Grand Jury's term of service, the Foreman of that panel urged other California grand juries to support Senate Bill 1261 concerning the use of force by law enforcement officers. The position paper included a copy of the proposed legislation and concluded with a suggestion that, "If you concur in the position adopted by the San Diego County Grand Jury, perhaps you would adopt a similar position and advise your legislators accordingly."

Responding to that position paper, the Foreman of the Sonoma County Grand Jury of 1992 wrote, "The Sonoma County Grand Jury's policy is to maintain a neutral position on any and all political proposals. We feel that this attitude helps us preserve our professional objectivity."[8]

Another Grand Jury included in its final report a reference to its interest in legislative matters and reported that the functions of its Legislative Review Committee included "reviewing legislation which will affect the County" such as "regional planning, regional government, and growth-management issues."[9]

Though they themselves may not exert pressure directly on state or federal officials, grand juries occasionally issue recommendations urging local officials to apply pressure to federal or state officials or agencies. For example, one Grand Jury urged that

> Trustees of Placer County school systems notify federal officials of their support for proposed reforms [in funding programs for libraries].[10]

Similarly, a Southern California panel revealed in its final report that it urged County Supervisors to

> encourage Governor Wilson to appoint a judge for [the Blythe Municipal Court] now, instead of waiting for election.[11]

Another type of jurisdictional problem is making recommendations about municipal or superior courts. Despite an opinion by a County Counsel to the contrary, a Central Valley Grand Jury included in its final report a lengthy account of an investigation into a municipal court. Although the Grand Jury may have been aware of the opinion adverse to its investigation, it did not refer to that opinion in its final report. The Grand Jury, however, conceded early in its report that

> accusations aimed at the judiciary are appropriately investigated by the State Commission on Judicial Performance. Therefore all complaints and subsequent data relative to the judiciary [the judges, rather than support staff] have been forwarded to that official state agency.[12]

Although the County Counsel's opinion concluded that the Grand Jury had no jurisdiction in matters pertaining to municipal court nonjudicial staff, the Grand Jury nevertheless reported a long list of allegations pertaining to one or more nonjudicial municipal court staff members, including purported "misuses of funds," "harassment of county employees," "violations of the Fair Labor Standards Act," and "willful misconduct that promoted distrust, fear and intimidation."[13]

The next type of jurisdictional problem we shall consider is intervening in matters currently being tried in court or commenting about outcomes of civil and criminal trials. In addition to the absence of statutory authority, common sense suggests that grand jury commentary about those matters could hinder the orderly conduct of a trial. Grand juries that intervene in judicial matters establish themselves, in effect, as a parallel tribunal. Nevertheless, some grand juries occasionally address matters under consideration in the courts, as these summaries indicate:

- Commentary regarding a lawsuit between two school districts concerning a purported inequity between the newly formed district and other districts; according to the Grand Jury, its predecessor's intervention in this matter resulted in a school district paying attorneys to prepare "an extensive 26-page response to the 1990–1991 Grand Jury's four-page report on the lawsuit. The cost of the highly legal response only added to the cost of the lawsuit."[14]
- Expression of "concern regarding adjudication against the appropriative water rights holders in Upper Basin brought by Solano Irrigation District and Solano County Water Agency."[15]

Another jurisdictional problem is created by the absence of authority for grand juries to issue pronouncements about broad social, political, or economic issues or policies. In colonial and later times, American grand juries often expressed their views about slavery, immigration, economic and political conditions, and related matters.[16] Today, no statutory authority exists in California for reporting expressions of concern such as "The Injustice of Illegal Immigration," or investigating "why businesses are leaving and what local government agencies can do to mitigate the problem and assist businesses to remain within Los Angeles County."[17]

Occasionally, grand juries attempt to justify their incursions into broad social, political, or economic problems by defining their purpose beyond what the statutes designate. For example, one Grand Jury Foreman declared that the Grand Jury on which he served:

> decided to approach our assignment somewhat differently than previous Grand Juries. In addition to responding to complaints presented by citizens, we decided to function as an instrument of education for the citizens.[18]

This conception of the grand jury's role resulted in a long, rambling report about water supplies and their distribution that bordered on policy issues. It touched on governments over which the Grand Jury had no jurisdiction and entangled the panel in legislative issues. Curiously, the report had no stated purpose, nor did its authors justify the basis of the Grand Jury's intervention into so broad a matter. The result was a puzzling digression that must have consumed many hours of time that the Grand Jury could have used for a purpose related to its statutory powers. One of the lessons the Grand Jury claimed it learned from its analysis was:

> Water Defined:
>
> Water, H_2O, the most widely used of all compounds, occurs in the solid, liquid and gaseous states. It covers three fourths of the earth's surface. In its solid state (ice) water floats and without this particular aspect much of the life as we know it would be possible [*sic*]. The purest of water falls as rain. However, in falling through the air, it dissolves and collects small quantities of fine particles of minerals and air and other gases. When the rain reaches the earth's surface, some of it flows into ponds, streams, rivers and lakes (surface water) and some sinks into the ground (ground water) and some evaporates into the atmosphere.[19]

This "educational" report ends with the following comment by the investigating committee emphasizing the importance of its work:

> We further recommend that if this committee is to remain effective as a body representing the water rights of citizens of Colusa County, the County should give future thought to the budgetary needs for counsel, materials, time and energy to pursue those rights.[20]

Independence

The exercise of the grand jury's independence does not by itself ensure effective investigations and reports. A strong, positive sense of independence is required, however, for a grand jury to fulfill its statutory responsibilities. In the many relationships a grand jury might establish during its term, it must achieve a balance between guarding its independence and its need to receive advice, assistance, and support from other institutions and persons.

Historically, controversy about grand jury independence often involves its relationship with the office of the district attorney. In California today, this issue is not as crucial as it once was, because of a recent statute that allows the creation of a separate, "criminal" grand jury.[21] Grand jury final reports nevertheless reveal occasionally that grand jury ties to district attorneys still exist in some counties. As examples, a photograph of the district attorney staff member assigned to it was included in the final report of the 1991–1992 Los Angeles County Grand Jury, and two other Grand Juries acknowledged the work of their "in-residence legal advisor" and the "assigned representative" of the district attorney's office.[22] Another Grand Jury expressed its relationship to the district attorney's office in even closer terms:

> During the past year as the grand jury conducted business by visiting agencies, answering complaints, *as well as serving under the District Attorney's office* one thing has become quite apparent; [*sic*] many citizens within Lassen

County have forgotten the definition and the use of the word "accountability" [emphasis added].[23]

In another Northern California county, a Grand Jury provided an example of a different type of independence problem: abdication of grand jury responsibility by deferring to public officials. In his "Overview," the Foreman recommended that the Grand Jury not respond to complaints about schools unless certain school officials make the complaints:

> Public education throughout our county is represented by elected citizens within school districts and by an elected county superintendent representing the entire county. Each school district is responsible for hiring its own personnel, providing academic instruction, and maintaining facilities according to the various California Codes and laws. Local school districts may request assistance from the County Office of Education on problems that arise. Further, school districts have access to legal services when needed. It seems appropriate and a better use of Grand Jury time if they [the Grand Jury] concentrated on County Government investigation *and only became involved in education issues at the request of the County School Board.* At that time an Ad Hoc Committee may be formed [emphasis added].[24]

Another type of independence problem might occur when grand jurors or local-government officials serve on each other's committees or when panels recommend that county employees be selected for grand jury service for the purpose of providing technical assistance:

> The Audit/Finance Committee met almost every week beginning July 19, 1991 until the audit was completed in late October 1991. [The] Auditor-Controller of Stanislaus County presided at those meetings.[25]

> To assist the Grand Jury in its functions, we also recommend that an attorney from the county always be included as a member of the Jury. The complexity of laws, regulations, statutes, etc., governing the functioning of the Jury and governmental bodies within its purview are so complex and open to interpretation [that] the common layman appointed to the Jury is overwhelmed and intimidated. The efficient functioning of the Jury was often hampered by lack of immediate access to counsel.[26]

The relationships between some grand juries and county government is close enough to be described as social:

> The orientation [conducted by the county counsel] was followed by a reception held by the Board of Supervisors. The reception enabled the Grand Jury members to meet the supervisors in an informal setting and get to know each other.[27]

One implication of grand jury independence is that only grand juries may decide what, within their statutory framework, they shall and shall not investigate. In deciding whether a complaint is within their jurisdiction, grand juries may elect to confer with legal advisors for assistance. The final determination to conduct an investigation, however, lies with the grand jury, not with a legal advisor, as the wording of this comment implies:

> The Educational Committee investigated 3 citizen complaints during the year. One was determined by Counsel to be out of the Grand Jury's jurisdiction.[28]

This wording, combined with the listing of county supervisors' names and the county seal on final reports, might suggest to citizens that grand juries are county departments rather than independent institutions. Just as grand juries must be careful to preserve their independence in their relationships with local-government officials, they also must avoid alliances with private persons or organizations. In some counties, for example, sitting grand juries refer openly to their associations with former grand jurors. Grand juries occasionally cite such relationships in their final reports and in brochures distributed to their communities:

> In an effort to make citizens aware of the work done by the Grand Jury, the Contra Costa County Grand Jury Alumni Association, with the cooperation of the sitting Grand Jury, sponsors an essay and art contest for high school seniors and juniors.[29]

> How Can the Public Contact the Grand Jury? Contact may be made to the Kern County Grand Jury to submit a complaint or request more information about the grand jury system. Arrangements may be made for present and former Grand Jurors to speak to schools or civic organizations concerning the Grand Jury system.[30]

The last example of actual or potential threats to grand jury independence is represented by foremen who report that they exercised powers not granted to them by statutes. For example, one grand jury procedures manual enumerates the duties of the foreman, including:

> 4. To appoint all standing and special committees as may be deemed necessary

> 12. To assign investigations to the proper committees[31]

One final report included three references to the usurpation of grand jury powers by a foreman:

> I assigned the committees the task of investigating these topics, not so much to uncover problems but to write reports that explain to our citizens the extent of county and citizen efforts being made to meet the challenges and solve the problems in these areas.

> At the inception of this year's Grand Jury it was decided and declared by the Foreman that this committee should concentrate efforts on several requested activities, rather than all departments in general.

> The Grand Jury Water Committee, the first ever for Colusa County, was appointed by the foreman … to look into the Colusa County water situation.[32]

FAIR COMMENT

Although the Legislature defines the jurisdiction of the California grand jury with words such as "methods" and "operations," grand juries should not hesitate to identify local-government officials by name if good cause exists to do so. For grand juries, the problem of referring specifically to public officials in final reports is a matter of how it should be done fairly. As one writer observed, "The authority to reveal violations of the public trust without initiating a prosecution remains one of the most controversial functions of the modern grand jury."[33]

The writer's comment applies to states whose legislatures have not enacted statutes authorizing grand jury civil investigations and reports. In California, however, the Legislature has authorized grand juries to investigate and report about designated local governments. That grant of authority is balanced by Penal Code Section 930, which denies grand jurors immunity from lawsuits for improper comment in reports of civil investigations.

It is possible for grand juries to issue effective reports about investigations without publishing names of elected and appointed officials and public employees. This cautious approach reduces the possibility of lawsuits by omitting names in grand jury reports unless an indictment or accusation is involved. This approach has the merit of forcing grand jurors' attention on organizations and their processes rather than on the people who work in them. In some cases, however, a final report would be weakened by not identifying a public official who, for example, willfully failed to comply with a regulation or law, who neglected to protect employees or citizens from unsafe or unhealthy conditions, or who refused to institute modern accounting procedures.

In considering the reporting of these matters, the crucial issue for grand juries is how they identify public officials or employees. If a panel provides a fair (factually documented and judiciously expressed) basis for its criticism, a lawsuit against the panel would not likely be successful for several reasons.

First, a long line of court cases upholds the principle that "Public officials owe a fiduciary duty to the public and therefore must comply with a more demanding standard of conduct than that required by the criminal law."[34] Related to this principle is the expectation in a democracy that public officials must tolerate a certain amount of citizen criticism for committing administrative errors, whether real or imaginary.

Second, justified criticism of public officials not only is permitted in our form of government but is actually essential, and the laws and traditions of California and the United States encourage public oversight and commentary about government and the people who operate it.

Third, the California Legislature, by enacting Penal Code Section 933, has nullified a traditional objection to grand jury reports—namely, that public officials have no forum or method for responding to them. In brief, our political values and laws support grand juries and other citizens in what they may say or write about public officials, provided that the commentary does not constitute libel or slander.

Considering the large number of investigations summarized in the database for the study period, one would expect to find many references to local-government officials either by name or by their offices. Early in this project, however, I did not include a code to capture the number of times those references appear in final reports. Had this been possible, the percentage of these references that were "fair comment" problems could be calculated. The percentage of fair-comment problems in the database is, I estimate, less than 5 percent of the number of times officials were named or otherwise identified in final reports during the study period.

The first and largest category of fair-comment problems is concerned with one of the most serious criticisms about grand juries in the literature: that they imply in final reports that public officials have committed wrongful acts but offer no evidence to support such claims, nor do they issue accusations or indictments based on such allegations. The following examples vary in the nature of their allegations, the number of individuals involved, and their possible consequences. Nevertheless, they each represent broad, sweeping, but undocumented accusations.

> A great deal of business within [—] County is conducted by mutual agreement behind closed doors, with little understanding of the rules, including the knowledge or application of the Brown Act. Officials state one thing to the public and then do another.

> In view of the many uncertainties involved in the controversy surrounding [a named local government] and its administration, the Grand Jury feels that even though the District Attorney's office has found no criminal liability, the volume of smoke produced by this investigation indicates fire somewhere. The seeds of doubt have been planted.

> The Grand Jury discovered that council members (past and present) have stretched, if not broken, the tenants [*sic*] of the Brown Act.

In the following example, a grand jury has not named individuals but has broadly maligned a legislative body by using terms such as "criminal misuse" and "misfeasance, malfeasance, and nonfeasance" in reference to "some" of its members—whom it does not name. The use of the terms "border on" and "apparent characteristics" does not exempt the panel from criticism for making such broad condemnatory statements out of the context of an accusation or an indictment.

> Some individuals appointed to the Board of Directors feel they need give little regard to the purpose of the district and to the regulations and laws applicable to their operations. Instead, their activities appear to be self-indulging and to

border on the criminal misuse of public funds.... Misfeasance, malfeasance, and nonfeasance are the apparent characteristics of the operation of the Board of Directors of....

Another grand jury also accused an elected body of willfully violating the law but did not report that an indictment or accusation was made against any of the members of the body:

Even though the Board of Supervisors have previously been made aware of this law, its members have chosen to ignore it, perhaps because it has always been done that way.

A similar example is a statement a grand jury made concerning derelictions ascribed to persons identified vaguely as "upper management" but did not then report that it had initiated criminal proceedings in the matter. As a result, the public is left with an impression of the existence of corruption that resulted in neither accusations nor indictments, and which therefore remains unresolved:

An Ad Hoc Committee was formed to investigate allegations of moral misconduct, lack of ethics and misuse of county funds by an individual or individuals in upper management of [—] County Government.

The next example concerns a grand jury that alluded to the existence of corruption but did not report why it filed no charges against an unnamed, but easily identified official, implying only that the investigation will be continued. Notice, however, that the Grand Jury did not name the agency or individual it claimed would continue the investigation:

In the course of investigating certain actions of the County Superintendent of Schools and the [—] County Office of Education ... the Grand Jury became aware of possible improprieties in purchasing equipment and in mileage expense claims made by the Superintendent of Schools. COMMENT: The matter continues under close scrutiny and review.[35]

Another fair-comment problem is represented by a grand jury that accused an official of misconduct in office and threatened to file an accusation if the person did not resign from office, commenting:

If the County Clerk does not voluntarily resign Office, the 1991–1992 Grand Jury with the help of the District Attorney shall prepare an accusation against the County Clerk accusing her of misconduct due to omission of duty.

Only a trial could determine whether the examples we have just reviewed constitute libel. In such a trial, consideration would be given to the principle that a grand jury report is "a threat to the public official's right to due process of law because it denies the procedural safeguards of a criminal prosecution, yet results in the same harm to reputation as a criminal accusation." This principle would be weighed against the need for legitimate public debate in a free society and the concept that "the grand jury's reporting authority [promotes] democracy by publicly exposing government wrongdoing." In weighing the merits of these competing ideals in a given case, some consideration also might be given to the principle that public officials must tolerate a certain level of criticism.[36]

If public officials must tolerate, by virtue of their office, a certain amount of public censure by grand juries or other citizens, it is well established that private persons need not be so tolerant.[37] Nevertheless, final reports sometimes include the names of private persons or corporations in a manner that could affect them adversely. In the following example, naming a law firm was unnecessary for reporting the investigation:

> On August 8, 1991, the contract with this law firm was revised to allow the Personnel Director unlimited access to, and utilization of, the firm's legal services. The result being that the Personnel Director had his own "private" County Counsel. His utilization of this firm was extensive and exhaustive. It appears that over the last twelve (12) months, [a named law firm] has billed the County for fees in excess of $250,000.00.

Elsewhere, another Grand Jury unnecessarily identified a private corporation that it claimed had managed a facility under contract with the county. During the contract period, the Grand Jury claimed that an "irregularity" occurred:

> [—] is a private corporation which contracts with three county departments: Mental Health, Social Services, and Probation. It provides group housing facilities for at-risk populations served by these three departments. The grand jury was not able to schedule a thorough study even though there was at least one publicized irregularity involving one of the homes. While there are needed services provided by this private agency, the huge budgetary cost to the taxpayers indicates a study by the 1992–93 grand jury would be very useful.

In the following example, three problems may exist. *First,* the Grand Jury reported about a matter alleged to have occurred in a private organization. *Second,* the Grand Jury repeated an allegation that something that might have been criminal in nature ("patient chemical abuse") occurred. *Third,* having made both statements, the Grand Jury declined to take action in the matter, claiming a lack of jurisdiction. This leaves the named private organization at the mercy of competitors who could use out-of-context quotations from the final report to discredit the company.

> The [—] County Grand Jury received a citizens [*sic*] complaint dated October 29, 1991, concerning alleged patient chemical abuse at [—]. Upon review of the complaint, it was the opinion of the Grand Jury that [—] is a private entity, receiving no county funds and, therefore, not within the jurisdiction of this body.

Final reports occasionally include derogatory remarks about unnamed but easily identifiable persons. Grand jurors sometimes mistakenly believe that making critical comments about people is permissible provided that they do not name these individuals. In this example, a grand jury made the following critical, undocumented comment about an unnamed person whose job title was clearly identified:

> [The coordinator of an educational program] showed an almost complete lack of knowledge of the very program he was to coordinate. The information finally supplied by the District was incomplete, evasive, and contradictory.

CONDUCTING JUSTIFIED INVESTIGATIONS

The reason for the criterion "conducting justified investigations" was to examine final reports for signs of "fishing expeditions"—investigations prompted by idle curiosity, vague suspicions, or whims. The data revealed no obvious evidence of this problem in final reports during the study period. Nevertheless, I noted two problems relating to "conducting justified investigations": (a) not explaining the reason for undertaking investigations, and (b) signs of conflict of interest, or possible conflict of interest, within grand juries.

Only rarely do grand jury investigative reports include clear statements of why panels began the investigations. For example, few grand juries reported that they conducted an investigation because one of the "shall" statutes mandated it or because a public official or some other citizen requested it. Similarly, no grand jury reported that an investigation into a public offense began because a grand juror brought the matter to the attention of the rest of the panel, as a Penal Code Section permits.[38] These examples from the State's least and most populated counties, respectively, typify how most reports of investigations began with a vaguely stated purpose or no statutory justification:

Summary

> The Chamber [of Commerce] is open and offers information regarding the County to the public seven days a week. They are actively pursuing ideas to promote tourism in Alpine County.[39]

Introduction and Summary

> The focus of this study is the growing perception that Los Angeles has become less competitive with other regions and is stifling its ability to maintain and attract new businesses.[40]

In the absence of clear statements about the statutory basis for grand jury investigations, some readers of final reports might wonder why they were initiated or whether they were lawful. By connecting an investigation closely to one or more sections of the Penal Code, grand jurors enhance the validity of reports, thereby assuring citizens that the institution has exercised its powers wisely and for good cause, and allaying suspicion and possibly antagonism among public officials.[41]

Documenting investigations with citizens' complaints also assures readers that grand juries are responsive to their communities. Similarly, when grand jurors make their first contact with a public official or department they intend to investigate, their careful explanation of the institution's statutory authority in the matter will avoid surprise, unnecessary antagonism, and the needless expenditure of effort. In a Southern California county, for example, a private attorney challenged a grand jury investigation on behalf of a local-government client and demanded to be informed

> by what authority [the Office of Auditor-Controller] or the Grand Jury have to examine the accounts and records of a special district.[42]

The inquiry resulted in a two-page written justification by the County Counsel regarding the lawful basis for the Grand Jury and the County Auditor-Controller to audit the financial records of special districts.[43]

Occasionally indications of possible self-interest appear in final reports. When former grand jurors recall attempts by members of their panels to use the grand jury's prestige and powers to achieve personal objectives, they cite examples of grand jurors who

- as supporters of candidates for public office, tried to persuade fellow panel members to investigate persons opposing their candidates in forthcoming elections.
- as recently retired elected officials of local governments, attempted to discourage fellow grand jurors from investigating complaints about matters with which they had been deeply involved in their previous public service.
- were directors of nonprofit corporations and who attempted to persuade fellow jurors to discredit competing nonprofit agencies that had contracts with the county.[44]

The term usually used for this sort of attempt is "ax-grinding," the essence of which is the possibility that self-interest within the grand jury will be served by intervening in a matter. Some grand juries have adopted codes of ethics that include provisions against ax-grinding or against its appearance.[45] Ax-grinding sometimes presents difficult challenges for grand jurors who wonder why their family connections, business interests, or professions might jeopardize an investigation in certain situations. Evidence of ax-grinding in final reports would be difficult to detect.

The following comment from a final report, however, illustrates how conflict of interest arises in grand jury service. In this case, a grand jury foreman identified himself in the "Foreman's Report" as a practicing attorney in the county and in that report broadly praised local judicial officials:

> As a member of the California State Bar, a special interest was taken in the review of the status and operations of the court system within the county. Without any doubt, the low point in this review remains, and embarrassingly so, the trailer used for court facilities at the South County Municipal Court building located in Oroville. Recognizing that the absence of funds for the

county is more severe than when the same absence justified only the use of a trailer for court procedures, some assistance at whatever level or with a combination of efforts must be made to alleviate the use of the trailer.

On the brighter side, the judges and staff of the municipal court system, overworked by all state-wide standards, must be complimented for their on-going efforts at expediting the court process and, at the same time, extending a quality of justice and assistance to members of the public.[46]

Emphasizing Systems, Procedures, Methods, and Equipment

Grand jury statutes include no words granting jurisdiction to panels in policy issues. Nevertheless, a variety of examples of incursions into policy matters were entered into the computer for the study period.

School districts are the local governments in which grand juries seem most likely to trespass on policy matters, such as making recommendations about homework assignments, articulating the needs for new programs, and even urging the adoption of studies and reports promulgated by national educational commissions, as these examples show:

- "The recommendation includes requiring each student to obtain a notebook that must be taken home each evening. All assignments, daily schedules, and an academic calendar are included in the notebook that parents are required to read and initial daily."[47]
- "The committee recommends that the Hanford Elementary School District seriously consider implementing a computer program in each of its schools. This district seems to be lacking in this area of instruction."[48]
- Discussion of public education and the need to adopt the recommendations of "America 2000," President Bush's "Education Strategy."[49]
- "That in the future, secondary schools in the County develop stronger and more varied vocational training programs along lines consistent with American educational values of flexibility in choice and equal opportunity for all students." And later: "School Districts should refocus their guidance activities to better address the academic and vocational needs of students."[50]
- "NVC [Napa Valley Community College] should seek ways to expand programs, such as Telecommunications, which place graduates in viable jobs within their fields."[51]

Many of the findings or recommendations in these five examples concerned policy issues. As examples, the adoption of year-round schooling, adding new academic or vocational courses, and the desirability of supporting or opposing a nationally promoted educational-reform program are matters for elected school-board members to decide.

Because of the high interest of many American citizens in public education, grand juries often are under considerable pressure to intervene in educational matters. One Grand Jury, for example, claimed on the one hand that it had "no opinion on the proposed Voucher System" but reported on the other hand that:

> All the districts are adamantly opposed to the proposed State Voucher system. Their concern is not the loss in income that might result, but a reduction in the quality and standard of education available with our present system. The proposed voucher system is scheduled to be included in the 1994 State of California ballot.[52]

One explanation for the ambivalence in this example is that one or more grand jurors who were public-school employees could have exerted pressure on the panel to take a position with respect to the then-forthcoming school-voucher election. Realizing that such a position would be improper, but perhaps not wanting to offend or disappoint colleagues who urged the Grand Jury to become involved in the matter, the panel tried to find a middle ground. As a result, some readers might see a contradiction in the example and wonder why the Grand Jury did not explain its need to refer to an issue over which it had no jurisdiction, claimed it had no opinion about it, but nevertheless included a "finding" that school districts were "adamantly" opposed to the proposed legislation.

Examples of other infringements on local-government policy making include questioning a decision by a local-government body, urging a district attorney to bring more indictments before the grand jury, recommending increases in fees, making a plea for more economic development in a county, and other matters, as these summaries or quotations indicate in whole or in part:

- Increase fees in Building Department to expand services.[53]
- The District Attorney should use the grand jury for more indictment proceedings resulting in a possible savings to the taxpayers in court costs.[54]
- Review of the County's Statement of Investment Policy for internal consistency and "philosophy" of the County's basic investment practices; review of conformance of policy to applicable laws.[55]
- "The City [should] formulate a plan to augment their budget, such as implementation of special taxes, benefit assessment districts, and recruitment of low impact-high/volume industry."[56]
- "The Board of Supervisors [should] take the lead in developing a plan of action with the Hollister Downtown Association, Economic Development Corporation, Chamber of Commerce, and other related agencies to attract more businesses and industries to the County to generate much-needed revenues. This effort will enable the County to maintain the present level of services as well as increase the effectiveness of services within the County."[57]
- Review of a resolution of the San Diego City Council regarding the nature and siting of a new central City library.[58]

- "The Police Department should establish an educational incentive program to encourage continuing police education and training. The educational incentive programs should include a provision for the partial funding of tuition, books and out-of-county transportation expenses."[59]
- "The past Grand Jury recommended that a second counselor be hired. The 1991–1992 Grand Jury concurs with this recommendation, even if it is a part-time position, if and when funding can be found. Due to the gender-sensitive issues, this Grand Jury suggests the possibility that the person be a female."[60]
- Report of a review of the Office of District Attorney; some improvement in morale; need for more investigators; wisdom of coercing employees to sign manual; reason why the District Attorney has not used the indictment function of the grand jury; work of Family Support Unit, and other matters.[61]

VALIDITY

One of the most striking validity problems in recent grand jury history occurred during the study period. Because of the secrecy and confidentiality of grand jury proceedings, citizens will not learn why this problem occurred. The episode, however, attracted considerable public attention when several newspaper stories revealed that the Merced County Grand Jury of 1991–1992 plagiarized an investigative report that the San Diego County Grand Jury had published previously.[62]

In publishing plagiarized material, the Merced County Grand Jury violated Penal Code Section 939.9. The Superior Court was not reported to have applied sanctions against any of the one-term members of the panel, its carry-over members, or the panel at large. One judge stated that the Merced County Grand Jury actually did conduct its own investigation but made the mistake of "trying to use someone else's work as [its] own."[63]

An interesting feature of this case was that the language of the plagiarized report differed markedly from that of other reports in the final report. During the deliberative process for this report, one might have expected that even a modestly perceptive grand juror would have questioned the proposed text. Nevertheless, the Grand Jury issued and distributed its final report widely before the news media revealed that it contained large amounts of plagiarized text from a previously issued San Diego County Grand Jury investigative report.[64]

One of the consequences of the Merced County Grand Jury's incorporating plagiarized material into its final report was that the Merced report contained several derogatory remarks about public officials in San Diego County. Because the San Diego final report referred generally to the officials by their titles, and not their names, some readers of the Merced County report might have believed that the remarks applied to officials in Merced County.[65]

Other problems with validity occurred in final reports during the study period. Some grand juries, for example, published findings and recommendations based mostly on tallies of questionnaires sent to local-government employees. People who are experienced in using survey-research techniques to study organizations rarely regard uncorroborated questionnaire data as conclusive evidence. These data by themselves have no more validity than rumors and hearsay. Nevertheless, one Grand Jury introduced the findings and recommendations of many of its investigative reports with conclusions it drew from a "Grand Jury Employee Questionnaire," as this example shows:

> City of Portola
> Response rate was 20%, morale is high, communications is [*sic*] excellent and very open, always receive updated instructions, career advancement is good and the work environment is good.
>
> Findings:
> Everything is running well.
>
> Recommendations:
> None.[66]

A more frequent error was publishing undocumented statements of purported fact. In the absence of proper citation, a reader cannot verify the figures on which the Grand Jury has based statements such as:

> The legislature … enacted AB 8 in response to Proposition 13, and then Butte County was frozen into a position of receiving only 23% of the property tax which is split among local agencies. The average California County receives 33%.[67]

Another validity problem is represented by statements using words such as "large" or "small" but that provide no evidence to justify the use of such adjectives; for example:

> Overall, the investigation [reported in one-half page] established that, considering the amount of cases handled, a small percentage of error occurs.[68]

The Grand Jury provided readers with no data to support the phrase, "considering the amount of cases handled" and provided no comparative figures to justify its statement that "a small percentage of error occurs." A similar example of an undocumented finding cited neither a rate nor its source, but nevertheless claimed that "the City has a remarkably low delinquency rate in the collection of utility bills."[69]

Similarly, final reports sometimes recommend additional staff or funds but provide no substantiating evidence. For example, a Grand Jury offered no workload statistics, crime statistics, productivity data, or any other similar facts to support a recommendation that "Funding for the Office of District Attorney should receive high priority" and "Staff should be increased to authorized level."[70]

The validity of findings and recommendations is also jeopardized by basing broad statements on interviews with only one or two people, not providing corroborating evidence, or conducting inspection tours of facilities in which individuals from only one level of an organization are interviewed. The following statement, for example, apparently was based on meeting with only the chief of police and one lieutenant of a police department. No other substantiating information was offered.

> The department has excellent morale and a high degree of cooperation with other law enforcement agencies. [It has] recently upgraded with the acquisition of a new vehicle. Crime within the city has not had any great changes. A steady amount of crime is noted, but few are major felonies.[71]

Elsewhere in its final report, the same panel conceded that, although it had conducted no investigation of the matter, it nevertheless was obliged to offer this recommendation with no supporting facts:

> LIBRARIES: Although this Committee did not focus on our County Libraries, we recognize the limited funding and services. We strongly recommend there be no further cuts and commend our Librarians and staff for their fine efforts.[72]

One Grand Jury investigated an allegation that two corrections officers at a State prison used undue force to subdue an inmate. A section of a report titled "Procedures Followed" stated:

> The [Grand Jury] Committee contacted the Warden's office at [the State prison]. Due to the absence of the Warden, a telephone interview with the Associate Warden was arranged.[73]

Citing no other evidence than a telephone interview, the Grand Jury concluded:

> The [officials] properly handled the incident according to the policies and procedures of the California Department of Corrections and the California State Personnel Board.

The investigation might have been improved by
- interviewing the allegedly assaulted inmate
- reviewing the staff reports written about the incident
- interviewing the corrections officers who allegedly used undue force
- interviewing the officers' supervisors
- interviewing other witnesses or providing a statement about the availability of such witnesses
- examining the department's official written procedures for using physical force
- reviewing the training that corrections officers receive in using force to restrain inmates

Although grand juries occasionally receive complaints about matters of potentially great importance, they at times fail to inform readers about the extent or significance of their findings or conclusions. One Grand Jury, for example, provided readers with only limited information about its investigation of a complaint about the possibility of

> falsifying attendance records of certain employee's [*sic*] children at Thomas Downey High School in past years, and that a student received pay checks for work not performed, while attending an out of state university.[74]

Although the allegations of the complaint suggest the absence of adequate accounting procedures, the possible theft of public funds, poor administrative and supervisory procedures, and other deficiencies, the Grand Jury's report does not include commentary about these investigative possibilities. For example, readers are not informed whether the first part of the complaint (concerning falsification of attendance records) involved one or more persons other than those involved in the second part of the complaint (receiving paychecks for work not performed).

With respect to the first allegation, the Grand Jury reported that it was unable to prove or disprove the charge because certain records were destroyed at the end of the year. The Grand Jury, however, did not report what it might have done to determine the extent and duration of the practice. For example, the panel might have conducted a random sample of current records to determine whether the practice continued. Similarly, because the alleged misappropriation of funds seems to have been institutionalized, the Grand Jury might have inquired into other school districts within its jurisdiction to determine whether similar inadequate accounting and supervisory systems existed. Nor did the Grand Jury comment about the financial, ethical, or other implications of falsification of school records.

Similar investigative deficiencies characterize the report concerning the second part of the complaint. Although only one person seems to have been involved in what the Grand Jury termed as the "Pay for Work to be Performed Later Concept," the panel did not report what it did to determine how widespread the practice was or how much money was misappropriated. Nor did the Grand Jury report what had been done, if anything, to recover the misappropriated money. Finally, the Grand Jury expressed satisfaction that school officials reported they were conducting "disciplinary proceedings," but the panel did not report why it did not return an indictment for embezzlement.

A Grand Jury in the lower Central Valley provides another example of referring to a serious complaint but not describing its investigation sufficiently to justify its conclusion of no wrongdoing. In this example, the Grand Jury reported that someone complained to it that school administrators improperly used public funds to hold "lavish" parties.[75] A Grand Jury committee claimed that the party in question was a special reception celebrating the dedication of a new public-school facility. The committee further reported that the event featured a buffet dinner for out-of-town guests as well as school administrators.

Expressing satisfaction that "the funds were used wisely," the Grand Jury provided no additional information about its investigation; for example:
- Who authorized and planned the "party"?
- When and where did the "party" occur, and how long did it last?
- How often do events of that nature take place?
- How many people attended?
- Who paid for the "party"?
- Who were the out-of-town guests, why were they invited, and how many of them attended?
- Was the "party" open to the public?
- How much did the "party" cost?
- Out of which fund were costs paid?
- What was served, who prepared it, how was that person or business paid, and how much?

Lack of documentation sometimes takes the form of not citing the code sections of laws that purportedly were broken. In the following example, a reader who desired to verify the Grand Jury's statement about the "state housing law" would have difficulty finding the referenced statute using only the information provided:

> The state housing law requires that fees charged for building permits ... "shall not exceed the amount reasonably required to administer or process such permits ... or to defray the costs of enforcement required ... and shall not be levied for general revenue purposes...." The county is clearly in violation of state law.[76]

The final example of validity is not about the absence of documentation, facts, or citations but is of a broader scope: how grand juror absenteeism may affect the validity of a final report. This problem arises from the difficulty many grand juries claim they have in maintaining consistent attendance. Because grand jurors may vote only on matters in which they have participated from start to finish, inadequate attendance could reduce the number of grand jurors legally required to approve a grand jury position.[77] One grand jury reported that 13 grand jurors resigned during the 1991–1992 term, including five carry-over grand jurors. The list of grand jurors in the final report shows the names of only 16 persons; evidently, the year ended with three grand jurors not having been replaced.

This much turnover, coupled with possible absences for vacations, health problems, and other reasons, suggests the likelihood that the same 12 persons may not have participated in all grand jury investigations from beginning to end. In fact, the Forewoman reported that "there were times as a grand jury we lacked a quorum. This caused frustration and hardship on the remaining jurors." In view of such extensive absenteeism, some readers might ask whether a quorum was always present to vote on approving investigations.[78]

A similar question could be raised about another grand jury. The Tuolumne County Grand Jury sat for 18 months to accommodate a change from a calendar-year term of office to a fiscal-year term. In that time, the Grand Jury reported that of the 29 grand jurors who served during that period, only 12 remained in Grand Jury service for the entire 18-month term.[79]

These two examples might be unusual cases. They do, however, suggest the desirability of better documentation of grand jury attendance to ensure the validity of grand jury investigations and reports.

LEGALITY AND EFFECTIVENESS OF FINDINGS AND RECOMMENDATIONS

The number of recommendations in the individual grand jury investigative reports studied varied from 1 to 40, depending on the complexity of an investigation. Assuming that the average number of recommendations for each report was five, the investigations in the database might have produced as many as 4,500 recommendations Statewide. Because grand juries often do not identify findings as explicitly as they identify recommendations, no estimate is offered about the number of findings that grand juries developed during the study period.

Penal Code Section 916 expresses the California Legislature's concern with the soundness of grand jury findings by specifying two requirements: first, that "all findings included in … final reports are supported by documented evidence"; and second, that findings in final reports must be based on interviews "attended by no fewer than two grand jurors." A third requirement could be added, though the statute does not connect it specifically to findings or recommendations. Penal Code Section 916 also directs grand juries to develop procedures to ensure that "all problems identified in a final report are accompanied by suggested means for their resolution, including financial, when applicable."

With respect to the third requirement, grand juries in the study period rarely provided cost estimates concerning "problems identified," either in the text of their reports or in their findings and recommendations.[80] One Grand Jury, however, roughly estimated the costs of a "collections office" it recommended for recovering certain public defender, district attorney, and probation costs:[81]

> [S]uch function would cost approximately $30,000 the first year, and 12–18 months would be required to recruit, locate and establish procedure before any organized effort could be productive. The "Up-Front" $30,000 would include base salary plus the 25–30% benefit package of one person.

Few final reports routinely include statements certifying that at least two grand jurors were present for interviews on which findings were based. The absence of such statements does not necessarily mean, however, that grand juries failed to comply with the two-person-interview requirement.[82]

In commenting about final reports, public officials need address only findings and recommendations. Because public officials must prepare those comments, it follows that of all the sections in an investigative report, these two categories should be most carefully deliberated, written, and presented. Unfortunately, many findings and recommendations are written ineffectively, as the following examples illustrate.

Problems with Findings

In enacting Penal Code Section 933, the Legislature might have expected grand jurors to understand the term "findings" as accountants or management analysts employ it. In writing final reports, though, grand jurors often use the term "findings" more loosely. For example, the term "finding" could denote "conclusion," "opinion," or "recommendation." The term also might be used for vague, conjectural comments or simple descriptive statements about local-government offices. As the term is used in various investigative fields, "findings" are derived from evidence that investigators have observed, collected, and analyzed in the fact-gathering phases of their investigations.[83]

In many final reports, the terms "findings," "conclusions," and sometimes "recommendations" are used with no distinction or are used interchangeably. An even less-precise use of "findings" is to use the word for prosaic descriptions of organizations, departments, or functions:

> The office of the assessor is comprised of the Assessor who is elected and one full-time employee.[84]

Another Grand Jury presented the following "finding" as a basis for a recommendation. The "finding," however, was merely a description of an existing practice:

> The Board of Supervisors appoints three commissioners from each zone who act as an advisory group. Each zone is self-supported and taxes must be spent in the zone in which they are raised.[85]

Without describing what problems this practice created, the same Grand Jury recommended that

> The advisory group should monitor more closely the fiscal management of the district in regard to both requests and expenditures.

By providing no empirical basis for the recommendation, the Grand Jury might have caused some readers to ask questions such as: Does the recommendation mean that someone is overspending or underspending? If so, by how much and for what? What is meant by "requests"? Are these expenditures? Is there something wrong with self-supporting zones and the requirement that taxes must be spent in the zones? To what kinds of taxes does the Grand Jury refer?

Some grand juries offer conclusions as findings with no supporting information, as these examples show:

Salary structure is notably lower than salaries of surrounding cities of comparable size.[86]

There are no toxics in the soil of the Del Monte site.[87]

In these two examples, grand juries presented conclusions about existing conditions but neglected to give readers substantiated findings as the basis for each conclusion. The absence of such data leaves unanswered questions such as: Compared to what? Which surrounding cities? How did the Grand Jury define "administrative salaries"?

Problems with Recommendations

If grand juries do not label recommendations as such or otherwise do not display them conspicuously, officials and other readers might overlook them. Panels that understand that many readers of final reports have limited time to read them list recommendations separately in final reports. For example, the San Diego County Grand Jury continued its tradition of including a separate, detailed listing of page numbers of its recommendations in the front matter of its final report. For additional emphasis, the panel repeated recommendations presented throughout its report in a 24-page "Restatement of 1991–92 Grand Jury Recommendations."[88]

One can imagine that public officials react to grand jury findings and recommendations with a variety of motivations and intentions. Some elected officials, for example, read them from the perspective of their possible effects on their careers at the next election. Other officials are deeply interested in finding new methods and procedures to improve public services. Still other officials resent the notion that citizens, particularly grand jurors, have invaded their domains. Some of these officials, and others with still different motivations, see poorly conceived recommendations as threatening, useless, harmful, or contrary to the public interest.

Like public officials, grand jurors view comments by public officials to grand jury findings and recommendations from a variety of perspectives. Grand jurors might interpret negative, patronizing, or supercilious comments about findings and recommendations as arrogant or politically inspired. On the other hand, grand jurors might view findings and recommendations that local-government officials commend, support, or implement as measures of the value of the grand jury.

Chapter 5 includes more discussion about the give-and-take between grand juries and local-government officials with respect to findings and recommendations. For now, this much should be clear: Soundly conceived and well-written recommendations are more likely to be implemented than recommendations that are vague, trivial, confusing, or unfounded. Although poorly written recommendations are of many types, in this section we shall consider only 10 categories:

1. Conclusions identified as recommendations
2. Inconsequential or trivial recommendations
3. Vague recommendations
4. Recommendations based on undocumented opinion rather than on known standards
5. Recommendations about policy issues
6. Recommendations without findings to support them
7. Equivocating recommendations
8. Observations, comments, or criticisms mistakenly identified as recommendations
9. Recommendations not based on independent grand jury investigation
10. Inappropriately addressed recommendations

LABELING CONCLUSIONS AS RECOMMENDATIONS

In investigating a complaint titled "Inmate Questioning Medical Procedures," a Grand Jury listed seven findings that were either vague descriptions of organizational procedures or undocumented conclusions. The one recommendation the Grand Jury presented from its investigation was worded like a conclusion developed from a finding:

> The county receives very adequate medical advice/attention through the contract with Dr. [—] and his PA's. The county pays $2,916.66 per month for this contract with the Adult Detention Facility.[89]

INCONSEQUENTIAL OR TRIVIAL RECOMMENDATIONS

Considered in the context of the many social, economic, and political problems facing local-government officials and their communities, recommendations such as the following examples inspire charges that grand juries are unable to address significant issues in their investigations and reports:

> The renovation of the Police Stables should include adequate boxstalls for all horses, water in each stall, and sufficient paddocks for non-working horses.[90]

> A rubber gasket is needed to protect wires where two-way radios are being recharged.[91]

The basis for the first recommendation was, "Each year the veterinarian treats at least one horse for impaction colic which is caused by dehydration." Although the Grand Jury's concern for the well-being of animals is commendable, the City and County of San Francisco has issues of a more pressing nature that might have benefited from the Grand Jury's intervention.[92] The second recommendation was the only suggestion for improvement that the Kings County Grand Jury developed from its tour of the City of Corcoran.

VAGUE RECOMMENDATIONS

When it recently amended Penal Code Section 916 to emphasize evidence, the Legislature probably intended that the revised statute would increase the factuality of grand jury reports. Undocumented and vague recommendations, after all, provide little assistance to local-government officials. The following example concerns an issue that was highly publicized in California during the study period as county governments began charging city police departments for the costs of booking arrested persons into county jails.

After expressing its concern that the imposition of booking fees by the county requires "arresting officers [in cities to be] cognizant of booking fees when they make an arrest," a Grand Jury recommended "that an alternative solution be explored."[93] In doing so, the Grand Jury ignored the words of Penal Code Section 916, which requires panels to identify "suggested means for [the] resolution" of the problem; instead, the Grand Jury wrote nebulously about "an alternative solution" but offered no suggestions about what such a solution might be.

The recommendations of two other grand juries show similar vagueness:

> The County and the community should continue to look for alternative revenue sources.[94]

> Continued recruitment of professional personnel should be an ongoing priority.[95]

In both examples, the grand juries addressed major local-government problems with which elected and appointed officials have struggled for years. The recommendations, however, provide little more than emotional support for those officials. If, on the other hand, the grand juries had provided specific examples of possible solutions, as Penal Code Section 916 requires, local-government officials might have been more motivated to include in their comments a discussion of the advantages and disadvantages of each grand jury's recommendations.

RECOMMENDATIONS BASED ON UNDOCUMENTED OPINION RATHER THAN ON KNOWN STANDARDS

One Grand Jury waived responsibility for basing its recommendations on known, approved standards and practices by expressing the superiority of its own judgment and deferring to the wisdom of agency staff:

> The Grand Jury did not research the legal or administrative standards that govern the conditions in the jails. However, the jury relied on its own judgment

on what is acceptable based on general understanding of what is humane and what is affordable, and on the attestations of Sheriff's Department personnel.[96]

RECOMMENDATIONS ABOUT POLICY ISSUES

Besides being vague, the following recommendation concerns a matter that is within the discretion of an elected board and therefore is outside the jurisdiction of the grand jury:

> Consider youth guidance and rehabilitation programs on the same level and as important as adult criminal apprehension and incarceration. This consideration should be given in the allocation of funds.[97]

Citing as evidence "Discussions with experienced individuals within the criminal justice system," a Grand Jury urged a district attorney to adopt a policy of not charging, "or if charged, [to] strike for sentencing purposes only, prior prostitution convictions more than five years old, so that a subsequent prostitution conviction does not necessarily require time in jail."[98]

RECOMMENDATIONS WITHOUT SUPPORTING FINDINGS

Readers familiar with the standards of objective reporting expect recommendations to be connected to findings that, in turn, are linked directly to documented facts. Recommendations also should be designated as such, rather than being termed "Areas that need correcting," as was the case with this comment: "There should be a policy or standard procedure for acquiring classroom materials, supplies, furniture, etc."[99] If it was intended as a recommendation, the statement lacks substantiating information. For example, the Grand Jury did not report whether it attempted to find a standard procedure, where it would have expected to find it, or why none existed. Similarly, the Grand Jury did not cite examples of ineffective methods "for acquiring classroom materials, supplies, furniture, etc." Missing also was any reference to the extent of the problem, how long it had lasted, and the costs of its consequences.

EQUIVOCATING RECOMMENDATIONS

Some recommendations are of the covering-one's-bets variety; this example provides for the possibility that the recommendation may be unnecessary:

> When fire districts provide medical aid to persons from counties other than Yolo County, the fire district should charge those persons for the expense of medical assistance (if they do not already).[100]

Mistakenly Identifying Observations, Comments, or Criticisms as Recommendations

For a recommendation to be effective, it should be clearly identified and should address a specific improvement. Occasionally, readers find text identified as recommendations that has no apparent purpose or direction. The following recommendation, for example, was a gratuitous, unsubstantiated criticism of someone whom grand jurors evidently observed during a tour. The comment was designated as a recommendation and, as stated, would be a challenge for any local-government official who might attempt to comment about it:

> While none of us were experts in education, we could not help but notice that the teacher, which is currently in place to educate children from kindergarten to high school, was not particularly youth oriented.[101]

This recommendation also is an example of a fair-comment problem. The Grand Jury did not define what it meant by "not particularly youth oriented," did not provide examples of this purported deficiency, and did not explain how not being "particularly youth oriented" related to the Grand Jury's jurisdiction.

Recommendations Not Based on Independent Grand Jury Investigation

An example of the reliance of some grand juries on the reports of their hired experts is exemplified in an acknowledgment in a final report of a Southern California grand jury:

> The Grand Jury's special thanks go to ... our contract auditor, and his dedicated team whose disciplined research and literate composition led to many of the conclusions and recommendations which we were pleased to adopt in those reports for which they were retained.[102]

If the apparent conflict between Penal Code Sections 939.9 and 916 were contested in court, one issue that might be addressed is whether a distinction should be made between two types of circumstances in which grand juries adopt as their own the reports, findings, conclusions, and recommendations of other persons or organizations: (a) the reports of professionally trained experts whom grand juries have hired, and (b) the reports of "experts" who volunteer their services to grand juries. One example of the latter case is reported in the final report of a Northern California grand jury:

> The grand jury requested [a local expert] to review and critique both the high school and elementary school geothermal wells. Dr. [—] is one of the preeminent geologist [*sic*] in California.... We would like to thank Dr. [—] for his time that he volunteered for this report. It is greatly appreciated.
>
> Facts and Findings: Dr. [—]'s report will stand as our facts and findings.[103]

Inappropriately Addressed Recommendations

Grand juries occasionally misdirect their recommendations to officials who have no authority to correct the problems specified. For example, one grand jury recommended that a board of supervisors require other elected officials in County government to receive training in various County policies and procedures. The Grand Jury apparently did not realize that boards of supervisors exert no direct policy control over elected officials such as the sheriff, auditor, or district attorney.[104]

Confidentiality and Secrecy

Breaches by grand juries of confidentiality and secrecy, if they occur, are not so identified in final reports. If grand jurors or other persons commit such acts, they more likely would occur outside final reports, such as during investigations or at social events.[105] Only six examples of revealing matters that should not have been publicized entered the database for the study period. One example concerned a grand jury comment that might have implications for lawsuits against a county; the remaining five were not breaches of confidentiality or secrecy as the law defines them. They were, rather, matters that should not have been published because of the potential hazards they present for the physical security of local-government employees or other citizens. Because these may continue to be potentially sensitive examples, their source is not documented.

The first example is a statement followed by a recommendation:

> There have been a number of deputy-involved traffic accidents resulting in injuries and/or the loss of life. Recommendation: It is recommended that the Sheriff provide a refresher course in defensive driving. It would not only benefit the Sheriff's personnel by improving their driving skills, but reduce the liability to the County.

This example contains several problems. First, it is not supported by facts. Instead, the recommendation refers vaguely to "a number of deputy-involved traffic accidents" but fails to state how many of these accidents involved negligence by deputy sheriffs rather than by other drivers.[106] If other drivers caused some of the accidents, few of them would have been prevented by the improved driving skills of deputy sheriffs. Second, the grand jury provided no information about the severity or costs of the problem. Third, the panel's statement offers the reader no insight about the procedures the sheriff's department routinely used to collect data about duty-related accidents in which deputy sheriffs were involved.

The fourth, and possibly most important, problem is that by making this statement, the grand jury unwittingly could support a plaintiff's attorney in a civil suit against the county. Because the statement occurs in what presumably is an authoritative grand jury report, a plaintiff's attorney could use it to influence jurors, as this hypothetical statement illustrates, by asserting that:

> Not only was the deputy in this case negligent in injuring my client, but even the grand jury report of 1991–1992 noted that the department is riddled with unsafe drivers and pointed out that the deputies are poorly trained. Ladies and gentleman of the jury, here is what the grand jury reported:

> "There have been a number of deputy-involved traffic accidents resulting in injuries and/or the loss of life. Recommendation: It is recommended that the Sheriff provide a refresher course in defensive driving. It would not only benefit the sheriff's personnel by improving their driving skills, but reduce the liability to the county."

The remaining examples represent a more immediate problem: informing burglars, robbers, and even possible rapists about the vulnerability of local-government buildings and employees. For example, one grand jury recommended that "the security system [in a public building] should be expanded by installing a TV monitor for the front lobby and check-processing room."

Another grand jury, whose members claimed that they frequently worked evenings and weekends at the main county-government building, expressed concern in its final report that "there was no apparent building or parking lot security." This observation resulted in an investigation into "the level of security, or lack thereof" at the site. Although it sent a separate "confidential report" to the board of supervisors describing other security problems, the grand jury's final report included a six-page report of the investigation that listed many other security problems throughout the building, including:

> The public has direct access to offices via the atrium back stairs.

> Offices are left unlocked at night, presenting potential risk to sensitive material.

> Many keys are pass keys and door locks are easily breachable.

> There are no anti-escape locks on courtroom doors.

> No security exists in the Vehicle Service Center where frequent vandalism occurs to County and Sheriff's vehicles.

Another grand jury issued a report of its findings and recommendations concerning the office of treasurer and tax collector, including:

> The combination to the vault has never been changed.

> The vault is not alarmed.

> The Treasurer and Tax Collector makes daily bank deposits but requests a security escort only "sometimes."

In an investigation of a special district, a grand jury included a copy of a Telephone Transfer Service Agreement authorizing a bank to transfer funds between checking and savings accounts or loan accounts by telephone. The copy showed the name of an official, her Social Security number, and her mother's maiden name. Few citizens would welcome having that information revealed in a publicly distributed grand jury report.[107]

COLLEGIAL AND CORPORATE NATURE OF THE GRAND JURY

Examples of this problem in the database are a small portion of its actual frequency in final reports. At least one example occurred in every final report, and in some final reports, the problem abounds. The examples of the problem we shall consider are of two types: (a) emphasizing grand jurors rather than the institution, and (b) usurpation of the institution's powers by individual grand jurors. The examples show that some grand juries do not function as the Legislature and case law intend them to function: as deliberating bodies of peers rather than as aggregations of individual grand jurors, some of whom have more authority than others. Instead, the examples create in many readers' minds the image of a loosely organized assemblage that exists for the convenience and aggrandizement of individual members or committees.

Misunderstanding the Foreman's Role

The principal statutory distinction between a foreman and other grand jurors is that Penal Code Section 912 requires the court to appoint the grand jury foreman or his replacement. No statute grants a foreman the authority to designate committees, assign grand jurors to them, appoint other grand jury officers, decide which investigations to conduct or not conduct, accept or reject citizens' complaints, and the like. It would seem possible, though ill-advised, under Penal Code Section 916 for grand jurors to delegate power and authority to the foreman to make those decisions. In no instance did final reports reveal that the required number of grand jurors voted to permit their foreman to execute powers or authority that otherwise reside only in the panel.[108] Final reports, however, occasionally reveal statements by foremen who early in their terms made decisions that only the grand jury has power to make, and who provided no indication that the grand jury delegated such powers, as the following example shows:[109]

> I assigned the committees the task of investigating these topics, not so much to uncover problems, but to write reports that explain to our citizens the extent of county and citizen efforts being made to meet the challenges and solve problems in these areas.

In the same report, the Audits and Administration Committee of the Colusa County Grand Jury recalled that:

> At the inception of this year's Grand Jury it was decided and declared by the Foreman that this committee should concentrate efforts on several requested activities, rather than all departments in general.[110]

Still later in the same document, a committee report disclosed that "the Grand Jury Water Committee, the first ever for Colusa County, was appointed by foreman ... to look into the Colusa County water situation."[111]

Two Mother Lode grand juries disclosed other examples of foremen deciding the organization of newly impaneled grand juries:

> The foreman suggested six committees be established and appointed the chairmen of five.[112]

> The grand jury was convened in January 1991 under its first foreman [who] structured the jury into four major committees and assigned chair-persons and personnel. Each committee had specific areas of concern to investigate along with the flexibility for excursions into unexpected developments.[113]

Emphasizing Committees Rather than the Grand Jury

In most institutions, committees exist temporarily to accomplish tasks delegated to them. Under Penal Code Section 916, grand juries may establish committees or any other kind of lawful arrangement for investigating complaints, conducting tours, reviewing drafts of grand jury final reports, and the like. As sometimes is the case in bureaucracies, however, grand jury committees often assume an identity apart from that of the parent body. Consequently, the cohesiveness of many grand jury final reports is diminished by practices that exalt committee identity.

During the study period, for example, the Ventura County Grand Jury Final Report listed committee assignments for all grand jurors, displayed conspicuously the names and signatures of committee chairmen on each committee report, and presented investigations in the name of committees rather than the Grand Jury. Other examples of emphasizing committee names and assignments are the following:

> It is the Law Enforcement Committee's finding that in most cases the reimbursements have been limited to this $50.00 fee levied at the time the case is accepted by the Public Defender's Office.[114]

> The Committee believes that the County may be better served without the County Constable position.[115]

> In the course of the year, the Administration Committee responded to 17 complaint letters. The Committee wrote a letter to the Board of Supervisors recommending a national search for the appointee to the position of County Administration Officer. In addition, the Committee issued three reports.[116]

The format of many final reports also reinforces the reader's impression that grand jury committees discharge the responsibilities of the body. For example, one final report consisted of collections of committee reports, each prefaced by a one-page summary of the committee's workload, history, and complaints, signed by the "Chair" of the committee, and titled with the name of the committee in large type—for example, "PUBLIC ADMINISTRATION COMMITTEE."

The same final report emphasized committees by displaying in the front matter the committee assignments of grand jurors. The Roster of Members included each grand juror's name, the community of residence, and "committee service," in this manner:

> [JUROR'S NAME] — Madera
> Chair: Public Services
>   Library
> Member: City of Madera
>   Editorial
>   Public Safety and Welfare[117]

In some cases, the tradition of representing reports as committee products, rather than products of the grand jury, is so strong that different-colored paper and separate page numbering systems are used for each committee. One grand jury listed colors, rather than page numbers, in its table of contents to designate committee sections; for example:

Administration and Audit Committee	Blue
Law and Justice Committee	Cream White
Special Assignments Committee	Lavender[118]

Using colored paper to designate separate committee reports has several disadvantages: Colored paper is more costly than white paper; some colors make the reports more difficult to read because they do not contrast well with certain inks; the use of different colors requires more steps in the printing process; and some colors photocopy poorly.

Emphasizing Grand Jurors Rather than the Grand Jury

Many grand juries traditionally list the names of individual grand jurors in the first few pages of final reports. Sometimes the names of grand jurors are listed with the names of their communities. This practice is appropriate. Although final reports are the products of the entire body, citizens should be assured that their communities are represented proportionately on the panel. In the few counties whose grand juries listed only the names of the entire panel, the name of the foreman is included alphabetically in the list of names.[119]

Beyond this single listing of names and communities of residence, the spirit of the institution is thwarted by repeatedly listing names and committee assignments of grand jurors, listing the names of grand jurors on dividing pages of committee reports, and, in some cases, listing the names of grand jurors on each investigative report. Going one step further, some grand juries provide photographs of the entire panel, of committees, and in one case, a picture of the panel at the start of its term and another picture of the panel at the end of the term.[120]

Southern California grand juries in two adjoining counties have developed the photographic tradition to the point that most grand jurors in each of the two counties were displayed in final reports at least three times. Table 16, "Photographs of Grand Jurors in the Los Angeles County Grand Jury Final Report of 1991–1992," lists the number of photographs of grand jurors in the Los Angeles County Grand Jury Final Report of 1991–1992. Table 17, "Photographs of Grand Jurors in the Orange County Grand Jury Final Report of 1991–1992," shows how grand jurors of that county displayed photographs of themselves and other persons.[121]

TABLE 16
Photographs of Grand Jurors
in the Los Angeles County Grand Jury
Final Report of 1991–1992

Description of Photograph	Number of Jurors Depicted
Entire group photograph	23
Grand Jury officers	6
Foreman	1
Audit Committee	6
County Administrative Office Committee	4
Cost Effectiveness Committee	3
Criminal Justice Committee	5
Editorial Committee	2
Eldercare Committee	2
Exit L.A. Committee	6
Gangs Committee	6
Jails Committee	7
Juvenile Services Committee	6
Pension Plan Committee	3
Save Our Water Committee	1
Sludge Disposal Committee	5
Social and Human Services Committee	8
Ad Hoc Committee	2
Total	96

Use of photographs by the Orange County Grand Jury is similar to the Los Angeles practice. In addition to a full-page photograph of the Grand Jury and a half-page photograph of Grand Jury officers in the front matter of the final report, half the area of the dividing page of each committee report is occupied by a photograph of the committee members. Thus, the images of some individual grand jurors may be included as many as five times in the final report. The dividing page of the Human Services Education Committee section of the Orange County Grand Jury Final Report showed one grand juror (wearing a straw-hat of 1890s style) seated before an old typewriter; another grand juror sat before the same desk, holding a telephone of an earlier era. The connection between the work of the committee and the attempt at levity conveyed by the photograph was not discussed.

TABLE 17
Photographs of Grand Jurors in the
Orange County Grand Jury Final Report of 1991–1992

Photograph Number	Description
1	Photograph and names of panel and staff secretary
2	Photographs and names of Judge, Deputy County Counsel, Deputy District Attorney, staff secretary
3	Photograph and names of the six officers of the Grand Jury
4	Photograph and names of the five members of the Administration Committee on the page divider introducing the Administration Committee report
5	Photograph and names of the six members of the Criminal Justice Committee on the page divider introducing the Criminal Justice Committee report
6	Photograph and names of the six members of the Environment/ Transportation Committee on the page divider introducing that committee report
7	Photograph and names of the five members of the Human Services/Education Committee on the page divider of the Human Services/Education Committee report
8	Photographs and names of the six members of the Juvenile Services/Education Committee on the page divider introducing the Juvenile Services/Education Committee report
9	Photographs and names of the six members of the Special Issues Committee on the page divider introducing the Special Issues Committee report
10	Photographs and names of the seven members of the Editorial Committee on the page divider introducing the Editorial Committee report

One Northern California county grand jury devoted six pages of the front matter of a 50-page report to individual photographs of grand jurors—usually four portraits to a page. Preceding these photographs was a portrait of the "Grand Jury Presiding Judge." The first page of the report displayed a list of the names of grand jurors and their home communities.[122]

Budget restrictions may prevent some grand juries from including photographs of grand jurors in final reports. Instead, the repeated listing of grand jurors' names serves a similar purpose. For example, the front matter of a Northern California county grand jury final report showed three lists of names: (1) a list of Grand Jury officers, (2) the 1991–1992 Membership List of grand jurors, and (3) the 1991–1992 County Grand Jury Committees, including the names of committee members.[123]

Individual Grand Jurors Acting Alone

Penal Code Section 916 requires that "all findings included in … final reports are supported by documented evidence … [such as] interviews attended by no fewer than two grand jurors." Although these words do not preclude individual grand jurors from conducting some activities, they do exclude from final reports evidence obtained during interviews conducted only by individual grand jurors.

Few grand jury final reports referred to actions of individual grand jurors. In one example, however, a grand juror, identifying himself as a committee member and signing a three-page letter on behalf of the Chairman of the Audit Committee, requested a County department head to provide a lengthy list of documents and other materials pertaining to a matter under investigation.[124] In the same final report, the "County Departments, Commissions and Directors Committee" issued a report of an inquiry into a citizen's complaint "dealing with property belonging to the County Fair Grounds." The method of reporting its investigation was to include in the final report a copy of a memorandum from one grand juror to another, concluding with the comment, "My observations were that there was no wrongdoing or intent."[125]

Implications

The lack of effective internal grand jury procedures caused many of the problems discussed in this chapter. In Chapter 6, I offer suggestions to reduce, if not altogether eliminate, problems of this nature. In Chapter 8, I discuss how certain characteristics of grand jurors might create deficient final reports. Because temperament of the grand jurors often is at the base of the problems cited in this chapter, however, I briefly offer several examples of how certain attitudes of grand jurors can affect the spirit of the institution.

Several years ago during a Grand Jury Exchange Seminar, a member of our Planning Committee took me aside and commented:

> I think we're spending too much time on grand jury law. We're going to get them so tied up in red tape, they'll be afraid to do anything. You can't accomplish anything that way. When I was president of [a large commercial enterprise], I didn't ask anyone whether I could or could not do something; I just did it. And I didn't hire anyone who didn't have the same attitude.

The comment surprised me on several counts. *First,* the speaker indeed had been the president of a large, Statewide commercial enterprise of a type that State and federal governments regulate thoroughly. In that type of organization, a free-wheeling management style would seem unlikely. *Second,* the speaker had been a grand jury foreman; however, nothing in the bland final report of the grand jury on which he served suggested the influence of a "man of action." *Third,* I had assumed that given the man's sophistication, education, and experience, he would understand that the goals and methods of the California grand jury were dissimilar to those of private enterprise, and that what might work in one sphere would not necessarily be suited for the other. *Fourth* and finally, the speaker had participated in Grand Jury Exchange Seminars for several years, and he had heard a variety of judges, district attorneys, county counsels, and former grand jurors recount grand jury controversies they experienced, most of which could be attributed to "shoot first and ask questions later" attitudes.

The speaker's comments certainly were not new to me. I have seen similar sentiments in written evaluations of the Seminars. On one occasion, the complaint took a somewhat unusual form: "I'm not going to recommend this Seminar to our Grand Jury for next year. Who needs to hear a lot of outdated legal historical stuff?" The comment puzzled me until I realized that the writer probably was referring to an hour-long session concerning grand jury case law. Like some grand jurors I have met, the writer probably regarded a detailed consideration of the legal foundation of the institution a boring waste of time and a subject the study of which grand jurors should defer to legal advisors.

The impatience of some grand jurors with learning grand jury law provides an interesting example of a classic problem of curriculum development: how to reconcile the contradiction between what students or trainees *think* they should learn with what objective analysis of job requirements discloses they *should* know. Each year, the contradiction is raised anew by examples of problems in grand jury investigations and reports.

I can think of no better explanation for the recurrence of these problems than Tocqueville's explanation of the dislike "men living in democratic ages" have for "forms," by which he meant something akin to the "rules of procedure" specified in Penal Code Section 916. In democracies, Tocqueville stated that people "do not readily comprehend the utility of forms." In fact, he claimed, citizens "feel an instinctive contempt for them." Leading the many causes of this disdain is that in their pursuit of "the object of their desires .... [T]he slightest delay exasperates them."[126]

"Red tape" is a mixed blessing. If it unnecessarily thwarts public officials or other citizens in their lawful activities, it is undesirable. If it prevents the abuse of power in public or private bureaucracies, it is justified. In the case of the grand jury, the stricture against interfering with the legitimate policy decisions of public officials prevents panels from infringing on the legislative function. Similarly, Penal Code Section 933 is useful red tape because it requires grand jurors to submit final reports to judges before releasing the reports to the public. This form enables courts to review reports for jurisdictional compliance and thereby protects the institution, public officials, or private persons.

Problems in grand jury investigations and reports are, with few exceptions, signs of ineffective internal procedures. Moreover, the problems are what might be expected from individuals who are ignorant of procedure, who are contemptuous of it, or who desire to exploit the prestige and influence of the grand jury for self-serving purposes. Whatever the causes of these problems, they have important consequences for the institution, some of which I shall now discuss. By doing so, I hope to demonstrate how the disdain for procedure that Tocqueville described can discredit or distort the grand jury in the eyes of the several publics interested in its work: public officials, the news media, and other citizens.

WASTING GRAND JURY ENERGY AND RESOURCES

Conducting inquiries into public or private matters not within the grand jury's jurisdiction diverts grand jurors from issues that should be investigated. Consider the example of the grand jury that reported its investigation into allegations of impropriety on an Indian reservation. Judging by the panel's account of its inquiry, it spent considerable time and effort on issues it had no authority to investigate. While grand jurors of that county investigated matters for which no jurisdiction existed, one wonders whether a special district, city, or school district was in greater need of the panel's attention. Similarly, one wonders how many people who read the report of the inquiry, or who otherwise knew of it, were confused by what must seem the curious paradox of a grand jury inquiring into matters that it conceded were not within its jurisdiction.

CONTRIBUTING TO CONFUSION ABOUT THE INSTITUTION

Recall that several panels issued recommendations concerning legislation. Among citizens who read the reports of these panels, what impression must they now have of the grand jury's identity and purpose? Is it connected somehow to the State of California or to the federal government? Is it a lobbying body? Suppose that one or two citizens who read the report eventually become grand jurors on a subsequent grand jury. What kinds of problems will arise if, recalling that a previous panel issued such recommendations, they importune their colleagues to take stands on legislative issues? How much time will be spent discussing whether the recommendations are lawful? Will someone argue that even if no statutes authorize recommendations for legislation, "Last year's grand jury got away with it, so why can't we?"

Similarly, what will citizens conclude from the statement by a grand jury that it "worked under" the district attorney? Does this mean that the district attorney controls the grand jury? If a citizen believed he had been improperly arrested and confined by a law enforcement agency, what would his perception be of the likelihood that a grand jury, subordinated as it is to a law enforcement body, would accept and investigate his complaint fairly? Finally, to what extent did the panel's comment add weight to the long-standing criticism that district attorneys control the institution?

Raising Doubts About the Institution's Objectivity and Integrity

Two examples in the previous section described grand jury investigations in school districts. In both cases, the panels provided information that suggested misappropriation of public funds. The panels, however, failed to provide information about crucial investigative leads that a well-planned investigation into each matter would have identified.

In one case, the grand jury reported that officials would take appropriate action concerning the mishandling of funds. The grand jury, however, provided no proof that the action was taken, nor did the grand jury report that it attempted to find out if the lax controls that had allowed the mishandling of funds in one school district also existed in others, or whether school-district officials had developed procedures for preventing recurrence of the problem.

In the second instance, the panel declared that it found no evidence of wrong-doing. The investigative issues the panel left unanswered, however, probably puzzled citizens reading the report who had even a rudimentary knowledge of the proper conduct of public affairs.

Creating Bad Law by Bad Practice

Every finding or recommendation that is unsupported by one or more facts increases the prospect of legislation hampering the institution's independence. This is particularly true if the findings or recommendations affect the careers of elected or appointed local-government officials. In Chapter 6, I describe attempts in the California Legislature to enact laws that would have allowed public officials, in effect, to censure final reports before courts released them to the public. Those attempts are strengthened by subjective statements, undocumented findings, and defamatory language. The intentional or unintentional failure to abide by Penal Code Section 916—particularly its requirement for documentation—therefore subverts the institution, comforts its opponents, and inspires legislation to curtail its independence.

Diminishing Institutional Prestige and Dignity

In the absence of effective procedures to prevent them, inconsequential investigations and reports detract from the institution. A grand jury final report of 150 pages that contains little more than servile commendations of public officials and their activities, tedious descriptions of visits to local-government offices, and numerous photographs of grand jurors inspires contempt in the news media, public officials, and other citizens who understand the institution's traditions, achievements, and potential.

Embroiling the Institution in Unnecessary Controversy

Even well-documented investigations and reports can result in controversy. Political systems are not the lifeless abstractions represented by organization charts in civics textbooks. Local governments consist of complex networks of formal and informal relationships, accommodations between the reality of human abilities and motives and the idealism of statutes, and internal compromises and alignments that have existed for many years. A grand jury report that identifies irregularities in these systems might not be welcome to persons benefiting from them. Thus, no matter how meritorious they might be, findings and recommendations to improve systems and procedures that clash with internal political realities often result in controversy. In a sense, controversy, then, might be unavoidable but is indeed essential for change.

The institution will survive controversy if investigations have been conducted and reported effectively. Controversy created by blunders, though, diminishes the institution's standing. The grand jurors who committed plagiarism in the Central Valley county gave the persons who were adversely affected by grand jury reports in that county, and possibly in others, ammunition for years to come in discrediting future panels, no matter how effective they might be.

By their nature, few pragmatists can be persuaded that the ends rarely justify the means. If—to return to the example of the report about immigration—men or women "of action" responsible for the report were commended by their friends and associates for issuing it, the report "worked," lawful or not. Other citizens reading the report might have concluded that characterizing the grand jury as an Anglo-Saxon institution has more than historical significance. Similarly, if the grand juror who urged school-district trustees to endorse a federal education proposal was pleased to see his name in a newspaper story of the event and no one in the community realized that a blunder had occurred, he will conclude that his strategy "worked." Of course, the report might not have comforted citizens in community who suspected that grand juries are pawns for special interests who benefit from expanding federal-government interference with local matters.

Perhaps the most serious consequence of the problems reviewed in this chapter is that they discredit the institution and thereby prevent it from contributing to public confidence in government. As Tocqueville pointed out, the early colonists attempted to create forms of government that would prevent some of the abuses of absolute power that they had experienced in their native land.[127] Years later, the authors of our founding charter incorporated some of these safeguards, including the grand jury, into the Constitution of the United States. Indeed, one scholar argues that the idea of the jury is "at the heart of the Bill of Rights. The Fifth [Amendment] safeguards the role of the grand jury; the Sixth, the criminal petit jury; and the Seventh, the civil jury."[128]

In this context, the manner in which California citizens create and manage the grand jury is of more than theoretical and historical significance: It is a measure of how well citizens today understand and perpetuate many of the principles of government that the colonists and framers of the Constitution dedicated their lives to create. It, therefore, is tragically ironic for grand jurors to create a panel that is procedurally defective when its statutory purpose is to evaluate the procedures of local government.

Summary and Conclusion

Three types of problems uncovered in final reports accounted for 39 percent of the examples of law-related problems in the database: jurisdiction and independence, legality and effectiveness of findings and recommendations, and validity. Grand juries reported few clashes with public officials. The few intemperate comments were in reference to unnamed but possibly identifiable persons. Thus, criticism that grand juries frequently malign the careers or private lives of public officials is, at least during the study period, without foundation.

Final reports revealed few obvious examples of fishing expeditions—using grand jury powers without good cause. Grand juries could do much to reduce allegations of "fishing" by clearly stating in their reports the statutory basis for each investigation. Identifying (within the limits of secrecy and confidentiality) the types of complainants requesting investigations (such as whether citizens, public officials, or grand jurors themselves filed complaints) also will allay suspicions about "witch hunting."

Issuing findings and recommendations about policy occurs occasionally, despite the lack of statutory authority to do so. Grand jury reports rarely described the measures that panels used to ensure the validity of their investigations. Examples of lack of validity include failure to document sources and report findings, conclusions, and recommendations without providing substantiating facts. Almost all grand juries ignored the statutory requirement to suggest means (including financial, when applicable) for resolving problems identified in final reports.

If grand jurors were to correct 10 types of problems affecting findings and recommendations, public officials would be more likely to consider implementing a larger number of grand jury recommendations. Although Penal Code Section 939.9 prohibits grand juries from adopting the recommendations of any other person, consultant, or report, grand jurors in the study period occasionally did so. Only one instance of plagiarism, however, was reported to have occurred in the study period, but it drew Statewide attention. No violations of secrecy by grand juries were apparent in final reports, but the reports did yield several examples of matters that otherwise should not have been revealed.

Just as the criminal grand jury is intended to be a deliberating body of peers, so, too, does that quality characterize its civil counterpart. Nevertheless, many final reports included practices that threaten the nature of the institution as a cohesive body of peers (for example, emphasis on committees, references to individual grand jurors, and recommendations issued in the names of foremen).

In assessing grand juries during the study period, I emphasized legal criteria. Nevertheless, even well-conceived and conducted investigations will be useless if grand juries do not communicate them effectively to their communities. In the next chapter, I evaluate how well grand juries convey the results of their work to citizens who read final reports.

5

Evaluating Investigations and Reports Using Other Criteria

The only insight that most California citizens will ever have into their county civil grand jury is what they acquire by reading its final reports. Except in limited circumstances, no one except grand jurors may observe panels in their formal meetings. Even experienced news-media representatives rarely obtain significant information about the institution from interviews with grand jurors because the latter, early in their terms, usually have learned well the statement, "Our report will speak for us." Most news or feature stories about grand juries, therefore, are written with interim or final reports as the sole source of information.

Because final reports are the principal means by which most citizens learn of the work of grand jurors, the quality of those documents is important to the standing of grand juries in their communities. In Chapter 4, I used legal criteria to assess reports of the study period and discuss certain recurring substantive problems in them. In this chapter I use two additional groups of criteria (community and technical) to assess final reports along less legalistic, but no less important, lines.

Community Criteria

The three community criteria for assessing grand jury investigations and final reports in this chapter are the *significance* of these investigations and reports, *accountability* of the grand jury to the community, and *continuity* in successive grand juries. These criteria and the grand jury tradition are closely related. For example, the lofty language that some writers use to portray the independence and jurisdiction of the institution implies that it deals with matters of profound import.[1] When grand jury investigations and reports fall short of these ideals, some citizens, news-media representatives, local-government observers, and legal scholars ridicule the institution and depict it disparagingly.[2]

The significance of a grand jury's investigations and reports is of great importance to a panel's relationship to its community. If, for example, a grand jury each year issues insignificant reports, citizens will see the institution as irrelevant. Given the serious social, economic, and political issues confronting California citizens daily, they will have little interest in a final report if its most serious issue is, for instance, to deplore the inadequate directory of the various offices in the county courthouse.

Even if grand juries investigate and report only highly significant matters, citizens will be unaware of them if grand jurors fail to account for them adequately in final reports. Similarly, grand juries that omit from their reports summaries of their workloads, achievements, and discussions of unusual problems they encounter, contribute to a problem that grand jurors often complain about: citizens' lack of knowledge about the institution and its work. Accountability to citizens therefore is important for obtaining community support without which independence has little meaning.[3]

Continuity refers to the lawful methods a sitting grand jury uses to create or maintain links between it and its predecessors and successors. Although each grand jury is independent, some institutional continuity is useful. For example, two statutes (Penal Code Sections 925 and 928) require that grand juries conduct investigations of designated local governments, respectively, on "some selective basis each year" and "selectively each year." If a grand jury does not know which departments its predecessors investigated, some local-government functions or agencies will escape review.

Similarly, if sitting panels ensure that local-government officials have, as the law requires, commented about the findings and recommendations of previous grand juries, they uphold the institution in the community by calling to account officials who challenge or ignore that duty. In providing continuity, grand juries must use care to ensure that routine follow-ups of previous investigations do not become, or appear to become, ax-grinding campaigns. Finally, although extensive files and records might be useful for planning investigations, grand juries should regard them as merely investigative leads and not as information they can rely on without corroboration.

SIGNIFICANCE

Of the three criteria, significance is the most subjective for several reasons. *First,* no objective standards exist to help readers distinguish between trivial and significant investigations. It is a matter of opinion, for example, whether investigating the procedures that juvenile-hall officials use to discipline their charges is more important than reviewing procedures that law enforcement officials provide for investigating citizens' complaints against peace officers. Most people, however, would agree that each of these hypothetical subjects is more important than reporting tedious details about tours through public buildings; praising the desserts that school cafeteria staff serve; or denouncing an unsightly drinking fountain, filthy doormats, and dirty windows in a public building.

Second, poor reporting practices can hide the import of a significant investigation. If, for example, a grand jury has not explained how an ineffective procedure or practice it has investigated could harm people, readers are deprived of a sense of the importance of the issue.

Third, grand jurors occasionally withhold some or all details of investigations from the public for various reasons. To illustrate, a grand jury may decide not to publish information about allegations of a public official's wrongdoing with an understanding that the official will resign from office. Similarly, grand juries occasionally withhold information that could strengthen the validity of reports.[4] Whether grand juries should censor themselves is, of course, debatable. In any case, my assessment of the significance of investigations must be in terms of what grand juries reported rather than what may have happened behind the scenes.

In one instance, a Grand Jury alluded briefly to what might have been a significant investigation but provided no additional information about it. Although this "report" occupied only half a page, it raises a number of questions about the panel's conception of its purpose, its independence from public officials, its sense of accountability to citizens, and the validity of its investigative methods. In this instance, the Grand Jury included in its final report a brief but curious reference to an investigation it claimed it conducted at the request of the Board of Supervisors:

> The specific purpose of the committee was to develop a plan of action for a limited inquiry of the training and operational policies, procedures and practices used by the Sheriff's Department.

The Grand Jury provided no other details about what it discovered in the investigation, why it chose to conduct it secretly, or what its findings and recommendations addressed, with the exception of terse comments about its investigative methods: "Questions for the inquiry were solicited from members of the Grand Jury. They were organized into twelve topics of information." The Grand Jury emphasized that the Los Angeles County Sheriff assisted in this inquiry. The Sheriff and several members of his staff appeared before the Grand Jury and provided a detailed response to each topic of information. The findings of the inquiry were documented in a report and submitted privately to the

Board of Supervisors.[5] Among the questions that could be asked about the investigation are:

• Why was it not publicly reported?
• How valid can it be if it relied only on oral testimony of a few people?
• Why did the Grand Jury inquire into policies when no statutory authorization exists to do so?
• How objective can an investigation be that draws its information principally from the top administrative component of the organization?

Although circumstances might have justified this unusual use of grand jury powers, the Grand Jury offered no explanation. Moreover, because no statutory authority permits local-government officials to use grand juries as management auditors who issue no public report of their findings and recommendations, this episode is a striking example of trivializing the institution.

Another problem makes assessing investigations for their significance difficult: Well-planned and conducted investigations might be hidden in final reports among many pages of information about routine tours; unsubstantiated, flowery commendations of officials or employees; or summaries of interviews with public officials that resulted in no findings or recommendations. After tiring of reading dozens of pages of this sort of material, some readers overlook investigations of greater significance. Two types of examples of these problems in final reports are:

1. Including many pages of inconsequential and tedious reports of meetings with selected local-government officials. For example, one Grand Jury devoted 9 pages of a 40-page final report to vague, undocumented reports of this kind:

STATEMENT:

The District Attorney ... met with the entire Grand Jury late in September 1991 to explain the duties of his office.

The District Attorney advises in legal matters, investigates, and brings requests for indictments. His office would defer to the County Counsel if any conflict arose.

FINDINGS:

The staff of this department appears to work efficiently and in a professional manner. The office of the District Attorney was most helpful and cooperative with the Grand Jury.

RECOMMENDATION:

The level of work is an asset to Mono County and its continuance will be beneficial.[6]

2. Lengthy descriptions of tours or visits to local-government offices, services, or departments that result in trivial findings or recommendations, or none at

all. Much of the Kings County Grand Jury Final Report during the study period consisted of brief accounts of tours through State prisons, local-government offices, various special districts, and other sites. Reports of tours of school districts occupied nearly half of the report (pages 35–130). A few of the tour reports resulted in useful findings and recommendations, but many pages were devoted to comments such as these:

> The committee watched the cooks prepare for the next day's meal which included turkey and fresh baked rolls.
>
> The committee thanks [a school superintendent] and all the friendly staff members for giving them such an interesting tour. The luncheon was delicious!
>
> The committee "sampled" delicious cinnamon rolls which were being prepared for lunch.
>
> The committee was grateful for the enjoyable and educational tour given to them. The administration and staff were most hospitable. The new cafeteria/gym is a wonderful addition to this campus. The spaghetti was great!![7]

Although it contained several significant civil investigations, the Tehama County Grand Jury Final Report during the study period included many perfunctory descriptions of local-government services, departments, or agencies that ended with neither findings nor recommendations. For example, the section headings of a one-page report about the Corning City Council were ambitiously expressed as: Duties, Qualifications, Needs, Projects, and Long Range Plans (p. 9). Following this, a two-page report about the "Department of Agriculture/Weights and Measures" was divided into these section headings: Department Responsibilities, Major Changes, Projects in Progress, and Personnel (pp. 10–11). Following the latter report was a two-page description of an Air Pollution Control District divided into four sections: Responsibilities, Major Changes, Projects in Progress, and Personnel (pp. 12–13). Neither these reports nor the many reports like them in the final report ended with findings or recommendations.

The examples we have just reviewed characterize at least one-third of the text of many of the grand jury final reports reviewed for this study. Conducting tours and inspections of local-government facilities is, certainly, an essential part of a grand jury's civil-investigation function. During tours and inspections, grand jurors might develop important insights about local governments' needs, problems, and objectives. Nevertheless, lengthy, detailed reports of pedestrian activities that yield only vacuous findings and recommendations cause citizens, journalists, and local-government officials to wonder about the judgment, motives, and diligence of grand jurors.

ACCOUNTABILITY

A question that citizens frequently ask about grand juries is, "What do they do?" Unfortunately, many grand jury final reports do not answer this question. Although statutorily imposed secrecy restricts grand juries from describing some of their work, no law forbids grand juries from reporting routine summary information about matters such as the numbers and types of complaints they received, investigated, or resolved; why grand juries rejected some complaints; how many tours and visits grand jurors conducted; or how many committee meetings and full-panel meetings the members attended.

Grand jury reports vary in the amount of detail that is revealed about workloads. During the study period, no grand jury comprehensively reported information about the entire scope of its activities. The "Secretary's Report" of a Northern California grand jury is an example of a brief overview of the grand jury workload:

> To date, the Grand Jury has received 35 letters regarding various complaints. The Grand Jury also received 54 form letters, each bearing several signatures, requesting an inquiry into the unsolved … homicide case.
>
> There have been 26 separate investigations conducted by the committees of this Grand Jury.
>
> Twenty-three (23) investigations have been completed by this Grand Jury. Several investigations are pending….
>
> To date, there have been 30 regular Amador County Grand Jury sessions and more than 300 committee meetings.[8]

Another Grand Jury briefly described some of its workload under a section of its final report titled "Statistics":

> There were seventeen general meetings conducted.
>
> The Final Report includes 12 areas of investigation.
>
> Eleven citizen complaints were received, investigated and answered by letter. Each complaint was assigned to a committee depending on the nature of the complaint.
>
> Over 17 reams of paper was [*sic*] used by the Grand Jury.[9]

The most frequently reported grand jury workload data in final reports were numbers of complaints and, in a few cases, their types and how grand juries disposed of them. The Santa Cruz County Grand Jury included, at the beginning of each committee report, a table called "Complaint Status" to account for the disposition of complaints assigned to each committee. In this report, the Health and Human Services/Special Districts Committee listed its "Complaint Status," for example, as:

Citizen's Complaints	Committee-Instigated Investigations	Resolved	Pending
12	1	11	1

Although this method identifies the complaint workload of each committee, it deprives readers of a view of the workload of the entire panel and contributes to citizens' perceptions of grand juries as loosely coordinated autonomous committees.[10] The most complete accounting of a grand jury's work during the study period was provided by a Northern California county Grand Jury:

The following is a list of the 1991/92 Grand Jury's activities:
- Held 26 meetings of the full jury and 76 committee meetings
- Met 12 times for indictment/accusation hearings
- Issued 14 Final Reports
- Responded to 72 requests for Grand Jury Complaint Forms
- Dealt with 45 formal complaints
- Responded to seven complaints referred from the 1990/91 Grand Jury
- Followed up on two specific recommendations contained in the 1990/91 Grand Jury Final Report
- Wrote six letters of appreciation
- Issued four Final Reports as the direct result of public complaints
- Investigated 36 complaints without issuing a report
- Referred one complaint to the California Attorney General
- Updated the Grand Jury Procedures Manual
- Continued the Joint Audit Committee with the Shasta County Board of Supervisors
- Reviewed the Budgets, Financial Reports, Audits and Management Letters of the City of Anderson, the City of Redding and Shasta County
- Reviewed the following audits: Burney Basin Mosquito Abatement District, Shasta County Fire Protection Area #1, County Service Area #2—Sugarloaf, County Service Area #6—Jones Valley, County Service Area #15—Street Lighting, County Service Area #17—Cottonwood, County Service Area #20—Ox Yoke Road, Shasta County Court System—1990 and 1991[11]

Examples of how other grand juries reported their complaint workloads during the study period are shown in these summaries from the project database:
- Summary of complaints the Grand Jury received; disposition of complaints.[12]
- Dispositions of complaints concerning law enforcement, the superior court, the district attorney, and other criminal justice officials.[13]
- Summary of 45 complaints the Grand Jury received.[14]
- Summaries of complaints the Grand Jury received from citizens; includes miscellaneous recommendations.[15]

- Summary of complaints handled by the Criminal Justice Committee and their outcomes.[16]
- Summary of complaints and their dispositions.[17]

CONTINUITY

The one-year life of the grand jury, its limited or nonexistent office facilities, and its meager resources create one of the institution's most pressing problems: the lack of an institutional memory. Although many grand jurors deplore these constraints on grand jury service, it is a consequence of the statutory and common-law logic of the institution. If the grand jury were intended to be a permanent bureaucracy, file clerks, filing cabinets, and indexing systems would be provided to serve its information-storage and management needs. Because of the grand jury's nature, however, the lack of an institutional memory imposes certain limits on the effectiveness of grand jury reports.

One consequence of inadequate grand jury archives is the time wasted on investigating complaints filed by the same person year after year. Although a panel should not dismiss any citizen's complaint arbitrarily, its decision to accept or reject a complaint should take into account how previous grand juries have dealt with it, particularly if the repeated complaint is bizarre or has psycho-pathological overtones.

Another problem for some grand juries is the unavailability of predecessors' final reports. Without a collection of final reports of past years, grand juries cannot determine when predecessors reviewed given local governments. Examples of other documents that are important research tools, if they are systematically indexed and filed, are:

- preliminary and final budgets of local governments
- financial and performance-audit reports
- selected publications of California State agencies, such as reports from the Office of the State Controller of California that pertain to local-government budgets and expenditures.

No statute prohibits grand juries from developing methods or systems to create an institutional memory.[18] Panels therefore may experiment with any lawful means to create continuity. Five of these means are: recommending investigations to successors, using manual and computerized systems for inventorying investigations and their outcomes, analyzing comments by public officials to grand jury investigations, using "wrap-up" investigations, and establishing a grand jury library.

Recommending Investigations to Successors

No final reports during the study period informed readers how grand juries established priorities for deciding which local-government agencies, services, departments, or functions to investigate. Thus, most grand juries provided no information about whether they complied with the Penal Code requirements to conduct certain kinds of investigations on some selective basis each year.[19] Instead, final reports may include other kinds of references to investigations and reports of predecessors.

Toward the end of their terms, grand juries often realize that an investigation they started or a complaint they received late in their terms could not be completed before the end of the grand jury year. Panels therefore may recommend that their successors complete such investigations. Although by law succeeding grand juries need not comply with such recommendations, some do. As a result, grand juries could investigate the same department or local government several years in succession. Examples of investigations that have continued for two or more recent years include:

- Investigation into why the County morgue has not been completed; reiteration of concerns of the 1990 Grand Jury about the morgue, including lack of security, possible alteration of physical evidence, sanitary storage of bodies, and related matters.[20]
- Review of the need for a revised contract between the City of Loyalton and Sierra County for law enforcement services.[21]
- Follow-up of the 1990 and 1991 Grand Juries' recommendations about the Community Development Agency's compliance with applicable codes; expression of concern that agencies hired an "outside firm" to respond to the Grand Jury.[22]

One grand jury conspicuously displayed recommendations for its successor in the front section of the final report, explaining that because of

> time constraints, the Grand Jury was not able to investigate all complaints and departments. As illustrated in the attached exhibit, several agencies of the City and County have not been investigated in several years. In addition, some of our findings warrant further investigation and follow-up.[23]

Manual and Computer-Assisted Follow-Up Studies of Investigations and Their Outcomes

Penal Code Sections 925 and 928 include, respectively, the phrases "investigations may be conducted on some selective basis each year," and "Such investigation and report shall be conducted selectively each year."[24] To comply with these statutes, some grand juries have developed procedures for tallying the investigations of predecessors. Varying in complexity and sophistication, these procedures allow grand juries to identify local-government agencies or functions that have been investigated too often or not at all.

Hand-Tally Systems

Some grand juries develop simple, hand-tallied charts or tables to identify local governments that their predecessors might have overlooked or to identify local governments that have not been reviewed recently. Collecting data for maintaining tallies is time consuming, and in some counties grand juries delegate this task to editorial or continuity committees. An example of a hand-tally system is shown in part below:[25]

Special Districts in San Joaquin County	'84	'85	'86	'87	'88	'89	'90	'91
Boggs Tract Fire Department	Y							
Eastside Fire Department			Y		Y			
Tuxedo Fire Department				Y	Y			

One grand jury published in its final report a "Combined Table of Contents" listing titles of investigations between 1980–1981 and 1990–1991. A portion of this document shows how the Grand Jury listed the title of the investigation, the page number, and the year of the final report:[26]

Lake Cachuma Private Docks	137	1983–84
Landfill, Foxen Canyon	24	1989–90
Legal Representation, Sheriff's Department Before Civil Service Board	83	1983–84

In an eight-page report, a former grand juror in a Northern California county provides another example of manually tallying comments by public officials. The author of the report, a foreman during the study period, completed his study just after the expiration of the statutory response period.[27]

Although the format of the study and its brief list of comment categories is a good example for grand jurors to consider, two important flaws limit its usefulness. The first problem is that the study does not make clear whether it is about comments to findings or comments to recommendations. The title of the report, "Responses to the Findings and Recommendations in the 1991–1992 Placer County Grand Jury Final Report," implies that its concern is with findings and recommendations. Yet the title of the table that displays the project's data reads, "1991–1992 Placer County Grand Jury Final Report Summary Tabulation of Responses to Findings." The one-page text accompanying the report does not explain the discrepancy but, instead, confuses the issue even more with the sentence, "Sometimes the respondent would agree with part of the final report's finding/recommendation and disagree with another part." I will assume that the focus of the report is, as its main table states, findings rather than recommendations.

The study by the former Placer County grand juror presented data according to the main chapter headings in the final report and displayed beneath them (in most cases) the titles of the persons from whom comments were required. Each finding was represented by the number shown for each finding in the final report. Under each number was an abbreviation representing one of nine categories of comments; for example:

County Assessor's Office and Personnel Department

	1	2	3	4	5
Board of Supervisors	A	D	D	A	N/C
Assessor	A	U	A	A	A

This segment of the table shows that the Board of Supervisors agreed (A) with findings 1 and 4 and disagreed (D) with findings 2 and 3, and that either no response was required for finding 5 or the Supervisors claimed that it did not apply to them (N/C). The Assessor agreed with findings 1, 3, 4, and 5 but was said to be unresponsive (U) to finding 2.

The second major problem with the study was that it did not include totals of its data. Therefore, when I finished reading it, an important question remained unanswered: To what extent overall did local-government officials agree, disagree, or ignore the Grand Jury's findings? Using data in the report, citizens reading it could perform the necessary calculations to answer this question themselves, but an hour of hand-tallying and double-checking would be required.

This is the kind of project for which spreadsheet programs are well suited. If the former Foreman had entered the codes and the associated numbers into a spreadsheet, he could have pressed one or two buttons at the end of the project and produced a table of considerable interest. I hand-tallied the comments for each of the categories in the study, and this is what I found:

Frequency Count of Comments to Findings

Comment Types		Frequency	Percentage of Total
A	Generally agree with the finding.	186	37.2
A*	Generally agree, but present funding will not permit implementation.	19	3.8
B/I	Idea, policy, or program is in the process of being implemented.	62	12.4
D	Generally disagree with the finding.	23	4.6
E	This idea, policy, or program is being evaluated at this time.	13	2.6
I	Idea, policy, or program has already been implemented.	38	7.6
N/C	No response is required, or finding or recommendation does not apply to us.	128	25.6
T	Thank you for your complimentary remarks.	4	.8
U	Unresponsive to the ideas in the finding.	27	5.4
	Total	500	100.0

This table shows that the highest percentage (37.2 percent) was for the "generally agree" category. The next highest (25.6 percent) was for "no response is required, or finding or recommendation does not apply to us." The third highest (12.4 percent) was for "idea, policy, or program is in the process of being implemented." Only 5.4 percent of the responses were characterized as "unresponsive."

Findings of these kinds can be useful for grand jurors who wish to evaluate the effectiveness of their grand jury service. For example, 25.6 percent would seem to be too high for the "no response is required, or finding/recommendation does not apply to us" category. Possibly the figure is inflated because the two concepts in the category ("no response is required" and "finding/recommendation does not apply to us") are two different ideas. Merging the two concepts can result in a misleading picture. Another possibility is that many findings were inappropriate, irrelevant, or misdirected. Similarly, by studying the differences between findings that had concurrence and findings with which officials disagreed, grand jurors could acquire a better understanding of the characteristics of well-researched and well-presented findings.

COMPUTER-ASSISTED TALLYING SYSTEMS

Although a hand-tallied chart or table serves a useful purpose, it has substantial limitations. In a large county, for example, the number of local governments within the grand jury's jurisdiction might be so large that a manually prepared system is cumbersome. Similarly, if the hand-tally shows only departments or functions investigated in a recent period and does not include information about the comments of local-government officials to findings and recommendations, it has only limited use. A well-designed computerized system, on the other hand, will quickly yield answers to questions such as the following, which hand-tally systems reveal only with much time and effort:

- Which special districts have not returned comments in each of the past five years?
- Do certain types of findings and recommendations meet with greater or lesser compliance than others?
- During the past 10 years, in which year was a grand jury the most successful in obtaining favorable comments to findings and recommendations?

Grand jurors with computer skills understand that creating a complex hand-tally chart requires about the same time and effort needed to enter data into a computer. Once the data are in the computer, one can print as many different kinds of reports as desired. For this reason, occasional examples of the use of computers for workload management and evaluation are found in grand jury reports.

For example, a grand juror with extensive data-processing experience prepared for the Amador County Grand Jury of 1991–1992 a computerized "Five Year Study of Amador County Grand Jury Recommendations and Their Responses."[28] Table 18, "Number and Percentage of Implemented or Not Implemented Recommendations Made by the Amador County Grand Jury: 1986–1987 to 1990–1991," displays only part of the information the project developed—namely, numbers and percentages of recommendations implemented and not implemented by year:

TABLE 18
Number and Percentage of
Implemented or Not Implemented Recommendations
Made by the Amador County Grand Jury:
1986–1987 to 1990–1991

Year	Recommendations No.	Percent.	Implemented No.	Percent.	Not Implemented No.	Percent.	Other No.	Percent.
90–91	43	16.6	9	20.9	11	25.6	23	53.5
89–90	45	17.4	15	33.3	17	37.8	13	28.9
88–89	14	5.4	5	35.7	8	57.1	1	7.1
87–88	85	32.8	32	37.6	32	37.6	21	24.7
86–87	72	27.8	37	51.4	21	29.2	14	19.4
Totals	259	100.0	98	37.8	89	34.4	72	27.8

Several other grand juries have conducted computer-assisted research into the dispositions of grand jury recommendations. For example, the 1989–1990 Kern County Grand Jury Final Report claimed that officials "Generally agreed [with 38 percent of the recommendations in a two-year period but claimed that they had] already implemented [them] in whole or part"; officials "Generally agreed, will comply, etc." with 22 percent of the recommendations, disagreed with 21 percent, and would "consider further" 18 percent. Officials did not respond to one percent of the recommendations.[29]

Analyzing Comments by Public Officials to Grand Jury Investigations

Although Penal Code Section 933 requires affected local-government officials to comment about findings and recommendations concerning them or their departments, readers will find few such comments in final reports. If, for example, a fiscal-year grand jury issues a final report two weeks before its discharge, governing bodies and other elected county officers and agency heads must comment within 90 and 60 days, respectively, about findings and recommendations in the report.[30]

Officials send their comments directly to a judge, but typically judges do nothing with the comments except send them to grand juries. Few newspaper reporters and even fewer citizens, therefore, read these comments because they are not distributed as widely as grand jury reports. Penal Code Section 933(c) names only three types of persons with whom responses must be filed: the clerk of the public agency, the office of the county clerk, or the mayor, when applicable.

Because grand jury findings and recommendations and comments about them rarely are published in the same document, citizens have few opportunities to study the exchanges between grand jurors and public officials. Reading only a final report or only comments about it does not reveal the drama, complexity, or subtleties of the linguistic give-and-take between grand juries and public officials.[31]

Scholars who study how people in organizations use the written language will not be surprised to learn that comments public officials make in response to findings and recommendations affecting them are not simple statements such as "Agree" or "Disagree." In commenting about findings and recommendations, public officials have discretion in how they express themselves; beyond requiring them to comment, Penal Code Section 933 does not mandate local-government officials to be accurate, specific, or truthful.[32]

TYPES OF COMMENTS
BY LOCAL-GOVERNMENT OFFICIALS

Most comments can be grouped into types. Table 19, "Eighteen Types of Comments by Local-Government Officials," shows the variety of comments that one grand jury reported it found after analyzing comments concerning 259 recommendations that grand juries made in the county between 1986 and 1991.[33]

COMMENTS ABOUT COMMENTS

Grand jury final reports reveal little information about how sitting grand jurors assess comments of local-government officials in response to findings and recommendations in reports of preceding grand juries. Several grand juries, however, examined the comments carefully during the study period. For example, one panel recommended a process for improving the submission of comments to the judge; a Southern California grand jury conspicuously listed the names of local governments affected by its findings and recommendations and indicated when required comments were due; and one grand

TABLE 19
Eighteen Types of Comments by Local-Government Officials

1.	Implemented	The recommendation was carried out or done as recommended.
2.	Being Implemented	The recommendation is in the process of being done.
3.	Partially Implemented	Part of it was done and part was not done.
4.	Already in Place	The item was being done before being recommended.
5.	No Response Requested	The Grand Jury did not request a response.
6.	No Longer Applies	Situation has changed, things done differently, etc.
7.	Still Pending	It is still planned to do but has not been started, etc.
8.	Agreed	The Board agreed it was a good idea, whether it was done or not.
9.	Not Implemented	The recommendation was never acted upon.
10.	Agreed, Not Done	The Board agreed it was a good idea but did nothing about it.
11.	Disagreed	The Board was opposed to the idea.
12.	Disagreed, Not Done	The Board was opposed to the idea.
13.	No Response Found	There may have been a response but it could not be found.
14.	No Response; Not Done	The Board (or whoever) did not respond to the recommendation.
15.	Did Not Apply	The recommendation was incorrect and facts did not fit.
16.	A Non-Response	The response did not apply to what was recommended.
17.	A Repeat	This recommendation was already made in this final report.
18.	Being Considered	Response indicates that this is being considered, and no decision has been made as yet.

jury expressed dissatisfaction with comments it reviewed, as these summaries from the database show:

- Review of responses by local government to recommendations of the 1990–1991 Grand Jury.[34]
- Review of implementation of responses to prior final report.[35]
- Description of an improved process by which local-government officials shall respond to grand jury reports; need for improved facilities for the Grand Jury.[36]
- Review of responses by City of Mendota to previous Grand Jury recommendations.[37]

- Expression of concern that the Board of Supervisors gives inadequate attention to recommendations of grand juries; concurrence by department heads does not always result in implementation; related matters.[38]
- Listing of local public agencies and the recommendations to which they should respond.[39]
- Follow-up of 1990 and 1991 Grand Juries' recommendations about community development agencies complying with applicable codes; expression of concern that agencies hired an outside firm to respond to the Grand Jury.[40]
- Review of how County administration responded to the interim Grand Jury report about purchasing procedures.[41]

Only one Grand Jury reported that it had reviewed the quality of comments by local-government officials and assessed the "adequacy of each comment." The Grand Jury assigned the task of reviewing comments about findings and recommendations in the previous Grand Jury report to a "Grand Jury Follow-Up Committee" whose objectives were:

> (1) to verify that the appropriate departments provided responses, (2) to evaluate the adequacy of the initial responses, and (3) to confirm that the agreed upon recommendations had, in fact, been implemented, or, if not, to determine the reason why they had not been implemented.

The Follow-Up Committee explained its procedure for reviewing

> the 1990–91 Grand Jury Final Report and the responses received from the appropriate agencies, departments, and special districts. The Committee determined whether the responses received to the findings and recommendations of the 1990–91 Grand Jury were adequate. For those responses that were incomplete, unclear, or nonexistent, information was requested from the appropriate agency by telephone, letters, or interviews. Members of the previous Grand Jury were consulted regarding some of the responses.

Among other conclusions the Grand Jury reached from the work of the Follow-Up Committee was that "problems with the evidence locker at the Truckee Substation still exist."[42]

Ensuring Compliance with Comment Requirements

Grand juries have developed a number of techniques for reminding local-government officials of their obligation to comment about findings and recommendations. In one county, final reports in recent years have conspicuously displayed, usually in the first three or four pages, a letter the presiding judge of the Superior Court signed and addressed to "Affected Governmental Agencies and Officers." The letter reminds the officials of the requirements of Penal Code 933(c) and further adds, "Those having questions concerning their responsibilities to respond to the Grand Jury's recommendations should contact County Counsel or their agency's general counsel."[43]

Examples of expressions of concern or approval by grand juries regarding comments include these summaries:

- Review of comments to prior final report; expression of concern that the "[—] School District did not answer specifics."[44]
- Grand Jury reviewed comments it received upon impanelment from the City of Mendota to findings and recommendations of the 1989–1990 Grand Jury; comments appear acceptable.[45]
- Board of Supervisors gives inadequate attention to recommendations of grand juries; concurrence by department heads does not always result in implementation; related matters.[46]

A Central Valley Grand Jury compiled an inventory of comments by local officials to the 29 recommendations in its predecessor's final report. The Foreman reported the results of the study in a letter he wrote to accompany the submission of the final report to the presiding judge of the Superior Court. The Foreman expressed concern that "of the 29 recommendations made by the 1990–1991 Grand Jury, only 19 of them received responses." Accordingly, the Foreman urged the judge to

> take immediate steps to obtain responses to the 10 unanswered recommendations made by the 1990–1991 Grand Jury. Further, we ask that you monitor responses submitted in answer to all recommendations made by this Grand Jury to ensure that all recommendations receive an adequate response.[47]

Expressing concern about the quality and timeliness of comments by local-government officials, one Grand Jury proposed a method for the officials to use in commenting about findings and recommendations in its final reports. The Grand Jury described its recommended process this way:

> [T]he El Dorado County Board of Supervisors and other local public agencies [should] adopt a prescribed uniform format for responses to Grand Jury reports ... [including the distribution of] these responses to current and immediate past Grand Jury members, affected County department heads, and the County public libraries ... [and that] the Board of Supervisors [should] adopt a specified procedure for preparing responses to Grand Jury reports.[48]

With one exception, the board of supervisors reported that it implemented the Grand Jury's recommendation for a systematic process for commenting about findings and recommendations "although not through the adoption of an ordinance or resolution."[49]

COMMENTS AND WORD CHOICE

One of the questions the law leaves unanswered regarding comments by local-government officials in response to grand jury findings and recommendations is, "Who actually should write the comments?" Typically, elected officials delegate the preparation of "comments" to their administrative staffs. Many career administrators, as experienced writers, can draft comments that seem to address a grand jury's recommendations but sidestep their intent. For example, a grand jury expressed concern in its final report about an unusual approach to the handling of children (juveniles in a juvenile hall). Although the Grand Jury did not condemn the method, it recommended that "an independent group of professionals from the field should review and evaluate the effectiveness of the Juvenile Services Center's approach."

The comment the Grand Jury received in response to this recommendation takes advantage of its use of the prepositional phrase "group of professionals from the field" to assert that the recommended evaluation has been completed.

> [T]he wisdom of the approach has been repeatedly validated by professionals in the field. In fact, the facility's design and operating concept has been replicated over and over again across the country. This concept is precisely what has made the facility a national model since it opened in 1981. Many individuals and groups consisting of professionals in the field continue to tour the facility to see if the concept still works. Their conclusions have consistently been that it does continue to work. Additionally, Probation Department staff, principally the Chief Probation Officer, have worked with their peers on the type of ongoing program evaluation recommended by the Grand Jury and have also concluded that the facility and program are based on a sound and effective operational concept.[50]

This comment illustrates how a grand jury's choice of words can defeat its purpose. The comment to the recommendation might have been different if it had been worded, "The program should be studied by an objective, qualified evaluator whose career and income do not depend on the outcome of the investigation."

Using "Wrap-Up" Investigations

Before they begin to conduct investigations, investigative reporters sometimes obtain as much information as possible about their intended "targets." By carefully reviewing, for example, financial or performance audits, publicly available internal memoranda or correspondence, and justifications for budgets and agendas, investigative reporters often develop useful ideas for their investigations.[51] Of all the historical materials investigative reporters acquire, past news stories from their own newspapers or other newspapers are frequently the most promising sources of insights and information for current investigations.

Similarly, some grand juries find previous grand jury investigations of a specific topic valuable as sources of investigative leads and for saving investigative effort by not duplicating all or part of earlier investigations. The following is a summary of a wrap-up investigation that served a number of purposes, including determining which recommendations of previous grand juries had been implemented:

> An investigation of the state of emergency preparedness in Orange County, with particular reference to "thirty-nine preparatory actions which were identified as a result of reports on the same subject from predecessor grand juries."[52]

The Sonoma County Grand Jury frequently reviews the work of its predecessors for investigative leads and to determine the status of previous recommendations; for example:

> The 1991 Grand Jury and previous Grand Juries in 1987, 1988, 1989, and 1990 have made certain recommendations regarding the abatement process. To date, none has been implemented by the affected departments.

> A review of the 1987, 1988, 1989, 1990, and 1991 Sonoma County Grand Jury Final Reports unfolded an overall lack of data processing systems management control in the building permit process, planning permit process, building abatement procedures, Community Hospital, Sonoma County management and contracts administration.

> In the 1989 Grand Jury Final Report, there was specific mention of the lack of communication with outside emergency services in case of power failure. The report further indicated that the phone system becomes inoperative without electricity and does not have a backup system.[53]

Establishing a Grand Jury Library

Grand jury reports occasionally provide information about the work of grand jurors whom the panel has assigned the task of developing a grand jury library. Depending on the extent of the library's holdings, the panel might appoint one grand juror as a librarian whose duties include:

- collecting and maintaining previous grand jury reports
- cataloging and indexing other materials, publications, and reports
- maintaining a log of materials that grand jurors have borrowed and returned
- clipping and filing newspaper articles of interest to the grand jury
- obtaining needed reference materials that grand jurors may request[54]

Technical Criteria

Making broad conclusions about grand jury reports is as perilous as making general statements about how grand jurors are selected, how they conduct their investigations, and how grand jurors define their roles. As in all such matters, California's 58 grand juries show wide variation. Some final reports are poorly written, organized, and bound, and are burdened with sections of unexplained or unreferenced photocopies of budgets, organization charts, or sections of the California Penal Code. Other final reports are well-edited, organized, indexed, and printed but contain many trivial investigations; effusive commendations; and many photographs of grand jurors, judges, and grand jury staff members. Some final reports feature superficial refinements such as expensive binding, colorful covers, artwork, and high-quality paper generally found in fine books. Even these costly embellishments do not enhance mediocre investigations.

Still other reports are mixtures of these characteristics. Some contain accounts of investigations that equal the work of professional management analysts. A few final reports each year are so carefully conceived and prepared that they would make excellent textbooks for college or university civics courses. Some grand juries with few resources reported extraordinary investigations that might have benefited from a few imaginative typographical techniques, better reproduction, and more careful editing.

The variation in final reports has many causes, including the education, training, and motivation of individual grand jurors; whether grand juries create editorial committees to review and edit reports and how much authority these committees have; the traditions that have developed in certain counties regarding the preparation of reports; and the latitude that statutes give grand jurors for deciding their procedures. In some counties, judges carefully review drafts of reports and tactfully point out problems, suggest improvements, and offer strategic and logistical advice to facilitate the production and distribution of reports. In other counties, judges avoid involvement in the process of producing reports to the extent that some grand jurors perceive them to be aloof or uninterested.

Although much could be said about the design and production of final reports, I limit my assessment in the remainder of this discussion to certain features that make final reports easy or difficult to read and to what grand juries reported about the distribution of reports.[55] In particular, my purpose is to recommend inexpensive improvements to help grand jurors prepare final reports that citizens can read and understand more easily; to determine whether the formats of final reports exemplify the independence of the grand jury; and to describe how grand jurors ensure that final reports circulate within the community.

EXTERNAL FEATURES

The appearance and size of any document can affect a reader's desire to read its contents. The color of the cover stock, the artwork, if any, and the typeface can determine whether a public official or any other citizen decides to read the final report immediately or sets it aside. Similarly, if the document contains unnecessary material merely for the purpose of adding to its bulk, some readers defer reading it indefinitely.

Artwork and Binding

Final report covers were of three general types:

1. Twenty-seven bore the name of the grand jury and the image of the county seal.
2. Twenty-five displayed only the name of the grand jury and were printed on plain cover stock or paper or had artwork such as county-outline maps, pictures of courthouses, eagles, or forest or downtown scenes.
3. Four featured the grand jury name and year and specially designed grand jury seals or symbols.

Almost all final reports had permanent or semi-permanent binding. The spines of nine of the final reports were printed with the grand jury's name and year of the report.[56]

With respect to binding, the most serious defect was the display of the county seal and the names of county supervisors on the cover or in the front matter. These practices detract from the independence of the grand jury and imply to readers that grand juries are adjuncts of county government under the direction of boards of supervisors.

Size of Reports

All grand jury final reports were printed or photocopied on 8½-by-11-inch paper, with the exception of six grand juries that distributed final reports in newspaper format.[57] Final reports varied in length from 7 pages (Plumas, newspaper format) to 257 (San Diego). The average number of pages was 95, excluding reports in newspaper format and those with pages not consecutively numbered. Table 20, "Frequency Count of the Number of Pages in 55 Final Reports," shows the variation in size of the final reports.

TABLE 20
Frequency Count of the
Number of Pages in 55 Final Reports

Number of Pages	Number of Grand Juries
49 or fewer	15
50–99	22
100–149	11
150–199	2
200+	5
Total	55

(Excludes three grand juries that did not number pages consecutively.)

Some final reports contained only relevant material. Others were unnecessarily bulky, causing readers to speculate why they had to read material presented in a disorganized manner and with no obvious connection to investigations. Some grand juries added unnecessary size to their reports by including pages of photocopied text that is readily available from other sources. The Colusa County Grand Jury Final Report, for example, contained 30 unnumbered pages (half of the report) of photocopied routine statistical information about public welfare. That material was referred to in a sketchy, three-page report of an inquiry into the County Welfare Department that ended with four recommendations, including: "Purchase a new copy machine for overall cost effectiveness." The panel offered the charts, tables, and graphs to readers with no analysis of this statistical information, merely the comment, "you will find the following graphs which indicate where Colusa County falls in comparison to the State."[58]

In the 1992 Marin County Grand Jury Final Report, 62 of the 109 pages constituted material that, if summarized, would have significantly reduced the size of the final report. For example, eight pages of a Municipal Code were included. By citing only applicable portions of the Code or advising readers where the Code might be obtained, the Grand Jury could have reduced the size of its report substantially. Similarly, 11 pages of a franchise agreement and 5 pages of miscellaneous material would have been more useful to readers in summarized form.

INTERIM REPORTS

Grand juries serving for the fiscal year (July 1 through June 31) usually issue final reports during the last three weeks of their terms. Citizens can expect grand juries serving the calendar year (January 1 through December 31) to issue final reports between Thanksgiving and Christmas. Some grand juries, however, issue interim reports during their terms. Issuing interim reports has the advantage, provided they are issued early enough, of allowing grand jurors, while still impaneled, to review local-government officials' comments about findings and recommendations. If, however, a report is designated as an interim report and not a final report, local-government officials have no statutory obligation to comment about the findings and recommendations in it.[59]

To require that local-government officials comment about findings and recommendations, some grand juries refer to any report they issue before the end of their terms as a final report. The wording of the pertinent statutes supports this practice. During the study period, several grand juries released more than one final report during their terms. The Fresno County Grand Jury, for example, issued two separate reports: Final Report #1 and Final Report #2. The latter report evidently was the last report the panel issued; it is dated July 1, 1992. Unfortunately, the report does not include information about what was in Final Report #1, so some readers who did not receive that report may wonder if it contained important information of which they should be aware.

In some cases, grand juries revise previously issued interim reports and incorporate them in final reports. And grand juries occasionally issue interim reports but do not include them or refer to them in final reports. For these reasons, some grand jury investigations during 1991–1992 might not be represented in this study.

INTERNAL FEATURES

Just as the external features of documents affect a reader's impression of them, certain internal features can make reading documents easy or difficult. Features such as tables of contents, the quality of printing or photocopying, and internal organization convey grand jurors' concerns, or lack thereof, for their readers.

Tables of Contents and Indexes

The Mendocino County Grand Jury Final Report of 1992 provided no page numbers in the table of contents for the various topics of the report. Other final reports did not include tables of contents but provided only divider tabs to identify committee reports. To illustrate, the Santa Barbara County Grand Jury Final Report had no table of contents or index for its 116 pages but used divider tabs for the various sections of the report. Readers who were particularly interested, for example, in the Santa Barbara County Grand Jury's report of "Occupational Safety Policies and Procedures," were required to browse through the entire report to find that investigation unless they knew that the Grand Jury had included it in the section titled "Public Safety."

As a general rule, documents exceeding 15 to 20 pages should have tables of contents, and documents exceeding 50 to 70 pages also should provide indexes for readers. During the study period, none of the final reports included an index, although the average length of final reports was 95 pages.[60]

Typography and Quality of Printing or Copying

In general, type styles were adequate in most final reports. Only rarely did grand juries use type styles that hindered readability. The Tuolumne County Grand Jury, however, used a dot-matrix printer to print its inch-and-a-half-thick report, double-spaced in unusually large and difficult-to-read print. The use of single spacing and a simple, readable type style would have presented a more inviting appearance and reduced the number of pages in the report, consequently lowering the costs of reproducing, binding, and distributing it.[61] Many final reports seem to have been printed professionally. In general, the quality of printing or photocopying of most final reports ranged between adequate and excellent.

Organizing Individual Investigative Reports by Categories

Most grand juries use specific categories to organize each of their investigative reports. For example, the Solano County Grand Jury used these categories in its final report to designate the several sections of each investigative report: "Charge," "Focus," "Findings," "Recommendations."[62] Using categories as subheadings to organize individual investigative reports is a fairly recent development and was not found widely in grand jury final reports until the late 1970s.[63] By using a standard format for individual investigations throughout final reports, panels hope to improve the readability of reports in several ways:

- A standard format requires all investigations to contain the same type of information. For example, if the format includes the category, "Investigative Methods," each investigative report will provide at least some information about that topic.
- Standard formats force investigative committees to collect and record certain types of information throughout their investigations, thereby facilitating the later writing of the report.
- As readers become accustomed to report formats, their reading time and comprehension improves because they need not adjust to the different formats in each investigation.

Table 21, "Organization of Investigative Reports in the Final Reports of 1991–1992," shows report categories in each final report during the study period. At first glance, it might seem to be a bewildering collection of categories. Closer inspection of the table, however, yields two kinds of useful insights into grand juries of the study period:

1. A tally of the frequency of occurrence of each category in final reports reveals that although many of the categories appear only once in Table 21, 10 categories were used considerably more frequently.
2. The names of the categories might explain, even if only partly, why certain problems persist from one year to the next in many grand jury final reports, as I shall discuss below.

FREQUENCY OF CATEGORIES

Table 22, "Frequency of Categories in Investigative Reports," was prepared from data in Table 21. The table shows that 15 of the 38 categories appeared only once in final reports of the study period. Notice in Table 21, for example, that only one grand jury (Ventura County) used the term "groundwork." On the other hand, 10 categories were each used 10 times or more; for example, 19 grand juries used "conclusions" as one category in their investigative reports.

TABLE 21
Organization of Investigative Reports in Final Reports of 1991–1992

Alameda

Name of Committee
Subtitle: Subject of Investigation
Analysis
Finding and Recommendation

Alpine

Title of Investigation
Summary
Findings
Recommendations

Amador

Name of Committee
Subject of Investigation
Reason for Investigation
Matters Investigated
Procedures Followed
Findings
Conclusions
Recommendations
Responses Required

Butte

Name of Committee
Introduction
Facts and Findings
Comments
Recommendations
Conclusion

Calaveras

Title of Investigation
Finding
Condition
Criteria
Effect
Cause
Recommendation

Colusa

Final Report of the [—] Committee
Title of Investigation
Findings
Conclusion

Contra Costa

Summary
Findings
Conclusions
Recommendations

Del Norte

Committee Name
Title of Investigation
Reason for Investigation
Background
Findings
Conclusions
Recommendations
Response Required

El Dorado

Committee Name
Title of Report
Reason for Investigation
Background
Findings
Conclusions
Recommendations
Response Required

Fresno

Committee Name
Introduction
Findings
Recommendations

Glenn

Summary
Sources of Information
Introduction
Findings
Conclusions
Recommendations
Response Requested

Humboldt

Title of Investigation
Introduction
Background

(Table Continued)

TABLE 21, *Continued*

Humboldt, *continued*
Findings
Conclusions
Recommendations

Imperial
Name of Committee
(No other categories)

Inyo
Name of Committee
Title of Report
(No other categories)

Kern
(Various)
Name of Committee (on dividers)
Name of Committee (at head of
    report)
Name of Investigation
The Situation
Facts Bearing on the Situation
Findings
Conclusions
Recommendation

Kings
Grand Jury Report Form
Area of Inquiry
Reporting Committee
Inquiry Purpose
Findings
Recommendations
Comments

Lake
(Various)
Name of Committee
Introduction
Recommendations

Lassen
Name of Committee
Title of Investigation
Findings
Recommendation

Los Angeles
(Various)
Introduction and Summary
Background
Procedure
Findings
Recommendations
Citizen Complaints
Persons Interviewed
Contacted

Madera
(Various)
Name of Committee
Background
Summary of Concerns and
    Allegations
Initial Overview
Conclusion
Recommendation
Documents Reviewed
Distribution

Marin
(Various)
Name of Committee
Abstract
Background
Issue
Findings
Recommendations
Request for Response

Mariposa
Area of Review
Background
Method of Investigation
Findings
Recommendations

Mendocino
Title of Investigation
Summary
Findings
Recommendations
Comment

(Table Continued)

TABLE 21, Continued

Merced

(Various)
Title of Investigation
Methodology
Findings
Recommendations

Modoc

Topic
Committee Purview
Areas of Study
Introduction
Facts and Findings
Conclusion
Recommendation

Mono

Statement
Findings
Recommendations

Monterey

Name of Committee
Title of Report
Concern/Complaint
Discussion
Recommendations
Witnesses
Documentation

Napa

Title of Report
Procedures Followed
Findings and Recommendations
Responses Required

Nevada

Title of Investigation
Reason for Investigation
Background
Procedure Followed
Findings
Conclusions
Recommendations
Responses Required

Orange

(Various)
Committee Name
Title of Report
Background
Purpose
Method of Study
Findings

Placer

Name of Government
Introduction
Discussion
Finding
Recommendation
Respondent

Plumas

Name of Government
Findings
Recommendations
Response Required

Riverside

Name of Government
Background
Findings
Recommendation

Sacramento

Name of Committee
Summary and Findings
Recommendations

San Benito

(Various)
Name of Committee
Title of Investigation
Background
Procedures
Information
Overview
Findings
Conclusions
Recommendations

(Table Continued)

TABLE 21, *Continued*

San Bernardino
Name of Committee
Name of Government
Background
Findings
Recommendations

San Diego
(Various)
Name of Committee
Name of Government
Introduction
Area of Concern
Background Discussion
Findings
Recommendations

San Francisco
(Various)
Title of Investigation
Background
Findings
Recommendations

San Joaquin
(Various)
Title of Investigation
Summary
Background
Investigation
Findings
Recommendations

San Luis Obispo
Name of Committee
Summary
Reason for Investigation
Condition
Criteria
Procedure
Findings
Conclusions
Recommendations

San Mateo
Name of Committee
Title of Investigation

San Mateo, *continued*
Background
Findings
Recommendation

Santa Barbara
Name of Committee
Introduction
Background
Investigative Procedures
Findings
Recommendations

Santa Clara
Title of Investigation
Summary
Introduction
Criteria
Investigation
Findings
Conclusions
Recommendations
Source Documents and Materials

Santa Cruz
Name of Committee
Purpose
Overview
Areas of Investigation
Findings
Recommendations
Conclusion
Response Required

Shasta
Title of Investigation
Subject of Investigation
Background
Method of Investigation
Findings
Recommendations
Responses Required

Sierra
Name of Government
Findings
Recommendations

(Table Continued)

TABLE 21, Continued

Siskiyou
Title of Investigation
Subject
Background
Findings
Recommendations

Solano
Name of Committee
Charge
Focus
Findings
Recommendations

Sonoma
Title of Report
Reason for Investigation
Background
History
Procedures
Documents Reviewed
Findings
Conclusions
Recommendations
Response Required on Findings and
    Recommendations

Stanislaus
Name of Committee
Introduction
Comment
Recommendations

Sutter
Name of Committee
Introduction
Recommendations
Findings

Tehama
Name of Committee
Title of Investigation
Recommendation

Trinity
(Various)
Name of Committee
Purpose
Background
Method of Investigation
Finding
Recommendation
Conclusion

Tulare
Name of Committee
Introduction
Finding
Reference
Recommendation

Tuolumne
Title of Investigation
Purpose
Methodology
Analyses and Findings
Recommendations

Ventura
(Various)
Name of Committee
Title of Investigation
Groundwork
Findings
Conclusions
Recommended Action

Yolo
Title of Investigation
Findings
Recommendations

Yuba
Name of Committee
Introduction
Area Investigated
Findings
Recommendations
Comment

NOTE: The categories shown for each county are the formats that grand juries used most often in their final reports. Some final reports used a variety of formats, as the word "various" in several lists suggests.

TABLE 22
Frequency of Categories in Investigative Reports

Category	Frequency
Analysis	2
Area of inquiry (allegations, concern, etc.)	8
Background (overview, etc.)	24
Cause (complaint, etc.)	1
Charge	1
Citizen complaints	1
Comment(s)	5
Committee name	35
Conclusions	19
Condition	2
Criteria	3
Discussion	2
Distribution	1
Documents reviewed (documentation, source, etc.)	4
Effect	1
Facts	3
Finding(s)	47
Focus	1
Groundwork	1
History	1
Information	1
Introduction	14
Investigation	2
Issue	1
Name of government	6
Persons interviewed (contacted, etc.)	2
Procedures (methods, methodology, etc.)	14
Reason for investigation (allegations, concerns, etc.)	11
Recommendations	54
Reference	1
Responses required or requested	11
Situation	1
Sources of information	1
Statement	1
Subject of investigation (matters investigated, etc.)	6
Summary (abstract, etc.)	10
Title of investigation (name of investigation)	27
Witnesses	1

Table 21 reveals certain similarities among grand juries in organizing individual investigative reports. Table 23, "Ten Categories Most Frequently Used for Investigative Reports," shows the categories that were used at least 10 times in the final reports of the study period. In the order in which they are listed in Table 23, these categories constitute a reasonably serviceable format for reporting investigations in almost any field. In fact, the 10 categories in Table 23 are roughly similar to how scientific, academic, or business reports and studies are often organized. Of course, the categories in Table 23 are merely a composite; no grand jury in the study period used all 10 categories in the exact order presented in the table. The Nevada County Grand Jury, however, used a format that, with one exception (Summary) resembled the categories in the order shown in Table 23.

TABLE 23
Ten Categories Most Frequently Used for Investigative Reports

Category	Frequency
Title of investigation	27
Summary (abstract, etc.)	10
Introduction	14
Background (overview, etc.)	24
Reason for investigation (allegations, concerns, etc.)	11
Procedures (methods, methodology, etc.)	14
Finding(s)	47
Conclusions	19
Recommendations	54
Response required or requested	11

If one ignores the rarely used categories, one can conclude that the fairly frequent use of certain categories means that a standard format for reports of individual investigations might be acceptable to grand jurors. Such a format also would assist readers of grand jury final reports.[64] In Chapter 6, I therefore recommend a format for investigative reports that includes some of the categories in Table 23.

RELATIONSHIP OF CATEGORIES TO PERSISTENT PROBLEMS

For some time I have wondered why grand jurors are preoccupied with county government to the near exclusion of other types of local government. One explanation might be found in a theory of language that maintains that words affect how we see the world and how we behave in it.[65] The theory might explain, to some extent, the persistent recurrence of subjectivity in grand jury final reports. As Table 22 shows, only 3 grand juries of the 58 used a category called "facts." Four grand juries, however, used a "documents" category, although documents are only one source of facts.

Of course, the absence of a category for facts or evidence does not necessarily mean that a given investigation is devoid of such material. In reviewing grand jury final reports, one might find facts or evidence, but if they are present, they frequently are interwoven with opinions, conclusions, or judgments, and thereby obscured. Whether the infrequent use of a category called "facts" in investigative reports signifies the lack of saliency of the concept in grand jurors' minds, I do not know. Nevertheless, including a "facts" category in a report format might add to the objectivity of final reports.

Table 21 also shows some variation in the use of two categories: "findings" and "recommendations." The Lake, Madera, Monterey, and Stanislaus County Grand Juries, for example, employed only the category "recommendation(s)." In contrast, the Orange County Grand Jury provided a separate category for "findings" but not for "recommendations." Also significant is that the Butte, Kern, and Modoc County Grand Juries used both "facts" and "findings" as one category.

This usage illustrates the confusion that has arisen about the terms "facts" and "findings," a matter that I shall address in Chapter 6. Table 21 shows that several grand juries used the four categories in the "chain of reasoning" graphic shown in Figure E, Chapter 6. For example, the Kern and Modoc County Grand Juries used all four links: facts, findings, conclusions, and recommendations, in that order.

Given that Penal Code Section 933 requires public officials to comment about both findings and recommendations affecting them, one would expect the frequency of use for each category to be identical. Table 22, however, shows that grand jury final reports used "findings" less often (47 times) than "recommendations" (54 times). All but one of the grand juries that included both "findings" and "recommendations" displayed the categories in that order; only Sutter County presented "recommendations" before "findings."

Committee Names and Number of Categories

The use of committee names in grand jury final reports was the third most frequent category, as Table 22 shows. The Kern County Grand Jury, as Table 21 reveals, displayed committee names not once but twice. In some cases, grand jurors displayed both the names of committees and the titles of reports (for example, Del Norte, El Dorado, and San Mateo). Other final reports, however, either subordinated the titles of investigations to committee names or used only committee names instead of titles (such as Amador, Lake, and Yuba).

The number of categories in individual reports ranged from a high of 10 (Sonoma County) to Imperial County with only one category (the names of committees). Fourteen grand juries used formats that varied throughout their reports. Eleven grand juries had a "response required" category. This practice might be useful for alerting public officials to their statutory obligation to file comments about findings and recommendations affecting them.

SOME IMPLICATIONS

Other than occasional brief recommendations in their charges to grand juries, judges do not specify detailed formats for grand jurors to follow in reporting their investigations. Even if the judiciary were to require or recommend specific formats, they would not entirely prevent the recurring problems I have identified throughout this study. For example, one can tell a novice writer that using paragraphs helps people read and comprehend text. If, however, a would-be writer does not understand the conventions behind the use of paragraphs or chooses not to use them, little will be accomplished.

Similarly, a standard format for individual investigative reports will not improve the final reports of grand jurors who do not understand or who are unwilling to respect the spirit of the institution. Thus, a grand jury consisting of mostly passive citizens might issue a final report in which the categories have been employed correctly but in which the investigations are insignificant and contribute little to the community. Nevertheless, if a standard format were to improve only moderately the quality of grand jury investigations and reports, its adoption would be justified. In the next chapter, I therefore propose a format that, if closely followed, would significantly reduce or eliminate the recurring problems with which this study is concerned and thereby nurture the spirit of the institution.

One problem with using a standard format is that if a grand jury adopts one that excludes an important category, all reports in the final report will be deficient in this respect. For example, during the study period, the Marin County Grand Jury published several significant investigative reports, but the panel used a format that did not require an explanation of the purpose of the investigation, nor did it provide a brief description of the social, economic, or political implications of the matter under investigation. As a result, readers who wished to know why the Grand Jury undertook its investigations would have found many of its investigations for that year silent in that regard. Likewise, an investigation of certain practices of local law enforcement agencies did not discuss the "harm" to citizens or officers the existing procedures might cause. The lack of a description of "harm" also weakened the panel's investigation of a funding program for medical emergency services.[66]

Titles of Investigations

Forty-four grand jury final reports in one way or another emphasized names of committees rather than titles of investigations. For example, the Colusa County Grand Jury designated each investigation as the "Final Report of the [—] Committee." In some cases, several major or minor investigations were confusingly included in one report titled by committee name. In such reports, a public official or news-media representative must scan the entire report before finding an investigation of interest unless that person happens to know that the investigation could be found in a certain committee section. Although this tradition is followed widely, its effects are to produce a final report that seems to be a collection of committee reports rather than a cohesive document representing a single institution. In other cases, dividing pages between sections of investigative reports featured committee names and repeated the names of committees at the heading of each investigative report.[67] With one exception, the 14 grand juries that titled reports by the subject of the investigation (such as "Investigation of Animal Control Shelter"), rather than by name of committee, were in Northern California.[68]

Readability

The increased use in recent years of grand jury editorial committees has improved some internal and external features of final reports. Still, writing problems such as misplaced modifiers, passive-voice ambiguities, pronoun-reference problems, and logic and consistency problems are found occasionally. For example, the first sentence of a paragraph titled "Facts and Findings" read:

> $20,000.00 was allocated for cattle guards. After spending some of this money, the County wants it returned.[69]

The Grand Jury offered no explanation of who allocated the money or who received it, why the issue was a problem, and who should return the money to whom and why. Notice also that the County would not be likely to spend the money if it "wants it returned."

Grand jury final reports generally are free of unusual abbreviations, jargon, and bureaucratese. This sentence, however, suffers from law enforcement jargon and a modifier problem suggesting that the police are a danger to themselves and to others:

> For example, if a person brought in on a 5150 by the police (a danger to themselves and others) is a Tuolumne County resident, the county will pay....[70]

Similarly, a reader must be familiar with aviation terminology to understand this statement:

> Mr. [airport staff member] says that he has application ready for IFR or AWOS system if the state grant is available.[71]

Language usage sometimes reveals insights into the possibility that one individual dominated the drafting of one or more investigative reports. The following example illustrates the legalistic use of "same" throughout a final report, suggesting domination of the report by one author, and that the Grand Jury did not review drafts of the report carefully to eliminate idiosyncratic locutions:

> Whereas generally these Federal funds must be expended within a limited time period following receipt of same, this limitation has been removed....[72]

An example of language usage as a sign of possible ax grinding was provided by the Central California grand jurors who received Statewide publicity for reproducing without attribution in their final report large portions of the work of another panel. Although this second example of the panel's work may or may not be plagiarized, it is distinctive in another respect: The peculiarity of its style suggests domination of an investigation by one person. Both the plagiarism of another panel's work and the idiosyncratic manner of expression of the following material could not have occurred in a panel that emphasized objectivity, collegiality, and thorough review and deliberation concerning every step of an investigation:

> This apparent restructuring is inconsistent with current research regarding organizational systems. The structure being put into place is based on old orthodoxy. It is the old top down Roman military model. It assumes the old prejudice that the further up you are the more you see. It assumes that strategic decisions are made higher up in the organization and that middle managers are out in front of the lower level front line employees. The old triangles within triangles have never been effective. Today's trial courts and other governmental agencies require enlightened methods. Research tells us clearly that falsely created layers of management reduces the effectiveness of the worker and decreases, if not eliminates, the upward flow of information absolutely necessary to survival in the 21st century.
>
> The paradigm has shifted. The question that must be answered is how does the organization motivate the employee to care about his/her work and its quality. This requires a motivational strategy. A horizontal strategy that treats employees fairly and fosters justice and equality. None of these appear to be present in the Municipal Court Administration.[73]

DISTRIBUTING FINAL REPORTS

The most effective report of a grand jury investigation has little value for a community if only one copy is available publicly. The statutes do not specify by name or title (except the judge and county clerk) the public officials or other citizens who must receive grand jury reports. Deciding who shall receive grand jury reports is one of many matters that Penal Code Section 916 permits grand juries to decide. Budget restraints, of course, limit how many final reports to print. In some counties, grand juries publish only a few copies of final reports; in other counties, they have developed extensive distribution lists and in a few cases, publish these lists in their final reports.

Distribution Lists

The Calaveras County Grand Jury listed the organizations, public officials, and other persons it intended to receive the 88 copies of its final report. Current grand jurors and each member of the succeeding panel accounted for about half this number. Fifteen final reports were designated for the Office of County Clerk, and the Commissioner of Historical Records was assigned one copy.[74]

In its distribution list, the Mendocino County Grand Jury emphasized the news media. The panel listed 20 local radio stations and newspapers that it decided should receive a copy of its final report. The Mendocino panel's list also showed that copies were sent to complainants, and the remaining copies were sent to local-government officials. The panel did not reveal the total number of final reports it printed and distributed.[75] The San Benito County Grand Jury placed its final report distribution list immediately after the cover of its final report; names of public officials dominated the list.[76] An extensive distribution list at the end of the San Joaquin County Grand Jury Final Report shows that the Grand Jury Staff Secretary received the largest number of reports (50); designated local-government officials and the news media were allocated the remainder of the reports.[77]

Final Reports as Newspaper Inserts

A recent trend for grand juries is to publish reports in tabloid form as inserts in newspapers.[78] During the study period, the Grand Juries of Del Norte, El Dorado, Humboldt, Inyo, Marin, and Plumas Counties followed this practice. Because tabloid-like final reports usually are paid-for inserts in widely distributed newspapers, grand jurors hope that the number of citizens who read them will be larger than the number of citizens who read traditionally printed and distributed reports and who learn about grand jury activities only by reading newspaper accounts of them. No systematic assessment of this practice was discussed in final reports of the study period. Some grand jurors say they believe that including final reports as inserts in newspapers increases readership of final reports. Disadvantages of the practice include:

- The size and shape of tabloid final reports make them difficult to file in libraries.
- Newsprint often discolors in one or two years and often becomes brittle, making storage difficult.

- The smaller print size associated with newspaper formats is more difficult for many older citizens to read.
- Conventionally printed and bound reports are more likely to be retained than are ephemeral-appearing, newspaper-like publications.
- Some copy machines reproduce copies of newsprint that are too dark to read.

Summary and Conclusion

Only grand jurors can ensure significance, accountability, and continuity for the grand jury, its investigations, and its reports. Second only to the grand jury's relationship with district attorneys, triviality ranks as the most frequently expressed criticism of the institution. Some criticism of the triviality of grand jury investigations has merit. Occasionally, however, public officials accuse grand juries of triviality as an effective strategy for discrediting the institution. This strategy may be effective if final reports are so difficult to obtain that citizens cannot judge them independently for their significance and are forced to rely on newspaper stories and editorials for their information about grand jury activities.

The absence of even simple accounts of grand jury workloads in final reports prevents citizens from acquiring knowledge about the institution. Given grand jurors' concern for lack of citizen understanding about the grand jury, one might expect final reports to include more information about grand jury achievements, problems, and workloads, but this sort of information is scarce. Grand jurors, however, have expended considerable effort to devise procedures and techniques for providing institutional continuity. The study identified five internally developed methods for passing information from one grand jury to the next, all of them lawful, provided that they exclude certain types of information about the indictment function.

The external appearance and internal organization of final reports vary. Penal Code Section 916 allows grand juries to exercise judgment in almost every aspect of designing and producing final reports, and grand juries may organize and report investigations in any lawful manner. Penal Code Section 916 places the burden, therefore, on grand jurors to decide how carefully they document the facts in their final reports. In the absence of documentation, public officials and other citizens are deprived of information they need to judge the validity of civil investigations.

Rigid adherence to an ineffective category system of reporting causes some deficiencies in final reports. Categories by themselves offer little assistance for answering two crucial questions that every writer of a factual report must confront: "How much is enough?" and "What is too much?" For the answers, grand jurors must depend on the panel's collective resources and on their own individual education, training, experience, wisdom, and independent thinking.

Although designing covers for final reports and writing titles for investigations might seem to be merely mechanical or editorial issues, they have important implications for the independence of the institution. For example, displaying the names and electoral districts of county supervisors on covers or inside title pages suggests that the grand jury is subordinate to elected officials of the executive branch of local government. These practices portray the grand jury as merely one of many local-government departments rather than as an independent arm of the judiciary. And using names of committees as titles of investigative reports suggests that final reports are collections of committee investigations rather than a comprehensive, cohesive report of grand jurors to fellow citizens. Distributing final reports also has implications for grand jury independence. If few reports are distributed and the grand jury has not established regular channels for communicating its reports to the community, independence serves no purpose.

This chapter and the one preceding it were concerned with current grand jury final report practices dealing with, respectively, substance and structure. In the next chapter, I offer suggestions to improve both of these qualities of final reports.

6

Improving Grand Jury Investigations and Reports

In this chapter, I offer suggestions to help grand jurors eliminate recurring problems in their final reports that detract from the spirit of the institution. The first group of suggestions I offer will eliminate certain organizational barriers to better investigations and reports. The second set of suggestions is presented in the order of the legal criteria discussed in Chapter 2. Following this section are recommendations concerning community and technical criteria described in Chapter 2.

Grand Jury Controversies and Their Legislative Consequences

I can think of no better way to introduce the chapter than to describe the consequences of an incident to which I alluded in the "Bureaucratic Encounters and Conflicts" section of Chapter 3. Although the incident began as a local controversy during the study period, it eventually led to several Statewide legislative attacks on grand jury independence that I shall describe later. For the purposes of this chapter, the incident and its consequences demonstrate how grand jury independence and objectivity are related and why grand jurors must protect them diligently by improving their investigations and reports.

The incident described in Chapter 3 involved a conflict between a Northern California grand jury of 1991–1992 and a district attorney.[1] According to the grand jurors' account of the matter, the District Attorney had assured the panel at the beginning of its term that he would assist it in its work. In their final report, however, the grand jurors claimed, "His assistance ... often proved to be a hindrance for the reasons stated in the findings below."[2] Thus, the final report included several sharply worded findings and recommendations concerning what the panel believed to be the District Attorney's intransigence. When grand jurors did not receive written comments from the District Attorney concerning their findings and recommendations about his office, they asked the Presiding Judge to intervene on their behalf.

In a letter, the District Attorney informed the Presiding Judge of the Superior Court that the findings and one recommendation in contention had already been "discussed and explained to the foreman [and] members of the grand jury ... at the time of the decision. Therefore, further comment is not warranted. Finding 5 is not worthy of comment. The stated recommendation, if it is a recommendation, is not worthy of comment."[3]

Not satisfied with the comments the District Attorney sent to the Judge, the former Foreman, after the end of his term, pursued the matter further. He obtained the assistance of a legislator who requested an opinion from the Office of Attorney General of the State of California concerning the legality of the District Attorney's comments. In particular, the former Foreman wished to determine whether the District Attorney's unwillingness to file written comments complied with Penal Code Section 933, the statute that requires public officials to comment about findings and recommendations affecting them in grand jury final reports.

A letter opinion of the Attorney General stated that Penal Code Section 933 did not prohibit the District Attorney's response.[4] Frustrated by the letter opinion, the former Foreman thereafter found a legislator who agreed to prepare a bill requiring public officials to use one or more comments from a prescribed list of options when responding to findings and recommendations affecting them. This provision, the former Foreman hoped, would prevent the recurrence of the "no comment" problem.[5]

Three Legislative Proposals

In 1994, a member of the California State Senate sought passage of Senate Bill 2000, thereby starting the following chain of events. Although Senate Bill 2000 originally contained only the prescribed-comments requirement, it eventually acquired an amendment similar to previous legislative attempts to restrict grand jury independence.[6] The amendment that was added to Senate Bill 2000 specified:

> Prior to adopting a final report required pursuant to Section 933, each grand jury shall meet with any person or entity entitled to comment on the report pursuant to Section 933, and shall provide an opportunity for that person or entity to comment on the draft findings and recommendations.[7]

Although Senate Bill 2000 did not become law,[8] some of its language would reappear in two subsequent legislative sessions. To help readers understand how Senate Bill 2000 led to subsequent legislative attacks on grand jury independence, I shall discuss certain details concerning two other bills introduced into the

California Legislature after the study period. To understand the circumstances surrounding Senate Bill 2000 and its successors, however, one also must understand certain problems that arose in several of the State's 58 county grand juries during the same period.

In describing these events, I hope to demonstrate the connection between grand jury independence and several of the institution's most persistent recurring problems, including subjectivity, issuing reports about policy matters, and internal conflict of interest. A summary of these events also is relevant for the objectives of this book by documenting another phenomenon that may be found in the political world at large: how an attempt to introduce corrective legislation may backfire on its proponent.[9]

The pre-publication disclosure-to-officials requirement for the institution had been dormant in the California Legislature for years but was revived with Senate Bill 2000. Indeed, on an earlier occasion it was reported to have been introduced unsuccessfully as a bill at the behest of a public official who believed that a grand jury had criticized his office unfairly for several years.[10] Although Senate Bill 2000 failed to become law, its author resurrected it in 1996 as Senate Bill 1457. In addition to the prescribed-comments requirement, Senate Bill 1457 contained a provision that would have permitted grand jurors to invite public officials to "verify" findings in draft reports. The bill would also have required grand jurors to distribute reports affecting public officials to those officials two days before the release of the reports.[11] When Senate Bill 1457 finally became law, it included the prescribed comments and the disclosure-to-officials provisions, the latter being at the grand jury's discretion.[12]

CONTROVERSIES BETWEEN GRAND JURIES AND PUBLIC OFFICIALS

While Senate Bill 1457 passed through the Legislature, a political imbroglio was under way in a county that was part of the constituency of the author of that Bill. Late in 1995, the San Mateo County Grand Jury released a final report that included a 13-page investigation it described as an "in-depth analysis of the transportation agencies that affect San Mateo County with the purpose of reducing cost and enhancing service."[13] Of the 13 pages, 8 were devoted to "Findings," but much of this text was descriptive material with few full citations to original sources. The report ended with four recommendations into which were mixed several policy issues including:

> That the San Mateo County Board of Supervisors and the San Mateo County Transit District ... withdraw immediately from the BART/SAMTRANS agreement to extend BART to San Francisco International Airport or any further into San Mateo County.[14]

Shortly after the distribution of the Grand Jury final report, the sponsor of Senate Bill 1457 publicly and emphatically expressed his dissatisfaction with that document. In particular, the Senator wrote a guest column in which he stated,

> The [San Mateo County] Grand Jury's wildly inaccurate and irresponsible Nov. 7, 1996, report, "Rail Transportation," compels me to refute point by point the innumerable errors contained in that unfortunate document.[15]

The report also angered another elected official: a San Mateo County Supervisor who was, at the time of the release of the controversial report, President of the California State Association of Counties: "[The County Supervisor] said many grand juries 'have more of a lynch mob mentality' and called the grand jury system 'out of control.'"[16]

In his role as President of the California State Association of Counties, the County Supervisor assembled a study group whose purpose was to propose legislation to ensure for California grand juries "the optimum chance of delivering a useful final report." Eventually, the study group released a report recommending passage of "The Civil Grand Jury Training, Communication and Efficiency Act of 1997." Included among eight principal recommendations in the Act was a new version of the disclosure-to-officials requirement offered in the spirit of "a collaborative component to the grand jury process":

> The grand jury shall, at some time during the investigation, and prior to the grand jury's approval of the report, meet with the chief executive or head of the agency under investigation to discuss the nature of the investigation and receive input from the chief executive or department head.[17]

In February 1997, the proposal of the California State Association of Counties was introduced into the California Legislature as Assembly Bill 829. This bill included language somewhat similar to that quoted in the preceding paragraph, including the word "shall":

> A grand jury shall request a subject person or entity to come before the grand jury for the purpose of reading and discussing the findings of the grand jury report that relates to that person or entity in order to verify the accuracy of the findings prior to their release. [and] During the investigation and prior to final approval of the report, the grand jury shall meet with the chief executive or department head of the investigated agency to discuss the nature of the investigation and to receive the comments of the chief executive or department head.

Besides the San Mateo County incident, several other controversies arose during the period of Senate Bill 2000 and Assembly Bill 829. These conflicts, added to those I cited earlier in this study, would have been known to many legislators who deliberated about these several bills. The most widely publicized controversy concerning grand juries, the Yuba County Grand Jury incident discussed in Chapter 1, continued to be publicized during the several legislative efforts described above.

Another controversial episode occurred in mid-1995 and also has been discussed briefly in Chapter 1: the indictment attempts by the Mariposa County Grand Jury of 1994–1995.[18] Whatever the merits of this incident might have been, from the perspective of the affected public officials, or the grand jurors who attempted to issue indictments, or the institution itself, it was widely publicized and certainly must have influenced some legislators' perceptions of the institution as they considered mandatory disclosure-to-officials amendments.

Likewise, the Tulare County Grand Jury of 1994–1995 had attracted considerable attention by issuing a controversial final report concerning a police department. Although this episode drew less Statewide attention than did the problems of the Mariposa County Grand Jury, it nevertheless involves important issues that are treated in this chapter and elsewhere in this study.

For example, in a letter to the Foreman of the Grand Jury investigating the Police Department, the Chief of Police claimed that a member of the Grand Jury committee conducting the investigation was married to an employee of a business firm that had filed a complaint about the organization. In his letter, the Chief commented, "It would seem unnecessary to point out that the spouse of a person who is employed by the party initiating the Grand Jury investigation lacks objectivity. Surely someone on the Grand Jury has considered the potential that a personal agenda may be fueling this probe."[19] According to an attorney representing the City, despite requests by city officials to do so, the person thought to have a conflict-of-interest was not removed from the Grand Jury committee as a result of the Chief's letter. Nevertheless, a formal demand to the Foreman and Presiding Judge later resulted in the removal of that person from the committee.[20]

Still another episode could have shaped legislators' views of the grand jury as they considered the mandatory disclosure-to-officials amendment in the last bill in the series discussed here: A judge discharged an entire grand jury because of irreconcilable internal conflicts within a panel. According to one news account of this matter, "This year's panel was fundamentally divided over what they perceived were appropriate grand jury rules."[21]

It would be incorrect to claim that a direct cause-and-effect relationship existed between the legislative activity I have described and the recurrence of the problems I have cited in this section and discussed elsewhere, yet the accumulative effect of publicized recurring grand jury problems each year must lead some legislators to believe that the institution requires corrective legislation. In any case, legislators and other public officials who support the institution will find it difficult to do so if grand jurors are unable or unwilling to discharge their powers responsibly. Survival of the institution, after all, depends almost entirely on how well grand jurors manage it.

Organizational Issues to Be Resolved Early in the Grand Jury Year

After ending their year of service, former grand jurors occasionally regret that they did not begin conducting investigations immediately after impanelment. Frequently, one or two months pass before grand jurors organize themselves well enough to conduct their first investigation. The first weeks in the grand jury year need not be wasted, though. If grand jurors use this time effectively, they can create a cohesive, well-organized panel for the remaining months. Ineffective use of that time, of course, can burden the panel with defects that impede it for the remainder of its year.

In proposing organizational issues and their solutions, I do not suggest that grand jurors consider only these matters early in its term. Under Penal Code Section 916, grand jurors are free to discuss and decide almost all organizational matters except appointment of the foreman. I have selected the issues for discussion in this chapter because they directly affect the quality of investigations and reports and because they recur persistently each year. Also, these are issues that the entire panel must consider. They provide an early experience in developing the deliberation and decision-making skills needed for effective grand jury service.[22]

CREATING AND MAINTAINING COLLEGIALITY

Each year, every grand jury faces the same problem: Many of its members begin their year not understanding that the grand jury is an institution unlike any they have experienced previously. In particular, the implication of collegiality might be unfamiliar to people whose only experience has been in hierarchical organizations. Unfortunately, modern society offers few opportunities for most citizens to learn how to be members of collegial, deliberating bodies.[23]

If grand jurors are unfamiliar with collegial bodies, they might not understand that in these groups, members have equal status, that one person is not more or less important than another, and that each member is therefore a peer among peers. In a grand jury, for example, no one is an assistant, an associate, or a master grand juror; nor do collegial bodies have seniority or tenure systems. Members of collegial bodies manage themselves; they have no "directors," "supervisors," or "bosses." Grand juries, like all other collegial bodies, are "flat" rather than pyramidal organizations. Thus, the principal distinction between the foreman and other grand jurors is what Penal Code Section 912 requires—namely, that the courts, not grand jurors, designate who shall serve as foreman. Beyond that statute, foremen have only those powers that their peers grant them.

Because grand juries, like trial juries, are collegial bodies, their decisions are legitimate only if each member has participated fully in them. Although all grand jurors need not agree, two statutes specify the minimum number of votes required for a decision to be legitimate (Penal Code Sections 916 and 940). During the "getting started" phase of its existence, grand jurors therefore should begin to fashion their panel as a collegial body. For that purpose, various methods have been used successfully and therefore are recommended.

Conducting an Experience-and-Skills Inventory

To create an effective organization, members must become acquainted with each other to some extent. For this reason, some grand juries early in their terms distribute questionnaires that members can use to inform their colleagues of their backgrounds. Questionnaires typically ask for information about grand jurors' skills, interests, experience, and involvement in local government. Discussing each other's interests and backgrounds assists grand jurors in developing cohesion and in blending their individual skills and experiences into an effective body.

Biographical information can serve another purpose: assisting grand jurors to identify potential conflicts of interest within the panel. For example, grand jurors who have relatives working in local government should disclose these relationships fully and frankly. And grand jurors who have friends or acquaintances in local government should declare those relationships to their colleagues. As a precaution, grand jurors also should make certain that no member is exempted by statute from grand jury service.[24]

Less obvious potential conflicts of interest also might be identified. For example, in a Northern California county, the sheriff's department was investigating a grand juror's relative. When her fellow grand jurors decided that the grand juror should not serve on the law enforcement committee, she resigned, disappointed because the panel did not see the wisdom of her chairing a committee that might become involved in an investigation of the sheriff's department.

In some counties, "get acquainted" questionnaires include lists of committees that grand jurors can use to express their preference for assignment. If the foreman or some other person decides upon the names and tasks of committees before the entire panel has deliberated about them and appoints grand jurors to the committees, the panel has lost its independence at its inception. Other information that might be requested in "get acquainted" questionnaires includes:

- Information about grand jurors' skills in using computers for writing and research
- Experiences grand jurors have had in organizing, collecting, and analyzing data

- Descriptions of management skills that grand jurors may have, such as budgeting, planning, organizing and controlling projects, or financial analysis
- A general summary of grand jurors' work experience, particularly past employment in local government
- Questions about relatives or friends of grand jurors who work in local government or who are elected or appointed officials
- Information about experiences that grand jurors have had within the most recent 10 years as campaign workers or managers for local-government elected officials, whether grand jurors have completed economic disclosure forms before grand jury service, and, if so, for what purpose
- Descriptions of advisory bodies or commissions of local government on which grand jurors currently serve or have served
- Descriptions of experience as directors or volunteers in nonprofit organizations
- Declarations of particular interest that grand jurors might have in specific local-government services, organizations, practices, and the like
- Suggestions that grand jurors might have for investigations or studies of local-government matters that the panel should consider

Reading and Discussing the Clinton Case

Another technique for building collegiality and cohesion is to read and discuss the *Clinton* case.[25] Despite its brevity, this case makes clear the collegial nature of the grand jury and the relationship of individual grand jurors to the body. The case also is important because it points out the consequences of one grand juror's attempts to force fellow grand jurors to conduct an investigation. Examples of topics this case suggests for grand jurors to discuss concerning investigations and reports are:

- How the case might affect the organization and procedures of the grand jury
- The need for all grand jurors to be informed fully about each investigation
- The relevance of the case to the role of the foreman
- The significance of the case for the validity of final reports
- The concept of the "rights" of individual grand jurors with particular reference to their initiating civil investigations

Developing Peer-Review Procedures

An important characteristic of collegial bodies is that they resolve disputes internally, including, if necessary, disciplining their members. Similarly, grand juries may wish to develop procedures for dealing with internal problems that inevitably arise in grand jury service, such as absenteeism, lack of participation by members, and possible misconduct by grand jurors (such as attempting as individuals to conduct investigations or otherwise abusing grand jury powers). Other important issues include discussing the limits of grand jurors' participating in local elections, considering the types of cases in which conflict of interest could arise based on the backgrounds of grand jurors, and reviewing hypothetical examples of breaches of confidentiality and secrecy. Panel members also may discuss the value of adopting codes of ethics to encourage high standards of conduct.[26]

DEFINING THE FOREMAN'S ROLE

An early discussion by the grand jury of the foreman's role will assist the panel in creating an organization that will function effectively as a deliberative, collegial body. Suggested issues for the grand jury to discuss with respect to the foreman's role are:

- Thoroughly reviewing the foreman's role described in the grand jury's procedures manual; making certain that the manual does not assign the foreman powers that only the current panel may delegate (for example, naming grand jury committees and appointing grand jurors to them; establishing investigative priorities; accepting or rejecting complaints without the grand jury's review and approval)

- Deciding which powers the foreman may exercise at his discretion

- Deciding what responsibility the foreman may exercise for making public statements about grand jury matters; discussing the limits of the foreman's responsibility in reviewing and editing drafts of final reports and for arranging the printing of the report; designating what kinds of correspondence the foreman may initiate upon his own discretion and what kinds of correspondence he may initiate only with grand jury approval

REVIEWING THE PROCEDURES MANUAL

Early in its term, grand jurors should thoroughly review their procedures manual or other written procedures and policies concerning panel operations. Every statement in the procedures manual affecting the collegial nature of the body and its independence should be read closely and deliberated. If questions arise concerning the information, the grand jury should consider assigning the revision of the manual to an appropriate committee. Revision of the manual should start early in the grand jury's year so time is available for the necessary legal research, consultation with legal advisors, and participation of the grand jury's editorial committee.

CREATING ORGANIZATION AND MANAGEMENT PRACTICES THAT FOSTER DELIBERATION

When internal disputes arise in grand jury service, they often occur early in the grand jury year. A foreman, for example, may not understand that the role of the grand jury foreman is unlike that in an industrial setting. On a factory production line, a foreman can order subordinates to start, discontinue, or modify a project. In grand jury service, only the entire body can decide those matters.[27] Similarly, several grand jurors might decide immediately after impanelment to conduct an investigation on their own initiative despite the wishes of the rest of the panel. Having made their decision before they understand the nature of the institution, they might be unwilling to rescind it. Thus, an internal, often bitter, dispute is born. Because the institution is created anew each year, its survival depends crucially upon whether citizens appointed to it have the forbearance and intelligence needed to develop in a collegial manner a work schedule consistent with the spirit of the institution.

DEVELOPING A GENERAL WORK SCHEDULE

A discussion of a general work schedule early in the grand jury year will help grand jurors prepare for many of the challenges they will face. Developing a general work schedule also identifies important administrative tasks that must be delegated and accomplished. One important technique for developing the schedule is to decide early in the year the date for submitting the final report to the court. When this has been established, other dates can be determined by working backward from the submission date to the month in which the grand jury was impaneled.

The general work schedule cannot precisely foresee the exact date when draft reports of given investigations must be circulated within the panel or when specific investigations should be started or concluded. These are examples of matters that depend on when the grand jurors receive complaints, how many they receive, how many they accept for investigation, and the like. Nevertheless, many important events that will occur during the grand jury year can be foreseen. The following activities, for example, are selected tasks from a general work schedule toward the end of a grand jury year; tasks like these probably will arise in roughly the same sequence in many California grand juries. An early discussion about the suitability of a general work schedule such as the one from which these activities were taken will assist panels in planning their year and provide an early exercise in collegial decision making.

Month	Week	Activity
May	2–3	Final reports must be completed by committees and given to the editorial committee
	4	Jury approves preliminary draft of final report and changes
June	1	Completed report ready for review by grand jury
	1	Program planning for impanelment of new jury
	1–4	Review of all files for destruction or retention for new jury
	1–4	Preparation of briefing materials for new jury, its officers, and committees
	2	Jury approval of final report
	2	County counsel or other legal authority reviews report for legality, grand jury jurisdiction, possible defamatory wording[28]

Grand juries should make certain that the procedure they use to establish their workload supports independence and cohesion by involving the entire panel. Neither an individual grand juror (including the foreman) nor a committee should control the establishment of grand jury priorities. Early in their term, grand jurors should discuss what method to use for determining their workloads. Various methods are available for involving all members of groups. For example, one method begins with each member of the panel suggesting at least two investigative topics. When the panel has produced a list of about 40 topics, it discusses each one until it reduces the list to 10 by using screening criteria that it has agreed upon previously. Several successive meetings of the body may be needed until the panel reduces the list to 10 items (or any other agreed-upon number).

Another method involves developing a questionnaire containing a list of potential investigative topics. After grand jurors have rated each topic in the questionnaire, they calculate the response score for each topic. Next they organize the list of topics according to their scores, the highest-scoring topic being at the head of the list. The grand jury then decides how many of the topics it wishes to investigate.[29]

DECIDING COMMITTEE ORGANIZATION AND PROCEDURES

One of the most serious mistakes that newly appointed grand jurors make is perpetuating the committees of predecessors or otherwise creating committees before the investigative workload has taken shape. This error is exacerbated if a foreman has created committees on his own initiative in the mistaken belief that he has the authority to do so. Often grand jurors will not realize early in their terms that in doing so, the foreman has overstepped his authority. As the year progresses and grand jurors become more familiar with the institution, however, they realize that the foreman, if only unwittingly, has usurped the powers of the body. If the foreman is flexible, he may gracefully retract his decisions so the body can begin again in the proper manner. By the time grand jurors have resolved their differences, though, valuable time may be lost.

Equally serious is the panel itself creating investigative committees before it receives citizens' complaints. For example, establishing a law enforcement committee prematurely implies that grand jurors should conduct investigations of law enforcement agencies. Grand jurors therefore may begin perfunctory tours and visits of law enforcement agencies that eventually consume much time unnecessarily. When the panel begins to receive complaints from citizens about other topics, so many grand jurors might be involved in routine inspections corresponding with committee names that the body does not have sufficient members available to inquire into citizen complaints about more serious matters.

One form of committee structure avoids the problems arising either from perpetuating committees of predecessors or from molding the grand jury work-load to correspond to committee names. Committees bearing the names of the major entities specified in the statutes governing grand juries would ensure that panels spread their efforts over a variety of local governments rather than concentrating, say, on county or city government. Such a committee structure would accommodate almost any kind of legitimate complaint a panel might receive. Table 24, "Suggested Grand Jury Line and Administrative Committees," shows two suggested types of committees: line committees (those named according to grand jury jurisdiction over designated local governments) and administrative committees (those to which grand jurors can assign important institutional-maintenance tasks).

TABLE 24
Suggested Grand Jury Line and Administrative Committees

Line	Administrative
• Cities and county	• Continuity, comment analysis, and resources
• Housing, nonprofits, and redevelopment	• Grand jury procedures, review, and internal affairs
• Jails, prisons, and other correctional institutions	• Editorial and case management and control
• Education and special districts	
• Joint Powers Agencies and the Local Agency Formation Commission (LAFCO)	

The five line committees include the local-government entities over which grand juries have statutory jurisdiction. The committee names also accommodate mandatory and discretionary grand jury investigations. I have grouped the committees roughly according to the nature of the local-government organizations, functions, and services. For example, in a broad sense, cities and counties are more similar to each other than they are similar to Joint Powers Agencies and Local Agency Formation Commissions.

The three administrative committees perform the principal institutional-maintenance tasks that grand juries require to ensure their independence, stability, and effectiveness. The Continuity, Comment Analysis, and Resources Committee, for example, maintains a list of completed past investigations and identifies local-government functions or services that previous panels might have overlooked. The Committee also ensures that affected local-government officials have filed their comments to previous grand jury reports as required by Penal Code Section 933. This Committee also monitors grand jury resources and trends in expenditures.

The Grand Jury Procedures, Review, and Internal Affairs Committee keeps the panel's code of ethical conduct current and ensures that the procedures manual is accurate, current, and appropriate for the spirit of the institution. Early in the grand jury term, this Committee recommends to the panel a flexible, yet comprehensive, procedure that the body may use to conduct its meetings and record its minutes. This Committee also may convene in cases of internal disagreements among grand jurors, to investigate actual or potential conflicts of interest within the panel, and to advise the panel of its findings.

The Editorial and Case Management and Control Committee reviews drafts of investigative reports; develops a schedule for the production, printing, and distribution of interim and final reports; and makes certain that the final report is well designed and effective. This Committee also develops and sends to the grand jury for approval a system of receiving and accounting for complaints from the community.

This suggested committee structure has several advantages over many of the committee arrangements grand juries have traditionally used:

1. It can exist from year to year with revisions required by statutory changes only.
2. The names of line committees are general rather than those of specific local-government topics, services, or functions; they do not thereby predispose grand jurors ritualistically to continue investigations that previous grand juries conducted—for example, of "The Sheriff's Department" or "Mental Health." Instead, the committee names remind grand jurors of their jurisdiction and, in doing so, encourage them not to overlook local-government functions that may not be sensational but nevertheless are worthy of grand jury review.

3. The committee structure is flexible enough to accommodate almost all types of complaints.
4. The number of committees is fewer than what many grand juries now create.

To the extent that committee structure is fragmented and complex, management problems increase; these might be status-related internal conflict, arguments over jurisdiction, and competition for resources. Moreover, the proliferation of committees limits the number of committees on which grand jurors can effectively serve and thereby contributes to the fragmentation of the institution.

Understanding Grand Jury Resources

A grand jury's independence and effectiveness are closely related to its resources. Early in their term, grand jurors should review how their budget is established each year, who has that responsibility, and how the board of supervisors decides each year's grand jury budget request.

Using information provided by the Continuity, Comment Analysis, and Resources Committee, panels can study current and past grand jury appropriation and expenditure trends; whether previous grand juries have stayed within their budgets or exceeded them (see Penal Code Section 914.5) and, if so, why; whether the grand jury or the district attorney bears the costs of indictments; and under what circumstances grand jurors can request judges to issue an order directing the payment of grand jury expenditures authorized by Penal Code Section 931. A complete understanding of these matters is necessary to ensure that the grand jury's budget is not reduced capriciously or for political reasons and that the person establishing the budget has sufficient status and knowledge to understand its importance in terms of the grand jury's independence and has the motivation to justify and defend it if necessary.

Suggestions Based on Law-Related Criteria for Improving Investigations and Reports

Although the legal criteria I described in Chapter 2, and that are used in this chapter, are expressed as separate categories, they are interdependent. They may support each other directly or indirectly, but in their entirety they constitute the spirit of the institution. Serious defects in only one of the criteria could result not only in grave harm to grand jurors or public officials but also to the future of the civil grand jury itself.

Independence and Jurisdiction

Except for a few statutory requirements, grand jurors enjoy autonomy in making decisions about their investigations and reports. If several generations of creative, energetic, and independent grand jurors have institutionalized effective procedures, reliance on the past may be the formula for success. If, however, grand jurors have been apathetic, unmotivated, and ill-informed about the institution, the patterns of mediocrity could be so firmly established that "radical surgery" is required to eliminate them.

Independence

The most important step that newly impaneled grand juries may take in understanding the institution's independence is to read and discuss thoroughly Penal Code Section 916. Although this statute is relatively brief, its implications for grand jury service are profound. Using Table 4, "An Analysis of Penal Code Section 916" (Chapter 2), grand jurors can use one or two meetings productively for reviewing and discussing the implications of that statute for the foreman's role, the organization of the grand jury, conducting investigations, and all other facets of grand jury service.

Grand juries also should discuss early in their term their relationships with elected and appointed public officials and with local government itself. For example, the fact that a local-government official nominated someone for grand jury service must not require that the latter owes the former any allegiance. Similarly, that the grand jury is housed in a county building does not mean that the panel is a department of county government. Grand jurors also should avoid associating the institution with the names of any public officials other than judges. Examples of practices that convey the mistaken impression that grand juries are county departments rather than independent bodies are: listing the names of county supervisors on front covers of final reports, displaying the seal of the county board of supervisors on a final report, and addressing final reports to county supervisors, rather than to the judge.

Grand jurors also should consider carefully their relationship with the district attorney even if that official does not involve the grand jury in indictments. Although the district attorney is one of the grand jury's legal advisors (Penal Code Section 934), grand jurors should attach no special significance to the role of that office with respect to the panel. Because the district attorney–grand jury relationship often has been criticized by the press, the bar, and civil libertarians, grand juries should make certain that their panel does nothing to justify the criticism.[30]

Even if grand jurors do not expect to be involved in indictments, they may wish—if only for educational purposes—to invite the public defender to meet with them to discuss the latter's role in the criminal justice system and to understand what the defense bar might find objectionable about indictment procedures. These informational meetings with the public defender also might be useful if it becomes necessary to inquire into a complaint about that office or into the office of the district attorney.

The relationship between grand juries and the superior court is rarely the subject of criticism in legal circles, but for grand jurors, if not judges, it can be confusing. Early in their term, therefore, grand jurors might wish to ask their advisor judge to visit with them to discuss his or her perception of that relationship. Before that visit, panel members may wish to review and discuss that portion of the judge's charge that discusses grand jury–judicial relations. Similarly, reading and discussing two cases in particular will assist grand juries in further developing their understanding of judge–grand jury relationships.[31] Grand juries should also read and discuss an opinion of the Attorney General of the State of California regarding the panel's lack of jurisdiction in the judicial system.[32]

Other practices that detract from the grand jury's independence are:

- assigning grand jurors to serve on committees of local government
- including in reports glowing, unsubstantiated compliments about public officials or local-government departments, services, and functions
- citing brand names, manufacturers' names, or trademarked names as preferred products in final reports
- adopting, without independent verification, the findings and recommendations of previous grand juries

Jurisdiction

Perhaps the greatest threat to the existence of the grand jury lies in its exceeding its jurisdiction. For this reason, grand juries should be thoroughly acquainted with the limits and boundaries of their authority. A thorough review and discussion of Table 3, "Civil Jurisdiction and Methods of the California Grand Jury, with Applicable Code Section(s)" (Chapter 2) may assist panels in accomplishing this goal. Throughout their year, grand juries should make certain that every complaint they receive is directly related to one or more statutes. As grand jurors receive and deliberate about complaints, they should keep in mind that the jurisdiction of the institution is limited to specific powers in designated local governments and their functions. Of course, if a complaint involves a possible criminal act, a grand jury may have criminal jurisdiction in public institutions in which it has no civil powers.

Understanding their jurisdiction thoroughly, and explaining it simply and clearly when contacting elected and appointed officials, administrators, and employees, might help grand jurors avoid unnecessary conflict in their relations with those persons. Therefore, while planning investigations, grand jurors should decide how to explain their jurisdiction to people they could interview. In some cases, sending a letter to a department head explaining the grand jury's decision to conduct an investigation, and its jurisdiction for doing so, is helpful. In other cases, an informal visit, or even a telephone call to a local-government official, may provide an opportunity to discuss the applicable Penal Code sections authorizing an investigation. By carefully explaining the need for the investigation, emphasizing the full involvement of the grand jury in the decision to conduct it, and citing the specific statute or statutes authorizing the investigation, grand jurors might prevent the initial antagonism of public officials upon their learning of an impending visit by the panel.

FAIR COMMENT

Fair-comment problems in grand jury final reports might have inspired some political support for the near enactment into law of the restrictive legislation I discussed earlier. These problems, however, were rare in final reports during the study period. Nevertheless, in certain circumstances, only one libelous comment in a final report could be sufficient incentive for the Legislature to eliminate the grand jury or to curtail its jurisdiction severely. Although grand jurors must exercise great care when naming persons in final reports, they should not hesitate to criticize officials if the criticism is documented properly and thoroughly. The Legislature has granted grand juries the authority to investigate specified matters in designated local governments; that authority implies that grand juries may discover irregularities or inefficiencies in local government.

In some circumstances, naming specific individuals who are responsible for ineffective management, administration, or supervision is appropriate. In most cases, however, focusing on well-documented ineffective methods, procedures, or systems is more likely to result in improvement than naming individuals. If grand jurors have deliberated about these matters thoroughly, they, and only they, will know and decide which strategy is correct in a given situation.

No legal advisor is statutorily required to instruct grand jurors about libel and slander. Grand jurors themselves must ensure that they have acquired a suitable understanding of the laws concerning defamation of character, particularly its written form—libel. Suggestions for providing appropriate training include:

- Inviting legal advisors to explain to grand jurors the statutes and case laws about libel and slander and what grand jurors can do to prevent it
- Reading and discussing Penal Code Section 930 and its implications for grand jury service
- Reading and discussing the facts and implications of the only California case to date that on appeal held that a grand jury had committed libel (*Gillett-Harris-Duranceau & Assoc., Inc., v. Kemple* (1978) 83 Cal.App.3d 214 [147 Cal.Rptr. 616])
- Assigning the Editorial Committee to read the sections about libel in the most recent edition of the *Associated Press Style Guide* and in *American Jurisprudence*.[33]

During internal training sessions discussions about libel also should include consideration of fair-comment problems such as those that arose during the study period; for example:

- The possibility of a libel lawsuit if a grand jury were to include in its final report a threat that it would file an indictment unless a named public official were to discontinue a specific practice
- Statements in final reports that a law enforcement agency was investigating a named person and that the grand jury therefore would not conduct its own investigation or that it was waiting for the results of the criminal investigation before proceeding with its own
- Including vague, unsubstantiated, conclusionary comments about the professionalism, competency, or motives of private persons or public officials or employees
- Writing with no substantiation broad condemnations of unnamed but identifiable public officials or alleging without proof that fraud, graft, and corruption was rampant in local government

Appendix B, "Twenty Suggestions for Avoiding Libel Suits," presents a list of topics that grand jurors can use for planning a training program in cooperation with their legal advisors. Appendix B provides only a brief listing of discussion possibilities concerning the law of libel. Grand jury legal advisors might have different perspectives on this complex and rapidly changing body of law. In any case, avoiding libelous comment will not be difficult for grand jurors who are thoroughly committed to developing and following procedures that will produce soundly conceived, factual investigations.

CONDUCTING JUSTIFIED INVESTIGATIONS

In this study, I have distinguished between justified investigations and jurisdiction, though the two criteria are closely related. An investigation outside the grand jury's jurisdiction cannot, by definition, be justified; however, an investigation within the grand jury's jurisdiction might seem to be unjustified if a reader is uncertain about the origins of the investigation. Unfortunately, many investigations in final reports during the study period included no information about their origins. Because no statute forbids or requires grand juries to document the origins of complaints, the decision to do so is within the grand jury's discretion—assuming that no consideration of secrecy or confidentiality dictates otherwise. Of course, grand jurors should not identify complainants in final reports unless those persons have given them permission to do so, and provided that no violation of the legal requirements of secrecy thereby occurs.

Several considerations argue for final reports including information about the origins of grand jury investigations. Some citizens, including public officials, believe that grand juries forage indiscriminately for matters to investigate.[34]

This viewpoint is sometimes expressed by the term "fishing expeditions." To avoid perpetuating the idea that grand jurors roam about looking for people and issues to investigate, panels should state in their reports the origins of, and reasons for, each investigation. Citing the statute or statutes that required or permitted the grand jury to conduct an investigation allows readers to examine the statute and judge for themselves whether it provided a sufficient basis for the investigation. Citing the statute is not sufficient by itself; the grand jury also should describe why it believed the statute applied to the particular facts in the matter.

If the grand jury began the investigation upon its own initiative, it should describe why panel members thought the investigation was needed and that the necessary number of grand jurors approved it. If a public official, such as a county supervisor or a city council member, requested the investigation, grand juries should identify the person and describe what procedures the panel used to make certain that the investigation was not politically motivated.

Documenting the origins of investigations also helps grand juries account more fully to their communities for their actions. To the extent that citizens read in final reports that panels undertook investigations in response to citizen complaints, citizens will see the grand jury as an institution serving their interests rather than those of local-government officials. Thorough documentation of the origins of investigations serves another purpose: If a grand jury explains in detail why it believes an investigation was needed, readers can judge for themselves the validity of its report. Sufficient news stories occur each year about possible ax-grinding, conflicts of interest, and other self-serving motives of grand jurors to persuade some citizens that grand juries fall short of the spirit of the institution.[35] Accordingly, grand juries should do everything possible to show that each investigation was conducted with full justification on behalf of the community.

Each investigative report also should describe how the grand jury explained its jurisdiction and the need for the investigation to the official or officials who were investigated. This practice has two advantages:

1. It assures citizens that grand juries proceeded with care in first approaching public officials in the investigation.
2. It prevents public officials from attempting to obstruct an investigation after it has begun by challenging the grand jury's jurisdiction.

Grand jurors might find this five-point test useful for deliberating about the merits of conducting an investigation:

- Is it directly related to at least one statute?
- Will its outcome advance the self-interest of one or more grand jurors?
- Will its outcome benefit the self-interest of the complainant?
- How will the problem affect the rest of the grand jury's workload?
- If allowed to continue, whom will the problem harm, and in what way?

EMPHASIZING SYSTEMS, METHODS, AND PROCEDURES

Although I designated the policy-procedure problem as a separate category, it actually is a matter of jurisdiction. As a careful reading of Table 3 in Chapter 2 reveals, no statute authorizes grand juries to investigate, challenge, or criticize policy matters. The terms the statutes use in defining grand jury jurisdiction are words such as *procedures, books, records, accounts,* and *methods.* Differentiating policy and procedure, however, is not always easy. In their charges to grand juries, judges rarely distinguish between the two terms. The distinction, however, is implied in admonitions such as this: "Your task is not to second-guess the lawful decisions of public officials."[36] Examples of such "lawful decisions" (those concerning policy matters) were illustrated in Chapter 4. They included a grand jury that demanded an explanation for why a district attorney did not involve them in more indictments, another panel that criticized a city council for the site it selected for a new building, and grand jurors who recommended changes in the curriculum of public schools.

During the first few weeks of the grand jury year, panel members can use several methods to learn the difference between procedures and policies; for example:

- Inviting experienced administrators such as city managers or county executive officers to discuss their understanding of the differences between the two terms
- Reviewing and discussing definitions of "policy" and "procedure" in several dictionaries
- Reviewing past grand jury final reports to identify possible examples of incursions into policy matters and discussing the examples
- Reading and deliberating about a county counsel's opinion concerning the jurisdiction of grand juries in public school districts, with particular reference to the cautionary language concerning the difference between procedure and policy[37]

During the study period, the largest number of examples of grand juries commenting about policy matters was about public-education issues. For this reason, grand jurors should learn early in their term to distinguish between educational policies and procedures.

One method to learn the distinction is to prepare a list of issues about public education and use the list for deliberating about educational issues. Table 25, "Policy-Detection Exercise," contains summaries of grand jury inquiries into California public schools in previous years. The exercise has been used several times at Grand Jury Exchange Seminars to help grand jurors learn to differentiate policies and procedures. In some cases, the distinctions are decided easily; in other cases, grand jurors decide that more information is required before a decision is possible. In these latter cases, grand jurors should discuss what kinds of additional information are required.

TABLE 25
Policy-Detection Exercise

Example	Policy?	Procedure?
1. Allocation of lottery funds	☐	☐
2. Develop after-school extended day-care program	☐	☐
3. Review of bidding practices in a school district	☐	☐
4. Review of bus-stop safety and supervision	☐	☐
5. Adequacy of purchasing procedures	☐	☐
6. Assign school district personnel to inter-agency Children's Protection Services	☐	☐
7. Need for a latchkey or extended-day-care program	☐	☐
8. Explore possibility of contracting for substance-abuse program training for teachers	☐	☐
9. Develop appropriate sex-education program	☐	☐
10. Develop a mission statement and re-examine goals	☐	☐
11. District should revise policies and procedures manual	☐	☐
12. Hire counselors for intermediate schools	☐	☐
13. High school should adopt closed-campus status	☐	☐
14. Each school should provide newsletter for parents	☐	☐
15. Give attendance caseworker expense reimbursements similar to those of other employees	☐	☐
16. Identify reasons for high dropout rates in high schools of the county	☐	☐
17. Discover reasons for poor school-grounds maintenance	☐	☐
18. Complaint concerning sick time granted to a school employee	☐	☐
19. Review of pay raise granted to a superintendent	☐	☐
20. Propriety of buy-out clause in a superintendent's contract	☐	☐

To obtain your policy-detecting score, multiply the number of correct answers by five.

Grand jurors might improve their ability to distinguish between procedure and policy by developing, early in their terms, criteria such as the following to assist them in making those distinctions:

- Is the matter something about which elected officials would deliberate and vote at a public meeting?
- Does the question being considered involve broad social, political, or economic issues or values?
- Is the matter concerned with why, rather than how, something is being done or not being done?
- Would the topic be something that a candidate would include in an election campaign platform?

If the answer to each of these criteria is "yes," the matter under consideration probably is a policy issue. Of course, no list of criteria for distinguishing between policies and procedures will be perfect in every circumstance.

VALIDITY OF INVESTIGATIONS AND REPORTS

Lack of validity of grand jury final reports motivates some legislators and other public officials to support limitations on grand jury independence. Independence of the institution, however, would be better served if grand jurors themselves were to review their draft reports for lack of facts, incorrect or illogical findings, or unlawful or unrealistic recommendations. Early in their terms, grand jurors should make certain that their training prepares them adequately for conducting and writing objective investigations. The first step in developing investigative skills would be to identify examples of validity problems in previous grand jury reports. Chapter 4 discloses several types of subjectivity problems in grand jury investigative reports, findings, and recommendations, including:

- Using uncorroborated questionnaire data as the basis for findings, conclusions, and recommendations
- Making conclusionary statements without providing proof, citations, or documentation for those statements
- Not providing sufficient information about the method of an investigation so readers can judge whether its procedure was objective
- Using adjectives such as "understaffed," "overstaffed," "small," or "large" without providing the basis of such judgments
- Writing reports based solely on telephone calls with no reference to any other attempt at fact-gathering, or basing findings or conclusions on interviews of an unspecified number of members in only one level of an organization

If a sufficient number of impaneled grand jurors have the necessary background, some or all of the following suggestions may be unnecessary. If, however, few panel members have the necessary background, grand jurors, early in their terms, should develop training within their ranks to acquire an adequate understanding of the characteristics of objective investigations and report writing.

Factuality in Investigative Report Writing

Many of the weaknesses in investigative reports cited in Chapter 4 demonstrate a lack of understanding of the differences between facts, conclusions, and opinions. In Chapter 8, I discuss several possible causes of this problem and its implications for citizenship. Here, however, I cite one of these causes: not understanding the nature of a fact. For example, the statement "The department is overstaffed" is not in itself factual; it is a conclusion. The statement might be acceptable if, for example, a chart or table were to accompany it, listing staffing figures for the department in question compared to similar figures for a number of similar departments. Assuming the figures were valid, they would document the conclusion.

One might ask, of course, "How accurate was the method for collecting the figures?" Or, "How do we know the figures were copied accurately?" Or, "Have the departments used for comparison been selected fairly, who was responsible for selecting them, and how old are the figures?" These are matters of corroboration, verification, and substantiation—all basic topics for an introductory training program about investigation.

Suggestions for Internal Training

Besides legal advisors to the grand jury, local government employs many different kinds of people who have extensive investigative experience. Although grand jury civil investigations rarely lead to prosecutions, some concepts and methods of criminal investigation are useful for civil investigations. For example, grand jurors must understand that not all evidence is of equal quality, that evidence should be tested against some standard, and that different tests must be applied to different kinds of evidence.

Because grand jury investigations are similar in many respects to the work of performance auditors, grand jurors should acquire some of the basic skills and knowledge of management auditing such as analyzing budget and work-load trends, sources of information concerning local-government services, and how performance auditors define organizational effectiveness. Grand jurors also might require training in how to organize an investigative report, what kinds of citations must be used for what kinds of evidence, and how to comply with the provision of Penal Code 916 requiring that "all problems identified in a final report are accompanied by suggested means for their resolution, including financial, when applicable."

To obtain this training, grand jurors could invite local-government employees in a variety of fields to meet with them to discuss the investigative concepts, methods, and techniques they use in their work. Examples of people to invite are:

- welfare-fraud investigators
- internal auditors employed by county auditors
- internal-affairs investigators in city police departments
- budget analysts in the offices of county superintendents of schools
- salary and wage specialists in civil-service departments
- experts in the use of databases and spreadsheets and in the effective display of numerical data

Other individuals who might be willing to offer brief presentations to grand jurors about evidence, factuality, documentation, and related topics, include:

- investigative reporters
- journalism instructors at community colleges
- certified public accountants who are familiar with local government

Suggestions for Investigative Procedures

Early in their terms, grand jurors should create procedures for receiving and investigating complaints. The first sentence of Penal Code 916 places that responsibility upon grand jurors: "Each grand jury ... shall determine its rules of proceeding." Among the many "rules of proceeding" a grand jury may create, none is more important than those governing civil investigations. An investigation that develops haphazardly, with no plan, goals, or system will fail. Worse, unplanned investigations are risky for grand jurors, public officials, and other citizens. In grand jury service, a systematic investigative procedure will improve

- the processing of complaints
- the collecting of and accounting for evidence
- the process for writing investigative reports

A sound investigative procedure also will

- coordinate investigations to eliminate duplicated effort and conserve time and resources
- provide corrective measures to regulate and control every phase of an investigation
- produce accurate, fair, and objective findings and recommendations
- involve each grand juror in considering and voting upon crucial decisions in planning and conducting investigations

Figure D, "A Suggested Investigative Process," is one way of depicting the steps in investigations. The 21 steps in the flowchart can be consolidated into seven major phases of an investigative process:

1. Receiving and acknowledging complaints
2. Screening complaints and establishing investigative priorities
3. Assigning complaints to investigating committees
4. Conferring with legal advisors
5. Notifying agencies or officials
6. Conducting the investigation
7. Preparing for report writing

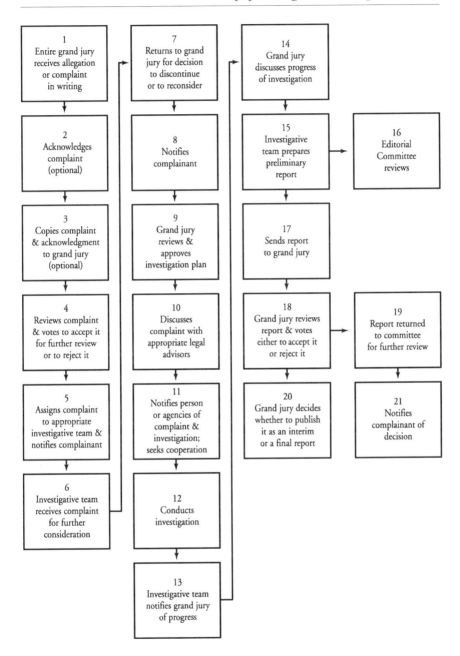

FIGURE D
A Suggested Investigative Process

The suggested flowchart might not be suitable for every grand jury in all circumstances. Nevertheless, it can provide a basis of discussion for grand jurors who wish to develop a more appropriate procedure to help their panels avoid problems that arise each year in grand jury investigations. Examples of these problems are:

- Not precisely defining investigative issues
- Not seeking appropriate legal advice before taking action
- Not realizing when a civil investigation has disclosed, or may disclose, a criminal matter
- Attempts by individual grand jurors or committees to exercise powers residing only in the panel
- Failure of investigating teams to keep the panel informed
- Not taking adequate notes of investigations
- Inadequate management of complaints and cases

Although many grand juries follow some or all of the steps in Figure D, no statute requires them to adopt the process the figure depicts. Grand juries have complete discretion in developing their investigative process. Indeed, controversy surrounds some of the steps in Figure D. For instance, in some counties, grand juries are not the first recipients of citizen complaints (step 1). In those counties, county employees such as staff secretaries are the first to see citizen complaints, as step three implies. In some counties, foremen originally receive complaints, as has been noted elsewhere, and reject or assign complaints as they please. Grand juries also differ in their practices of how and when they notify officials of an impending investigation (step 11), how often investigative teams inform the entire panel of their progress (step 13), the extent of involvement of editorial committees in reviewing draft reports (step 16), and whether they should notify complainants that they will investigate their complaints (step 5) or inform them of the progress of the investigation (step 21).

A carefully developed, succinctly expressed description of the grand jury's investigative procedures serves another important purpose: By including in their final report a brief description of how the panel decided the objectives, issues, and scope of its investigations, grand jurors assure citizens that the panel's procedures were fair. This description should include the process the grand jury adopted to ensure that the entire body reviewed, approved, and edited reports of investigative teams; the date the grand jury approved each investigation; and a statement that at least the statutory minimum number of assenting jurors approved each investigative report.

LEGALITY AND EFFECTIVENESS OF FINDINGS AND RECOMMENDATIONS

Issuing findings and recommendations in final reports is the most important means a grand jury has to achieve its civil-investigative objectives. Because the local-government officials who are affected are required to comment about them, well-conceived findings and recommendations might result in significant improvements in local-government services. Ineffective findings and recommendations, in contrast, discredit the institution, create unnecessary work for local-government officials, and eventually disillusion grand jurors.

Despite their crucial importance for the civil function, many findings and recommendations in final reports during the study period suffered from a variety of defects, as I discussed in Chapter 4. These shortcomings in findings and recommendations no doubt contributed to legislative attempts to curtail grand jury independence, which I described earlier in this chapter. If the statutory purpose of grand juries is to expose irregularities in local government, panels themselves must abide by statutes governing them. Accordingly, grand jurors should exert every possible effort to ensure that findings and recommendations in final reports are lawful. Findings and recommendations also must be improved in other respects. In this section, therefore, I offer suggestions to assist grand jurors to comply with the two provisions in Penal Code Section 916 concerning (a) accompanying problems identified in final reports with "the suggested means for their resolution, including financial," and (b) supporting "all findings included in [final reports with] documented evidence."

Obtaining Training in Estimating Costs and Documenting Findings

During their first weeks, grand jurors should request someone skilled in the subject to show them how to estimate the costs of recommendations they may make concerning local-government services, procedures, organizations, and the like. Examples of specialists who could provide assistance are:

- internal auditors
- staff members in city or county managers' offices
- performance auditors with whom the grand jury might have contracted for services

Many grand jurors also will benefit from training in how to distill findings from facts. Because Penal Code Section 916 does not define the meaning the California Legislature intended the word "findings" to convey, grand jurors must do so themselves, well before they conduct investigations and write draft reports.[38]

In this study, I use "finding" to mean a statement that has been inferred from a fact. To illustrate, consider the following numbers from a table in an annual report of the California Department of Justice. The Department of Justice report[39] shows that of 17,468 citizen complaints about police officers that local law enforcement agencies claimed they received, 1,745 concerned possible criminal matters. The table shows how many complaints about possible criminal matters were for felony crimes and how many were for misdemeanor offenses. It also reveals how many of the felony and misdemeanor complaints were "sustained" (administratively determined to be true).

For this discussion, assume that the numbers in the Department of Justice report are "facts."[40] The text accompanying the table from which these data were taken included no "findings." I present five findings, however, to illustrate how I use the term in this study. Consider first these figures from the table in the report:

Criminal Classification of Complaint	Number of Complaints	
	Reported	Sustained
Felony	782	110
Misdemeanor	963	200
Total	1,745	310

From the "facts" shown, we might infer these findings:

Finding #1: 45 percent of the 1,745 complaints were for felony offenses

Finding #2: 55 percent of the complaints were for misdemeanor offenses

Finding #3: 18 percent of the felony and misdemeanor complaints were sustained

Finding #4: 14 percent of the felony complaints were sustained

Finding #5: 21 percent of the misdemeanor complaints were sustained

In one sense, these findings are conclusions, but they are closely connected to the facts. Indeed, one might think of them as paraphrased facts. Where the facts are merely raw numbers, the findings elevate the numbers to the level of analysis. In this case, they help the reader begin to understand what the facts might imply. A conclusion, on the other hand, is more than analysis. In this example, a conclusion might speculate about causation; for example: "It seems to be more difficult to prove citizen allegations against police officers about felony matters than it is to sustain citizen complaints about misdemeanor offenses."

Of course, if the same kinds of data were available for, say, 15 police departments and 10 sheriffs' departments, one could develop far more interesting findings and conclusions about the data. For example, one might find significant differences between large and small police departments, differences between sheriffs' departments in urban and rural counties, and differences between the two types of departments. In any case, the differences would constitute findings inferred from the data. Our judgments or opinions about their implications would be conclusions, and the remedies we prescribe to deal with the problem would be recommendations.

Other Suggestions for Improving Findings and Recommendations

The example illustrates several important characteristics that apply to many findings and recommendations in final reports of the study period, namely that findings

1. should be specific, not vague;
2. should not be routine descriptions of or comments about local governments or services. Findings should be about serious matters rather than, "The desserts we sampled in the school cafeteria were delicious";
3. and conclusions, though closely connected, are different: A conclusion speculates about the implications of findings;
4. must be supported by documented evidence, as Penal Code Section 916 requires, and cited in a manner that permits readers to consult the materials if they desire; and
5. should be conspicuously numbered so readers can quickly find them in masses of text.

Recommendations suffer from many of the same deficiencies affecting findings. The examples in Chapter 4 showed that they also may be confused with findings and sometimes with conclusions, and they may be vague and difficult to identify in text. Just as some findings were not connected to documented evidence, some recommendations were not connected to findings. Some recommendations were trivial, and some were about policy matters. Many findings and recommendations were not directed to a specific person or department, and a few were misdirected. Some were lengthy, rambling statements, often as long as two or three paragraphs, and many lacked a positive, constructive tone.

An editorial committee can do much to eliminate problems affecting findings and recommendations in final reports. For example, the committee could assume the role of "devil's advocate" and, from the viewpoint of a public official, imagine the various kinds of reactions each finding or recommendation might elicit. In doing so, grand jurors might be able to correct flaws that are otherwise not obvious. The editorial committee also should ensure that recommendations represent the consensus of the panel and that none of them serves the personal interests of grand jurors.[41] The committee should not, of course, have authority to change the meaning of findings and recommendations. Only the panel has that authority.

In reviewing draft reports, grand jurors might find it helpful to think of facts, findings, conclusions, and recommendations as links in a chain, as Figure E, "Facts, Findings, Conclusions, and Recommendations: A Chain of Reasoning for Grand Jury Investigations," illustrates. In this illustration, findings are based on facts; conclusions logically flow from findings; and recommendations are supported by facts, findings, and conclusions. Thus, no recommendation should be reported unless the other links in its chain are also reported.

FACTS   FINDINGS   CONCLUSIONS   RECOMMENDATIONS

FIGURE E
Facts, Findings, Conclusions, and Recommendations:
A Chain of Reasoning for Grand Jury Investigations

CONFIDENTIALITY AND SECRECY

Because the grand jury is a deliberating body, it occasionally must discuss complaints about public officials that are bizarre, outrageous, or malicious. If grand jurors were required to deliberate in public about such matters, the reputations of many people could be damaged before the panel established the falsity of the claims. For these and other reasons, the courts consistently have upheld the secrecy of grand jury proceedings in criminal and civil matters.[42]

If "leaks" and other breaches of confidentiality and secrecy occurred during the study period, they were not obvious in the final reports. Concerns about them have arisen, however, on occasion.[43] Because of the damage such incidents can inflict on the orderly conduct of investigations, the lives of involved persons, and the independence and validity of the grand jury, grand jurors must thoroughly understand the special meaning of secrecy and confidentiality in grand jury service, including such matters as:

- types and causes of breaches of secrecy and confidentiality that may occur
- their implications (for example, suits for libel and slander, findings of contempt, and effects on people's lives and careers)
- the statutes relating to them[44]
- why confidentiality applies not only to criminal matters but also to civil investigations
- whether confidentiality ends with discharge from grand jury service
- the circumstances under which grand juries may or may not invite officials to review drafts of grand jury reports, findings, recommendations, and conclusions for accuracy before releasing a report of a civil investigation to the public[45]
- whether grand jurors may retain their notes after grand jury service
- why the names of complainants should not be included in final reports unless permission to do so has been obtained

- reviewing the grand jury code of ethics to make certain that it includes adequate provisions for secrecy and confidentiality requirements in grand jury service[46]

Grand jurors should be especially familiar with the discussion of secrecy in the *McClatchy* case.[47] In a few pages, the court summarized the historical and contemporary implications of secrecy for grand jury service. Familiarity with this discussion will help grand jurors explain to the community why the courts have consistently upheld grand jury secrecy provisions. Some citizens conceive of grand jury secrecy as being for the procedural convenience of the grand jury, for conducting sinister inquisitions outside public scrutiny, and for other unsavory purposes. In particular, members of the news media are often opposed to secrecy in any sphere of governmental activity. False charges of official misconduct that self-serving, misguided, or deranged complainants sometimes make in civil grand jury meetings would be, of course, the stuff of circulation-building news stories. The courts, however, repeatedly have emphasized the importance of secrecy in grand jury proceedings.[48]

Editorial committees should make certain that grand jury reports exclude breaches of confidentiality and secrecy. Examples of breaches that have been discussed previously are jury commentary in final reports that may expose local-government employees to physical risks, disclosures of Social Security numbers, and references to the vulnerability of local-government buildings or other places.

Practices Supporting or Jeopardizing the Collegial Nature of the Grand Jury

Earlier in this chapter, I proposed that grand jurors should devote the early weeks of their term to creating the organization and procedures that are appropriate for the collegial, deliberative nature of the institution. Many of my suggestions are presented in general terms as topics that grand juries themselves can develop. Because the grand jury is an independent body, I believe it is important that grand jurors accept responsibility for making the specific decisions that will promote careful deliberation.

Many different forces and influences will attempt to obstruct the emergence of collegiality. The person appointed as foreman, understandably, might wish to "hit the beach running"—a phrase I have heard often at Grand Jury Exchange Seminars. So motivated, the foreman immediately might create and name committees, appoint grand jurors to them, designate committee chairmen, and appoint a variety of grand jury officers. Ambitious but disappointed persons whom the court did not appoint as foremen might contend for other forms of recognition.

Occasionally, the resulting proliferation of "co-corresponding secretaries," "vice chairmen," and "assistant foremen" in a body of 19 people reminds one of military organizations in comic operas. Some people strive to attain what they consider to be the second best rank, that of foreman pro tem., and those who fail to attain that honor might settle for appointments as committee chairmen. In some cases, committee chairmen will attempt to operate their committees as small-scale grand juries. As the year progresses, committees will insist that their work be recognized, by organizing the final report as a collection of committee reports.

As these and other pressures for personal recognition develop, grand jurors who were not chairmen or officers also will want recognition for their work. To satisfy these needs, some final reports include photographs of grand jurors in committees on the first page of investigative reports. In these "vanity" final reports, the titles of the investigations are the names of committees. Similarly, in many final reports, the first information that readers see are lists of committees and their members.

The very existence of foremen's reports provides another indication of the extent to which the grand jury has failed to become a collegial body. In some cases, foremen's reports are small final reports, some even containing findings and recommendations. Similarly, and most particularly in highly fragmented grand juries, a few grand jurors even demand that they be permitted to issue "minority reports."[49] These examples are symptomatic of panels in which members failed to understand and implement the spirit of the institution embodied in its statutes and case law, and thereby thwarted the conditions conducive to independence and validity.

Community-Criteria-Related Suggestions for Improving Investigations and Reports

The qualities I selected for evaluating investigations and final reports as community documents are significance, accountability, and continuity. These are discretionary criteria; they are absent or present in final reports to the extent that grand jurors desire them.

SIGNIFICANCE

Deciding how to report the significance of an investigation is a matter of judgment. What is significant for one grand jury is insignificant for another. Some investigations during the study period were insignificant on their face. Others could have been significant but were reported sketchily and therefore seemed trivial. If grand juries neglect to explain the significance of investigations, the news media might ignore them, and public support will not develop. I do not suggest that grand jury reports be sensational, dramatic, or exciting; however, grand jurors should at least explain what social, economic, or safety, health, and security risks might have arisen if the investigation had not been reported. In a later section, I offer suggestions for designing the organization and format of a final report so grand jurors can convey in it the potential "harm" of a complaint to the community.

ACCOUNTABILITY

Several years ago, a grand jury asked me to assist it in a major civil investigation. Following administration of the oath of secrecy, I helped the panel plan and conduct a complex investigation.[50] As I worked with the grand jurors, I noticed that the investigation increasingly dominated their attention. The scope of the investigation became so large and its implications so compelling that it consumed most of the grand jury's energies and resources.

During the investigation, however, the panel assigned several of its members to conduct what some people might regard as minor investigations. One of these investigations arose from a complaint an elderly man made to the grand jury. The man's house was next to a field office of a local government, and he complained that for several years, public employees working in the field office drove across his lawn, threw trash on his property, and otherwise made his life miserable. He also claimed that when he tried several times to talk about the problem to the supervisor of the employees, that person was unresponsive. Moreover, the citizen said, the employees became hostile when he pleaded with them to be better neighbors.

Several grand jurors verified the complaint, found most of its particulars to be true, and resolved the problem with the assistance of higher-level administrators of the public agency. Later, while I assisted the grand jury in editing its draft final report, I noticed that no mention was made of this or many other so-called minor investigations. I urged the grand jurors to include at least a summary of these matters in their final report. Nevertheless, they decided not to include any reference to them, believing it would detract from the major investigation.

Later, in defending themselves against the findings and recommendations of the larger investigation, the public officials who were affected charged that grand jurors had ignored legitimate complaints from the community to complete what the officials claimed to be a "witch hunt." By not reporting details of its minor investigations, grand jurors lost an opportunity to show that though the major investigation was important, the panel also conducted other investigations that affected the lives of citizens in the community. Important though the single-topic final report was, it failed to inform citizens of their panel's efforts to improve their lives in other ways.

This incident illustrates that grand jurors should account, in final reports, for the institution's resolution of all citizen complaints unless an issue of confidentiality or secrecy prohibits this. Not only does this practice affirm the institution's traditions, but it yields another advantage: preventing the recurrence of inappropriate practices in local government. Suppose, for example, that the department head in the above incident retires, and a new administrator is hired. If no public record of the incident exists, employees might resume their earlier practice of harassing the complainant. The new administrator would be unaware of the previous incident and therefore would be unable to deal with its recurrence in a fully informed manner.

Final reports also should explain to citizens how the grand jury spent its time. Each final report therefore should include a section, preferably in the beginning of the document, briefly summarizing major grand jury activities of the year. Following is a composite list of information grand juries reported in final reports during the study year. Although reporting all this information may not be appropriate for each grand jury, much of the data would give readers a comprehensive view of how panels spent their time. Almost all the information can be reported in numerical form and may be routinely accumulated as part of the grand jury's internal case-management control system.

Examples of grand jury workload statistics are:

1. Number of investigations by origin of complaint (e.g., citizens, public officials, grand jurors)
2. Number of complaints by type of complainant and disposition of each complaint
3. Number of investigations initiated at the discretion of the grand jury
4. Number of statutorily required investigations completed
5. Number of complaints referred without further investigation to another authority
6. Number of indictments sought by the district attorney
7. Number of witnesses heard during indictments
8. Number of days the grand jury met for indictments
9. Number of true bills endorsed
10. Disposition of indictments the grand jury heard
11. Disposition of accusations the grand jury heard
12. Number of panel meetings
13. Number of hours of investigation by committee
14. Number of investigative committee meetings
15. Average number of committees on which each grand juror served
16. Number of persons interviewed during civil investigations
17. Number of reimbursed miles traveled
18. Average number of local-government meetings each juror attended
19. Average amount of witness fees each grand juror received

20. Number of interim and final reports issued
21. Number of public appearances grand jurors made
22. Number of grand jurors who served the entire term; number of resignations
23. Number of inspections, tours, and visitations conducted
24. Total number of days of attendance by all grand jurors
25. Number of hours grand jurors spent in training and source of training

CONTINUITY

Survival of the grand jury institution depends on grand jurors' distinguishing between desirable and undesirable forms of continuity. Grand jurors cannot, for example, adopt without independent investigation the findings and recommendations of their predecessors (Penal Code Section 939.9). They may, however, use that material as investigative leads or to create a system to study local-government officials' comments about findings and recommendations affecting them. Grand jurors also should not continue the committees of predecessors without careful deliberation. Continuity, then, is not desirable solely for its own sake. Some forms of continuity are appropriate; others subvert the institution.

Penal Code Section 924.4 permits panels to transmit "records, information, or evidence" of a noncriminal nature from one grand jury to the next that pertains to their civil investigations. Grand juries also have the discretion to destroy notes, draft reports, and other documents concerning civil investigations that they may have accumulated during their year. This discretion is part of the logic of each grand jury being an independent body of citizens. During their term of service, many grand jurors also learn, however, that transmitting some information from one panel to the next might improve the effectiveness of investigations and grand jury internal procedures. Each grand jury, therefore, faces the challenge of deciding what information it shall retain for its successor and what it should destroy. Examples of how grand jurors could provide continuity from one year to the next with respect to the civil function are:

- reviewing and analyzing findings and recommendations of previous grand juries, and studying and reporting public officials' comments concerning them
- verifying the achievements of predecessors and including them in final reports
- listing in procedures manuals the types of grand jury files, magazines, articles, budget documents, and the like, that should be considered for retention from one year to the next
- obtaining each year from one of its legal advisors a written opinion about what kinds of information may be retained permanently in grand jury files

- developing a manual or computer-assisted system for tracking findings and recommendations
- making certain that at least one public library receives and stores at least one copy of each final report and that a reference to the location of this archive is included in each final report

Technical Criteria

In previous chapters, the content of final reports was my concern. In this section, I offer suggestions to improve the physical features of final reports—in particular their appearance and the arrangement of their parts. Because final reports are the principal means by which most citizens learn of the work of the institution, the first impression these documents evoke in citizens' minds could determine whether final reports are read carefully or scanned indifferently. The suggestions I offer in this section therefore are based on the assumption that citizens are the primary audience for final reports and that reports must be designed for quick and easy reading and comprehension. The technical criteria are based on principles of document design and generally accepted and advocated principles of technical writing.[51]

The suggestions in this section are presented in keeping with the sequence of the 10-section format I propose for final reports rather than the relative importance of each section. Thus, the sixth, seventh, and eighth sections of the format are its heart, though the remaining sections also contribute to it. An important characteristic of the suggested format is that reports of major investigations are separate from and precede reports of minor investigations, inspections, tours, and visitations. Similarly, the format provides for including bulky supporting material in a separate section so citizens can read the text without being obstructed by such material.

A SUGGESTED 10-SECTION FORMAT FOR FINAL REPORTS

The suggestions I offer in this section for organizing individual investigative reports and the final report embody the spirit of the institution. The suggestions also will help grand jurors prevent many of the recurring problems that have been identified and discussed in previous chapters. Therefore, the suggested internal and external formats are, so to speak, devices for quality control. For example, each section of the recommended format reminds grand jurors with editorial responsibilities about the kind of information they must obtain from their fellow grand jurors as the latter proceed in their investigations. By discussing at one of their first meetings the implications of each section and subsection of the 10-part format, grand jurors also will have taken an important step in answering for themselves the question, "How do we get started?"

The suggested format conforms to established requirements of investigative reporting and is adapted to the institutional needs of the grand jury and its statutes. Some grand juries now use most of the ideas in the suggested 10-section format, though no grand jury during the study period followed the format entirely. Examples of the appearance of each section of the format will assist readers in comprehending its sequence.

Section 1: Cover and Binding

The cover of the final report should be of heavy stock. As is the case with the entire document, the cover should convey the decorum, independence, and dignity of the judiciary. The color of the cover therefore should not be garish, and the typeface should be distinctive but not ostentatious. Cartoons, amateurish artwork and photographs, and poorly designed computer art should not appear on the cover. Any seal or other symbol used should depict the grand jury or the judiciary, not the county board of supervisors or other local-government officials or agencies. The binding should permit the name of the grand jury and the year of the final report to be printed on the spine so the document can be found quickly among other publications on a bookshelf. A simple, dignified format for the cover of the final report has three elements:

1. *Title* of the final report, the year and name of the county grand jury
2. A distinctive *symbol* representing either the grand jury or the superior court
3. *Text* stating that the final report was prepared in and for the superior court of [—] County, State of California.

Section 2: First Inside Page

The first printed page of the final report displays two elements:

1. *Title* of the final report
2. *Date* of issuance

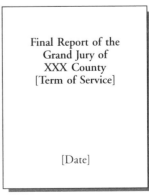

Section 3: Judge's Acceptance Statement

Signed by the current advisor judge, this statement attests that the final report complies with Title Four of the Penal Code and instructs the county clerk (Penal Code Section 933(a)) to accept it for filing as a public document. The statement supports the spirit of the institution in three ways:

1. It signifies that the judiciary has reviewed the report and approved it for publication, thereby adding validity to the document.
2. The statement emphasizes the connection between the grand jury and the judiciary, thereby separating it from county government in the public mind.
3. The statement conveys to readers that the final report is a public document and therefore is available for citizens to read.

An example of how the judge's acceptance statement might be worded is, "I certify that the XXX County Grand Jury Final Report complies with Title Four of the California Penal Code and direct the County Clerk to accept and file the final report as a public document."

Section 4: Contents and Page Numbers

This section shows each of the main sections of the report. Neither the contents section nor any other section of the report should contain committee names. As I shall discuss later, the titles of the investigations, instead, should refer to some important facet of each investigation (such as principal finding or recommendation or the name of the local-government departments, services, or functions the grand jury investigated). The titles of investigations and other divisions in the contents should correspond exactly to those used for the investigations and other divisions of the report. If the final report contains fewer than 40 or 50 pages, the contents section might be sufficient and an index may not be necessary. If an index is provided, the contents section may be less detailed.

Contents

Page
Judge's Acceptance .... [p]
Preface .... [p]
Major Investigations .... [p]
   ABC investigation .... [p]
   XYZ investigation .... [p]
Minor Investigations,
Routine Inspections, etc. ... [p]
   Inspection of XXX .... [p]
Report to the Community . [p]
Supplementary Materials ... [p]
Index .... [p]

[p]

Section 5: Preface

This one-page statement signed by the foreman on behalf of the grand jury certifies to the court and the community that each investigation received the statutorily required number of votes (Penal Code Sections 916 and 940). The suggested preface replaces what traditionally is called the "Foreman's Report." To emphasize the cohesiveness of the panel, each grand juror's signature also could be included in the lower portion of the preface. The list of signatures should not include committee assignments, titles of officers, or any indication of which grand juror was the foreman. The preface also should exclude recommendations and any other comments made in the name of the foreman or any other individual grand juror.

Section 6: Major Investigations

The two main sections of each major investigative report are the summary and the narrative section. The summary is for busy readers who wish to read only the highlights of an investigation. The narrative section provides a more complete account of the investigation, excluding bulky supporting materials that are reproduced in a later section. The summary immediately follows the title of the investigation. Thus, the order of the sections and subsections of each major investigative report is:

> Title
> Summary
>> Synopsis
>> Findings
>> Conclusions
>> Recommendations
>> Comment Requirements
> Narrative
>> Origin of the Investigation
>> Authority for the Investigation
>> Description of Local Government
>> Chronology of the Main Issues of the Investigation
>> Methods and Validity of the Investigation
>>> Principal Methods
>>> Review Process
>>> Jurisdiction
>>> Validity
>> Conclusion

Title

Just as professional auditors do not use the names of their companies or audit team members for titles of investigative reports, the titles of grand jury investigative reports should exclude names of committees and individual grand jurors. Instead, report titles should summarize some important feature of each investigation. Depending on the impression that grand jurors wish to create in the minds of readers, a title could emphasize a particularly significant finding, recommendation, conclusion, or some other feature of the investigation. Examples are as follows:

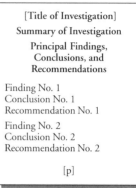

[Title of Investigation]
Summary of Investigation
Principal Findings,
Conclusions, and
Recommendations

Finding No. 1
Conclusion No. 1
Recommendation No. 1

Finding No. 2
Conclusion No. 2
Recommendation No. 2

[p]

- The principal finding of the investigation
  Example: "The Fire Chief Permitted Unauthorized Persons to Operate Official Vehicles"
- The principal recommendation of the investigation
  Example: "The Board of Supervisors Should Authorize Two More Field Officers for the Animal Control Shelter"
- The principal conclusion of the investigation
  Example: "Sheriff's Department Property Room Lacks Adequate Security"
- The principal method used in the investigation
  Example: "A Comparative Analysis of Trustees' Travel, Meal, and Entertainment Expenses in Four School Districts"
- The main emphasis of the investigation
  Example: "T-bone Steaks Are Frequently Served to the Inmates at the Vollmer Men's Facility"
- The scope of an audit
  Example: "A Review of the Smithson Unified School District's Procurement Practices and Controls Over Property"
- The name of the agency or organization investigated
  Example: "Office of the Hamilton County Superintendent of Schools"

Summary

The purpose of the summary is similar to that of executive summaries in business reports: to communicate to busy readers the principal findings, conclusions, and recommendations of an investigation separate from its supporting details. The summary may be placed in one of two locations in a final report.

1. Summaries of all investigations could be placed in a separate section at the beginning of a final report for readers who wish to review all of them at once.
2. Each summary could be placed at the beginning of the respective investigative report. Persons requiring more information about the method of the investigation, its validity, the process or organization that was studied, and similar information will find it in the narrative section of the report.

The suggested summary should be as short as possible with the following five subsections: (a) Synopsis, (b) Principal Findings, (c) Principal Conclusions, (d) Principal Recommendations, and (e) Comment Requirements.

Synopsis:

The synopsis summarizes in several sentences, as does the lead paragraph in a newspaper story, important elements of the investigation, such as who, what, why, where, and when. The synopsis is a succinct overview of the investigation and assists readers by orienting them to the remainder of the report. Busy readers also might find the synopsis useful for deciding whether to continue reading the report.

Findings:

Findings follow the synopsis and should be:
- presented in order of importance
- written concisely in one sentence each
- numbered sequentially
- displayed conspicuously
- supported in the narrative section by documented evidence (Penal Code Section 916)

Conclusions:

Although no statute requires conclusions, they help readers who wish to know the grand jury's analysis of the implications of its findings.

Recommendations:

Recommendations can follow conclusions or findings. They should be:
- presented in order of importance
- written concisely, preferably one sentence each
- logically related to at least one finding and assigned a number corresponding to the number designating the findings on which they are based
- displayed conspicuously

Comment Requirements:

Each investigation should identify the local-government official from whom comments must be received and when the comments are due. This section should include a reference to Penal Code Section 933 to help affected local-government officials understand their statutory duty to prepare comments.

NARRATIVE

The narrative section is chronological; it provides details about the investigation from start to finish. This section should be complete enough that readers could repeat each step of the investigation if they were to choose to do so—except for information that should not be revealed for confidentiality, secrecy, and security reasons. The narrative section is intended for readers who have time to read investigative details and for those who have read the summary section and wish to know how the grand jury developed its findings, conclusions, and recommendations.

Supporting materials for each investigation may be included as Section 7 of the narrative, or they may be included in a separate section of the final report following Section 7, "Reports of Minor Investigations and Routine Inspections, Tours, and Visits." This section consists of seven subsections if it includes pertinent supporting materials, or six subsections if it does not:

Origin of the Investigation:
This subsection describes how the need for the investigation came to the panel's attention—for example, whether grand jurors began the investigation on their own initiative or whether a citizen, public official, or some other person or agency filed the complaint that started it. This section, like other sections of investigative reports, should not include confidential or secret material.

Authority for the Investigation:
The grand jury describes how it concluded that it had sufficient justification to conduct the investigation; identifies the statute or statutes upon which the investigation is based; describes how the grand jury notified the person or local government of its authority to conduct the investigation; certifies that the entire grand jury voted to proceed with the investigation and that it had obtained the required number of votes to do so.

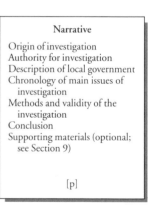

Narrative

Origin of investigation
Authority for investigation
Description of local government
Chronology of main issues of
    investigation
Methods and validity of the
    investigation
Conclusion
Supporting materials (optional;
    see Section 9)

[p]

Description of Local Government (department, agency, process, function):
This description includes sufficient information so the reader can understand the setting of the investigation—for example, a brief description of the statutory authority of the local government, agency, or function; revenue and expenditure information; staffing trends; workload information; systems, procedures, or methods relating to the purpose of the investigation.

Chronology of the Main Issues of the Investigation:
The largest of the subsections in the narrative section, the chronology provides information about the major phases of investigations, including possible causes of problems under investigation; discussion of the possible consequences of the investigation such as harm to citizens, unnecessary expenditures, potential property damage, and implications for employee morale and turnover; obstacles the grand jury may have encountered in the investigation.

Methods and Validity of the Investigation:
The grand jury informs readers of the procedures and methods it used to ensure that its findings and recommendations were developed soundly. This section has four subsections:

- Principal methods: Describes briefly but inclusively the main methods used to collect information on which findings and recommendations were based.
- Review process: A brief description of the process the grand jury adopted for reviewing, approving, and editing reports of investigative teams, and the date the grand jury approved each investigation.
- Jurisdiction: An account of how the grand jury determined that the complaint or investigation it conducted on its own initiative was within its jurisdiction. Vague statements such as "Pursuant to 925 of the Penal Code ..." are insufficient explanations.
- Validity: A summary of steps taken to ensure and verify the accuracy of facts and findings and the legality of recommendations—for example:
  - verification of facts by at least two independent sources
  - consultation with legal advisors
  - steps taken to eliminate hearsay or unsubstantiated information obtained from interviews, questionnaires, and the like
  - identification, using a standard method of citation, of the source of each fact taken from documents, publications, and so forth

CONCLUSION

The conclusion reveals the grand jury's opinion about the significance of what it found, implications for the community, and related matters.

Section 7: Reports of Minor Investigations and Routine Inspections, Tours, and Visits

Following the suggested format for major investigations is a section for minor investigations and other routine activities that resulted in either a few minor findings or recommendations or none. Advantages of providing this material in a separate section immediately following major investigations include:

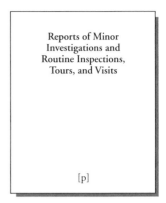

Reports of Minor
Investigations and
Routine Inspections,
Tours, and Visits

[p]

- Conserving the time of citizens who read final reports but who, for one reason or another, may not be interested in reading accounts of relatively minor matters
- Reducing the size of final reports, thereby conserving grand jury resources and encouraging citizens to read reports by making them seem less formidable
- Demonstrating to readers that grand jurors understood the need to present investigative reports in the order of their importance to their communities

An example of a format for this section is:

Name of Local Government	Date and Time of Visit	Site of Visit
City of Montmorency, Office of City Manager	October 19, XXXX 10:30 a.m. – 12 p.m.	City Hall
Green Island Irrigation District; Tour of Business Office	November 15, XXXX 3:00 p.m. – 5:00 p.m.	G.I.D. offices
Rutherford Union High School District	November 22, XXXX 2:00 p.m. – 4:40 p.m.	RUHSD Superintendent's Office

Section 8: Grand Jury Activity Report

A brief statistical summary of selected grand jury activities is the principal component of this section. Examples of activities that grand jurors could discuss for possible inclusion in this section were listed under Accountability earlier in this chapter. A brief description of the grand jury's complaint-deliberation and investigation process, significant problems the grand jury encountered, and results of grand jury assessments of public officials' comments concerning findings and recommendations in previous reports also may be included in this section.

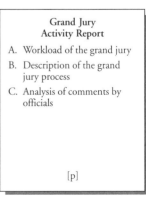

Grand Jury
Activity Report

A. Workload of the grand jury
B. Description of the grand jury process
C. Analysis of comments by officials

[p]

Section 9: Supporting Materials

Because grand jury final reports must be documented carefully, decisions about where to place lengthy tables, charts, graphs, copies of statutes, ordinances, business correspondence and memoranda, and the like must be considered. In some circumstances, grand jurors decide to place these materials within investigative reports. For example, a copy of a certain document could be placed as close as possible to a related principal finding. In this case, care must be taken to ensure that the supporting material does not interfere with readers' ability to proceed smoothly through the report.

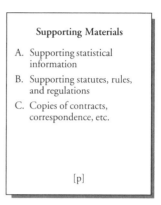

Supporting Materials

A. Supporting statistical information

B. Supporting statutes, rules, and regulations

C. Copies of contracts, correspondence, etc.

[p]

In other circumstances, bulky substantiating material also may be important, but readers do not necessarily need to inspect it within the investigative report. Material of this nature may be included in the end matter of a final report. If the material is unusually voluminous, it need not be included within a final report; however, grand jurors should state somewhere in the narrative where the material can be reviewed (for example, the grand jury office, the office of a city finance director, the office of a special district official).

Section 10: Index

Final reports longer than 40 or 50 pages should include an index. The index assists readers in quickly finding the page numbers of specific investigations; specific topics within investigations; references to local-government services, functions, and agencies; main sections of reports; references to statistical materials, and the like. The index should be placed at the end of the report, as is the customary practice.

Index

- A -
aaa, [p]
axx, [p]
- B -
bbb, [p]
bbx, [p]
bxx, [p]
- C -
ccc, [p]

- D -
ddd, [p]
dxx, [p]
- E -
eee, [p]
exx, [p]
- F -
fff, [p]
ffx, [p]

[p]

A SUGGESTED ALTERNATIVE TO TABLOID FORMATS

In the 1990s, some grand juries revived an old practice of publishing final reports as sections of newspapers or as separate inserts. The justification given for this practice is that more citizens will read final reports they find in their newspapers than will read conventionally bound and distributed copies. This is a debatable premise and one that has never been systematically evaluated.[52] A less-expensive and more readable alternative to the cumbersome and costly tabloid format is for grand jurors to abstract the principal findings and recommendations of their final report, organize them in an attractive format, and publish this document in a newspaper or at an Internet web site. The summary of the final report should include instructions to help citizens obtain the complete report if they desire to do so. Figure F, "Example of a Summary of Principal Findings and Recommendations for Publication in a Newspaper," illustrates an inexpensive alternative to publishing an entire grand jury final report in tabloid format.

EDITORIAL ORGANIZATION AND PROCESS

A well-conceived editorial process ensures that investigative reports conform to pertinent statutes and case law and adhere to grand jury policies and procedures. If grand jurors establish internal controls over their investigations early in their terms and each grand juror is fully involved in deliberating about them, the production of a final report will be a relatively effortless and effective byproduct of a well-integrated and smoothly functioning panel.

Suggested Editorial and Case-Management Tasks

Establishing an editorial and case-management-and-control committee is one method for coordinating the entire panel in its review of each detail of investigative plans, field contacts, and drafts of investigative reports. Duties of the group include:

- developing a plan and schedule for the production and distribution of the final report so it is released before the panel is discharged
- planning the internal and external organization of the final report and presenting the plan to the entire body for deliberation
- reviewing draft reports for unfair commentary, libelous statements, and unfounded allegations
- acquiring knowledge about the uses and limits of minority and interim reports if the need for considering such matters arises
- coordinating with the continuity, comment-analysis, and resources committee to track and account for all grand jury activities; documenting achievements and preparing summaries of them for publication in the final report; preparing for inclusion in the final report an analysis of comments by local-government officials to findings and recommendations of previous grand juries; and preparing for the final report a review of past budgets, expenditures, and resources of grand juries

A Report to the Community
by the
[—] County Grand Jury of [Term of Service]

Introduction

The California Legislature authorizes and requires grand juries of each county to inquire each year into the books, records, accounts, methods, systems, and procedures of designated local governments. By diligently completing its civil function (sometimes known as the "watchdog function"), your grand jury encourages local-government officials to use your tax dollars fairly and effectively. Although the Legislature does not allow grand juries to manage local government, many local-government officials carefully review and sometimes implement the findings and recommendations in grand jury final reports.

Your grand jury's final report about local-government issues this year is _____ pages long. It contains many findings and recommendations that directly concern you as a taxpayer and citizen. You may obtain your copy of the final report by [explain]. Meanwhile, here are some of the principal findings and recommendations your grand jury offered local-government officials in this year's final report to the citizens of _____ County:

- Inventory of joint powers agencies in the County; lack of accountability of such entities to electorate; recommendations to County Clerk to improve system for keeping list of such entities current.
  Finding #1:
  Recommendation #1:

  Finding #2:
  Recommendation #2:

  Finding #3
  Recommendation #3a:
  Recommendation #3b:

- Report of a survey to identify how many boards, commissions, and board-appointed special districts exist and how County officials oversee them.
  Finding #1:
  Recommendation #1:

  Finding #2:
  Recommendation #2:

  Finding #3:
  Recommendation #3a:
  Recommendation #3b:

- Report of an investigation into a citizen's complaint concerning the method of creating a redevelopment advisory committee.
  Finding #1:
  Recommendation #1:

FIGURE F
Example of a Summary of Principal Findings
and Recommendations for Publication in a Newspaper

The editorial committee must not have the authority, without panel approval, to remove material from drafts of final reports, rewrite drafts of reports, or add material to final reports. The committee, however, should have the authority to suggest changes to the panel about these matters. The editorial committee also should review draft reports for readability, documentation, and objectivity. Specifically, the committee should ensure that the writing tone of the final report is mature, objective, and dignified. Table 26, "Contrasts Between Objective and Subjective Writing Styles," depicts writing practices that support or impede objective, reader-oriented reports:

TABLE 26
Contrasts Between Objective and Subjective Writing Styles

Objective	Subjective
Respects readers' need to know sources of facts	Expects readers to accept unfounded statements on the basis of grand jurors' authority, status, and prestige
Fully cites sources of facts used in report	Does not understand documentation or believes it is unnecessary
Understands differences between facts, findings, opinions, and conclusions	Dismisses as trivial the distinction between facts, findings, opinions, and conclusions
Provides illustrations, uses examples; explains unusual words, terms, acronyms, jargon, and abbreviations	Advocates that if readers cannot understand text, they have no business reading it
Understands that the citizens of the community are the "audience" of final reports	Believes that grand jurors should write each investigative report in the jargon of public officials
Writes in a calm, dispassionate tone	Prefers emotional terms, adjectives, adverbs, invidious comparisons, etc.

Use of a Checklist for Improving Reports and Investigations

Appendix C, "One Hundred Suggestions for Improving Civil Grand Jury Investigations and Reports," incorporates many of the problems and solutions discussed in previous chapters. The suggestions in Appendix C are presented in the order of the legal, community, and technical criteria developed for this study. By familiarizing themselves with the checklist early in their terms, grand jurors can plan and conduct civil investigations that will serve the broad community interest, avoid unnecessary controversy, and defend the institution from legislative attempts to restrict its authority and independence. Public officials and other citizens also could use the checklist to determine whether grand jurors have conducted themselves in the best traditions of the institution.

Summary and Conclusion

Early in their terms, grand jurors should create procedures for conducting and reporting responsible, constructive, and valid investigations. In so doing, grand jurors will prevent legislative restrictions on grand jury independence. In the absence of collegiality, an important grand jury process—deliberation— is not possible. When deliberation is not possible, thorough consideration of facts, findings, and recommendations cannot occur.

The internal organization of grand juries should create subgroupings of panel members that are flexible enough to permit the investigation of any type of lawful complaint the grand jury receives. Grand jury internal organization also should be structured sufficiently to ensure that the panel distributes its resources evenly among the local governments within its jurisdiction.

A crucial question for grand jurors to answer before beginning any investigation is: "Do we have the necessary statutory authority?" By recognizing that no authority exists to malign or defame public officials and other citizens, grand jurors will prevent lawsuits for libel arising from final reports. Preventing libel suits will occur only if grand jurors develop a strong sense of evidence and deliberate thoroughly each word and phrase in their draft final reports.

As a community document, the final report should be a tool for greater public knowledge of the institution and account for panel activities throughout its year of service. Poorly organized reports, in which significant and trivial investigations are interspersed and that have inadequate tables of contents and no indexes, will perplex and confuse the institution's intended readers.

Although some well-planned and executed investigations were reported during the study period, the percentage of insignificant, ineffective investigations is sufficiently large to raise questions about the abilities of citizens who serve as grand jurors to create the necessary institutional arrangements for effective grand jury service. In the next chapter, I discuss several causes of ineffective final reports and propose legislative remedies to assist grand jurors in using the institution's powers to benefit their communities more fully.

7

Legislative Suggestions for Improving the Civil Grand Jury

When civil grand juries in California function well, they do so in the context of the same statutes that govern ineffective panels. Citizenship, rather than statutes, chiefly determines the quality of grand jury investigations and reports. Although statutory reform by itself will not improve grand jury investigations and reports, it will remove some of the obstacles that thwart the spirit of the institution each year. If—as I am convinced they now are—many statutes pertaining to the civil grand jury in California are disorganized and unnecessarily complex and ambiguous, they obstruct the effective exercise of citizenship in grand jury service for even the most inspired panel members. Statutory reform therefore is the central concern of this chapter, and if my proposals do not guarantee a more congenial climate for the spirit of the institution, they will at least allow grand jurors with a strong sense of citizenship to strive for it.

Later in this chapter, I offer legislative proposals to align the California grand jury more closely to the spirit of the institution. Many of these proposals augment suggestions in the previous chapters; others are about issues that have been treated only briefly elsewhere in this study but nevertheless are significant—for example, selecting grand jurors. Therefore, to help readers understand the concept of citizenship underlying each legislative proposal, I provide in the next section additional commentary about matters that were discussed previously: the spirit of the institution, its history and culture, the problem of subjectivity, certain social changes affecting the institution, and the selection of grand jurors. Stated as separate categories, these topics might seem unrelated. They will come together, however, in the legislative proposals I recommend to strengthen the California grand jury and the practice of active citizenship upon which it relies.

Institutional Origins and Characteristics

The civil grand jury often is caught between the spirit of the institution and the culture that grand jurors, public officials, and other citizens create for it. In this section, I describe how these two influences frequently clash.

THE SPIRIT OF THE INSTITUTION

The phrase "spirit of the institution" is used in this study to characterize the essential features and ideals of the grand jury set forth in its history, the case law and statutes affecting it, and its literature. Unfortunately no scholarly publication is available that distills from English and American history the spirit of the institution in both countries. Nonetheless, something of its essence can be inferred from its literature, particularly the titles of publications, catchphrases in them, and the use of expressions such as "ombudsman" and the "great equalizer."[1]

Even though the statutes granting the California grand jury its civil investigating and reporting authority in local government do not employ fanciful figures of speech, one can understand why grand jurors and other citizens might use them. Unfortunately, these idealized characterizations can shape the expectations of newly impaneled grand jurors in unproductive ways. Indeed, it has been my experience that many grand jurors are content to derive their understanding of the institution entirely from these romanticized expressions rather than from reading pertinent statutes, judicial charges, or case law. Thinking of the grand jury in idealized terms might be inspiring, but it can damage the institution by raising citizens' hopes beyond the ability of grand jurors to fulfill them.

Despite their imprecision and romanticism, these idealized words and phrases convey an important historical truth about the institution: Its purpose never has been to advance the interests of grand jurors, public officials, or the state. To the contrary, the grand jury won its place in history by intervening between the citizenry and abuses of governmental power, by fighting corrupt political systems, and by advocating changes in the administration of justice.[2]

The words and phrases that legal scholars, judges, news media staffs, and other citizens have invented to symbolize the institution are curious in this respect: None of these terms appears in the statutes that grant the institution its powers. Thus, in the absence of a clear statutory definition of institutional purpose, many grand jurors, public officials, and other citizens define the grand jury to suit themselves. Some county supervisors, for example, think of the institution as a device they can use to bestow honors upon friends or political and business associates. This is why many local-government officials are startled when a grand jury unexpectedly releases a final report inimical to their political interests: The institution has not "behaved" in the expected manner, and it therefore could be spoken of as a "runaway" panel.

Similarly, the lack of a statutory statement of the institution's independence explains why some district attorneys even today use the phrase "my grand jury." Statutory vagueness as to its nature also might explain why some grand jury foremen early in their terms attempt to fashion "their" grand jury along the lines of organizations in which they spent their careers. The spirit of the institution, however, is not to be found in the fancies or aspirations of grand jurors, public officials, or other citizens but, rather, in the history behind its statutes.

THE GRAND JURY IN HISTORY

As might be expected in so old an institution, the grand jury has changed considerably through the centuries. Its first stage of development began in twelfth-century England and lasted through the fifteenth century.[3] In this period, people whom today we call grand jurors were loyal to the monarchy—that is to say, the regime. Accordingly, the expression "grand jury independence" would have sounded strange to them. These early grand jurors seem to have been people of a higher social status than their modern counterparts, and though they often participated in the criminal-justice process of their time, their role was somewhat different from that of grand jurors before whom indictments are brought today.

For example, grand jurors of the early era were truly "rubber stamps" for ruling interests, whereas grand jurors today are more inclined to speak of their "independence."[4] Toward the end of the early era, grand juries in parts of England began exercising what we today call the local-government oversight function, but not to the extent that this function now exists in California. Usually, the discharge of this function was at the command, directly or through subordinates, of the monarch.

In the second stage of its history, the England of the sixteenth, seventeenth, and eighteenth centuries, several important changes occurred in the institution. *First,* it became more involved than it had been in the administration of justice and acquired its own terminology (for example, "accusation," "presentment," "indictment"). *Second,* although grand jurors seem not to have been as high-born as their predecessors, they probably were somewhat higher in the social order than are contemporary grand jurors in California. Grand jurors in more vulnerable social rankings would not have possessed the social-class advantages needed to assert their independence in the several dramatic episodes that distinguished the institution in this era.[5]

Third, the allegiance of grand jurors in the second stage shifted from the monarchy to the judiciary. This change seems to have accompanied the growing independence of the judiciary itself. *Fourth,* the civil function broadened. In some places, for example, grand jurors inspected roads, jails, public infirmaries and bridges, made payments to contractors and officials such as "courthouse keepers," and even kept books and accounts of certain public services.[6] The most important change, however, was that the grand jury became, at least on some notable occasions, more assertively independent:

> It is thus clear that a functional revolution in the grand jury occurred in the six centuries between the Assize of Clarendon and the adoption of the Fifth Amendment to the United States Constitution. By the time of the latter, the institution had evolved in its purest form: a citizen's tribunal, set resolutely between the state and the individual.[7]

In the United States, the third stage of grand jury evolution began early in the nineteenth century. During this era, the panel continued its formal relationship with the court, but it slowly and informally became dependent upon the prosecuting attorney. As the information replaced the indictment for initiating prosecutions, grand jury indictments were reserved for certain types of crimes, particularly those of high community interest.[8] The increased use of the information made the grand jury less a part of the routine administration of criminal justice than it had been in its first and second stages. When grand juries exercised their indictment power, it usually was in connection with investigations initiated by prosecuting attorneys of highly sensational and politically significant cases. This relationship eventually created the image of the grand jury as a puppet of prosecutors.

During this period, another trend further diminished the stature of the grand jury. In many American states, legislatures enacted statutes replacing the common law as a source of the institution's powers. In doing so, legislatures stripped the grand jury of many of its ancient common-law functions and authorized it in some American states to perform only a few minor local-government oversight tasks. Thus, the grand jury survived in some states but only as a considerably scaled-down version of what it had been in England. In California, however, the Legislature gradually broadened the panel's range of so-called watchdog powers beyond that which now exists elsewhere in the United States.[9]

In the early years of its third stage, grand jurors continued to be somewhat higher in social status than citizens at large. In this period, the term "blue ribbon" grand jury therefore often was associated with the institution. In the social order of England and the United States until the 1900s, critics who condemned the institution for its elite character enjoyed little success in changing the methods used to select grand jurors.[10] Since the end of World War II, however, legal scholars and social scientists began writing, and continue to write, critically about the undemocratic nature of grand jury selection.

Several other changes in the grand jury of recent times are of interest. For example, grand juries now are involved less frequently in investigations of fraud, graft, and corruption in state and local government than they were in the late 1800s through World War II.[11] One explanation for this diminished activity is that, unlike their predecessors, district attorneys today rarely use the grand jury to advance their political careers. Accordingly, no reason exists for seeking the publicity surrounding grand jury indictments that was so essential between the late 1800s and the late 1940s for prosecutors who aspired to higher office.[12] Contemporary grand juries therefore are less often involved in what are now referred to as "public integrity" offenses than they were before World War II.

Another explanation for the institution's formerly more active involvement in prosecuting fraud, graft, and corruption offenses is that these were topics of intense interest among the so-called Progressive reformers of an earlier time, many of whom served as grand jurors. For a variety of reasons, fraud, graft, and corruption in local government today arouse less public concern than they did in previous decades, perhaps because citizens have come to accept them as ineradicable facts of civic life. Many of the elements of the "good government" principles that Progressives espoused in the 1900s (for example, home-rule charters, the measurement of productivity, viewing nepotism as a corrupting influence) are rarely issues that citizens discuss today.[13]

The rise of a professional class of public administrators, internal auditors, performance auditors, and government researchers and analysts also has made inroads on the institution.[14] Fifty or 60 years ago, for example, few California counties and cities employed "county administrators," "city managers," or persons with similar titles. Grand jurors therefore often recommended in final reports the kinds of changes or improvements in local-government administration that later became the province of professional administrators. Indeed, grand juries sometimes urged boards of supervisors or city-council members to hire chief administrative officers to manage daily governmental operations.[15]

As this brief sketch of the institution's history has shown, the idealized view of the grand jury has a foundation. Indeed, in California, the range of its authority, jurisdiction, and case law defines the grand jury as a potentially formidable instrument for civic improvement. Nevertheless, one of the institution's greatest shortcomings is that citizens impaneled as grand jurors often are uncertain as to its true nature. Thus, the statutory ambiguity that surrounds the institution together with a grand jury culture are often more potent in defining what the institution becomes at the hands of newly appointed grand jurors than are the spirit of the institution, its statutes, or its case law.

GRAND JURY CULTURE

A striking quality of many grand jury final reports year after year is their mediocrity. If, for example, one studies 10 successive final reports of the same grand jury, one might find that only one of them is relatively free of the problems revealed in this study. I have never been able to obtain the information needed to explain conclusively how it happens that effective grand juries are so infrequently impaneled.[16] An equally interesting question is why in some of California's largest and most affluent counties the amount of money a grand jury spends[17] has no consistent relationship with the quality of final reports.[18]

Among possible explanations for these variations, one stands out as particularly useful: the grand jury culture. By "culture" I refer to the mostly unrecorded beliefs, attitudes, and expectations that constitute the social, economic, and political environment of any institution. A grand jury culture, of course, can be beneficial if it comports with the spirit of the institution. If it does not, we would expect to find that it serves less worthy purposes. Good or bad, the culture is maintained and transmitted by a variety of means, including:

- the tone in which handbooks or procedures manuals are written; how these documents express the powers of the institution and describe its limitations, and what might be intentionally or inadvertently omitted from them[19]
- how well informed the county employees are who are assigned as support staff to the grand jury and upon whom newly appointed grand jurors rely for their initial orientation and information, and whether these persons understand and respect the institution
- formal and informal relationships with public officials, former grand jurors (either as individuals or members of associations), local civic groups, other interest groups, and the news media
- whether the local judiciary regards the grand jury as an annoying anachronism or as a vital element in the civic life of the community, how the court's point of view is communicated in its charge to newly impaneled grand jurors, and what kinds of relationships an impaneling judge wishes to maintain with the grand jury he or she has appointed

The culture of a grand jury is shaped by another force: the discrepancy between the spirit of the institution as embodied in statutes and case law and what newly appointed grand jurors want the institution to be. Depending on how closely their expectations align with the spirit of the institution, grand jurors will create either a panel that fulfills the institutional ideal or that serves other purposes. Of course, subversion of the institution in any year might begin well before a court impanels grand jurors. For example, citizens might volunteer for grand jury service for a self-serving objective.[20] Or, as the grand jury year proceeds, persons identifying themselves as former grand jurors may make public statements implying that their prior service cloaks them with a special relationship to the sitting grand jury.[21]

In counties where former grand jurors have, or seem to have, close ties with sitting grand juries, the institution could be compromised by becoming a pawn in a political battle.[22] Former grand jurors or other people who exploit, or attempt to exploit, the institution may claim that they do so for a worthy purpose. Nevertheless, when their efforts are publicized, they become part of the lore of the community and add to any reservations citizens might have about the tradition of grand jury independence in their county.

Some types of assaults on the integrity of the institution are less direct than the foregoing examples. They become apparent only after one has observed individual grand juries over a span of time. For example, years ago a grand jury began to sponsor an essay contest among the school districts of its county. The stated purpose of the contest was to help students learn about the institution, and the public at large therefore would be better informed about it. Each year, the final reports of that county included students' prize-winning essays, most of which portrayed a shallow understanding of the institution.

Given the longstanding emphasis in this county on the ceremonial features of grand jury service, the essay contests seemed to serve more than an educational purpose. Final reports often included several photographs of grand jurors, students, and public-school teachers and administrators attending the award ceremonies for the essay winners. I also noticed that the grand jury sponsoring the contests rarely reported factual inquiries into the county's school districts but often included glowing commendations of various public-education practices, general statements about the need for more funds for school districts, and assurance to citizens of the county that, despite severe budget problems, schools continued to provide "quality" education. The high point in this grand jury–school district partnership occurred several years ago when a final report included an admiringly written "profile" of a school district official who was running for office during the panel's term. In short, the grand jury had slowly evolved into an advocacy body for public education as a consequence of its institutionalized ceremonial nature.

Final reports do not reveal directly how practices such as the essay contest become part of a grand jury culture. In some cases, however, important clues can be found outside of final reports. Several years ago, for example, I was unable one year to obtain a grand jury final report from a certain county despite several mailed requests. This was a grand jury whose final reports interested me each year for several reasons:

1. Although the grand jury is in a large, urban county that is often plagued by news media reports of various local-government controversies, grand jury final reports of that county rarely address these problems.

2. Considering the intellectual resources in this county, one would expect grand jury final reports to rival those of performance auditors. Yet, few investigations in the final reports of the grand jury of this county are of substantial content.

3. Final reports focus almost entirely on county government, despite the existence of several large cities and special districts in the county.
4. The formats of final reports vary little from one year to the next. The documents are always of about the same thickness, typestyles, and text formatting, and the names of the categories that designate different sections of each investigative report change little each year. Typographically, it would seem that somewhere in a county computer, a software template exists into which each year someone types the grand jury final report.

A plausible explanation for this unremitting uniformity and mediocrity presented itself when, after being sent from one county-government office to the next during the several hours of my search for the grand jury office, I finally found someone who thought it might be in a building several blocks away from the main county complex. Upon entering the structure to which I was referred, I saw on the building directory no mention of the grand jury, but a floor number was shown for a branch of the district attorney's office. I took the elevator to the designated floor, and as I left the elevator, a sign on the wall directly ahead of me read:

> OFFICE OF THE DISTRICT ATTORNEY
> Grand Jury

Of course, a sign on a wall is not conclusive proof that grand jurors think of themselves as being subordinate to the Office of the District Attorney. The sign does, however, raise the question of whether grand jurors or the judiciary in that county understand its implications for independence of the institution.

In any county, one also can find clues to the grand jury's status in the location, design, and furnishings of its meeting room. In one county, the grand jury meeting room was for many years in the main county building. Following several well-publicized conflicts between the grand jury and the Board of Supervisors, the latter body caused the grand jury meeting room to be moved from the central courthouse complex to a site some 15 miles distant. In still another county, one of the largest in the State, the grand jury has no permanent meeting room, no file cabinets, and no permanent telephone number or mailing address. Each time the grand jury desires to meet, its members must seek a suitable vacant room in the courthouse or some other location.

The temperament of the county employee, if any, whom the courts have assigned to the grand jury also can have an important influence on its culture. Several years ago, a foreman in a small, mid-State county was successful during his term of service in obtaining a permanent office and a part-time secretary for the grand jury. After he and his fellow grand jurors moved into the office, the newly hired part-time secretary informed the foreman where his desk would be. Using a marking pen, she drew a line on the wainscoting to designate what portion of the room the grand jury could occupy and what floor space would be hers. For several months, the foreman and his fellow grand jurors had to contend with similar behavior, and the foreman later recalled that the secretary's conduct added to the many problems besetting the panel. Fortunately for the institution, the secretary's impolitic behavior eventually resulted in her assignment to another county office. Her replacement had better social and technical skills, and in recent years, final reports have included favorable comments about her management of grand jury files, her word processing skills, and her knowledge of county business procedures. Indeed, grand jury final reports sometimes refer to "the grand jury administrator" as "our twentieth grand juror," a practice that raises questions of another order about panel independence.

Selected Institutionalized Problems and Their Solutions

In offering these examples of grand jury culture, I have attempted to illustrate how the social context within which the institution must function affects it. Equally important are two additional sets of problems closely related to the concept of citizenship: (1) subjectivity and (2) grand jury selection. A consideration of these two topics will assist readers in evaluating the statutory reforms I offer in the next section.

THE PROBLEM OF SUBJECTIVITY

The common-law grand jury of the past and the statutory grand jury of today share at least one characteristic: Both were intended to be deliberative fact-finding bodies. In California, this conception of the institution is implied in various statutory requirements such as retiring "to a private room … [to] inquire into the offenses and matters of civil concern cognizable by it" (Penal Code Section 915) and ensuring "that all findings included in its final reports are supported by documented evidence" (Penal Code Section 916).

Examples of Statutory Vagueness and Ambiguity

Unfortunately, the words I have just quoted from Penal Code Section 916 are almost the only guidance for grand jurors with respect to conducting and reporting factual investigations. The same statute authorizes grand jurors to establish their "rules of procedure," but it does so only vaguely and thereby exposes the institution, grand jurors, and public officials to considerable risk. To encourage grand jurors early in their terms to consider carefully what rules of procedure might enhance objectivity and therefore institutional effectiveness, the Legislature could have included in Penal Code Section 916 additional examples of specific procedures, such as

> guidelines for preventing and resolving conflicts of interest within each grand jury, the retention and destruction of documents at the end of the grand jury term, and the method each grand jury adopts to ensure that all correspondence, complaints, and other communications are received at the same time by the entire panel and are properly considered and deliberated.

In offering this suggestion, I do not advocate that the Legislature should attempt to provide all the institution's rules of procedure. I merely suggest that adding several more examples of such rules to the existing statute will emphasize the need for comprehensive procedures to ensure objectivity and thereby prevent many of the problems disclosed in this study.

Penal Code Section 916 contains another serious oversight. Although it requires that all "findings included in ... final reports are supported by documented evidence," it fails to define what is meant by "findings." For some people, "findings" are synonymous with "facts." For others, "findings" are the inferred implications of "facts." In some settings, "findings" means the entire report of an investigation or refers to the results of a judicial or administrative proceeding. It seems likely that in Penal Code Section 916 the Legislature intended "findings" to refer to the implications of the facts, not to facts themselves. Otherwise the phrase in Penal Code Section 916 that requires "all findings included in its final report [to be] supported by documented evidence" would be equivalent to saying that all facts should be supported by facts.

As I shall discuss in the "Raw Evidentiary Material" section below, however, some confusion arises each year in grand jury service about the difference between "facts" and "findings." The Legislature could correct this confusion by making clear in pertinent statutes the meanings it wishes the word "findings" to convey.

The wording of Penal Code Section 930 (denying grand jurors immunity from prosecution for their comments in final reports about unindicted persons) is another example of statutory vagueness. For example, the statute does not use the words "libel" or "slander," or even the phrase "defamation of character." Therefore, anyone who wishes to know what statutes govern unfair comment in grand jury service would not find them indexed under those words or phrases. Although Penal Code Section 930 would have meaning to persons trained in the linguistic subtleties of the law, many grand jurors would begin to understand the implications of the statute only after some months of grand jury service.[23]

By enacting Penal Code Section 930, the Legislature left grand jurors with essentially three options in deciding whether to conduct an investigation:

1. Avoid the possible consequences of a libel suit by not conducting it.

2. Conduct and report the investigation in a trivial manner so it offends no one.

3. Proceed with it and hope that no lawsuit arises.[24]

Suppose, for example, that grand jurors decide to investigate what seems at the outset of a complaint to be a routine issue. As the investigation proceeds, grand jurors begin to wonder if what they have discovered is evidence of one or more crimes, whether it is a breach of ethics short of being a crime, or whether the case is some form of "willful or corrupt misconduct" (Government Code 3060). Assume, also, that for some reason no legal advisor is willing to assist grand jurors in the investigation, as sometimes is the case. In this example, grand jurors would be left to their own devices to decide how to conduct the investigation. Unless one or more panel members has the necessary knowledge to guide the body, chances are that no mention of the matter will be found in its final report.

Nothing illustrates the troubling uncertainty of grand jury service better than an incident that occurred in a Northern California county about midway in the grand jury year. Faced with the possibility of conducting a politically risky investigation, several grand jurors sought from their legal advisors assurance that, if anyone were to sue the Grand Jury, the County insurance program would include them and that the County would pay for their legal expenses. When no public official would provide such assurance, one grand juror resigned because of "the possibility of being sued and left high and dry."

In commenting about this issue, the Grand Jury Foreman observed, "There is something inherently wrong with the notion that you would be denied representation by the very county you are working for." The Foreman also noted that the procedures manual for the Grand Jury emphasized that grand jurors are neither employees of the County nor judicial officials; rather, they are "vendors."[25] I cite this example because the issue of insurance coverage for grand jurors arises year after year, and no statute addresses this problem in the context of grand jury service.

Taken together and in combination with the confusion concerning "raw evidentiary material" that I discuss below, Penal Code Sections 916 and 930 provide little guidance to help grand jurors decide what may or may not be libelous in their final reports. For example, if no statute specifically requires findings to be based on documented facts in final reports, what implications does this have for issuing reports about inept or dishonest public officials? Suppose a grand jury has proof that Department Head Smith in a 10-year period repeatedly drove a County vehicle to another state for recreational purposes. Perhaps, for example, the panel has obtained motor-pool trip tickets documenting these excursions. Would some legal advisors consider this evidence to be "raw evidentiary material" and advise grand jurors to exclude it from their final report and include only the undocumented "finding" that

Department Head Smith misused county equipment? In this case, how would citizens, including Department Head Smith, know whether the grand jury was justified in publishing its "finding"?

Deciding when evidence may be reported lawfully in final reports often requires legal advice. If, however, legal advisors decline to assist grand jurors in the example I have described, what recourse does the panel have? If it publishes such material, and Department Head Smith threatens to sue the panel for libel, to whom do grand jurors turn for legal assistance? If, before they publish their final report, grand jurors attempt to search the Penal Code statutes pertaining to the grand jury but find no reference to libel, what will they conclude? That if no statute expressly addresses libel, its omission means that the panel members are exempt from prosecution for committing it?

Of course, much more could be written about the problem, but I wish only to make this point: From the perspective of a reasonably intelligent citizen impaneled for grand jury service, the statutes offer little guidance for preventing libel and many other troublesome issues that persistently arise every year. Given that few people, grand jurors included, do not relish the thought of a lawsuit, one might expect that panel members faced with such uncertainties would conduct only shallow investigations. This response could explain the triviality of many grand jury final reports, just as the same uncertainty about libel laws has a chilling effect on newspapers.[26]

Later in this chapter I offer several suggestions for eliminating statutory vagueness—a source of considerable confusion for grand jurors in conducting investigations. Before doing so, however, I believe readers will be better able to assess the feasibility of my legislative proposals if they understand another example of the uncertainties that grand jurors must face in conducting investigations and issuing reports.

The "Raw Evidentiary Material" Problem

In 1988, a California court published a case in which it held that a grand jury could not reveal in its final report certain "raw evidentiary material" it acquired in an investigation conducted under the guidance of a district attorney.[27] The case was a quasi-criminal matter rather than a routine civil investigation. As the court described the proceeding in its ruling, the panel's involvement in the investigation resembled grand jury hearings conducted by district attorneys into suspected criminal matters, including obtaining information from sworn witnesses in secret "closed door" sessions. Nothing in the case, however, suggests that the fact-finding hearings reached the indictment stage. Nevertheless, an appellate court upheld a superior court judge who had expunged certain material concerning the investigation from the grand jury final report before its release, arguing that publication of the material would have been improper.

Expungement of the material seems to be a reasonable exercise of judicial authority in this instance. I believe, however, that the appellate court's use of the phrase "raw evidentiary material," without explaining clearly what the term meant, inadvertently created confusion about what grand jurors may or may not include in final reports. The principal holding of the case was that grand jury reports must contain only findings, not "raw evidentiary material," and the court defined "findings" vaguely and without example as something distilled from evidence.[28] After the "raw evidentiary material" stricture entered the grand jury culture, many grand jurors (and perhaps their legal advisors) seem to have concluded that even routine civil grand jury investigations must not contain facts, but only findings inferred from facts. This ruling might explain to some extent why final reports often are devoid of the documentation that Penal Code Section 916 requires.

Although the subjectivity problem is not entirely attributable to the *McClatchy* case, the use of facts in reports about routine civil investigations seems to have decreased since its publication. Thus, many reports of routine civil investigations contain only statements of opinion, undocumented conclusions, or "findings" not supported either by reported facts or citations to them, thereby depriving readers of any means for judging their validity. Besides being contrary to the general principles of factual investigation and reporting in almost every profession or discipline, this trend contravenes Penal Code Section 916, requiring each grand jury to adopt procedures to "ensure that all findings included in its final reports are supported by documented evidence." In developing its position, the court regrettably did not reconcile its "raw evidentiary material" holding in the *McClatchy* case with the "documented evidence" requirement of Penal Code Section 916.

After the court issued its "raw evidentiary material" holding, I noticed that the incidence of subjectivity in grand jury reports increased. Apprehensive that this trend eventually would result in a successful libel case against grand jurors, thereby further eroding the legitimacy of the institution, I tried to obtain opinions from legal advisors to grand juries about the effects of the court's holding on grand jury investigations and reports. None of them offered an opinion about my analysis. As persons well trained to distinguish fact from opinion, legal advisors might not understand why citizens serving as grand jurors would not understand these concepts. It also is possible that legal advisors think that because they review drafts of grand jury reports, grand jurors need not be concerned about such matters. As the following quotation from a final report shows, however, the implications of *McClatchy* also were confusing for some legal advisors. Shortly after issuance of the *McClatchy* case, a final report included a statement of "thanks" to legal advisors who tried to

> help the grand jury understand as best we could the case of *McClatchy Newspapers v. Superior Court* (1988) 44 Cal.3d 1162. As a result, we have not

included in any of the reports the names of people interviewed or the names of the committee members doing the investigation. This is a departure from past practice, but is done in the spirit of protecting those who come before the jury.[29]

Excluding the names of persons interviewed may or may not be consistent with *McClatchy*, depending on the nature of the interviews. The *McClatchy* case, however, does not address the issue of when grand jurors' names should not be revealed.

Eventually, the confusion concerning the "raw evidentiary material" holding resulted in passage of Penal Code Section 929 in 1998, a decade after the issuance of *McClatchy*. The irony of this "corrective" legislation is its narrow focus on the peculiar circumstances of the *McClatchy* case and its failure to address directly the central problem of the statutes concerning the California civil grand jury: the lack of emphasis on factuality. To some extent, the subjectivity problem can be corrected statutorily, and in a later section I offer legislative suggestions to improve the factuality of final reports. No amount of corrective legislation will succeed, however, if judges do not impanel fair-minded, impartial, and knowledgeable citizens for grand jury service. To understand why the quality of the grand jury "manpower pool," so to speak, is so important for the institution, we must consider the effects of certain social trends on it.

THE EXPERIENCE-AND-RESOURCE PROBLEM

Grand jurors typically conduct civil investigations in one of two ways. The first method, which is rarely used, is for grand jurors to wait for other persons (for example, public employees, the news media, and other citizens) to present to them, in a formal hearing, evidence, facts, documentation, and so forth, about matters of concern. In this method, grand jurors presumably would retire after these proceedings to their "private room" to deliberate about the evidence, sift fact from fiction, detect bias, identify additional needed documentation, and request subpoenas to obtain it, if necessary.[30]

Having assessed the evidence at hand, the panel would deliberate and vote in secret about its findings and recommendations and issue a public report about them. If a sufficient amount of the evidence brought before grand jurors is lawful and otherwise adequate for the investigation, their task is relatively simple, particularly if the district attorney has guided them through the process.

The method just described is roughly similar to how a trial jury obtains and considers information. The work of civil grand jurors in California, however, is usually unlike that of their counterparts in the criminal-justice system. The second, and most often used, method to conduct civil investigations is for grand jurors to obtain evidence through their own efforts, unlike trial jurors who examine verified facts that trained investigators have brought before them.[31] In some ways, therefore, the knowledge and skills that citizens impaneled as civil grand jurors require for conducting successful fact-finding missions are of an even higher order than that which trial jurors need.

In the rarely reported cases in which a district attorney, a county auditor, or a hired professional analyst has assisted grand jurors in conducting investigations, issues such as the quality of evidence, what kinds of evidence to use, and how facts are verified, are attended to by specialists. About all grand jurors must worry about in these circumstances is that the skills of the persons who assist them are sufficient to protect panel members from publishing risky final reports. Unfortunately, grand juries rarely enjoy throughout an investigation the help of independent professional investigators. As a result, the quality of most grand jury final reports is the direct consequence of the citizenship skills that grand jurors do or do not possess.

Decline of the "Blue Ribbon" Grand Jury

One reason the institution in the several decades before World War II acquired prestige and fame is that grand juries of that time usually were "blue ribbon" panels. Because grand jurors often were drawn from a certain social stratum, that of the business world, they were familiar with financial matters, writing objective reports, and the like. For these individuals, examining columns of figures, drawing conclusions from them, and inferring logical and practical findings and recommendations from facts are conventional business skills, easily transferable to grand jury service.

It may well be, as some critics claim, that blue-ribbon panel members used these skills selectively, avoiding investigations that might harm their friends, business interests and associates, and their political allies. When they did conduct investigations into matters of import, however, they generally did so more effectively than do their counterparts today. It is no accident that the era in which the American grand jury accumulated its greatest prestige was during its blue-ribbon stage, judging by accounts of grand jury activity of that time.[32]

For better or worse, blue-ribbon grand juries, during their heyday, also had closer ties with district attorneys than is the case today. With trained investigators and lawyers routinely assisting them, grand jurors faced fewer risks in conducting investigations than they do today when they often plan and undertake civil investigations without professional assistance.[33] In short, the democratization of the institution, while worthy in many respects, has not been without costs. For example, some California panels include large numbers of currently employed or retired public employees. These people may be hard-pressed to undertake vigorous, impartial investigations into the local governments employing them or from which they retired. They either might wish to protect their past or present colleagues from grand jury inquiry, or they might believe they have grievances to settle with supervisors, administrators, or elected officials.

The inability of the courts to find sufficient numbers of business owners and managers to impanel is a recurring problem. This is especially true for small private businesses in which the hour-by-hour involvement of owners or managers is crucial. The presence of large numbers of elderly people on grand juries also is a chronic problem, both in terms of demographic balance and ability to serve. Unfortunately, the debilities of age sometimes offset the experience and wisdom that senior citizens can bring to grand jury service. Of course, every civil grand jury can accommodate a small number of aged and infirmed members, but when they dominate a panel, the spirit of the institution could suffer.

Changes in Education

Another problem that restricts the institution in the current era consists of certain changes in educational philosophy. The rise of specialized high school and college courses in "critical thinking" is the result of those changes and the widespread concern that fewer and fewer Americans have the ability to reason effectively. Although a sizable body of literature has developed around this problem, I shall describe its consequences using only a few examples of my experiences in training grand jurors.[34]

In the late 1970s through the mid-1980s, when several former grand jurors and I began training newly appointed grand jurors, we created a number of small group sessions dealing with specific public services. During this period, grand jurors who enrolled in our 2½-day programs selected 4 or 5 sessions to attend from a list of 30 or more choices. For example, the agenda for the August 1985 Grand Jury Exchange Seminar included 35 different small-group sessions; among the topics were:

- How to Study a Police Department
- How to Read a School District Budget
- Foster Care and Adoption Problems
- Welfare Departments and Their Management
- Child Abuse: the County Government Response
- County Health Department Problems and Solutions
- Purchasing Issues and Problems in Local Government
- Environmental Health Issues
- Treasury Cash Management
- How to Study Sheriffs' and Coroners' Departments

As the years passed, the persistence of problems in final reports convinced me that, although some grand jurors benefited from the general information they acquired in the subject-matter sessions, many of them needed training in conducting factual investigations (for example, how to interview; how to find, verify, and corroborate information; how to design questionnaires; how to design tables, charts, and graphs). Accordingly, the Seminar began to de-emphasize small-group sessions about specific local-government services. In their place, we developed workshops and forums about the information and skills needed to conduct and report civil investigations. Despite the increased number of investigative-methods presentations in the Seminars, however, subjectivity continued to characterize many grand jury final reports.[35]

Comments that grand jurors often made at the Seminars began to illuminate some of the causes of the subjectivity problem. Frequently, for example, grand jurors expressed impatience at the emphasis we placed on the painstaking efforts they must exert to verify facts. To illustrate the difficulty that grand jurors often have in understanding the concept of proof, I shall cite only one example from many. During a Seminar, a group of grand jurors objected to several sentences from a final report I displayed to illustrate a possibly libelous statement. Although I did not identify in my presentation the source of the example, the grand jurors recognized that the quotation was from the final report of the panel preceding theirs. They objected strongly to my comment that the statement ("several county employees in the … department complained that their supervisor drank alcoholic beverages on duty") could have exposed the panel to a libel suit. In defense of their predecessors, the grand jurors argued that if only one employee had complained about the alcoholism of a supervisor, the statement might be questionable. They insisted, however, that because several interviewees made similar claims about the same person, further efforts to verify the assertions were unnecessary.

To help grand jurors acquire a sense of evidence, we tried another training strategy: We invited professional management or performance auditors to speak at the Seminars. We thought that if grand jurors were to become familiar with some of the fact-finding techniques that auditors use, new panel members would acquire at least the rudimentary skills of documentation, verification, corroboration, and validation. We realized, of course, that several hours of training were not equivalent to the much more extensive time required to train expert investigators.

One result of exposing grand jurors who attended the Seminars to the work of performance and management auditors became evident in final reports. Many grand juries adopted the format for organizing their investigative reports that performance and management auditors often use for organizing their reports. Thus, sections of grand jury investigative reports might be designated by terms such as: "Findings," "Condition," "Criteria," "Effect," "Cause," and "Recommendations." Although some grand juries used these formats effectively, too many final reports confirmed that organizing a report in a highly structured format does not by itself ensure objectivity.

Frequently, the text in sections of final reports bore little resemblance to the titles of the sections of the reports. A section titled "Findings," for example, might actually contain undocumented opinions, and the text under the heading "Recommendations" might contain findings, and so on. Even worse, some grand jurors might have interpreted the absence of a section labeled "Facts" in the reporting format that auditor-presenters advocated at the Seminars as a justification for excluding facts from reports. Although we eventually abandoned training grand jurors in using this format, it entered into the grand jury culture and often is now used in final reports (see Table 21, Chapter 5).

Attitudes Toward Government

As the Seminars added more and more information about fact finding and reporting, we gained new insights into how well citizens were prepared for grand jury service, their expectations about their work as grand jurors, and their grasp of the spirit of the institution at the beginning of their terms. The comments that some of them made in the evaluation forms we asked them to complete at the end of each annual Seminar illustrate some of the attitudes among grand jurors with which the spirit of the institution must contend and how some grand jurors define citizenship:

> I'm too busy to learn all this stuff about the law. If we need to know about the law, our [county employee serving as the] secretary will tell us. That workshop about how to use the law library was a waste of time. If we need to know how to investigate something, we'll ask the department head.

> [Local government officials] are poorly paid and grand juries should do everything possible to give them the support they need. Leave the criticisms to the experts. Grand juries should spend more time complimenting public officials and public employees for the fine work they do.

> Someone must think we're supposed to be junior G-men. Citizens have no business asking government officials questions about what they're doing. That's why we have elected officials.

> You spend too much time on the law. That's the problem with government today, too much regulation. All that time you spent on libel you must think your job is protecting bureaucrats and public officials.

> Your approach is too conservative. If we spent all that time planning investigations and double-checking everything, we'd never get anything done. Let the chips fall where they may!

Of course, it is difficult to say how many of the approximately 1,000 grand jurors who are impaneled each year in California would agree with these sentiments. If a grand jury has several people who strongly hold such attitudes, their more objective colleagues likely will have trouble initiating and conducting impartial investigations. Moreover, if consensus concerning findings and recommendations is sought among a quorum of grand jurors who hold such views, a vague, superficial, and subjective final report would be the likely result.

The examples I have offered are a small sample of similar statements I have encountered among grand jurors at Seminars. Short of conducting survey research into the extent of such beliefs, I cannot offer empirical evidence concerning their representativeness and their effect on grand jury procedures and practices. I believe, however, that these attitudes account for many of the persistent problems I have discussed previously. The existence of viewpoints such as these also emphasizes the importance of grand jury selection for the spirit of the institution.

Selecting Grand Jurors: Some Problems and Solutions

Articles about grand juries that appear in the press and in scholarly journals sometimes criticize how the courts select citizens to serve on panels. Although much of the criticism pertains to the indictment function, selecting grand jurors for the civil function is also a matter of occasional concern for grand jury observers. As one expressed it:

> If some sectors of the community ... are systematically underrepresented on our grand juries, then the grand jury's activities will be skewed. The interests of all will not necessarily be served. The body can be an instrument for partisan decisionmaking or be subject to governmental manipulation.[36]

Here is another example of how commentators see the importance of selecting civil grand jurors: "Wielded by an energetic and conscientious panel of jurors, [the civil grand jury] is probably the people's biggest deterrent to and most powerful weapon against malfeasance in office."[37]

An Example of Criticism

Although little research has been reported about selecting civil grand jurors, the observations of one writer more than 50 years ago typifies the criticism found today in legal periodicals and newspaper articles. Edwin Lemert, a sociologist, reviewed grand jury final reports issued between 1929 and 1945 in Los Angeles County. Lemert concluded that the "businessman outlook of the grand juries has been very obvious in their reports with reference to such things as government economy, real estate assessments, taxes, labor unions, and relief, welfare and school expenditures."[38]

Lemert's analysis of the selection of Los Angeles County grand jurors followed the sociological fashion of its day, including the proposition that one's source of income affects one's outlook on life. Unfortunately, Lemert did not extend his analysis to the implications of impaneling the employees of local governments within the jurisdiction of the grand jury. Thus, his concern about self-interest and objectivity was restricted to only one economic category.

Although Lemert urged judges to impanel more representative grand juries, he did not describe in detail the selection procedure the courts used during the period of his study, nor did he assess that procedure in terms of pertinent statutes. Consequently, Lemert's principal objection to how the courts selected grand jurors was not that unlawful selection procedures were used but only that a certain class of citizens became grand jurors. Although Lemert's study is now a half-century old, its main theme is still current, judging by newspaper feature stories that occasionally are written concerning the Los Angeles County Grand Jury and other panels in California.[39] Because the selection of grand jurors is the subject of criticism so frequently, some reform is necessary to ensure the integrity of the institution. Before I present my suggestions pertaining to grand jury selection, a review of current statutes concerning this matter will be helpful.

Statutory Provisions

The most important feature of the Penal Code sections that govern the selection of grand jurors is that they grant superior court judges great discretion. In the same county, for example, a judge could use one method for selecting grand jurors one year and a different method the next year. In the same county, then, the superior court could impanel successive grand juries:

- in which half the jurors are replaced every six months (Penal Code Section 908.2)[40]
- that consist of some grand jurors who, like trial jurors, have been selected randomly and some grand jurors whom the court has chosen from a list of people compiled by elected and appointed local-government officials
- that are drawn completely at random (except for those persons statutorily exempted)

It also is lawful for a grand jury to consist entirely of individuals who have volunteered for grand jury service.[41] Further, the flexibility of existing statutes allows a grand jury to consist of persons who are all close relatives of one local government official. Given the vagueness of the existing selection statutes, these statements pertaining to the character and quality of panel members may be made:

- No statutory requirement exists for objectively assessing prospective grand jurors for their knowledge of local government and pertinent statutes, nor for their intelligence, thinking and writing ability, or any other knowledge or skill relevant to grand jury service.[42]

- No statute requires full public disclosure of the method used to select grand jurors.
- The same 10 individuals may be grand jurors year after year, provided that they do not serve for a year following their second term.
- No exemptions preclude from grand jury service persons who work for local governments within the institution's jurisdiction, or who are related by blood or marriage to elected or appointed public officials, or who may have current business dealings with local government.
- The optional requirement for randomness in grand jury selection governs only the manner by which names are drawn from the final pool of grand jury candidates; therefore, grand jurors may be men and women whose names have been drawn randomly from a carefully selected group of political allies and associates of the local-government officials whose operations panel members will inspect.

Penal Code Section 903.4 provides another example of the wide latitude that judges enjoy in selecting grand jurors. This statute permits judges to ignore "any names from the list returned by the jury commissioner" and instead "make all or any selections from among the body of persons in the county suitable and competent to serve as grand jurors regardless of the list returned by the jury commissioner."

Statutory vagueness permits judges to select individuals for grand jury service who have actual or potential conflicts of interest, multiple convictions for misdemeanor crimes, and inadequate physical or intellectual capabilities. Of course, a judge who desires to do so can use the same statutes to select grand jurors with excellent backgrounds, who are highly motivated citizens, and who fairly represent a cross-section of the population of the county. In practice, however, the manner in which grand jury selection was conducted in a central California county in a recent year illustrates procedures used, in whole or in part, for grand jury selection in many counties.

A Case Study of Grand Jury Selection

The Stanislaus County Superior Court each year sends to local news media a 10- to 15-page description of its procedure for selecting civil grand jurors. The document features pie-charts, tables, and lists of figures. Throughout the text of a recent version, the word "randomness" appears several times. Busy news media reporters and other citizens quickly reading the document might assume that the profusion of graphically displayed data signifies a straightforward process for recruiting grand jurors randomly from a broad base of citizens. A close inspection of the figures, however, leads to a different conclusion.

For example, the description of how grand jurors for the panel of 1996–1997 were selected stated that 400 citizens' names were obtained randomly from the trial jury list but, of these citizens, fewer than 10 percent were interviewed as prospective civil grand jurors. Almost all of the citizens who eventually became grand jurors had been nominated by "community leaders" (mayors, county supervisors, school-district trustees, and so on) for grand jury service.[43] This process resulted in a body of citizens who almost entirely were nominated by local-government officials. Even more striking was the small number of citizens drawn from the random trial-juror pool whom judges deemed qualified for grand jury service:

> Number of citizens nominated by "community leaders" 61
> Number of citizens' names in the master trial-jury pool 400
> Number of citizens nominated by "community leaders" who
>   became grand jurors 16
> Number of citizens from the master trial-jury pool who
>   became grand jurors 3

Although the process I have described is legal, its official description implies more randomness than actually occurs in the selection of grand jurors. The claim of randomness may be accurate with respect to the 400 citizens' names drawn from the trial-juror pool. "Randomness" also may be correct to describe the *act* of drawing slips of paper on which are written the names of prospective grand jurors from the "grand jury box" (the container specified in Penal Code Section 902). "Randomness" cannot, however, characterize the entire method used to reduce the 461 names of citizens to the much smaller group of names that eventually are placed in the grand jury box. Thus, as the above list shows, citizens had a much greater chance of becoming grand jurors if they had been nominated by "community leaders" (public officials responsible for entities within the jurisdiction of the grand jury) than did citizens whose names were in the master trial-jury pool.

In brief, the overall process violates the essential feature of randomness as a statistical concept—namely, that every element in a sample had an equal chance of becoming part of the sample.[44] The document from which the above figures were taken did not reveal another important fact about the grand jurors impaneled in that year: Almost half of them were currently employed or recently retired local-government employees.

The Public-Employee-As-Grand-Juror Problem

Impaneling currently employed or recently retired local-government employees poses difficulty for the legitimacy of the institution as an independent investigating body. If the argument is valid that socio-economic status predisposes members of the business community to certain viewpoints, perspectives, biases, and prejudices, the same claim can be made about currently employed or recently retired local-government employees. Until the promulgation of an attorney general's opinion about this issue, the courts rarely impaneled such persons.[45] Indeed, the practice of impaneling currently employed or retired public employees is occasionally met with skepticism by the press:

> In general, insiders—those who are close to government officials—should be avoided. It also might be wise to avoid picking former county employees—or former employees of any level of government.[46]

The main reason I recommend excluding currently employed or recently retired local-government employees from grand jury service has nothing to do with the motives, integrity, or intelligence of these citizens. The practice is objectionable because it violates the principle that oversight bodies should not include persons who are overseen. Consider one type of the problem this practice could create, as one grand juror expressed it:

> The judge appointed a county employee to our grand jury who was accused of serious misconduct at work. The process for resolving the accusation had been extended for many months, with no end in sight. What happens now if we issue a report about the agency employing the person? Everyone in our county knows about this controversy. If our report should be favorable to the organization, we've conducted a white-wash. If it isn't favorable, we've conducted a witch-hunt.

Permitting currently working or retired public employees and officials to serve on grand juries also could expose those people to strained or compromised relationships with friends, acquaintances, or relatives still employed in local government. Public employees in many local governments have a variety of relationships with public employees in other local governments. In small communities, two, three, or more members of the same family sometimes work for the same local government. If one family member is a grand juror, that person would be in an awkward position if he were serving on a panel that is investigating a local government that employs a relative. Even if grand jurors are retired public officials or employees, they still might maintain relationships with colleagues in one or more local governments.[47] This comment in a foreman's transmittal letter in a final report raises questions about the validity of the document:

> Now, having been a public official of ... Sutter County for 20 years, I find the Board of Supervisors, Department Heads and their employees doing a good job of running our county. We can always make improvements but basically our county is being administered in an acceptable fashion.[48]

Additional examples of this practice that, according to former grand jurors, caused difficulties during their term of service are the following:

- A grand juror who was a county mental-health worker was married to an administrator in the welfare department about which a complaint had been filed.

- A grand juror who was employed in the county assessor's office was the mother of a county employee of an agency that a grand jury investigated until the conflict-of-interest problem became public, causing the panel to discontinue its investigation.
- The court appointed as foreman a recently retired public-works director who, owing to his former position, continued to enjoy extensive relationships as a private consultant with elected and appointed officials of the special districts of the county.
- A recently retired police officer was impaneled who held a grudge against a special unit of a probation department but who insisted that he remain on a committee that reviewed the department's operations.
- A former superintendent of schools became the foreman of a grand jury that published in a final report numerous commendations of named public-school officials.

These examples are not uncommon.[49] Of course, if more grand jurors were impaneled whose understanding of the practice of citizenship enabled them to foresee the consequences of those relationships, conflict-of-interest problems would arise less frequently than they now do. The most effective solution to the public-employee-as-grand-juror problem would be to add references to persons such as these to the statute that exempts certain types of citizens from grand jury service (Penal Code Section 893). Because a statute now exempts "elected public officer[s]" from grand jury service, extending the exemption to retired or currently employed public employees should not be objectionable.[50]

With respect to actual or potential bias of grand jurors who are members of the business community, or who are currently employed or recently-retired local government employees, some comments about the limitations of the "economic self-interest" argument should be made. First, the argument assumes that economic interest and political beliefs are consistently and predictably related. This is not always so. As examples: Some capitalists are liberal Democrats, and some public employees are Libertarians. Some police officers oppose capital punishment, and some welfare workers would endorse reducing welfare budgets sharply. Some conservative Republicans are ardent environmentalists, and some Democrats would support harvesting the last stand of old-growth redwood trees. Nevertheless, if a case may be made that members of one category filter their grand jury service through a screen of self-interest, the same must be said for members of other categories of grand jurors.[51]

If the effects of self-interest on investigations and final reports cannot be prevented by statute, full public disclosure of the past or current employment of grand jurors would assist citizens to appraise the possible influence of employment status on grand jury investigations. Finally, in the present era, it is by no means certain that wealthy, conservative grand jurors dominate panels. For example, in commenting about a grand jury investigation into "numerous reports of assaults on and abuse of inmates by jail staff," a sheriff "said he noticed a liberal view in some areas of ... the Butte County Grand Jury's report of its investigation of the County Jail." In a sidebar story, a newspaper reporter claimed, "[O]f the 18 grand jury members, eleven, or 61 percent, are registered Democrats."[52]

The Problem of Carrying Over Grand Jurors

The presence of carry-over grand jurors on a panel is, I believe, a "red flag" indicating corruption of the institution, intentional or otherwise.[53] In the abstract, the idea of having experienced grand jurors serve a consecutive term is appealing, but it nevertheless is contrary to the spirit of the institution. As is sometimes the case with theoretically good ideas in public service, the gap between principle and practice is wide.

During the study period and subsequently, several superior courts abandoned or modified longstanding practices of impaneling jurors for a consecutive term. For example, following a rancorous controversy within the Contra Costa County Grand Jury, the Superior Court of that County, "in a rare but deserved move, [permitted] no members of the Contra Costa Grand Jury [to be retained]" on the succeeding panel.[54]

In 1993, the Superior Court of Kern County, following a series of newspaper stories about internal grand jury problems, seems to have gradually discontinued impaneling carry-over grand jurors. In fact, an inspection of the list of grand jurors in its Final Report of 1996–1997 shows none of the names that were in the list of grand jurors of the immediately preceding year.[55] The presence of three carry-over grand jurors on the Santa Cruz County Grand Jury of 1996–1997 did not deter dissension that eventually led the Superior Court to disband the panel several months before the end of its term.[56]

If the carry-over statute was intended to improve grand jury service by impaneling citizens with previous grand jury experience, no evidence other than occasional anecdotes by carry-over grand jurors themselves validates the practice. Indeed, many of the problems documented in this study were found in final reports issued by grand juries that often include carry-over grand jurors. For example, the grand jury that published the notorious plagiarized report described in Chapter 4 included two carry-over panel members. One of the two grand jurors had been a foreman on the preceding panel, and the foreman of the panel that committed the plagiarism also was a carry-over grand juror. The shame this blunder brought to the spirit of the institution is accented by this ironic twist to the incident: The final report containing the plagiarized material included a recommendation endorsing the carry-over system.[57]

The carry-over provision in the Penal Code is a questionable selection practice that has been so recognized by critics and supporters of the institution throughout its existence.[58] For many of the same reasons that long terms in office for elected officials encourage corruption, impaneling grand jurors for two consecutive terms can create more problems than it solves. Citizens who have served on grand juries with one or more carry-over jurors have offered the following reasons for eliminating the practice of carrying over grand jurors:

- Because even novice grand jurors often understand and respect the idea of independence of the institution, they might resent attempts by carry-over grand jurors to offer a new panel the benefits of their experience.

- If carry-over grand jurors are friends, acquaintances, or business associates of local-government officials, they might use their experience to thwart aggressive grand jury investigations.

- If carry-over grand jurors are ax-grinders, they might use their grand jury experience to persuade new grand jurors to continue investigations of the previous panel or to undertake investigations that the previous panel was unwilling to support but that would serve the purposes of the special-interest grand jurors.

- The arguments favoring term limits for elected officials apply to term limits for grand jurors: "No matter how well-intentioned, honest or experienced they may be, incumbents who become careerists in office tend to develop a proprietary attitude toward the job and, by extension, the agency they govern."[59]

- The appointment of carry-over grand jurors violates the principle that, in a democratic society, as many citizens as possible should participate in public affairs.

Desirability of Strict Randomness in Grand Jury Selection

Random selection often is advocated as a means for impaneling civil grand jurors who represent the general population as fairly as possible.[60] Of course, a grand jury drawn at random in the purely statistical sense is undesirable and unlawful. If everyone in a California county were to have an equal chance of impanelment, infants, felons, and insane persons would have the same opportunity to become grand jurors as would eminently qualified citizens. Penal Code Section 893 obviates this possibility, for it specifies the kinds of persons who are "competent" to be grand jurors.

True randomness, even within the statutory exemptions, also is difficult to achieve because many citizens are unwilling or unable to devote hours of unpaid work to serve as grand jurors. Thus, many self-employed men and women, single parents, emergency service workers and other types of citizens would suffer severe economic or other hardships if they were forced to serve as panel members. For these reasons, a broad-brush condemnation of the courts for not using completely random methods to select grand jurors is unfair and unreasonable.

No matter how fairly the judiciary attempts to impanel citizens, grand jury selection probably will always be a contested issue. Even a cursory analysis of the demographic characteristics of civil grand jurors in most California counties would reveal that few panels would survive the kind of legal challenge that might be raised about the composition of a criminal grand jury.[61] Challenges, of course, are more likely to arise against a grand jury that has indicted someone than against a grand jury that has issued a perfunctory final report. Nevertheless, a grand jury that consists largely of political allies, business associates, and relatives and friends of persons who have nominated them does not embody the spirit of the institution.[62] If pure random selection is neither desirable nor lawful, and if it is corrupt for grand jurors to be hand-picked by the public officials over whom they have jurisdiction, how can the problem of selecting civil grand jurors be resolved as honestly as possible, if not perfectly?

A Proposal for Open Grand Jury Selection

As they now are written, the statutes governing grand jury selection do not prevent judges from selecting ineffective, apathetic, or ignorant persons to be grand jurors. On the other hand, the vagueness of the statutes permits judges to select grand jurors in a manner that supports the spirit of the institution. I do not believe that statutes could be written that would guarantee selection procedures compatible with that spirit. Although severe penalties could be added to the statutes to discourage subversion of grand jury selection, the problem of who would initiate the prosecution of such corruption would remain.

The best that can be done to improve the selection of civil grand jurors is to create a system designed so citizens, if they wish to do so, can inspect it and decide whether grand jury selection in their county conforms to the spirit of the institution. The system I propose therefore would be open in two important respects:

1. It would permit any statutorily qualified person to volunteer for grand jury service.
2. It would be thoroughly documented and open for citizens to review.[63]

Elements of the system include:

- Encouraging as many people as possible to apply for grand jury service by methods such as (a) seeking volunteers from among citizens on the trial juror list; (b) inviting members of all the legitimate civic organizations in the county to apply for grand jury service; (c) posting announcements in libraries and other designated public places throughout the county to inform citizens about how they may apply for grand jury service; (d) urging the news media to publicize the manner in which citizens submit applications for grand jury service.

- Requiring all volunteers for grand jury service to complete a comprehensive questionnaire that includes information about their occupations, political affiliations, familial and business connections with local-government officials and employees, and other matters that might affect their independence and objectivity of judgment.
- Placing responsibility on a designated public official (for example, a senior member of the court administrative staff) to declare under oath that the process for selecting civil grand jurors has been described fully and accurately in an annual "Grand Jury Selection Plan" available for public review in the Office of the County Clerk.

Requiring the method of selecting grand jurors to be thoroughly documented and publicly accessible would not prevent the deliberate or unintentional corruption of the selection process. Judges who prefer to impanel grand jurors who pose no threat to local political establishments could do so within the guidelines I have suggested. The main difference between the legislation concerning selection that I recommend in the next section and what now takes place in some counties is that my proposal would create a transparent procedure that the news media and other citizens could use to assess legitimacy of the process.

Suggested Grand Jury Legislation

If there were no other explanation for the subjectivity and triviality of many grand jury final reports, the obscure language and patchwork organization of the nearly 100 statutes governing the civil grand jury would be reasons enough. Even a panel of intelligent, motivated, and energetic grand jurors would be hard-pressed to make sense of the opaquely drafted, vague statutes with which they must work. Indeed, the confusingly written nature of certain grand jury statutes could provide a strong defense for an attorney representing grand jurors in a libel lawsuit.[64]

As I commented previously, grand jurors should not be expected to understand the implications for final reports of Penal Code Section 930 when it does not include either the phrase "defamation of character" or the words "libel" and "slander." And should not the Legislature make mandatory rather than permissive the authority and responsibility of the courts to expunge from grand jury final reports any material that is clearly libelous? After all, if the judiciary is to be a legal advisor for grand juries in more than name only, should it not be authorized to prevent grand jurors from committing the one act that is their most potentially serious error?

Moreover, now that the Attorney General of California has issued one opinion stating that the civil grand jury has jurisdiction in public school districts and another opinion holding that the institution has no jurisdiction in the judicial system, should not the statutes incorporate these important clarifications of the institution's authority?[65] And if the civil grand jury is to be a fact-finding institution, should not the word "fact" appear at least once in an appropriate statute?[66]

A comprehensive revision of the statutes pertaining to the grand jury's civil function is necessary for another reason: The patchwork accumulation of statutes and cases concerning the grand jury that evolved since statehood is a body of law that sometimes is inconsistent, often confusing, and illogically organized. Consequently, among the safeguards for grand jurors, public officials, and other citizens that are missing from the statutes are a clear statement of what the Legislature intends the institution to be, a description of the limits of its jurisdiction and powers, and a clarification of how the Legislature defines grand jury independence.

For example, a comprehensive reorganization and revision of the statutes that incorporates case law and relevant opinions of the State Attorney General would result in consistent, simplified, and organic statutory guidelines and requirements. As a result, neither grand jurors nor their legal advisors would be required to engage year after year in a struggle with the present statutory disorder and confusion that drains their energies and otherwise obstructs the spirit of the institution.

A full exposition of the needed changes in the statutes governing the grand jury is beyond the scope of this chapter. Instead, the suggestions I offer illustrate the types of improvements the Legislature might consider to articulate more clearly and logically its grant of authority to the institution. The legislative changes I propose are of several types:

- Creating a declaration of legislative intent that includes a clear statement of the objectives, goals, and limitations of the institution
- Organizing the statutes pertaining to the grand jury more logically
- Improving and making more explicit the method the courts use in each county to select grand jurors
- Adding, deleting, or modifying grand jury statutes to correct certain problems represented by the criteria described in Chapter 2
- Incorporating into the statutes certain appellate court rulings and opinions of the Attorney General that support independence, fair comment, and the observance of grand jury jurisdiction

The legislative suggestions I offer are consistent with the spirit of the institution as I have described it in previous pages. Some suggestions will result in higher standards of proof in grand jury final reports and thereby protect public officials and other citizens from abuses of civil grand jury authority. Other suggestions might encourage public officials to challenge findings and recommendations in final reports, but this will inspire grand jurors to issue final reports that correspond more closely to the spirit of the institution and its lawful authority. Finally, the statutory suggestions I offer will affirm the willingness of the Legislature, the judiciary, and local-government officials to endow the institution with the resources and tools necessary for the institution to be an effective citizens' body.

LEGISLATIVE INTENT AND STATUTORY REORGANIZATION

The suggestions in this section will do much to eliminate the problems that arise from confusion regarding the nature of the California grand jury. Into the first suggestion, a declaration of legislative intent, I have compressed solutions to problems of jurisdiction, collegiality, and subjectivity. The suggested declaration of legislative intent is largely a blend of case-law principles and should not require extensive legislative debate. The second suggestion, reorganizing grand jury statutes, will require more legislative attention, but the amount of time and effort it eventually will save grand jurors, their legal advisors, public officials, and other citizens who wish to consult the statutes governing the institution is great.

Legislative Intent

Perhaps the most serious defect in the statutory scheme of the California civil grand jury is that no clear statement expresses its mission, methods, or limitations. In effect, the California Legislature has set adrift an institution with a vaguely defined destination, no compass, and no rudder. In the absence of a clear statement of purpose, it is not surprising that grand jurors sometimes lose their bearings. A declaration of legislative intent[67] immediately preceding the grand jury statutes in Title 4 of the Penal Code would:

- Assist courts in deciding contested grand jury issues
- Provide a unifying framework for the statutes governing the grand jury
- Assist grand jurors in comprehending the purpose, methods, and limitations of the institution.

The following statement illustrates the wording of a declaration of legislative intent for the institution. Some of the language in the example paraphrases case law; some repeats and thereby emphasizes words or phrases already in the statutes; and some of the text represents what I consider to be the spirit of the institution:

> The civil grand jury may exercise only those powers, responsibilities, and authority the Legislature has granted it. As a deliberative body of citizens with equal status, the grand jury shall issue only reports based on documented facts. In issuing reports of their facts, findings, and recommendations, grand jurors shall not infringe upon the lawful policy-making function of elected officials. The Legislature declares that every civil grand jury shall be impaneled in the most representative manner possible and that documents accurately

and completely describing the processes and methods of selection and impanelment shall be available for public inspection without charge in the place designated by law. Although the grand jury is an independent body, it is an arm of the judiciary, and as officers of the court, its members are entitled in the lawful execution of the institution's authority to all privileges and indemnification the judiciary itself enjoys.

In whatever form it may take, the declaration of legislative intent should be the first statement at the beginning of that section of the Penal Code in which the powers, responsibilities, and limitations of the grand jury are enumerated.

Statutory Reorganization

The most recent year in which the California Legislature addressed grand jury statutes as a body of law was 1959. Since that time, several important California Supreme Court and appellate court cases have been published, and the Attorney General of the State of California has issued a number of important opinions concerning the civil grand jury. The lawful and effective functioning of the institution would be enhanced if the principal holdings of these decisions and opinions were incorporated into statutory law.

Problems that grand jurors, public officials, and other citizens have in finding, reading, and understanding grand jury statutes are compounded by the relative disarray of the statutes. Statutes pertaining to similar topics are scattered throughout Title 4 of the Penal Code, and several statutes affecting the civil grand jury are found in codes other than Title 4. A thorough reorganization of civil grand jury statutes, and a comprehensive reconciling of the statutes with case law, is beyond the scope of this chapter. Nevertheless, I offer suggestions to illustrate some of the changes that would assist grand jurors, public officials, and other citizens to understand more readily the institution's powers, limitations, and spirit.

The most important structural improvement that could be made to the statutes would be to group them logically according to the natural sequence of selecting grand jurors, organizing the civil grand jury, and issuing reports, as this list of section headings suggests:

- Legislative Intent
- Selection, Impanelment, and Discharge of Grand Jurors
- Organization, Resources, and Legal Counsel
- Jurisdiction and Independence of the Grand Jury
- Investigative Powers, Limits, Methods, and Standard of Evidence
- Reports and Presentments
- Indictment and Accusation

The Legislature also should move statutes pertaining to the civil grand jury from the Penal Code to a more appropriate code. By doing so, the Legislature would make clearer the distinction between the civil grand jury and the criminal grand jury. Because the civil grand jury has no enforcement powers, no logical reason exists for placing its statutes in the Penal Code. The term "civil" also should be abandoned in referring to the grand jury that has been the subject of this study, and "civic" used instead in the pertinent statutes. "Civic" more aptly describes its function and further distinguishes the institution from "civil," which has another meaning in the law.[68]

SELECTION, IMPANELMENT, AND DISCHARGE OF GRAND JURORS

Reforms in procedures for selecting grand jurors could be accomplished in one of two ways:

1. The Legislature could issue a resolution to the Judicial Council of California (the official organization serving the California judiciary) urging that body to develop standards for the selection of citizens to serve as civil grand jurors. Because the grand jury is a branch of the judiciary, the courts would be an appropriate body to develop selection standards.
2. If the courts do not wish to accept this responsibility, the Legislature could enact statutory reforms upon its own initiative.[69]

In either case, statutory improvements in the selection of civil grand jurors should include these provisions:

- Each superior court of every California county shall prepare an "Annual Plan for Selecting Civil Grand Jurors" no later than three months before impaneling a grand jury; the plan shall be available for inspection without cost by citizens in the Office of each County Clerk; the court also shall forward a certified copy of the annual plan to the Judicial Council, where it also shall be available for public inspection at no cost.
- Each annual plan for selection shall include at least the following information about every person whose name appears in the final pool of names from which civil grand jurors are randomly selected:
  - A description of the occupation of each person, using standard U.S. Bureau of Census terms or other authoritative terms to describe occupations[70]
  - The name of the public or private entity that employs each person
  - The name of any person in the final pool of names who is a retired federal, State, or local-government employee, public official, or public officer, together with the name of the public entity from which the person is retired, and any other relevant information that would permit citizens to assess the representativeness of each grand jury and actual or potential conflicts of interest of grand jurors; similar information shall be available concerning persons retired from private enterprise

- The names of any person, persons, or organizations to whom the court has delegated in whole or in part the responsibility of establishing and executing the method for selecting grand jurors
- The names of every person in any "pool" from which grand jurors have not been drawn by statistically sound random selection procedures
- Identification of the supervisorial district in which each person in the civil grand juror "pool" resides
- A copy of every completed questionnaire or other data-gathering document used to obtain information from civil grand jurors who have been impaneled
- Information revealing the relationship of each person in the civil grand juror pool to local-government public officials or employees by blood, business, marriage or any other manner that could affect the objectivity of grand jurors

Several additional suggestions for grand jury selection, the appointment of foremen, and the discharge of grand jurors are to:

- Eliminate the statute (Penal Code Section 901(b)) authorizing impanelment of carry-over grand jurors, and add to an appropriate statute a provision forbidding any person from serving as a civil grand juror more than once in any seven-year period.
- Eliminate Penal Code Section 908.2, which permits half of each grand jury to be appointed every six months.
- Add a statute that permits a grand jury, by a vote of the number of assenting grand jurors specified in Penal Code Section 940, to recommend to the court the discharge of any grand juror; include in the same statute a clear statement of the authority for the court on its own initiative to remove a grand juror.
- Amend Penal Code Section 916 to permit the superior court to invite civil grand jurors within two months of their impanelment to nominate one or more persons whom the judge may consider to appoint as foreman.[71]

With respect to the public-employee-as-grand-juror problem, a straightforward solution would be to create safeguards to lessen the potential for conflicts of interest or other problems that individuals might encounter in grand jury service; for example, a statute that reads:

No one may be a grand juror who is currently employed or who has been employed within the last five years by one or more of the public entities in the county over which the grand jury has jurisdiction.

Finally, the Legislature could reduce markedly the burden of grand jury selection on the courts by enacting a statute to exempt grand jurors from filing "Statement of Economic Interests" forms. This change should occur, however, only if the employment-disclosure requirement (or a similar requirement) I have recommended as part of the annual plan for selecting civil grand jurors is enacted into law. Obliging grand jurors to complete the same economic-interest disclosure forms required of elected and appointed local-government officials demonstrates a misunderstanding of the institution. Unlike elected and appointed local-government officials, grand jurors have no policy-determining authority. The authority of grand jurors is limited to issuing findings and recommendations about non-policy matters—a limitation that several proposals in this chapter emphasized.

On the other hand, public disclosure—for example, of the fact that a county supervisor derives substantial income from his real estate business—is important because county supervisors can make important policy decisions about land use. If conflict of interest among grand jurors is the issue, public disclosure of the information I propose in the annual plan for selecting grand jurors would be more useful than the information in their economic-interest disclosure forms. In addition, the proposed exemption would do much to broaden the base for recruiting civil grand jurors.[72]

Legislative Suggestions Based on Law-Related Criteria

In this section I offer legislative proposals to correct the nine types of problems represented by the law-related criteria in Chapter 2. In some cases, the suggestions can be implemented with new statutes. In other cases, deletions of statutes or amendments to existing Penal Code sections are required.

Grand Jury Jurisdiction

The number of problems arising each year from confusion and disputes about the jurisdiction of grand juries can be reduced significantly by several statutory changes. Notwithstanding two opinions maintaining that civil grand juries have the same jurisdiction in public-school districts that they have in special districts, confusion about this matter arises every year. For example, one Grand Jury foreman claimed that the county counsel advised his colleagues that "even reporting of facts which have been published by the school districts themselves, without comment by the Jury, could subject us to potential liability for violating the Grand Jury's scope of inquiry."[73]

By consolidating the statutes that specify grand jury authority in designated local governments, emphasizing the limits of grand jury powers, and removing several statutes that are used rarely, the Legislature will help grand jurors, public officials, and other citizens understand the institution's jurisdiction more easily. The most important change that should be made to clarify and emphasize the jurisdiction of civil grand juries is to incorporate into one provision the various statutes pertaining to the specific local-government entities within the grand jury's purview, as this suggested language proposes:

> The grand jury may at any time examine the books, records, and accounts of any city, city and county, county, housing authority, joint powers agency, local agency formation commission, nonprofit agency providing services on behalf of any entity designated in this section, public school district and special district of any kind, and every redevelopment agency. In addition to any other investigative powers granted by this Chapter, the grand jury may investigate and report upon the operations, organization, functions, and the methods, systems, and procedures of performing the duties of any entity designated in this statute, and report any such lawful facts, findings, and recommendations pertaining thereto as it may deem proper and fit, provided that such facts, findings, and recommendations do not address the lawful substantive policy matters of the elected or appointed officials of any such entity.

The advantages of consolidating in the above manner the current statutes pertaining to the grand jury's jurisdiction include:

- emphasizing that the grand jury has the same jurisdiction with respect to each entity
- specifying in one place the jurisdiction for each entity, thereby reducing the number of statutes pertaining to the jurisdiction of the civil grand jury
- using "may" rather than "shall" in the consolidated statute, thereby enhancing the independence of the institution and allowing each grand jury more latitude in establishing its investigative and visitation priorities
- clarifying the authority pertaining to nonprofit corporations
- incorporating public school districts into the statutes, thereby aligning the consolidated statute with relevant case law and attorney general opinions concerning the grand jury's jurisdiction in public school districts
- making explicit the prohibition against grand juries interfering with the lawful policy decisions of elected bodies

With regard to the suggestion forbidding grand jurors from encroaching upon the policy-making authority of local-government officials, one more comment should be made: If the California Legislature intended to confine civil grand juries to matters of procedure, systems, methods, and the like, it failed to declare that intention explicitly in a statute. This is unfortunate; the limitation is desirable and should be stated clearly and emphatically.

Incursions into policy matters is second only to unfair comment as the most significant threat to the institution's existence. Condemning, criticizing, or supporting the lawful policy-making function of elected and appointed local-government officials places the grand jury, and therefore the judiciary, in an awkward constitutional position. Moreover, the mistaken belief that grand juries have the authority to criticize, challenge, or support the lawful decisions of public officials attracts applicants for grand jury service who are ax-grinders, power seekers, and aspirants to political office.

"Policy poaching" also embroils the institution in controversies in which it has no lawful role and thereby drains its resources for conducting investigations into matters that grand jurors should investigate. Given the size of local government and its immense significance for the political economy of California, the institution has formidable enough challenges without grand jurors' attempting to transform it into a fourth branch of government. For this reason, I recommend the repetition of language restricting grand jurors from entering the domain of public policy. This restriction, therefore, should appear in the declaration of legislative intent and in the consolidated statute of jurisdiction I have proposed.

Other suggestions pertaining to jurisdiction include:

- Changing Penal Code Section 919(b) to permit grand jurors, upon their own initiative, to inspect public prisons rather than to make such inspections mandatory.
- Removing Penal Code Section 920 pertaining to the grand jury's involvement in escheat proceedings.[74]
- Changing Penal Code Section 927, concerning the mandatory study by a grand jury of the salaries of elected and appointive officials at the request of the board of supervisors, to permit the grand jury at its own option to study those matters in any entity within the grand jury's jurisdiction. The amended statute should confine grand juries to the *method* used to establish salaries and other benefits rather than issuing recommendations about salary *amounts*. As a policy issue, the latter would not be within the jurisdiction of grand juries.

I offer one additional change concerning the jurisdiction of grand juries: I believe that grand juries, as bodies of citizens, must ensure that local government is administered not only effectively, but honestly. Because of the widely publicized concerns of citizens about the integrity of governmental officials, every possible effort should be made to assure citizens that fraud, graft, and corruption in State and local government are investigated and prosecuted vigorously.

A review of newspapers from different parts of California on any day reveals examples of allegations against or trials of public officials and employees for embezzlement, sexual harassment, extortion, falsification of expense accounts, and other abuses of power and authority. No official State agency collects, analyzes, and reports data about these matters. As an established, official institution in each county, the grand jury is well situated to play a significant role in this regard. For that reason, I offer the following legislative proposal to require that prosecutions of public-integrity crimes alleged to have been committed by elected and appointed officials, public employees, and other citizens be initiated only by indictment:

> The district attorney shall, by indictment only, initiate prosecutions against any elected or appointed public official, officer, or employee or any other persons suspected of committing fraud, embezzlement, or any other form of corruption or abuse of power involving any local public entity over which the grand jury has jurisdiction or that involves any State employee or official suspected of committing any such offense within the county of the jurisdiction of any civil grand jury.

Involving the institution in prosecuting State and local-government officials and other persons suspected of committing public integrity crimes would contribute, in the long run, to the restoration of public confidence in government. By this involvement, civil grand juries would represent the community's interest in those matters. If a grand jury believes that a district attorney is seeking an indictment for political purposes, the panel could refuse to authorize it.[75] By thwarting the plans of district attorneys who might use their office for political purposes, the institution would assure the community that the machinery of justice has not been subverted.[76]

The proposed involvement of the civil grand jury in prosecuting public-integrity crimes also would be the first step in a uniform Statewide public-integrity crime-reporting system. For the system to be effective, a means of collecting and disseminating information Statewide about those crimes must be created at the level of State government. The California Department of Justice, with relatively little effort and expense, could track public-integrity crimes from the decision to indict to the final disposition of the offenses.[77] The system I propose also would include accusation proceedings initiated under California Government Code Section 3060. In several years, the accumulation of data about fraud, graft, and corruption in State and local government would provide answers to questions such as:

- How many public-integrity offenses by type are reported and investigated each year Statewide and by jurisdiction?
- To what extent is the public treasury diminished by these offenses, and what efforts are made to recover money and property that have been appropriated improperly?
- What are the characteristics of those who are found guilty of these offenses?
- To what extent do decisions to prosecute these offenses vary among district attorneys in California's counties?
- What forms of criminal sanctions are applied against those found guilty of these offenses, and how does the levying of sanctions vary?

My final recommendation concerning grand jury jurisdiction is to remove from several Penal Code Sections (e.g., 888, 925(a), and 928) a phrase that is inconsistent with the principle that grand juries have no jurisdiction in public policy: "including the abolition or creation of offices." Penal Code Section 888 applies this phrase to "county matters of civil concern." Penal Code Section 925(a) employs the phrase in reference to joint powers agencies but uses the word "agencies" rather than "offices." Penal Code Section 928 applies the phrase to "all county officers in the county."

The elimination of local governments or their functions or departments by merger, consolidation, or unification usually requires, depending on the type of local government, either the votes of elected officials or approval by voters. For grand juries to intrude into these matters embroils them in political decisions contrary to the principle that the institution has no jurisdiction in policy issues.[78] If the Legislature intended this phrase to apply only to the procedural matters incident to merger, unification, consolidation, or the elimination of functions or departments of local governments, the statutes should be written more clearly to express that limitation.

Enhancing Independence

Properly employed, independence of the grand jury is an essential element of its spirit. Independence, however, is a hollow ideal if grand juries do not have the same access as public officials to qualified legal advice, if decisions about grand jury financial resources are made exclusively by the public officials over whom the institution has jurisdiction, if grand jury funds are used to maintain alliances with politically motivated organizations, and if grand jurors have no control over the institution's indictment function. The following statutory changes should prevent these problems:

- Enacting legislation requiring the judiciary to provide special counsel for grand juries requesting it if the statutorily designated legal advisors for any reason declare their inability or unwillingness to do so.[79]
- Modifying Penal Code Section 931 to require that the authority to establish the grand jury budget for each year resides only in the court, and that grand jury revenue and expenditure amounts be included in county and city-and-county published budgets.
- Forbidding grand juries from using public funds of any kind to pay for memberships in associations or organizations that engage directly or indirectly in legislative advocacy, and prohibiting grand jurors from making gifts of public funds in the form of prizes, awards, commemorative plaques, and the like.
- Clarifying statutes pertaining to the indictment function to make its use entirely a matter of grand jury discretion.

Fair Comment

Essentially, resolving the fair-comment problem in grand jury final reports requires a balance between two objectives: (a) ensuring that public officials or other citizens are not maligned or impugned unfairly, and (b) ensuring that grand jurors can conduct civil investigations without the needless fear of being sued for libel. Citizens other than grand jurors and public officials also have an interest in this issue—namely, the right to be informed of the results of grand jury civil investigations, provided that the latter have been conducted and reported properly. Statutory safeguards such as the following might achieve the needed balance:

- A statute requiring that every final report would include a declaration signed by the superior court judge who impaneled the grand jury that the document complies with applicable sections of Title 4 of the Penal Code; the signing of such declaration thereby shall confer upon every member of the grand jury the same privilege accorded to the judiciary and other State and local appointed and elected officials for their lawful acts.[80]

- Authority for the superior court to expunge any material in a grand jury report that the court deems libelous or that does not otherwise comply with Title 4, provided that the court issues a written explanation for its reason for doing so, and that the grand jury may, at its option, include the court's written explanation in its final report, if no secrecy or confidentiality provisions are thereby violated.

- An amendment to Penal Code Section 930 to provide that no person shall be identified by name or be otherwise identifiable in any civil grand jury report for criticism or condemnation unless the grand jury has voted to do so, in which case the recorded votes of the panel shall be sealed and opened only upon an order of the court; the court may destroy such records of sealed votes at any time after the expiration of the statute of limitations pertaining to criminal or civil suits for defamation of character or other abuses of grand jury authority.

- An amendment to Penal Code Section 930 allowing grand jurors to include in a final report criticism or condemnation of a named or otherwise identifiable public official only if such commentary is about a matter factually proven to be directly connected to "the public official's non-criminal failure to discharge his public duty."[81]

Conducting Justified Investigations

Citizens and other public officials are entitled to know what statute or statutes authorize a grand jury to conduct an investigation and report it. Few grand juries provide this information in their final reports. As a result, needless controversy, ill will, and skepticism about grand jury authority might be created. To avoid these problems, a statute such as the following is suggested:

In issuing a report of any investigation containing at least one fact, finding, recommendation, or finding and recommendation, every grand jury shall include a justification of such investigation citing one or more statutes authorizing the investigation. In doing so, the grand jury must describe clearly the reason or reasons it believes that the statute or statutes it cites are directly connected to any facts, findings, and recommendations issued in its final report.

Issuing Reports About Policy

Two opinions, one issued by the Office of Attorney General of the State of California and one by a County Counsel, have declared that grand juries do not have jurisdiction in matters of "substantive public policy." The opinions are well founded; no statute confers such jurisdiction on grand juries. This limitation of grand jury authority, however, is explicit in no existing statute. If, as I proposed in the "Grand Jury Jurisdiction" section, the several statutes that grant the civil grand jury jurisdiction in designated local governments are combined, the wording of the consolidated statute also should forbid grand jurors from commenting about and issuing findings and recommendations concerning public policy. Because of its importance, the same restriction should be included in the statement of Legislative intent, as I proposed in the "Legislative Intent" section, above.

Validity

To the extent that grand juries issue factual and otherwise lawful reports, the spirit of the institution is upheld.[82] The statutory changes I propose in this section would help grand jurors prevent subjectivity in final reports in several ways:

1. The distinction between facts and findings would be emphasized more clearly in the pertinent statutes; moreover, both would be required in any investigative report a civil grand jury issues.
2. Any uncertainty and confusion that the term "raw evidentiary material" might have created would be eliminated.
3. Grand jurors would be required to observe a standard-of-evidence provision in their deliberations and reports.
4. Additional examples of documented evidence that must be cited in final reports to satisfy the standard-of-evidence provision are specified.

Suggested additions to or modifications of the Penal Code with regard to validity are:

- A statute authorizing the superior court to expunge from any final or interim report before its publication any fact, statement, finding, conclusion, recommendation, or other material the publication of which would constitute a breach of secrecy or confidentiality.
- A statute requiring that no grand jury shall report any material from any interview it has conducted under any authority granted by Title 4 of the

Penal Code unless such material is substantiated by at least two facts independent of the interview, the publication of which does not constitute a violation of secrecy or confidentiality.

- A statute specifying that every fact, finding, recommendation, and conclusion presented in a final report must be documented sufficiently to permit a reader to verify whether the facts are correct and whether findings, recommendations, and conclusions are logically derived from and supported by the facts.
- Revising Penal Code Section 916 to emphasize that grand jurors must base their findings, recommendations, and conclusions on disclosed facts (unless consideration of confidentiality and secrecy precludes such publication); for example, more illustrations of what "documented evidence" means could be provided, as this proposed revision suggests: "documented evidence such as budgetary and staffing data, statistical reports, research reports, correspondence, memoranda or other official records or other data not exempted by statute."
- A statute that denies privilege (see Glossary) to grand jurors individually and collectively serving on any civil grand jury that adopts and reports as its own without attribution and independent verification the facts, findings, conclusions, recommendations, or other text or data obtained from other sources.
- Strengthening the intention of Penal Code Section 939.9 to emphasize that adopting and reporting facts, findings, conclusions, or recommendations of any other grand jury or other source without independent investigation shall negate the statutory requirement of any affected public official to comment about such report.
- Amending Penal Code Section 916 to allow a grand jury, by the vote required in Penal Code Section 940, to invite a public official to its meeting room to discuss with that person any facts qualified for public disclosure, but not findings, recommendations, and conclusions or other text pertaining to any investigation a grand jury has conducted concerning the office or functions of that official; the foreman of the grand jury must admonish any such official that revealing any information discussed in the grand jury room is punishable as a felony.
- A statute requiring each grand jury to maintain a book of procedure that it shall review each year for accuracy; grand juries shall distribute copies of these books to the county law library and every county public library and its branches within each county where the documents shall be available for public inspection; every grand jury book of procedure shall include a complete description of grand jury complaint-processing and investigative procedures, excluding any information that would constitute a violation of confidentiality or grand jury secrecy statutes.

- A requirement that, in issuing an investigative report of any person, department, or organization, every civil grand jury shall include in any such report a statement affirming that the required number of grand jurors heard and deliberated about all evidence included in the report.
- Modifying Penal Code Section 939.5 to make explicit for civil grand jurors their duty to declare any actual or potential conflict of interest they may have in connection with a civil investigation and report thereof, including a requirement that each grand jury shall include a discussion of these matters within one of the first four general meetings of its year; every final or other report a grand jury shall issue must include a signed declaration by the foreman that this provision was followed.
- Adding a subsection to Penal Code Section 939 forbidding grand jurors from participating in any investigation involving a relative; for example:

> No grand juror may participate in deliberations about any matter concerning a public official or public employee of any of the public entities over which the grand jury has jurisdiction if such grand juror is related within the sixth degree by blood or marriage to such person.

Two more suggestions might enhance the validity of grand jury investigations and reports:

1. A statute should require civil grand jurors to employ a standard of proof in their deliberations and reports. The statute could permit grand jurors to adopt any such standard that its legal advisor recommends. To support a standard-of-proof provision, judges also should be required to include in their charges to civil grand jurors an explanation of standards of proof and their implications for civil investigations. Other than the "diligently inquire into and true presentment make" phrase of the grand juror's oath (Penal Code Section 911) and the few examples of "documented evidence" cited in Penal Code Section 916, no statute explicitly obliges grand jurors to base their findings and recommendations on anything more substantial than opinion, conjecture, or whim.[83]
2. Judges should also be required to include in their charges to civil grand juries instructions concerning the meanings of "facts," "findings," and "conclusions" as these terms are used in judicial proceedings.

Legality and Effectiveness of Findings and Recommendations; Comments by Public Officials

The following statutory provisions are offered to improve findings and recommendations issued in final reports. The first suggested statute would encourage grand jurors to ensure that their final reports comply with all sections of the Penal Code governing their investigating and reporting function. The second suggestion provides a sanction for public officials who willfully ignore their duty to comment about properly reported findings and recommendations. The third proposed statute fixes responsibility for the proper filing of comments on elected or appointed public officials even if those persons delegate their preparation to subordinates.

1. No public official has a duty to comment about any grand jury report, fact, finding, conclusion, or recommendation that does not comply with Title 4 of the Penal Code. In declining to comment on any such report, fact, finding, conclusion, or recommendation, officials must fully explain in writing to the judge impaneling the grand jury their lawful reasons for so declining.

2. Every public official required to comment under Penal Code Section 933(c) to any lawful civil grand jury report, fact, finding, and recommendation shall address the comments to the Presiding Judge of the Superior Court; any judge of the superior court may issue an order of compliance to any public official who has not commented in good faith about any lawfully reported grand jury fact, finding, and recommendation; any judge of a superior court may issue an order to the county auditor or other local-government disbursing authority to withhold payment of wages of any local-government public official whom the judge has determined not to be in compliance with Penal Code Section 933(c).[84]

3. Elected and appointed officials required to comment under Penal Code Section 933(c) to any lawfully reported fact, finding, and recommendation may delegate the preparation of such comments to any appropriate subordinate, but the comments shall be presumed to be the official position of the elected or appointed official or officials required to file the comments.

Confidentiality and Secrecy

Most of the violations of confidentiality and secrecy in civil grand jury proceedings that have come to my attention have been committed by people other than grand jurors. One such problem occasionally arises when county employees open mail addressed to grand juries and discuss what they have read with other employees. A somewhat different problem is reported to occur, if only rarely, when a county official or employee intercepts a grand jury final report in the county printing department and orders the document to be printed with portions of one or more investigations excised or altered. Finally, confusion occurs every year among some civil grand jurors concerning what correspondence, statistical data, and the like pertaining to an investigation may be acquired from predecessors or given to successors. Statutory provisions such as the following could correct these problems:

- Any unauthorized person who alters or causes to be altered any grand jury final report or other document, or who obstructs the timely publication or distribution of any grand jury final report or other document, or who reveals any portion of any grand jury document, correspondence, or any final report prior to publication shall be guilty of a felony.

- Only the grand jury as a whole may receive and consider written complaints addressed to the body; authority to do so may not be delegated to the foreman, a committee of grand jurors, individual grand jurors, or any public official or employee; anyone who obstructs the delivery of such complaints or other forms of communication to the grand jury, or who otherwise intimidates, or attempts to intimidate, grand jurors is guilty of a felony.

- Other than evidence or other materials pertaining to indictments, or materials that otherwise could violate confidentiality or secrecy, each grand jury may decide which, if any, documents, reports, studies, or other material it has acquired in the discharge of its civil function it wishes to transmit to its successor.

Collegiality

Early in their terms, grand jurors must create collegiality within their panel. To encourage this essential ingredient for effective deliberation, I propose several additional statutes and amendments to existing statutes concerning the civil grand jury. The first suggestion incorporates into the statutes a principal holding from an appellate court case.[85] The remaining suggestions affirm main points of the *Clinton* case—namely, that the grand jury is a body of peers[86] and that individual grand jurors have no authority to conduct investigations the panel has not authorized.[87]

- No grand jury shall issue a minority report unless the number of grand jurors specified in Penal Code Section 940 has voted to issue that report.
- The foreman of every grand jury shall have only the authority that a quorum of grand jurors has delegated to him or her under Penal Code Section 916.
- Every grand jury may organize itself in any lawful manner it deems to be appropriate, provided that no individual grand juror, or two or more grand jurors constituting any subdivision of the panel, may exercise any authority the panel has not delegated to the member or members, or withhold from the panel any information or materials acquired on its behalf.

OTHER LEGISLATIVE POSSIBILITIES

In the preceding proposals I have generally confined myself to the problems represented by the criteria in Chapter 2. In doing so, I have not addressed two suggestions for legislation that grand jurors occasionally propose. Instead, I offer comments about these matters in this section for two reasons:

1. They are examples of proposals that, in the context of other types of institutions or organizations, might be appropriate. Both ideas, however, are invalid with respect to the civil grand jury for the same reason: They are contrary to the spirit of the institution.

2. My reservations about these proposals are more appropriately discussed apart from previous suggestions.

Perhaps the suggestion that grand jurors most frequently propose is that the Legislature should authorize a two-year term for grand jury service. Grand jurors, the argument holds, could use their first year to acquire skill and experience; in their second term they would apply their superior knowledge to conduct more effective investigations. Extending the grand jury term beyond one year is unwarranted for these reasons:

- Many superior courts are hard-pressed to find competent, energetic, and dedicated citizens to serve one term as grand jurors. To recruit grand jurors for two-year terms would be even more difficult.

- Term length and grand jury effectiveness are not necessarily related. Some grand juries are effective, whereas others are ineffective during the same one-year term. During the study period, the Tuolumne County Grand Jury served an 18-month term and, as the Foreman Pro Tem. stated in the final report, three different people served as Foremen, and many members resigned during the extended term.[88] Indeed, the quality of the final report of that 18-month panel was indistinguishable from final reports of previous grand juries of that County.

- Time management has more promise for improving grand jury investigations and reports than merely adding more months to the grand jury term. A "Grand Jury Investigative Report" of a county grand jury in Georgia was at least as comprehensive as final reports from half of the grand juries of California during the study period, but the Georgia grand jury was impaneled for only two months and accomplished its work without carry-over grand jurors.[89]

The second idea that grand jurors and other citizens advance occasionally is to enact legislation that forces public officials to implement grand jury recommendations. This proposal has no merit. *First,* even if such a law were passed, it would be challenged immediately and declared unconstitutional as an attempt to assign executive power to the judiciary. *Second,* many grand jury recommendations are unrealistic or unlawful. A forced implementation of such recommendations would be folly. *Third,* a large number of recommendations each year either are so poorly written that they cannot be understood or are so vague as to have no meaning. Public officials obviously would object to a requirement to implement unrealistic, unlawful, or incomprehensible findings and recommendations.

Two other suggestions that grand jurors occasionally propose might be useful. One proposal that could correct a number of problems associated with the institution is to reduce its size.[90] History, rather than empirical evidence, has dictated the number of grand jurors the Legislature authorized for the institution.[91] A recent law (Penal Code Section 888.2) that permits judges to impanel 11-member grand juries in counties with a population of 20,000 or fewer persons provides an opportunity to study the effectiveness of smaller-sized panels.

In one county, the first grand jury impaneled under the recent law authorizing an 11-member body was unable to maintain a quorum and therefore did not issue a final report for 1996–1997.[92] Assuming that in other counties the use of the new law was positive, though, the Legislature could designate 11 members as the maximum size for all grand juries, including Los Angeles. By reducing the size of grand juries, selecting grand jurors would be simpler and less expensive than it now is for the judiciary. Reducing the size of grand juries also might allow judges to spend more time selecting more competent citizens for grand jury service. Any legislation to reduce the size of the civil grand jury, however, should be accompanied by the elimination of the carry-over statute.

Another proposal that is expressed occasionally is to create a civil grand jury for State government. This idea sometimes is accompanied by the suggestion that only former members of county civil grand juries should be appointed to that body. Although I have confined this study to the county civil grand jury in California, I offer several comments and questions about the proposal for a State civil grand jury. First, I concede that civil grand juries in California occasionally rise above mediocrity. Some citizens who served on these panels might, indeed, serve effectively on a State civil grand jury. The fact that a grand juror served on a meritorious county civil grand jury, however, does not necessarily mean that, as an individual, he or she was competent. Even if a sufficient number of effective former civil grand jurors could be found for a State panel, how many of them could donate many consecutive weeks of their time to serve as grand jurors at the State Capitol where, presumably, the State civil grand jury would be seated?

Also, what would be the relationship of a State civil grand jury to the various law enforcement departments, regulatory bodies, and other oversight agencies in State government? How large a budget would a State civil grand jury require, and what would be the source of its funds? Finally, in which branch of government would a State civil grand jury be located, and what would be the relationship of the institution to the culture of its host?

These are only a few of the questions that might be raised about creating a State civil grand jury. They can be answered, though, and I think the idea is worth exploring. As one experienced investigator of public-integrity crimes observed, the leading problem in public bureaucracies is not fraud, graft, or corruption but, rather, "staggering inefficiency."[93] Assuming that an adequate number of competent citizens could be recruited for a State civil grand jury and a statutory framework could be created that is consistent with the spirit of the institution, the idea of a civil grand jury for State government deserves serious consideration.[94]

Restoration of the Presentment

For hundreds of years, the term "presentment" was associated with the grand jury in England and early America. I recommend that the concept be revived, but with safeguards to prevent a recurrence of the abuse that caused its demise.[95] As I use the term, a presentment would be a formal report to the community, similar to the final report that has been the subject of this study. Except for restoration of the term "presentment," nothing is unusual about this recommendation; "presentment" would merely be used in the titles of reports that civil grand juries would issue in the exercise of one or more of the four categories of existing statutory powers. Issuance of any of the four types of presentments discussed below would not occur without review and authorization by the superior court.[96] Returning the presentment to the grand jury tradition would serve several purposes:

- Using "presentment" in the titles of the four types of reports invests them with equal importance, thereby helping grand jurors and other citizens acquire a more concrete, consistent, and cogent impression of the institution's nature and purpose.
- The term "presentment" emphasizes that the grand jury initiated an action, thereby enhancing and affirming the institution's independence.
- The term "presentment" conveys, as the term "final report" does not, a sense that the institution has accounted for its activities and findings to the citizenry at large and in doing so has expressed the will of the community.

Depending on local circumstances, grand juries could issue one or more of each type of presentment at any time during their terms. The safeguards I have proposed elsewhere in this chapter and in this section would ensure that grand jurors would not use the historic presentment power capriciously or malevolently.

THE PRESENTMENT OF FINDINGS AND RECOMMENDATIONS CONCERNING LOCAL GOVERNMENT

The presentment of findings and recommendations concerning local government would replace the "final report" as the document by which grand juries promulgate their civil investigations. For some time, the term "final report" has seemed unsatisfactory to me. "Final report" implies that at least one previous report has been issued. Although Penal Code Section 933(a) permits a panel to submit to the court more than one final report during its term, issuing two or more successive reports about the same or different subjects, each identified as a "final report," is confusing. The term I suggest in this section would eliminate confusion and also help readers unfamiliar with grand jury matters understand that the presentment has a specific purpose: It is a report the grand jury presents to its community about investigations, facts, findings, conclusions, and recommendations concerning one or more local governments of a county.

The process of releasing a presentment would be similar to how a final report is issued now. The grand jury would send its draft of the presentment to the judge who impaneled it. The judge would review the document to ensure that it complies with the law. In addition, judges should be explicitly authorized, as I previously proposed, to expunge from a presentment libelous material, material that violates confidentiality and secrecy requirements, and material outside of the institution's jurisdiction. Upon approving the presentment, the judge would direct the county clerk to release it immediately to the community.

THE PRESENTMENT OF INDICTMENT

Grand juries would issue the presentment of indictment in one of two ways. The first process for the presentment of indictment would be identical to that of the traditional indictment; it would involve both the district attorney and the grand jury.

The second presentment of indictment process would occur only if the district attorney were to decline to assist a grand jury in preparing one. This process recognizes that the indictment is a discretionary function of the grand jury, as a court recently affirmed:

> The decision whether or not to indict, i.e., to initiate a criminal prosecution, resides entirely with the grand jury. Once the grand jury has voted an indictment, the process admits of no opportunity for the district attorney to intercede, and calls for the immediate presentment of the indictment directly to, and its filing with, the superior court, thereby commencing a criminal prosecution .... [T]he authority of the grand jury independent of the district attorney to conduct investigations culminating in indictment cannot be gainsaid.[97]

The presentment of indictment not involving the district attorney would require a somewhat different process than would the indictment involving that official. The process would begin with the grand jury seeking authorization from the superior court to obtain special counsel. If the court authorizes counsel, the court would issue an order to the board of supervisors to provide the money required for that purpose. The responsibility for drafting any indictment arising from the investigation by the grand jury and the special counsel would be that of the latter.

The grand jury would be authorized to include in its presentment of findings and recommendations concerning local government a statement that it requested, but was denied by the court, authorization to employ a special counsel. The grand jury, however, would not be permitted to report any of the details of the requested-but-denied indictment. The grand jury also would be authorized to publish the court's written refusal to approve an indictment. Similarly, the grand jury would be authorized to reproduce in its presentment a statement by the district attorney explaining why he or she refused involvement in the indictment. Neither the court nor the district attorney would be permitted, in its written justifications of refusal, to include information that would embarrass, humiliate, or defame the character of any person specified in a grand jury indictment that did not survive judicial review. The grand jury also would be forbidden to include any such material in its report.

The second form of indictment would relieve tension that arises occasionally between grand juries and district attorneys. This second procedure would allow a district attorney who has a legitimate reason to step aside from the indictment process to do so with little political risk. Too often, when district attorneys refuse to assist grand juries in filing accusations or indictments against public officials or employees, grand jurors assume that prosecutors are doing so for improper reasons. Unfortunately, even if a district attorney has a legitimate reason for declining to assist the grand jury in these matters, the legal nuances of his or her justification might clash with grand jurors' "common sense" understanding of the issues in dispute. Under the process I propose, district attorneys would have an opportunity to explain in writing the legal basis for their refusal to assist the grand jury in the indictment.

The second option also could lessen citizens' distrust about government. As matters now stand, if a grand jury believes it has sound evidence of some form of fraud, graft, or corruption, and a district attorney refuses to assist it in proceeding in the matter, some panel members return to their communities after grand jury service with grave doubts about the integrity of the district attorney in particular and government in general. Because the second option allows district attorneys to "go on the record" when they decline to assist grand juries in initiating indictments, it should reduce misunderstandings between them and grand juries.

THE PRESENTMENT OF MALFEASANCE, MISFEASANCE, OR NONFEASANCE

The name of the third type of presentment is more specific than the term now used for the purpose it would serve: to initiate an accusation. As its title implies, the presentment of malfeasance, misfeasance, or nonfeasance would be used in three types of suspected noncriminal wrongdoing by public officials (see "accusation" in the Glossary). The proposed title also would eliminate the confusion between the term "accusation" described by California Government Code Section 3060 and the term "accusation" used in criminal law.[98] In other respects, this proposed presentment would be identical to what the statutes now provide for the accusation.

THE PRESENTMENT TO RECOVER PUBLIC MONIES OR PROPERTY

The presentment to recover public monies or property would serve the purposes of Penal Code Section 932. By issuing this presentment, the grand jury would notify citizens that it and the district attorney seek to recover public monies or property they believe to have been used, allocated, or appropriated improperly. The procedure for issuing this presentment would begin when the grand jury sends a draft of it to the court for review. If the court determines that the presentment is valid on its face, it would authorize the grand jury to send it to the district attorney. If the district attorney declines to proceed with a suit for recovery, that official would be required to send to the judge a written explanation for not doing so. Upon receiving the district attorney's explanation, the court would decide whether to authorize special counsel to assist the grand jury. With the approval of the court, the grand jury would be permitted to include in its Presentment of Findings and Recommendations Concerning Local Government the district attorney's verbatim explanation for declining to assist it in executing a suit for recovery. With respect to the district attorney's explanation, or the grand jury's comments about the matter, the court would be authorized to expunge inappropriate statements from the presentment.

Summary and Conclusion

The California civil grand jury descends from the English juries of the early medieval era. When, in the seventeenth and eighteenth centuries, the English grand jury achieved a degree of independence from the crown and the courts, it began a new line of development: It changed from an institution of the monarchy into a citizens' tribunal. Above all other considerations, the spirit of the institution depends crucially on the type of citizenship that grand jurors practice during their term of service. As is the case with other public or private institutions, traditions, beliefs, and practices create a culture that is as important in shaping institutional destiny as any official mandate, statute, or purpose. Culture is, of course, a human product and, in the case of the grand jury, grand jurors are its principal creators.

The ingredients of the grand jury culture are many, but among them are the clarity of grand jury statutes, the means used to identify and select grand jurors, and the relationships that grand jurors have with their legal advisors and other public officials. This chapter offers more than 50 legislative proposals to enhance the spirit of the institution. Still, the quality of citizens who serve as grand jurors will always be the institution's most important asset. For this reason, the next chapter concludes this study with an exploration of citizenship in grand jury service.

8

Citizenship and the Future of the Civil Grand Jury in California

Throughout this book I have cited examples of the persistent problems that burden the California civil grand jury each year. The legislative suggestions in Chapter 7 and the procedural suggestions in Chapter 6, if they are implemented, will eliminate many obstructions the spirit of the institution faces yearly. Under the discretion that Penal Code Section 916 confers upon them, grand jurors can implement many of the improvements I have suggested with only minor costs, if any.

Taken as a whole, all of the suggestions I propose would constitute an organic revitalization of the institution; most of them complement, reinforce, and sustain each other. Legislative reform by itself, though, will not improve the investigations and reports of the civil grand jury. If statutory improvements are to succeed, grand jurors must also exercise a strong sense of active citizenship. It is with this subject that I conclude this book.

The Importance of Citizenship for the Spirit of the Institution

In social science, one tries to identify the fewest facts that explain the most variation in the subject under review. The present study, of course, was not meant to be a carefully controlled experiment. Therefore, I cannot claim to have identified conclusively the one most important cause of variation in the quality of grand jury investigations and reports during the study period. Nonetheless, if a more rigorous analysis of grand jury investigations were conducted, I would nominate pathologies of "citizenship" as the most powerful cause of the persistent problems this study has disclosed. Stated more precisely, the style of citizenship that grand jurors practice is what most strongly affects each criterion discussed in Chapter 2.

Despite its importance, grand jurors rarely think of grand jury service in terms of how they practice citizenship. And newspaper stories about the California grand jury rarely are so expressed. For example, one of the most thorough feature stories about California civil grand juries in recent times bore the headline, "Grand Juries Crippled by Lack of Experience, Skills."[1] Absence of the word "citizenship" before "skills" suggests that the author of the story missed the point of his own analysis.

Likewise, legal scholars writing about indicting or civil grand juries rarely consider the institution from a perspective of citizenship theory.[2] When, therefore, grand jury observers urge improvements to the institution, their remedies are merely for structural, monetary, or procedural changes such as larger budgets, better grand jury meeting rooms, permitting grand jurors to contract for legal counsel, allowing courts to empanel an ever-larger number of carry-over grand jurors, increasing jurors' fees, authorizing public officials to review grand jury reports before publication, and so on.[3] None of these solutions confronts the institution's central problem: finding at least a minimum number of citizens who are appropriate for its purposes.

Some structural-procedural improvements, of course, are worth considering. The suggestions for legislation in Chapter 7 contained several applicable examples. Indeed, if the California Legislature were to debate comprehensive reform legislation for the civil grand jury, every reasonable suggestion to improve grand jury investigations and reports must be evaluated. Grand jury investigations and reports will improve little, however, unless the "variable" that affects the institution most significantly also improves: the nature of citizenship in modern society and its relationship to grand jury service.

Citizenship, the Spirit of the Institution, and Its Persistent Problems

Simply stated, the civil grand jury in California has a severe staffing problem. Too few citizens who become grand jurors have the citizenship skills needed to achieve the institution's potential and the will to do so. Although I do not claim that the grand juror behaviors I have described so far and discuss further in the remaining pages constitute a complete profile of grand jurors, they illustrate defects in the practice of citizenship that obstruct the spirit of the institution every year. In this section I illustrate how the lack of a sense of assertive citizenship is revealed in day-to-day problems that arise among civil grand juries in California.

RESOURCES AND BUDGETS

As Chapter 3 revealed, grand jury budgets are declining Statewide, and some grand jurors do not have meeting rooms dedicated solely for their use, or office space, or even telephones. Limitations such as these unquestionably hinder grand jury service. On the other hand, some grand juries function well with budgets far smaller than those of persistently mediocre panels. Moreover, grand jurors with a strong sense of the spirit of the institution will ensure that the necessary resources are available. Exercising this kind of statesmanship, however, requires a certain form of citizenship, as the following episode illustrates.

Several years ago a newly appointed grand jury foreman volunteered to speak at a Grand Jury Exchange Seminar. His credentials were impressive: He retired with high rank from military service and had acquired, during his military career, an advanced academic degree. When I learned of these achievements, I looked forward to inviting the foreman, after his year of grand jury service, to help plan and present future seminars. My enthusiasm quickly subsided, however, when he told me that his first act after a judge appointed him as grand jury foreman was to cancel the grand jury post office box and telephone. When I asked him why he had done so, he said, "Well, budgets are really tight in our county and I wanted to help our county supervisors save money."

Apparently his attitude affected fellow grand jurors. The final report the panel issued a year later under his leadership was even less effective than those of past grand juries of that county. This incident is even more striking when one realizes that the foreman of the previous year had persuaded the board of supervisors to obtain, for the first time in that panel's history, a grand jury post office box and telephone. Although I was not able to learn why the foreman who was the retired general made such a blunder and expressed pride in committing it, I concluded that impressive credentials do not guarantee a conception of citizenship consistent with the spirit of the institution.

AMBIGUOUS AND INADEQUATE LAWS

In research terms, the statutes and case law governing the California civil grand jury are a "constant." In theory, the statutes govern all civil grand juries equally. Consider, however, the *Clinton* case. Notwithstanding its brevity, no other California appellate case is more concerned with the logic and identity of the institution. One would think that as old as the *Clinton* case is, it would have changed the civil grand jury culture in California years ago, particularly in the county of its origin. Ironically, however, a Superior Court judge in that county severely chastised a grand juror in 1997 for behavior reminiscent of that which created the *Clinton* case 60 years ago.[4]

The incident had another ironic twist to it. In their final report, grand jurors of the same year complained that no one had informed them of the case law governing the grand jury. The panel therefore urged the "assigned Legal Advisor from the District Attorney's staff" to ensure that succeeding grand juries acquire such information.[5]

Thus, the California panel that leads other grand juries in expenditures, corporate self-esteem, and the size of the population from which grand jurors are selected, conceded, in effect, that none of its members could find the County Law Library. How shall we reconcile such a helpless form of citizenship with the panel's longstanding tradition of publishing color photographs of its members, accepting helicopter rides from law enforcement officials, and including the seal of the county board of supervisors on the front cover of its final reports?

One answer to the question lies in the out-of-date, obscurely written, and poorly organized nature of the statutes pertaining to the California civil grand jury. In their present state, the statutes are a barrier to any grand juror, public official, or other citizen who wishes to comprehend them. In the absence of more coherent statutory direction, grand jurors and others try to find guidance in the admixture of rumor, speculation, and wishful thinking that pervade the grand jury culture. That culture, in turn, nurtures the annually recurring problems that stain the spirit of the institution.

Ax-Grinding, Policy Poaching, and Civility

While I was writing this chapter, grand jurors in a small California county asked me to conduct a two-day training program for them. The county is one of several in its region well known for its part in a decades-long dispute with other jurisdictions concerning a natural resource. After the first day of working with the panel, I decided it was blessed with grand jurors of unusual talents, life experiences, good will, and motivation. Three grand jurors of the previous year, however, were on the panel. Toward the end of the second day, the grand jurors asked me to comment about the final report of the previous year. At the end of my critique, I said that one investigation in the report strayed perilously close to public policy. I also said that the language of the report suggested that someone with a certain occupational background was its principal author. My third comment was that some of the recommendations in the report were confusingly written, trivial, and unconnected to any facts in the body of the report. The combination of these problems, I concluded, could portend difficulties in the coming year, to say nothing of the fact that the subject of the grand jury inquiry was already in the courts.

Upon hearing my evaluation, one of the carry-over jurors objected angrily that I was mistaken in stating that the institution has no jurisdiction in policy. The juror then sketched on a blackboard an intricate, if somewhat arcane, argument to justify his position. He became even more upset when I would not immediately retract my comments about the policy issue and concede that I was mistaken in my understanding. I replied that the matter would be easy to settle: All that was required was for the panel to request from its legal advisors a written opinion about the validity of the juror's position. The grand juror loudly retorted, "Written opinions box you in. When you think you're right, don't ask for legal opinions—just go ahead and do what you think is right."

The juror's demeanor and some of his other comments suggested that I had unwittingly trespassed on his plans to continue an investigation he had conducted in the previous year and in which he had a considerable emotional investment. In itself, this would not be objectionable. Sooner or later, the rest of the panel would vote on whether to continue the investigation. Nevertheless, his strident unwillingness to seek legal advice about his theory concerning grand jury intervention in policy matters could present a problem if he were to persuade fellow panel members, as he said, to "shoot first and ask questions later." The episode reminded me of how close Tocqueville came to saying that the American conception of citizenship extols pragmatism over principle.[6]

CONFLICT OF INTEREST

In training grand jurors, I have learned that one of the most reliable predictors of the quality of grand jury investigations and reports is how panel members react when I present to them examples of actual or potential conflicts of interest. As a concept, conflict of interest is either received agreeably by grand jurors or is dismissed as an academic nicety. For example, I often point out during training that public employees who are selected for grand jury service have an unusual problem. Because the jurisdiction of civil grand juries is local government, sooner or later currently employed or recently retired local-government employees serving on panels will either experience an actual conflict of interest or be troubled by one that other citizens who read final reports might perceive to be so.

To illustrate my point, I refer to studies in final reports concerning the salaries and fringe benefits of public employees.[7] Some grand-juror public employees quickly see that their self-interest could taint grand jury recommendations to improve the salaries and benefits of public employees. Other grand-juror public employees deny the possibility of conflict of interest and begin discussing the injustice of the inequity between salaries in the public and private sectors.

On occasion I have cited another type of example, a highly controversial incident that arose from an attempt by a grand jury "that jumped into the middle of a dispute between the Deputy Sheriff's Association and the county administration over staffing levels [that indirectly involved] a dispute between several supervisorial candidates and the county administration." In rebuking the Grand Jury for its involvement in this affair, a newspaper editorial emphasized that an officer of the Grand Jury was married to a deputy sheriff who was a member of the Deputy Sheriff's Association.[8] In my training programs, some public employees who are grand jurors dismiss as meaningless even this blatant example of conflict of interest.

Conflicts of interest are often subtle and might require careful analysis before they can be resolved. For this reason, I frequently present hypothetical issues of conflict of interest that test grand jurors' willingness to forego during their term certain types of citizenship activities. In general election years, for example, I ask them to discuss the ramifications of the following possibility:

> You are known in your community as a strong supporter and worker for your political party. You have served twice as party chairman and are a person whom political candidates of your party rely on for fundraising. This year while you serve as a grand juror, several candidates of your party ask you for permission to use your name and grand jury affiliation in their newspaper political advertisements. What will you do?

Some grand jurors quickly state that they will forbid the use of their names for those purposes and that they will otherwise refrain from political activities during their term of service. More often than one might expect, however, I receive a reply such as this:

> When I became a grand juror, I did not abandon my civil rights. No one is going to tell me who I can or cannot campaign for, and you can bet that if I am asked to help out in any way during a campaign, I'll do everything I can for my party, grand juror or not.

When, on another occasion, a grand juror made a similar comment, I asked her whether she knew that judges have developed codes of professional conduct to help them deal with such problems. I asked her to consider whether, as officers of the court, grand jurors should not be as careful as judges in avoiding involvement in political campaigns. She replied:

> What the judges do is their business. I've got two hats. One for the grand jury and one for my work for the party. Everyone knows when I've got my grand jury hat on and when I've got my party hat on. It's not a problem.

Strong convictions based on sound principles are an asset for any undertaking. When, however, grand jurors refuse to open their minds to the possibility that grand jury service could require them for one year to set aside certain of their enthusiasms or emotional needs, the spirit of the institution alone pays the price.[9]

SUBJECTIVITY AND TRIVIALITY

Many grand jurors I have trained object to learning about factuality, documentation, verification, and corroboration of evidence, referring to these matters as "unnecessary," "busy work," or "nitpicking." Although I often have wondered why people holding such convictions would agree to serve on a fact-finding body, I do not believe a lack of intelligence explains their views entirely. With the abandonment of the "blue ribbon" grand jury and the recruitment of grand jurors from a broader base of the general population, fewer and fewer of them likely have learned about what used to be called "logic," "rhetoric," "the scientific method," or similar subjects in high school and college.[10]

It is one thing when citizens have sufficient insight to realize that grand jury service requires fact-finding and analysis skills they do not possess. They might ask legal advisors or other qualified persons to help them acquire those skills. It is another matter when citizens impaneled as grand jurors dismiss these topics as useless, theoretical, or impractical. In grand jury service, these skills are more than mere refinements of reasoning. They are the best protection a grand juror has against a libel suit.

In a libel suit, topics such as evidence, facts, verification, and the like are no longer busy work or nitpicking. They are now what concern the court, trial jury, plaintiff, and defendants as the case proceeds to judgment. From a grand juror's perspective, these concerns also underlie the need to determine whether one's homeowner's insurance policy includes coverage for damages in a suit for libel. One also may worry about whether it is too late to file a declaration of homestead.

Finally, the former grand-juror defendants might speculate about whether the trial jury will take into consideration, as extenuating circumstances, contradictions between the "raw evidentiary material" holding of the *McClatchy* case and the requirement in Penal Code Section 916 for documentation that was discussed previously. All of these issues, and many more, will loom large as the trial participants assess the implications for their financial well-being of the varieties of subjectivity listed in Appendix D.[11] A pressing question from the perspective of citizenship is whether grand jurors considering such matters in a libel suit will resent an educational system that has failed to prepare them for the kind of fact finding and deliberation necessary for grand jury service in particular and for self-government in general.

One cannot be certain merely from reading grand jury final reports why subjectivity occurs so often. Almost everyone commits logical fallacies occasionally or is tempted to leap to conclusions. To expect every member of a panel to be a logician would be unrealistic. Even if this were so, grand jurors would be susceptible to another shortcoming that affects people in organizational settings: group think. Group-think theory contends that maintaining the emotional equilibrium of the group is, for many people, more important than deciding issues on the basis of reasoned deliberation.[12]

Thus, fact finding, inference drawing, and principle itself may, because of social pressure, take a back seat to what group members believe is necessary for the psychological needs of their colleagues. Consequently, decisions that groups make may be less creative and objective than the decisions of individuals.

Another tenet of group-think theory is that group members will be suspicious of any group member who is more intelligent than themselves. In these circumstances, quick-witted, energetic panel members might be regarded with suspicion by their less mentally able colleagues. Thus, what should be an asset for the institution becomes a liability.

The obstacles that poor thinking skills and social conformity pose for the spirit of the institution are formidable. If the evidence in final reports for the effects of these related influences is only circumstantial, one must remember that, as Thoreau said, "Some circumstantial evidence is very strong, as when you find a trout in the milk."[13] Persuasive circumstantial evidence also can be found in grand jury final reports about another strong force related to citizenship: the extent to which grand jurors defer to public officials.

GRAND JURY SERVICE AND SOCIAL STATUS

Some scholars claim that, in earlier times, grand jurors and public officials were from the same social class. Because of this similarity, one writer contends that, contrary to criticism about their ineffectiveness, the "benevolent paternalism" of grand juries in the seventeenth century often improved local-government practices.[14] Of course, the similarity in social standing of grand jurors and local-government officials probably worked both ways in earlier times, as it does today. Although the parity of their status with public officials permitted grand jurors to influence some local-government practices, it might also have made them reluctant to criticize others.

With the democratization of the institution in recent times, civil grand jurors often find themselves interviewing public officials they believe to be of higher social rankings. Impressive titles, conspicuously displayed professional credentials on office walls, and the costly trappings and furnishings of bureaucracy therefore might intimidate some panel members. Moving freely for the first time in their lives among political elites, grand jurors could sense that they have acquired a heightened social status. In these circumstances, they would want to protect their newly found importance. One way to do so is to avoid disturbing the local-government political system.

The profuse display in final reports of colored photographs of themselves, the frequent repetition of their names in final reports, and paying newspaper publishers to print final reports as tabloid inserts enables grand jurors to broadcast their rise in social rank to their fellow citizens. For some citizens, grand jury service therefore is important chiefly for its prestige value. For example, obituaries occasionally list the years of service and committee assignments among the other social achievements of deceased grand jurors. On one occasion, I found a reference to grand jury service listed among other cultural achievements of a local symphony director.[15]

Even grand jurors who already have some standing in their social circles might be grateful to local-government officials for having made them privy to the political intrigues and inner workings of the county political establishment. This is why tension between a county supervisor and a grand jury in one of California's most affluent counties is of interest. The grand jury in question rarely issues final reports that criticize county officials. Indeed, during the study period, the Foreman expressed in a final report his gratitude and that of fellow grand jurors for a reception that County Supervisors staged early in the panel's term.[16]

When a grand jury of that County in a more recent year displayed unaccustomed independence in addressing a local issue, one of the County Supervisors, working through a Statewide association, caused The Civil Grand Jury Training, Communication and Efficiency Act of 1997 to be introduced into the California Legislature. Some time later, the same Supervisor announced his intention to change by legislation the name of the California civil grand jury to "Citizen Review Committee."[17]

Exploiting the institution to enhance social status might seem to be merely a mild form of corruption. It becomes serious, however, when grand jurors, not wishing to offend "their betters," decide against conducting an investigation that could threaten the local political system. Status concerns therefore may explain why ceremonial panels rarely conduct significant investigations. Even if circumstances force a ceremonial grand jury to conduct a potentially controversial investigation, status-minded grand jurors do everything possible to ensure that reports of their investigations do not disturb the local balance of political power. This practice might explain why some investigations summarized in Chapter 4, which should have been conducted and reported vigorously, were downgraded to minor incidents. Thus, grand jurors who wonder why other citizens know so little about the institution might well ask the question in another way: What have grand jurors accomplished in the community that should command the attention of its citizens?

The carry-over statute, Penal Code Section 901(b), also has implications for status-minded grand jurors and the institution. If one term of grand jury service is a mark of distinction, two terms inflate one's status doubly. Ironically, far from ensuring the presence of skilled active citizens on a panel, the sociology of the carry-over statute fosters mediocre investigations and reports for several reasons:

1. Novice grand jurors on a panel are, as a group, likely to be suspicious of the more "experienced" panel members, particularly if the latter insist that the grand jury continue an investigation of the previous year.

2. Many carry-over grand jurors serve a second term because they have little else to do. This might imply a lack of initiative that irks more dedicated grand jurors.

3. The carry-over system often attracts status-seeking citizens who will be reluctant to offend those who nominated or appointed them.

These are only a few examples of the tensions that can arise between carry-over grand jurors and their colleagues who have no previous grand jury service. Unfortunately, the consequences of the carry-over statute too often are dissension and the resulting dilution of purpose, effort, and effectiveness.

Social-status concerns also underlie the much-criticized deference that grand jurors often extend to district attorneys. The novelty of associating with a public official known as "the county's chief law enforcement officer" is, for many citizens, a rare opportunity. The district attorney is, after all, the gatekeeper for the exciting, risky, and sinister world of the criminal justice system. With the possible exception of the sheriff or a chief of police, the district attorney is the only public official who can take grand jurors behind the scenes of the daily drama of crime and social disorder.

For some grand jurors, indictment proceedings offer cultural opportunities that are even more alluring than the civil function is. In Los Angeles County, a former grand jury Foreman complained that were it not for the opportunity to hear indictments, there would be no point to grand jury service. An indictment hearing afforded him an opportunity, after all, to meet pop-culture celebrity Cher, who was a witness in a drug-related case.[18]

Thus, a term of grand jury service yields many interesting stories for impressing friends, neighbors, and relatives whose own life circumstances would not otherwise allow them access to the corridors of local-government political power. None of these benefits can be obtained if the relationship between the grand jury and the district attorney is strained or indifferent. This could explain why, during the study period, grand jurors rarely reported investigations of district attorneys' offices. Status enhancement, the carry-over statute, and the need for equilibrium in local political systems therefore affect complementarily the sense of citizenship that guides some grand jurors during their term of service.

What Kind of Citizenship Does the Institution Require?

The preceding section offered several examples of how different conceptions of citizenship can affect the spirit of the institution. Although ideology, self-interest, status insecurity, and the like no doubt influence grand jury investigations and reports, a broader analysis of the practice of citizenship in grand jury service would include additional matters. For example, one might consider how educational institutions prepare Americans for the kind of active citizenship required, not only for grand jury service but also for participation in government affairs in general.

Increasingly, commentators of the left and right ends of the political spectrum express concerns about the objectivity of "government schools" in providing civics education. Whereas educational theorists 30 years ago were loath to allow business interests to influence consumer education curricula, the question now being asked is whether civics education designed and dispensed by government schools realistically can be expected to produce independent-thinking, active citizens.[19]

The decline in investigative reporting of local-governmental affairs by the news media also should be examined as it affects how citizens conceive their civic responsibilities.[20] With "news you can use" and booster journalism replacing traditional investigative reporting, an important citizenship value is being forgotten: Government functions most effectively and honestly when its affairs are open to rigorous public scrutiny.[21] If journalists abandon their First Amendment rights and their responsibilities as citizens to report public affairs critically, will their readers conclude that oversight therefore must be unnecessary? If so, will they lose the skills and motivation necessary for active citizenship?

Moreover, what significance does this trend in journalism have for recruiting citizens for grand jury service? Does the "news blackout" of local-government activities and practices create a citizenry that does not understand the concept of accountability, much less have the will to demand it in public affairs? Finally, if is it true, as some critics fear, that the news media decide what to publish or broadcast exclusively in terms of their economic self-interest, how does this practice affect citizenship?

Intellectual fashions and trends in social science are also promising fields of inquiry for the study of citizenship. Political scientists, historians, and economists, for example, write the textbooks that often are used in secondary education. Thus, to some extent, the fads of the social science disciplines define what young American citizens learn about the governments that soon will affect their lives and careers so profoundly. Therefore, to understand why Americans know so little about their government, one must consider the politics of the social sciences. The complexity of this subject requires more discussion than I can accord it here, except for one observation: Social scientists, like most other citizens, are concerned with their careers and economic status. Unfortunately, studying citizenship and improving the practice of self-government offer few incentives for research. Government contracts and foundation grants for research into establishment-approved projects are far more abundant.

A study of the social forces that affect citizenship, and thereby the grand jury, would be incomplete if it were to ignore the legal profession. In California, the statutorily designated advisors for the institution are, after all, lawyers. Moreover, the grand jury is an arm of the judiciary. Accordingly, the extent to which the legal profession has developed a body of literature to support the institution contributes to how effectively grand jurors discharge their duties and, by extension, how well the institution achieves its legitimate objectives.

The combination of education for citizenship, the work of the news media, and the scholarly legal resources and social science knowledge available for grand jurors directly shapes the kind of citizenship that grand jurors practice during their term of service. Many influences besides those that I have briefly discussed affect the kind of citizenship that Americans exhibit throughout their lives and careers. Comprehensive treatment of this subject would include, for example, research into what Americans learn about citizenship from television, their family members, and from friends and acquaintances. The economics of earning a living no doubt also has much to do with the practice of citizenship.

With respect to grand jurors, other issues, such as judges' knowledge about the grand jury and their attitudes concerning it, also must be included in a thorough inquiry into how citizens define their responsibilities as grand jurors. Such a broad-gauged examination of citizenship is not feasible in these closing pages. Instead, later in the chapter I review some of the implications of a more fully elaborated citizenship project by discussing in greater detail the four influences I have treated briefly. Before doing so, however, we first must consider the form of citizenship implicit in the statutes and case law that are the foundation of the civil grand jury in California.

Aristotle's "Serious Citizen"

In his *Politics*, Aristotle discussed citizenship but refrained from defining the "ideal" citizen. To answer the question, "What kind of citizen does the spirit of the institution require?" Aristotle might have replied, "The grand jury requires the kind of citizenship suited to its purpose." Aristotle used the term "serious citizens" for individuals who were willing and qualified to conduct themselves according to what the regime in which they lived required of its citizens. Thus, absolute monarchies required not active citizens but, instead, compliant subjects.

In the case of representative government, one who is actively engaged in the conduct of public affairs would be the regime's appropriate, that is to say, serious citizen. That person, therefore, would be not merely one who is ruled but who also rules: "The citizen, simply speaking, is defined by nothing else so much as by his having a share in judgment and rule or office."[22]

The "Serious" Grand Juror

Several years ago I wrote a "job description" for grand jury service. This was an experiment. I thought it might assist judges in their annual efforts to recruit grand jurors. As they are used in civil service, job descriptions typically consist of lists of skills, experience, and educational qualifications that a particular function requires—for example, that of a police officer or a welfare director. When I reviewed the draft of the grand juror job description, I realized it lacked something important. The missing element, moreover, was that which personnel technicians rarely include in job descriptions: the values required for effective job performance. Without a statement of desirable values, a job description for the office of grand juror consisting only of tasks, skills, and knowledge would not distinguish grand jury service significantly from other positions in local government.

In almost every local government in California, for example, some local-government officials and employees would qualify for a job statement with specifications such as, "Must have knowledge of statutes related to grand jury service," "Must be able to plan, conduct, and report investigations," and "Must understand California local government." The spirit of the institution requires something different in a citizen serving as a grand juror: a cast of mind that, in some respects, is contrary to that found in civil service.

Active citizens serving as grand jurors understand that, in our form of government, citizen participation means more than merely supporting their political party, voting, or paying taxes. They believe that the practice of "deep citizenship" is necessary to preserve government as a common good, and that citizens must constantly observe, maintain, and repair the state.[23] Questioning public officials about their practices, examining their answers carefully, and insisting on verification and corroboration of facts imply a citizen activism that causes discomfort for some public officials and employees and, indeed, other citizens. Skillful citizens, however, know how to ask pointed questions with courtesy and respect, and, if rebuffed, they are willing to employ the necessary lawful techniques to obtain answers. In the words of a prominent student of citizenship, the serious grand juror is willing to "pay attention" to public affairs and knows how to do so.[24] Thus, a serious grand juror is not a "cocoon" citizen but, rather, believes that in representative government, passive citizens have neglected their duties and responsibilities and therefore are subversive of the social order.[25]

Serious-citizen grand jurors would consider it a personal failure to complain in a final report that public officials failed to inform the panel of the location of the county law library, a facility that in most California counties is either in the same building as the chambers of the superior court or within a few blocks of them. They also would be embarrassed if they could think of nothing more imaginative to conserve tax dollars than to urge county supervisors to disconnect the grand jury's telephone and discontinue its post office box. They would understand the symbolic implications of such an act for the independence of the grand jury. Indeed, grand jurors committed to the spirit of the institution would, as the foreman described in Chapter 7 did, arrange for the panel to acquire its own meeting room, computer, file cabinets, and the other necessities of an active and productive office.

The attitude of the serious citizen serving as a grand juror would be neither blindly supportive of the state nor needlessly antagonistic to it. This perspective would foster neutrality in conducting investigations, the nurturing of civility, and the persistence, energy, and will necessary for understanding that to create effective solutions, one must aggressively seek the root causes of problems. These citizens also would conceive of grand jury service not as a status-enhancing right but, rather, as a duty and responsibility to be performed on behalf of their community. They also would believe that if grand jury service is a school for citizenship, the community is well served by having as many "alumni" grand jurors as possible. Therefore, the idea of carrying over grand jurors would be understood as contradictory to the spirit of the institution, corrupting, and an ill-advised limitation on the number of citizens in a community who have had the privilege of exercising an important civic duty.

Additionally, serious grand jurors would recognize the wisdom of the institution's lack of jurisdiction in policy matters. They would understand, for example, that if grand jurors took a strong position in their final report against a particular policy issue, the subsequent panel would be equally justified in adopting the opposite position. The panels therefore would nullify each other. Conversely, serious grand jurors know that exposing corrupt or ineffective local-government systems, procedures, or methods often arouses a community to correct those practices. Serious grand jurors also would comprehend that paying a newspaper money to reproduce in its entirety a grand jury final report is not a triumph for the institution but, rather, a surrender to the evils of the commercialization of the news media.[26]

In this discussion I do not use "serious" in the sense that grand jurors should be dour, puritanical, or self-righteous. The institution is burdened enough by critics who wish to associate it with grim Star Chamber proceedings. Consider, however, the grand juror I referred to in Chapter 4 who posed for a photograph that appeared on the dividing page of a final report. Recall that he wore a straw hat and held an antique telephone. What purpose do such highjinks serve, and what meaning do they convey about the grand jury culture of the county? What shall we conclude about the grand juror's view of himself? of his fellow grand jurors? of the institution? of American civic life? To be a "serious" citizen in the sense that Aristotle used the term means that, in representative government, one conceives of his relationship to his community in a mature, active sense rather than as child-like subjecthood.

Although much more could be written about characteristics of the serious citizen as grand juror, this brief account shows why a value statement about citizenship for the "position" of grand juror would not be found in a local-government job description written in traditional personnel administration terms. Another way to understand the nature of citizenship that the spirit of the institution requires is to consider examples of investigations that serious grand jurors might conduct.

Grand Jury Investigations and Active Citizenship

Many examples of behavior by grand jurors that I discussed in previous chapters involve civic values—by which I mean bedrock attitudes and beliefs about citizens' rights and duties with respect to government. Although the California Legislature enacted statutes authorizing the jurisdiction of the civil grand jury, they say little about why grand jurors should investigate local government, what they should look for, or how they should judge what they find. Of course, in exempting itself from grand jury oversight, by excluding the word "policies" from the statutes, and by using words such as "operations," "methods," "books" "records," and "accounts," the Legislature expressed its own values about the institution. In general, however, California lawmakers evidently intended grand jurors to draw upon their own values, within statutory limits, in deciding what to investigate or not to investigate, how to conduct investigations, and what to report about them.

From the institution's perspective, the discretion the Legislature allows grand jurors is a mixed blessing. If a panel consists of citizens who know only that local government exists but understand little more about it, the "Cook's Tours" final reports described in Chapter 5 will be the limits of their skills. One might argue on the one hand that being ignorant about something and having or not having values concerning it are different issues. On the other hand, the "value" in the case of grand jurors who know little or nothing about local government is that they apparently believe citizens should be ignorant about an important part of their lives.

Some grand jurors are well informed about local government but also are biased in what they believe its purpose should be. Grand jurors, for example, of the "Businessman's Outlook" that concerned the sociologist who studied Los Angeles County Grand Juries five decades ago would select somewhat different investigative topics than would grand jurors who are public employees.[27]

One must concede that, at best, inferring civic values from final reports is risky. Perhaps some Cook's Tours final reports come about not because of ignorance of local government or the presence or absence of certain values, but, instead, because grand jurors are so preoccupied with indictments that they have no time to conduct significant civil investigations. Another possibility is that irreconcilable conflicts in values arose among grand jurors. As a result, they reported trivial investigations because they could not agree on more important topics. In other panels, perhaps the turnover of grand jurors during the year was so frequent that too few of them were present from the beginning of investigations to their conclusions. The fact-finding nature of the grand jury would seem to require that grand jurors vote only on investigations they deliberated about from start to finish. Even if this were not required, grand jurors would be ill-advised to identify themselves with investigations with which they became involved after the grand jury concluded the evidence-gathering phase.

Grand jurors rarely include in final reports explicit statements about their civic values. For instance, the grand juror referred to in Chapter 4 who urged county school-district trustees to adopt President Bush's Goals 2000 initiative, or the grand jurors who wrote a vacuous treatise about water in their county, or the grand jurors who formed an alliance with a local grand jurors' association to "get" a local public official, did not state in their final reports why they did so. In the absence of candid statements about their motives, one can only speculate about matters such as these.

Later in this chapter I explain how civic values can affect grand jury investigations. Before doing so, I offer examples of civic values that are, so to speak, drawn from the lore of governance upon which our political system rests. Obviously, these precepts do not constitute the entire body of belief about governance. Nor do I claim that all citizens accept them either as I have stated them or in any other form. Indeed, each of these civic values has an opposite counterpart. What is important for grand jury service is not whether the value is expressed positively or negatively but, rather, whether it supports or subverts the spirit of the institution. For example, if one accepts the premise that we should leave government to the professionals and let them manage public affairs without being accountable to citizens, the grand jury would have no reason to exist. That position, of course, would conflict with a longstanding civic value in American government that professionalism often is important in the management of public affairs but that it must be responsive to the citizenry.

Although the following discussion presents individual examples of civic values, they often do not stand alone and, of course, neither the Constitution of the United States nor, possibly, any of the other documents associated with the nation's birth expresses them as I do in my discussion. Depending upon their presence or absence and the proportions of their mix, they nevertheless affect the grand jury culture in each county, and therefore they may be inferred from many grand jury investigations and reports.

Examples of Civic Values

One might argue that the statutes creating the California civil grand jury themselves express a prime American civic value—that public affairs must be open to the scrutiny of citizens. Or, to state the postulate differently, government must not conduct the public's business behind locked doors.[28] A related civic value also asserts that citizens are entitled to information in public records not exempted from public oversight by statute.[29]

Both civic values—open public meetings and access to public records—are intertwined with the spirit of the institution. Without those principles, the grand jury has no reason to exist, nor, for that matter, do the news media. Actually, much of our Constitution would be meaningless if citizens were to permit government to operate on its own terms and with no involvement by citizens. Assuming that the Legislature intends grand jurors to conduct investigations not merely for appearances, the authority of the grand jury to issue findings and recommendations about its deliberations implies another civic value: Representative government requires institutions and procedures through which citizens can legitimately influence public affairs. This premise underlies the First Amendment of the United States Constitution, thereby connecting grand juries with the news media, libraries, the Internet, public-interest groups, and countless other civic institutions.

The right and duty of citizens to examine government operations and seek changes in them connote still other civic values. For one, citizens must be permitted to attend legislative meetings and have access to public records. Neither type of access to government would have meaning if public bodies were authorized to meet at irregular times and places, if they were to charge citizens exorbitant fees for copies of public documents, or if they otherwise were to create difficulty in obtaining them. Thus, procedures must be provided to ensure that public meetings occur at regular times and at designated locations and that advance notices of the meetings are posted in public places.

Further, reasonable and effective procedures must be devised so citizens can easily obtain records of meetings and all other information not lawfully exempted from public review. Charges for copies of public records must be modest, and no physical or procedural barrier should intimidate citizens who desire access to those materials. Even the design of meeting rooms, the ease of entering and occupying them, and the demeanor of elected officials and their staff in responding to citizens who request assistance are issues derived from the civic values of open meetings, freedom of information, and responsive public officials.

Another civic value that differentiates our form of government from other political regimes is that government officials must not use public resources for any purpose other than the common good. Making gifts of public funds, for example, is counter to this principle.[30] And, if public officials use tax funds to create citizen support for bond elections, if they use tax funds to augment their campaign funds, or if they use the funds to benefit only narrow classes of citizens, they have offended two basic civic values:

1. Money in the public treasury is collected for the common good and therefore must be spent fairly and honestly for that purpose.
2. Citizens are at a disadvantage if government uses their taxes to oppose or support elections for bond measures, tax-rate increases, and the like.

Other examples of civic values include the belief that no one should have preference in obtaining public employment because of their family, business, religious, or fraternal connections. Similarly, public officials must not restrict their appointments to advisory boards or commissions to business associates, political allies, or their friends. Nepotism and "packing" boards or commissions are practices long considered to be examples of the "bossism" that breeds corruption in government.[31]

CIVIC VALUES AND THE REPUTATION OF THE CIVIL GRAND JURY

Many civic values associated with grand jury service can be classified under one of three beliefs inherent in our form of government:

1. Public officials should be accountable for their acts.
2. Public officials must use the power and authority of the state as carefully, honestly, and humanely as possible.
3. The resources of the state should be used for the common good rather than for the personal benefit of privileged individuals or groups.

Without these values, explicit or implicit, grand jury investigations and reports have little substance, and public officials, the news media, and other citizens may properly criticize grand jurors for their pointlessness, insignificance, and shallowness. To the extent that news-media staffs perceive the institution in this light, they do not regard grand jury activities as newsworthy. Citizens, in turn, do not learn about grand jury accomplishments, and the enemies of the institution are comforted. Therefore, this sequence of opinions about the institution explains why—as many grand jurors ask when they are first impaneled— citizens so frequently are ignorant about grand juries and their purposes.

Civic Values in Grand Jury Investigations

In this section I present five examples of civil grand jury investigations. My purpose in doing so is to illustrate grand jury investigations that I believe are attuned to the spirit of the institution. The examples represent the types of investigations that grand jurors who have at least a rudimentary grasp of longstanding civic values would conduct. For each example I describe one or more civic values that it implies and discuss how grand jurors' conceptions of citizenship might affect those values. The topics are consistent with grand jury statutes; they concern local-government activities within the jurisdiction of grand juries, and they do not intrude into policy matters but, rather, involve procedures, systems, methods, and so on. They also are within the conceptual grasp of knowledgeable, active citizens. Moreover, grand jurors can conduct them with the resources usually available to panels.

Although some grand jury final reports in the study period have touched on one or two of the topics I discuss below, I never have read a report of a grand jury investigation into any of these matters that was as comprehensive as each description suggests. In discussing each topic, my purpose is not to present them as examples of model investigations but, rather, to illustrate the civic values and conceptions of citizenship implicit in each topic and to discuss its significance for community well-being.

Example A: Identify and describe the extent of use of quasi–local-government agencies in the county, their purposes, and organization and administration.

Observers of public affairs are concerned increasingly about the rapid growth of quasi-governments that local-government public officials create for a variety of purposes.[32] Although these entities were formed for sound reasons in certain circumstances, some commentators claim that public officials use them occasionally for questionable purposes.[33] To the extent that citizens do not know how many entities like these exist in their counties, the size and scope of government theoretically could expand far beyond what citizens might believe or desire it to be. Equally important, because elected officials often appoint themselves or are required by law to be policymakers for these nontraditional governments, they could become the public-sector equivalent of the interlocking directorates that many observers of massive corporatism and monopolistic systems in private enterprise have long deplored.

Quasi–local governments also offer opportunities for political patronage. For instance, quasi–local governments could permit elected officials to expand greatly the number of friends, relatives, business associates, campaign contributors, and others they can reward with political appointments. As is the case in the next example, the information that certain State agencies collect and publish about quasi–local governments is only as accurate as the creators of those entities permit it to be. Grand juries therefore could provide a valuable service to their communities by ensuring that the agencies comply with State reporting requirements. To do so, however, grand jurors first must obtain or compile an accurate inventory of all such entities in their counties. Conducting the inventory or verifying one that some other agency has compiled would do much to notify public officials that quasi–local governments are subject to public scrutiny not merely in theory but also in practice. An investigation of this nature also would support the civic value of open government.

Example B: Determine whether the county has a single, accurate source of information about the extent of indebtedness of each local government.

Although several agencies of the State of California collect and publish information they receive from local governments concerning their indebtedness, the agencies necessarily rely on local officials for the accuracy, completeness, and timeliness of the information. The California Debt and Investment Advisory Commission, for example, qualifies the data it periodically publishes about local-government indebtedness with these words: "[This report] is based on information reported to the California Debt and Investment Advisory Commission...." If, therefore, a local government has not reported data about its indebtedness to appropriate State agencies, that information will not appear in reports from State sources. Similarly, if local government sends inaccurate indebtedness data to a State agency, the agency may not have sufficient staff to detect errors or omissions, or possess any statutory authority to do so. Recognizing the importance of collecting timely and accurate information about public indebtedness, the California Debt and Investment Advisory Commission is attempting to improve the method it uses to collect such information.[34]

Grand jurors could play an important part in this effort by assessing in their own counties the systems, procedures, and methods that local governments have developed to collect such information and forward it to appropriate State agencies. As uninteresting as that project might sound, in the present economic climate of California, few grand jury inquiries exceed its importance. This investigative topic, therefore, is an example of the prime civic value of *accountability.*

To the extent that local-government indebtedness data are incomplete, no one knows exactly how much debt public agencies have accumulated either in individual counties or Statewide. Most citizens are unaware that they are the guarantors of the debt that their local governments incur. In effect, citizens are liable for the indebtedness that funding creates: examples are major public-works projects such as sports stadia, buildings for public schools and other government functions, redevelopment projects, and the like. In the absence of accurate systems and procedures for compiling and reporting this sort of information, California could reach and exceed the point at which a large-scale public-finance disaster occurs. Yet, even in the largest county in California, no local-government agency is responsible for monitoring public indebtedness.[35]

Examples of questions that grand juries could ask in conducting a study of this nature include:

- What is the total local-government indebtedness for the county?
- How large is the indebtedness on a per-capita basis, and how does the county's per-capita indebtedness compare to that of similar counties?

- Are the indebtedness data that local governments report to State agencies consistent with that available locally?
- Have any professional auditors recently tested the accuracy of the data collected locally, and, if so, what was discovered?
- What is the ratio of indebtedness to general-fund revenues, and how might credit ratings and future borrowing costs within the county be thereby affected?

Aristotle's "serious citizen" would understand that, to some extent, the amount of indebtedness of a local government is a measure of its social, economic, and political soundness. For this reason, some lending institutions publish indebtedness ratings of local governments, and these ratings may affect their ability to obtain future loans. Moreover, in the absence of accurate and timely information about public indebtedness, citizens would not know whether their communities are on the brink of a financial debacle similar to what took place in Orange County, California, in the mid-1990s. Thus, grand jury inquiries into whether local-government agencies comply fully with statutory requirements to report their indebtedness to designated State agencies could have profound implications not only for one county but for the entire State and possibly the nation as well.

Example C: Evaluate the method the county library uses to select periodicals.

Grand juries occasionally receive complaints from citizens about the content of one or more periodicals in public libraries. Fearing that complaints of this nature might subject them to charges of comstockery, grand jurors typically refuse to conduct such investigations. If they are unaware of laws governing the civil grand jury, citizens filing complaints about library periodicals might interpret grand jurors' refusals to investigate them as a "government cover-up." A grand jury investigation into such a complaint, however, could be undertaken without implications of censorship.

Periodical collections are among the valuable cultural resources that libraries provide to serve the reading interests of many different kinds of people. Although grand jurors have no jurisdiction in judging as a policy matter which magazines libraries should or should not subscribe to, panels could inquire lawfully into the *methods* that libraries use to decide which magazines to place in the periodical collection. Among the issues that grand jurors could address are:

- What procedures have library officials developed to ensure that magazine titles serve the broadest possible public?
- How do libraries decide the "mix" of periodicals (as examples, newsletters, scholarly publications, news magazines, do-it-yourself and other self-help publications)?

- Is the existing system for deciding which magazines to acquire consistent with standards that recognized library associations and authorities recommend?
- If a citizen library advisory group is involved in selecting periodicals, who appoints that body, for how long do they serve, and what interests do they represent?

The "systems, methods, and procedures" approach that I have described can do much to assure citizens that nothing jeopardizes the common-good character of one of any community's most important intellectual assets: the public library. Although grand jurors do not have, nor should they have, power to order libraries to subscribe to specific periodicals, they do have the authority to determine whether the library complies with the civic value of developing fair and equitable acquisition procedures rather than making decisions along ideological or partisan lines. Whether a proposal for such an investigation would survive in a grand jury that includes current or retired librarians or other grand jurors with strong political, religious, or cultural commitments is a question of citizenship.

Example D: Investigate the extent to which local governments employ internal auditors or contract for such work.

Given the expansion of government in recent decades, opportunities for ineffective use and management of public resources, for embezzlement of public funds, and for misuse of publicly owned equipment and related abuses have increased commensurately. If these matters are too technical for grand jurors or require expenditures of time and effort that are not available to them, they can at least ensure that local-government officials have created adequate systems and procedures to prevent the theft and misuse of public resources. In public administration it is axiomatic that the extent to which fraud, graft, and corruption are prevented or detected is a function of how much effort is exerted for those purposes.[36]

Grand jurors are in an unusually favorable position to investigate the extent to which local governments in their county employ internal auditors or contract for those services. If the use of internal auditors by local governments has declined, the reason should be determined. If internal audits have been conducted in local governments in recent years, grand jurors should discover what the subjects of the audits have been, what important issues have not been addressed, and which agencies have been frequently audited and which have been infrequently or never audited. Similarly, grand jurors could conduct an inventory of audit reports, discover where they are filed, and determine whether citizens have ready access to them.

Just as grand jurors should follow up on the outcomes of their own findings and recommendations, they also should conduct research into the implementation of findings and recommendations in internal auditors' reports. Finally, if local governments contract with private consulting firms for internal audits, grand juries should determine which firms are hired, for how long, and what bidding procedures exist for contacting prospective auditing firms. By conducting such an investigation, grand jurors would demonstrate their willingness to nurture within their communities the civic values of account-ability and the effective use of public monies.

Example E: Inquire into the procedures that local-government officials created for assessing how the "millennium bug" problem affected the provision of public services.

In 1998 and 1999, the so-called millennium bug or Y2K problem received worldwide publicity. Some computer experts predicted that because many software programs could not recognize the digits needed to express the year 2000, numerous computers would not function after the beginning of that year. Forecasts of the consequences of this problem ranged from a complete collapse of social, economic, and political systems to minor discomfort and inconvenience for some segments of the populace.

Given the extensive speculation and gloomy forecasts that preceded its arrival, one might have expected the millennium-bug problem to have been the topic of many grand jury investigations. Curiously, none of the grand juries of the study period, and few since then, addressed it.[37] For the civil grand jury and local government, the millennium-bug problem was essentially an issue of disaster preparedness. The civil grand jury is well suited to address this issue even in its aftermath, for a review of the matter involves the efficiency of emergency planning systems, procedures, and methods.

A retrospective study of the millennium-bug problem also lends itself to the productive use of a civil grand jury power that is rarely invoked: holding public sessions to obtain testimony concerning an issue affecting the "general public welfare."[38] To my knowledge, the only two uses of the public-session statute in the past decade involved the Madera County Grand Jury in 1989 and the Santa Clara County Grand Jury in 1996. Its use in Madera County arose from a rancorous public controversy concerning salary increases for the County Board of Supervisors.[39] In 1996, the statute was used to hold a public hearing about a deputy sheriff who was accused of shooting and killing a citizen in a foot pursuit after a high-speed automobile chase.[40]

The public-session statute permits civil grand jurors in a "town hall" setting to take statements from public officials and other citizens concerning their positions about a controversial issue. By holding an orderly, well-planned public session, grand jurors could decide whether local governments prepared adequately for the problem, what they believed its extent was, and the extent to which citizens were concerned about its consequences. A civil grand jury inquiry would also reveal what local-government officials learned from their inspections of computers and software, including the efficiency and integrity of data processing systems beyond the issue of the Y2K problem. A "town meeting" inquiry into the millennium-bug problem would also affirm a crucial civic value in an open political system: the need to ensure not merely that the state has taken the steps to prevent a civil disaster, but that its procedures to do so were effective.

Citizenship and the Five Examples

To some extent, each of the examples I have discussed exemplifies the characteristic of the institution that distinguished it in history: intervening between citizens and the state. Thus, each example tests whether grand jurors are willing as citizens to exercise their right and duty to ensure that the government they and their forebears created is used for the common good rather than for private purposes. The principle of accountability is also present in each example, as is the civic value of openness in government. Each example also shows why the institution's lack of jurisdiction in policy matters is not a defect but is, rather, an asset. To the extent that investigations into systems, methods, procedures, and the like are well planned, conducted, and reported, they will accomplish far more than subjective harangues about the wisdom, say, of public indebtedness, or whether magazines in libraries undermine public morality, or whether government is too large or too small. The chief effect of investigations of the type I have described will be to place these matters squarely in the public arena for informed debate by the electorate who, after all, are the proper judges of the policy implications of such issues.

In varying degrees, each investigation also raises important questions about the ethical and technical limitations of professionalism. If elected officials and their staffs create quasi-governments solely as strategies to evade citizen oversight, what does this say about their integrity? If no one knows the extent of public indebtedness in a county, what does this imply about relationships between public employees who are the stewards of indebtedness data and the private financial institutions that benefit from indebtedness? If trained and credentialed librarians are reluctant to involve citizens in decisions about an institution that exemplifies the common good in our communities, what does this say about their professionalism? If public officials have not hired internal auditors at a rate proportionate to the expansion of government, what may citizens conclude about the willingness of those officials to be effective guardians of the public treasury? Finally, how did it happen that thousands of professional programmers for decades permitted the millennium-bug problem to lie dormant? If citizens serving as grand jurors can find answers to these questions, they will have well served their communities and the spirit of the institution.

Each of the five examples poses another question about citizens in grand jury service: To what extent do investigations of the type I have described challenge the citizenship skills and values of panel members? For example, to be conducted effectively, each of the investigations demands that grand jurors ask difficult questions of public officials. If grand jurors are unwilling to ask these questions, or if they believe that the questions might offend public officials, one need not wonder why the news media pay little attention to the institution. Likewise, several of the topics might be disturbing to people because they suggest distrust of elected and appointed public officials. Grand jurors so inclined not only misunderstand the spirit of the institution but also have not learned one of the foundational civic values of our political system: the right and duty of citizens to demand accountability in government.

The subjects of the investigations also challenge the ability of citizens to rise above self-interest. For example, grand jurors who depend upon real-estate development or financial institutions for their incomes might be uneasy with inquiry into public indebtedness. They might believe that an investigation of this kind will raise the consciousness of citizens about a matter that is best left undisturbed. Similarly, several of the investigations might pose problems for currently employed or recently retired public employees. Some of them, for example, might have spouses or other relatives who are employed by quasi-governmental agencies. They therefore would be concerned about the outcomes of the investigations. Other former or current public employees, such as educators and librarians, might object to grand jury inquiries into library affairs, arguing that only professionally trained persons are qualified to evaluate those matters.

Finally, if, through collegiality and open-minded deliberation, grand jurors eliminate internal barriers to civil investigations, they will confirm one of the most basic civic values in our form of government: the sovereignty of its citizens—a subject that brings us to the question posed in the next section: What kind of citizen does the spirit of the institution require, and what is it about the larger civic culture that impedes development of responsible, active citizenship?

What Is to Be Done?

The plot of "Stopover in a Quiet Town," a 1964 *Twilight Zone* episode, is a useful metaphor for discussing American citizenship. The main characters in the story are a high-living, self-centered, hedonistic wife and husband. The story begins with a scene of the wife driving her inebriated husband home from a party. The young woman is only slightly more sober than her husband. As they are about to crash, a cloud envelops their car. Upon awakening, the couple discover that they are apparently the only inhabitants of a small town.

"Quiet Town" reminds one of scenes in the Thornton Wilder play, *Our Town*: lovely homes surrounded by white picket fences, quaint lampposts, and clean, shady streets. Slowly, the couple in the *Twilight Zone* episode realize that something is wrong: Although they can see no one, they occasionally hear the tolling of a church bell and the laughter of an unseen child. Puzzled, the husband leans against a tree to contemplate the situation. The tree falls over, and as it lies on the ground, the husband sees that it is fake. Startled, he drops a cigarette on a lawn, which ignites immediately. Trying to extinguish the flame, the husband discovers that the "grass" is also artificial. Suddenly the couple see a train stopped at the town depot. They enter an unoccupied passenger car, and the train immediately moves forward, picking up speed rapidly. Relieved at escaping from the pseudo-village, the couple happily discuss how wonderful it will be to return home. After some time, the train loses speed and then stops. Looking out the train window, the couple, to their horror, see that the train has returned to the town they thought they had left. The show ends with the revelation that just before the pair crashed, a spaceship transported them to a planet of gigantic men and women. The couple are no longer adults moving happily and freely in their lives. They now are merely the horror-stricken "toys" of a gargantuan child. As this is disclosed, the viewer realizes that throughout the drama, the couple, despite their predicament, never looked skyward.

Although no gigantic child stands over the county of my residence, equally massive forces are at play. More than a dozen local-government legislative bodies meet throughout the week, often committing citizens to millions of dollars in expenditures, large-scale public-works projects, and the consequences of extensive reorganizations of public agencies and services. Even during meetings at which elected officials make significant decisions about their communities, only a handful of citizens attend. If one were to see large numbers of townspeople at a public meeting of, say, a city council, their purpose probably would be to oppose increases in golf-course green fees or to demand a new baseball field or ice-skating rink.

After members of a militant tax-protest group viciously assaulted the County Clerk of my County, only a few citizens wrote letters to newspapers expressing their concern or their support for her. Evidently, citizens did not understand that the incident was as important, if not on the same scale, as the bombing of the government building in Oklahoma City. During a period when a city council of the same County committed blunder after blunder in a poorly planned but far-ranging redevelopment project, few people attended city council meetings to voice their opinions. In the five years following a sales-tax increase promoted by the County library, no information has been reported publicly concerning how much money the new tax raised or whether it was spent for its intended purpose.

As similar issues come and go in my community, neither the local press nor any civic organizations or the County Grand Jury has raised important questions that should have been asked about these and other matters. Just as the couple in "Stopover in a Quiet Town" failed to look upward, few citizens in a trade area of nearly half a million residents seem concerned about, or are aware of, the enormous public-policy forces that, like the child in the television drama, loom over them. The decay of citizenship I have described is not by any means peculiar to the Central Valley of California. It is everywhere.

What, as Lenin memorably asked, is to be done? How can citizens be convinced to "look up" from time to time? What kinds of institutional and cultural changes must be instituted to replace somnolent subjecthood with a sense of active citizenship? What skills and values must we learn, or relearn, to avoid being cocoon citizens in Quiet Towns?

A Proposal for "Civic Revitalization"

At no time in the history of the United States, with the possible exception of the "town hall era" in New England, have citizens routinely filled the meeting rooms of legislative bodies.[41] No historical evidence supports the notion that even at the founding of our country many citizens devoted much time to participating actively in public affairs. Indeed, only a small percentage of citizens were involved directly in the American Revolution. Citizen apathy, except for brief periods following disclosures of fraud, graft, and corruption, historically is a "normal" political condition. From time to time, though, the electorate stirs itself. Between the American Revolution and the beginning of the twentieth century, for example, citizens' organizations such as the "Know Nothing," Granger, and Women's Christian Temperance movements waxed and waned.[42] During the Progressive Era and for some time thereafter, crime commissions, taxpayers' associations, citizens' public-expenditure councils, and the like flourished.[43] Following one or two initial victories, however, groups like these typically were short-lived.

Speaking of the brief lifespan of citizens' movements, Bryce commented, "Nowhere is the saying so applicable that nothing succeeds like success." Americans, Bryce continued, "have what chemists call low specific heat; they grow warm suddenly and cool as suddenly." Upon achieving their goals, or some measure of them, most citizens' movements vanish or coalesce with other movements that themselves soon disappear.[44]

If some political scientists lament the decline in voluntary associations of citizens, others claim that groups such as these are more numerous today than ever before.[45] To the extent that voluntary associations are declining, we are experiencing a loss in what many scholars claim are "schools for citizenship."[46] No one knows for certain, of course, whether the number of citizens' associations today is proportionate to what it was at the founding, whether it is declining, or whether it is increasing. One commentator pointed out, somewhat ironically but astutely, that the only voluntary associations that seem to be increasing are self-help groups such as Alcoholics Anonymous.[47] Counting only raw numbers of voluntary associations is a questionable measure of the vitality of citizenship. The Communist Party in Russia spent much time and effort creating various kinds of associations of citizens, but it cannot be reasonably claimed that, as Americans think of free association, these groups were truly voluntary.[48] Moreover, in terms of what used to be called the "common good," the existence of large numbers of aggressively competing special-interest citizens' groups has destructive consequences.[49]

In the city of my residence, the few voluntary associations that consistently maintain an interest in governmental affairs are concerned with environmental issues or in promoting self-interests. Important though these issues are for their proponents, they do not define the limits of what should concern citizens about their governments. The much broader common-good question of whether local government at large functions effectively and honestly is rarely asked in public meetings by local print media or by any nonpolitical voluntary association of concerned citizens. Thus defined, a general state of citizen disengagement from the daily operations of local government prevails not only in one California community but throughout the nation.

One would be naive to expect that in a nation of a quarter billion people, every adult man and woman would be citizens in the active sense of the word that effective civil grand jury service connotes. If the infamous bell-shaped curve is valid with respect to intelligence, a segment of the population is conceptually unsuited to practice vigorous, participatory citizenship at any level of government. Military service creates another block of the populace that cannot be active citizens in their communities of origin. A small percentage of other citizens often are physically unable to attend city hall regularly, intelligent though they may be.

Many other reasons could explain why expecting to find in the adult American population large numbers of active citizens is unrealistic. Therefore, I do not raise the question, "Why are not all Americans active citizens?" but, rather, "What can be done to encourage as many citizens as possible to participate more fully in public affairs?" The brief answer to the latter question is that if active citizenship is to be an important civic value in more than name only, a large-scale, nationwide debate must be undertaken to define what active citizenship means and what must be done to nurture it.

FOUR INTERDISCIPLINARY EXAMPLES

In the remaining pages of this book, I do not describe a comprehensive campaign to attack the problem of non-participating citizenship in the United

States. Instead, I restrict my attention to merely a few possibilities for such a program. By discussing selected elements of a more fully developed program, I hope to illustrate the broad scope that a comprehensive project to foster more active citizenship would require, the many social, psychological, and economic boundaries it must cross, and the interconnectedness of its elements. Although a comprehensive project would affect many citizens, not all of them will become active citizens in the sense that civil grand jury service requires. Just as an expectation that every pupil in the public education system can be transformed into a dedicated scholar is unrealistic, the expectation that every pupil will become an active citizen is naive. Nevertheless, a mass-education approach will at least ensure that everyone who wishes to move from "cocoon" to "active citizen" status will have an opportunity to do so.

Education

The single most potentially effective means to increase the number of active citizens in American communities is education. Because tax-funded schools dominate the educational landscape, I confine my observations to that system, realizing, of course, that private schools also could play a role in education for citizenship.[50] If public education is to accept more responsibility for preparing young men and women for more active citizenship, it first must resolve at least two important issues.

First, public schools are governmental institutions. They are, in effect, the arm of the state that develops, controls, and delivers most of the educational services in the United States. In this context, one might reasonably ask whether a governmental institution can be a disinterested party in educating citizens about the organization, procedures, and services of government. As I commented earlier, both ends of the political spectrum have reservations about this question, but no doubt for different reasons. The issue is akin to reservations that public-education theorists have raised from time to time about the propriety of "business interests" influencing curricula. It is not proper, so the argument runs, for commercial interests to use public education to instill anti-taxation and anti-government attitudes into young minds. Commercial interests would argue, of course, that using tax-supported educational resources to advocate anti-business economic or government policies is likewise objectionable.

Although the influencing-the-curriculum argument comprises many more issues, the principal question to be resolved is what must be done to produce responsible, active citizens whose sense of citizenship is as little tainted by either influence as possible? So framed, the question is not merely academic or theoretical. It is at the core of the current debate about public education, including concerns about the demise of civics in the curriculum. To the extent that public education theorists and administrators are willing to recognize relevant criticism and eliminate its causes, they might succeed in opposing changes such as school vouchers, home schooling, and privatizing education.

The *second* issue that government schools must face if they are to accept responsibility for fostering the skills and knowledge of active citizenship is to resolve the thorny question of what a revitalized civics curriculum would look like. An answer to this question may be found in a restatement of an important restriction on the jurisdiction of the California civil grand jury: It has no jurisdiction in policy matters. Thus, the institution is confined to assessing the systems, procedures, and methods of operation of local government. Before I explain how the relationship of this restriction on the jurisdiction of the California civil grand jury is related to a revitalized civics curriculum, a brief summary of the history of civics education in public schools will be helpful.

A review of American civics textbooks of the late nineteenth and early twentieth centuries shows that "citizenship" often was discussed in the context of personal hygiene, patriotism, community sanitation and aesthetics, the building of highways, the enactment of laws, the responsibility to vote regularly, the need to support public education, and the like.[51] As is the case today, civics textbooks rarely included information about corruption in office, ineffective government practices, and related abuses of power. Moreover, the information about government in civics textbooks almost always was about its formal structure rather than how it actually works. This focus continued through World War II. Like the apparatus of taxation, though, the emphasis shifted from local government to state government to federal government.

Even the sequence of information in civics textbooks revealed a changing emphasis. In earlier decades, material about local government typically appeared in the first half of civics textbooks, usually after a chapter or two about community and family life. Gradually, information about local government shifted to the concluding chapters. Conversely, descriptions of state and federal governments moved from the concluding pages of civics textbooks to their opening chapters. As this happened, subjects such as the nature of communities, family life, and city, county, or township government became incidental or disappeared. Here, for example, are several chapter numbers and headings from a textbook that some citizens who were grand jurors during the study period for this book might have read in their school years:

> III.   Origin of the Federal Constitution
> IV.   The Federal System of Government
> VI.   Expressed and Implied Powers of Congress
> XXXII.   County and Township Government[52]

As the focus of civics textbooks changed, local-government topics waned and a "problems of democracy" emphasis increased. Only rarely, however, did problems of democracy include discussions of dysfunctions in governance such as abuse of power, nepotism, fraud, or references to specific civic values such as the undesirability of one person holding two or three public offices simultaneously. In the index to the textbook cited in the previous paragraph, the words "fraud," "graft," and "corruption" do not appear. Several pages are devoted to the "Corrupt Practices Act," but this information pertains to campaign funding, a concern that Tocqueville and Bryce expressed decades ago but that has never been satisfactorily resolved. Just as information about local government diminished, references to concepts such as honesty, loyalty, and other moral issues also disappeared.

The responsibility for designing curricula for what used to be called "civics" courses falls within the purview of social studies teachers, a professional group that has almost exclusive jurisdiction in defining what its pupils learn. A "Civics and Government" themed issue of one social science journal reveals insights into how social science teachers think about designing civics curricula.[53] The authors of the articles in the issue were, generally, elementary school or high school teachers, social science coordinators and consultants, and professors of education. Without exception, the articles present a static, descending-power view of civic life with no references to abuse of office or ineffectiveness in any branch of government. Nor do the authors offer recommendations for dealing with the widespread dissatisfaction with governance that characterizes the present era. Considerable time, however, was devoted to praising the National Standards for Civics and Government and the Goals 2000 Educate Americans Act of 1994.

Scholars and practitioners in public administration occasionally advocate more involvement by their colleagues in citizenship education. One writer recommends that city managers, department heads, and elected local-government officials become part-time instructors in public school systems. In this manner, officials can assist citizens in acquiring an identity of togetherness with appointed and elected officials rather than holding a we-they attitude.[54] The expected result of this involvement is that citizens will become more confident in the ability of government to solve problems. The "identity of togetherness" objective, by definition, connotes a "steady-state" civic education curriculum. In the context of descending governmental authority, citizens, unfortunately, can hope to be little more than junior partners.[55]

The inattention to local government and an "all is well in city hall" perspective continues today. The document that prescribes what pupils in California learn about public affairs includes only one or two brief references to local government. When that topic is mentioned, it is part of a relatively minor "unit" in the curriculum titled "Federalism: State and Local Government." Moreover, the only reference to the possibility that anything untoward might arise in governmental administration is a brief comment about "corrupt big city machines [of the Progressive Era] that delivered services to the immigrant poor in exchange for votes."[56] In short, nothing in the curriculum will prepare young people to exercise the vigilant citizenship needed for effective review of the procedures and operations of the form of government that is the largest system of public administration in which they will live, rear their families, and pursue their careers.

Even more ironic, local government also is that manifestation of the state that citizens may, by direct action in their communities, influence in any significant manner. Thus, the jurisdiction of the civil grand jury in the systems, procedures, and operations of local government is an ideal framework for an improved civics curriculum. What could be more important civic knowledge and skills for students to acquire than the ability to assess the effectiveness, fairness, and integrity of the public services upon which they will depend for decades as citizens of their communities?

A thorough consideration of reforming civics education must consider many more issues than those I have sketched briefly. But the question of whether that function of government we call "public education" can rise above its self-interest to design an active-citizenship curriculum must be resolved before the much-lamented problem of citizen apathy can be addressed. Unless some way can be found to develop a curriculum for citizenship that is independent of self-interest of any variety except that of citizens themselves, most Americans likely will be little more knowledgeable about the role of government in their lives than the fifth grader who assumes that anyone wearing a uniform must be a public employee.[57] Fortunately, it is possible to create a larger number than now exists of citizens with a more mature sense of citizenship, as I soon shall propose. This goal, however, cannot be attained solely by improving the civics curriculum in public schools. Reform in citizenship also must proceed along other fronts.

The News Media

Even if the public-education establishment were to accept no responsibility for nurturing a more active sense of citizenship in American communities, the news media could offset that deficit to some extent. To do so, however, they must change certain current practices. For many years, investigative journalism was an important source of information and inspiration for active citizens. By exposing ineffective and corrupt local-government practices, the news media aroused the community sentiment needed to prevent and correct those abuses. In its heyday, investigative journalism was so much a part of community life that the fearless, independently minded investigative reporter became a prominent Hollywood theme.[58] Several recent trends in the news-media industry have seriously crippled the contributions that investigative reporting made in the past to fostering active, participatory citizenship in American civic life.

Several decades ago, many of their owners discovered that newspapers could become highly profitable "industries." Because enlarging profits in any commercial enterprise is often a matter of reducing production costs, newsroom budgets became frequent targets of cost cutting. Investigative reporting, in particular, can be an expensive form of journalism. In an investigative project of even modest scope, finding facts and checking them requires costly "legwork."[59]

Newspaper stories about fraud, graft, corruption, and waste in government also can lead to lawsuits or threats thereof. To avoid these problems, newspaper owners in previous times often retained law firms to review investigative stories before their publication. The more sensitive and comprehensive the story, the greater were the costs of prepublication review by lawyers. The professional services of lawyers also were required at times after publication. Hard-hitting investigative stories might result in jail or prison sentences, fines, or removal from office for public officials. Therefore, even public officials who were caught "red-handed" had considerable incentive to initiate lawsuits. Thus, legal expenses became a consideration in the quest for profits.

Legal expenses were not the only "cost center" in investigative reporting. The salaries and expenses of investigative reporters could be eliminated by abandoning the tradition of investigative reporting. Moreover, the good will of advertisers was a consideration because they sometimes were the political supporters of elected officials or friends of highly placed appointed officials. Gradually, profit-seeking led to a decline in the traditions of investigative reporting, and revenue-producing advertisements filled the space of what was once referred to as the "news hole."

These are merely a few of the reasons why investigative reporting declined in American communities. In the long run, sadly, the costs that citizens pay for this trend do not appear in stockholders' reports: No accounting category captures the dollar value of apathetic citizenship.

Just as the public-school establishment might justify eliminating civics in the curriculum by arguing that pupils have no interest in the subject, newspaper owners and managers sometimes claim that government is too complicated for readers to understand.[60] One might counter that citizens have no interest in government affairs because they know so little about them, either as students or voters, owing to the local-government news-media and educational "blackout." As the blackout expanded, newspaper owners began to realize that American's respect for and confidence in newspapers as community institutions were declining.[61] This trend posed a problem for profit-minded news-media executives: If citizens hold the news media in contempt, they will decline to buy newspapers or watch television. To counteract this trend, the news media created a new form of reporting now known as "news-you-can-use journalism," "civic journalism," and similar terms.[62]

Many corporations that own newspapers widely embrace civic journalism. It fills news holes cheaply and is less risky politically than traditional investigative reporting. Threats by business owners who are allies of public officials to discontinue full-page advertisements are often an effective means for discouraging investigative reporting.[63] "Soft journalism" stories, on the other hand, about "kids in chaos," "visions for our future," "troubled neighborhoods," and the like are relatively inexpensive to produce, and they rarely result in angry "targets" and legal expenses.[64] The new journalism also costs less than investigative journalism because of the large amounts of "canned" information available from interest groups concerned with influencing public opinion about, for example, abortion, euthanasia, gun control, international affairs, race, and "sexual politics."

Further, revelations about the private lives of celebrities are considerably less expensive to produce than labor-intensive inquiries into allegations of corrupt or wasteful governmental practices. For example, reporting the details of a fatal car accident of a prominent figure can be accomplished by remaining seated at a desk and paraphrasing stories from other publications. This could explain why accounts of one such death were reported to have received more news-media coverage "in England than any single event that happened in all of World War II."[65]

Compounded by the shallowness of citizenship education in public schools, the effects of these news-media trends on American citizenship have been profound. As is the case with civics textbooks that promote an "all's well" view of local government, "booster journalism" implies that, because nothing is wrong in city hall or the county courthouse, nothing needs repairing. Therefore, because local-government officials must be inerrant and scrupulously honest, citizens assume that they need not pay attention to their local governments.[66]

Sooner or later, public officials conclude that if citizens are unconcerned about accountability in government, the latter have tacitly permitted the former to manage public affairs to suit themselves. In time, public officials become unaccustomed to citizen inquiries about their practices, and eventually citizens who ask questions about local government are regarded as impertinent, derogating, or even perverse. Thus, the civic value of openness and responsiveness in government passes into oblivion, arrogance of office abounds, and the civic virtue of "accountability in office" fades.

The disappearance of news stories written in the tradition of investigative reporting also contributes to a decline in the skills of objective thought and discourse among citizens. Because reporters can canvass people more cheaply by telephone for opinions about public issues than they can dig independently for leads and evidence, citizens lose their understanding of what factual reporting looks like. A 1998 article about the status of civil grand juries in California illustrates this trend.[67] The story consisted mostly of quotations or paraphrases of quotations from people who repeated many stereotypical beliefs about grand juries but who provided little evidence to support their opinions. This reporting technique—sometimes known as "he said, she said" journalism—requires little more expenditure than a telephone bill and buying a filing cabinet from which one can extract clippings of previously published newspaper stories about the topic under "investigation." Thus, despite its length, the story contained no new facts acquired from independent research about grand juries but was merely a recitation of some erroneous statements and many oft-quoted clichés about the institution.

Because it relies almost entirely on opinions from the "usual suspects" concerning the issue being reported, journalism by telephone contributes to what has been described aptly as "the argument culture."[68] Thus, the interplay of ineffective citizenship education and cost-cutting journalistic strategies adds to the growing incivility and subjectivity of public discourse in society. Unlike the case of public education, however, a hopeful note can be found in contemporary journalism: The latter profession is more frank about its shortcomings than is the former. This comment, for example, is attributed to a highly placed newspaper executive:

> Some of us tend to forget why we have [First Amendment] privileges. It's so we can have informed citizens who know what's going on, and can debate and participate in government. We have these privileges to use in trust.[69]

Although the news media, particularly the print media, often are refreshingly candid in their self-criticism, the same cannot be said about another field of intellectual inquiry whose inattentiveness to modern American citizenship is a serious shortcoming.

Social-Science Disciplines

By "social-science disciplines" I refer chiefly to anthropology, economics, political science, psychology, and sociology. Each of these disciplines has distinct methods and perspectives well suited for research into how Americans conceive their citizenship responsibilities and duties. Considering the widespread contemporary concern about citizens' apathy, declining voter-turnout rates, disaffection with government, and related matters, it is difficult to imagine a more important subject than citizenship for social scientists to address. As one political scientist said of his discipline, however, it "has been diminished by the extent to which it has veered from the central questions of democratic governance." Moreover, previous generations of political scientists "were more acutely aware of the fragility of democracy [and] had a greater appreciation of the potential for abuses of political power." The focus of political scientists of the previous generation was therefore "on the structures and processes for exercising power, for restraining those who abuse it, and for holding governors and citizens alike accountable."[70] These concerns are, or should be, central to a continuing program of research into citizenship. Unfortunately, social science has abandoned any interest it had in those matters in previous years.

Although social science has great potential for broadening our understanding of citizenship, its practitioners must overcome two important obstacles for this to happen. *First,* as I commented earlier about civics textbooks, the scholarly shift of focus in the social sciences generally has been from the local to the global. As this shift from the specific to the abstract progressed, scholars lost sight of the concrete foundations of civic life, community, and citizenship.[71] Meanwhile, centralization of government, corporate monopolization, fusion of the public and private, and many other contemporary social trends stunted that part of their personal identity that Americans usually refer to as "citizenship." A research-for-action citizenship project therefore must begin at the community level where, if it is practiced at all, Americans are most inclined to display their skills of active citizenship.

Starting at the foundation and working toward the roof in conducting the research needed to reform the practice of American citizenship has another advantage. Local government is where many state and national legislators begin their political careers, exporting what they have learned in local government to the capitals of the states and the nation. If elected officials in local government become accustomed to citizens' indifference in their home communities, there is little reason to expect that their own sense of citizenship will be improved by transferring to a larger, and more distant, form of government.

The *second* problem that social science must overcome if it is to conduct research worthy of its name into citizenship is its distaste for so-called normative analysis. I do not mean that the methods or findings of social science should be tainted by the researcher's ideology. Research design and methods should, of course, be as objective as possible. When the findings from comprehensive investigations into citizenship have been distilled from the data, however, one would hope that the several disciplines of social science would offer recommendations about what must be done to eliminate any dysfunctions of citizenship that have been revealed.[72]

The findings I have developed from the present study suggest many promising lines of social-science research into the formation of one's identity as a citizen. For example, in working with grand jurors, I often have wondered why so many of them seem to be unacquainted with what I have referred to as "civic values." I do not expect all grand jurors or other citizens to exhibit consensus about what these values should be, but the spirit of the institution in particular and governance in general would be better served if more grand jurors were to understand that these values exist. They are, after all, the basis for statutes that, for example, require open public meetings or access to public records or the disclosure by public officials of financial assets that could affect their official duties or responsibilities.

In the absence of some notion that—as is the case within one's household—certain principles must be observed as social norms, grand jurors and citizens in general have no criteria to use for assessing government operations. A brief anecdote from my work in training grand jurors will illustrate this point. A newspaper in Northern California during the study period published a feature story about the backgrounds of newly appointed grand jurors in its county. Without further comment, the story stated that the new foreman of the panel was also an elected official serving on a multi-county special district. Thinking that the newspaper must be in error, I called the new foreman to verify whether he was, in fact, the same person identified as a special-district trustee. The foreman acknowledged that he currently was an elected official but said he saw no problem with his dual role. When I told him that California Penal Code Section 893 forbade this practice, he said that he would bring the Code section to the attention of the impaneling judge. When I later asked the foreman what the judge had said about the matter, the foreman replied, "Oh, he knows about it, but he said not to worry about it. No one would probably know the difference anyway."

On occasion, I have told this story to grand jurors to help them understand that if one of their fellow panel members is currently an elected official, this violation of the law could be troublesome under certain circumstances. The variety of comments that grand jurors make about this incident range from, "Well, that's silly. If someone wants to be a grand juror, why shouldn't he?" to "What difference does it make?" Of course, some grand jurors understand the significance of the statute and state that it should be observed. During training sessions I have conducted, grand jurors have made similar responses about other precepts of governance. Some grand jurors, for example, do not know what the term "nepotism" means; others contend that having large numbers of the same family employed in one local government creates organizational cohesion. Still others argue that nepotism saves money by reducing recruitment costs.

It is conceivable, of course, that certain civic values of the past now require revision, refinement, or perhaps even elimination. For these reasons, a national debate about citizenship principles suited to contemporary governance needs should precede a civic revitalization project.[73] An understanding of these principles, a respect for them, and an insistence on their observance by all citizens, including grand jurors, public officials and employees, and the news media, determines whether government functions lawfully, fairly, and effectively.

Grand jury final reports would yield many valuable insights into new principles of governance and modifications of those that might be outdated. In this regard, poorly conducted and reported grand jury investigations are as valuable as those that are well conducted and reported. Good or bad, grand jury investigations and reports are the records of encounters that grand jurors have with the state. As such, final reports reveal much about the assumptions of governance that have shaped these encounters. Considering the rapidly changing social, cultural, and economic character of the United States, few issues are more important for its future. Thus, social scientists who wish to find new ways to govern will discover that the grand jury is an ideal institution to study.

Social science also could contribute significantly to the study of active citizenship by examining thoroughly the interaction between public officials and citizens. Some citizens argue that questioning local-government practices is futile because "they're going to do what they want to do no matter what people want." When one asks these people how they became so discouraged, they cite examples of being refused information when they asked for it, of being appointed to local-government advisory commissions that were "stacked decks," or finding it difficult to attend meetings of legislative bodies that allow citizens to speak only for three minutes during a half-hour period after 10:00 p.m. on Friday.

To what extent do practices such as these create beliefs in citizens that they are trapped in systems of government that are beyond their control? What other practices contribute to that perception? How do these practices originate, and how might they be eliminated? These are examples of research into citizenship that must be undertaken if questions about the withdrawal of American citizens from political participation are to be answered fully.

Another phenomenon of citizenship that deserves the attention of social scientists is the use of public power to discourage or intimidate the participation of citizens. In the county of my residence, I often discuss local-government affairs with fellow citizens. Invariably, in any such discussion, remarks of the following kind are made: "I know I should do something about this, but my business would suffer," or, "Once you stick your neck out, you're branded." In some jurisdictions citizens are required as they enter meeting rooms to sign their names to "attendance rosters" held by uniformed police officers. Few citizens, including, apparently, some elected officials, know that in some states "open meeting" laws forbid this practice.[74]

Just as the intimidation of jurors is a civic wrong, the intimidation of citizens should be.[75] Of course, fear of retaliation by public officials often is groundless. But, fear based on what *might be* is as palpable as fear based on reality. A comprehensive study of citizenship therefore must explore the effects of intimidation, real or imagined, on citizen participation. Among the questions that should be raised in this connection are:

- To what extent do citizens believe that retaliation may ensue if they openly support or oppose public officials in their communities?
- To the extent that fear exists, what are its specific forms?

- Do sufficient statutory safeguards exist to prevent intimidation of citizens?
- How extensively are Strategic Lawsuits Against Public Participation (SLAPPs) used and what circumstances created them?[76]
- What have been the effects of these strategies on the practice of citizenship, and do similar legal processes impede public discourse?

Social scientists also could develop a large national database about Americans who attempt to practice active citizenship in their communities but who thereafter reap painful consequences for their activism. For example, a retired accountant in a small county requested revenue-and-expenditure information from a legislative body about an income-producing enterprise it operated. As a result of his request, the citizen was named as the defendant in several SLAPP-like lawsuits that public officials filed against him. Fortunately, sufficient community support developed to assist this citizen through a difficult ordeal. A thorough case study of incidents like this and their community-wide effects would provide valuable insights into the practice of active citizenship.

Not far from the community in which the episode of the prior paragraph occurred, a woman attempted to obtain information from public officials about why they had authorized the dumping of hazardous materials on property near hers. Although this citizen had no previous experience as a citizen activist in local government, her successful efforts in this incident prevented a possibly significant environmental calamity. Thorough documentation of this episode would yield important information about the transformation of a formerly passive citizen into one who successfully challenged an elected body, its legal staff, and a variety of local-government department heads and their subordinates about an issue of broad significance for a community.

Case studies of the experiences of responsible citizen activists would identify many important issues of governance for interdisciplinary social-science research at, so to speak, the local level. How, for example, did the experiences of the citizen activist in the preceding paragraph affect her life during and after the episode? What recommendations would she offer concerning education for citizenship in school curricula? How did she acquire the knowledge and skills during this incident to obtain information that initially was denied her? To what extent did access to Internet resources assist her? Two years after the incident, what suggestions would she offer other citizens who attempt to intervene on behalf of their communities into the actual or potential mismanagement of public resources?

One far-reaching contribution that social scientists could make to establishing active citizenship as a field of study would be to create a body of literature about the subject. As matters now stand, little research is available for textbook authors or social-science teachers concerning the experiences of responsible citizen activists in local government. This limitation accounts to some extent for the static nature of civics textbooks, bereft as they are of concepts such as openness in government, accountability in public office, fraud, graft, corruption, and other abuses of power. The absence of a body of literature concerning active citizenship seriously obstructs the efforts of educators who wish to help their students learn, not merely in theory but in practice, how government responds to citizens who attempt to evaluate its performance. For this purpose, scholarly assessments of responsibly conducted and reported grand jury inquiries into local-government affairs would be valuable.

If, either by intention or neglect, men and women are conditioned to be apathetic citizens, no incentive exists to create a body of knowledge about active citizenship. Neither teacher-training institutions nor textbook publishers therefore have any monetary incentive for developing courses of study or teaching materials for a "product" that has no "customers." The marketplace concept of education for citizenship may be stated another way: If citizens are encouraged to think of themselves as "individual customers [or] collective consumers of public services," there is no need for "owners' manuals" pertaining to the apparatus of government.[77] Maintaining the tools of production is, after all, someone else's responsibility.

The marketplace conception of citizenship is limited in many respects. In particular, it provides no governmental Better Business Bureau, so to speak, to deal with scale tampering, false advertising, and price gouging. Even worse, this passive conception of citizenship requires no courses in consumer education for citizens, rare though they may be, who responsibly seek redress for shoddy public services they have "purchased." Thus, manufacturers of the "products" have much to gain by encouraging "consumers" to be uninformed. In these circumstances, the disappearance of civics from the curriculum explains why civics textbooks, monographs about the evaluation of public services, and scholarly journals devoted to the assessment of governmental practices are rare.

If social science is to accept responsibility for helping Americans define citizenship as something more than passive consumerism, it first must decide what citizens themselves must decide: whether citizenship can continue to be what it has been in the last half of the twentieth century, or whether the advent of the twenty-first century demands a form of citizenship closer to the Tocquevillian ideal of a "civic community marked by an active, public-spirited citizenry, by egalitarian social relations, [and] by a social fabric of trust and cooperation."[78] Of course, creating this form of citizenship would first require— to use a term of the 1960s—a "consciousness raising" among citizens and social scientists alike. To achieve this end, a "civic rearmament" project, designed and conducted by social scientists, would be essential. Among the kinds of questions the project should raise and answer are:

- What educational experiences cultivate or impede development of the civic values and skills that citizens must possess to undertake effective inquiries into the workings of the state such as this study has reported?

- To what extent does the pursuit of issues of self-interest distract citizens' attention from broader concerns about the objectives, integrity, and effectiveness of government?
- How many styles of citizenship exist, and how do these vary by the circumstances of citizens' lives?
- Do regional differences affect the expression and practice of citizenship and, if so, in what way?
- Given the press for a global society and economy, the strain for centralization among governments, and the radical changes in communications media, what form of citizenship is needed to help men and women deal with the consequences of these trends on their lives?

These are merely examples of research that I believe will lead to solutions for the widely deplored pathologies of citizenship and governance that command the attention of present-day social commentators such as those listed in "Additional References." My preference for a strategy to guide a project like this would be to conceive of it as research into the development of identity. To ask how one's conception of his or her duties and responsibilities as a citizen—one's civic identity—is formed is, after all, a question of one's identity as a member of the human race. In working with grand jurors and other citizens, I frequently wonder how many different styles of citizenship exist and, of these, why so many of them seem contrary to, if not downright destructive of, the civic ideal of self-government. The few anecdotes about grand juror behavior and attitudes that I have described to illustrate various points in this book are not isolated incidents, nor are they the most extreme of what I have observed. Although they are merely illustrative, they suggest why civic self-concept is a promising focus for research into citizenship.

How one becomes what one becomes and how social forces affect that process are, of course, classic concerns of social science. One thinks, for example, of a landmark study of how young students progressed through medical school and how the stresses of that experience affected their emotional development.[79] Just as medical students must reconcile cynicism and idealism during their training, many citizens face similar challenges in developing a personal ethic for the practice of citizenship. What sentiments other than cynicism and idealism are, after all, more important for studying that portion of our consciousness that we refer to as citizenship?

A large social-science project during World War II also has relevance for contemporary research into citizenship.[80] Just as it was important to find ways to help soldiers deal with the effects of combat on their lives, it is equally important to discover how the strains of modern social forces affect citizenship. The research findings from a history-making inquiry into military morale therefore may be applicable to finding solutions for problems of uncertainty, frustration, and anxiety in the body politic. Another milestone social-science project of a previous generation could be helpful in at least two respects for establishing objectives for a contemporary inquiry into citizenship:

1. The project generated large amounts of data that could provide valuable insights into how Americans' conceptions of citizenship have changed in the past 40 years.

2. The project yielded important data about citizenship self-concepts in other countries.

These findings would add breadth and depth to contemporary inquiry into the practice of American citizenship.[81]

As I stated earlier, the examples I have offered are merely illustrative. I selected them because they represent different social-science disciplines, because each of them affected social-science research for years after their publication, and because in different ways they were concerned with the interplay between citizens and their institutions. Each of the projects also stimulated much debate about their validity and theoretical soundness. Thus, the shortcomings that their critics exposed could improve the methods and the concepts for an investigation into the practice of citizenship in contemporary America.

The projects I have described briefly were innovative and provocative in their scope and design when they were first published. Similarly, research into citizenship that goes beyond conventional inquiries into voter turnout, membership in voluntary associations, political-party affiliation, and the like must include a line of inquiry that has never been studied exhaustively: What happens when citizens and their public servants meet face to face in contexts similar to those that this study has disclosed? Or, to frame the question as Aristotle might have asked it, what kind of citizenship should citizens practice in a mass culture that is buffeted by the sometimes antagonistic and sometimes mutually accommodating forces of rampant monopolistic corporatism and an expanding pervasive state? The answers to this question will be useful not merely for the grand jury as one institution, but for society at large.

Before social scientists can benefit from the many opportunities that the civil grand jury offers for research into governance and citizenship, they first must recognize that the institution exists. Possibly because of their lack of interest in local government in general, or because the indicting grand jury has a certain unsavory reputation in their ranks, social scientists generally ignore the institution. One example of how social scientists have overlooked the institution is provided by a distinguished scholar who wrote a thoughtful book in which he suggested certain "reforms" that would promote civic participation. One of his suggestions was to create neighborhood assemblies. In offering his suggestion, he commented, "It's one of the ironies of the American form of government that no uniform nationwide system of local participation has ever been institutionalized or even considered."[82] The California civil grand jury, of course, does not exactly fit his specifications, but to my knowledge, no other local institution comes closer to what his suggestion implies.

If the educational establishment, the news media, and social scientists have neglected the study of citizenship and the search for solutions to its many problems, does the literature of the legal profession yield a richer harvest of knowledge about active citizenship? The authors of our Constitution, after all, were concerned with finding answers to a basic legal-philosophical question: What institutional arrangements will allow citizens to prevent the power of the state from intruding unnecessarily into their lives? One would therefore expect legal scholars to be debating this question continuously. If this were the case, it would also seem that legal theorists long ago would have recognized that the grand jury, embedded as it is in common law, statutes, and case law, is a significant focal point of inquiry.

The Law

Although the law usually is not considered a social science, its methods and subject matter are crucial for the study and practice of active citizenship. The legal profession, however, rarely addresses citizenship in its literature, as the term is used in this book. Some idea of the meaning of citizenship for legal scholars may be inferred from the key words under the main entries and "see also" sections for "citizenship" in recent issues of the *Current Law Index*:[83]

adopting	domicile	minorities	naturalization
aliens	dual citizenship	national identity	race
deportation	migration	nationality	taxation

Typically, legal scholars develop citizenship in the context of rights. For example, they write law-review articles about how the law has been used or may be used to protect a given class of people from the standpoint of a civil-rights violation or to seek damages for applicable injuries,[84] or they may explore a legal issue related to environmental litigation,[85] or they may attempt to reconcile various legal theories or philosophies about a social issue of the day.[86] Thus, other than the topics listed in the preceding paragraph, the field of citizenship in the vast body of legal scholarship is generally limited to issues concerning property rights; environmental statutes, rules, and regulations; and related class-action suits against government. Indeed, one is more likely to find in the *Current Law Index* more references to law-review articles about animal welfare than to articles about self-governance.

The irony of this "blackout" by legal scholars is that, unlike the professions I discussed earlier in this section, members of the bar are the custodians of knowledge about the few tools a citizen might use independently to offset the immense power and resources the state has at its disposal. If more members of the bar were to construe *pro bono publico*[87] beyond property-rights or environmental issues, publications of the following kind might be available for grand jurors and other citizens who wish to practice active citizenship:

- Descriptions and explanations of legal processes that citizens can initiate to obtain information that public officials deny them, to petition public officials to comply with laws or regulations they have ignored, to restrain public officials from engaging in unlawful activities, and the like[88]
- Case studies describing and assessing how the justice system responded to proceedings that citizens initiated successfully or unsuccessfully to intervene in unlawful, dangerous, or improper local-government activities
- Legal analyses of crucial issues that may arise in citizen-government confrontations, such as public-policy implications of the advantage that public officials enjoy with respect to the availability of legal counsel, their custodianship of public records and documents, and their use of public funds to develop countermeasures against citizen intervention
- A nationwide study of whistle-blower laws, including commentary about intimidation of public employees who attempt to invoke them, the outcomes of trials involving them, and how effective whistle-blowers' activities have been in changing government practices
- Descriptions of research techniques and sources of information that active citizens can use to search legal literature for information concerning local-government issues

For many years, legal scholars provided a fairly constant and sizeable stream of publications about the grand jury. Most of these studies concerned the indictment function; however, the former stream, in the last decade, has become a mere trickle. Consequently, citizens, for either adversarial or supportive reasons, who desire current information about grand jury affairs are hampered by its scarcity. Examples of publications that legal scholars could produce to assist grand jurors, public officials, and other citizens who seek current, authoritative information about the institution include:

- A monograph for laymen describing the historical origins of the indictment, trends in its use in the United States, the constitutionality of grand jury–district attorney relationships during its proceedings, and the public-policy implications of permitting grand juries to issue indictments at their sole discretion
- A publication for laymen describing the accusation, its use throughout the United States as revealed by case law, its similarity or dissimilarity to impeachment proceedings, and its significance for citizenship and the civic culture
- A nationwide study of statutes and case law concerning civil grand juries, suggestions for statutory reform of the civil function, and an analysis of similarities and differences in the civil function among the states[89]

- An annotated, classified bibliography of publications concerning the grand jury in the United States since 1976[90]
- A publication explaining in laymen's terms the concept of factuality, evidence, proof, corroboration, verification, and other related terms as they are used in legal proceedings, but explaining how these concepts apply to civil grand jury service in particular and active citizenship in general.

Conclusion

In Chapter 1, I summarized the libel lawsuit against the Yuba County Grand Jury of 1993–1994. As interesting and instructive as it might be, a complete account of that proceeding is unnecessary for the point I wish to make here: The incident illustrates how inadequate knowledge and skills of citizenship can cause unnecessary grief, effort, and financial loss. Several proposals for legislation in Chapter 7, particularly those relating to documentation and factuality, could reduce the possibility of similar lawsuits in the future. As I stated previously, however, legislation by itself will not ensure effective and lawful civil grand jury investigations. Assertive, responsible citizenship most decisively explains variations in the quality of grand jury investigations cited in previous chapters.

Effective grand jury final reports of the study period were generated within the context of the same statutes and case law in which trivial, subjective final reports were published. Moreover, equal access without charge to three different kinds of official, and presumably expert, legal advisors is available to every civil grand jury each year in California. Whether grand jurors avail themselves of those resources is a matter of their discretion, and how they exercise their discretion depends on the nature and quality of that portion of their identity that they reserve for their sense of citizenship. Because the same laws apply equally to every California civil grand jury, one is hard-pressed to avoid the conclusion that, in the end, the give and take among grand jurors in the privacy of their meeting rooms determines how well they serve their communities. The internal, unseen dynamics of citizenship in grand jury service are, after all, products of grand jurors' character, experience, and education.

If one insists on assigning blame for the Yuba County episode to anyone or anything, it should be attached to whatever impedes development of the mature citizenship that grand jury service in particular, and our form of government in general, demands. Aristotle was right: The nature of a regime defines the kind of citizenship it requires. Sadly, as the Yuba County episode demonstrates, and the other citizenship problems revealed in previous chapters suggest, merely creating the constitutional framework for self-government does not guarantee that it will be practiced effectively.

With few exceptions, existing laws permit any citizen, grand juror or not, to undertake most of the grand jury inquiries referred to in previous chapters. In practice, few citizens in the present era single-handedly initiate such projects. This is a pathological condition in a free society. If we insist on exporting democratic self-government to other nations, we first must learn to practice it ourselves. One objective of the civic revitalization program I have proposed would be to find ways to inspire American citizens to learn how to practice independently the skills of self-government that our Constitution allows. If we succeed in doing so, we will have solved the problem of finding competent citizens for civil grand jury service. Even more important, we will have created an adequate supply of citizens who are not merely "good enough" but who are the appropriately skilled and motivated citizens that self-government requires.

GRAND JURY SERVICE: SHOULD IT BE A SCHOOL FOR PUBLIC AFFAIRS?

For many years, trial and grand jury service has been praised as a school for public affairs. I know of no other fallacy that has inflicted more mischief on the institution. For all his genius and enthusiastic endorsement of the jury as a uniquely "republican" institution, even Tocqueville saw jury service as a tuition-free "public school [that is one of] the most efficacious means for the education of the people which society can employ."[91] The school-for-citizenship theory bespeaks contempt and condescension for the institution and for citizens in general. Neither the grand jury nor government at large can function well under conditions of shallow citizenship. If the high honor and prestige associated with civil grand jury service is to have meaning, judges should impanel only exceptionally well-prepared, civically mature, and highly dedicated men and women as grand jurors.

The school-for-public-affairs view of the institution is precisely the kind of myth that people who wish to immobilize the institution would perpetuate. What every grand jury needs badly are citizens who enter their year of service well equipped with the knowledge, skills, and motivation appropriate for the exercise of active citizenship. Similarly, any political system that purports to be a regime of self-government also needs such citizens.

Previously I offered examples of how our educational system, the several social-science disciplines, our legal profession, and the news media could contribute to civic revitalization. I use the term "revitalization" with some reservation. Never in the United States was there a time when all adult Americans were fully developed citizens in the sense that I have used the term in this study. One could argue that at no time has even a sizable minority of such citizens existed. Throughout our history, however, some Americans occasionally have stirred themselves to active citizenship. Indeed, the writing of the Declaration of Independence was achieved in that spirit.

After the American Revolution, the Progressive Era was the next outbreak of root-and-branch active citizenship. The spirit of that period lasted many years. Even today one sometimes learns about a citizen who, against great odds, single-handedly has exposed an ineffective, corrupt, or wasteful practice in governmental affairs. The national news media also occasionally report the successes of whistle-blowing public employees. As some examples in this book have shown, civil grand jurors from time to time likewise achieve the institution's potential. When citizens initiate remedies for unjust, corrupt, or ineffective uses of the power of the state, they reinforce the civic value of self-government that is the heart of the United States Constitution. To the extent that we have a sufficient recruitment pool of citizens to achieve such victories, we have solved the problem not only of creating a free society but also of maintaining it.

At this writing, about 34 million men, women, and children populate California. If only one-quarter of these individuals are eligible for grand jury service, the California courts should easily find each year among so vast a recruitment pool 1,000 highly qualified and motivated adult citizens for civil grand jury service. The challenge is even less formidable. All that would be required to improve grand jury investigations and reports significantly Statewide is half that number of authentic citizens. The presence of even several dedicated, skilled, and intelligent citizens on each panel would be sufficient to improve grand jury final investigations and reports substantially. If, given the resources we spend each year for our public and private educational systems, we cannot find enough citizens to operate a small-scale civic institution effectively, how shall we find a sufficient number for government at large?

"A POLITICAL CULTURE OF DEEP DISSATISFACTION ..."

It will be tragic enough if we continue to ignore the causes of ineffective citizenship in view of the apathy, discontent, and anger concerning government that, according to an unending torrent of surveys, abounds in American society.[92] It will be even more tragic if we continue to ignore the relationship between ineffective citizenship and the decline in citizen trust of and support for local, state, and federal government. Unfortunately, the people who wrote the Constitution of the United States, the Bill of Rights, and the Declaration of Independence did not enshrine in these texts a mandate for cultivating and practicing the form of citizenship necessary for maintaining the political system they so brilliantly created.

Perhaps the framers were weary from years of Revolutionary warfare, or perhaps they assumed that citizenship education was essentially a moral proposition and that a sufficient number of traditional institutions always would exist to accomplish that task. What they understood to be "public schools" were, after all, generally church-related institutions in which civic virtue was "taught across the curriculum." The framers also were accustomed to a different kind of newspaper subculture than that of today. They therefore might have assumed that profit-seeking never would inhibit a free press from advocating and practicing the kind of citizenship that republican government requires. The First Amendment was, to some extent, conceived for this purpose. The founders also may have concluded that a sufficiently large number of citizens during each generation would accept responsibility for acquiring the civic skills, beliefs, and values necessary for self-government. These are possible explanations for how we inherited the ideal of a free society but, in terms of the day-to-day practice of citizenship, failed to develop the skills to maintain it. One important cause of the somnolent citizenship that has thwarted the founders' prescription for self-government is easy to identify but difficult to correct—namely, that humankind has been molded for generations into subjecthood rather than active citizenship.

The founders themselves grappled with the difficulty of casting off certain customs rooted in thousands of years of living under descending rather than ascending governments. Social-psychological conditioning, when it is applied over the ages and infused thoroughly into the social fabric, is difficult to change. Even George Washington, shortly after becoming the first President of the United States, was importuned by several advisors to cloak himself with regal "dignity."[93] Thus, although the framers of the Constitution had the historical, political, and economic knowledge necessary for drafting a charter for freedom, they did not include in it provisions to eliminate the effects of eons of social and psychological indoctrination for subjecthood. Although the Constitution fosters ascending government, it speaks little about the means and ends required to maintain it.

American citizens always have had to work out the details of popular self-government. This is why some commentators refer to our regime as a work in progress. The Constitution provided the broad outline of freedom, but its particulars were for us to fashion. In working on the details of governance, we face constant tension between ascending and descending political power. Legislation such as public-records acts, open-meeting laws, and term-limits statutes reveal that tension. Most Americans assume that once enacted, these laws will maintain themselves. This is not the case. The passage of laws for ascending governance, and for their maintenance and modification, is frequently deprecated or ignored by those who wield the power of descending government. Similarly, the beneficiaries of power, being largely in control of legislative processes, are conveniently situated to initiate legislation to protect their interests.

Consider, for example, the recent legislative attempts to "improve" grand jury proceedings that I cited previously. Recall that one bill would have required grand jurors to show draft reports of their local-government investigations to the officials responsible for the affected departments or agencies.[94] An association of public officials struck another blow at the independence of the institution with a bill beguilingly titled, "The Civil Grand Jury Training, Communication, and Efficiency Act of 1997." Recall also that the former president of that group later expressed his plans to introduce legislation to eliminate the designation "grand jury" and substitute for it "Citizens' Review Committee." The rationale for this proposal was that "grand jury" conveys an unrealistic sense of power. These are examples of legislation with regard to the institution that only a descending conception of citizenship would have conceived, promoted, and enacted. The failures of citizenship referred to in previous chapters unfortunately provided much of the impetus for that legislation.

Just as the passage of laws will not by itself entirely eliminate the abuse of grand jury powers, legislation also will not fully eliminate ineptitude, corruption, or abuse of authority by public officials. To paraphrase Karl Popper, legislation accomplishes little more than limiting the amount of damage that incompetent or malevolent persons can inflict on our political institutions.[95] As I stated earlier, I do not expect the statutory reforms I proposed in Chapter 7 to eliminate all the problems this study revealed. The suggested changes, however, might reduce their frequency and severity. Some of the proposed statutes also will make it difficult for grand jurors or their legal advisors to ignore, excuse, or defend certain kinds of abuses of the spirit of the institution.

For example, the repetition in several statutes of the word "fact" may convey the essential idea of the grand jury's character to even the most obdurate citizen impaneled for grand jury service. Similarly, if it prevents only one professional reputation from being damaged unfairly, ample justification is present for the passage of a statute that requires every finding, conclusion, and recommendation in a final report to be supported by documented evidence that has met a specified standard of proof.

Statutory changes alone cannot correct the social trends that continue to stultify a mature sense of citizenship from developing in the populace. The erosion of investigative reporting, the abandonment of civics education and research by educational and social-science establishments, the inattention of the legal profession to problems of citizenship and governance, and related matters continue to foster the quiescent brand of citizenship that we Americans now practice. Considering the emphasis in our founding documents on freedom and liberty, one might wonder how we arrived at our present state of civic somnambulism. It is unrealistic to expect that even the active citizens who conceived the Declaration of Independence and the United States Constitution could have accurately foreseen the demographic, economic, and political character of their country 200 years after their time. Had the framers predicted these problems, they might have debated the question, "What kind of citizenship skills, knowledge, and attitudes shall we embed in the Constitution to permit freedom and liberty to survive in the United States notwithstanding future social and economic conditions?"

Except for certain passages from which we might infer one or two answers to this question, no language can be found in the Constitution that directly addresses it. The Declaration of Independence, however, is another matter, but it is not part of the formal "basic law" of the United States. This could explain why, for the most part, many Americans know so little about it.[96]

A debate of sorts is under way about modern citizenship and the future of the United States. The books cited in "Additional References" are a fraction of the publications that social commentators have written about this issue in recent years. Unfortunately, I have yet to find in such literature a treatment of the nature of citizenship in the sense that I have used the term in this study. As far as the practice of citizenship defined as "responsible direct intervention and participation in governance" is concerned, the subject well deserves to be characterized by a term such as "the Lost Continent" or the "blind eye" of social science, jurisprudence, journalism, and educational philosophy.

NOTES FOR A NEW UNDERSTANDING OF "CITIZENSHIP"

As I began to write this chapter, a new book about citizenship, *The Good Citizen,* was published.[97] Subtitled "A History of American Civic Life," the book began with an anecdote about the proprietor of a Colonial American coffee house who, in 1690, wanted to publish a newspaper. Failing to obtain permission from the government to print his paper, the aspiring publisher abandoned the project. The episode was a fitting beginning for a book about citizenship. It illustrated why the framers included in the Constitution the civic value of freedom of the press. The story also emphasized the self-government precept of freedom of assembly; coffee houses have a long tradition as important institutions in the civic life of English-speaking communities. The remainder of the chapter was devoted to the history of newspapers in public life. By the middle of the first chapter, I was encouraged by the author's down-to-earth approach to citizenship, an expectation that continued to Chapter 2.

Chapter 2 offered a thought-provoking discussion of "private associations" in civic life and the first of many later references to the "informed citizen." In the remaining chapters, the combination of the history of public-affairs journalism, the role of private associations in communities, and further references to an informed citizenry marked the book as unusual in the contemporary literature of citizenship. In particular, the author's development of the term "informed citizens" suggested that he eventually might propose a genuinely active conception of citizenship, something beyond conventional admonitions to vote, serve on juries, or work as volunteers in community organizations.[98] My anticipation therefore increased as I proceeded to the final chapter of the book and its epilogue titled, respectively, "Widening the Web of Citizenship in an Age of Private Citizens" and "A Gathering of Citizens."

As I approached the final pages of *The Good Citizen*, I looked forward to reading the author's answer to the questions he posed for himself in his introduction: "What kind of citizenship, of the kinds that may be possible, should we strive for? What kinds of standards, of the kinds that can resonate with people's life experiences now, should be held up as ideals?" The words, "of the kinds that may be possible," suggested that the author, in the manner of Aristotle, eventually might discuss the varieties of citizenship and recommend that which he believes is best suited for our form of government and our present civic condition. The considerable promise of the preceding chapters of *The Good Citizen*, however, lost momentum in its conclusion, with one exception: the introduction of the "Monitorial Citizen." "Monitorial" was an inspired choice of adjectives. The term suggests something of the vigilant, active citizenship implied in the Declaration of Independence and the kind of citizenship that a majority of the framers probably entertained as they debated drafts of the Constitution.

The Latin root of "monitor" means "to warn." Given its etymology, "monitorial" goes beyond Professor Bellah's advice that American citizens should "pay attention" to what is happening in their communities.[99] For instance, one might pay attention to something because of idle curiosity, but "monitorial" suggests that the citizen has a duty to make certain that public affairs are in good order, and if they are not, fellow citizens must be notified. In contrast, terms such as "informed" suggest merely the acquisition of information, a condition that describes many citizens today who spend hours passively watching television news but whose conception of their duties as citizens is limited to voting.

As is often the case in the contemporary literature of citizenship, the author of *The Good Citizen* cited no examples of what truly active citizens might accomplish in courthouses, city halls, or school-board meetings. This is how he defined the monitorial citizen:

> All that is required [of the monitorial citizen] to criticize the present state of affairs is to know that some serious injustices persist, that some reasonable conditions that limit human possibility lie before us, and that resources for reconstituting ourselves can be found.[100]

The only illustration the author offered to describe monitorial citizens in action is that of parents at a community pool where their children are swimming: "They are not gathering information; they are keeping an eye on the scene." Puzzled by the lack of public-affairs examples of what monitorial citizens might accomplish, I was reminded of a comment an English professor made years ago in an undergraduate course: "The author took you right up to the bedroom door and slammed it in your face."

Despite this shortcoming, *The Good Citizen* is by no means a failure. Up to its concluding pages, it is a valuable record of the interplay between journalism, political-party politics, voluntary associations, and what the author described as three stages of American citizenship. The book is well documented and entertainingly covers 200 years of American political history. In view of the author's skill in developing the first five chapters of his book, I wondered why he did not expand further his concept of the monitorial citizen. A clue to an answer to that question appears early in the book.

In his introduction, the author—possibly to illustrate his definition of active citizenship—described how he volunteered to serve briefly as a county "election inspector." Although his illustration of his civic spirit is commendable, if he offered it as an example of active, autonomous citizenship, it fell short of the mark. Volunteer work in highly structured bureaucratic circumstances implies almost no independent action, initiative, or thought. Puzzled by the anecdote, I wondered why someone with an otherwise good grasp of his subject was unable to cite a better example, perhaps something like the incident of the woman I referred to earlier who was concerned about the dumping of toxic waste near her farm. I concluded that, as is so often the case in the literature of citizenship, the author's practical experience in citizen activism fell short of his theoretical understanding of it. Anyone who has been a citizen activist in local government could provide much more compelling examples of what monitorial citizens might accomplish than performing semi-clerical tasks as volunteer workers in a governmental office.

The author's example of what active citizens could achieve in their communities differs little from what can be found in civic journalism, modern civics texts, and "puff-pieces" that local-government officials distribute at downtown booster-club luncheons. Even though the lack of active-citizenship examples is a shortcoming of his book, the author nevertheless coined a useful term to describe the kind of citizenship needed for the present era. The appeal of the term "monitorial" is its suggestion of something more assertive than the passive variety of citizenship associated with descending government. It also implies that its originator agrees with what many other commentators have concluded about American civic life: Something must be done to help Americans develop a valid sense of involvement, achievement, and trust in their dealings with government.

Educating citizens for subjecthood may be appropriate for regimes of descending power, but it has led only to civic demoralization in contemporary America. It is little wonder that one citizen of international stature who survived a totalitarian regime has cautioned us that "the principal challenge of our time" is that "the modern era has reached a point of culmination, and if we are not to perish of our own modernness we have to rehabilitate the human dimension of citizenship as well as of politics."[101]

"They Will Call Us Citizens, but We Will Be Something Less"

Earlier in this chapter, I proposed a project for civic revitalization and offered examples of contributions that several disciplines and professions could make to it. I conclude this book with an observation about the semantics of the word "citizenship" in such an undertaking. In Chapter 1, I referred to a friend who expressed surprise that the title of this book included the word "citizenship." "What," he asked, "have grand juries got to do with immigration?" Consider, also, the comments I made about conditioning citizens to define citizenship only in terms of obeying laws, defending the nation, and paying taxes.[102] Though these activities are important, they exclude what should be a constant, primary concern of every adult American: Is the power of the state used fairly, justly, and effectively?

This is a question that not everyone committed to a descending conception of citizenship would conceive, much less ask. Nor is it a question that the news media, social-science scholars, or the legal profession often pose. It is, however, a question that every one of Aristotle's "serious" citizens serving as a grand juror should raise, and one that other citizens must ask, not merely occasionally, but daily. It also is the central question that our educational establishment must address if its purpose is to create the kind of citizenship that our founding charter implies. As one commentator warned, education for citizenship is a "messy business," but it is an enterprise that "liberal theory would be foolish to ignore."[103]

The most important asset in any undertaking to revitalize citizenship is the United States Constitution. One of its prime concerns, after all, are the power alignments between the state and the citizenry. Because the spirit and laws of the civil grand jury are similarly concerned, I often have thought of the institution as the afterglow of the civic "Big Bang" of the American Revolution. Most assuredly, a project to resurrect the spirit of citizenship that the signing of the Constitution liberated would be a massive undertaking. Fortunately, Americans today can avail themselves of many technological and social innovations to renew the ideal of self-government even if it is now little more than the relic radiation from the enormous political explosion that created our charter for ascending government 200 years ago.

Rapidly advancing electronic technology for exchanging information almost instantly is available to every citizen. The widespread demand for educational reform is encouraging new thinking about education for citizenship. Concepts such as alternative schools, charter schools, and school vouchers threaten the monopolistic advantage of public education and create the possibility for curricular research and experimentation on behalf of active citizenship rather than subjecthood.

Above all, and weak though they now may be, the roots of self-government reach throughout our social, economic, and political foundation. They therefore are within easy grasp for a project of civic revitalization. All that is required for their renourishment are citizens with the will to demand it. Even the contemporary emphasis on the Self could serve the goal of citizenship renewal. The psyche, after all, is diminished if one's identity as a citizen is stunted. To decide what kinds of human beings we wish to be, we must learn to practice a form of citizenship consistent with the ideal of self-government. No truly freedom-loving people can accept the alternative:

> If we are not willing to rule in our turn, other men (Hegel's Civil Servants, professional politicians, and professional revolutionaries, corporate bureaucrats, and so on) will rule in theirs. They will call us citizens, but we will be something less.[104]

APPENDICES

Some Notes About the Study and Its Method

Twenty Suggestions for Avoiding Libel Suits

One Hundred Suggestions for Improving
Civil Grand Jury Investigations and Reports

Examples of Subjectivity in a Civil Grand Jury
Investigative Report

Endnotes

Glossary

Additional References

Index

APPENDIX A

Some Notes About the Study and Its Method

In social-science terms, this originally was an exploratory study. For many years I have wanted to develop a method for compiling an annual index of investigations in final reports of California civil grand juries. Occasionally, grand jurors ask me if anyone publishes such an index. Often these people are seeking suitable topics for investigations that their grand juries might conduct, or they wish to read investigations that grand juries elsewhere in California have conducted about certain subjects. Newspaper reporters also request this sort of information. For example, an investigative journalist recently asked me if any grand juries in the past five years have reported investigations of solid-waste management issues. Although I recalled several applicable investigations, a comprehensive index to final reports might have identified others.

The potential value of an annual index was obvious, but I had misgivings about how much time the project might require. Therefore, the original purpose of this study was to determine how many hours would be needed each year to compile an index and what kind of format was best. As matters turned out, I cannot report exactly how much time the index required. As I began to read the 58 final reports for the study period, my attention became diverted to something I had suspected for many years: Grand jury final reports are a rich source of information about the practice of citizenship. The import of final reports for this purpose is not apparent, however, if one examines these documents from only one or two counties. As is often the case with institutions, comparative analysis is more fruitful than single-case research.

As my interest in the citizenship implications of civil grand jury final reports grew, the original goal became secondary, although I still pursued it. As the data-processing phase of the project ended, I had answered one of my original project questions: How many investigations did California civil grand juries conduct Statewide each year, and what were the subjects of such investigations? As Table 13 in Chapter 3 reveals, during the study period, grand juries conducted about 1,000 investigations into 70 topics. The printed listing of the summaries of those investigations was 98 pages.

A Statewide View of Grand Jury Final Reports

If my attention during the project had been confined only to compiling an index to investigations, perhaps no more than a month of reading and data entry would have been needed. A variety of concerns developed, however, that attracted my attention beyond the index. For example, the problem of triviality of grand jury investigations and its attendant problem of subjectivity could be dismissed as idiosyncratic if one were reading final reports of only several counties. As the database grew, it became apparent that these defects were widespread.

Similarly, although I have long suspected that California grand jurors are pre-occupied with county government and rarely study other forms of local government, the database revealed the actual extent of the problem. Other examples of trends and patterns that are not obvious from reading final reports of only a few counties are the following:

- In contrast to final reports of large and small counties, those of medium-sized counties generally are, with some exceptions, more varied and well written.
- Statewide, public officials have little to fear from grand juries in terms of unfair comment or criticism.
- To the extent that they report such data, grand juries in medium-sized counties seem to receive more complaints from citizens than do panels in larger or smaller counties.

The question of why certain practices seem to become institutionalized in some counties but not in others also became more striking as I proceeded through the 58 final reports. A Statewide perspective also raised questions about citizenship and grand jury service. For example, what accounts for the patterned occurrence of jurisdictional errors in final reports? Do some citizens serving as grand jurors not understand that the institution has statutory limits? Or, if they do understand the limits of the institution's authority, why do they ignore them? And why do the judges who review grand jury final reports not find such errors and order them to be expunged from final reports?

These are only a few examples of how the original goal of the project, developing an index to civil grand jury final reports, broadened into questions about the practice of citizenship in the modern era.

Development of the Coding Guide

Even if I had confined my reading of 58 civil grand jury final reports to compiling an index, a computer would have been useful. As I became more interested in final reports as insights into the practice of citizenship, however, using a computer to organize this information became not only useful, but necessary. Using a computer to study large amounts of textual materials requires an important preliminary step: planning and testing a coding guide to collect and store information such as quotations, numbers, and personal observations in a consistent, easily retrievable manner.

For example, to create an inventory of grand jury investigations classified by subjects, I eventually developed a list of 70 local-government topics—those shown in Chapter 3, Table 13. Considerable time was required to refine the categories so they did not overlap. Similar experimentation and refinement was required for all the other computer codes that were created as the study objective widened. Thus, the project coding guide grew from an original three pages to nearly 12 pages.

Not starting the project with a well-tested and refined coding guide created certain problems for the accuracy of some data in this study. For example, it was necessary to separate some codes into two, three, or more subcategories as the study progressed. In some cases renaming them meant that Statewide tallies of some problems are incomplete. On the other hand, some original categories in the coding guide (such as those used to prepare the summaries reported in Chapter 3) were constant throughout the project. In other cases, I added categories to the guide after having read several final reports or more. In these instances, I did not go back to the final reports to find examples of the new categories. The sums of entries into some categories, therefore, are smaller than they would have been if their codes had existed from the beginning of the project.

One example of a category that remained constant was "grand jury achievements." The coding guide began with that category, and it never was altered or modified. Another example of a code that remained constant throughout the project was "jurisdiction." In the revised coding guide, however, that topic now has been separated into a code for each type of jurisdictional problem the study revealed—for example, "courts," "federal government," "legislation." If the project is repeated in the future, it now will be possible to identify not only the total Statewide number of jurisdiction problems that occur in one year but subtotals for each of their types as well. This information would be useful for judges who review final reports of civil grand juries before their publication.

In contrast, about halfway through the project, I created and used a code for favorable or unfavorable comments grand jurors made about their legal advisors. This category occurred to me only after I had read two such comments in final reports involving the district attorney of one county and the county counsel of another. Thus, the number of such problems in the database probably is undercounted.

The code for negative comments about public officials or employees is an example of a category name change during the project. Originally I had created a "libel" code for these comments, but I eventually renamed "libel" to "fair comment" for three reasons. *First,* realizing that what is or is not libelous can be determined only by a trial, I decided to use a less legalistic name. *Second,* I found comments that, although they might not be adjudicated as libelous, were otherwise unfair. Eventually, therefore, the "libel" code became "fair comment," a term with which I still am not satisfied.

A *third* problem arises about the factual basis of derogatory comments. On occasion, a grand jury issues an undocumented statement about a person that, on its face, seems libelous. For example, a final report might include the statement, "Mr. Jones has mismanaged public funds." Such a statement is, of course, conclusionary as it is expressed. It may or may not be justified and, in the absence of any reported supporting facts, a reader would not know whether it is based on solid evidence or whether it is merely a scurrilous, and possibly libelous, comment.

When I have had the opportunity to discuss such statements with former grand jurors who served on panels that reported them, I have been told occasionally that the panel did, in fact, have the documented evidence to support the statement but, for one reason or another, did not publish it. In the case of Mr. Jones, for example, perhaps he realized that the grand jury could support its conclusionary statement with facts and therefore decided not to sue for libel. In these cases, grand juries sometimes make "deals" with public officials: Resign, keep your retirement pay and medical benefits, and no indictment will be filed. It is also possible that grand jurors made the comment without sufficient evidence as lawyers understand the term. What a panel of laymen might think is solid evidence could merely be rumors or hearsay commentary. Nevertheless, for a reason known only to himself, Mr. Jones might have decided not to sue the grand jury even though, on its face, the statement could be the basis for a libel suit.

Suppose a grand jury had included these words in a final report: "Mr. Jones is not very careful with his handling of public funds." This is somewhat different from the statement in the preceding paragraph. It could mean almost anything, such as the petty cash in Mr. Jones' department is kept in a hatbox. Even if a court were to rule that the statement was not libelous, it would be unfair if the grand jury had no factual basis for it. To the extent that such statements were in final reports during the study period, I classified them in the "fair comment" category and left it to the courts to decide whether they were libelous.

Faced with ambiguities of this sort about defamation as a legal concept, I decided to rename the "libel" code to "fair comment." Although I made this change fairly early in the project, I did not go back to the final reports I had read already to collect examples of statements I might have missed when I focused more narrowly upon the more technical concept of libel. Thus, the tally of fair-comment problems might understate their actual extent during the study period.

The Accuracy of Coding Decisions

Consistency in coding decisions is important. For example, three different people could disagree about whether a grand jury comment should receive a fair-comment code. To the extent that coders might disagree about coding decisions, the validity of research findings, conclusions, and recommendations could be jeopardized. The consistency of coding decisions may, of course, be measured using certain statistical procedures. From these calculations, conclusions might be drawn about the validity of coding decisions.

For this exploratory study, I chose not to use such rigorous tests principally because of the cost involved in hiring coding technicians and training them to code independently the hundreds of computer entries for the project. With the exception of several fair-comment examples, however, the citations to original documents in this study allow readers to decide for themselves the accuracy of the project data.

Format of Summaries of Investigations and Other Notes From the Database

Chapters 3, 4, and 5 include many quotations, summaries of investigations, and other materials from final reports. The summaries are abstracts of investigative reports that ranged from 2 or 3 paragraphs to 8 or 10 pages in length. This is an example of a summary:

> Investigation into allegations of theft of cocaine from a Sheriff's Department sub-station; grand jury received investigative assistance from the Office of Attorney General; review of internal procedures for prevention of theft of evidence; Placer, 1991–1992, 8:5.

The last part of the summary identifies the county grand jury and the year of its report. The number of pages of each investigative report and the number of its recommendations, respectively, are the figures on both sides of a colon, such as "8:5." Thus, these two numbers mean that the original report was eight pages long and had five recommendations. In some cases (for example, quotations), the numbers of pages and recommendations are not shown; instead the page numbers on which the examples appeared in final reports are cited.

Occasionally a question mark instead of the number of recommendations appears in a summary. The question mark means that I was not certain whether the report contained one or more recommendations. This might denote that a grand jury did not clearly designate its recommendations or that the recommendations were otherwise difficult to discern. In a few cases, a plus mark (+) or the word "Appendix" follows the number of recommendations. These notations mean that a grand jury attached supporting material to its report but did not number the pages.

Generally, I did not create notes for perfunctory descriptions of local-government services, offices, or agencies not accompanied by at least one recommendation, or one or more significant or unusual observations or comments. Many pages of "Cook's tours" ruminations appear each year in final reports. Although I excluded most of this commentary from the study, I included a few examples to illustrate the significance criterion discussed in Chapters 2 and 5.

Cases and Opinions of Legal Advisors

California appellate and supreme court cases concerning the civil function of the grand jury are few; and, in most cases, the courts have supported the institution. California grand jury case law generally has been about the indictment or accusation functions. Because my focus in this study was the civil function, I did not cite case law concerning either accusations or indictments. I also restricted my citations of published opinions of the Office of Attorney General in California only to matters involving the legal criteria described in Chapter 2.

With respect to appellate and supreme court opinions, an attorney verified my interpretation of the conclusions I have drawn about each case. Similarly, the cases cited in this study have been examined to make certain that their holdings have not been negated by subsequent statutory law, and therefore are consistent with previous or subsequent cases. It is possible that new case law or statutes have been created between the end of the project and publication of this book. An attorney in the Office of the California Attorney General reviewed Chapter 2 and informed me that nothing in it contradicts his understanding of relevant statutes, case law, or opinions of the Attorney General of the State of California.

Grand Jury Expenditure Data

Most of the data in this study pertaining to grand jury expenditures and expenditures of county boards of supervisors are from the *Annual Report of Financial Transactions Concerning Counties in California* for the years shown. The Office of Controller for the State of California collects these data from the county auditors of California under State law. To the extent possible, the staff of the State Controller verifies the accuracy of the data. In one case, I discovered a million-dollar error in grand jury expenditure data that the Controller's office reported one year for a large California county. The Executive Officer of the Superior Court of that county kindly sent me revised figures upon my request.

In a few cases, expenditure data for several grand juries in small counties were missing from the Controller's reports for certain years. Grand jury foremen in these cases sent me the needed expenditure data. The foreman of one small county was unable to supply such data for each of six years. The magnitude of the missing data, however, was so small that Statewide totals would be affected only slightly.

Expenditure data also are missing for the City and County of San Francisco, a local government that is subject to different rules of accounting than those affecting other counties in the State. Despite several attempts, I was unable to obtain the missing expenditure data for the City and County of San Francisco.

For grand juries and boards of supervisors, I used expenditure data, not the amounts appropriated for grand jury budgets at the beginning of each fiscal year. Budgetary information also would make an interesting study. For example, comparing grand jury budget data to expenditure data might reveal how often grand juries exceeded their budgets in the study period. This could happen for good reasons, as when a grand jury finds that it must conduct an unusually expensive investigation and receives the court's approval to do so. Likewise, it might be possible to determine how often grand juries exceed their budget because of poor internal management and whether, in doing so, they have violated Penal Code Section 914.5, the provision that requires panels to stay within their budgets unless they receive judicial approval to exceed them.

The following expenditure data for the boards of supervisors pertain only to the legislative bodies themselves, not other elected or appointed officials. These expenditures pay for items such as salary, fringe benefits, postage, travel and conferences, meals, and the like. The data for civil grand juries and boards of supervisors exclude capital outlay expenditures.

The Statewide data in Chapter 3 depicting the expenditures of grand juries and boards of supervisors are based on the following data from the aforementioned annual reports of the Office of Controller of the State of California.

In Chapter 3 I refer in the Statewide trends section to "best-fit" lines. These are, in effect, "smoothed-out" versions of the jagged lines that represent actual expenditures. Best-fit lines allow one to examine the general long-term trend in a set of data. The references I make in Chapter 3 to comparing individual counties to counties in comparable population-size groups are based on data I have not, because of their volume, published in this book. I plan to release the data in monograph form before the year 2000 ends.

Term	Grand Jury Expenditures	Board of Supervisors' Expenditures	Grand Jury Expenditures as a Percentage of Supervisors' Expenditures
1996–1997	$4,605,453	$56,788,998	8.1
1995–1996	4,414,273	54,230,753	8.1
1994–1995	4,463,765	56,414,069	7.9
1993–1994	4,546,484	53,312,011	8.5
1992–1993	4,427,092	54,764,833	8.1
1991–1992	4,467,805	55,041,027	8.1
1990–1991	4,294,105	51,398,971	8.4
1989–1990	4,772,879	47,697,086	10.0
1988–1989	3,826,012	43,443,108	8.8
1987–1988	3,617,989	38,106,172	9.5
1986–1987	3,748,159	36,580,318	10.3
1985–1986	3,362,605	33,157,566	10.1
1984–1985	3,195,653	30,299,821	10.6
Percent Change	44.1	87.4	

Archives of Grand Jury Final Reports

One of the consequences of the master's thesis I wrote in the early 1960s about the California grand jury was that the library of the University of California at Davis (UCD) began collecting final reports from California grand juries. The collection was started at the behest of a grand jury foreman I had met while conducting interviews for my thesis project. When I expressed to the foreman the difficulty in obtaining final reports from certain counties, he urged a librarian at the UCD library to start the collection.

Although the collection now is quite large, it is not complete. Counties send final reports to the library voluntarily, and some counties send reports intermittently or not at all. Originally, the collection was in the main UCD library. Later it was transferred to the University of California at Berkeley, where accessing the collection now is possible. A somewhat less complete collection of grand jury final reports also is available at the Maps and Government Information Library of the University of California at Los Angeles.

Future Research

Scholars and others interested in governance, citizenship, bureaucracy, and similar topics, will find the final reports of California civil grand juries an unending source of insights. A growing consensus is developing that the pressing citizenship issue for this century will be how to reconcile democratic principles and ideals with the imperatives of citizenship in a mass culture and global economy. The civil grand jury in California is an excellent research focus for persons with such concerns. Many of the leading issues of the day can be seen at work within the California civil grand jury and, no doubt, within grand juries of a similar nature in other states. For example, the institution's counterpart of the "term limits" debate is the controversy about the carry-over grand juror statute. For those who are interested in the idea that the form of government we have created in the United States is out of control and beyond the ability of most Americans to understand, issues about how well our educational systems prepare citizens for self-government can be explored in grand jury final reports.

The California civil grand jury offers research possibilities in another respect. A longstanding concern for social scientists is how the size of an institution affects the people it employs or serves and the quality of its products. For example, are small schools superior to big schools in terms of the emotional health of students, their educational attainment, or teacher-administrator ratios? Is there a size or form of local government in which citizens participate most actively in civic affairs? In the case of the grand jury, are the population characteristics of a county related in some way to the recruitment of effective citizens for grand jury service? Answers to questions such as these might result in new knowledge about the forms of government that most encourage citizen participation.

Another topic that merits research is the legislative history of the California civil grand jury. This should include an examination of transcripts of the deliberations of the Constitutional Convention at the founding of the State. Research might reveal answers to questions such as what purpose the framers of the California Constitution thought the grand jury might serve, who supported or opposed it and why, and what kinds of compromises occurred in debates about the institution before it was enshrined in the California Constitution. Answers to these questions would be valuable for people who are interested in reforming the California civil grand jury.

The study objectives excluded information about the grand jury accusation process in California for removing from office without criminal penalty public officials who are guilty of malfeasance, misfeasance, or nonfeasance. Although this process has been little used in recent years, a fairly large number of appellate court cases in previous times describe its successful application in cases of conflict of interest, theft of public property, and various other abuses of power. An inspection of case law concerning the accusation process in California and elsewhere could yield important information about preventing and controlling fraud, graft, and corruption in government.

Grand jury selection provides interesting opportunities for studying how local political regimes use the institution as an instrument of social control. Students of socio-linguistics will find many new insights into the political uses of language by studying how grand juries word their findings and recommendations in contrast to the language strategies that public officials use to comment about them. Similarly, persons interested in mass communications might wish to study how the news media report grand jury investigations. For example, a close examination of the contrast between what final reports contain and what the news media ignore or emphasize in them could reveal much about the role of the press and television in government.

Political scientists or legal scholars interested in reforming the civil grand jury will find many leads for corrective legislation by conducting a national survey of grand jury statutes and case law pertaining to the civil function. Of particular importance in this respect would be a comparative study of statutes and case law concerning judicial review of final reports, statutes that ensure objective investigations and reports, provisions for grand jury independence, and a clearer definition of jurisdiction for civil grand juries. Although I did not develop these matters extensively in this study, statutes in other states merit review for civil grand jury reform in California.

Another issue that deserves attention is what caused the grand jury in England to be eliminated. I have read several different explanations for its demise but found nothing definitive. A comprehensive analysis of the parliamentary history leading to the elimination of the grand jury in England is of interest for several reasons:

1. Contemporary social scientists in England often express concerns about citizen apathy. In view of this concern, it would be useful to discover why legislators of a previous generation in England struck down an institution deeply rooted in Magna Carta.
2. An inquiry into the passing of the grand jury in England might shed light on the question of whether direct citizen intervention in government is antithetical to the growth of professionalism that accompanies the expansion of the welfare state.
3. By identifying the causes of the elimination of the grand jury, it might be possible to resurrect it in a form more suited to contemporary social conditions in emerging and established democracies.

I offer one more suggestion for future research: When I first read years ago the *Clinton* case that I described in Chapter 2, I regrettably assumed that Mr. Clinton must have been engaged in an ax-grinding mission for self-serving purposes. Although this is not stated explicitly in the case now bearing his name, the tone in which the court expressed its opinion conveyed this impression. The principal holdings of the case are consistent with the spirit of the institution, but the unfortunate implication of the wording of the court's opinion is that Mr. Clinton tried to use the Los Angeles County Grand Jury for his own, possibly nefarious, purposes. Since then, I have learned that Clifford Clinton was attempting, as a citizen, to expose governmental corruption. Although the case reports none of this information, Mr. Clinton was, at the time of his grand jury service, the leader of a group of citizens who were attempting to expose fraud and graft in Los Angeles city and county government in the 1930s and 1940s.

Despite his reputation as a citizen activist, Clifford Clinton somehow had been appointed to the Los Angeles County Grand Jury. While serving as a panel member, he tried to persuade his fellow grand jurors that they should investigate certain corrupt activities in Los Angeles County and City government. History shows that Mr. Clinton had ample reason for urging his grand jury colleagues to investigate "his case"—to use the court's words. Unfortunately, when Mr. Clinton and several other grand jurors asked their fellow panel members to hear their evidence, an internal struggle ensued.

The result of Mr. Clinton's efforts was the appellate court case that now bears his name and portrays him as something he was not: a meddling eccentric. To the contrary, Clifford Clinton was one of a vanishing breed of citizens who understood and practiced the civic virtue of the common good. His error as a grand juror was that he had not taken the time to understand thoroughly the spirit of the institution and develop a strategy for encouraging his fellow grand jurors to use the institution's powers for a laudable purpose. Thus, the irony of the *Clinton* case is that collegiality, which ordinarily is a virtue of the institution, was used for a malevolent purpose: to block a legitimate and much-needed investigation.

As for its research implications, the *Clinton* case offers unusual opportunities. Now that 60 years have passed since its publication, the case should be studied in the context of the news accounts, police investigations, and other publications of the time concerning the corruption that Mr. Clinton eventually uncovered. For example, it now should be possible to determine which, if any, of Mr. Clinton's fellow grand jurors had been nominated for grand jury service by the public officials who were implicated in the matter. Further, it now is possible to determine whether the antagonistic relationship between Mr. Clinton and the then-district attorney resulted in voters subsequently removing that official from office. Moreover, what does history disclose about the judge who impaneled the grand jury that refused to conduct an inquiry into Mr. Clinton's concern? Occasionally, judges direct grand juries to initiate investigations into controversial issues in local government. Was this option possible during the Clinton episode, and, if so, is archival material available that reveals why the judge did or did not exercise that option?

A thorough historical study of the events surrounding the *Clinton* case would reveal valuable information for scholars interested in the mechanisms and processes of the corruption of public institutions. Finally, such a study would vindicate a man and his family who paid a high price for their integrity, to say nothing of affirming the spirit of the institution.

Twenty Suggestions
for Avoiding Libel Suits

To become familiar with the concept of defamation of character, grand jurors should ask their legal advisors early in their term to conduct a workshop about defamation of character, with emphasis on understanding and preventing libel. The following topics may assist in planning the workshop.

1. Read the *Gillett-Harris-Duranceau and Assoc., Inc. v. Kemple* case ((1978) 83 Cal.App.3d 214 [147 Cal.Rptr. 616]) before your legal advisor conducts the workshop. If you have questions about the case, ask your legal advisor to clear them up for you at the workshop.

2. Also before your legal advisor presents the workshop, read Penal Code Section 930. This is the statute that, in certain circumstances, removes the immunity of grand jurors from adverse lawsuits. Make certain that you understand exactly what the statute means and that the concept of "privilege" is clear to you.

3. Ask your legal advisor whether your County would defend grand jurors if a libel suit were to arise, whether the County's insurance would cover grand jurors in the event of a successful lawsuit, and to quote and explain the language in the County's insurance policy that specifically provides protection for grand jurors.

4. Before you begin an investigation that might lead to allegations of wrongdoing, ask your legal advisor to advise the grand jury where potential pitfalls might be in such an investigation.

5. Exercise great care if an investigation enters areas that traditionally have resulted in libel suits, such as allegations of criminality, abuse of power or wrongful use of office; sexual misconduct; conflict of interest; and allegations of alcoholism, mental incompetence, impotence, professional misconduct, or guilt by association.

6. Have a group of grand jurors play "devil's advocate" with a draft of a report containing negative statements about named or unnamed but identifiable persons; for example, the jurors should figuratively tear the report apart and try to imagine how named or identifiable persons, corporations, or groups might react to it.

7. Avoid adjectives and adverbs; these parts of speech are almost always the offending words in libel or slander suits.

8. Avoid naming people but, rather, focus on procedures and policies. Do not, however, conclude from that statement that you must never use names or otherwise identify people, even in a negative sense.

9. Do not play lawyer unless you are one. If you are not a lawyer but have heard terms such as "negligent," "malicious intent," or "reckless," make no assumptions about what they may mean in libel law without qualified legal advice.

10. Business and professional groups such as engineers, medical personal, attorneys, and school teachers are geared up to suing for libel. Be especially careful where such people are concerned. But don't fall into the trap of predicting who will and who will not sue. You may be in for a surprise.

11. Undocumented news stories should not be the basis for drawing conclusions; make certain you check, double-check, and triple-check original sources.

12. Cartoons, photographs, paintings and the like can be the basis for libel in some circumstances.

13. Make certain that you can back every finding and conclusion with a documented fact, and that you understand the precise meanings of concepts such as facts, evidence, conclusions, and findings.

14. Private businesses, unions, nonprofit corporations, products, and groups can be libeled in certain circumstances just as an individual can. Don't drop your guard with these entities just because they aren't live people; they can be "hurt" or "damaged" in a legal sense, and you might end up paying the bill.

15. Conducting an investigation with persistence, enthusiasm, and energy is one thing. Getting wrapped up in it so completely that you lose objectivity is another. If this happens, watch out!

16. The biggest trap you can fall into is believing that truth is the best, unassailable, and always perfect defense against libel. Ask your legal advisor to comment about that statement.

17. Ask your legal advisors to explain the differences between criminal and civil libel, and the implications of those differences for grand jury service.

18. If you repeat a libel, you could be just as guilty of libel as the person who originated it. Ask your legal advisor to define and illustrate "re-publication" as the concept pertains to libel.

19. Look within yourself. If something is saying to you, "Hang 'em high," or "Go get the rotten so-and-so," you're a good candidate for a successful libel suit.

20. Be careful about advice from "guard-house lawyers," of which this guide is a product. Always, always, always, confer with the proper legal advisors.

A Formula For ...

CONSTRUCTIVE GRAND JURY SERVICE

Established jurisdiction +
Objective and careful investigation +
Fair-minded, collegial deliberation +
Factual, accurate reporting =
Constructive change and positive community support

DESTRUCTIVE GRAND JURY SERVICE

Vague or unclear jurisdiction +
Unwillingness to function as a corporate body +
Hearsay evidence, opinions, assumptions, careless investigation +
Undeclared conflict of interest +
Subjective, self-serving reporting =
Lawsuits, rancorous conflict, and damage to the grand jury institution

APPENDIX C

One Hundred Suggestions
for Improving Civil Grand Jury
Investigations and Reports

Law-Related Criteria

JURISDICTION AND INDEPENDENCE

1. Issue final reports that show a balanced grand jury workload and focus rather than concentrating on only one type of local government.

2. Exclude findings and recommendations about the courts, existing or proposed legislation, State or federal agencies, private persons or corporations, plea bargaining, matters currently in court, and other matters for which no statutory authority exists.

3. Exclude investigations, findings, and recommendations about matters of broad social, economic, or political policy within the province of federal, State, or local legislators.

4. Do not permit grand jurors to serve as voting or honorary members on committees, task forces, or advisory groups of local-government organizations or services within the panel's jurisdiction.

5. Establish policies and procedures that require grand jurors to disclose familial, political, fraternal, and business relationships that could jeopardize their impartiality in grand jury service.

6. Exclude from final reports brand names, manufacturer's names, and trademarked names.

7. If the court so requests, include in each final report a review of grand jury expenditures and finances for the past five years, an assessment of the suitability of meeting rooms, office supplies, equipment, and other resource matters that could enhance or hinder grand jury independence and effectiveness.

8. Use only symbols, logos, or artwork depicting the independent nature of the grand jury. Do not use local-government logos, symbols, names, and titles of elected or appointed officials or their offices that imply that the grand jury is an arm of a body other than the court.

9. Exclude references in final reports that imply that the grand jury is associated with or dependent upon private institutions, educational institutions, public officials (other than the courts), groups advocating legislation, political or civic groups, former grand jurors either as individuals or associations, and the like.

10. Do not imply that succeeding grand juries will continue investigations or are otherwise bound by the decisions, interests, or findings and recommendations of sitting panels.

FAIR COMMENT

11. Document commendations about public officers or employees with facts. Express them with dignity and tact, and avoid broad, sweeping, sycophantic praise.

12. If the report includes information about indictments, particularly the names of individuals, ensure that the grand jury complies with applicable statutes and case law for reporting this information.

13. Omit references to persons who have been charged in some other tribunal with a criminal offense or dereliction of duty or who otherwise are being investigated by some lawful body.

14. Request legal advisors to present training in the statutes and case law governing defamation of character.

15. Exclude all comments about the professionalism, competency, morality, or motives of private persons, public officials, public employees, or corporations unless a legal advisor has reviewed that material and informed panel members of its possible legal consequences. If critical references to public officials are necessary, ensure that they are documented by evidence, expressed factually, and provide no basis for a libel suit.

16. Recognize that no legal advisor or other person has a statutory obligation to protect grand jurors from committing libel, although the court has the discretionary authority to order the grand jury to delete that material from its report.

CONDUCTING JUSTIFIED INVESTIGATIONS

17. Identify the citizen, official, grand juror, or other person requesting an investigation only if that person granted permission to disclose his or her identity unless the disclosure violates secrecy and confidentiality provisions.

18. Include in each investigative report a statement informing readers whether specific statutes required the investigation or whether the grand jury initiated it and why it believed sufficient cause was present to do so.

19. Describe how and when the grand jury explained to department heads, elected officials, or other persons the statutory justification and other important reasons for the investigation.

EMPHASIZING SYSTEMS, PROCEDURES, METHODS, AND EQUIPMENT

20. Report only investigations that emphasize systems, procedures, books, records, accounts, and methods, and that exclude references to substantive policy matters.

21. Early in the grand jury term, develop criteria for distinguishing policy from systems, methods, and procedures. Use the criteria for deliberating about complaints, establishing investigative priorities, and reviewing drafts of reports.

VALIDITY OF INVESTIGATIONS AND REPORTS

22. Using a standard method of citation, identify the source of each fact in each final report that was taken from other reports, documents, and publications unless confidentiality or secrecy requirements bar disclosure.

23. Document the sources of information reported in tables, figures, and graphs unless confidentiality or secrecy requirements bar disclosure.

24. Do not report as facts uncorroborated data from interviews, questionnaires, documents, or other sources.

25. Include a statement in the final report assuring readers that no grand jurors were allowed to serve on any investigative teams or were not informed of the progress of any investigative team concerned with a topic that presented a real or potential conflict of interest for the jurors.

26. Provide information about the attendance record of grand jurors to assure readers that a sufficient number of grand jurors deliberated about each phase of every investigation and voted on it.

27. Do not use conclusionary words such as "large," "small," "overstaffed," "understaffed," "scarce," and "abundant" unless the facts are cited upon which the opinions are based.

28. Publish investigative reports only if they are the product of the grand jury's independent investigation and were not adopted without independent investigation or verification by the panel.

29. Include in orientation programs a discussion of the definition and consequences of plagiarism and its consequences for grand jury service.

30. Regard equivocating phrases such as, "It would appear that," "Informed sources say," and "It is our perception that" as signs of subjectivity or uncertainty, and remove this material from grand jury reports.

31. Publish enough information about the methods used in each investigation so that a reader could reproduce it in its essential details.

32. Describe briefly the principal methods used to verify information reported in each investigation.

33. Exclude from final reports information not obtained from interviews attended by at least two grand jurors. To the extent possible, verify, with facts from other sources, information obtained from interviews.

34. Make certain that each grand juror is impaneled lawfully and that his or her status is not included in the statutory exemptions for grand jury service.

35. In a section of the final report, describe the editorial process and how it ensured the validity of each investigative report.

36. If consultation with persons other than grand jurors was necessary in conducting an investigation and writing a report, describe it unless a confidentiality issue precludes doing so.

37. Cite letters, memoranda, and written opinions by legal advisors that explain actions the grand jury took or did not take pertaining to investigations or reports.

38. Include a statement in the front of the final report, signed by all grand jurors, affirming that the entire panel reviewed and discussed all drafts of the final report and each phase of the investigation, and that at least the statutorily required number of grand jurors approved its publication.

39. Document steps taken to eliminate hearsay and unsubstantiated or uncorroborated information from reports.

40. Ask the judge who reviews the final report before its publication to provide a written statement for inclusion in the document affirming that it complies with laws governing the grand jury and therefore is acceptable for filing with the county clerk and subsequent distribution to the community.

LEGALITY AND EFFECTIVENESS OF FINDINGS AND RECOMMENDATIONS

41. Include only one topic in each finding and recommendation.

42. Make certain that the terms "facts," "findings," "recommendations," and "conclusions" are used consistently throughout final reports.

43. Make certain that findings, recommendations, and conclusions are connected logically to each other.

44. Base each finding on at least three facts and report them in each investigation unless a legal prohibition exists against publishing such facts.

45. Include a statement in the front of the final report describing Penal Code requirements for comments by affected local-government officials to grand jury findings and recommendations.

46. Omit findings and recommendations from the foreman's letter, if any, as this practice implies that they are the product of only one person.

47. Include in the front or back of each final report a numbered list of principal findings and recommendations organized according to the name and title of the local-government official or officials from whom comments are expected.

48. In issuing an interim report, inform affected public officials that the law does not require comment to findings and recommendations in interim reports.

49. Make certain that all problems identified in a final report are accompanied by suggested means, including financial, for their resolution, when applicable.

50. Display and number findings and recommendations conspicuously in the text of each investigation.

51. Before including a recommendation in a final report, make certain that it has not been implemented already.

52. Express findings and recommendations emphatically and constructively, without qualification, uncertainty, or malice.

53. Direct findings and recommendations in an investigative report to a named, specific person, official, organization, or agency.

54. Make certain that findings and recommendations in each investigative report are as conspicuous as possible to assist public officials in identifying them and referring to them in their comments.

55. Write findings and recommendations simply, concisely, and concretely, avoiding jargon, abbreviations, and judgmental and conclusionary words.

56. Exclude recommendations and findings that the grand jury did not develop from its independent investigation.

57. Limit findings and recommendations to sentences no longer than 25 words each and list in order of importance.

CONFIDENTIALITY AND SECRECY

58. If the *McClatchy* case requires deletion of essential information from a report, explain the need for the deletion unless some consideration of secrecy or confidentiality prevents the explanation.

59. Exclude specific references to safety and security weaknesses, problems, or hazards in local-government agencies, departments, or facilities that might encourage criminal acts or otherwise harm citizens or other public employees.

60. In an appropriate place in the final report, explain applicable laws specifying whether grand juries are authorized or required to permit public officials or other persons to review drafts of grand jury reports, findings, recommendations, and conclusions for accuracy before publication.

61. Make certain that the inclusion of names in final reports complies with any statutes or case law pertaining to the publication of names.

PRACTICES SUPPORTING OR JEOPARDIZING THE COLLEGIAL NATURE OF THE GRAND JURY

62. Develop an internal process that the grand jury can use to resolve disputes, disagreements, allegations of conflict of interest among grand jurors, and related matters that could impair the institution's effectiveness.

63. Publish no minority reports that the required number of grand jurors has not approved.

64. If the creation of committees or other subgroupings is necessary, regard them as temporary administrative conveniences rather than as permanent identified subdivisions of the grand jury.

65. Include only findings, recommendations, and conclusions issued in the name of the entire grand jury rather than by foremen or other individual grand jurors or investigative teams.

66. Document how the grand jury deliberated as a body about the objectives, issues, and scope of each investigation and decided the panel's work schedule for the year.

67. Describe briefly in the final report the process the grand jury adopted to ensure that the entire body reviewed, approved, and edited reports of investigative teams; report the date the grand jury approved each investigation; include a statement that approval was supported by at least the statutory minimum number of assenting jurors, but do not disclose the voting of individual grand jurors.

68. Devote at least one panel session to reviewing and deliberating about the *Clinton* case and its implications for all facets of grand jury service.

69. Involve all grand jurors early in the year in deliberating about the powers, authority, and responsibility of the foreman, the names and objectives of grand jury investigative teams, the form and content of the procedures manual, and all phases of the investigative process.

Community Criteria

SIGNIFICANCE

70. Describe the possible consequences of the subject of each investigation such as harm to citizens, wasteful expenditures, employee safety, morale and turnover, possible lawsuits, diminished confidence in government, and the like.

71. Present major investigations in the front of the final report, and at the end of the document briefly report minor inspectional tours, visitations, or other activities that resulted in no findings or recommendations.

72. In each investigative report provide sufficient information about the mission, workload trends, staffing patterns, and expenditure and revenue history of local-government organizations or services to assist readers in understanding the importance, scope, and context of the investigation.

ACCOUNTABILITY

73. No statute requires grand jurors to do so, but if they wish to identify themselves in interim or final reports, list names alphabetically, identify communities, but show no titles of officers or committee assignments.

74. Describe the method the grand jury used to avoid possible "leaks," conflict of interest, and prejudice that might have arisen from the presence of specialists, experts, and retired or currently employed local-government employees serving on the panel.

75. Publish in each final report a brief summary of major grand jury activities of the year, such as the number and type of complaints and their disposition,

number of general and investigative-team meetings that grand jurors attended, number of miles that jurors traveled in connection with grand jury activity, number of meetings of local-government legislative bodies attended, and similar information.

76. If the panel is used for indictments, account for the number and type of indictments, their disposition, the amount of grand jury time spent on each, and a brief description of effects of the indictment function on the civil function.

77. Include in each final report a tactful, accurate, and brief account of the achievements of the preceding grand jury and, if they are known, the current panel.

78. Include a reference in final reports to where interested persons can obtain and review nonconfidential grand jury guides, manuals, handbooks, and the like.

CONTINUITY

79. Consider including in the final report at least one "wrap-up" report concerning two or more investigations of the same topic by panels in the preceding five years.

80. Include in each final report a section that discloses the status of investigations, findings, and recommendations issued by grand juries in the five years preceding the current panel.

81. Include in final reports any findings and recommendations of consequence to which affected local-government officials have not yet commented, but issue no position on those matters without independent investigation.

Technical Criteria

EXTERNAL AND INTERNAL GUIDES
FOR PREPARING AND DISTRIBUTING FINAL REPORTS

82. Include in their entirety, or summarize in final reports, interim reports, if any, issued during the year.

83. Omit from reports voluminous, undigested material; summarize and cite relevant, lengthy material rather than include it in final reports; provide information in final reports about where citizens can obtain copies of supporting materials such as consultants' reports, sections from government codes, tables from budget documents, and the like.

84. Print and distribute at least 50 final reports in an 8½-by-11-inch page format for permanent filing in selected locations such as city and county libraries, university libraries, law libraries, historical archives, and the office of the county clerk.

85. Include in final reports a list of persons, organizations, news media, and the like to which final reports have been distributed.

86. Each report should present a businesslike, professional appearance without ostentatious distractions such as expensive paper, lavish and unnecessary typesetting, costly artwork, and expensive methods of designating sections.

87. Immediately following the title of an investigative report, present a general synopsis of the investigation that summarizes key features such as who, what, why, where, and when, and that clearly expresses the main focus of the investigation.

88. Develop a two-part investigative report format; the first section should be no longer than four pages and is a summary for busy readers of the main points of the investigation; the second section includes the details supporting the main points of the first section.

89. In general, if tables, charts, or graphs are longer than one page, present them as an appendix to the report.

90. Write reports in plain English for citizens rather than in the terminology of specialists, experts, or public officials.

91. Explain and define acronyms, abbreviations, and unusual words, terms, and phrases in the narrative section of the investigation or in a glossary in the appendix.

92. Organize the narrative section of the report chronologically.

93. If investigative reports are organized into named categories, headings, or blocks of text, use a consistent format for each major investigation.

94. Minimize adjectives and adverbs; emphasize factuality.

95. Do not use desktop publishing embellishments that impair ease of reading, such as ornate typestyles, shading, clip art, extensive use of boxes, underlining, italicizing, and the like.

96. Make certain that the report is printed or photocopied so it can be easily read.

97. Write titles of investigative reports to emphasize key issues of the investigation, such as principal facts, findings, or recommendations, rather than names of investigative teams or names of governmental departments.

98. Emphasize the unity, cohesiveness, and independence of final reports by excluding foremen's reports, names of committee members, commendations for and photographs of individual grand jurors and investigating teams, investigative-team assignments, photographs of judges, county staff, bailiffs, prosecuting officials, and related matters.

99. Write reports in a positive and constructive problem-solution tone rather than a problem-condemnation style.

100. Final reports should have tables of contents. If final reports are longer than 50 pages, indexes are also helpful.

APPENDIX D

Examples of Subjectivity in a Civil Grand Jury Investigative Report

- Using vague terms (for example, numerous, inadequate, very seldom, poor communication, erratic, several occasions) but reporting no factual basis for those judgments.

- Using qualifiers such as "appears to," "seems to," and "apparently" instead of unqualified statements based on facts that something did occur, something was stolen, someone harassed someone else, and so on.

- Overgeneralizing comments; for example, stating that "supervisors in this department are inefficient" in a report based on an investigation of a complaint about one or two supervisors in a department that might have more supervisors.

- Not describing in detail the nature and circumstances of statements obtained from interviews; readers are not told whether a specific comment was made by someone in sworn testimony or whether it was made informally in the workplace.

- Developing findings, conclusions, and recommendations from routine interviews but not providing any information about what the grand jury did to verify any "facts" from the interviews.

- Referring in a report to records, forms, memoranda, receipts, or other public documents but not providing proof of their existence and informing readers where they can be checked.

- Reporting that a specific number of persons was interviewed but not reporting how they were selected, what portion of the workforce they represent, or other information about the generalizability of findings from the interviews.

- Reporting information obtained from interviews but not reporting what questions were asked, the attitudes of interviewees, the circumstances under which interviews were conducted, and other information that might support the validity of information obtained.

- Referring vaguely to someone's failure to act but not providing proof of failure, dates on which the purported failure occurred, examples of consequences, who witnessed the event, and the like.

- Asserting that an unlawful condition exists and that a named or identifiable person is responsible for it but providing no independent proof of its existence, frequency of occurrence, dates of occurrence, and so on.

- Accepting and reporting findings derived from sworn testimony but offering no information about attempts the grand jury made to verify or corroborate the findings.

- Stating that official procedures were ignored but not offering proof of the existence of the procedures (where they might be found, how current they are, who authenticated them).

- Asserting or implying impropriety but offering no documentation that it exists.

- Referring to the examination or review of records but not specifying which records were examined, who conducted the examination, or how information from them is linked to findings and conclusions about violations.

- Asserting that an illegal transaction may have occurred but that verification of it was not available at the time of writing the report.

- Committing the "missing link" error: discontinuity between facts, findings, conclusions, and recommendations.

- Stating that contradictions, discrepancies, and inconsistencies occurred in interviews, records, and the like, but not resolving these differences or assuming without reporting supporting evidence that one viewpoint is correct.

- Alleging that faulty systems, procedures, and methods exist but providing no substantiating evidence.

- Committing the error of unverified informal testimony: If "A" says "X" is so, and "B," "C," and "D" agree, this agreement is sufficient proof that "X" occurred.

- Not describing investigative procedures, methods, and strategies sufficiently for readers to have a basis for judging their validity.

Endnotes

Chapter 1

1. Strictly speaking, California has only 57 counties. The local government known as San Francisco is officially a combined city and county (*Blum v. San Francisco* (1962) 200 Cal.App.2d 639 [19 Cal.Rptr. 574]).

2. Chapter 2 addresses the legal basis for the California civil grand jury.

3. Much of the information in this section was obtained from articles published about the Mariposa County Grand Jury controversy by the *Mariposa Gazette* between April and August of 1995.

4. Interim Report, Mariposa County Grand Jury, February 23, 1996, p. 17. According to information received from a reporter for the *Mariposa Gazette* on February 14, 1997, no lawsuits had been filed to that date by any person involved in this episode.

5. Although the Attorney General did not address the facts involved in the Mariposa case, the opinion did make clear its principal finding that the California grand jury has no jurisdiction in the judicial system of which it is itself a part (Office of the Attorney General, State of California, Opinion No. 92-1204, May 4, 1993, Vol. 76, p. 70).

6. My purpose in making this observation is to illustrate an example of some unsettled aspects of grand jury law. If, as the courts have held repeatedly, grand juries can investigate only what they have been authorized to investigate, a grand jury inquiry into the work of another grand jury must be unlawful, for no statute authorizes such inquiry. The leading cases restricting the grand jury's jurisdiction to what the statutes authorize are cited in Chapter 2.

7. *San Francisco Chronicle*, December 14, 1994, p. B-1.

8. "Review of Orange County Treasurer/Tax Collector Investment Function," Orange County Grand Jury Final Report, 1984–1985, pp. A-49–A-51.

9. See John E. Petersen, "Tending the Municipal Garden," *Governing*, October 1996, p. 94. One scholar who thoroughly studied the Orange County financial disaster concluded that "it sounds a warning that there is a disturbing trend toward

a lack of civic participation that can have profound implications for the future of U.S. communities" (Mark Baldassare, *When Government Fails,* Berkeley and Los Angeles: University of California Press, 1998, p. 236). Another scholar, a resident of Orange County, calculated that his share of the loss created by the County's "sophisticated" investment scheme was $3,500 (Philippe Jorion, *Big Bets Gone Bad,* San Diego: Academic Press, 1995, p. ix).

10. Depending on the size of the grand jury, the courts may hold over as many as 10 grand jurors from one grand jury to the next. See, for example, Penal Code Section 901(b). More information about this practice is provided later in this study.

11. San Joaquin County Grand Jury Final Report, 1992–1993, p. 2; Tehama County Grand Jury Final Report, 1992–1993, p. 3. I excluded from the latter quotation a summary of the advantages and disadvantages of the carry-over statute that was offered before the statement beginning, "Having just spent...." I provided the emphasis in the two quotations to assist the reader.

12. "[T]he integrity of the entire research enterprise rests on the honesty with which the data are collected, analyzed *and* reported [italics in original]. Suppressed tables, selective discussion of relevant findings, soft-pedaling of negative data, and similar tactics have no place in responsible survey reporting" (Donald P. Warwick and Charles A. Lininger, *The Sample Survey: Theory and Practice*, New York: McGraw-Hill Book Company, 1975, p. 326).

13. This summary is based on the following news stories in the *San Jose Mercury News*: December 4, 1998, p. B-2, "Third grand juror quits: judge calls for meeting"; December 5, 1998, p. B-1, "Confrontation postponed"; December 11, 1998, p. B-7, "Grand jury still divided"; December 23, 1998, p. B-6, "Verdict on the grand jury"; December 30, 1998, p. A-1, "Grand jurors dismissed"; January 7, 1999, p. B-2, "Ex-grand jurors vow battle for system reforms."

14. Yuba County Grand Jury Final Report, 1993–1994, pp. 3–17. The panel did not explain why its final report contained separate sections about the same public agency and two of its administrators.

15. *Larry F. Brooks et al., v. Douglas F. Binderup et al.,* Court of Appeal of the State of California, Third Appellate District, C026607, May 29, 1998. Because they are not germane to my summary, I have omitted from my discussion important issues that both parties raised in the Appellate hearing.

16. According to one legal scholar, depublication is peculiar to the California judicial system and seems to have originated in the early 1970s (Stephen R. Barnett, "Depublication Deflating: The California Supreme Court's Wonderful Law-Making Machine Begins to Self-Destruct," *Hastings Law Journal,* Vol. 45, 1993–1994, pp. 519–568). Although the criteria for deciding which cases to depublish are not officially articulated, former California Chief Justice Rose Byrd is reported to have said that the Supreme Court depublishes a case "with which the court does not agree in lieu of accepting the case for hearing" (p. 523). Other California Supreme Court justices have been quoted as saying that depublication occurs when the Supreme Court disagrees with the conclusion of a case or all or some of the legal reasoning upon which the conclusion was based (p. 524). Depublication therefore prevents the case from influencing subsequent rulings.

17. Bruce T. Olson, *The California Grand Jury: An Analysis and Evaluation of its Watchdog Function*, Master's thesis, University of California, Berkeley, 1966.

18. "To see a World in a Grain of Sand / And a Heaven in a Wild Flower / Hold Infinity in the palm of your hand / And eternity in an hour," "Auguries of Innocence," *The Complete Poetry and Prose of William Blake*, David V. Erdman, ed., Berkeley and Los Angeles: University of California Press, 1982, pp. 490–493.

19. For a discussion of the problems encountered in constructing a theory of citizenship, see Will Kymlicka and Wayne Norman, "Return of the Citizen: A Survey of Recent Work on Citizenship Theory," *Ethics*, 104, January 1994, pp. 352–381.

20. For an example of an expression of concern about writers who neglect to define what they mean by citizenship, see Kim Rubenstein, "Citizenship in Australia: Unscrambling Its Meaning," *Melbourne University Law Review*, Vol. 20, No. 2, 1996, pp. 503–527. The writer speaks of three different views of citizenship: citizenship as a legal status, citizenship as participation and membership in a democratic community, and citizenship as a desirable (i.e., normative) activity.

21. A sample of the recent literature concerning citizenship, governance, citizen apathy or disengagement, and the like is provided in "Additional References."

22. Mark Pisano, "Federal Policy and Community Involvement," *National Civic Review*, Vol. 84, No. 1, Winter 1995, p. 31. Many current and former high-ranking public officials are aware of this growing distrust. For example, during a C-SPAN broadcast on April 13, 1995, Lloyd Cutler, in an address to the University of Virginia Law School, said that public disdain for public officials, the U.S. Congress, and Washington DC is at an alarmingly high level.

23. Emile Durkheim, *The Division of Labor in Society*, trans. George Simpson (1893); reprint, New York: MacMillan, 1993; Alexis de Tocqueville, *Democracy in America*, New York: Everyman's Library, 1994; Richard D. Younger, *The People's Panel: The Grand Jury in the United States, 1634–1941*, Brown University Press: American History Research Center, 1963. Younger is the only author I have found who has documented the American grand jury's civil function throughout much of this nation's history. In view of his interest in local matters, it is surprising that Tocqueville wrote so little about the American grand jury. Nevertheless, he offers occasional insights into the institution, including passing references to its civil function: "The grand jurors [of Massachusetts] are bound to inform the court of the bad state of the roads" (Alexis de Tocqueville, *Democracy in America*, New York: Alfred A. Knopf, 1994, p. 78, fn. 33).

24. Bryan S. Turner, "Outline of a Theory of Citizenship," *Sociology*, Vol. 24, No. 2, May 1990, p. 196.

25. Pamela Johnston Conover, Ivor M. Crewe, and Donald P. Stearing, "The Nature of Citizenship in the United States and Great Britain: Empirical Comments on Theoretical Themes," *Journal of Politics*, Vol. 53, No. 3, August 1991, pp. 800–832. Two reasons the writers offer to explain the differences in the conception of citizenship between the two nationalities are: (a) a strong constitutional tradition in the United States enhanced by a written Constitution and Bill of Rights that creates a "contractual bias," and (b) a strong welfare-state tradition in England that leads to a communal orientation among citizens.

26. Robert D. Putnam, *Making Democracy Work: Civic Traditions in Modern Italy*, Princeton NJ: Princeton University Press, 1993.

27. Michael Walzer, *Obligations: Essays on Disobedience, War, and Citizenship*, Cambridge: Harvard University Press, 1970, p. 230.

28. See Robert D. Putnam, "Tuning in and Tuning Out: The Strange Disappearance of Social Capital in America," *PS: Political Science and Politics*, Vol. 27, No. 4, December 1995, pp. 664–683.

29. Geraint Parry, "Democracy and Amateurism—the Informed Citizen," *Government and Opposition*, Vol. 24, No. 4, Autumn 1989, p. 491.

30. Adrian Oldfield, "Citizenship: An Unnatural Practice," *Political Quarterly*, Vol. 61, No. 2, April–June 1990, pp. 177–187.

31. Robert A. Dahl, "The Problem of Civic Competence," *Journal of Democracy*, Vol. 3, No. 4, October 1992, p. 46.

32. Ibid., p. 48.

33. I do not disparage political theorists who deal only in high levels of abstraction about their subjects. Without these persons, we would be deprived of seminal works such as Karl R. Popper, *The Open Society and Its Enemies*, Princeton NJ: Princeton University Press, 1950. My point is that few social scientists today regard local government in the United States as an important field of inquiry. Thus, to the extent that social science is a source of information for the news media, teachers of civics, and other citizens, only meager academic information is available about the form of United States government that most pervasively affects our daily lives. The scholarly attention of most social scientists is fixed on the federal and state governments and international affairs. This intentional or inadvertent lack of interest in local government by public-policy analysts, political scientists, economists, sociologists, and members of other academic disciplines is curious. On many scales of measurement (public expenditure, numbers of public employees, numbers of individual governments), American local governments far outnumber state governments and the various agencies of the United States government. One report, for example, shows that of the 511,039 local, state, and federal elected officials in the United States, 96 percent are local-government representatives. Similarly, of the 85,006 governments in the United States, only 51 are at federal and state levels (U.S. Bureau of the Census, *Popularly Elected Officials in 1992*, preliminary report, U.S. Government Printing Office, Washington DC, 1994, Table A).

34. Michael X. Delli Cardini and Scott Keeter, "Stability and Change in the U.S. Public's Knowledge of Politics," *Public Opinion Quarterly*, Vol. 55, No. 4, Winter 1991, p. 607. *See also* Richard Moring, "Tuned out, tuned off: Millions of Americans know little about how their government works," *Washington Post* (national weekly edition), February 5–11, 1996, pp. 6–8. The song referred to is, "What a Wonderful World," by Cooke, Albert, and Adler.

35. Ronald F. Wright, "Why Not Administrative Grand Juries?" *Administrative Law Review*, Vol. 44, No. 3, Summer 1992, pp. 465–521. In expressing my support for Professor Wright's proposal, I note with some concern that he has not clearly restricted his administrative grand juries from inquiring into matters of policy.

36. Jean Bethke Elshtain, *Democracy on Trial*, New York: Basic Books, 1995, p. 118.

37. Michael Walzer, *Obligations: Essays on Disobedience, War, and Citizenship*, Cambridge: Harvard University Press, 1970, p. 205.

38. R. M. MacIver, *The Web of Government* (revised ed.), New York: Free Press, 1965, p. 327.

39. Citizens who wish to obtain copies of grand jury final reports should contact their county clerk or the administrative office of the Superior Court in their counties. It is possible that a small number of grand jury investigations are not included in this study if any grand juries issued interim reports during their terms but did not include them in their final reports. More will be said about interim reports in later chapters.

40. Penal Code Section 905.5 requires a fiscal-year term of service for grand juries unless a board of supervisors provides that the grand jury "shall be impaneled and serve during the calendar year." In practice, boards of supervisors invoke this provision only at the request of grand juries.

41. More information about typographical and other problems with recommendations is discussed in Chapter 4.

42. Grand juries are not the only institutions that are studied in terms of their documents rather than their behavior. Research into newspapers, for example, often is based on the analysis of text rather than on observations of newspaper reporters at work. Journalism has a fairly large body of research about the factuality of news stories. I know of no examples of research that have been conducted by observing reporters at work. In my experience, newspaper reporters are reluctant to speak candidly about their investigative techniques. Nevertheless, some research into the types of errors in news stories has been reported. The inaccuracies, as might be expected, are similar to those that abound, grand jury critics often claim, in final reports (inaccurate quotations, omitted facts, over- and under-emphasis, etc.). See William A. Tillinghast, "Source Control and Evaluation of Newspaper Inaccuracies," *Newspaper Research Journal*, Vol. 5, No. 1, 1983, pp. 13–24. In an earlier article, Tillinghast writes that reporters dispute four-fifths of the errors that "sources" (those they interview or about whom they have written) attribute to them (William A. Tillinghast, "Newspaper Errors: Reporters Dispute Source Claims," *Newspaper Research Journal*, Vol. 3, No. 4, 1982, p. 21). The difference between studying grand jurors during their deliberations and newspaper reporters at work is that the law prohibits the former. The infamous "bugging" by university researchers of a federal jury sitting in Wichita some years ago was the last known public outcry concerning using illicit research methods to study jurors (Warren E. Burger, "Tampering with the Anglo-American Jury System," *Vital Speeches of the Day*, Vol. 22, No. 3, November 15, 1955, pp. 78–80). Note that Penal Code Section 891, prohibiting the recording or observing of grand juries in California, was enacted in 1959; under this statute, such activities are misdemeanors.

43. See, for example, Kenneth Ellingwood, "Grand Jury Duty—An Exercise in People Power or a Maddening Foray into Monster Government?" *Pasadena News*, January 4, 1991, n.p. This article includes most of the topics that capture the attention of reporters who inquire into the California civil grand jury: secrecy of panel deliberations, problems with selection, and anecdotes of former grand

jurors. Examples of other revelations elsewhere in the press about grand juries include reports that county officials "steer[ed grand jurors] from their course," thereby blocking an investigation; that racial dissension prevented a grand jury from completing its work (*Paradise Post*, August 11, 1994, p. A-9); and that "more than a few public officials consider [the Kern County] grand jury a bunch of pests in over their heads, blinded by a thirst to embarrass bureaucrats" (*Bakersfield Californian*, July 3, 1994, p. B-1).

44. "I am not a lawyer, thank Heaven," Joe Doctor, *The Sun, Herald, Echo*, May 4, 1988.

45. "Ex-official Rips Grand Jury Ethics Call," *Modesto Bee*, June 5, 1991, p. B-1.

46. For example, in 1992, California law enforcement agencies reported making 564,416 felony arrests (*Crime and Delinquency in California, 1992*, Law Enforcement Information Center, Division of Law Enforcement, California Department of Justice, p. 34). Of 284,810 dispositions of those arrests in 1992, 540 arrests (0.2 percent of the total felony arrest dispositions during 1992) resulted in indictments (*1992 Offender-Based Transaction Statistics; Disposition of Adult Felony Arrests, Statewide*, Law Enforcement Information Center, Department of Justice, November 14, 1994). For a recent 13-year period, the indictment function nearly vanished in California, because of a California Supreme Court case, and I know of no reported evidence that curtailment of the indictment function affected the crime rate one way or another during this period. A discussion of this case and its effect on grand juries in California can be found in Robert D. Coviello and Richard J. Lynch, "Grand Jury System Modified: *Hawkins v. Superior Court,*" *Western State University Law Review*, Vol. 6, No. 2, 1979, pp. 343–353.

47. In an opinion, the Attorney General of the State of California addressed the question of whether a grand jury could limit a district attorney to presenting criminal matters (indictments) to a 10-day period in a month. The opinion concluded that, "A county grand jury may not limit the district attorney to a period of ten days each month for the presentation of criminal matters to the grand jury." The opinion cites one statute and one case for its assertion that the initiation of prosecutions in California must be by the district attorney (Office of the Attorney General, State of California, Opinion No. 91-103, October 8, 1991, p. 186). See, however, Chapter 7, "The Presentment of Indictment," for another perspective about the district attorney's authority to initiate indictments.

48. Only one final report during the study period included a reference to an accusation: "The jury sat as a body with the foreman on a hearing with the district attorney to determine if sufficient evidence was presented for an accusation for the removal of a county elected person" (Calaveras County Grand Jury Final Report, 1991–1992, p. 6). In 1994, however, a grand jury prepared to file an accusation resulting in part from an investigation conducted by a grand jury included in the study period. The 1994 panel did not file the accusation because the public official resigned from office (Mendocino County Grand Jury, 1994).

49. The statutorily designated number of grand jurors for California counties is 19, with two types of exceptions: In counties with fewer than 20,000 people, 11 grand jurors may be selected; in Los Angeles County, 23 grand jurors are impaneled. See Penal Code Sections 888.2 and 908.

50. "Grand jury: the great white watchdog sleeps," *Journal-Register*, July 23, 1991, p. A-5; "Grand jury makeup criticized: Critics: Panel's lack of Hispanics hurts," *Salinas Californian*, January 3, 1991, p. C-4; "Alameda judges give kin the nod for grand jury duty," *Oakland Tribune*, May 28, 1990; p. 1; "Grand jury: Free, white—and 51," *Willows Journal*, July 12, 1992, n.p.; "Public defender calls grand jury racially skewed," *Contra Costa Times*, September 25, 1992; p. A-21. The practice of "stacking the deck" in selecting grand jurors has long been documented. For example, one New York public official years ago was reported to have noticed that certain persons seemed to have a better chance than others of being drawn "at random" for grand jury service from a box containing the names of prospective panelists. To determine how this might happen, the official attended a ceremony at which grand jurors' names were to be drawn. Also attending the ceremony was a variety of public officials, including the mayor, a presiding judge, and other dignitaries. Apparently undeterred by the presence of such persons, the official inserted his hand into "… the wheel and found that some of the slips were heavier and of a different texture than the others and could be easily separated by the sense of touch. The inference was obvious. Undoubtedly the opportunity [to choose] between the sheep and the goats had been made good use of" (Arthur Train, *The Prisoner at the Bar: Sidelights on the Administration of Criminal Justice*, New York: Scribner's Sons, 1904, p. 112).

51. Only in the statute establishing so-called criminal grand juries does the Legislature express its intent that such grand jurors must be randomly selected: "[A]ll persons selected for the additional criminal grand jury shall be selected at random from a source or sources reasonably representative of a cross section of the population which is eligible for jury service in the county" (Penal Code Section 904.6).

52. During the study period, for example, only seven of the foremen of the 58 grand juries had women's names.

53. Later chapters provide more information about final reports not including information concerning grand jury achievements.

54. Citations to these cases are provided in Chapter 2.

55. "Lilies That Fester," C. S. Lewis, *The World's Last Night and Other Essays*, New York: Harcourt, 1960, p. 36.

56. S. I. Hayakawa, *Language in Thought and Action*, San Diego: Harcourt Brace Jovanovich, 4th ed., 1978, p. 33.

57. The number of grand jurors who must concur in voting about a matter is at least 14 of the 23 members of the Los Angeles County Grand Jury and 12 and 8 in counties that impanel 19 and 11 grand jurors, respectively (Penal Code Section 940).

58. Chapter 2 includes more information about statutes and case law concerning the review of grand jury reports by judges.

59. Penal Code Section 933(c).

60. James Q. Wilson, *Bureaucracy: What Government Agencies Do and Why They Do It*, New York: Basic Books, 1989, p. 373.

61. Readers who prefer more legalistic definitions may consult sources such as *Black's Law Dictionary*.

62. For discussion of the "disease of allness" problem in human discourse, see Irving J. Lee and Laura L. Lee, *Handling Barriers in Communication*, New York: Harper and Row, 1956, pp. 21–39.

63. See, as an example of the indiscriminate use of "county government" for "local government," the 1992 edition of the "Stanislaus County Grand Jury Handbook," Section V, p. 1: "Most citizens do not understand that it is the responsibility of the Grand Jury to examine the conduct of county government officials and that such civil investigations do not necessarily imply malfeasance." The grand jury's jurisdiction in malfeasance extends beyond officials of county government.

64. *Monroe v. Garrett* (1971) 17 Cal.App.3d 280, 284 [94 Cal.Rptr. 531]. The term "spirit of the institution" is neither my invention, nor is it modern. See endnote 58, Chapter 7, for an example of its use in reference to the English grand jury of the eighteenth century.

Chapter 2

1. Sidney and Beatrice Webb, *The Parish and The County*, North Haven, CT: Archon Books, 1963, Vol. I, p. 449. Kennedy and Briggs (see endnote 5, below) offer evidence that the origins of the civil investigation and reporting functions of grand juries are considerably older than the examples the Webbs offer. I have not found a comprehensive historical study of California grand juries, but occasionally references can be found in law-review articles and similar publications. For example, two writers (Lawrence M. Friedman and Robert V. Percival, "The Processing of Felonies in the Superior Court of Alameda County, 1880–1984," *Law and History Review*, Spring 1987, Vol. 5, No. 1, p. 416) reported that a California grand jury was exercising its civil function in the 1880s:

> It looked into scandals and misconduct in office and it could recommend reforms in the system of justice. One grand jury, which filed its final report in December 1882, castigated Oakland for allowing pools of stagnant water near schools, analyzed the way the Sheriff ran his office, complained about disgraceful conditions among insane people housed in the county jail (e.g., "The English language does not contain the words sufficiently strong to express our abhorrence of this … criminal neglect."), and recommended that a law be passed to "Set up a State School of Industry for young offenders."

2. The courts have emphasized repeatedly the California grand jury's dependence on the Legislature for its powers. One case expresses this principle in the following way: "The grand jury can function only as a body under and according to and within the limitation of its legal authority" (*Clinton v. Superior Court* (1937) 23 Cal.App.2d. 342, 345 [73 P.2d 252]). Even more pointedly, a later court wrote, "Although its powers are broad, they are carefully defined and limited by statute, and the grand jury has no inherent investigatory powers beyond those granted by the Legislature" (*Board of Trustees v. Leach* (1968) 258 Cal.App.2d 281, 285 [65 Cal.Rptr. 588]). More recently, and even more pointedly, a court held that "Broad though they are, the grand jury's powers are only those which the Legislature has deemed appropriate"

(*McClatchy Newspapers v. Superior Court* (1988) 44 Cal.3d 1162, 1179 [245 Cal.Rptr. 774, 751]).

3. No statute authorizes grand juries from different counties to hold joint meetings as entire bodies. When, in 1954, 23 grand juries met to draft a joint statement deploring certain aspects of the administration of public welfare programs, the Legislature later passed Penal Code Section 939.9 forbidding grand juries from adopting recommendations not based on independent investigation. (Research Note, "Some Aspects of the California Grand Jury System," *Stanford Law Review*, Vol. 8, July 1956, p. 632).

4. Office of the Attorney General, State of California, Opinion No. 83-903, February 24, 1984, Vol. 67, p. 58.

5. This is a simplified treatment of a complex concept. For more information about the common-law origins of the grand jury, see Harold W. Kennedy and James W. Briggs, "Historical and Legal Aspects of the California Grand Jury System," *California Law Review*, Vol. 43, No. 2, May 1955, pp. 251–267.

6. Briefly stated, by depriving the grand jury of the common law as the source of its authority, the Legislature substituted statutes for custom. Occasionally, however, courts will refer to common law in deciding contested issues concerning grand juries. See, for example, page 608 of the reference cited in endnote 22.

7. This chapter excludes from discussion several infrequently used grand jury powers such as escheat proceedings (Penal Code Section 920); the requirement for grand juries, upon request of the board of supervisors, to examine the salaries of certain officials (Penal Code Section 927); and the authority to order the district attorney to sue for the recovery of money due to the county (Penal Code Section 932). Nor does the chapter discuss several statutes in other codes pertaining to grand juries (e.g., Government Code Section 12552; Code of Civil Procedure Sections 203 and 229; Government Code Sections 54953.1 and 68094; Penal Code Section 148.5(d); and Revenue and Taxation Code, Section 408.2).

8. The last major legislative review of grand jury statutes seems to have occurred in 1959; any success that undertaking enjoyed has been diminished by subsequent patchwork additions of grand jury laws or amendments to the Penal Code.

9. Penal Code Section 919(b), however, authorizes grand juries to inspect public prisons. This statute is the one exception to the principle that grand juries have no civil jurisdiction in State government; in California, prisons and jails are, respectively, State and local institutions.

10. "Charge to the Grand Jury of Placer County," Hon. Richard L. Gilbert, July 7, 1989, pp. 12–13. In the period immediately following the Revolution, judges, in charging federal panels, often expounded on their philosophy of government and the desirability of citizens finding a middle ground between anarchy and despotism; David J. Katz, "Grand Jury Charges Delivered by Supreme Court Justices Riding Circuit During the 1790s" (*Cardozo Law Review*, Vol. 14, Nos. 3–4, January 1993, pp. 1045–1087). Katz also reveals that, particularly in Georgia, grand juries often delivered presentments about contemporary matters such as the need to repeal the excise laws, the desirability of a federal bankruptcy statute, the passage of stay laws for preventing the "collection of pre-war debts owed to British creditors," and inadequate compensation for jury duty.

11. James P. Botz, County Counsel, County of Sonoma, "Grand Jury Civil Jurisdiction Over School Districts," July 6, 1990, p. 2., citing Office of the Attorney General, State of California, Opinion No. 81-1015, December 29, 1981, Vol. 64, p. 900:

> Procedural considerations, however, are to be carefully distinguished from substantive concerns. Thus, the parameter of operational *procedure* [emphasis in original text] does not extend to an inquiry as to the merit, wisdom, or expediency of substantive policy determinations which may fall within the jurisdiction and discretion of a particular district.... It is concluded that a grand jury is authorized to investigate the method or system of performing the duties, i.e., the operational procedure, of any special purpose assessing or taxing district located wholly or partly in the County.

12. For an example of the concern among school district officials regarding the grand jury's jurisdiction, see "When the Grand Jury says, 'Let's go Fishing' ... Just say No!" in the newsletter of the *Small School Districts' Association*, Vol. 6, No. 11, November 1989, p. 5. The article summarized without citation some of the findings of *Board of Trustees v. Leach,* (1968) 258 Cal.App.2d 281 [65 Cal.Rptr. 588] but otherwise seems to conflict with the opinions of many county counsels and the Attorney General of the State of California about the grand jury's jurisdiction (see, for example, Office of the County Counsel, County of Sonoma, "Grand Jury Jurisdiction Over School Districts," July 6, 1990; Office of the Attorney General, State of California, Opinion No. 95-113, September 13, 1995, Vol. 78, p. 290: "A grand jury may investigate and report on the manner in which a school district performs its duties and functions").

13. The original version of Section 925 of the Penal Code was derived from Stats. 1851 Ch. 29, p. 235.

14. The statute that authorizes grand jury civil jurisdiction in only one aspect of State government (Penal Code Section 919(b)) was enacted two years after the Gold Rush (Stats. 1851 Ch. 19, Sec. 214). Note, however, that although the grand jury's civil investigating and reporting powers do not extend to State government, its indictment powers are not similarly restricted.

15. If grand juries allocated their investigative efforts proportionately to the magnitude of expenditures for the several types of local governments subject to their jurisdiction, one would find in final reports more investigations into city and special-district matters than now occurs.

16. The practice in some California counties of inviting local-government officials to recommend friends, business associates, or political supporters for grand jury service has little to commend it from a broad, public-interest perspective; but, of course, it fulfills many practical, if self-serving, political needs.

17. That grand jurors and other citizens should be so ill-informed about local government is not difficult to understand. Few California high school, community college, or four-year college students receive more than meager instruction in local government. The lack of understanding of most citizens regarding local government leads to blunders in final reports such as, for example, a grand jury addressing an interim report about a city police department to the chairman of the county board of

supervisors rather than to the city council having authority over the police department. Realizing that "so little is known and taught about the government most easily accessible to individuals—local government," one California organization recently published a teacher's guide emphasizing local government for civics teachers in various grades (*Participating in Local Government*, Sacramento: Institute for Local Self-Government, 1991, p. iv.).

18. The inclination of some grand jurors to think of themselves as county-government officials is interesting to observe, particularly among grand jurors in counties with a tradition of local-government officials nominating the same citizens year after year for grand jury service. For a discussion about the employment status of grand jurors, see Office of the Attorney General, State of California, Opinion No. 55-40, April 14, 1955, Vol. 25, p. 259.

19. To my knowledge, no California court has addressed the question of the jurisdiction of the civil grand jury in policy matters. If one were to do so, it would no doubt cite precedent in other states that restrict grand juries from such matters. See, for example, *Application of Lundy* (1955) 208 Misc. 833 [148 N.Y.S.2d 658]; see also *In Re Grand Jury* (1953) 173 Pa. Super. 197 [96 A.2d 189].

20. Grand juror's oath (Penal Code Section 911); requirement to retire to a private room "and inquire into the offenses and matters of civil concern cognizable ... by the grand jury" (Penal Code Section 915); grand jurors must not disclose evidence adduced before the grand jury (Penal Code Section 924.1); grand jurors may not disclose information about their deliberations and discussions (Penal Code Section 924.2). See, however, Penal Code Section 924.2, which permits "any court [to] require a grand juror to disclose the testimony of a witness examined before the grand jury" for specified purposes. Note, also, that Penal Code Section 924.4 permits a grand jury "or, if the grand jury is no longer empaneled, the presiding or sole judge of the superior court [to] provide the succeeding grand jury with any information or evidence acquired by the grand jury during the course of any investigation conducted by it during its term of service, except any information or evidence which relates to a criminal investigation or which could form part or all of the basis for issuance of an indictment."

21. San Joaquin County Grand Jury Code of Ethical Conduct adopted by the 1989–1990 Grand Jury, p. 4.

22. California grand juries are restricted from hiring investigators or other experts for criminal investigations (*Allen v. Payne* (1934) 1 Cal.2d 607 [36 P.2d 614]) but may employ persons for designated purposes in civil investigations; see Penal Code Section 926.

23. For example, one editorial, titled "Shallow Critique," included this comment: "That's how it went for the anecdotal evidence employed by the grand jury. Also, the jury didn't help itself with ambiguous phrases such as, 'It appears that there may be a tendency to jump to an unwarranted conclusion,' and in saying that the integrity and mission of the department 'appear to be questionable.' College freshmen who write like that should get Fs" (*San Jose Mercury News*, July 26, 1993 p. B-8).

24. Penal Code Section 933(a). In many counties, grand juries customarily submit their final reports to the judge who impaneled them. No statute requires

the grand jury to submit its final report before publication to the county counsel, but this also is customary in some counties.

25. *Ibid.*

26. *People v. Superior Court of Santa Barbara County* (1975) 13 Cal.3d 430 [119 Cal.Rptr. 193].

27. Penal Code Section 939.9.

28. Penal Code Section 929.

29. In the last sentence of Penal Code Section 933(a), use of the passive voice makes unclear who shall file the report with the county clerk, but the preceding sentence refers to the presiding judge. In practice, most grand juries distribute 100 to 300 copies of the final report throughout the community, some using mailing lists maintained by superior court staff for this purpose. Title 4 of the Penal Code contains most of the statutes regulating the grand jury's civil function.

30. During the period of this study, six grand juries issued final reports in newspaper formats: Del Norte, El Dorado, Humboldt, Inyo, Marin, and Plumas. This practice will be discussed in a subsequent chapter.

31. Penal Code Section 933(c). Section 933 requires local-government officials to comment about findings and recommendations no later than 60 or 90 days (depending on the type of official) after receiving final reports. See Penal Code Section 933.06(b) for an exception to Penal Code Section 933.

32. I know of no instance of using the writ of mandate for this purpose.

33. See *Newsletter of the Grand Jury Exchange Seminar,* American Grand Jury Foundation, Vol. 10, No. 2, December 1992, p. 6, for a summary of a conflict between a grand jury and a district attorney in which the former accused the latter of not commenting properly about grand jury findings and recommendations. More information is provided about this incident in later chapters.

34. Alameda County Grand Jury Final Report, 1991–1992, p. 49: "The Response Committee would like to point out that the response time for interim reports starts with date of issue." Local-government officials have no statutory obligation to comment about findings and recommendations in reports designated as "interim."

35. See Yuba County Grand Jury Final Report, 1991–1992, p. 68, for a local-government official's complaint that "it is sometimes difficult to isolate jurors' findings and recommendations from general comments, leaving question as to which items require response."

36. An example of a minor restriction on grand jury discretion is Penal Code Section 928 requiring grand juries to conduct and report certain investigations "selectively each year." As worded, however, the statute allows grand jurors to decide the extent to which they will inquire into county matters.

37. *People v. Sperl* (1976) 54 Cal.App.3d 640, 663 [126 Cal.Rptr. 907]; cert. denied 429 U.S. 832, 50 1. Ed.2d 97, 97 S. Ct. 95 (1976).

38. Final Report of the Imperial County Grand Jury, 1991–1992, p. 42.

39. Final Report of the Yuba County Grand Jury, 1991–1992, p. 14.

40. *Unnamed Minority Members etc. Grand Jury v. Superior Court* (1989) 208 Cal.App.3d 1344 [256 Cal.Rptr. 727]. In its decision, the court did not forbid minority reports but ruled only on the issue that a judge acted properly in not approving a minority report because the entire panel had not reviewed it. Since this

ruling, the question of filing minority reports seems not to have arisen among grand juries, whereas the issue arose at least once or twice a year, sometimes rancorously, before this case.

41. *McClatchy*, see endnote 2. This case discusses at length the historical and public policy reasons for grand jury secrecy. For more commentary about grand jury secrecy, see also *Farnow v. Superior Court* (1990) 226 Cal.App.3d 481 [276 Cal.Rptr. 275].

42. Penal Code Section 929 reads in part: "As to any matter not subject to privilege, with the approval of the presiding judge of the superior court or the judge appointed by the presiding judge to supervise the grand jury, a grand jury may make available to the public part or all of the evidentiary material, findings, and other information relied upon by, or presented to, a grand jury for its final report in any civil grand jury investigation provided that the name of any person, or facts that led to the identity of any person who provided information to the grand jury, shall not be released."

43. I have not attempted to find libel suits that grand jurors might have filed against public officials or against each other.

44. *Gillett-Harris-Duranceau & Assoc., Inc. v. Kemple* (1978) 83 Cal.App.3d 214 [147 Cal.Rptr. 616], in which an engineering firm sued the Grand Jury for $1.8 million for damages to its professional reputation and $3.6 million for punitive damages (*Lake County Record-Bee*, Wednesday, January 7, 1981, p. 1). In expressing its satisfaction with the appellate court's ruling against the Grand Jury, counsel for the plaintiff observed that this was the only known instance in the United States in which a grand jury issued a retraction for libelous remarks in a report and paid damages for libel. Many law-review articles have argued the case for and against grand juries issuing reports in which private citizens or public officials are criticized but no indictment occurs. For example, a case in New York State held that the grand jury could not rely on common law to issue such reports; the New York Legislature, however, later enacted statutes to permit such reports under limited conditions (*Wood v. Hughes* (1961) 9 N.Y.2d 144 [212 N.Y.S.2d 33]). In California, the existence of a number of statutes authorizing civil investigations and reports places the grand jury's civil investigating and reporting powers on a firmer basis than in other states. What grand juries may or may not write in final reports concerning local-government officials is the subject of an extensive, if somewhat inconclusive, study: Barry Jeffrey Stern, "Revealing Misconduct by Public Officials Through Grand Jury Reports," *University of Pennsylvania Law Review*, Vol. 136, No. 1, November 1987, pp. 73–140. Penal Code Section 930, the statute that deprives grand jurors from immunity against lawsuits for what they have written in their final reports, states, "If any grand jury shall, in the report above mentioned, comment upon any person or official who has not been indicted by such grand jury, such comments shall not be deemed to be privileged." For a discussion of libel in lay terms, particularly a section about "Public Officials, Public Figures, Public Issues," see *The Associated Press Stylebook and Libel Manual*, New York: Associated Press, most recent edition.

45. *People v. Superior Court of Santa Barbara County* (1975) 13 Cal.3d 430 [119 Cal.Rptr. 193]. Penal Code Section 929, enacted in 1998, now permits superior

court judges to "require the redaction or masking [in final reports of] materials of a defamatory or libelous nature."

46. One court noted that the California grand jury must not "initiate investigations *not specifically enjoined* upon it without probable cause [emphasis added]" (*Board of Trustees of Calaveras Unified School Dist. v. Leach* (1968) 258 Cal.App.2d 281 [65 Cal.Rptr. 588]). The import of the emphasized words seems to be that a grand jury must conduct investigations into only those matters for which it has authority. The term "fishing expedition" therefore seems to refer to incursions into areas not authorized. In the writings of the legal profession, "fishing expedition" usually refers to using the power of the law merely on the basis of whim, curiosity, rumor, suspicion, or vague charges. For example, using a search warrant beyond its stated purposes might constitute a fishing expedition. One theory regarding the origin of the fishing-expedition doctrine as it applies to grand juries is that it "may have been established in a charge of Mr. Justice Field in 1872 to a federal grand jury sitting in California. He stated that subjects proper for inquiry should be those which are founded upon knowledge which comes to [grand jurors] 'not by rumors and reports' but by knowledge acquired from the evidence before them or from their own observations" (Harold W. Kennedy and James W. Briggs, "Historical and Legal Aspects of the California Grand Jury System," *California Law Review*, Vol. 43 No. 2, May 1955, p. 264, citing: *Charge to Grand Jury*, "Case No. 18,255," 30 Fed. Cas. 992 2 Sawy. 667 [1872]).

47. An Attorney General's opinion cautions, however, that the grand jury's jurisdiction in special districts (and, presumably by inference, school districts) is limited to procedural matters, not "substantive policy determinations" (Office of the Attorney General, State of California, Opinion No. 81-1015, December 29, 1981, Vol. 64, p. 900). A more recent Attorney General's opinion also emphasizes that the grand jury has no authority in policy matters and offers examples in the context of public education to distinguish between policies and procedures (Office of the Attorney General, State of California, Opinion No. 95-113, September 13, 1995, p. 290).

48. Penal Code Section 911.

49. Penal Code Section 918.

50. *Clinton v. Superior Court* (1937) 23 Cal.App.2d 342 [73 P.2d 252].

51. The Legislature has specified the minimum number of assenting grand jurors needed to approve a grand jury action or decision. Because the court must impanel 23 grand jurors in Los Angeles County, at least 14 assenting grand jurors are required; in counties authorized to impanel 11 grand jurors, the number of assenting grand jurors is at least 8; in counties authorized to impanel 19 grand jurors, the assenting number is at least 12. The Legislature's use of the phrase "at least" suggests that under Penal Code Section 916, grand jurors could vote to require a larger number of assenting votes (See Penal Code Sections 888.2, 916, and 940).

52. Although many county counsels use public funds to support the computerized storage and indexing of their written opinions, citizens are not permitted access to this system. The Office of Attorney General of California, on the other hand, regularly publishes its opinions.

53. Among his other accomplishments, such as writing *Tom Jones* and being instrumental in creating the English police service, Henry Fielding, an English magistrate, delivered a lengthy charge that his judicial colleagues insisted he publish as a pamphlet. Fielding's charge stands today as a valuable insight into English jurisprudential history; see *Henry Fielding: His Life, Works, and Times*, F. Homes Dudden, Hamden, CT: Archon Books, 1996, pp. 740–745.

54. Bruce T. Olson, *The California Grand Jury: An Analysis and Evaluation of Its Watchdog Function*, Master's thesis, University of California, Berkeley, 1966, p. 124. For a brief history of charges to early American grand juries, see George J. Edwards, *The Grand Jury*, New York: AMS Press, Inc., pp. 124–128.

55. Hon. Patrick J. Morris, Judge of the Superior Court, San Bernardino, California; n.d.

56. In re: Matter of the Court's Charge of the 1989–1990 Grand Jury, Hon. Richard A. Gilbert, Judge of the Superior Court in and for the County of Placer, July 7, 1989. This was an unusually clear charge. Many of the charges to California civil grand juries suffer from the same defects found in trial jury instructions: ponderousness, lack of clarity, and much jargon. For a discussion of these problems and how they affect trial jurors, see Joel D. Lieberman and Bruce D. Sales, "What Social Science Teaches Us About the Jury Instruction Process," *Psychology, Public Policy and Law*, Vol. 3, No. 4, 1997, pp. 589–644.

Chapter 3

1. For suggestions that grand jurors may use to start their year, see Bruce T. Olson, *Getting Started*, American Grand Jury Foundation, 1992, No. 0109.

2. An example of the "professional grand juror" viewpoint is provided by a grand juror who applied for worker compensation payments, reasoning that having been a grand juror several times in a five-year period, he was, in effect, a county employee.

3. A frequent problem in procedures manuals is the loose use of the term "county government" as a synonym for "local government." For example, one manual claims that grand juries have jurisdiction in "all aspects of county government." This statement is misleading and incorrect. *First,* grand juries do not have jurisdiction in "all aspects" of any local government but may exercise only designated powers. *Second,* the context of the statement suggests that the term "designated local governments" rather than "county government" would have been more accurate. The grand jury, after all, has jurisdiction in other local governments besides county government. Another example of a statement with no legal basis in some grand jury manuals is the claim that grand jurors cannot be sued for what they may have reported in connection with an accusation under Government Code 3060; in fact, no statute grants such exemption. *Third,* some grand jury manuals are updated so infrequently that they contain the earlier version of the grand jurors' oath that ends with, "So help me God."

4. The Penal Code section defining the grand jury's jurisdiction in city government (925(a)) is a *may* statute. The section defining grand jury jurisdiction in county

government (925) is a *shall* statute; however, the same statute permits grand juries to conduct county-government investigations on "some selective basis each year." Therefore, a grand jury could investigate only one or two county departments, spend the rest of its time on other local governments, and nevertheless comply with Penal Code Section 925.

5. The handbook of the Santa Barbara County Grand Jury during the study period, for example, included a six-page description of the "scope" and "duties" of the various committees it recommended: Government Administration, Audit/Finance, Continuity, Criminal Justice, Editorial, Education, Health and Social Services, Grand Jury Review, Community Relations, Public Safety, and Natural Resources Committees (Santa Barbara County Grand Jury Procedures Manual, June 1992, pp. 12–17).

6. The data in Table 5 are from grand jury final reports of the respective years. Some grand jury committee names include only one topic (e.g., "Law Enforcement"); others include two or more topics (e.g., "Audit and Financial"). In creating Table 5, I counted only the first topic (the primary committee name) if committee names included two or more topics. Although many grand jury committee names included only one topic, enough combinations of topics existed that I decided to tally only the first-named topic to avoid creating a more cumbersome table. I excluded primary committee names that occurred fewer than five times in each of the two years. Table 5 and Table 7, "Trends in Grand Jury Committee Organization: 1991–1992 and 1992–1993," are based on grand jury final reports from each California county in 1991–1992. The tables, however, exclude data from four final reports of 1992–1993 that were unavailable.

7. Bruce T. Olson, *The California Grand Jury: An Analysis and Evaluation of Its Watchdog Function,* Master's thesis, University of California, Berkeley, 1966, p. 134.

8. The trend of not publishing the names of committees and their members could be attributable to discussions at the Grand Jury Exchange Seminars in 1992 and 1993. The discussions arose because the District Attorney of San Diego County issued subpoenas to former grand jurors identified in their final report as committee members of the 1991–1992 San Diego County Grand Jury (*In re. matter pending before the 1992–1993 San Diego County Grand Jury; Superior Court of the State of California for the County of San Diego,* June 10, 1993).

9. Persons interested in determining whether a grand jury has preserved the collegial principle may wish to review their county's grand jury procedures manual; the section describing the duties of the foreman could be of particular interest. In one manual, "Duties of the Foreman" includes the power "to appoint all standing and special committees as may be deemed necessary" (Kern County Grand Jury Procedures Manual, n.d., p. 53). See also the Merced County Grand Jury Procedures Manual, June 1990, p. II-3: The foreman's duties may include: "Establishing all standing and special committees on the basis of the Jurors' interests." The San Diego County Grand Jury Procedures Manual, June 1986, p. 76, displays a "Complaint Process Flow Diagram," which specifies that only the foreman can accept or reject complaints, but if he rejects a complaint, he "briefs jury on rejection." None of these provisions, or many others like them in other manuals, has a statutory basis.

10. *Clinton v. Superior Court* (1937) 23 Cal.App.2d 342 [73 P.2d 252].

11. Judging by references in reports to the persons who originate such complaints, complaint topics that citizens initiate more often than grand jurors do include planning, land use, zoning, building departments, and code enforcement. Other types of people who file complaints with grand juries are public employees (sometimes as whistle-blowers), prison inmates, welfare recipients, former grand jurors, and elected or appointed officials; even judges and news-media reporters have been known to request grand juries to initiate investigations.

12. Penal Code Section 918 provides that a grand juror who "knows, or has reason to believe, that a public offense, triable within the county, has been committed ... may declare it to his fellow grand jurors, who may thereupon investigate it."

13. For a discussion of historical events that have contributed to the characterization of the grand jury as a "court of last resort," see Harold W. Kennedy and James W. Briggs, "Historical and Legal Aspects of the California Grand Jury System," *California Law Review*, Vol. 43, No. 2, May 1955, pp. 251–267.

14. One of the most controversial and well-documented grand jury investigations in recent times originated when a foreman noticed that the word "Confidential" was stamped on a memorandum prepared by a county administrator for his employer, the Board of Supervisors. When the Grand Jury challenged the official for attempting to classify information as confidential that the panel believed was the public's business, events unfolded that developed into a 31-page report, which eventually was reported widely in the United States and in at least one foreign periodical (Stanislaus County Grand Jury Final Report, 1990–1991, Part One, March 15, 1991).

15. Indictment data for the years shown are from the Criminal Justice Statistics Center, California Department of Justice, Sacramento, California. The agency cautions that the data for 1993, 1994, and 1995 are "preliminary counts" (letter, May 20, 1997, from Program Manager, Criminal Justice Statistics Center, Department of Justice, State of California).

16. "The average California grand jury is in session 15 full days during its term. Many more hours are spent in committee activity. Of this investment in time and energy by the grand jury, 83 percent is devoted to the role of 'watchdog' over county affairs" (Research Note, *Stanford Law Review*, Vol. 8, No. 4, July 1956, p. 648).

17. Santa Clara County Grand Jury Final Report, 1991–1992, Foreman's letter, n.p.

18. San Benito County Grand Jury Final Report, 1992, Foreman's Report, p. 7.

19. In my experience, grand jurors do not usually oppose the indictment as a criminal-justice process; however, some of them object to district attorneys who are unwilling to consult the grand jury about when it is to be used and for what purpose. An opinion of the Office of Attorney General of the State of California holds that, "A county grand jury may not limit the district attorney to a period of ten days each month for the presentation of criminal matters to the grand jury" (Office of the Attorney General, State of California, Opinion 91-103, October 8, 1991, Vol. 74, p. 186).

20. "Problems of the Grand Jury System," Assembly Interim Committee on Criminal Procedures, September 30, 1964, p. 24. An amusing account of a struggle between a grand jury foreman and a New York district attorney is quoted in Bruce T.

Olson, *The California Grand Jury: An Analysis and Evaluation of Its Watchdog Function,* Master's thesis, University of California, Berkeley, 1966, p. 152. George Putnam, a New York publisher *circa* 1914, tells how he suspected a "leak" in the District Attorney's Office and requested the District Attorney to leave the grand jury room while testimony was being taken. When the District Attorney objected, Putnam appealed to the Court to resolve the matter. Putnam wrote that when the Judge asked the District Attorney for his account of the dispute, the District Attorney explained at length how his ancestors had raised the first American flag on Manhattan Island. When the Judge interrupted the District Attorney and demanded that he get to the point, the District Attorney answered by describing in some detail how close he had been to being present at the Battle of Gettysburg. By this time, the Judge's patience was exhausted and, telling the District Attorney to sit down, he ruled in favor of the Grand Jury.

21. Butte County Grand Jury Final Report, 1991–1992, p. 2.

22. Imperial County Grand Jury Final Report, 1991–1992, pp. 4–5. See also, San Joaquin County Grand Jury Final Report, 1991–1992, Foreman's letter, n.p.: "The 1991–1992 Grand Jury was disappointed that no criminal cases were brought before it for possible indictments."

23. The expenditure data for grand juries and boards of supervisors are from, for the respective years, the *Annual Report of Financial Transactions Concerning Counties of California,* Office of the Controller, State of California. This report does not include grand jury expenditures each year for the City and County of San Francisco.

24. Resources Survey, February 24, 1992; Grand Jury of the City and County of San Francisco, June 22, 1992.

25. Calaveras County Grand Jury Final Report, 1991–1992, pp. 13–15.

26. In many California counties, elaborate familial relationships exist in local government, and, for example, some time may elapse before grand jurors learn that the department head they are investigating is a blood relative of a county employee who has access to grand jury files and reports. Judging by the infrequent comments in grand jury reports about the potential consequences of these dual-loyalty relationships, grand jurors rarely seem to be concerned with potential problems such as conflicts of interest, possibilities of leaks of information and documents, and the occasional pressure that local-government employees receive from department heads who may wish to "keep abreast" of the grand jury's activities.

The dual-loyalty problem is especially troublesome for grand juries that require legal advice from persons who are employees of local government. Professor Wright, noting that the Constitution of Hawaii provides for the appointment of independent counsel for grand juries, observed that, "There is … a real danger that the grand jury could become overly deferential to any permanent government employee who advises [it]. Hence, it may be wisest to give the grand jury power to hire and supervise its own staff, possibly by giving it funds to hire lawyers or other experts drawn from a list of qualified candidates for the duration of their term of office" (Ronald F. Wright, "Why Not Administrative Grand Juries?" *Administrative Law Review,* Vol. 44, No. 3, Summer, 1992, p. 516).

27. Historians, sociologists, economists, and other social scientists often face the challenge of summarizing large masses of information. Creating typologies is one method for expressing, in a few words or phrases, different functions, objectives, or classes of institutions, people, systems, or processes. An important characteristic of typologies is that they represent only what the people who develop them think they see as patterns in masses of information. Several people examining the same information might, therefore, create different typologies. Nevertheless, typologies can be useful for studying social, political, or economic patterns, trends, or activities. For a discussion of the uses and limits of ideal types as "temporary harbors in the sea of empirical facts," see Ahmad Sari, *Max Weber's Sociology of Intellectuals,* New York: Oxford University Press, 1992, pp. 11–26.

28. Penal Code Sections authorizing grand juries to contract for auditing services are 925, 925(a), 933.1, and 933.5.

29. The Marin County Grand Jury Final Report of 1992 included a report of a lengthy investigation into how police departments in that County respond to complaints by citizens against police officers. Individuals desiring to obtain a copy of the responses to the report by police officials would have had to pay the County Clerk 50¢ a page, a total of $30 for the entire document.

30. Sonoma County Grand Jury Final Report, 1992, p. 11.

31. Sonoma County Grand Jury Final Report, Foreperson's letter, January 8, 1992, n.p.

32. Butte County Grand Jury Final Report, 1991–1992, p. 3.

33. Yuba County Grand Jury Final Report, 1991–1992, p. 14.

34. Professor Wright comments on the professionalism problem and the rise of the administrative state at several points in "Why Not Administrative Grand Juries?" *Administrative Law Review*, Vol. 44, No. 3, Summer 1992.

35. Keynote Speech by the Honorable Don L. Chapman, Judge of the Superior Court, Inyo County, for the Seventh Annual Grand Jury Exchange Seminar, Davis, California, August 22, 1986, p. 2.

36. El Dorado County Grand Jury Final Report, 1991–1992, especially pp. 8–10.

37. Sierra County Grand Jury Final Report, 1991–1992, p. 33.

Chapter 4

1. San Bernardino County Grand Jury Final Report, 1991–1992, pp. 3–5.

2. Amador County Grand Jury Final Report, 1991–1992, p. 135. The Amador County Grand Jury Final Report of 1993–1994 continued to express its support of a State agency, a Youth Conservation Camp, and recommended that the facility "is a valuable asset to the community at large and the State of California. These specialized services should be continued" (Amador County Grand Jury Final Report, 1993–1994, p. 14). Traditionally, one or more employees of California Adult Correctional or Youth Authority institutions serve on Amador County grand juries.

3. San Joaquin County Grand Jury Final Report, 1991–1992, p. 44.

4. Kings County Grand Jury Final Report, 1991–1992, p. 138.

5. Ventura County Final Report, 1991–1992, p. 62.

6. Orange County Grand Jury Final Report, 1991–1992, pp. AH-1–AJ-2.

7. San Diego County Grand Jury Final Report, 1991–1992, p. 230.

8. Sonoma County Grand Jury Final Report, 1992, Foreman's Report, n.p.

9. Solano County Grand Jury Final Report, 1992, p. 18. This quotation is another example of how the use of the term "county government" rather than "designated local governments" confines a grand jury's perception of its responsibilities to one form of local government at the expense of others.

10. Placer County Grand Jury, 1991–1992, p. 123.

11. Riverside County Grand Jury, 1991–1992, p. 52.

12. In an opinion dated three months before the end of the fiscal year, the Merced County Counsel advised a municipal court judge concerning a grand jury's lack of jurisdiction in municipal court matters (Opinion by Office of the County Counsel, April 3, 1992).

13. Merced County Grand Jury Final Report, 1991–1992, p. 1. Other than the opinion the Merced County Counsel issued, I found no evidence that any State agency or official notified grand juries about the statutory reorganization of municipal and superior courts that occurred during the study period and the implications of that massive change for grand jury jurisdiction. In the absence of such information, final reports of 1991–1992 contained a number of inquiries into judicial matters. The Sacramento County Grand Jury, for example, directed recommendations to the Superior Court and a municipal court (Sacramento County Grand Jury Final Report, 1991–1992, pp. 16–17).

In the next year, the Attorney General of the State of California published an opinion stating that "the grand jury no longer has oversight of the trial courts and their officers since that now reposes in state officers, the Judicial Council, and the Legislature itself" (Office of the Attorney General, State of California, Opinion No. 92-1204, May 4, 1993, Vol. 76, p. 70).

14. Kern County Grand Jury Final Report, 1991–1992, pp. 1–10.

15. Lake County Grand Jury Final Report, 1991–1992, pp. 16–17.

16. Richard D. Younger, *The People's Panel: The Grand Jury in the United States, 1634–1941*, Providence, Rhode Island: Brown University Press, 1963; see, for example, Chapter 7, "The Slavery Question."

17. Los Angeles County Grand Jury Final Report, 1991–1992, pp. 193 and 65, respectively.

18. Colusa County Grand Jury Final Report, 1992, Foreman's Letter to the Court, n.p.

19. Colusa County Grand Jury Final Report, 1992, pp. 22–23.

20. Colusa County Grand Jury Final Report, 1992, p. 32.

21. Penal Code Section 904.6.

22. Alameda County Grand Jury Final Report, 1991–1992, p. i, and Ventura County Grand Jury Final Report, 1991–1992, p. xii, respectively.

23. Lassen County Grand Jury Final Report, 1991–1992, p. iv.

24. Trinity County Grand Jury Final Report, 1991–1992, p. v.

25. Stanislaus County Grand Jury Final Report, 1991–1992, p. 16.

26. Colusa County Grand Jury Final Report, 1992, Foreman's Letter to the Court, December 31, 1992, n.p.

27. San Mateo County Grand Jury Final Report, 1992, Foreman's Letter, n.p. In this example, the Grand Jury did not discuss the cost of the reception, who paid for it, where it was held, or whether a quorum of the Board of Supervisors attended. Later in its final report, the Grand Jury Foreman referred to the number of complaints the Grand Jury received during its year.

For the size of the County's population, the number of complaints is unusually low: "During the year, the Grand Jury received 17 letters of complaint from citizens of San Mateo County. All were looked into by the appropriate committee. Many of these investigations did not result in a report and recommendation contained in this report" (San Mateo County Grand Jury Final Report, 1992, Foreman's Letter, n.p.).

Perhaps the apparent close relationship of the grand jury to the board of supervisors discourages citizens in that County from seeing the panel as an independent body. Two much smaller counties reported they received 35 "inquiry requests" and 11 complaints, respectively, during their terms (Amador County Grand Jury Final Report, 1991–1992, Foreman's Letter, n.p., and Trinity County Grand Jury Final Report, 1991–1992, p. iv).

28. Stanislaus County Grand Jury Final Report, 1991–1992, p. 29.

29. Contra Costa County Grand Jury Final Report, 1991–1992, p. 101.

30. *Facts About the Kern County Grand Jury,* a brochure produced by the Kern County Grand Jury, n.d.

31. Napa County Grand Jury Procedures Manual, July 1, 1991, p. 22. One procedures manual, in contrast, emphasizes that "it is important that the Foreperson of the Grand Jury remember that he/she is one of nineteen equal Jurors." Even this manual, however, suggests that one of the foreman's responsibilities is "to assign investigations to the proper committees" (Santa Barbara County Grand Jury Manual, June 1992, p. 7).

32. Colusa County Grand Jury Final Report, 1992, Foreman's Letter; n.p., p. 4, and p. 22, respectively.

33. Barry Jeffrey Stern, "Revealing Misconduct by Public Officials Through Grand Jury Reports," *University of Pennsylvania Law Review*, Vol. 136, No. 1, November 1987, p. 139.

34. Stern, "Revealing Misconduct," p. 74.

35. A conversation with a former grand juror from the County later revealed that the words "continues under close scrutiny and review" referred to the continuing investigation of the case by the District Attorney. Even if this were so, the Grand Jury would have no authority to assure readers that the District Attorney was committed to bringing the case to prosecution. Eventually, the public official referred to resigned from office before the Grand Jury issued an accusation specifying 12 counts of alleged willful or corrupt misconduct in office.

36. Stern, "Revealing Misconduct," pp. 76 and 79, respectively. Although it does not present a clear-cut standard for guiding grand juries in making lawful but adverse comments about public officials, grand jurors and public officials would benefit equally from reading Stern's article. Note that Penal Code Section 939.91 requires grand jurors to omit from reports references to individuals they have investigated but have not indicted, provided that those persons make such requests and the courts approve them.

37. Ibid., p. 76, fn. 5, citing William P. Cannon, "The Propriety of a Breach of Grand Jury Secrecy When No Indictment is Returned," *Houston Law Review,* Vol. 7, No. 3, January 1970, p. 352.

38. Penal Code Section 918: "If a grand juror knows, or has reason to believe, that a public offense, triable within the county, has been committed, he may declare it to his fellow jurors, who may thereupon investigate it."

39. Alpine County Grand Jury Final Report, 1991–1992, p. 6.

40. Los Angeles County Grand Jury Final Report, 1991–1992, p. 65.

41. For an essay by a former grand juror about "reasonable cause," see Edwin Limond, "Reasonable Cause to Believe: What Is It?" 1989; American Grand Jury Foundation Research Bibliography, No. 0221.

42. Imperial County Grand Jury Final Report, 1991–1992, p. 43.

43. "Audits of Special Districts by the Auditor Controller and/or The Grand Jury," Thomas M. Fries, County Counsel, County of Imperial, April 1, 1992. The County Counsel emphasized that only the "full Grand Jury" can request such an audit; in this case, an individual grand juror apparently had requested the County Auditor to conduct the audit.

44. Final reports do not often reveal such internal conflicts of interest, and newspapers rarely report them; however, exceptions do occur. See, for example, "Grand Jury apparently dipping into politics: Campaign plug written on county Grand Jury stationary [*sic*]," *The Ventura County Star Free Press,* March 23, 1990, p. A-1.

45. See, for example, "Code of Ethical Conduct," Santa Clara County Grand Jury, 1988–1989; American Grand Jury Foundation Research Bibliography, No. 0212.

46. Butte County Grand Jury Final Report, 1991–1992, p. 1. It included additional comments regarding the need for "video cameras and a closed-circuit system," and satisfaction with "an energetic program to obtain visiting judges."

47. Tulare County Grand Jury Final Report, 1991–1992, p. 77.

48. Kings County Grand Jury Final Report, 1991–1992, p. 80.

49. Trinity County Grand Jury Final Report, 1991–1992, pp. 40–46. The Grand Jury included in its final report a copy of a speech that grand jurors made during their term to a meeting of Trinity County Superintendents of Schools, urging the school officials to adopt what it referred to as President George Bush's "Education Strategy." This is a curious matter in view of a recommendation early in the final report, presumably written by the Foreman, that the Grand Jury defer to the professionalism of County educators and "only become involved in education issues at the request of the County School Board" (p. v).

50. Santa Barbara County Grand Jury Final Report, 1991–1992, pp. 48 and 50, respectively.

51. Napa County Grand Jury Report, 1991–1992, p. 24.

52. San Benito County Grand Jury Final Report, 1991–1992, pp. 51–52.

53. Calaveras County Grand Jury Final Report, 1991–1992; 1:1.

54. Inyo County Grand Jury Final Report, 1991–1992; 1:10.

55. Marin County Grand Jury Final Report, 1992; 8:2.

56. San Benito County Grand Jury Final Report, 1992, p. 43.

57. San Benito County Grand Jury Final Report, 1992, p. 49. Later in the same report, the Grand Jury expressed concern that population growth is an important problem for school districts (p. 51).

58. San Diego County Grand Jury Final Report, 1991–1992, 2:1.

59. San Francisco City and County Grand Jury Final Report, 1991–1992, p. 11.

60. Sierra County Grand Jury Final Report, 1991–1992, p. 13.

61. Siskiyou County Grand Jury Final Report, 1991–1992, 7:5.

62. See, for example, "Group Taking On Child Protective Services," *Sacramento Union*, August 8, 1992, p. A-6: "Merced County's grand jury criticized Child Protective Services in its 1992 annual report for inadequate investigations and disregarding rights of parents and children. But preparation of the report became as much of an issue as its contents when it was found that the Merced jurors had copied whole paragraphs from a similar report by the San Diego County grand jury." In the letter transmitting the Merced County Grand Jury Final Report to the judge, the foreperson declared that "The Grand Jury as a whole [has] reviewed and discussed all reports, and as such [has] approved the final version of the 1991–1992 Final Report" (Merced County Grand Jury Final Report, 1991–1992, p. II).

63. See *The Modesto Bee*, Friday, July 17, 1992, B-2. This grand jury was cited above in connection with its extra-jurisdictional comments about judicial matters; see endnotes 12 and 13, this chapter.

64. "Families in Crisis," Report by the 1991–1992 San Diego County Grand Jury, February 6, 1992.

65. None of the affected Merced County officials is known to have filed a libel suit in this matter.

66. Plumas County Grand Jury Final Report, 1991–1992, n.p. In this report, the Grand Jury commented that "Probation Department employees were reluctant to respond [to the "Grand Jury Employee Questionnaire"] due to the belief held by respondents that the 1991–1992 Grand Jury is thought to be influenced by the District Attorney and lacks independent thought and action" (n.p.).

67. Butte County Grand Jury Final Report, 1991–1992, p. 13.

68. Kern County Grand Jury Final Report, 1991–1992, p. 54.

69. San Benito County Grand Jury Final Report, 1992, p. 43.

70. Riverside Grand Jury Final Report, 1991–1992, pp. 58–60. Its summary of "District Attorney Hearings" (presumably indictments) and "Investigation Hearings Only" suggests that the panel might have drawn its conclusions from its frequent contact with the District Attorney's staff during its term (Riverside County Grand Jury Final Report, 1991–1992, pp. 3–4).

71. Colusa County Grand Jury Final Report, 1922, p. 19.

72. Colusa County Grand Jury Final Report, 1992, p. 17.

73. Amador County Grand Jury Final Report, 1991–1992, p. 125.

74. Stanislaus County Grand Jury Final Report, 1991–1992, p. 31.

75. Kings County Grand Jury Final Report, 1991–1992, p. 38.

76. Lassen County Grand Jury Final Report, 1991–1992, p. 9.

77. The number of grand jurors who must concur in voting about a matter is at least 14 of the 23 members of the Los Angeles County Grand Jury and 12 and 8 in counties that impanel 19 and 11 grand jurors, respectively (Penal Code Section 940).

78. Lassen County Grand Jury Final Report, 1991–1992, pp. i, ii.

79. Tuolumne County Grand Jury Final Report, 1991–1992, Letter of Foreman Pro Tem., 1991–1992, n.p.

80. Penal Code Section 916 does not explicitly require an estimate of the costs of "suggested means." The intent of the statute may merely be that a grand jury must provide suggestions about funding sources. One grand jury in an earlier year admitted its concern about not complying with this requirement: "A frustrating factor of our service involved our inability due to a lack of supporting professional staff to assign accurate fiscal costs to recommended changes in policies and procedures" (El Dorado County Grand Jury Final Report, 1989, p. v). Although use of the word "policies" is perhaps inadvertent, it shows the necessity for grand jurors to remove the term from their vocabularies during grand jury service.

81. San Benito County Grand Jury Final Report, 1992, p. 31.

82. Penal Code Section 916.

83. For a discussion of findings, see Ronell B. Raaum, "A Recipe for Writing Management Audit Reports," *The Government Accountants Journal*, Vol. 31, No. 2, January 1982, pp. 36–43.

84. Alpine County Grand Jury Final Report, 1991–1992, p. 3.

85. Riverside County Grand Jury Final Report, 1991–1992, p. 83.

86. San Benito County Grand Jury Final Report, 1991–1992, p. 42.

87. Sutter County Grand Jury Final Report, 1991–1992, p. 33.

88. San Diego County Grand Jury Final Report, 1991–1992, pp. 6–8 and 235–258, respectively.

89. Lassen County Grand Jury Final Report, 1991–1992, p. 14.

90. San Francisco City and County Civil Grand Jury Final Report, 1991–1992, p. 12.

91. Kings County Grand Jury Final Report, 1991–1992, p. 22.

92. Almost any issue of "alternative press" publications in San Francisco presents a broad range of issues suitable for grand jury consideration; see, for example, "Special Report, Ethics in [San Francisco] Politics," *CitiReport*, Vol. 15, No. 3–5, February 28, 1994.

93. Yuba County Grand Jury Final Report, 1991–1992, p. 38.

94. Alpine County Grand Jury Final Report, 1991–1992, p. 2.

95. Glenn County Grand Jury Final Report, 1991–1992, p. 44.

96. Stanislaus County Grand Jury, 1991–1992, p. 25. For example, the California Board of Corrections provides consultation services to grand juries, and other persons and organizations, regarding jail administration practices. Also, the Grand Jury Handbook for this panel includes a "facility report" (pp. 19–22) for conducting inspections of various types of local institutions. My objection to this recommendation is not merely that the Grand Jury chose to reject known standards for its own but that it did not state the basis for "its own judgment."

97. Kern County Grand Jury, 1991–1991, p. 15.

98. Civil Grand Jury Reports, City and County of San Francisco, 1991–1992, p. 2.

99. Lassen County Grand Jury Final Report, 1991–1992, p. 3.

100. Yolo County Grand Jury Final Report, 1991–1992, p. 26.

101. Imperial County Grand Jury Final Report, 1991–1992, p. 12.

102. Los Angeles County Grand Jury Final Report, 1991–1992, n.p.

103. Modoc County Grand Jury Final Report, 1991–1992, p. 13.

104. Kings County Grand Jury Final Report, 1991–1992. p. 7, *et seq.*

105. Public officials themselves sometimes improperly reveal grand jury testimony; see, for example, "Charges dropped for apology to grand juries," *Press-Enterprise*, March 14, 1992, page unknown, concerning a county staff member who, after apologizing to a grand jury, had contempt charges dropped against her for discussing grand jury testimony in public. The incident resulted in a revised "Grand Jury Secrecy Admonition/Order and Procedure" (American Grand Jury Foundation *Research Bibliography*, No. 0107).

106. Local law enforcement agencies routinely investigate duty-related traffic accidents involving officers and report such accidents just as they report vehicle collisions involving citizens; the grand jury did not report that it reviewed this process before making its recommendation. Such a review might have disclosed facts that would have added significantly to the investigation.

107. The Social Security Administration cautions citizens to do everything possible to avoid disclosing their Social Security numbers: "Our primary message is this: Be careful with your Social Security number and protect its privacy whenever possible" (*Understanding Social Security*, U.S. Department of Health and Human Services, Social Security Administration, SSA Publication No. 05-10024, January 1993, p. 9). Ruling in favor of a citizen who refused to reveal his Social Security number as a condition of registering to vote, a court emphasized that "the harm that can be inflicted from the disclosure of a Social Security number to an unscrupulous individual is alarming and potentially financially ruinous" (*Fresno Bee*, February 22, 1994, A-1). For an example of how Social Security numbers in the wrong hands can be "ruinous," see "Getting Extra Credit: [Modesto Junior College] instructor held in charge-card scam," *Modesto Bee*, January 11, 1996, p. A-1; using Social Security numbers obtained from fellow faculty members' pay stubs and students' Social Security numbers "which appear on the roll sheets instructors get for each class," the faculty member allegedly opened at least 35 spurious charge accounts throughout the nation.

108. Occasionally, grand jury handbooks imply that a foreman has powers the statutes have not authorized. See, for example, the Handbook of the Contra Costa Grand Jury for 1992, p. 105: "The Foreman announces the Foreman pro temp, selects a secretary, and a secretary pro temp. He announces his selection of the Chairmen and Vice-Chairmen of the standing committees and the committee members. He solicits two volunteers for the Social Committee." This statement in the Handbook conflicts with a statement by two of the Contra Costa Grand Jury's legal advisors that "each grand jury shall choose its other officers … (Penal Code Section 916)" (Victor J. Westman, County Counsel, and Gary T. Yancey, District Attorney, "The Grand Jury: Background and Functions; Powers and Limitations," Contra Costa County, p. 3). The 1992 edition of the Stanislaus County Grand Jury Handbook contains an example of investing the foreman and Grand Jury officers

with powers not authorized by statute: "[The foreman] meets with the Grand Jury officers to appoint standing and special committees and designate temporary committee chairpersons" (Section III, p. 1). See also, Section IV, "Committees," p. 1: "Each committee should perform the duties assigned to it by definition and referred to it by the foreperson."

109. Foreman's Letter to the Court, Colusa County Grand Jury Final Report, 1992, n.p.

110. Colusa County Grand Jury Final Report, 1992, p. 4.

111. Colusa County Grand Jury Final Report, 1992, p. 22.

112. Calaveras County Grand Jury Final Report, 1991–1992, p. 6.

113. Letter by the Foreman to the Judge, July 14, 1992, Tuolumne County Grand Jury Final Report, 1991–1992, n.p.

114. Siskiyou County Grand Jury Final Report, 1991–1992, p. 22.

115. Mono County Grand Jury Final Report, 1991–1992, p. 15.

116. Orange County Grand Jury Final Report, 1991–1992, p. 5.

117. Madera County Grand Jury Final Report, 1991–1992, p. 7.

118. Marin County Grand Jury Final Report, 1992, *passim; see also* the Tulare County Grand Jury Final Report, 1991–1992. Although each of seven committee report sections was a different color, the Grand Jury did not use a separate page-numbering system for each report.

119. The Modoc and Trinity County Grand Juries listed alphabetically the names of grand jurors in the front matter of their respective reports. Both reports also included the foreman's title but did not list any committee assignments.

120. Santa Clara County Grand Jury Final Report, 1991–1992, pp. 5, 6. The June 1992 photograph of the grand jury has a supernatural quality to it; the image of one of the jurors has been obliterated, and in its place is a black void, roughly in the shape of a human form. The same obliteration occurs in the July 1993 photograph. According to several County officials, the grand juror whose image was deleted was apprehensive about possible retaliation by indicted persons.

121. The Los Angeles County Grand Jury has not always been concerned with the self-laudatory aspect of grand jury service. For example, a comment in a final report of 32 years ago reveals a disdain for self-aggrandizement, arguing that a final report "which tersely and concisely calls for action cannot at the same time be the leisurely and pedestrian account of the year's activities. Gone from this report are the commendatory reports of committee chairmen regarding their secretaries. Gone, too, are the pages listing the hundred-plus institutions wherein conditions are often listed as 'clean and satisfactory.' Missing are multitudinous pages of statistics regarding cases heard, indictments returned, committee meetings held, days worked and other self satisfying, but non-motivating facts" (Los Angeles County Grand Jury Final Report, 1962, p. 3).

122. San Mateo County Grand Jury Final Report, 1991–1992, n.p.

123. Mono County Grand Jury Final Report, 1991–1992, pp. i, ii, iii.

124. Imperial County Grand Jury Final Report, 1991–1992, pp. 62–64. In a written opinion concerning the grand jury's jurisdiction in special districts, the Imperial County Counsel noted that "grand jury audits may be authorized only by

the full Grand Jury (i.e., not by individual members of the grand jury)" (Opinion by Thomas M. Fries, County Counsel, Imperial County, April 1, 1992, cited in Imperial County Grand Jury Final Report, 1991–1992, pp. 43–44).

125. Imperial County Grand Jury Final Report, 1991–1992, p. 11.

126. Alexis de Tocqueville, *Democracy in America*, New York: Alfred A. Knopf, 1994; fourth book, pp. 325–326. In the interest of brevity, I have presented only part of Tocqueville's explanation for citizens' dislike of "forms" in democratic societies. A leading American dictionary that was extant at the time of Tocqueville's tour of America defined "forms" as "stated method; established practice ... as the forms of judicial procedure" (Noah Webster, *An American Dictionary of the American Language*, New York: Johnson Reprint Corporation, 1970).

127. Alexis de Tocqueville, *Democracy in America*, New York: Alfred A. Knopf, 1994; Vol. 1, Chapters II–V, pp. 26–105.

128. Akhil Reed Amar, "The Bill of Rights as a Constitution," *Yale Law Journal*, Vol. 100, No. 6, April 1991, p. 1183. Several of Amar's observations suggest that his treatment of the jury includes its civil function (for example, "More broadly, the grand jury had sweeping proactive and inquisitorial powers to investigate suspected wrongdoing or coverups by government officials and make its findings known through the legal device of 'presentment'—a public document stating its accusations," p. 1184).

Chapter 5

1. Examples of titles of articles that extol the institution include: Irving R. Kaufman's "The Grand Jury: Sword and Shield," *Atlantic*, April 1962, pp. 54–60; Peter Megargee Brown, "Ten Reasons Why the Grand Jury in New York Should be Retained and Strengthened," *The Record*, Vol. 22, No. 6, 1967, pp. 471–478; Cornelius W. Wickersham, "The Grand Jury: Weapon Against Crime and Corruption," *American Bar Association Journal*, Vol. 51, December 1965, pp. 1157–1161.

2. Melvin P. Antell, "The Modern Grand Jury: Benighted Supergovernment," *American Bar Association Journal*, Vol. 51, February 1965, pp. 153–156; Patricia Mar, "California Grand Jury: Vestige of Aristocracy," *Pacific Law Journal*, Vol. 1, January 1970, pp. 36–64; "Our Toothless Watchdog," *Bay Guardian*, June 30, 1993, pp. 21–23, 25.

3. For an example of concerns by former grand jurors about citizen awareness of the institution, see "Grand Jurors wonder if anyone listens," *Marin Independent Journal*, January 2, 1988, n.p.; American Grand Jury Foundation Research Bibliography No. 0160. The Marin County Grand Jury Final Report of 1992 might explain why citizens in that County know little about their grand jury: "Our primary goal was to see that corrective action was taken and not to gain publicity" (Foreman's Letter, n.p.).

4. For example, grand jurors also occasionally are reported to have excluded information from reports because they fear that a local-government employee might experience embarrassment, reprisal, or harassment. "Council Answers Tax Tirade: Grand Jury Blasted for Its 'Innuendoes,'" *Modesto Bee*, August 17, 1993; p. 1: "A

former grand jury member, who did not want to be named, said the grand jury was aware of the memo but did not mention it in its report because it did not want to hurt [a city staff member's] career."

5. Los Angeles County Grand Jury Final Report, 1991–1992, p. 215.

6. Mono County Grand Jury Final Report, 1991–1992, p. 6.

7. Kings County Grand Jury Final Report, 1991–1992, pp. 74, 102, 111, and 120, respectively.

8. Amador County Grand Jury Final Report, 1991–1992, p. 30.

9. Trinity County Grand Jury, 1991–1992, p. iv.

10. Santa Cruz County Grand Jury Final Report, 1991–1992, p. 81, *passim*.

11. Shasta County Grand Jury Final Report, 1991–1992, p. 5.

12. Kings County Grand Jury Final Report; 1991–1992; 2:0.

13. Modoc County Grand Jury Final Report; 1991–1992; 3:0.

14. San Bernardino County Grand Jury Final Report; 1991–1992; 1:0.

15. San Joaquin County Grand Jury Final Report; 1991–1992; 6:4.

16. Stanislaus County Grand Jury Final Report; 1991–1992; 5:0.

17. Yolo County Grand Jury Final Report; 1991–1992; 1:0.

18. A grand jury has discretion in deciding what information it can leave for successor panels, "except any information which relates to a criminal investigation or which could form part or all of the basis for issuance of an indictment" (Office of the Attorney General, State of California, Opinion No. 88-703, August 3, 1989, Vol. 72, p. 128). See also Penal Code Section 924.4. The United States General Accounting Office is an example of an auditing agency that systematically monitors "the status of actions taken on the recommendations made in GAO reports." In particular, the agency tracks "open recommendations" and provides, on request, such recommendations on computer diskettes for interested citizens (U.S. General Accounting Office, Office of Public Affairs, *Reports and Testimony,* January 1996, p. 7).

19. Previous versions of the pertinent sections of the Penal Code required grand juries to conduct investigations of designated local governments at specified intervals (e.g., every four years). But the more general terms "on some selective basis each year" (Penal Code Section 925) and "shall be conducted selectively each year" (Penal Code Section 928) are used now, thereby allowing grand juries more discretion in deciding priorities. Some grand jury procedures manuals are not current in this regard; see, for example, *Procedures Manual,* Napa County Grand Jury, July 1, 1991, p. 5: "All Government agencies should be [reviewed] at least once every four years."

20. Monterey County Grand Jury Final Report; 1992; 3:3.

21. Sierra County Grand Jury Final Report; 1991–1992; 1:1.

22. Sonoma County Grand Jury Final Report; 1992; 8:5.

23. San Benito County Grand Jury Final Report, 1992, pp. 10–11.

24. An earlier version of Section 928 required that county departments be studied every eight years; perhaps the increasing growth and variety of local-government entities motivated the California legislature to allow grand juries more discretion in determining their investigative priorities.

25. San Joaquin County Grand Jury Final Report, 1991–1992, p. 77. Occasionally, grand juries include vague, undocumented comments in their reports about attempts to study the agreement or disagreement of public officials with grand jury recommendations: "A study by [—] in 1988, indicated that 85% of the Grand Jury recommendations had been acted upon; thus, there is evidence that there is no validity to the claim that nothing happens after the report is submitted" (San Benito County Grand Jury Final Report, 1992, p. 47).

26. Santa Barbara County Grand Jury Final Report, 1991–1992, p. 112.

27. Responses to the Findings and Recommendations in the 1991–1992 Placer County Grand Jury Final Report, November 7, 1992.

28. Amador County Grand Jury Final Report, 1991–1992, pp. 175–223.

29. Collecting official comments, summarizing and coding them for computer entry, entering them into a computer, and other necessary tasks required more than 80 hours of time for a study of recommendations and comments for a five-year period. More information about this project is reported in: Bruce T. Olson, *Grand Jury Recommendations and Their Responses: A Demonstration of a Computerized Tracking System*, American Grand Jury Foundation, 1989.

30. Penal Code Section 933(c).

31. An amusing account of an exchange between county supervisors and one of their department heads concerning the comment requirement is shown in the publication cited in Endnote 29. In this incident, a county department head attempts to explain to skeptical county supervisors why he has not implemented recommendations from a previous grand jury final report.

32. Penal Code Section 933 creates some confusion by using the word "responses" in Subsection C, where it addresses the filing of what otherwise is referred to five times elsewhere as "comments." The import of the terms "comments" and "responses" in Penal Code Section 933 is of considerable interest. Grand jurors sometimes express concern that comments they receive from local-government officials are vague or evasive. Although Penal Code Section 933 uses "comments" more frequently than "responses," most grand jurors and public officials use the term "responses" when discussing the findings-recommendations-comment cycle. A dictionary definition of the two words suggests that "comment" is more vague than "response"; in fact, one dictionary offers as definitions of "comment": "A remark, as in criticism or observation," "a brief statement of fact or opinion, especially one that expresses a personal reaction or attitude," "to talk, or gossip." For "response," the first three definitions by the same authority are: "To make a reply; to answer. To act in return or in answer. To react positively or cooperatively." See *The American Heritage Dictionary of the English Language*, New York: American Heritage Publishing Company, 1969. These definitions do not suggest a great difference in the meanings of the two terms except that a comment need not be a response; it may be merely a rumination. Even in its Latin root, "response" seems to be a more specific term in that it is derived from a Latin word meaning "to promise in return." A dictionary of legal words and phrases offers as a definition of comment, "The expression of the judgment passed upon certain alleged facts by a person who has applied his mind to them, and who, while so commenting, assumes that such allegations of fact are true.

The assertion of a fact is not a 'comment.'" Though this definition adds little to the discussion, a definition of "responsive" is more instructive: "Answering; constituting or comprising a complete answer" (*Black's Law Dictionary*, St. Paul, MN: West Publishing, 1991).

33. Amador County Grand Jury Final Report, 1991–1992, p. 176. This list somewhat resembles a classification of comments in the publication cited in Endnote 29. The wording of the list is that of the Grand Jury.

34. Contra Costa County Grand Jury Final Report; 1991–1992; 3:1.

35. Del Norte County Grand Jury Final Report; 1991–1992; 4:0.

36. El Dorado County Grand Jury Final Report; 1991–1992; 27:15.

37. Fresno County Grand Jury Final Report; 1991–1992; 1:0.

38. Monterey County Grand Jury Final Report; 1992; 2:5.

39. San Diego County Grand Jury Final Report; 1991–1992; 3:0.

40. Sonoma County Grand Jury Final Report; 1992; 8:5.

41. Tuolumne County Grand Jury Final Report; 1991–1992; 6:3.

42. Nevada County Grand Jury Final Report, 1991–1992, pp. 63–68.

43. Kings County Grand Jury Final Report, 1991–1992, p. ii; the Judge refers only to "recommendations," but Penal Code Section 933(c) requires comments about findings and recommendations.

44. Del Norte County Grand Jury Final Report; 1991–1992; 4:0.

45. Fresno County Grand Jury Final Report; 1991–1992; 1:0.

46. Monterey County Grand Jury Final Report; 1992; 2:5.

47. Foreman's Letter of Transmittal, San Joaquin County Grand Jury Final Report, 1991–1992, n.p.

48. El Dorado County Grand Jury Final Report, 1991, p. 25.

49. *Ibid.*, p. 26.

50. San Luis Obispo County Grand Jury, 1991–1992, pp. 80–81.

51. Some reporters refer to this process as "backgrounding." See, for example, John Ullman and Steve Honeyman, *The Reporter's Handbook: An Investigator's Guide to Documents and Techniques*, New York: St. Martin's Press, 1983, Chapter 5, "Backgrounding Individuals."

52. Orange County Grand Jury Final Report; 1991–1992; 14:2.

53. Sonoma County Grand Jury Final Report, 1992, pp. 9, 72, and 138, respectively.

54. The 1987–1988 Tehama County Grand Jury Final Report, pp. 66–76, included a study by a Grand Jury Files Ad Hoc Committee. The Committee was formed to determine "Whether sufficient information was available in the Grand Jury files system (particularly from the 1982–83 Grand Jury) to have [prevented] what proved to be a major embarrassment to this county." The Committee's report reads like a mystery story, including the possibility that certain sensitive missing files were replaced surreptitiously by someone who learned that the Committee was investigating the filing system. The Committee concluded that "the major problem … is that Grand Jury members are thoroughly intimidated by the [disorder of the] files: Members tend to regard the files as they would an Egyptian mummy's tomb—one with a heavy curse on it—full of forbidden things best left undisturbed."

The recommendations of the report addressed "Files System Security" and "Files System Efficacy."

55. For more information about the design, preparation, and editing of final reports, see Bruce T. Olson, *A Guide for Preparing Grand Jury Final Reports*, 2d edition; Modesto, CA: American Grand Jury Foundation, 1990.

56. Two final reports were received without covers.

57. Del Norte, El Dorado, Humboldt, Inyo, Marin, and Plumas Counties.

58. Colusa County Grand Jury Final Report, 1992, p. 17.

59. Penal Code Section 933, subsections a, b, and c, govern the promulgation of final reports, comments by officials about findings and recommendations affecting them, who maintains copies of comments, and several other matters. Neither this nor any other statute authorizes interim reports.

60. One former grand juror explained in a private conversation that the grand jury on which she served chose not to include a table of contents or an index because, "We wanted public officials to read the entire report and not just the section pertaining to themselves." Few officials have time to read sections of final reports that do not apply to them, just as few people read all sections of a newspaper. Moreover, the primary audience of final reports should not be public officials but, rather, citizens. Tables of contents and indexes help citizens find specific reports and provide a view of the contents of the entire report.

Finally, providing tables of contents or indexes is a matter of courtesy, convenience, and consideration of readers: "A book or periodical without an index has been likened to a country without a map, and it is now generally accepted that nearly every work of nonfiction is far more useful if provided with such a chart in the form of an index." G. Norman Knight, ed., *Training in Indexing*, MIT Press, Cambridge: Massachusetts Institute of Technology, 1969, p. 1.

61. Tuolumne County Grand Jury Final Report, 1991–1992. This Grand Jury sat for 18 months; therefore, the bulk of the report might have resulted from the panel's unusually long term of service.

62. Solano County Grand Jury Final Report, 1992, *passim*.

63. Bruce T. Olson, "The California Grand Jury: An Analysis and Evaluation of Its Watchdog Function," Master's thesis, University of California, Berkeley, 1966. See page 218 for examples of report formats then in use.

64. For example, using a standard format for individual investigations would simplify reading and understanding them. A sufficiently detailed standard format also would remind grand jurors of the types of information they must obtain in their investigations and similarly assist them in planning them.

65. John B. Carroll, ed., *Language, Thought, and Reality: Selected Writings of Benjamin Lee Whorf*, Cambridge, MA: MIT Press; 1956. I refer to Whorf's "principle of linguistic relativity, which states, at least as a hypothesis, that the structure of a human being's language influences the manner in which he understands reality and behaves with response to it" (p. 23).

66. "Harm" is used in the sense that one finds the term used in some performance audits—namely, to describe the social, political, or economic effects of sloppy

procedures or practices (lawsuits, wasted resources, loss of public support, resignations of effective employees, etc.). Other terms also are used for this purpose (e.g., "Statement of Effect"). See Ronell B. Raaum, "A Recipe for Writing Management Audit Reports," *Government Accountants Journal*, Vol. 31, No. 2, Summer 1982, pp. 36–43. Raaum describes a four-section "structured approach" for writing audit reports: Introduction, Results, Cause, and Conclusions and Recommendations. Although such systems can be useful for people who understand, for example, the differences between a finding and a conclusion, the structure of a report by itself will not produce effective reports unless those writing them understand terminology such as "criteria," "cause," and "findings."

67. Marin County Grand Jury Final Report, 1991, Law and Justice Committee, "Law Enforcement Internal Review Procedures," pp. 1–49, cream-white section; Health and Human Services Committee, "Study of the Emergency Services Fund Enacted by Resolution 90-262 of the Marin County Board of Supervisors," pink section, pp. 1–18.

68. Alpine, Contra Costa, Glenn, Humboldt, Nevada, Plumas, San Francisco, San Joaquin, Santa Clara, Shasta, Sierra, Sonoma, Tuolumne, and Ventura.

69. Modoc County Grand Jury Final Report, 1991–1992, p. 34.

70. Tuolumne County Grand Jury Final Report, 1991–1992, p. I-3.

71. Modoc County Grand Jury Final Report, 1991–1992, p. 36.

72. Colusa County Grand Jury Final Report, 1992, p. 11.

73. Merced County Grand Jury Final Report, 1991–1992, p. 9. This investigation also was cited in Chapter 4 as an example of unauthorized comment about judicial matters.

74. Calaveras County Grand Jury Final Report, 1991–1992, p. 57.

75. Mendocino County Grand Jury Final Report, 1992, p. 80.

76. San Benito County Grand Jury Final Report, 1992, pp. 1–4.

77. San Joaquin County Grand Jury Final Report, 1991–1992, pp. 78–81.

78. This trend is a revival of an old practice in many California counties. Mid-nineteenth century newspapers in the Mother Lode, for example, often included grand jury reports, as this example from page 125 of the commemorative issue of *The Mariposa Gazette*, 1854–1979, shows:

Report of Grand Jury

To the Honorable County Court of Mariposa County

We, the G.J., have been in session five days, during which time we have found seventeen bills. We have also visited the County Jail & found three persons awaiting trial for murder. Another person was also confined on the plea of insanity, but has since been pronounced sane by the visiting physician. The Jury, therefore, recommended his discharge. The condition of the jail was good, prisoners well fed & no fault found.

On visiting the County Hospital we found three patients ... as follows: Dropsy, 1; lung affection, 1; scrofula, 1. The rooms for sick and indigent are clean & the patients well fed & cared for. The building is very much out of order &

needs repairing, & we would recommend that immediate steps be taken to improve same.

John D. Tate

Foreman

January 6, 1865

Grand jury reports in other states have also been included in newspapers for many years; see Ronald F. Wright, "Why Not Administrative Grand Juries?" *Administrative Law Review*, Vol. 44, No. 3, Summer 1992, p. 471: "Grand jury reports were matters of public record and were often published in the newspaper at the request of grand jurors themselves [in the mid-eighteenth century]."

Chapter 6

1. Some of this story is told in "Grand Jury Frustration in El Dorado County," *Grand Jury Exchange Seminar Newsletter,* December 1992, pp. 6–7.

2. El Dorado County Grand Jury Final Report, 1991–1992, p. 8.

3. Memorandum, District Attorney of El Dorado County to Presiding Judge of the Superior Court, May 13, 1992.

4. Letter Opinion, State of California, Department of Justice, Office of the Attorney General, October 14, 1992.

5. One example of the prescribed comments that the former foreman proposed, and that eventually became legislation, is: "The recommendation has not yet been implemented, but will be implemented in the future." (Senate Bill 2000, Legislative Counsel's Digest, January 3, 1994, p. 2).

6. For example, in its first printing, Assembly Bill 1814 (March 5, 1987) would have required that "the grand jury shall present the county officer or agency with a draft of the report intended for public release 30 days prior to that release, and the county officer or agency shall have 30 days to prepare a response which will become a part of the grand jury report."

7. Senate Bill 2000, August 26, 1994. In the interest of brevity, I have not included in this account of Senate Bill 2000 and its progeny several amendments that were added to or deleted from the bills during their progress through the Legislature. The several bills also contained other provisions that I do not discuss here. Eventually, the requirement for grand juries to meet "with the subject of [an] investigation" during an investigation was added to Penal Code Section 933.05.

8. Governor's Office, State of California, September 28, 1994, veto Letter to the Members of the California Senate.

9. Essentially, Senate Bill 2000 began with legislative efforts by several associations of former grand jurors to force public officials to comment about findings and recommendations affecting such officials. After the demise of Senate Bill 2000, the associations continued to press for the prescribed-comment concept that had been part of that bill. As the two subsequent bills acquired or discarded amendments, persons originally supporting the bills sometimes became opponents later.

10. "Opponents of [Assembly Bill 1814] also noted that the bill was sponsored by the Orange County Department of Education, which has been the target of unfavorable reports by that county's grand jury" (*Los Angeles Daily Journal*, Monday, June 27, 1988, n.p.).

11. Senate Bill 1457, February 6, 1996.

12. Penal Code Section 933.05(d). The statute declares that the purpose of disclosing a draft report to a public official is to "verify the accuracy of the findings prior to their release." No definition of "findings" is offered, nor is a penalty provided for officials who ignore the prescribed comments provision.

13. San Mateo County Grand Jury Final Report, 1995, pp. 61–74.

14. *Ibid.*, p. 74.

15. "Grand Jury way off track on BART," *Peninsula Independent*, Dec. 12, 1995, n.p. This was only one of many newspaper stories, letters to the editor, and editorials about this controversy that were generated for several months after the release of the Grand Jury report. As might be expected, supporters and opponents of the Grand Jury and the other parties in this episode expressed, often heatedly, many opinions about this issue.

16. *San Francisco Chronicle*, April 1, 1996, n.p.

17. *CSAC Legislative Bulletin*, February 10, 1997, p. 5.

18. "Grand jury blasts board, top aides," *Mariposa Gazette*, August 10, 1995, p. 1.

19. Letter, April 7, 1995, by Chief of Police, Visalia Police Department, to the Foreman of the Tulare County Grand Jury of 1994–1995.

20. Letter, Law Offices of McCormick, Kabot, Michner & Foley, August 18, 1995.

21. *Santa Cruz County Sentinel*, "Beleaguered grand jury disbanded—internal conflicts lead to breakup," April 4, 1997, pp. A-1–A-4.

22. Portions of this section are taken from Bruce T. Olson, *Getting Started*, The American Grand Jury Foundation, 1992.

23. Collegial bodies include some college or university faculties, judicial bodies, and religious institutions such as the College of Cardinals. See Max Weber, *The Theory of Social and Economic Organization*, A. M. Henderson and Talcott Parsons (trans.); New York: Oxford University Press, 1947, p. 400.

24. Occasionally, elected public officers or trial jurors are impaneled on grand juries. Penal Code Section 893 excludes them from grand jury service. The presence of such persons could be the basis of a challenge to the legality of a final report.

25. See Chapter 2 for a discussion of the case.

26. Bruce T. Olson, *A Suggested Code of Conduct, Practices, and Policies for California Grand Jurors*; American Grand Jury Foundation *Research Bibliography*, No. 0098. The suggested code includes 15 topics—for example, attendance and absences; collegiality; confidentiality and secrecy; expenses and budgets; objectivity, impartiality, and the misuse of the grand jury name and power.

27. In one county during the study period, a judge appointed in succession three grand jury foremen. The first two resigned within four months after impanelment, during which time "eight grand jurors quit ... as well as three [alternates]." The first foreman who resigned conceded, "I'm a pushy sort of guy [and] I am

more results-oriented rather than procedures-oriented" (*Five Cities Times-Press-Recorder*, Nov. 6, 1992, p. 10).

28. Adapted from *General Grand Jury Work Schedule*, Grand Jury Exchange Seminar, 1987; American Grand Jury Foundation *Research Bibliography*, No. 0061.

29. Procedures for these two methods are described in Bruce T. Olson, *Getting Started*, 1992; American Grand Jury Foundation *Research Bibliography*, No. 0109.

30. A useful basis for a discussion about the grand jury's relationship to the district attorney is provided in *Authority of Grand Jury to Exclude District Attorney from [Grand Jury Sessions];* American Grand Jury Foundation *Research Bibliography*, No. 0141.

31. *McClatchy Newspapers v. Superior Court* (1988) 44 Cal.3d 1162 [245 Cal.Rptr. 774]; *People v. Superior Court* (1973 Grand Jury) (1975) 13 Cal.3d 430 [119 Cal.Rptr. 193].

32. "[T]he grand jury no longer has oversight of the trial courts and their officers since that now reposes in state officers, the Judicial Council, and the Legislature itself" (Office of the Attorney General, State of California, Opinion No. 92-1204, May 4, 1993, Vol. 76, p. 70).

33. The *Associated Press Style Guide* is available in most public libraries; it also can be purchased in many bookstores. *American Jurisprudence* ("A Modern Comprehensive Text Statement of American Law") is a standard reference work available in most county law libraries in California. In particular, the sections in *American Jurisprudence* concerning "elected or appointed government officials," "government employees," and "teachers, principals, and other educational officials or employees" will be of interest to grand jurors.

34. The impression that grand juries have broad, free-ranging investigatory powers in California local government or anything else, for that matter, is sometimes implied by people writing in law reviews; for example, "Grand juries have been given enormous power in our legal system: the power to demand information from anybody, the power to investigate anything, the power to indict any of us" (Jon Van Dyke, "The Grand Jury: Representative or Elite," *Hastings Law Journal*, Vol. 28, Sept. 1976, p. 62).

35. "F grade for jury report: This past week the Butte County Grand Jury posted an annual report that at best is pathetic" (*Oroville Mercury Register*, July 9, 1994, p. A-4).

36. One grand juror explained the difference this way: "In our house, our policy is to serve dessert after the main course. Our procedure is to eat dessert with knives or spoons, not with our fingers."

37. James P. Botz, "Grand Jury Civil Jurisdiction Over School Districts," July 6, 1990, American Grand Jury Foundation *Research Bibliography*, No. 0233. See also an opinion that the Attorney General of the State of California has published that provides specific examples illustrating policy and procedures (Office of the Attorney General, State of California, Opinion No. 95-113, September 13, 1995, Vol. 78, p. 290).

38. In *McClatchy*, the Court discusses the meaning of "findings," but its definition is abstract and not supported by examples (*McClatchy Newspapers v. Superior Court*,

44 Cal.3d 1162 [245 Cal.Rptr. 774]). A widely used law dictionary presents several definitions of "findings," of which one seems most suitable for this discussion: "A decision upon a question of fact reached as the result of a judicial examination or investigation by a court, jury, referee, coroner, etc." (*Black's Law Dictionary*, West Publishing, 1991 edition).

39. *Crime and Delinquency in California*, California Department of Justice, Division of Law Enforcement, Law Enforcement Information Center, 1992, p. 100. To conserve space, I have shown only a portion of the data in the report.

40. Some students of general semantics might argue that the facts are the actual events the numbers represent, but I shall not draw so fine a point in this discussion.

41. "In fairness, a lot of recommendations [in grand jury final reports] are not very good.... Some are someone's private agenda or they haven't got their facts right" (Statement by a "two-time former member" of the Santa Barbara County Grand Jury, *Open Agenda*, August, 1990, p. 2).

42. A discussion by the courts of the public policy implications of grand jury secrecy can be found in *McClatchy Newspapers v. Superior Court* (1988) 44 Cal.3d 1162 [245 Cal.Rptr. 774].

43. For example, "County blasted over handling of Floyd case" (*San Luis Obispo Telegram Tribune*, November 19, 1990, n.p.). In this story, a former grand jury foreman's public comments were reported to have "shocked some county officials who say he may be violating a state confidentiality law by speaking out." In another county, a county supervisor claimed that "a member of the county grand jury may have violated state law by publicly discussing details of an investigation that led to a 1993 report critical" of him. See "Carpenter accuses juror" (*The Press Democrat Empire News*, August 18, 1994, p. B-1). In Southern California, a newspaper reported an incident in which a county official was reported to have revealed details about a grand jury inquiry to other public officials. Contempt charges were said to have been dropped against the official after she apologized for her act ("Charges dropped for apology to grand juries," *Press-Enterprise*, March 14, 1992, n.p.). For another example of concern about public officials revealing information about civil investigations in final reports before they are available publicly, see "Don't Leak Our Reports, Grand Jury Says," *San Diego Tribune*, January 13, 1998, n.p.

44. In particular, Penal Code Sections 924.1 (disclosing evidence, proceedings, or votes), 924.2 (disclosing testimony on order of court), and 911 (grand juror's oath).

45. "Does Penal Code 933(c) subsection (a) authorize submission of a draft of a Grand Jury Final Report to an officer, agency, or department, which comment may lead to a revision of the report before release as a Final Report?" (Riverside County Counsel, September 10, 1992; American Grand Jury Foundation *Research Bibliography*, No. 0194). Penal Code Section 933.05(d) modified the import of this opinion.

46. "A Suggested Code of Conduct, Practices, and Policies for California Grand Jurors" (American Grand Jury Foundation *Research Bibliography*, No. 0089).

47. See endnote 31, above.

48. "Confidentiality and the Grand Jury," a letter from a Superior Court judge to a grand jury foreman, February 4, 1991; American Grand Jury Foundation *Research Bibliography*, No. 0020.

49. These reports are permissible if the required number of grand jurors votes to approve their issuance (*Unnamed Minority Members etc. Grand Jury v. Superior Court* (1989) 208 Cal.App.3d 1344 [256 Cal.Rptr. 727]).

50. Because of my obligation under the oath of confidentiality, I have altered certain details of this incident.

51. See, for example, Alice I. Philbin and John W. Presley, *Technical Writing: Method, Application, and Management*, New York, Del Mar Publishers, Inc., 1989.

52. For several reasons, I do not share the enthusiasm that some grand jurors express for distributing final reports as newspaper inserts. First, the institution would be better served if as few people as possible read the too-frequent final reports that are severely marred with the problems represented by the criteria used in this study. Second, the number of citizens who are interested in public affairs, unfortunately, is only a small proportion of the general population in any community. Most of the general public will ignore lengthy, but trivial final reports inserted in their newspapers. Thus, the unit cost of the inserts that citizens actually read is probably as high as the unit cost of final reports printed conventionally. That is why I recommend that grand jurors prepare a readable, well-planned one-page advertisement that displays the principal findings and recommendations from final reports. This method also is considerably less expensive than printing the complete final report as an insert. Third, even citizens who might read final reports will not be likely to accept the visual challenge of reading a 100-page final report that has been reduced to 30 pages of the dense print that the tabloid format requires. Fourth, the use of public funds to pay for reports of grand jury proceedings is no more justified than paying newspapers to report the meetings of boards of supervisors.

Chapter 7

1. "The Grand Jury's Ombudsman Function," Alameda County Grand Jury Final Report, 1988–1989, p. 1; "Grand Jury Fills Ombudsman Role," *Modesto Bee*, December 26, 1976, n.p.; "The Grand Jury is … the Great Equalizer of the Common Man," *The Christian American*, January–February 1992, p. 17.

2. For examples of how judges in appellate cases have described the grand jury, see *William S. Bradley v. Gary L. Lacy* (1997) 53 Cal.App.4th 883 [61 Cal.Rptr.2d 919]); e.g., the grand jury "sits as the great inquest between the State and the citizen"; the grand jury stands "between the prosecutor and the accused"; etc. For a discussion of how a political boss corrupted a California grand jury, see Jon Van Dyke et al., "*Quadra v. Superior Court of the City and County of San Francisco*: A Challenge to the Composition of the San Francisco Grand Jury," *Hastings Law Journal*, Vol. 27, No. 1, January 1976, pp. 594–595.

3. One author contends that the grand jury began to take form in the early fourteenth century, having arisen from the idea of "triers," that is, "a knightly jury representing the whole county and with a general function, as distinct from panels

of knights elected to hear cases submitted to the Grand Assize, in the eyres of" the reign of Edward I. (David Cook, "Triers and the origins of the grand jury," *Journal of Legal History*, Vol. 12, No. 2, Spring 1991, p. 104). Well before the Assizes of Clarendon, various mechanisms existed in Anglo-Norman and Anglo-Saxon England for resolving local conflicts of various kinds. The Assizes of Clarendon seem merely to have standardized these mechanisms and thereby created what we now call the grand jury to execute them. See W. L. Warren, *Henry II*, Berkeley: University of California Press, 1973, p. 282. More information about the evolution of the grand jury, including some of its abuses, can be found in *Encyclopedia of the American Judicial System*, Robert J. Janosik, editor, New York: Charles Scribner's Sons, 1987.

4. For a discussion of executive, judicial, and legislative controls of the grand jury, see Note, "The Grand Jury As an Investigatory Body," *Harvard Law Review*, 1961, Vol. 74, p. 590.

5. Richard D. Younger, *The People's Panel*, Providence, RI: Brown University Press, 1963. Younger comments on the social-class characteristics of grand jurors in his accounts of some of the institution's achievements in England and the United States. For a discussion of how grand jurors fit into the social order in England between the thirteenth and fifteenth centuries, see Gerald Harriss, "Political Society and the Growth of Government in Late Medieval England," *Past and Present*, No. 138, February 1993, pp. 28–57.

6. "Presentments Made on the County of Clare at Spring Assizes, 1828," Ennis: Printed at the Clare Journal Office, n.p. For evidence that the English grand jury in the early seventeenth century was issuing presentments about local-government problems, deficiencies, and achievements, see J. S. Morrill, *The Cheshire Grand Jury 1625–1659: A Social Administrative Study*, Leicester University Press, 1976.

7. *Reform of the Grand Jury System*, Hearing before the Subcommittee on Constitutional Rights of the Committee on the Judiciary, United States Senate, Ninety-fourth Congress, September 28, 1976; Washington, DC: United States Government Printing Office, p. 90.

8. For a history of the indictment in California, see Richard P. Alexander and Sheldon Portman, "Grand Jury Indictment Versus Prosecution by Information— An Equal Protection-Due Process Issue," *Hastings Law Journal*, Vol. 25, Nos. 1–6, 1974, pp. 997–1016.

9. A study revealed that in 35 states, grand juries exercise one or more of the following civil functions:

• Inspecting jails, prisons, or correctional facilities
• Inspecting public buildings and offices
• Examining records or books of designated officials
• Investigating public officials
• Inspecting local-government operations
• Commenting on public affairs, public safety, or welfare
• Inquiring into the corrupt acts of public officials

Few grand juries in the 35 states have more than one or two of these functions, the first in the list being exercised most frequently. David R. Rottman et al., *State

Court Organization, 1993, U.S. Department of Justice, Bureau of Justice Statistics, Washington, D.C., USGPO, 1995; Table 38, "Grand Juries: Composition and Functions," pp. 280–282.

10. Jeremy Bentham, "the great codifier and legal reformer," complained that the grand jury was a corrupt institution because panel members were of the upper classes "to the exclusion of the yeomen" (Younger, *The People's Panel,* p. 56, citing Jeremy Bentham, *The Elements of the Art of Packing, as Applied to Special Juries,* London (1821); pp. 14–28).

11. Use of the accusation, for example, has diminished in recent times to the point that on those rare occasions in California when the press reports its actual or possible use, reference to its infrequent application may be included in the news story: "This is the first time in more than 25 years that a Contra Costa politician has been so accused" ("Grand Jury: Bishop Unfit; Supervisor faces trial, says she will not quit board"; *Contra Costa Times,* March 21, 1996, p. A-1).

12. Thomas E. Dewey is an example of a prosecutor whose political career (culminating in an unsuccessful bid for the presidency) was assisted by publicity arising from his work with grand juries. See Richard Norton Smith, *Thomas E. Dewey and His Times,* New York: Simon and Schuster, 1982, especially the second section of the book, "The Gangbuster, 1935–1940," pp. 147–276. In California, the indictment function of the grand jury also was important to Earl Warren and Edmund G. Brown as prosecuting attorneys in the development of their careers. Warren and Brown had been district attorneys before becoming attorneys general and eventually governors of the State of California.

13. For an account of the progressive movement in California, see George E. Mowry, *The California Progressives,* Berkeley: University of California Press, 1951. Progressive reformers used the term "good government" so often that their critics referred to them as "goo-goos."

14. For a discussion of what one writer sees as a trend in local government's use of a "new breed of auditor" who evaluates public services, see Jonathan Walters, "Auditor Power!" *Governing,* April 1996, pp. 25–29.

15. Bruce T. Olson, "The California Grand Jury: An Analysis and Evaluation of its Watchdog Function," thesis for the degree of Master of Criminology, University of California, Berkeley, 1966, p. 288.

16. Among the possible causes of the one-in-a-decade phenomenon are (a) pure chance, (b) an especially skillful foreman, (c) the deliberate impanelment of an unusually high percentage of intelligent, civic-reform-minded citizens. In the county of my residence, the same judge impaneled the only two grand juries of the past 10 years that have issued reports of consequence.

17. See Chapter 3 for a discussion about grand jury expenditures and other resources. Appendix A, "Some Notes About the Study and Its Method," provides other information about grand jury expenditures.

18. For example, the final reports of the grand juries of Marin, San Diego, and Santa Barbara Counties are consistently superior to those of Alameda, Los Angeles, and San Mateo Counties. These differences are particularly striking because of the similarities in the socio-economic profiles and intellectual resources of these six counties.

19. In 1986, Los Angeles County grand jurors revised their procedures manual. The panel requested one of its legal advisors to review a draft of the revised manual. These are three examples of differences in the draft prepared by the Grand Jury and the draft that was adopted after review by the legal advisor:

Original text:

Mail addressed to the grand jury will be delivered to the office. Mail is stamped with the date of receipt; only the Foreman and the Committee chairmen are authorized to receive grand jury mail. (p. 6)

Revised text:

Mail addressed to the grand jury is picked up by the legal advisor and given to the staff secretary. The staff secretary will open all incoming mail, stamp it with date received and assign it a correspondence number. (p. 6)

Original text:

Routinely, legal advice is provided by the legal advisor. If higher authority is desired, grand jurors should consider asking for advice in written form, called opinions. Opinions are based on law and have its force and effect unless they are overruled. Grand jurors should consider opinions as confidential matters between them and their legal advisors unless the latter authorizes publication. (p. 13)

Revised text:

Routinely, legal advice is provided by the legal advisor. At the beginning of its term, the legal advisor schedules orientation by officials for general introductions to the operation of their offices and any suggestions they may have for the grand jury's consideration. (p. 12)

Original text:

Recommendations are each Grand Jury's most important product; they must not be allowed to be overlooked, ignored, or misinterpreted by local government officials to whom they have been directed. Copies of final reports and responses are on file for review and use, as required, by grand jurors. (p. 53)

Revised text:

Recommendations are each grand jury's most important product. Copies of final reports and responses are on file for review and use, as required, by grand jurors. (p. 50)

20. "Some of the motives people have for wanting to be on the grand jury don't necessarily coincide with the purpose of the grand jury.... There are people with personal agendas, and there are people who are unemployed and this is a means of employment, and there are people who are seeking to be one up on members of the community, [and] there are people looking for a social life..." (statement attributed to an official of the Los Angeles County Superior Court, Robert W. Stewart, "Grand Juries Crippled by Lack of Experience, Skills," *Los Angeles Times*, August 6, 1986, p. 20).

21. When a former grand jury foreman so identified himself in public as he requested a grand jury "probe" into a controversial land-use issue, a sitting grand jury released a statement emphasizing that "this Grand Jury is concerned that the

residents of the county may feel that former Grand Jury members have information not available to the general public concerning present activities, or a relative advantage in terms of successfully soliciting an investigation by this body" (*Appeal-Democrat*, January 28, 1993, p. A-9).

22. *Ukiah Daily Journal*, October 30, 1988, p A-1:

Not the troops but the leadership—that's what's wrong with the Sheriff's Department, an association of past and present grand jurors said Saturday.

Sheriff Tim Shea, in a letter published in Friday's Journal, said the Past Grand Jurors Association's interest in his department was a "personal attack on every employee and volunteer of the sheriff's office."

"That's crap, old politics," a current grand juror said. "We have no problems with the deputies, it's the management we want."

The association met Saturday in Redwood Valley to discuss their next course of action after claiming two victories—a five-day Department of Social Services workweek and the voluntary demotion of [the County Librarian]. The *Journal* was permitted to attend the meeting on the condition that members remain anonymous.

23. Although a statute requires judges to instruct grand jurors in their duties, it allows judges discretion in deciding how detailed that instruction shall be: "When the grand jury is impaneled and sworn, it shall be charged by the court. In doing so, the court shall give the grand jurors such information as it deems proper, or as is required by law, as to their duties, and as to any charges for public offenses returned to the court or likely to come before the grand jury" (Penal Code Section 914). In their charges, therefore, judges can provide as much or as little information as they desire about defamation of character.

24. In certain situations, other options might be possible, but these are the two that occur most frequently.

25. *The Union*, January 25, 1996, p. A-1.

26. Elizabeth K. Hansen and Roy L. Moore, "Chilling the Messenger: Impact of Libel on Community Newspapers," *Newspaper Research Journal*, Spring 1990, Vol. 11, No. 2, pp. 86–99.

27. *McClatchy Newspapers v. Superior Court* (1988) 44 Cal.3d 1162 [245 Cal.Rptr. 774].

28. The only definition of "findings" the court offered was that they are statements that "bridge the analytic gap between the raw evidence and ultimate decision" (*McClatchy*, above, p. 1180).

29. San Francisco City and County Grand Jury Final Report, 1988–1989, letter by Foreperson, n.p. For another example of problems in applying the "raw evidentiary material" principle, see "Testimony Taken by Grand Jury Protected," *Press-Enterprise*, October 4, 1991, p. B-1. In an unusual display of independence, the Los Angeles County Grand Jury commented at length in its final report of 1997–1998 on the confusion the "raw evidentiary material" stricture has created: "This was a pervasive problem, because it would impact the reporting of each and every civil investigation carried out by this grand jury" (Los Angeles County Grand Jury Final Report, 1997–1998, pp. 5-1–5-6).

30. The phrase "private room" is from Penal Code Section 915. Although the statute employs this term, it does not require the court specifically to ensure that a grand jury has such a room at its disposal.

31. In the final reports of the study period, few grand juries reported receiving investigative assistance from other persons such as county auditors, district attorneys, or county administrative officers.

32. See, for example, Richard Younger, *The People's Panel*, Providence, RI: Brown University Press, 1963, especially Chapter 8, "Municipal Corruption."

33. For a variety of reasons, including some that I described earlier, the gap in many counties today between the civil grand jury and the Office of District Attorney has widened in recent years. For example, during the dispute between the grand jury and a district attorney that was discussed in Chapter 3, the latter explained why he refused to assist the panel in an investigation. Noting that the office of the district attorney had been criticized previously for "steering grand juries," the district attorney observed, "This year we certainly solved that problem" (*Tahoe Daily Tribune*, July 22, 1992, p. 2A).

34. Why modern universities fail to impart to students the skills of reasoning, and some of the consequences of that failure for society in general and democracy in particular, is the concern of Allan Bloom, *The Closing of the American Mind*, New York: Simon and Schuster, 1987. Several decades ago, Dorothy L. Sayers asked, "Is not the great defect of our education today … that although we often succeed in teaching our pupils 'subjects,' we fail lamentably on the whole in teaching them how to think?" Dorothy L. Sayers, *A Matter of Eternity*, Grand Rapids: Eerdmans Publishing Company, 1973, p. 114. If these examples of concern about the thinking skills of citizens seem academic, see Steve Allen, *Dumbth*, Buffalo, NY: Prometheus Books, 1991, for a more entertaining exposition of the idea that "it is a matter of our society's survival that we begin to train our children, and ourselves, to think" (p. 195). The current concern about critical thinking is evidenced by the recent proliferation of suppliers of educational materials who specialize in the subject. See, for example, the catalog, *Critical Thinking Books and Software*, Pacific Grove, California, 1996.

35. Typically, only about half of the 58 California grand juries were represented at the Seminars, and of those counties attending, the average enrollment for each county was four grand jurors.

36. Jon Van Dyke, "The Grand Jury: Representative or Elite," *Hastings Law Journal*, Vol. 28, No. 1, September 1976, p. 62.

37. Nicholas J. Livak and Leon E. Panetta, "Criminal Indictment Function of the Grand Jury," *Santa Clara Lawyer*, Vol. 2, 1962; with regard to the grand jury "watchdog" power, the authors concluded:

> Ineffective as [the "watchdog"] power might be in the hands of a lethargic jury, its very existence is enough to arouse considerable consternation in any county office…. Wielded by an energetic and conscientious panel of jurors it is probably the people's biggest deterrent to and most powerful weapon against malfeasance in office. (p. 194)

One writer compared officials' comments to recommendations that the Santa Barbara County Grand Jury issued in two different periods: when it consisted only of volunteer grand jurors and an earlier period when grand jurors were generally drawn from a pool of names nominated by the courts. Public officials agreed more often with the recommendations of volunteer grand juries than with those of "conscripted" panels. The writer also concluded that the recommendations of volunteer grand juries made fewer blunders than those of the comparison group. The writer recommended that the courts should continue impaneling volunteer grand juries (M. Cash Mathews, "The County Grand Jury System: A Study in Reforms," *Justice System Journal*, Vol. 10, No. 1, 1985, pp. 110–119).

38. Edwin M. Lemert, "The Grand Jury as an Agency of Social Control," *American Sociological Review*, Vol. 10, No. 6, December 1945, p. 754. Other than some obscure passages about sociological theory, Lemert's article is worthwhile reading today. Although he disapproves of what he regards as the ideologically conservative bias of grand juries, he nevertheless cites a number of interesting accomplishments of the Los Angeles panel in the 1920s, 1930s, and 1940s. He also discusses how the district attorney of Los Angeles County controlled the grand jury during the period he studied it.

39. A Los Angeles County grand juror, identified in a news story as an African-American, complained that the Los Angeles County Grand Jury's "Anglo majority" of "older, wealthier people … were completely out of touch and really weren't aware of the problems of a lot of people who live in Los Angeles County [and whose] attitude was 'the sheriff's department is always nice to me'" (Sue Corrales, "Grand Jury's Composition Under Fire," *Long Beach Press Telegraph*, January 25, 1993, p. A-1).

40. To my knowledge, this section has been used only once, and, according to a member of that panel, the result was disappointing. The "staggered term" statute created, in effect, two grand juries within one. Thus, it spawned the same problems that are reported to arise in grand juries with carry-over panel members: suspicion, distrust, and status-based disputes (Edmond A. Limond, "Grand Jury Organization and Selection," American Grand Jury Foundation, Order No. 0097).

41. With regard to selecting trial jurors, a recent study urged the California courts to "reach out to the community through the Internet, public service announcements, juror appreciation weeks, and high school and college programs … to promote jury service as an important civic responsibility" (*Final Report of the Blue Ribbon Commission of Jury System Improvement*, San Francisco: The Judicial Council of California, circa May 1996, p. 29). The "blue ribbon" commission emphasized the relationship between the deliberative process and representative selection: "The jury's role in the justice system is to represent the community's wisdom, experience, values, and common sense in applying the law as given to it by the court to the facts as established by the evidence and found by the jury. To fulfill this role, the jury needs to reflect the diversity of the community and must consist of a fair cross-section of the community's population" (p. 49).

42. I do not propose that prospective grand jurors be required to complete "civic aptitude" tests for grand jury service; my intention is merely to emphasize that they, when first impaneled, may be, and sometimes are, "blank slates" with respect to the skills and knowledge needed to be effective panel members. Whether

this is a handicap, of course, depends on the intellectual capacity of grand jurors to learn quickly what they need to know.

43. The information in this section is taken from "1996–1997 Civil Grand Jury Selection Process," Superior Court, Stanislaus County, n.d. In previous years, the terminology "elected and appointed officials" was used instead of "community leaders."

44. For an introduction to sampling theory, see: Morris James Slonim, *Sampling*, New York: Simon and Schuster, 1960. The court appointed two carry-over grand jurors to the 1996–1997 Stanislaus County Grand Jury. Thus, only 17 persons had to be impaneled.

45. Office of the Attorney General, State of California, Opinion No. CV 77-137, March 3, 1978, Vol. 61, p. 88. The Attorney General cited as one argument for this opinion that Penal Code Section 939.5 requires the "withdrawal" of any grand juror who has a state of mind that may be biased. The logic of this opinion was developed in the context of a county employee not being involved in matters concerning his department. This is a narrow view of the problem. The opinion might have served a more realistic objective if it had specified that those individuals should not be involved in any matter concerning any division of the local governments that employ them, but even this falls short of fully addressing the problem.

46. *The County Telegram Tribune*, November 7, 1991, p. B-6.

47. Generally, conflict of interest in civil grand jury service is not a matter of a grand juror directly benefiting financially from an act or a report of a grand jury. A more common example is when conflict of interest, or its appearance, arises indirectly, as when a grand juror knowingly votes on a matter benefiting or harming a political ally, friend, fellow local-government employee, relative, or business associate.

48. Letter to Judge by the Foreman of the Sutter County Grand Jury, 1991–1992, n.p.

49. I have disguised these examples to some extent, but they are otherwise accurate accounts of some of the conflict-of-interest problems that grand jurors have reported.

50. As an example of one proposal to exempt public employees from grand jury service, see Assembly Bill 714 introduced by Assemblyman Milias in the 1968 regular session of the California Legislature.

51. For a study of how self-interest motivates public employees to vote on ballot issues affecting them, see Ronald N. Johnson and Gary D. Libecap, "Public Sector Employee Participation and Salaries," *Public Choice*, Vol. 68, 1991, pp. 137–150.

52. *Paradise Post*, May 2, 1996, p. 1.

53. For a condemnation of the practice of impaneling carry-over grand jurors ("it violates the theory that grand jurors should not be under the influence of others. Each grand jury should enter the arena with a clean slate."), see "County grand jury is under attack—may be on way out?" *Lindsay Gazette*, September 9, 1992, p. 4.

54. *Contra Costa Times*, July 7, 1994, n.p. This decision followed a series of newspaper articles describing internal dissension within the Contra Costa County Grand Jury. One such story carried this headline: "County Watchdog 'Impotent';

Grand Juror: 'We Should Quit'; Panel wracked by conflict, racial strife, reports of threats" (*Contra Costa Times*, November 5, 1993, n.p.).

55. *The Bakersfield Californian*, June 9, 1993, p. B-7. A review of the lists of grand jurors in the final reports of 1996–1997, 1995–1996, 1994–1995, and 1993–1994 shows that the Superior Court of Kern County continued to impanel some former grand jurors until the 1996–1997 term. Some of these panel members, however, are not, strictly speaking, carry-over grand jurors because the court did not impanel them for the year immediately succeeding their grand jury service but allowed the passage of one year before their next term.

56. "Beleaguered grand jury disbanded: Internal conflicts lead to breakup," *Santa Cruz Sentinel*, April 6, 1997, p. A-4. One of the three carry-over grand jurors was the foreman of the discharged panel (telephone conversation with Court official in Santa Cruz County, June 19, 1997).

57. Merced County Grand Jury Final Report, 1991–1992, p. 72. I base my conclusion about the presence of carry-over grand jurors on the panel on similarities in the names of grand jurors listed in the final reports of the two years in question.

58. Noting that in the jury lists of Lancashire County, the same names occurred frequently in a six-year period, an observer who later became the Lord High Chancellor of England commented:

> It is evident in these respects the spirit of the institution has altogether been lost sight of. Its beauty and excellence depend on the unquestioned impartiality, the perfect indifference with which the lists are formed; for, if a doubt arises in the commencement of a proceeding, before it is brought to a close, the doubt may ripen into suspicion; and the decision of juries must cease to command that confiding reverence which is at once the indispensable and the never-failing attendant of a pure administration of justice. (John Lord Somers, *The Security of Englishmen's Lives; of the Trust, Power, and Duty of the Grand Juries of England,* London: Effingham Wilson, 1821; p. vii [a reprint of the edition of 1681])

The practice of packing grand juries with jurors who are sympathetic to the social and economic interests of local politicians is not new. In 1835, a community reformer, one J. S. Ormerod, agitated successfully for changes in how judges selected grand jurors in an English borough. Later reflecting on the reasons for the demanded changes, Mr. Ormerod observed that he discovered that jurors in his community

> were men chosen by a class of individuals who were self-selected from men possessing precisely the same politics as themselves; [and] that these men were so ignorant as to boast of having been on that jury thirty years, some for more than twenty years, others for twenty. (*The Manor and the Borough,* Sydney and Beatrice Webb, Connecticut: Archon Books, 1963, p. 57)

59. Alameda County Grand Jury Final Report, 1991–1992, p. 28.

60. For a detailed study of how the Superior Court selected grand jurors some years ago for the City and County of San Francisco, see Jon Van Dyke et al., "Superior Court of the City and County of San Francisco: A Challenge to the Composition of the San Francisco Grand Jury," *Hastings Law Journal*, Vol. 27,

January 1976, pp. 565–636. The author recommended "random selection from some neutral list such as the list of registered voters" (p. 630). Only in this way, the author argued, can the San Francisco Grand Jury be truly independent and not a hand-picked body "by persons with close ties to city government" (p. 573).

As another example of a statistical study of grand jury selection and a similar argument that the selection of civil grand jurors should be as fair as possible to avoid "a sense of alienation from local government and the judicial process ... among members of the excluded groups," see William George Prahl, "The Civil Petitioner's Right to Representative Grand Juries and a Statistical Method of Showing Discrimination in Jury Selection Cases Generally," *UCLA Law Review,* Vol. 20, No. 3, February 1973, p. 600.

61. When a district attorney informed grand jurors that because they were not selected representatively he would not bring indictments before them, the panel sent the district attorney a letter demanding that he justify "why you consider this a 'Blue Ribbon' grand jury." The district attorney by letter carefully explained to the grand jurors that the method by which they were selected could result in a criminal case being "ultimately ... thrown out of court under a due process or equal protection argument even if the defendant had been convicted at a properly conducted trial" (correspondence between the Amador County Grand Jury and the District Attorney of Amador County, dated September 17, 1991, and September 24, 1991, respectively).

For an example of an attempt by a defense lawyer to dismiss indictments because "certain minority groups have been systematically excluded from [serving as] grand jury [foremen]," see "Indictments Challenged on Race Grounds," *Daily Journal,* February 27, 1993, p. 2.

62. During the study period, one news story reported that a superior court invited county supervisors to nominate grand jurors "to get an adequate representation of the county on the grand jury." So pleased were county supervisors with the new method that they recessed their regular meeting "to witness the 20-minute ceremony." Some local observers stated that the new selection method would have "other benefits including smoothing over some of the rough history between the two groups [previous grand juries and the board of supervisors]" (*Appeal-Democrat,* February 14, 1992, p. A-3).

63. During the study period, one grand jury reported that permitting citizens to volunteer for grand jury service resulted in a more positive approach by panel members to their responsibilities: "This jury enjoyed the privilege of knowing that, for the first time in Grand Jury selection, it was a body made up entirely of individuals who had come forward to volunteer their service. Realizing this distinction, not once did anyone complain about the necessity for so many meetings, so much travel or the requirement for so many interviews, investigations and reports" (letter from Foreman to Superior Court Judge, Shasta County Grand Jury Final Report, June 25, 1992, n.p.).

64. The maxim "Ignorance of the law is no excuse" seems to have lost some of its former potency. Occasionally public officials successfully evade accountability by pleading that they are not aware, for example, of the "open government" statute.

Using similar logic, grand jurors defending themselves in a libel suit could argue that, as citizens without a legal background, they could not understand the meaning of the obscurely written Penal Code Section 930. One grand jury declared that such an excuse is "unacceptable" but pursued no further the investigation of "a variety of complaints" about violations of the Brown Act (Yolo County Grand Jury Final Report, 1995–1996, p. 2).

65. "A grand jury may investigate and report on the manner in which a school district performs its duties and functions" (Office of the Attorney General, State of California, Opinion No. 95-113, Vol. 78, September 13, 1995, p. 290); "the grand jury no longer has oversight of the trial courts and their officers since that now reposes in state officers, the Judicial Council, and the Legislature itself" (Office of the Attorney General, State of California, Opinion No. 92-1204, Vol. 76, May 4, 1993, p. 77).

66. Penal Code Section 928 at one time contained the phrase, "and report as to the facts they have found, with such recommendations as they may deem proper and fit" (Statutes and Amendments to the Code [California], Extra Sessions 1911, p. 373).

67. Examples of expressly declared legislative intent in statutes with which grand jurors may become acquainted during their term include the Ralph M. Brown Act (Government Code Section 54950, concerning "open government"), the Public Records Act (Government Code Section 6250), and the Legislature's declaration of its intention that "all persons qualified for jury service shall have an equal opportunity to be considered for service as criminal grand jurors" (Penal Code Section 904.6(e)). In suggesting a clear expression of legislative intent, I do not claim that such a statement will correct all of the abuses of the institution. The statement I propose, however, will direct the attention of grand jurors and others who read it to important principles of case law underlying the spirit of the institution about which they might not otherwise learn. For a discussion of the concept of legislative intent, see Russell Holder, "Say What You Mean and Mean What You Say: The Resurrection of Plain Meaning in California Courts," *U.C. Davis Law Review*, Vol. 30, No. 2, Winter 1997, pp. 569–618.

68. The term "civil" jury is often used in legal circles to describe the kind of panel that is involved in trials concerning noncriminal matters. Unfortunately, this form of jury has lost prestige and public support recently. Thus, using another term to describe the type of grand jury that has been the subject of this study could prevent the institution from experiencing some of the public disdain directed at juries involved in civil suits. For a discussion of the reasons why "criticism of the jury has grown increasingly harsh in recent years," see "Developments—The Civil Jury," *Harvard Law Review*, Vol. 10, No. 7, May 1997, pp. 1411–1536.

69. One study reported that some judges of the largest county in California "do not consider nomination of potential grand jurors as one of their more important responsibilities" ("Final Report of the 1981–82 Los Angeles County Grand Jury on the Role and Effectiveness of the Grand Jury," Peat, Marwick, Mitchell and Company, January 1982, p. II-4).

70. See, for example, the *Dictionary of Occupational Titles*, U.S. Department of Labor; Lanham, MD: Bernan Press, 1991.

71. In recent years, Marin County grand jurors have, in effect, chosen their foremen. To do so, they inform the superior court of the name of the colleague whom they wish to be foreman. The judge, if he so desires, appoints that person as foreman. This practice seems to have started some years ago when in a letter to a superior court judge, a foreman recommended that "popular election of the foreman would strengthen the authority of the grand jury and make for better cohesion" (letter from the Foreman of the 1978–1979 Marin County Grand Jury to the Presiding Judge of the Superior Court of Marin County, June 5, 1979). One possible disadvantage of this practice is that it could transform the appointment of grand jury foreman into a political contest, a situation that one author described as a "violent" disease of ambition and avarice (Henry Fielding, *Tom Jones*, New York: Penguin Books, 1985, p. 190).

72. The document referred to is Form 700, "Statement of Economic Interests," State of California, Fair Political Practices Commission. An inquiry into the reasons for "the slow decline of grand juries" included a comment by a superior court judge that the Fair Political Practices Commission "ruling that grand jurors are required to reveal property holdings and business interests" has made the selection of grand jurors more difficult (B. J. Palermo, "Not So Grand Juries: Grand Jurors Must Tell About Their Finances," *California Lawyer*, February 1989, p. 22).

73. Letter to the American Grand Jury Foundation by the Foreman of the San Benito County Grand Jury, May 25, 1995. *See also* Lassen County Grand Jury Procedures Manual, 1986, p. 22, for an admonition that if grand jurors think of public-school districts as State agencies "which are not subject to Grand Jury review, the matter [the question of whether grand juries have such jurisdiction] should be cleared up."

74. Escheat proceedings may be instituted in the case of an estate that no one has been designated to inherit or for which no one has filed a claim. In the nearly 40 years I have been monitoring the California civil grand jury, I never have heard of a panel being involved in the execution of this statute.

75. One safeguard that could prevent political use of the indictment is to add to the statutes pertaining to that function a malicious-prosecution sanction for prosecutors and grand jurors found guilty of such abuse. For a discussion of how a statute similar to the one I propose works in a state in which the county grand jury has civil responsibilities similar to that in California, see R. Perry Sentell, Jr., "Georgia Local Government Officials and the Grand Jury," *Georgia State Bar Journal*, Vol. 26, No. 2, November 1989, pp. 50–58.

76. Involving the grand jury in the prosecution of crimes against the community at large is consistent with its spirit. Much of the institution's prestige was earned in the Progressive Era when it and reform-minded district attorneys fought civic corruption. In the present day, the image of the crime-fighting district attorney and grand jury has all but vanished. The failure of grand juries and district attorneys to continue the tradition of aggressively investigating and prosecuting public-integrity crimes therefore contributes to citizen distrust of government and cynicism about the value of the grand jury.

77. Quite likely, the costs of the proposed system could be met by imposing a modest assessment on fines levied against persons found guilty of public-integrity offenses. This method of defraying part or all of the costs of certain criminal-justice functions is not unusual in the United States.

78. Restricting grand juries from presenting recommendations to eliminate or combine local-government services or agencies occasionally places grand jurors in the awkward position of repudiating recommendations that predecessors have made. See "Disconnect housing authority from County, Grand Jury says," *Contra Costa Times*, March 25, 1995, n.p.

79. To accomplish this objective, Penal Code Section 936.7 might be a useful guide. This statute pertains only to the grand jury of Sacramento County and provides a process by which that panel can obtain, with court authorization, independent counsel for its civil investigations. For a discussion of some of the implications of the grand jury–county counsel problem, see the Contra Costa County Grand Jury Final Report, 1993–1994, pp. 1–3.

80. For a discussion of the kind of protection from suits for libel that grand jurors should have in exercising the civil function, see Note, "The Grand Jury As an Investigative Body," *Harvard Law Review*, 1961, Vol. 74, pp. 597–599. The practice in most states is for grand jurors to have "absolute immunity from liability for any defamatory statement made as part of their official duties" (Sarah Sun Beale, William C. Bryson, *Grand Jury Law and Practice*, Deerfield, IL: Callaghan and Company, 1986, Chapter 3, p. 39).

81. This concept is discussed in Frank W. Cureton, "The Reportorial Power of the Alaska Grand Jury," *Alaska Law Review*, Vol. 3, December 1986, p. 326. Article I, Section 8, of the Alaska Constitution provides that "the power of grand juries to investigate and make recommendations concerning the public welfare or safety shall never be suspended."

82. Some of the suggestions I offer in this section comport with a case decided by a New York court concerning the grand jury in that State (Application of Lundy (1955) 208 Misc. 833 [148 N.Y.S.2d 658]).

83. For example, preponderance of evidence might be a suitable standard for the civil grand jury. See California Evidence Code Section 502 for several illustrations of how courts shall instruct juries about preponderance of evidence.

84. Throughout the various codes of the State of California, provisions can be found for levying fines, withholding salary, or imposing other sanctions against State or local officials or agencies that do not comply with specified reporting requirements or fail to perform certain duties in a timely manner. See, for example, Education Code Sections 44030 and 45057 and Government Code Sections 12461.2 and 53895. Article VI, Section 19, of the Constitution of the State of California specifies that judges who do not act on "any cause" before them "for 90 days after it has been submitted for decision" may not receive their salaries.

85. *Unnamed Minority Members etc. Grand Jury v. Superior Court* (1989) 208 Cal.App.3d 1344 [256 Cal.Rptr. 727].

86. The absence of a clear statutory expression of the principal holding in the *Clinton* case is another example of how the statutes have not been brought up to

date with case law concerning the civil grand jury. Because no statute expresses the principal holding of the *Clinton* case, for example, at least one incident each year comes to light about one or more grand jurors who attempt, without panel approval, to conduct investigations. (As an illustration of this problem, see "2 county grand jurors ousted after meeting with TV reporter," *Monterey County Herald*, August 18, 1995, p. C-1.)

87. *Clinton v. Superior Court* (1937) 23 Cal.App.2d 342 [73 P.2d 252].

88. Grand Jury Final Report, County of Tuolumne, 1991–1992, n.p.; "A major problem for the grand jury, due primarily to the extended term, was turnover in personnel. From the original jury totaling 19 with 6 alternates, only 12 of the original group completed the full 18 months."

89. "Grand Jury Investigative Report," February/March, 1988, Investigative Grand Jury of Muscogee County, March 29, 1988. See "Handbook for Grand Jurors," Prosecuting Attorneys' Council of Georgia, Smyrna, Georgia, 1990, p. 10: "In order to prevent the development of professional jurors, the General Assembly has provided that any person who served as a juror (grand or petit) at the preceding term of court is disqualified from service as a juror at the next succeeding term of the court in which he has previously served."

90. In Los Angeles County the number is 23; in counties other than Los Angeles but with populations larger than 20,000 persons, the number is 19; in counties of 20,000 persons or fewer, the number is 11 (Penal Code Section 888.2).

91. In a case concerning grand jury procedures, a California court quoted an English legal authority who several hundred years ago commented about the number of grand jurors needed to vote for an indictment: "And it seemeth to me, that the law in this case delighteth herself in the number of 12; for there must not only be 12 jurors for the trial of matters of fact, but 12 judges of ancient time for trial of matters of law in the Exchequer Chamber. Also, for matters of state there were in ancient time 12 Counselors of State. He that wageth his law must have 11 others with him which think he says true. And that number of 12 is much respected in Holy Writ, as 12 apostles, 12 stones, 12 tribes, etc." (*Fitts v. Superior Court* (1936) 6 Cal.2d 230, 239 [57 P.2d 510], quoting Sir Edward Coke).

92. Letter, County Clerk, Alpine County, May 13, 1997. The law authorizing this practice was introduced as a result of a request by the Superior Court of this County.

93. Hon. Ian Temby, Q.C., Commissioner, The Independent Commission Against Corruption, Sydney, Australia; statement made at the Twelfth Annual Grand Jury Exchange Seminar, August 20, 1991, Santa Clara University, Santa Clara, California.

94. Although space does not permit a thorough discussion of this concept in this study, I believe it has considerable potential. One form that an effective State civil grand jury could take is to create it as a hybrid of the county civil grand jury and an independent commission against waste in government, fraud, graft, and corruption. For example, several existing State agencies (such as the Office of Auditor General, the Office of Legislative Analyst, and the Commission on California State Government Organization and Economy) could be consolidated into a State civil grand jury.

The State civil grand jury would consist of a designated number of former county grand jury foremen and forewomen appointed for one year and an equal number of persons with no previous grand jury service. Staff members would be on temporary assignment from the aforementioned, but now defunct, State oversight agencies. The State civil grand jury also would be authorized to draft for temporary service specialized investigators from local law enforcement organizations or other State agencies. Quite likely, the fines and penalties accruing from prosecutions initiated by a grand jury of the State of California would be more than adequate to finance it. For more information about hybrid agencies of this type, see Peter N. Grabosky, "Citizen co-production and corruption control," *Corruption and Reform,* Vol. 5, No. 2, 1990, pp. 125–151.

95. Renée B. Lettow, "Reviving Federal Grand Jury Presentments," *Yale Law Journal,* Vol. 103, No. 4, January 1994, pp. 1333–1362. Use of the term "presentment" perplexes even legal historians. Lettow defines it as "a charge the grand jury brings on its own initiative" and states that "in federal cases, a presentment cannot by itself initiate a prosecution" (p. 1134). At one time, "Jury of Presentment" was the term used for what later came to be known as the grand jury (Frances and Joseph Gies, *Life in a Medieval Village,* New York: Harper Collins Publishers, p. 174). Occasionally one finds examples of the use of the presentment preserved in literature. For example, the grand jury of the City of Dublin issued a presentment in 1724 concerning the circulation of counterfeit money. See Jonathan Swift, *The Drapier's Letters and Other Works,* 1724–1725, Oxford: Basil Blackwell, 1941, pp. 69–71.

96. In the sense that I use the word "presentment," grand jurors would not issue one without judicial review and approval. Judicial oversight would ensure procedural correctness of presentments and thereby prevent abuses that characterized them in the past. For a brief discussion of the history of the presentment in California, see *In re. Grosbois,* 1895 42 p. 444, 109 C. 445.

97. *William S. Bradley v. Gary L. Lacy* (1997) 53 Cal.App.4th 883, 892 [61 Cal.Rptr.2d 919].

98. Government Code Section 3060, *et. seq.* For a discussion of the grand jury's authority to institute removal proceedings against public officials and a comment about future use of this statute, see Gail Ehrlich, "Instituting '3060' proceedings after Steiner: Can a Public Official Ever be Removed for Misconduct?" *Public Law Journal,* Vol. 21, No. 3, Winter 1998, p. 5.

Chapter 8

1. Robert W. Stewart, "Grand Jurors Crippled by Lack of Experience, Skills," *Los Angeles Times,* August 6, 1986, p. 20.

2. One exception to this statement is a thoughtful discussion of the jury as a citizens' institution by Phoebe A. Haddon, "Rethinking the Jury," *William and Mary Bill of Rights Journal,* Vol. 3, Issue 1, Summer 1994, pp. 29–106.

3. See, for example, Stephanie A. Doria, "Adding Bite to the Watchdog's Bark: Reforming the California Civil Grand Jury System," *Pacific Law Journal,* Vol. 28, Issue 3, Spring 1997, pp. 1115–1155.

4. Michael D. Harris, "Ex-Juror is First to be Fined for Speaking to the Press," *Daily Journal,* July 23, 1997, p. 3.

5. Final Report, Los Angeles County Grand Jury, 1997–1998, pp. 5–8.

6. Alexis De Tocqueville, *Democracy in America,* New York: Alfred A. Knopf, 1994. See especially Volume 1, Chapter 17, "Principal Causes Which Tend to Maintain the Democratic Republic in the United States."

7. See Table 15, "Examples of Nine Types of Grand Jury Investigations," Chapter 3.

8. "The Grand Jury: Damaged Goods," *Stockton Record,* June 12, 1988, n.p.

9. For an account of how the "don't confuse me with the facts" attitude has lost lives, empires, and wars, see Barbara Tuchman, *The March of Folly,* New York: Alfred A. Knopf, 1984. Professor Tuchman (p. 7) calls this human shortcoming "woodenheadness": "[a form of] self-deception [that] consists in assessing a situation in terms of preconceived fixed notions while ignoring or rejecting any contrary signs ... [and] acting according to wish while not allowing oneself to be deflected by the facts."

10. Legal scholars complain about juror incompetence more often than they praise jurors for their competence. Of course, some of the reasons for the criticism lie in the tendency of members of professions to devalue the opinions of laymen about technical matters. With respect to the work of grand jurors, ineffective final reports are the consequences of a complex set of causes of which lack of basic legal knowledge is only one defect. The root cause is a lack of the citizenship skills to which I have referred throughout this book.

For a discussion of the "jury-as-icon/jurors-as-fools" problem, see Laura Gaston Dooley, "Our Juries, Ourselves: The Power, Perception, and Politics of the Civil Jury," *Cornell Law Review,* Vol. 80, No. 2, January 1995, p. 30.

For the viewpoint that civil grand jury service in California is beyond the resources that "even the most intelligent layman normally possesses," see Burton R. Brazil, "Investigation of Local Government by the Grand Jury: Notes From Santa Clara County," *Santa Clara Lawyer,* Vol. 2, No. 2, Spring 1962, p. 183.

Citing "non-legal" research, however, another writer concludes that "juries by almost any measure, out-perform judges [in] virtually any type of decision-making" (Kenneth S. Klein, "Unpacking the Jury Box," *Hastings Law Journal,* Vol. 47, No. 5/6, 1995–1996, p. 1366). Klein states that evidence concerning jurors' decisions of law is less clear. Of course, the advantage that trial jurors enjoy is that attorneys present facts to them, whereas civil grand jurors usually must develop facts for themselves. Observing that criticism that "grand jurors are not very bright [is] ... a bit harsh," another commentator argues that the problem is not dull-wittedness but that grand jurors often do not have fact-finding and analysis skills, a deficit that is responsible for their dependency on prosecutors (Judith M. Beall, "What Do You Do With a Runaway Grand Jury?: A Discussion of the Problems and Possibilities Opened Up by the Rocky Flats Grand Jury Investigation," *Southern California Law Review,* Vol. 71, No. 3, March 1998, p. 631).

11. I developed this list from the "Management and Personnel" section of the Yuba County Building and Planning report in the final report of the Yuba County Grand Jury, 1993–1994, pp. 3–17.

12. For an argument that group-think was an important cause of the Bay of Pigs blunder, see Peter Wyden, *Bay of Pigs,* New York: Simon & Schuster, 1979, pp. 313–316.

13. Henry D. Thoreau, *Journal,* Vol. 3, 1848–1851, Princeton, NJ: Princeton University Press, 1990, p. 139.

14. J. S. Morrill, *The Cheshire Grand Jury 1625–1659: A Social and Administrative Study,* Leicester University Press, 1976, p. 47.

15. *Program,* Modesto Symphony Orchestra, 1997–1998 season.

16. San Mateo County Grand Jury Final Report, 1992, Foreman's Letter, n.p.

17. "Grand juries' future at center of debate," *San Francisco Examiner,* September 6, 1998, p. C-7. "Like many other officials, Nevin argues for changing the panel's name from 'grand jury' to 'citizen review committee,'—a title he said better conveys its role without connoting grandiose authority." More information about passage of the Act is reported in Nick Warner, "AB 829 Changes Civil Grand Jury," *California County,* March/April 1998, p. 15.

18. Jean Guccione, "There're No Lines Around the Block for Grand Jury Work," *Daily Journal,* July 27, 1987, p. 5.

19. Referring to the vested interest the state has in preserving the *status quo,* one writer comments that, for this reason, persons of contrasting political ideologies occasionally share a concern about the state holding a monopoly on the education of citizens, particularly if the result of the education is "deference to the establishment" (Derek Heater, "A Remarkable Case of Sudden Interest," *Parliamentary Affairs,* Vol. 44, No. 2, April 1991, pp. 150).

20. Several times a week C-SPAN broadcasts conferences, forums, or other meetings sponsored by professional associations of journalists. Many of these presentations are about topics that directly affect citizenship as I use the term in this chapter. Recent examples of such broadcasts and their topics include C-SPAN, August 21, 1998 (James Carey, discussing how profit seeking has changed journalism); C-SPAN, January 15, 1997 (interpretive versus factual journalism); and C-SPAN, October 22, 1997 (Jay Rosen, when journalism became a profession, it lost touch with citizens). Journalism trade and professional magazines, too, are concerned with these and related issues. See, for example, Joe Nicholson, "Are Newspapers Abandoning Their Statehouse Coverage?" *Editor and Publisher,* September 12, 1998, p. 16.

For a discussion of the need to create an independent procedure for evaluating citizens' complaints about news coverage, see Alicia C. Shepard, "Going Public," *American Journalism Review,* April 1997, p. 25. An expression of concern about factuality in the news media can be found in "Fictitious Facts Have News Media Licking Wounds," *San Francisco Examiner,* June 21, 1998, p. A-9.

21. "Publicity is justly commended as a remedy for social and industrial diseases. Sunlight is said to be the best of disinfectants; electric light the most efficient policeman" (Louis D. Brandeis, *Other People's Money,* New York: Frederick A. Stokes Company, 1914, p. 92). Publicity also can be a "disinfectant" against venal business practices. In "relying on a governing concept as old as civilization: Shame," one California legislator announced his intention to introduce legislation to use the Internet to publicize the names of "business owners who owe business taxes ("A plan to shame deadbeat retailers," *San Jose Mercury News,* February 26, 1999, p. B-3).

22. Peter L. Phillips Simpson, trans., *The Politics of Aristotle,* Chapel Hill: University of North Carolina Press, 1997, Book 3, "Definition and Division of Regime," pp. 75–78.

23. See Paul Berry Clarke, *Deep Citizenship,* London: Pluto Press, 1996, p. 123: "To be a citizen is to be involved in political decisions at all times. And this is a condition that runs very wide indeed, for to be engaged in the world is to be political." Berry's use of "political" is much broader than its partisanship sense.

24. Robert N. Bellah, et al., *The Good Society,* New York: Vintage Books, 1992, p. 254.

25. For a discussion of cocoon citizenship, see William Fulton, *The Reluctant Metropolis,* Point Arena, CA: Solano Press Books, 1997, pp. 333–347.

26. For a discussion of support for and opposition to the practice in one community of paying newspapers to include final reports as inserts in newspapers, see "Grand Jury Paid $10,616 to Run Report," *Press Democrat,* January 23, 1994, p. B-1. Another newspaper declared its willingness to print without cost and insert a final report into one of its regular editions (*Auburn Journal,* May 7, 1992, n.p.: "Because we believe so strongly in maximizing public awareness of how its government works, the *Journal* is offering to insert and deliver the [final] report at no charge.").

27. Edwin M. Lemert, "The Grand Jury As an Agency of Social Control," *American Sociological Review,* Vol. 10, No. 6, December 1945, p. 754.

28. Exceptions to "open-meeting laws" in some American states permit public bodies in certain circumstances to meet privately to discuss specified matters.

29. The California Legislature incorporated this value into Penal Code Section 921: "The grand jury is entitled to free access, at all reasonable times [and] to the examination, without charge, of all public records within the county."

30. This is another example of a civic value that has been embodied in the law (Constitution of the State of California, Article XVI, Section 6).

31. See William L. Riordan, *Plunkitt of Tammany Hall,* New York: Penguin Books, 1991, for an account by a famous political boss of how "honest graft" depended on such practices.

32. Examples of these entities include downtown business improvement districts, joint powers agencies, and nonprofit corporations organized by one or more local governments (for example, cities, counties, and school districts). One commentator refers to the use of entities for "fiscal adaptation," meaning that public officials sometimes create them to circumvent voter-approved fiscal constraints (see John J. Kirlin, "The Impact of Fiscal Limits on Governance," *Hastings Constitutional Law Quarterly,* Vol. 25, No. 2, Winter 1998, pp. 207–208).

33. One observer of local government claims that 25,000 of these "microgovernments" exist in California (John E. Petersen, "The Blossoming of Microgovernments," *Governing,* October 1994, p. 78).

34. "Legislature sends outstanding debt reporting measure to Governor," *Debt Line,* Vol. 17, No. 9, September 1998, p. 1.

35. For a news story about the lack of oversight of local-government indebtedness in the largest county of California, see "L.A. debt out of control, study says," *San Francisco Chronicle,* February 7, 1998, p. A-15.

36. After one government agency installed a "fraud hotline," "130 legitimate tips of suspected fraud [were received] in the first four months" (W. Steve Albrecht, "Fraud in Governmental Agencies: The Perpetrators and Types of Fraud," *Government Finance Review,* December 1991, Vol. 7, No. 6, p. 30).

37. In the final reports I received for fiscal year 1997–1998, the table of contents of only one grand jury listed an inquiry into the millennium-bug problem: "The Year 2000 Ready or Not—Here It Comes," Contra Costa County Grand Jury Final Report, 1997–1998, n.p.

38. Penal Code Section 939.1. Note that the words following "general public welfare" in the statute are: "... involving the alleged corruption, misfeasance, or malfeasance in office or dereliction of duty of public officials or employees or of any person allegedly acting in conjunction or conspiracy with such officials or employees in such alleged acts...."

39. "In the Matter of the 1989 Madera County Grand Jury Request for Public Session," Hon. Edward E. Moffat, Judge of the Superior Court, September 9, 1989. It is difficult to understand how a salary increase for county supervisors, controversial though it may have been, qualified for the use of the public-session statute.

40. "Grand jury goes public in case of cop shooting," *San Jose Post Record,* May 23, 1996, p. A-1.

41. For a view that "town hall" meetings were not consistently well-attended gatherings of citizens of equal statuses, see Michael Schudson, *The Good Citizen,* New York: Free Press, 1998, pp. 16–19.

42. See Rogers M. Smith, *Civic Ideals,* New Haven, CT: Yale University Press, 1997, for examples of how citizens' associations in their respective heydays influenced American public policy.

43. For an account of the origins, purposes, and methods of such groups, see Lorin Peterson, *The Day of the Mugwump,* New York: Random House, 1961.

44. James Bryce, *The American Commonwealth,* London: MacMillan and Co., 1888, Book 2, p. 253.

45. Two authors argue that merely counting the decline in "old civics types" of voluntary associations results in the incorrect conclusion that civic activism is fading. To correct this oversight, participation by millions of Americans in the "new types" of volunteer associations must be recognized. Examples of these "new types" are 12-step groups such as Alcoholics Anonymous (Frank Reissman and Erik Banks, "The Mismeasure of Civil Society," *Social Policy,* Vol. 26, No. 3, Spring 1996, p. 3).

46. Political scientists often claim that, as Professor Dahl states, "Independent associations are a source of civic education and enlightenment. They provide citizens not only with information but also with opportunities for discussion, deliberation, and the acquisition of political skills" (Robert A. Dahl, *On Democracy,* New Haven, CT: Yale University Press, 1998, p. 98).

47. Robert N. Bellah et al., "Individualism and the Crisis of Civic Membership," *Christian Century,* Vol. 13, No. 6, May 8, 1996, p. 510.

48. See Philip Selznick, *The Organizational Weapon,* New York: McGraw Hill Book Company, 1952, *passim,* for an account of the central role that "voluntary" associations played as instruments of social control in Communist Russia.

49. See Jean Bethke Elshtain, *Democracy on Trial,* New York: Basic Books, 1995, *passim,* for a discussion of this concept.

50. The question of civics education in private schools is complicated by the religious affiliations of some of them. As interesting and important as this difference between public and private education is, I exclude it from this discussion to conserve space. One legal scholar points out that the American Civil Liberties Union (ACLU) does not object to civic-virtue topics in public schools, such as "honesty, good citizenship, sportsmanship, respect for the rights and freedom of others, respect for persons and their property, civility, the dual virtues of moral conviction and tolerance and hard work" if those subjects are not presented as religious principles. The cited list of acceptable civic virtues does not specifically include topics such as knowledge of local government but, presumably, the ACLU would find this topic acceptable if it were to exclude religious references (Richard S. Meyers, "Reflections on the Teaching of Civic Virtue in the Public Schools," *University of Detroit Mercy Law Review,* Fall 1996, Vol. 74, No. 1, p. 65).

51. Three examples of civics books from a previous era containing such material are: Arthur William Dunn, *The Community and the Citizen,* Lexington, MA: D.C. Heath and Co., 1914; Henry L. Smith, et al., *Our Government,* Chicago: Laidlaw Publishers, 1936; and Frederic P. Woellner, *How We Govern,* Sacramento, CA: State Printing Office, 1927.

52. Frank Abbott Magruder, *American Government: A Consideration of the Problems of Democracy,* Boston: Allyn and Bacon, 1945.

53. *Social Studies Review,* Vol. 35, No. 1, Fall 1995.

54. Edward C. Sembor, Jr., "Citizenship Education for the Community: The Local Public Administrator as Instructional Leader," *Public Administration Quarterly,* Vol. 17, No. 2, Summer 1997, pp. 227–231.

55. "Ascending" and "descending" are terms I have adopted from the work of a medieval historian. Using these terms, Professor Ullmann differentiates political power emanating from citizens in contrast to that wielded by theocratic, monarchical, or other authoritarian political systems (Walter Ullmann, *Principles of Government and Politics in the Middle Ages,* London: Methuen and Co., Ltd., 1961).

56. *History-Social Science Framework,* Sacramento: California State Board of Education, July 1987, pp. 105 and 94, respectively.

57. Stanley W. Moore, et al., *The Child's Political World: A Longitudinal Perspective,* New York: Praeger Publishers, 1985, p. 101.

58. *The Front Page* (1931) and *Deadline USA* (1952) are examples of this genre.

59. For example, an investigation by a newsman of how attorneys in San Francisco evaluated superior court judges began in June 1998 and was published six months later; Scott Winocur, "How justice is served in S.F.," *San Francisco Examiner,* December 13, 1998, p. A-1.

60. One writer claims that this attitude explains why the news media in Orange County, California, failed to "live up to their role as watchdog for the public" (Mark Baldassare, *When Government Fails,* Berkeley: University of California Press, 1998, p. 230).

61. For a discussion of citizen discontent with the news media, see Jay G. Blumler, "Origins of the Crisis of Communication for Citizenship," *Political Communication,* Vol. 14, No. 4, 1997, pp. 395–404.

62. The Pew Center for Civic Journalism is a leading source of funds for various professors of journalism, working journalists, and others who promote civic journalism.

63. The use of economic threats to kill investigative stories is well illustrated in the movie, *Deadline USA* (1952), and it is a reality that exists to this day.

64. These are examples of "public journalism" cited by one of its advocates, Jay Rosen, editor, "Rethinking Journalism: Rebuilding Civic Life," *National Civic Review,* Vol. 85, No. 1, Winter–Spring, 1996, p. 15.

65. Untitled news item, *Sonoma County Independent,* October 16–22, 1997, p. 6.

66. One writer discusses the complex process by which failure of the news media to promote active citizenship leads to citizens' withdrawing from political participation with, sooner or later, demagoguery and citizen distrust of government as the consequences: "The two basic sources of the problem are an inadequate supply of high-quality, independent reporting and a paltry demand for such news" (Robert H. Entman, *Democracy Without Citizens: Media and the Decay of American Politics,* New York: Oxford University Press, 1989, p. 129).

67. "Grand juries' future at center of debate," *San Francisco Examiner,* September 6, 1998, p. C-1. For other examples of "investigation by telephone" stories about the civil grand jury, see "Grand Jury: Playing Politics? Are grand jury reports the voice of the people—or a hunt for red herrings?" *Coast Weekly,* January 7–13, 1999, p. 16; "Citizens' Watchdogs or Useless Probers?" *Fresno Bee,* July 26, 1998, p. B-3.

68. Deborah Tannen, *The Argument Culture,* New York: Random House, 1995.

69. Richard Lambert, "Rebuilding Trust," *Columbia Journalism Review,* November/December 1998, p. 39. Almost every issue of *American Journalism Review, Columbia Journalism Review,* or *Editor and Publisher* includes at least one article about the topics I have reviewed in this section and many other critical comments about the news media.

70. Peter Aucoin, "Political Science and Democratic Governance," *Canadian Journal of Political Science,* Vol. 29, No. 4, December 1996, pp. 660, 654, and 659, respectively.

71. Consider, for example, this extract from a book whose title promises more than it delivers: "Community or collective life narratives, like individual life narratives, are open-criterion narratives that have as their rhetorical function the representation of the current status of desire with respect to its object" (Thomas Bridges, *The Culture of Citizenship: Inventing Postmodern Civic Culture,* 1994, Albany, NY: State University of New York Press, p. 192).

72. See Robert D. Putnam, *Making Democracy Work,* Princeton, NJ: Princeton University Press, 1993, p. 3, for a discussion about the reluctance of his colleagues to evaluate political systems.

73. A good beginning for such a debate would be a discussion of the validity of Professor Dahl's five standards for a democratic process in terms of citizenship

skills and competence: (a) effective participation, (b) voting equality, (c) enlightened understanding, (d) control of the agenda, and (e) inclusion of adults (Robert A. Dahl, *On Democracy,* New Haven, CT: Yale University Press, pp. 37–38).

74. See, for example, California Government Code Section 54953.3.

75. California Penal Code Section 95.

76. Matthew Heller, "Who's SLAPPing Whom," *California Lawyer,* November 1997, pp. 17–18.

77. Peter Aucoin, "Political Science and Democratic Governance," *Canadian Journal of Political Science,* Vol. 29, No. 4, December 1996, p. 646.

78. Robert D. Putnam, *Making Democracy Work,* Princeton, NJ: Princeton University Press, 1993, p. 15.

79. Howard S. Becker et al., *Boys in White,* New Brunswick, NJ: Transaction Books, 1961.

80. Samuel A. Stouffer, *The American Soldier,* Princeton, NJ: Princeton University Press, 1949.

81. Gabriel A. Almond and Sidney Verba, *The Civic Culture,* Princeton, NJ: Princeton University Press, 1963.

82. Benjamin Barber, *Strong Democracy: Participatory Politics for a New Age,* Berkeley: University of California Press, 1984, p. 284.

83. The *Current Law Index* contains abstracts of legal studies taken from more than 800 law-school journals, bar association magazines, and many other law-related publications in the United States and elsewhere.

84. Amy Lovell, "Other Students Always Used To Say, 'Look at the Dykes': Protecting Students from Peer Sexual Orientation Harassment," *California Law Review,* Vol. 80, No. 3, May 1998, pp. 617–654.

85. Ann E. Carlson, "Standing for the Environment," *UCLA Law Review,* Vol. 45, No. 4, April 1998, pp. 931–1004.

86. Linda B. Epstein, "What is a Gender Norm and Why Should We Care? Implementing a New Theory in Sexual Harassment Law," *Stanford Law Review,* Vol. 51, No. 1, November 1998, pp. 161–182.

87. *Pro bono publico* (more commonly known as "pro bono") legal services "for the public good" are provided without charge by lawyers. Recipients of these services usually are nonprofit organizations or individuals with limited means. Typically, the services rarely are provided for controversial issues such as a citizen who has proof of government fraud, graft, or corruption.

88. Petitions for writs of mandate and *qui tam* and *quo warranto* proceedings are examples.

89. See George J. Edwards, Jr., *The Grand Jury,* Philadelphia: George T. Bisel Co., 1906. This study was republished in 1973 by AMS Press. Edwards' book, if updated, would be a valuable reference work for lawyers, grand jurors, and social scientists.

90. For an example of a useful format for an annotated bibliography about grand juries in the United States, see Harry S. Martin, III, et al., "The Grand Jury: A Selected Bibliography with Exhibit Notes," *Tarlton Law Library Legal Bibliography Series,* No. 10, 1975, University of Texas School of Law.

91. Alexis de Tocqueville, *Democracy in America*, Book 1, New York: Alfred A. Knopf, 1994, p. 285.

92. One scholar claims that, "Citizen surveys in California reveal a political culture [of] deep dissatisfaction with government and a strong opinion that government wastes resources ... [and other attitudes] reasonably parallel to those elicited in national surveys" (John J. Kirlin, "The Impact of Fiscal Limits on Governance," *Hastings Constitutional Law Quarterly*, Vol. 25, No. 2, Winter 1998, pp. 204–205).

93. Willard Sterne Randall, *George Washington: A Life*, New York: Henry Holt and Company, 1997, p. 452.

94. Penal Code Section 933.05(e) now provides for such a meeting unless the court determines that it might be detrimental.

95. Karl Popper, *The Open Society and Its Enemies*, Princeton, NJ: Princeton University Press, 1950, p. 120.

96. Social-science instructors occasionally recount what might be an urban legend in their discipline concerning a colleague who asked students to solicit signatures from friends and relatives in support of the Declaration of Independence. Few people were willing to support the document, and some of the students expressed alarm at its "radical" language.

97. Michael Schudson, *The Good Citizen*, New York: Free Press, 1998.

98. These examples of "how individuals can become participatory citizens" are from the *History-Social Science Framework*, Sacramento: California State Board of Education, July 1987, p. 105.

99. Robert N. Bellah, et al, *The Good Society*, New York: Vintage Books, 1992, p. 254.

100. Michael Schudson, *The Good Citizen*, New York: Free Press, 1998, p. 313.

101. Václav Havel, *The Art of the Impossible: Politics as Morality in Practice*, New York: Alfred A. Knopf, 1997, p. 127.

102. These and similar illustrations of the "office of citizenship" are from a high-school civics textbook by James E. Davis et al., *Civics: Participating in Our Democracy*, Menlo Park, CA: Addison-Wesley, 1991, p. 48.

103. Meira Levinson, "Liberalism Versus Democracy: Schooling Private Citizens in the Public Square," *British Journal of Political Science*, Vol. 23, No. 3, July 1997, p. 3.

104. Michael Walzer, *Obligations: Essays on Disobedience, War, and Citizenship*, Cambridge, MA: Harvard University Press, 1970, p. 225.

Glossary

These definitions are not intended to replace the more detailed explanations of legal terms one can find in legal dictionaries. Many of the definitions will change with the passage of time, the enactment of legislation, or the creation of new case law. Similarly, legal definitions may vary among jurisdictions. Those who desire more precise explanations may wish to consult the most recent edition of *Black's Law Dictionary*, St. Paul: West Publishing, or Gerald N. Hill and Kathleen Thompson Hill, *Real Life Dictionary of the Law*, Santa Monica, CA: General Publishing Group, 1995.

accusation. A formal charge against someone, alleging the commission of a crime. Also, a non-criminal process under California Government Code Section 3060 that may result in removing a public officer from office (*see also* malfeasance; misfeasance; nonfeasance).

ad hoc. For a specific purpose and usually for a limited time, as an *ad hoc* committee of a grand jury.

advisor judge. A term used in some California counties to refer to a judge who answers grand jurors' questions, meets with them occasionally, and assists them, upon their request, with administrative details, obtaining resources, and so on.

allegation. The matter that a prosecutor attempts to prove in court; noun form of "allege."

appeal. To ask a higher court to review a decision of a lower court (verb form).

appellate court. A court with the power to review the decisions of lower courts.

audit(s). An examination and report of the financial condition (financial audit) or a review of the processes, methods, and systems (performance audit) of a local government.

Brown Act. A California State law that forbids certain local-government elected bodies from holding secret meetings and that also regulates the holding of executive sessions; named after former California Assemblyman Ralph M. Brown.

calendar year. *See* fiscal year.

case law. The law the courts create when they interpret or decide matters concerning statutes, constitutions, and the like; sometimes called "decisional law."

charge. To inform the jury about legal issues; in other contexts, another word for "accuse" (verb form).

civil investigation. *See* investigation, civil.

civil powers. The lawful authority to conduct civil investigations (*see* investigation, civil).

civil proceeding. In contrast to criminal proceedings, a court action initiated to correct a private wrong, usually where monetary damages are assessed or a court order is issued to achieve some form of relief.

collegial body; collegiality. A form of organization in which all members have equal status, power, and authority and in which decisions are made by general agreement rather than by one person.

common law. Judge-made laws based on custom, unwritten principles, and prior judicial decisions rather than laws created by legislatures.

complainant. One who complains; sometimes incorrectly pronounced "complain*t*ant."

complaint. A verified written accusation that a prosecuting official files in a local criminal court to charge one or more persons with committing one or more offenses.

conclusionary. Not factual; a statement expressing an opinion; inferential.

conclusions. An opinion about the social, political, and economic implications of findings.

confidential(ity). Something that is private and not available for publication or dissemination.

conflict of interest. The result when one's personal circumstances (income, livelihood, and the like) affect decisions he or she may make about public matters.

corrections. A term that refers broadly to places such as jails, prisons, halfway houses, and other institutions in which convicted persons are confined.

corroboration. Evidence that supports or verifies another's testimony; sometimes incorrectly pronounced "collaboration."

counsel. Another name for lawyer, suggesting that the basic function of the lawyer's role is to advise and otherwise guide the client.

county counsel. A lawyer whom a county has hired to provide elected and appointed officials with legal advice, support, and opinions.

court. The place where a judge administers justice, but sometimes the word is synonymous with "judge," as "May it please the court."

court of last resort. A court from which there is no appeal; in popular use, an institution to which a person may turn for a final attempt to obtain justice or relief.

criminal justice. The major institutions and processes by which the aims of the criminal law are attained; includes the police, prosecution-defense function, courts, and correctional agencies (including probation and parole).

criminal proceeding. A legal proceeding carried out in court, and which involves or could involve a specified punishment for the commission of one or more crimes.

criterion; criteria. The standard or standards against which something is measured or judged.

decisional law. *See* case law.

defendant. The accused in a criminal proceeding.

discretionary. Not mandatory; an act that a public official chooses to perform or not perform.

district attorney. *See* prosecutor.

documented evidence. Evidence supported by an exact description of its source or other reference.

due process. The orderly sequence of events by which a person's constitutional rights are safeguarded in a judicial proceeding.

entity(ies). "Local public entity" includes a county, city, district, public authority, public agency, and any other political subdivision or public corporation in the State but does not include the State (California Government Code Section 940.4).

escheat. Refers to property that has reverted to the state because no one has legally claimed it.

evidence. Legally accepted materials used in a trial to prove or disprove allegations.

examination. A synonym for "preliminary hearing," "preliminary examination," and "examining trial"; an inquiry conducted in a lower court to determine whether a crime has been committed, and whether a certain person should be held to answer to a charge against him or her in a higher court.

fair comment. A statement based upon facts rather than opinion, ill will, malice, or supposition, and which is said or written dispassionately rather than emotionally.

felony. A crime generally punishable by imprisonment in a state or federal prison or by death.

final report(s). The report a grand jury issues at the end of its term or during its term about its facts, findings, conclusions, and recommendations concerning matters within its jurisdiction.

financial audit. *See* audit(s).

finding(s). An objective, reasonable, and logical inference drawn from one or more facts. A finding differs from a conclusion in that the latter may speculate about the social, economic, political, or policy implications of the finding. A finding is devoid of value judgments.

fiscal year. A 12-month budget year, often beginning July 1 and ending June 30, in contrast to a year beginning January 1 and ending December 31 (calendar year). This word sometimes is incorrectly pronounced "physical year."

foreman. One member of a grand jury whom the court has so designated but who, except for several minor procedural statutory duties, may exercise only those powers the grand jury authorizes.

general session. A regularly scheduled meeting of the entire grand jury.

grand jury. A judicially appointed group of men and women with the power of indictment (*see* indictment) and, in some states, specific investigatory powers over designated public matters.

Hawkins decision. A decision of the California Supreme Court in 1979 that resulted in diminished use of the indictment between 1980 and 1990.

hearsay evidence. Generally, a statement other than that made by a witness while testifying that is not admissible as evidence except in extraordinary circumstances.

housing authority. A form of local government whose purpose is to provide housing for low-income persons.

immunity. Not subject, because of some special status, to prosecution, censure, or penalty.

impanel (impanelment). To draw a jury and qualify its members for service.

incorporated city. A city created under State laws governing incorporation.

indictment. A finding, in a secret meeting of the grand jury, using the standard of strong suspicion, that a named suspect committed a crime.

information. A method by which a district attorney may, without grand jury involvement, initiate a prosecution in a superior court for a felony.

inquisitorial. An inquisitorial body is one whose purpose is to seek the truth but not necessarily make judgments.

interim report(s). A report a grand jury issues about a specific topic during the grand jury year; the law in California does not require affected local-government officials to respond to it.

investigation, civil. A grand jury inquiry into books, records, accounts, and methods, systems, or procedures of designated local governments; less formally, a "watchdog" investigation.

jail(s). A city or county institution that confines persons found guilty of misdemeanors or in which persons are held for arraignment or during trial.

joint-powers agencies. Legal entities that two or more local governments may create by contract to perform a function common to both or all parties.

judgment. The court's decision regarding a case, including what should happen to the defendant, according to the law.

jurisdiction. Certain specific powers conferred on the court with regard to specific classes of cases. Types of judicial jurisdiction are (a) geographical area; (b) nature of proceeding; (c) nature of the case; (d) extent of punishment; (e) persons involved; and (f) whether exclusive or concurrent (whether two different types or levels of court can hear the same kind of case).

jurist. One who is eminently knowledgeable about the law but who may or may not be a judge. A person is a grand juror, not a grand jurist.

LAFCO. Local Agency Formation Commission; a local body in California appointed for a variety of purposes including the review of efforts to incorporate cities, change boundaries, and the like (pronounced "laff-co").

legal advisors. Persons lawfully empowered to provide grand jurors with legal advice, such as a judge, district attorney, or county counsel.

legislative intent. The purpose or goal of the legislature in enacting a law; sometimes stated explicitly in statutes.

liability. The risk borne by grand jurors for improper exercise of their powers.

libel. Written form of defamation of character (*see also* slander).

malfeasance. An abuse of official power or responsibility by a public officer (*see also* misfeasance; nonfeasance).

mandamus. A court order requiring an official to perform a specific act.

McClatchy case(s). One of two California Appellate Court cases about matters crucial to grand jury proceedings. One case is concerned with secrecy, "raw evidentiary material," and the authority of the courts over grand jury final reports. A second case deals with minority reports (see below).

minority report(s). A dissenting report by one or more grand jurors. Publishing such reports has no lawful basis unless the required number of grand jurors so authorizes.

misdemeanor. A violation punishable by a sentence to county jail for no more than a year.

misfeasance. Incorrectly or improperly executing a lawful duty, act, or responsibility (*see also* malfeasance; nonfeasance).

nonfeasance. Neglect or failure to discharge some official responsibility or to perform an official act (*see also* malfeasance; misfeasance).

nonprofit corporation(s). A corporation not organized for profit and whose directors or officers generally are not allowed to receive income from its activities.

oath. Generally, a declaration made by a person who swears to tell the truth; formal oaths often are made under penalty of perjury.

obstructing justice. An accusation made against a person that he or she has interfered with the lawful act of a criminal-justice official.

ombudsman. A person or agency that receives and investigates complaints or grievances from clients, customers, or citizens.

Open Meeting Law. *See* Brown Act.

opinion(s), legal. Oral or written advice from legal authorities regarding legal principles, issues, or questions, or the application of the law to a specific situation or set of facts.

ordinance. A city, village, township, special district, or county criminal statute, in contrast to a state law.

panel. The entire grand jury rather than one or more jurors or grand jury committees.

Penal Code. The statutes that specify crimes and their penalties.

performance audit/auditors. *See* audit(s).

perjury. Willfully making a false statement under oath.

plagiarism. Taking without permission and representing as one's own creation the writings or ideas of someone else. A form of intellectual theft.

plaintiff. A person who institutes a civil rather than a criminal lawsuit.

plea. An answer to an indictment or an allegation.

policy. The broad social, political, or economic reason for a decision by a legislative body, in contrast to procedure (*see also* procedure(s)).

precedent. A previous decision by a court that provides a basis for future decisions in matters similar to the original circumstance or set of facts.

preliminary hearing. *See* examination.

preponderance of evidence. A standard of proof used in civil cases that is less stringent than the level of evidence required for conviction of a criminal offense.

presentment. Written notice or comment by a grand jury of a matter of community concern or an alleged wrongdoing that it has learned about independently, without having been so informed by a bill of indictment brought before it.

presiding judge. The judge who is elected by colleagues to serve as the administrative head of the superior court for a year; sometimes informally called the "P.J."

prison(s). A state institution incarcerating persons found guilty of felonies.

privilege. *See* immunity.

probable cause. Facts and circumstances that would allow a reasonable person to believe that a crime has been committed.

probation. A sentencing option by which convicted offenders can remain out of prison, on terms of good behavior; probation can be revoked if the probationer violates the court-dictated terms of probation.

procedure(s). The means by which a policy is implemented; the steps taken to accomplish something rather than the reason (policy) for doing it.

prosecutor. An elected (in some states appointed) official who brings action against parties in the name of the government.

public defender(s). An elected or appointed lawyer charged with defending persons who have been accused of committing a criminal offense and who cannot afford to hire private counsel.

public-integrity offenses. A term used for crimes or other acts that lower public trust of government and that are abuses of power, authority, privilege, office, and so on.

recommendations. Prescriptions for desirable courses of action.

redevelopment agency(ies). A separate agency in city or county government charged with the responsibility of planning and supervising the renewal of buildings and other properties.

runaway grand jury. A jury that attempts to exercise powers it does not lawfully possess; or, disparagingly, a jury that exercises its independence contrary to the wishes of an official who desires to control it to achieve some private advantage.

school district(s). A form of special district organized for educational purposes (*see also* special district(s)).

sealing reports or records. To accomplish some desired purpose, the order by a court that certain documents, records, or reports be sealed with one or more provisions, such as instructions that the sealed material be destroyed at a specific time or that they can be opened only by a certain person.

slander. The spoken form of defamation of character (*see also* libel).

special district(s). A type of local government that usually has been established to provide a single service or function, such as a fire district, mosquito abatement district, or irrigation district.

statute(s). The written specification of a crime, including its elements, punishment(s), and other pertinent matters.

subpoena. An order to appear to give sworn testimony or to surrender records; "STD" is jargon for *subpoena duces tecum*, a specific type of subpoena.

superior court(s). The court of original or trial jurisdiction for felony cases and juvenile hearings; in California, these courts are associated with county government.

testimony. Evidence given by a person who is qualified and sworn as a witness.

true bill. A document affirming that a grand jury has found an offense indictable.

validity. The quality of something being what it purports to be, or being true, accurate, or factual.

verification. Making certain that a fact is true; testing something for its accuracy; confirming that something did or did not occur, and so forth.

warrant. A judicial written process requiring that specified action be taken in accordance with the law.

watchdog. A person or organization that monitors the acts of someone else or some other organization, usually to make certain that work is done lawfully, decisions are made correctly, and the like.

whistle-blower. Someone within an organization who publicly reveals actual or suspected unlawful or improper acts of other persons.

Additional References

Selected Works About
American Citizenship and Democracy

Bartlett, Ronald L., and James B. Steele. *America: Who Stole the Dream?* Kansas City, MO: Andrews and McMeel, 1996.

> The growing gap between those who have much and those who have little threatens the future of America.

Bellah, Robert et al. *Habits of the Heart: Individualism and Commitment in American Life.* Berkeley: University of California Press, 1985.

> Extreme individualism is destroying civic commitment and participation.

Bloom, Allan. *The Closing of the American Mind: How Higher Education Has Failed Democracy and Impoverished the Souls of Today's Students.* New York: Simon and Schuster, 1987.

> The decline of classical education undermines society and governance.

Bovard, James. *Lost Rights: The Destruction of American Liberty.* New York: St. Martin's Press, 1995.

> As the functions and structures of government expand, proportionately more American citizens are enmeshed in petty regulations, bureaucratic procedures, and large and small abuses of power.

Boyte, Harry C. *Commonwealth: A Return to Citizen Politics.* New York: Free Press, 1989.

> To restore citizenship, we must restore the commonwealth tradition.

Carter, Stephen L. *Civility: Manners, Morals, and the Etiquette of Democracy.* New York: Basic Books, 1998.

> Because democracy is a way of life rather than merely a product of contending political interests, an etiquette is required to make it work well. Without mutual respect, we cannot have the civil conversations upon which democracy is based.

Chickering, A. Lawrence. *Beyond Left and Right: Breaking the Political Stalemate.* San Francisco: Institute for Contemporary Studies, 1993.

Citizen alienation arises from a belief that government is unable to handle pressing social problems because of a stalemate caused by conflicts between freedom and order and rights and responsibilities.

Codevilla, Angelo M. *The Character of Nations: How Politics Makes and Breaks Prosperity, Family, and Civility.* New York: Basic Books, 1997.

The political regime in which one lives profoundly affects one's life. For example, as a result of its social policy, Sweden has become a nation whose citizens are so asocial that large numbers of them live alone.

Dionne, Jr., E. J. *Why Americans Hate Politics.* New York: Simon and Schuster, 1991.

Citizen distrust of liberal and conservative politics has created apathy.

Ehrenhalt, Alan. *The Lost City.* New York: Basic Books, 1995.

A difficult problem challenges American citizens: how to restore a sense of community in their lives without accepting limitations on personal autonomy.

Elshtain, Jean Bethke. *Democracy on Trial.* New York: Basic Books, 1995.

Democracy cannot survive a "politics of displacement" in which groups of "victims" contest each other for dominance.

Etzioni, Amatai. *The Spirit of Community: Rights, Responsibilities, and the Communitarian Agenda.* New York: Crown Publishers, 1993.

The Communitarian movement will restore citizens' control of their political institutions, but to do so, a balance must be found between rights and responsibilities.

Fallows, James. *Breaking the News: How the Media Undermine American Democracy.* New York: Pantheon Books, 1996.

Changes in media ownership, styles and techniques of reporting, the rise of the media "superstar," and similar changes have contributed to citizens' distrust of the press and political institutions.

Freedom Forum First Amendment Center. *Nothing Sacred: Journalism, Politics, and Public Trust in a Tell-All Age.* Nashville, TN: Freedom Forum First Amendment Center, 1994.

What must the news media do to regain public trust?

Geyer, Georgie Anne. *Americans No More: The Death of Citizenship.* New York: Atlantic Monthly Press, 1996.

The effects of uncontrolled immigration, costly political campaigns, and the like have changed the concept of citizenship.

Glendon, Mary Ann, editor. *Seedbeds of Virtue.* Lanham, MD: Madison Books, 1995.

Far more so than in other political systems, the American brand of democracy demands much virtue from its citizens. Whether recent changes in the form and nature of family life in America will weaken civic virtue is of great importance for the political future of the United States.

Greider, William. *Who Will Tell the People: The Betrayal of American Democracy.* New York: Simon and Schuster, 1992.

The gap between democratic idealism and its contemporary practice has caused citizens to think they have lost control of their lives.

Harwood, Richard C. *Citizens and Politics: A View from Main Street America.* Dayton, OH: Kettering Foundation, 1991.

Focus-group research shows that people feel severed from public officials and cast aside from politics.

Jacobs, Jane. *Systems for Survival: A Dialogue on the Moral Foundations of Commerce and Politics.* New York: Vintage Books, 1992.

Blurring of the distinction between business and government has consequences for society.

King, Anthony. *Running Scared: Why America's Politicians Campaign Too Much and Govern Too Little.* New York: Free Press, 1997.

Elected officials spend so much time and effort raising money for political campaigns that they neglect the purpose for which citizens voted them into office; as a result, citizens are profoundly dissatisfied with how government functions.

Marty, Martin E. *The One and the Many: America's Struggle for the Common Goal.* Cambridge, MA: Harvard University Press, 1997.

The proliferation of aggressively competing special interests has destroyed the possibility of social cohesion in America based on a "common story."

Monagan, Robert T. *The Disappearance of Representative Government: A California Solution.* Grass Valley, CA: Comstock Bonanza Press, 1990.

Monagan, a former speaker of the California Assembly, argues that among the causes of the lack of citizen participation in government are the high cost of political campaigns, politically inspired reapportionment schemes, frequent uses of the initiative, and excessive regulation.

Sandel, Michael J. *Democracy's Discontent: America in Search of a Public Philosophy.* Cambridge, MA: Harvard University Press, 1996.

Both political parties have contributed to the loss of community, citizen distrust of government, and erosion of the skills of self-government.

Saul, John Ralston. *The Unconscious Civilization.* New York: Free Press, 1977.

Loss of a sense of the common good and the will to participate in governance are caused by "corporatism," especially of the type developed in fascist Italy and Germany.

Schachtman, Tom. *The Inarticulate Society: Eloquence and Culture in America.* New York: Free Press, 1995.

The civic and political well-being of a democracy requires citizens who can think, read, speak, and write with precision. Asking well-thought-out questions, listening attentively, and speaking and writing effectively are important skills of citizenship. The decline in these skills will undermine our society.

Schlesinger, Arthur M., Jr. *The Disuniting of America.* New York: W. W. Norton and Co., 1992.

The author, a leading historian, questions whether the "cult of ethnicity" eventually will erode the American identity. Nevertheless, he is confident that Americans will solve the problem of how to balance the tensions created by a multicultural society with the form of citizenship that democracy requires.

Schudson, Michael. *The Good Citizen.* New York: Free Press, 1998.

American citizenship has changed as it passed through three eras and now is attempting to assume a new identity. The "new model" of citizenship will require Americans to be "monitors" of various trends in an "informational environment" and to be "posed for action if action is required."

Selznick, Philip. *The Moral Commonwealth: Social Theory and the Promise of Community.* Berkeley and Los Angeles: University of California Press, 1992.

The balance between rights and responsibilities and Communitarian theory must be restored.

Smith, Rogers M. *Civic Ideals: Conflicting Visions of Citizenship in U.S. History.* New Haven, CT: Yale University Press, 1997.

Civic identity in the United States is the product of legislative compromise between competing and contradictory political values (liberalism, republicanism, Anglo-Saxon racial supremacy, patriarchy, and so on).

Sullivan, William M. *Work and Integrity: The Crisis and Promise of Professionalism in America.* New York: HarperCollins, 1995.

The professions have turned away from a civic-minded, service orientation to acquisition and self-aggrandizement.

Selected References
Concerning the American Grand Jury

Edwards, George J., Jr. *The Grand Jury: An Essay.* Philadelphia: George T. Bisel Company, 1906. Republished by AMS Press, Inc., Foundations of Criminal Justice series, New York, 1973.

The author surveys the law governing English and American grand juries from their origins through the 19th century.

Younger, Richard D. *The People's Panel: The Grand Jury in the United States, 1634–1941.* Providence, RI: Brown University Press, 1963.

This account of the American grand jury during the nation's principal epochs ends with the beginning of World War II.

Index

American Grand Jury Foundation

Purpose and Objectives

The primary objectives of the American Grand Jury Foundation are to

- train newly appointed grand jurors
- conduct research into the grand jury system and related issues
- publish and distribute information about grand juries and selected local-government topics
- educate and train the general public and local-government officials about grand jury matters
- encourage research into the American grand jury system by providing internships, grants, and awards
- recognize and publicize achievements of grand jurors, governmental officials and employees, and other citizens who have contributed to improving the grand jury system

Program

The American Grand Jury Foundation restricts its activities to education, training, and research. It does not support or oppose legislation; nor does it endorse, support, or oppose candidates for political office. Foundation Directors believe that the historic independence of the grand jury is best served by not taking positions under the aegis of the term, "former grand jurors." Directors also believe that the Foundation's education, training, and research programs can be objective only if they are undertaken in a non-advocacy, non-political, non-partisan context.

EDUCATION AND TRAINING

The Foundation's principal work is training newly appointed grand jurors. The Foundation also has hired law-school students occasionally to conduct research into grand jury matters.

PUBLICATIONS

The American Grand Jury Foundation has undertaken a comprehensive publication program. The cornerstone of this program is a continually updated, published bibliography of grand jury materials. Interested persons may obtain information about ordering the bibliography and other Foundation publications by writing the Foundation's office. Among publications that are now available or will be released in the future are:

- The Accusation Power of the California Grand Jury
- Using a Computer to Track Grand Jury Recommendations
- A Survey of Case Law Affecting the California Grand Jury
- How to Conduct an Investigation

- How to Conduct an Informational Interview
- How to Write a Grand Jury Final Report
- Grand Jury Expenditures in California: A Comparative Analysis

History

The American Grand Jury Foundation was first known as the Grand Jury Exchange Seminar, a term still used to identify its principal annual training activities. The Seminars began in 1979, and the Foundation achieved nonprofit incorporated status in 1987.

Directors

A Board of Directors, consisting mainly of former grand jurors, governs the Foundation and establishes its policies. The Board supervises an Executive Director who is responsible for the Foundation's business affairs, maintaining its books and records, and implementing Board decisions.

For More Information

Interested persons are invited to write to the American Grand Jury Foundation for additional information about the Foundation or for information about ordering its publications.

The American Grand Jury Foundation
P.O. Box 1690
Modesto CA 95353-1690
(209) 527-0966
www.grandjuryfoundation.org

Order Form

The American Grand Jury Foundation
P.O. Box 1690
Modesto CA 95353-1690
Fax: 209-527-2287
www.grandjuryfoundation.org

Name: _____

Mailing Address: _____

_____

City: _____

State: _____ Zip Code: _____

Telephone: (_____)_____

E-mail address: _____

Quantity	Item	Unit Price	Total
	Grand Juries in California	$39.95	
	Sales Tax (California only)	7.375%	
	Shipping & Handling		
	TOTAL		

Shipping & Handling (U.S. Priority Mail):
$5.00   1 book
$7.00   2–3 books
+$.75   each additional book

Payment Type: ❑ Check   ❑ Money Order   ❑ VISA/MasterCard

Card No.: _____ Exp. Date: _____

Billing Address: _____

City: _____

State: _____ Zip Code: _____

❑ Please send information about other publications

Order Form

The American Grand Jury Foundation
P.O. Box 1690
Modesto CA 95353-1690
Fax: 209-527-2287
www.grandjuryfoundation.org

Name: _____

Mailing Address: _____

_____

City: _____

State: _____ Zip Code: _____

Telephone: (_____) _____

E-mail address: _____

Quantity	Item	Unit Price	Total
	Grand Juries in California	$39.95	
	Sales Tax (California only)	7.375%	
	Shipping & Handling		
	TOTAL		

Shipping & Handling (U.S. Priority Mail):
$5.00   1 book
$7.00   2–3 books
+$.75   each additional book

Payment Type: ❑ Check   ❑ Money Order   ❑ VISA/MasterCard

Card No.: _____ Exp. Date: _____

Billing Address: _____

City: _____

State: _____ Zip Code: _____

❑ Please send information about other publications